Anatolia, I

For Matina

Froh empfind' ich mich nun auf klassischem Boden begeistert,
    Vor- und Mitwelt spricht lauter und reizender mir.
Hier befolg' ich den Rat, durchblättre die Werke der Alten
    Mit geschäftiger Hand, täglich mit neuem Genuß.
Aber die Nächte hindurch hält Amor mich anders beschäftigt;
    Werd' ich auch halb nur gelehrt, bin ich doch doppelt beglückt.

Anatolia

Land, Men, and Gods in
Asia Minor

Volume I
The Celts in Anatolia and
the Impact of Roman Rule

STEPHEN MITCHELL

CLARENDON PRESS · OXFORD

Oxford University Press, Walton Street, Oxford OX2 6DP
Oxford New York
Athens Auckland Bangkok Bombay
Calcutta Cape Town Dar es Salaam Delhi
Florence Hong Kong Istanbul Karachi
Kuala Lumpur Madras Madrid Melbourne
Mexico City Nairobi Paris Singapore
Taipei Tokyo Toronto
and associated companies in
Berlin Ibadan

Oxford is a trade mark of Oxford University Press

Published in the United States
by Oxford University Press Inc., New York

© Stephen Mitchell 1993
First issued in paperback 1995

British Library Cataloguing in Publication Data
Data available

Library of Congress Cataloging in Publication Data
Anatolia: land, men, and Gods in Asia Minor/Stephen Mitchell.
Includes bibliographical references and indexes.
Contents: v. 1. The Celts in Anatolia and the impact of Roman rule
— v. 2. The rise of the Church.
1. Turkey—History.   2. Hellenism.   3. Paganism—Relations—
Christianity—Turkey.   4. Celts—Turkey—History.   5. Rome—
Provinces—Turkey—History.   6. Byzantine Empire—Civilization.
7. Christianity—Early church, ca. 30–600—Turkey.   I. Title.
DS155.M57 1993   956.1'01—dc20   92-29738
ISBN 0-19-815029-X

1 3 5 7 9 10 8 6 4 2

Printed in Great Britain
on acid-free paper by
St. Edmundsbury Press, Bury St. Edmunds

Designed by John Trevitt

Preface

THE writing of this book has spread over several years, and the preparation has lasted longer still. My first encounter with the historical world of Asia Minor dates back to 1970, when I began work on an Oxford D.Phil. thesis, *The History and Archaeology of Galatia*, which was completed in 1974. I owe much to the supervisors of that thesis, the late E. W. Gray, whose Oxford undergraduate lectures on Asia Minor provided me with notes which I still use with profit; and E. L. Bowie, who has constantly encouraged me to pursue the human and humane interest of even the driest material. The greatest stimulation in these years and later, however, came from constant contact with the inexhaustible wealth of historical and archaeological material in Turkey itself. Repeated visits for the purpose of travel or specific research, usually under the aegis of the British Institute of Archaeology at Ankara, converted me into one of the many scholars, and the far greater number of other travellers, who have fallen under Anatolia's powerful spell. Gradually, I venture to hope, the fascination has come to be matched by a measure of understanding of its complex history.

The book could not have been completed without the support of several institutions. The first part was written in the summer of 1981, during a term of sabbatical leave granted by the University College of Swansea. Swansea also gave me a year's leave of absence in 1983/4, which enabled me to accept an appointment as a visiting member of the School of Historical Studies, at the Institute for Advanced Study, Princeton. A Fellowship Grant from the Leverhulme Foundation as well as the support of the Institute itself helped to make this stay a financial possibility. I had optimistically hoped that the year's leave would suffice to complete the planned book. The foundations for Parts II and III were indeed laid in Princeton, but like many other visiting members of the Institute I found that the stay there served above all to broaden my historical horizons, and led me to ask questions of the evidence which lay well beyond the scope of the original plan. This was in no small measure due to the stimulus of working in an extraordinary constellation of ancient historians, including many with a special interest in Asia Minor, who gathered in Princeton that year under the guidance of Professors Glen Bowersock and Christian Habicht. Teaching commitments in Swansea and research on other topics prevented me from finishing the project quickly, but made it possible to take account of much new evidence that has come to light during an exceptionally productive decade of epigraphic exploration and other research activity in Turkey. In 1989 I was awarded a Research Readership by the British Academy, tenable from September 1990 to 1992, and I have completed the book, in complete freedom from the normal multifarious commitments of academic life, as a guest of the Althistorisches Seminar at the University of Göttingen. My stay in Germany was made possible in part by a generous grant from the Gerda-Henkel-Stiftung, Düsseldorf. My thanks are due to Professor J. Bleicken and to Christoph Boehringer for making this possible, but above all I am grateful to Professor Christopher Collard and my colleagues at Swansea, who inevitably have had to shoulder a heavy burden of extra teaching in my absence. Without relying on hidden support of this kind, no member of a humanities department in a British University under current conditions can reasonably hope to conclude a large-scale research undertaking.

Several people have read parts of the manuscript and made valuable suggestions and criticisms, notably Christian Habicht, Michael Speidel, Robin Lane Fox, Theresa Urbainczyk, and Stuart Clark. Fergus Millar has been a constant source of encouragement. I can recall few conversations with him which have not caused me to rethink my approach to one or another aspect of the subject matter. I must also express my warm thanks to the many colleagues who have sent me offprints of their work, at a time when a university library on the scale of Swansea's cannot hope to subscribe to all of the growing number of journals and specialized volumes where much of this work has been published. I am also much indebted to Dr O. Vacano and Dr R. Ziegler of the University of Düsseldorf, for their advice and help in selecting the coin illustrations from the Düsseldorf cast collection, and for supplying the photographs used for Figs. 18, 35, 36, and 39.

I would like in particular to thank three friends who have been among my closest colleagues during the period of the composition of this book. Barbara Levick has read the whole manuscript and offered a host of suggestions for improvement at all levels. Her level-headed good sense and boundless energy have been a constant inspiration and encouragement. I have also been privileged to spend long hours and days in the field with two of the finest archaeologists working in Turkey today, David French, the director of the British Institute at Ankara; and Marc Waelkens. What I owe to their publications may be judged from my footnotes; it is outweighed by what I have learnt at first hand from their efforts to make sense of the material legacy of Hellenistic and Roman Anatolia, which has only begun to receive the attention that it deserves in recent years. The documentary record of Anatolian history has been extensively and brilliantly explored over the last century; archaeologically most of the region remains *terra incognita*. It is certain that the picture of the culture and society of Anatolia offered in this book will require alteration in the light of new finds in the years ahead. I am certain that new archaeological discoveries and further appraisal of the non-documentary record will be the cause of the most drastic revisions.

The index is largely the work of Bill MacKeith and I hope that readers will be as grateful to him as I am.

I owe a debt of another kind to my family. My parents have been a constant source of moral and material support. The full brunt has fallen on my wife. Only she knows what the effort of composition has cost. I trust to Goethe's lines to express the feelings behind my dedication.

S.M.

Contents

Contents to Volume II   *page* ix

List of Maps   xi

List of Figures   xiii

Abbreviations   xiv

1   Introduction   1

I   **The Celts in Anatolia**   11

2   The Galatians in the Hellenistic World   13
    I   Invasion   13
    II   Settlement in Central Anatolia   19
    III The Galatians, Pergamum, and Rome   21

3   The Allies of Rome   27
    I   Tribal Organization and Political Structure   27
    II   Rome in Asia Minor, 133–63 BC   29
    III The Settlement of Pompey   31
    IV   Galatia during the Civil Wars   34

4   Ethnography and Settlement of the Anatolian Celts   42
    I   Tribes and Leaders   42
    II   Warfare   44
    III Clients and Slaves   46
    IV   Religion   47
    V   Language   50
    VI   The Settlement of Galatia   51

II **The Impact of Roman Rule**   59

5   *In formam provinciae redacta*: Annexation and the Framework of
    Roman Administration   61

6   The Pacification of the Taurus   70

7   City Foundations and Urban Growth   80
    I   The Graeco-Roman City   80
    II   Central Anatolia before Augustus   81
    III Augustan City Foundations   86
    IV   City Foundations from Tiberius to Hadrian: The North   91
    V   City Foundations from Tiberius to Hadrian: The South   94
    VI   Cappadocia: The Exception   97

8   The Imperial Cult   100

9   The Euphrates Frontier and the Impact of the Roman Armies:
    Garrisons, Roads, and Recruitment   118
    I   Garrisons   118
    II   Roads and the Impact of Military Traffic   124
    III Legionary Recruitment   136

10 Estates and the Land   143
    I   The Physical Setting   143
    II   The Pattern of Settlement   148
    III Estates in Galatia   149
    IV   Estates in Phrygia, Bithynia, and Lydia   158
    V   Estate Administration   162

11 Rural Anatolia   165
    I   Two Views from the City   165
    II   Ethnic Diversity   170
    III Villages and Rural Communities   176
    IV   Villagers in Consort: The Organization of Large Villages   181
    V   The Rule of the Gods: Authority, Order, and Morality in Village
         Life   187
    VI   Worlds Apart   195

12 The Development of the Cities   198
    I   Changing Characteristics of City Life   198
    II   Administration and the Civic Community   199
    III Civic Patriotism and Benefactions   206
    IV   Public Buildings   211
    V   Agonistic Festivals   217
    VI   Central Anatolia: An Exception?   225

13 Crisis and Continuity in the Third Century   227
    I   Introduction   227
    II   Militarization   228
    III Brigandage and Insurrection   234
    IV   Goths and Sassanians: The External Threat   235
    V   The Resilience of the Countryside   239

14 Tax, Grain, and the Economy   241
    I   Reconstructing the Ancient Economy   241
    II   City and Country: The Economic Relationship   243
    III Central Anatolia under Grain and the Problem of Transport   245
    IV   Supplies for Troops   250
    V   Grain Supply and Living Standards in Cities and Villages   253
    VII Local Coinage and Money Taxes   255
    VII Economic Growth and Urbanization   257

General Index   261

Contents to Volume II

Contents to Volume I   *page* ix
List of Figures   xi
List of Maps   xii
Abbreviations   xiii

III   The Rise of the Church   1

15   Christian Origins   3

16   Pagans, Jews, and Christians from the First to the Third Century   11
      I   Pagan Worship   11
      II   The Indigenous Cults of Anatolia   19
      III Jews   31
      IV   Christians   37
      V   One God in Heaven   43

17   From Pagan to Christian: Social and Civic Transformations in the
      Fourth Century   53
      I   Gregory the Wonder-Worker and the Age of Conversion   53
      II   Dominant Christian Groups before Constantine   57
      III Persecution, Martyrdom, and the Importance of Saints   64
      IV   Rural Christianity in the Fourth Century: Cappadocia   66
      V   Cities, Bishops, and Imperial Authorities   73
      VI   Pagan Culture in Fourth-Century Ancyra   84
      VII Julian   88
      VIII Christians in Fourth-Century Ancyra   91
      IX   The Novatian Church in Asia Minor   96
      X   The Epigraphy of the Anatolian Heresies   100

18   The Rise of Monasticism from the Fourth to the Sixth Century   109
      I   The Origins of Anatolian Monasticism   109
      II   The Spread and Impact of Monastic Christianity   114
      III Social Change in the Fifth and Sixth Centuries   119

19   Central Anatolia at the End of Antiquity: The Life of Saint Theodore
      of Sykeon   122
      I   The World of Theodore of Sykeon   122
      II   The Making of a Holy Man   134
      III Exorcism and Cure: The Saint in Action   139
      IV   Possession and Christian Belief   144

Appendix 1.   Provincial Boundaries in Asia Minor, 25 BC–AD 235   151
Appendix 2.   Provincial Boundaries in Asia Minor, AD 235–535   158

General Index   165

x CONTENTS TO VOLUME II

Index of Personal Names 174
Index of Non-Christian Cults 185
Index of Places and Peoples 188

List of Maps

1   Asia Minor: Physical features   *between pages* 1 *and* 2
2   The Galatian invasions of Greece and Asia Minor   *page*   14
3   Kingdoms and Roman provinces in Anatolia in
    the first century BC   *at end*
4   (*a*) Galatian settlements   *page*   52
    (*b*) The archaeological and historical evidence   53
5   The Pisidian Taurus   *at end*
6   The cities of central Anatolia from Augustus to Hadrian   *page*   99
7   The Roman military presence in western Anatolia   120
8   Roads, garrisons, and recruitment in central Asia Minor   130
9   The Euphrates frontier   131
10 Central Anatolia: Imperial and private estates   *at end*
11 Lydia and western Phrygia   *page* 190

List of Figures

1	Karaca Dağ	*page* 2
2	Demirözü Çay	2
3	North-East Galatia	6
4	Orcistus	6
5	The Lycus valley at Amaseia	8
6	The Bozova near Andeda	8
7	The Dying Gaul	46
8	Peium: The treasury of Deiotarus	56
9	Blucium: The palace of Deiotarus	56
10	Pisidian Antioch: Inscription for Caristanius Fronto	75
11	Pisidian Antioch: Inscription for St. Pescennius	75
12	Pisidian Antioch: Freedmen of the Caristanii	75
13	The imperial temple at Ancyra	101
14	The imperial temple at Pisidian Antioch	101
15	Pisidian Antioch: Garland frieze from imperial temple	106
16	Pisidian Antioch: Corinthian capital from imperial temple	106
17	Tavium: Acanthus frieze	106
18	Coin-types illustrating colonial foundations and the Imperial Cult	115
19	Inscription from *castellum* at Aulutrene	123
20	Gravestone at Ancyra for members of *cohors I Augusta Cyrenaica*	123
21	Gravestone at Ancyra for the centurion M. Aebutius Victorinus	123
22	Hadrianic milestone from north Galatia set up by A. Larcius Macedo	123
23	Roman highway in the Phrygian Pentapolis	125
24	The *via Sebaste* between Pisidian Antioch and Iconium	125
25	Roman road from Perge to Magydus in Pamphylia	128
26	Roman road at Cremna in Pisidia	128
27	Decorated tombstone from Koca Köy, north-west Galatia	171
28	Tombstone of a musician from Appia, upper Tembris valley	171
29	Marble tombstone of a priestly family from the upper Tembris valley	171
30	A Christian family in the marble business from Docimeium	171
31	Tombstone of Aphia, upper Tembris valley	186
32	Tombstone of an unmarried girl, upper Tembris valley	186
33	Tombstone with Phrygian curse formula	186
34	Uninscribed doorstone from Orcistus	186
35	Coins depicting civic concord, buildings, and cults	205
36	Coins depicting foundation legends and the impact of imperial politics	209
37	Aezani: Theatre, stadium, and temple	215
38	Nicaea: The north gate	215
39	Coins and festivals	223
40	Petition of the Aragueni	231
41	Dedication to Zeus Anpeleites by a villager of Aragua	231

Abbreviations

AASS	*Acta Sanctorum*
ABSA	*Annual of the British School at Athens*
AE	*L'Année épigraphique*
AEMÖ	*Archäologisch-epigraphische Mitteilungen aus Österreich*
AJA	*American Journal of Archaeology*
AJPhil.	*American Journal of Philology*
Alt. v. Perg.	*Altertümer von Pergamon* (1895–)
Anc. Soc.	*Ancient Society*
Ann. sc. it.	*Annuario di scavi italiani*
ANRW	*Aufstieg und Niedergang der römischen Welt*
Ant. class.	*Antiquité classique*
Anz. Wien	*Anzeiger der Akademie der Wissenschaften, Wien*
I (–VIII) Araş	*I (–VIII) Araştırma Sonuçları Toplantısı.* Reports of the Archaeological Research Symposia, published by the Turkish Directorate General of Antiquities, Ministry of Culture, Ankara, 1983–90
Arch. Anz.	*Archäologischer Anzeiger*
Armies and Frontiers	S. Mitchell (ed.), *Armies and Frontiers in Roman and Byzantine Anatolia* (1983)
AS	*Anatolian Studies*
ASBuckler	W. M. Calder and J. Keil (eds.), *Anatolian Studies presented to William Hepburn Buckler* (1939)
ASRamsay	W. H. Buckler and W. M. Calder (eds.), *Anatolian Studies presented to Sir William Mitchell Ramsay* (1923)
Ath. Mitt.	*Mitteilungen des Deutschen Archäologischen Instituts, Abteilung Athen*
Aulock, *Lykaonien*	H. von Aulock, *Münzen und Städte Lykaoniens* (1976)
Aulock, *Pisidien*	H. von Aulock, *Münzen und Städte Pisidiens*, i (1977) and ii (1979)
Aulock, *Phrygien*	H. von Aulock, *Münzen und Städte Phrygiens*, i (1981) and ii (1987)
Babelon, *Recueil général*	W. H. Waddington, E. Babelon, Th. Reinach, *Recueil général des monnaies grecques d'Asie Mineure* (1904–25)
BASP	*Bulletin of the American Society of Papyrologists*
BCH	*Bulletin de correspondance hellénique*
BIAA	British Institute of Archaeology at Ankara
BJb.	*Bonner Jahrbücher*
BJRL	*Bulletin of the John Rylands Library*
Blanchetierre	F. Blanchetierre, *Le Christianisme asiate au IIe et IIIe siècle* (1977)
BM	British Museum
BMC	*A Catalogue of the Greek Coins in the British Museum*
Bosch, *Ankara*	E. Bosch, *Quellen zur Geschichte der Stadt Ankara im Altertum* (1967)
Broughton, *Roman Asia Minor*	T. R. S. Broughton, *Roman Asia Minor*, in T. Frank (ed.), *An Economic Survey of Ancient Rome*, iv (1938), 499–918
Bull. ép	*Bulletin épigraphique*, published in *REG* (1938–84, J. and L. Robert; 1985 and since, various authors)
Byz. Zeitschr.	*Byzantinische Zeitschrift*
CIG	*Corpus Inscriptionum Graecarum*

CIL	*Corpus Inscriptionum Latinarum*
CJ	*Codex Iustinianus*
Class. Phil.	*Classical Philology*
CMG	*Corpus Medicorum Graecorum*
CMRDM	E. N. Lane, *Corpus Monumentorum Religionis Dei Menis*, i–iv (1971–8)
Coll. Wadd.	E. Babelon, *Inventaire sommaire de la Collection Waddington* (1898)
CQ	*Classical Quarterly*
CR	*Classical Review*
CRAI	*Comptes rendus de l'Académie des Inscriptions et Belles Lettres*
CSHB	*Corpus Scriptorum Historiae Byzantinae*
CTh	*Codex Theodosianus*
Deininger, *Provinziallandtage*	J. Deininger, *Die Provinziallandtage der römischen Kaiserzeit* (1965)
DOP	*Dumbarton Oaks Papers*
Ec. Hist. Rev.	*Economic History Review*
Eck, *Senatoren*	W. Eck, *Senatoren von Vespasian bis Hadrian* (1970)
Eighth Congress	*Eighth International Congress of Greek and Latin Epigraphy, Athens 1982* (1984)
Epigr. Anat.	*Epigraphica Anatolica*
Ét. celt.	*Études celtiques*
Fayer, *Dea Roma*	C. Fayer, *Il culto della dea Roma: Origine e diffusione nell' Impero* (1976)
FGrH	F. Jacoby, *Die Fragmente der griechischen Historiker*, I–III (1924–58)
FHG	C. and Th. Müller, *Fragmenta Historicorum Graecorum*, i–v (1874–83)
Forsch. Eph.	*Forschungen in Ephesos* (1906–)
Foss, 'Ankara'	C. Foss, 'Late Antique and Byzantine Ankara', *DOP* 31 (1977), 29–87
French, *Pilgrim's Road*	D. H. French, *Roman Roads and Milestones of Asia Minor*, i. *The Pilgrim's Road* (1981)
G&R	*Greece and Rome*
GIBM	*The Collection of Ancient Greek Inscriptions in the British Museum*, 4 vols. (1874–1916)
Gibson, 'Christians'	E. Gibson, *The 'Christians for Christians' Inscriptions of Phrygia* (1978)
Gött. Gel. Anz.	*Göttingischer Gelehrter Anzeiger*
GRBS	*Greek, Roman, and Byzantine Studies*
Habicht, *Gottmenschentum²*	C. Habicht, *Gottmenschentum und griechische Städte* (2nd edn. 1970)
Halfmann, *Senatoren*	H. Halfmann, *Die Senatoren aus dem östlichen Teil des Imperium Romanum* (1979)
Harnack	A. Harnack, *Mission und Ausbreitung des Christentums* (1906)
Haspels, *Highlands*	C. H. E. Haspels, *The Highlands of Phrygia* (1971)
Head, *HN²*	B. Head, *Historia Nummorum* (2nd edn. 1911)
Histoire des conciles	C. Hefele and H. Leclercq, *Histoire des conciles d'après les documents originaux*, i–ii (1907–8)
Hoben, *Kleinasiatische Dynasten*	W. Hoben, *Untersuchungen zur Stellung kleinasiatischer Dynasten in den Machtkämpfen der ausgehenden römischen Republik* (1969)
Holder	A. Holder, *Altceltischer Sprachsatz*, i–iii (1896–1913)
Holleaux, *Études*	M. Holleaux, *Études d'épigraphie et d'histoire grecques*, i–vii (ed. L. Robert, 1938–68)
Horsley, *New Docs.*	G. H. R. Horsley, *New Documents Illustrating Early Christianity*, i–v (1981–9)
HSCP	*Harvard Studies in Classical Philology*
IAMY	*Istanbul Arkeoloji Müzeleri Yıllığı*
I. Apamea	T. Corsten, *Die Inschriften von Apamea (Bithynia) und Pylai*, IGSK 32 (1987)
I. Delos	F. Durrbach, *Inscriptions de Délos* (1926–37)
I. Didyma	A. Rehm, *Didyma II: Die Inschriften* (ed. R. Harder, 1958)
I. Eph.	*Die Inschriften von Ephesos*, i–vii. 2, IGSK 11–17. 2 (1979–84)
I. Erythrai	H. Engelmann, R. Merkelbach, *Die Inschriften von Erythrai und Klazomenai*, i–ii, IGSK 1 (1972) and 2 (1973)
IG	*Inscriptiones Graecae*

IGBulg.	G. Mihailov, *Inscriptiones Graecae in Bulgaria repertae*, i–iv
IGLS	*Inscriptions grecques et latines de Syrie* (see H. MacAdam, *JRA* 3 (1990), 458–64)
IGR	R. Cagnat *et al.*, *Inscriptiones Graecae ad res Romanas pertinentes*, i, iii–iv (1906–27)
IGSK	Inschriften griechischer Städte aus Kleinasien
IGUR	L. Moretti, *Inscriptiones Graecae Urbis Romae*, i–iv (1968–90)
I. Hadr.	E. Schwertheim, *Die Inschriften von Hadrianoi und Hadrianeia*, IGSK 33 (1987)
I. Ilion	P. Frisch, *Die Inschriften von Ilion*, IGSK 3 (1975)
I. Iznik	S. Şahin, *Katalog der antiken Inschriften des Museums von Iznik (Nikaia)*, i, and ii. 1 and 2, IGSK 9, 10. 1–2 (1979–82)
I. Kios	T. Corsten, *Die Inschriften von Kios*, IGSK 29 (1985)
I. Klaudiupolis	F. Becker-Berthau, *Die Inschriften von Klaudiupolis*, IGSK 31 (1986)
I. Kyme	H. Engelmann, *Die Inschriften von Kyme*, IGSK 5 (1976)
I. Kyzikos	E. Schwertheim, *Die Inschriften von Kyzikos und Umgebung, 1. Grabtexte*, IGSK 18 (1980)
ILS	H. Dessau, *Inscriptiones Latinae Selectae*
I. Magnesia	O. Kern, *Die Inschriften von Magnesia am Mäander* (1900)
Imhoof-Blümer, *Griechische Münzen*	*F. Imhoof-Blümer, Griechische Münzen* (1890)
I. Miletupolis	E. Schwertheim, *Die Inschriften von Kyzikos und Umgebung, 2. Miletupolis*, IGSK 26 (1983)
I. Mylasa	W. Blümel, *Die Inschriften von Mylasa*, i–ii, IGSK 34–5 (1987–8)
I. Pergamon	M. Fraenkel, *Die Inschriften von Pergamon*, i–ii (1890–5)
I. Pessinus	J. Strubbe, 'The Inscriptions', in J. Devreker and M. Waelkens, *Les Fouilles de Pessinonte*, i (1984), 214–44
I. Priene	Hiller von Gaetringen, *Die Inschriften von Priene* (1906)
I. Prusias	W. Ameling, *Die Inschriften von Prusias ad Hypium*, IGSK 27 (1985)
I. Selge	J. Nollé and F. Schindler, *Die Inschriften von Selge*, IGSK 37 (1991)
I. Smyrna	G. Petzl, *Die Inschriften von Smyrna*, i, ii. 1–2, IGSK 23, 24. 1–2 (1982–90)
Ist. Mitt.	*Mitteilungen des Deutschen Archäologischen Instituts, Abteilung Istanbul*
I. Stratonikaia	M, Çetin Şahin, *Die Inschriften von Straonikaia*, i, ii. 1–2, IGSK 21, 22. 1–2 (1981–90)
I. Teos	D. McCabe, *The Inscriptions of Teos* (circulated from the Institute for Advanced Study, Princeton, 1985)
JAC	*Jahrbuch für Antike und Christentum*
JdI	*Jahrbuch des deutschen archäologischen Instituts*
JEA	*Journal of Egyptian Archaeology*
JHS	*Journal of Hellenic Studies*
JNG	*Jahrbuch für Numismatik und Geldgeschichte*
JÖAI	*Jahreshefte des Österreichischen Archäologischen Instituts*
J.öst.Byz.	*Jahrbuch für österreichischen Byzantinistik*
Jones, *CERP*[2]	A. H. M. Jones, *Cities of the Eastern Roman Provinces* (2nd edn. 1970)
Jones, *LRE*	A. H. M. Jones, *The Later Roman Empire: A Social, Economic, and Administrative Survey* (1964)
JRA	*Journal of Roman Archaeology*
JRS	*Journal of Roman Studies*
JSav.	*Journal des Savants*
JTS	*Journal of Theological Studies*
Karl	H. Karl, *Numismatische Beiträge zum Festwesen der kleinasiatischen und nordgriechischen Städte im 2. und 3. Jhdt.* (1975)
KP[1,2,3]	J. Keil and A. von Premerstein, *Erster (Zweiter, Dritter) Bericht über eine Reise in Lydien und der südlichen Äiolis*, Denkschrift der Akademie, Wien 53. 2 (1908), 54. 2 (1911), 57. 1 (1914)
Laum, *Stiftungen*	B. Laum, *Stiftungen in der griechischen und römischen Antike: Ein Beitrag zur antiken Kulturgeschichte* (1914)

Launey, *Recherches*	M. Launey, *Recherches sur les armées hellénistiques*, i (1949) and ii (1950)
Levick, *Roman Colonies*	B. M. Levick, *Roman Colonies in Southern Asia Minor* (1967)
Liebmann-Frankfort, *La Frontière orientale*	T. Liebmann-Frankfort, *La Frontière orientale dans la politique extérieure de la république romaine depuis le traité d'Apamée jusqu'à la fin des conquêtes asiatiques de Pompée (189–63)* (1969)
LW	P. le Bas and W. H. Waddington, *Voyage archéologique en Grèce et Asie Mineure pendant 1834 et 1844*, 6 vols. (1853–70)
MacMullen, *Soldier and Civilian*	R. MacMullen, *Soldier and Civilian in the Later Roman Empire* (1964)
Magie, *RR*	D. Magie, *Roman Rule in Asia Minor*, 2 vols. (1950)
MAMA	*Monumenta Asiae Minoris Antiqua*, 9 vols. (1929–88)
MEFRA	*Mélanges de l'École Française de Rome—antiquité*
Mendel, *Cat. Mus. Imp.*	G. Mendel, *Catalogue des Musées Impériaux Ottomans*, 3 vols. (1910–13)
Michel, *Recueil*	Ch. Michel, *Recueil des inscriptions grecques* (1897–1926)
Millar, *ERW*	Fergus Millar, *The Emperor in the Roman World* (1977)
Mommsen, *Ges. Schr.*	T. Mommsen, *Gesammelte Schriften*, 8 vols. (1905–13)
Mon. Ant.	*Monumenti antichi*
Moretti, *Inscr. agon. gr.*	L. Moretti, *Iscrizioni agonistiche greche* (1953)
Nachtergael, *Galates*	G. Nachtergael, *Les Galates en Grèce et les Sôtéria de Delphes* (1975)
Not. scav.	*Notizie degli scavi*
Num. Chron.	*Numismatic Chronicle*
Num. Zeitschr.	*Numismatische Zeitschrift*
OGIS	W. Dittenberger, *Orientis Graeci Inscriptiones Selectae*, 2 vols. (1903–5)
PBSR	*Papers of the British School at Rome*
Perrot, *Exploration*	G. Perrot and E. Guillaume, *Exploration archéologique de la Galatie et la Bithynie* (1862)
Peek, *GV*	W. Peek, *Griechische Versinschriften*, i (1955)
Pflaum, *CP*	H.-G. Pflaum, *Les Carrières procuratoriennes équestres sous le haut-empire romain*, 4 vols. (1960–1); *supplément* (1982)
PG	*Patrologia Graeca*
PIR²	*Prosopographia Imperii Romani*, 2nd edn.
PL	*Patrologia Latina*
PLRE	A. H. M. Jones, J. R. Martindale, and J. Morris, *Prosopography of the Later Roman Empire*, 2 vols. (1971–88)
P.Oxy.	Oxyrhynchus Papyri
Price, *Rituals and Power*	S. R. F. Price, *Rituals and Power: The Roman Imperial Cult in Asia Minor* (1984)
PCPS	*Proceedings of the Cambridge Philological Society*
RAC	*Reallexicon für Antike und Christentum*
Radt, *Pergamon*	W. Radt, *Pergamon. Geschichte und Bauten, Funde und Erforschung einer antiken Metropole* (1988)
Ramsay, *Galatians*	W. M. Ramsay, *A Historical Commentary on St. Paul's Epistle to the Galatians* (1899)
Ramsay, *HGAM*	W. M. Ramsay, *The Historical Geography of Asia Minor* (1890)
Ramsay, *CB*	W. M. Ramsay, *The Cities and Bishoprics of Phrygia*, i. 1 (1895), and i. 2 (1897)
RE	*Paulys Real-Encyclopädie der classischen Altertumswissenschaft*
REA	*Revue des études anciennes*
RECAM ii	S. Mitchell *et al.*, *Regional Epigraphic Catalogues of Asia Minor*, ii, *The Inscriptions of North Galatia* (1982)
REG	*Revue des études grecques*
REL	*Revue des études latines*
Rev. arch.	*Revue archéologique*
Rev. celt.	*Revue celtique*
Rev. hist. eccl.	*Revue d'histoire ecclésiastique*
Rev. num.	*Revue numismatique*

Rev. phil.	*Revue de philologie*
Rh. Mus.	*Rheinisches Museum*
Riv. arch. chr.	*Rivista di archeologia christiana*
Riv. fil.	*Rivista di filologia*
Robert, *Documents*	L. Robert, *Documents d'Asie Mineure* (1989)
Robert, *Ét. anat.*	L. Robert, *Études anatoliennes* (1937)
Robert, *Ét. ép. phil.*	L. Robert, *Études épigraphiques et philologiques* (1938)
Robert, *Gladiateurs*	L. Robert, *Les Gladiateurs dans l'Orient grec* (1940)
Robert, *Hellenica*	L. Robert, *Hellenica: Recueil d'épigraphie, de numismatique et d'antiquités grecques*, 13 vols. (1940–65)
Robert, *Noms indigènes*	L. Robert, *Les Noms indigènes dans l'Asie Mineure gréco-romaine* (1963)
Robert, *OMS*	L. Robert, *Opera Minora Selecta*, 7 vols. (1969–90)
Robert, *Villes²*	L. Robert, *Villes d'Asie Mineure*, 2nd edn. (1962)
Röm. Mitt.	*Mitteilungen des Deutschen Archäologischen Instituts, Abteilung Rom*
Rostovtzeff, *SEHHW*	M. I. Rostovtzeff, *Social and Economic History of the Hellenistic World*, 3 vols. (1953)
Rostovtzeff, *SEHRE²*	M. I. Rostovtzeff, *Social and Economic History of the Roman Empire*, 2nd edn., rev. P. M. Fraser (1957)
Ste Croix, *Class Struggle*	G. E. M. de Sainte Croix, *The Class Struggle in the Ancient Greek World* (1981)
Sb. Ak. Wien	*Sitzungsberichte der Akademie der Wissenschaften, Wien*
Sb. Berl.	*Sitzungsberichte der königlichen preussischen Akademie der Wissenschaften zu Berlin*
Sb. München	*Sitzungsberichte der bayerischen Akademie der Wissenschaften*
Schürer²	G. Vermes and F. Millar (eds.), E. Schürer, *The History of the Jewish People in the Age of Jesus Christ*, rev. edn. i–iii. 2 (1974–86)
Schw. num. Rundsch.	*Schweizerische numismatische Rundschau*
SEG	*Supplementum Epigraphicum Graecum*
SERP	W. M. Ramsay (ed.), *Studies in the History and Art of the Eastern Roman Provinces* (1906)
SGDI	H. Collitz, *Sammlung der griechischen Dialektinschriften* (1884–1915)
Sherk i	R. K. Sherk, *The Legates of Galatia from Augustus to Diocletian* (1954)
Sherk ii	R. K. Sherk, 'Roman Galatia: The Governors from 25 BC to AD 114', *ANRW* ii. 7. 2 (1980), 954–1052
Sherk iii	R. K. Sherk, 'A Chronology of the Governors of Galatia, AD 114–285', *AJPhil.* 100 (1979), 166–75
Sherk, *RDGE*	R. K. Sherk, *Roman Documents from the Greek East: Senatus Consulta and Epistulae to the Age of Augustus* (1969)
SIG³	W. Dittenberger, *Sylloge Inscriptionum Graecarum*, 4 vols. (3rd edn. 1915–24)
SNG	*Sylloge Nummorum Graecorum*
SP	J. G. C. Anderson and F. Cumont, *Studia Pontica*, i–iii (1903–10)
Stähelin, *Galater*	F. Stähelin, *Geschichte der kleinasiatischen Galater* (2nd edn. 1907)
Sterrett, *EJ*	J. R. S. Sterrett, *An Epigraphical Journey in Asia Minor*, Papers of the American School of Classical Studies at Athens, ii (1883/4, pub. 1888)
Sterrett, *WE*	J. R. S. Sterrett, *The Wolfe Expedition to Asia Minor*, Papers of the American School of Classical Studies at Athens, iii (1884/5, pub. 1888)
Stud. clas.	*Studii clasice*
Subs. Hag.	*Subsidia Hagiographica*
Swoboda, *Denkmäler*	H. Swoboda, J. Keil, and F. Knoll, *Denkmäler aus Lykaonien, Pamphylien und Isaurien* (1935)
Syme, *RP*	R. Syme, *Roman Papers*, 7 vols. (1979–91)
TAD	*Türk Arkeoloji Dergisi*
TAM	*Tituli Asiae Minoris*
TAPA	*Transactions of the American Philological Association*

Tenth Congress	*Proceedings of the Tenth International Congress of Classical Archaeology, Ankara and Izmir 1973* (1978)
TIB	*Tabula Imperii Byzantini*, ii, F. Hild and M. Restle, *Kappadokien* (1981); iv, K. Belke and M. Restle, *Galatien und Lykaonien* (1984)
TTAED	*Türk Tarih, Arkeoloji ve Etnografya Dergisi*
Waelkens, *Türsteine*	M. Waelkens, *Die kleinasiatischen Türsteine* (1986)
Welles, *Royal Correspondence*	C. B. Welles, *Royal Correspondence in the Hellenistic Period: A Study in Greek Epigraphy* (1934)
Wenzel, *Steppe*	H. Wenzel, *Die Steppe als Lebensraum: Forschungen in Inneranatolien*, ii (1937)
Wenzel, *Sultandagh*	H. Wenzel, *Sultandagh und Akshehir Ova: Eine landeskundliche Untersuchung in Inneranatolien* (1932)
Will, *Histoire politique*	E. Will, *Histoire politique du Monde Hellénistique*, 2 vols. (2nd edn. 1979–82)
Wörrle, *Stadt und Fest*	M. Wörrle, *Stadt und Fest im kaiserzeitlichen Kleinasien: Studien zu einer agonistischen Stiftung aus Oinoanda* (1988)
YCS	*Yale Classical Studies*
ZfN	*Zeitschrift für Numismatik*
Ziegler	R. Ziegler, *Städtisches Prestige und kaiserliche Politik. Studien zum Festwesen in Ostkilikien im 2. und 3. Jht. n. Chr.* (1985)
Ziegler, *Münzen Kilikiens*	R. Ziegler, *Münzen Kilikiens aus kleineren deutschen Sammlungen* (1987)
ZPE	*Zeitschrift für Papyrologie und Epigraphik*
ZNW	*Zeitschrift für die neutestamentliche Wissenschaft*

1 Introduction

Anatolia, the vast region of mountains and upland plateaux which extend across the interior of modern Turkey from the Mediterranean and the Black Sea coasts to the Euphrates and to the Syrian desert, is a land mass whose importance may easily elude casual enquiry. In historical times it never contained a great city; it has produced no major writers or thinkers whose works have made a decisive contribution to our collective culture, either in the Western or in the Islamic tradition; and, apart from three widely separated periods—that of the Hittite empire in the second millenium BC; the eleventh to thirteenth centuries AD, when the Seljuks controlled a great kingdom from Konya; and modern times, when Ankara has become the capital of Turkey—Anatolia has not been an independent political unit but part of a larger political structure. Its history has thus often been ignored while attention has focused on the imperial capitals, under whose control it lay. The story of Anatolia, under Persia, Rome, or Constantinople, is indistinct and ill-articulated. Indeed, like many provinces of larger empires, it is, in one sense, a land without history.

The landscape itself has contributed to this perception of the region's character. In the words of its most persistent explorer, 'the plateau is like a continuation of central Asia, vast, immobile, monotonous.' That description will be instantly familiar to anyone who has taken the night train from the bustle and colour of Istanbul and woken in the early morning to look over the bare, treeless, and dun-coloured steppe between Eskişehir and Ankara. Cicero, who travelled along the highway across the southern part of the Anatolia in 51/50 BC, had the same experience; and there have been many like him for whom the land and its people offer a dry and dusty monotone, and who cannot wait, if not for the turmoil of Roman republican politics, at least for the culture and variety of the classical cities of the Aegean and Mediterranean coastlines. But for others, who have stopped to observe and absorb, the vast horizons and subtle variations of the Anatolian landscape exercise a powerful spell. 'The tone everywhere is melancholy, but not devoid of a certain charm

which, after a time, takes an even stronger hold of the mind than the bright varied scenery of the Greek world.'[1] Charm seems too weak a word with which to describe the fascination, almost the compulsion of a country which, like the desert of Arabia or the steppes of central Asia, has powerfully captured the imagination of travellers and explorers. It is not strange that this should be so, for in one geographical perception the plateau of Anatolia represents the westernmost outpost of central Asia, a continental land mass rudely thrust into Mediterranean surroundings.

A prehistorian has no need to be convinced of the significance of Anatolia in the development of the social organization and material culture of the Old World. It is one of the paradoxes of archaeology that the most dramatic example of quasi-urban development at the beginning of the Neolithic Age should be found in this area, where cities have rarely flourished, at Çatal Hüyük. The centres of the prehistoric civilizations of ancient Turkey throughout the Bronze Age remained bound to the central plateau, moving from Hacılar in the south-west, to Alaca Hüyük, and, in a final culmination, to Boğazköy, the capital of the Hittite empire, in the north-east. In the early first millenium BC the focus of power moved west to Gordium in Phrygia, the centre of one of the major cultures of the Iron Age.

After the collapse of the Phrygian kingdom at the end of the seventh century BC, if we discount eighty years of Galatian independence between about 270 and 189 BC, no permanent and autonomous political power established itself on the Anatolian plateau until the end of the eleventh century AD. Indeed for the 300 years between the end of the old Phrygian kingdom and the time of Alexander the Great, neither written sources nor archaeological discoveries have much to tell us about its history. Under Persian domination, and in the Hellenistic Age, it was traversed by two famous overland routes, the royal road from Sardis to Susa, and the *koine hodos*, the common highway, which

---

[1] Ramsay, *HGAM* 23, for both quotations.

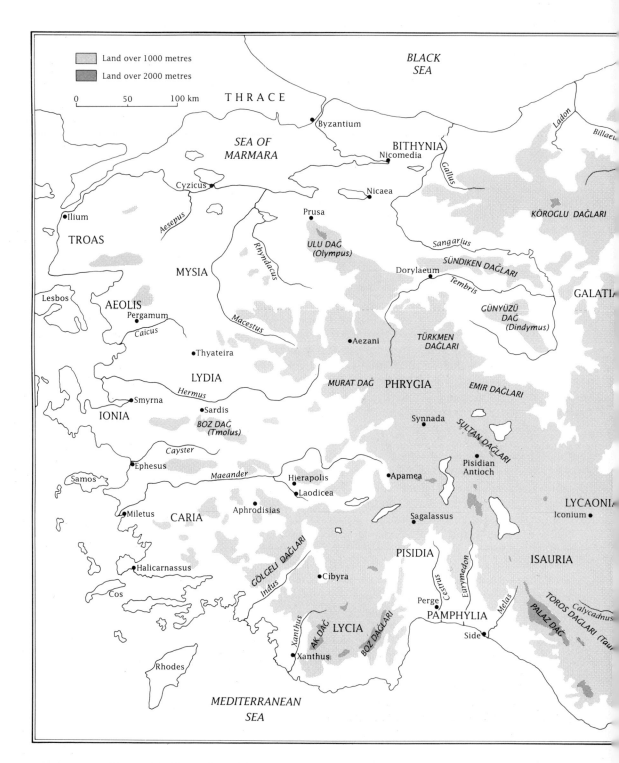

Map 1. Asia Minor: Physical features

KÜRE DAĞLARI

Sinope

Pompeiopolis

ILGAZ DAĞLARI (Olgassys)

Amnias

PAPHLAGONIA

Gangra

Halys

Amisus

PONTUS

Amaseia

Iris

Neocaesareia

Lycus

Nicopolis

Trapezus

ÇAKIL DAĞ

ARMENIA MINOR

Satala

YILDIZ DAĞ

Ancyra

Tavium

DEVECI DAĞ

Euphrates

MUNZUR DAĞLARI

ARMENIA

ÇALGAN DAĞ

Lake Tatta

Caesareia

ERCIYES DAĞ (Argaeus)

CAPPADOCIA

Melitene

BINBOGA DAĞLARI

MELENDIZ DAĞ

ALA DAĞ

COMMAGENE

KARACA DAĞ

Samosata

BOLKAR DAĞLARI (Taurus)

Pyramus

NUR DAĞLARI (Amanus)

Zeugma

MESOPOTAMIA

CILICIA TRACHEIA

Tarsus

CILICIA PEDIAS

Sarus

Aegeae

SYRIA

Seleuceia

Antioch

Fig. 1. The Anatolian Steppe. A view showing Karaca Dağ, south of Ankara and west of the modern town of Kulu. This probably belonged to the Proseilemmene, the region between north Galatia and Lycaonia which served as an extension to the original area of Celtic settlement. See Ch. 4 § vi nn. 115–18.

Fig. 2. The eroded hills and alluvial valley of the Demirözü Çay, an eastern affluent of the Sangarius, in the western part of north Galatia below the Byzantine castle of Taburoğlu Kale.

Anatolian landscapes

took a more southerly line from Ephesus to the river Euphrates and beyond.[2] The royal road linked the Persian court with its western satrapies, and the *koine hodos* was famous as an artery of trade, but neither couriers nor merchants will have spared much time for the empty expanses which they had to cross in the course of their business.

From the early third century BC the history of Anatolia begins to acquire more substance. From then until the beginning of the seventh century AD, the span of time covered by this study, historical documentation and archaeological evidence can be used to provide a far fuller account of the region, set against the background, first of the history of the Hellenistic kings who inherited the domains of Alexander the Great, and then, above all, of Rome and her empire. Indeed the shadow of imperial domination, whether cast from Rome or from Constantinople, dominated Anatolia's history for the best part of a millenium, and provided the essential—if changing—backdrop against which Anatolia's political and social development must be interpreted. But the relationship between a ruling power and its subject territories has never been one-sided. An empire without provinces is no empire, and while Rome, with her possessions in the western as well as the eastern Mediterranean, would have been a major power without Asia Minor, it is arguable whether the same could be said at an earlier period of Persia, still less afterwards of Byzantium and the Ottoman empire. All of Asia Minor's political masters drew constantly on its resources of manpower and rural economic strength. In the pre-industrial age Anatolia was the chief power house of the Levant.

A hundred years ago it seemed impossible even to Mommsen to make sense of the history of Asia Minor as a whole.[3] Anatolia duly received relatively scanty and superficial treatment in the two classic studies of Rome's provinces, Mommsen's own *The Provinces of the Roman Empire* (1886; English trans. 1909), and Rostovtzeff's *Social and Economic History of the Roman Empire* (1st edn. 1926). The yawning gap was handsomely filled with two formidable studies by American historians, T. R. S. Broughton's *Roman Asia Minor* (1938), and D. Magie's *Roman Rule in Asia Minor* (1950). Both drew together a prodigious quantity of material, but deliberately limited their historical perspectives, in the first case to the economic conditions of Rome's provinces in Asia Minor, and in the second to the spread of Roman power, influence, and administrative practices, with their direct and indirect consequences for the region's development.

Broughton and Magie took full account of the flood of new information concerning Anatolian history which had become available since Mommsen's day, above all the thousands of inscriptions discovered between around 1880 and 1914. Neither, however, could fully reflect the transformation of our understanding of the history and culture of Asia Minor which was due to the efforts of Louis Robert. Between the 1920s and the 1980s Robert devoted the best part of his genius and his scholarly energies, which were hardly inferior even to Mommsen's, to the study of Asia Minor. The historical documentation of the region in the Graeco-Roman period, in particular the epigraphic record, has always been remarkable for its richness and variety. Robert's achievement was to make sense of and realize the potential of this material, to a degree that would have been unimaginable to a historian of an earlier generation. What Robert has done for the study of ancient history can be fruitfully compared with the contribution of his contemporary, Fernand Braudel, to the study of early modern Europe. In all of Robert's enormous *œuvre* geography and the written record, 'la terre et le papier', are woven seamlessly into a single historical fabric. Just as Braudel's *Mediterranean* is an attempt to realize not the partial but the total history of the Mediterranean world of the sixteenth century, so Robert's life work, and indeed the studies of many who have been inspired and guided by his example, have transformed our knowledge of Asia Minor to such a degree, that so far from being the region which defied even Mommsen's historical ambitions, it is now perhaps the one part of the ancient world where the writing of a total history can at least be envisaged as a possibility. The richness of the material evidence, and the astonishing acumen and empathy of Robert's countless studies, offer a challenge to the historian to produce a book which measures up to the diversity, if not to the totality, of Anatolia's past.

In an attempt to bring some order to the complex variety of the subject, I have provided these volumes with three central themes, marked off from one another both by chronology and by the nature of their subject matter. The first part takes as its subject the invasion and the settlement of the Celts, who occupied the central Anatolian plateau in the second quarter of the third century BC, and remained the dominant ethnic

[2] See Herodotus 5. 52–3; Strabo 14. 2. 29, 663. There is room for argument about the course of both, especially the former. For discussion and references see Levick, *Roman Colonies*, 10–13.

[3] 'Ich möchte nicht gerne in diesen kleinasiatischen Dingen, die doch wenig mehr sind als der Holzwurm im Baum, viel weiter gehen; dem dummen Aristides bin ich absichtlich aus dem Wege gegangen . . . und vor allen Dingen: Ich verstehe davon zu wenig, und möchte möglichst wenig das übernehmen, was ich nur nachsprechen würde. Tarsos zum Beispiel — was soll ich da machen?', letter of Mommsen to Wilamowitz, cited by Ziegler, 11–12 n. 5 from J. Malitz, *Quaderni di Storia*, 17 (1983), 139.

group there at least until the end of the first century BC. The appearance of these Celtic tribes, the Galatians, and their impact on the cities of the Greek East, provides one of the most important and best-documented episodes in the great expansion and migration of Celtic peoples from central Europe between the fifth and third centuries BC. The account contains two substantial narrative chapters. Chapter 2 is concerned with the relationship, always uneasy and often violent, between the newcomers and the cities and indigenous peoples of Asia Minor; Chapter 3 documents their role during the first century BC, as Rome's principal allies at a period when Roman influence, or outright control, was extended over much of Anatolia for the first time. The final chapter of this first part is an attempt to sketch out an ethnography of these eastern Celts, and to show that although they were partially assimilated into the culture of Hellenized Asia Minor, they retained many of the distinctive characteristics of their kinsfolk in western Europe.

Under the first emperor Augustus, most of Anatolia was annexed to the Roman empire. Although Roman influence was already strongly marked in the region, provincial status in the new framework of the Roman principate was decisive in shaping the history and organization of Anatolia for the next three centuries. The chapters of the second part of the book are designed to identify, illuminate, and as far as possible explain the crucial changes which the region underwent under Roman rule. Obviously these included a new administrative structure and a permanent, well-defined military presence. More important, and more characteristic still, was the emergence for the first time of a network of cities in central Asia Minor, and the accompanying growth of urban institutions. With these came radical changes in the pattern of land-ownership and land exploitation, and the systematic integration of the region into the social and economic organization of the Roman empire.

The urban structure of the empire underwent a profound crisis in the third century, plain in Asia Minor as elsewhere, which led to a sharp decline in the visible prosperity and to radical changes in the organization of all but the largest cities. However, behind the appearance of disruption there are strong indications of continuity. Much that was important in the provincial life of the high Roman empire was transmitted over the third century crisis into the world of late Antiquity, first by an uninterrupted classical culture, and then, more crucially, by the resilience of rural institutions and the agricultural economy. The spectacular flowering of urban life between the first and third centuries AD should not be allowed to hide the fact that this had been built on vastly expanded and improved agricultural production, in the villages and on landed estates. The countryside, which appears to have been far less affected by the adverse conditions of the third century than the cities, remained the key to economic prosperity, and to imperial recovery in the fourth century.

The third part of the study is principally concerned with the culture of the late Roman and early Byzantine period from the third to the seventh century AD. The overriding theme is the emergence and rise of Christianity, which had been introduced to Anatolia by St Paul within a generation of the Crucifixion. To take this perspective does not entail losing sight of wider issues of social and political history. For one thing, the overwhelming majority of sources for this later period are, in one way or another, connected with the Church: ecclesiastical histories, the lives of saints, or the letters and sermons of bishops, which often touch on matters beyond the doctrinal or purely theological concerns of the Church. For another, and much more significantly, the lives of both communities and individuals were increasingly dominated by the Church, to the extent that it became not only the chief, but almost the only source of political power in a regional context, and provided by far the most important structures and principles according to which society was organized. With the decline of the autonomous civic life of the imperial period, the role of bishops and other church leaders became all-important, both in exercising authority locally over their congregations, and in establishing relationships between their communities and the emperors, who were now based in Constantinople.

The organization of the hierarchy of the early Church reflected the administrative structure of the Roman empire; authority was vested in bishops, who resided in the cities. The influence of a bishop was confined by the status and standing of his city. Even during the fourth century a bishop was hard-pressed to exercise control or moral authority over rural society, and conditions favoured the emergence of an independent, less political Christian tradition, whose moral strength was derived from conspicuous asceticism. The development of the monastic movement in Asia Minor, as elsewhere, reflected and was abetted by the decline of civic institutions.

The decline of the cities led to a renewed emphasis on the rural communities, and it is no coincidence that evidence from late antiquity brings us closer to the realities of rural life in Anatolia than almost any evidence that has survived from the Hellenistic or Roman periods. The chief resource of Anatolia has always been its land, which sustained the two principal occupations of the peasant population, agriculture and stock-raising. Fittingly, therefore, the work can end by analysing an account of the mid-seventh-century *Life of St Theodore of Sykeon*, which is richer in details about rural life, agricultural production, and village organization than any other single source for Anatolia in Antiquity. Theodore's *Life* also provides by far the most explicit illustrations of the nature of popular Christian belief and the power-structure of Christian society in an age where the authority of the bishops had greatly diminished.

Within a few years of the death of Theodore in AD 613 the Persians, under Chosroes, invaded Anatolia. According to one interpretation that invasion, and the Byzantine response to it, brought to an end the whole classical period of Graeco-Roman Antiquity in Asia Minor.[4] The truth of this theory is subject to debate, and it is doubtless facile and arbitrary to divide up the seamless fabric of history by eras and periods, but the Persian invasions of the early seventh century AD provide a stopping point that is more convenient and convincing than most. They herald, for Anatolia at least, a genuine Dark Age. During the rest of the seventh and eighth centuries almost the entire history of central Asia Minor remains impenetrably obscure.

The geographical scope of the book requires further definition. In Antiquity Anatolia was clearly differentiated from the Mediterranean and Aegean coasts. The Ionians of the fifth century BC looked on Anatolia as 'up-country', τὰ ἄνω τῆς Ἰωνίης χωρία, and the same terminology was used during the Roman empire to describe the interior parts of western Asia Minor by Luke in the Acts of the Apostles; and by a native of the region, Aelius Aristides, in his *Sacred Tales*.[5] Nevertheless, despite the obvious and recognized differences between the coastlands and the interior, it is virtually impossible to set a dividing line between the two, and thus establish a clear cut-off point for the material which has been included and studied. Neither administrative nor geographical boundaries will serve adequately.

The boundaries of Roman provinces have often been used to define areas of regional study in the ancient world. That is desirable where Roman provinces coincided with existing cultural or economic units, and particularly where the main object of investigation is the impact of a particular pattern of Roman administration on the region in question. It is inappropriate in this case, both because the Roman division of Asia Minor into provinces notoriously cut across cultural and other pre-existing boundaries (see below, Ch. 11 §II), and because the book as a whole is not

intended, except briefly in Chapter 5 and incidentally elsewhere, to illuminate the structure and pattern of Roman administration. Furthermore, in Asia Minor more than in any other part of the empire, provincial boundaries were frequently altered. This is true both for the late republic, when Roman provinces were acquired haphazardly in the course of war and diplomacy, and were in any case often better defined as areas of operations than as geographically distinct regions with fixed frontiers;[6] and more unusually for the imperial period, when provincial boundaries elsewhere in the empire usually remained stable, at least until the radical reorganizations of the third and fourth centuries AD. In Anatolia, however, except for the proconsular province of Asia which remained unaltered from the time of Augustus to around 250 AD, boundaries were frequently redrawn. I have attempted in Vol. II, Appendix 1 to establish the chronology and extent of these many changes, but have made no systematic attempt to explain them. The sources are largely silent about the reasons for these alterations, which may be sought in administrative practice, in the overall thrust of Roman foreign policy, or in the vagaries of local history.[7] Similarly, I have attempted no more than a bare record of the changing provincial boundaries of the late empire, until the time of Justinian, in Vol. II, Appendix 2. Although the sources preserve important information about the division of Cappadocia in AD 371 (see Vol. II, Ch. 17 §V at n. 196; App. 2 at n. 55), and for the new arrangements introduced by Justinian in AD 535 for Pontus, Paphlagonia, Cappadocia, Armenia, Isauria, Lycaonia, and Pisidia,[8] as a rule specific contemporary evidence about the reasons for these changes is as sparse as in the earlier period.

Natural boundaries have more permanence than administrative frontiers, and the basic geography of inland Anatolia changed little throughout Antiquity. There was no drastic geomorphological change in the interior, as occurred along the west and south coasts of Turkey, where the aggradation of river silt and changes in the sea level radically altered the fortunes of some coastal cities. As far as the limited evidence allows us to judge, the vegetation cover of the interior also remained broadly similar from the early Hellenistic

[4] C. Foss, 'The Persians in Asia Minor and the End of Antiquity', *English Historical Review*, 90 (1975), 721–47.

[5] Herodotus 1. 142; Acts 19: 1; Aelius Aristides, 50 (*Sacred Tales* 4), 12. 428 K; cf. also Appian, *Syr.* 12, 47.

[6] A. W. Lintott, *G&R* 28 (1981), 53–67 is clear and to the point. For the principle in Asia Minor, see A. N. Sherwin-White's admirable study, 'Rome, Pamphylia and Cilicia', *JRS* 66 (1976), 1–14.

[7] B. Rémy, *L'Évolution administrative de l'Anatolie aux trois premières siècles de notre ère* (1986) is a recent essay in interpretation. The results are not very revealing.

[8] Justinian, *Novellae*, 24 (Pisidia), 25 (Lycaonia), 27 (Isauria), 28 (Helenopontus), 29 (Paphlagonia), 30 (Cappadocia), 31 (Armenia).

Fig. 3. North-East Galatia. A Roman tomb cover in the shape of a lion stands guard over the stony bed of a tributary of the Halys north of Kalecik (ancient Malos). Dry in the summer and autumn, it can turn into a torrential flood after winter snow-melt and heavy spring rain. The bare hills and mountains in the background separated the Halys basin from Ancyra. For the topography, see S. Mitchell, *AS* 32 (1982), 95–100.

Fig. 4. Eastern Phrygia. The site of Orcistus. Ruins of an ancient building in the foreground. Only the trees around the village interrupt the monotony of the flat landscape of the upper Sangarius basin.

Anatolian landscapes

period until the end of Antiquity. Doubtless intensive agricultural exploitation and widespread timber cutting in the Roman imperial period brought previously untilled land under cultivation (see below, Chs. 10 §11 and 14 §111), and eroded the forest cover in specific locations, but not to the extent of fundamentally altering the landscape's appearance. The central Anatolian plateau was as treeless in Antiquity as it is today (Ch. 10 §1); despite the heavy exploitation of the timber forests of Bithynia, Paphlagonia, and Pontus in the north;[9] Mysia in the north-west;[10] and Lycia and Cilicia in the south,[11] the tree cover was not destroyed or significantly reduced.

Coastland and interior were separated not by clear divisions but by gradual zones of transition. In the north and south, it is true, the Pontic mountain chains and the Taurus range present formidable barriers between the sea and the central plateau, but to the east and west the limits cannot be so simply drawn. The land rises gradually from the Aegean in the west. The boundary between the Mediterranean zone and that of the continental interior is irregular since the low-lying basins of the major rivers, the Caicus, Hermus, Cayster, and Maeander, allow a Mediterranean style of cultivation far into the interior, while the hilly country that separates them brings the world of inner Anatolia close to the coast. Lydia, Mysia, and Caria occupy transitional geographical zones between the coastlands and the higher plains of Phrygia, many of which lie close to 1,000 metres above sea level. To the east, Galatia and Lycaonia form a basin in the centre of the peninsula at a slightly lower median altitude, whose terrain is for the most part flatter than that of Phrygia. This extends as far as the river Halys, where the country begins to climb again, through Pontus and Cappadocia, as far as the next major line of demarcation, the upper valley of the river Euphrates. Any line drawn across the unfolding interior of Turkey, as it rises in gradual steps from the west to the highlands beyond the Euphrates, is necessarily an arbitrary one.[12]

Culture and human settlement offer a third useful criterion by which to define the interior of Anatolia. The Phrygians, Mysians, Lydians, and other native peoples of the interior are distinguishable from one another (though often with difficulty), and can themselves be subdivided into smaller ethnic or tribal units. However, they had important features in common which set them apart in turn from the peoples of the Pontic mountain chains in the north and of the Taurus mountains in the south: settlement in agricultural villages (see below, Ch. 11 §§111–IV), linguistic similarities which are especially clear in the onomastic evidence (Ch. 11 §11), and a shared religious culture (Chs. 11 § v and Vol. II, Ch. 16 §§1–III). One negative cultural criterion is even more pronounced. Little of the interior of Anatolia was Hellenized before the emergence of Roman rule in the late Hellenistic and early imperial period. Apart from a handful of exceptional communities founded by Hellenistic rulers, which were designed to protect their territory in western Asia Minor or to establish the land route between the Aegean and Syria along the valleys of the Maeander and the Lycus and then across the northern edge of Pisidia, there were virtually no Greek cities in Phrygia, Lydia, Galatia, Lycaonia, or further east. This cultural criterion offers a valuable distinction between the world of inner Anatolia and, for instance, the highland communities of Pisidia, whose inhabitants, despite their reputation for barbarian intransigence, had been profoundly Hellenized during the third and second centuries BC.[13] Although central Anatolia was part of Alexander's empire, and was claimed as territory by his Hellenistic successors, it was in no sense integrated into the classical Greek world. The adventurous Macedonian settlers, who made a home on the fringes of the central plateau in the late fourth and third century BC, occupied isolated oases in what, for a Greek, was a cultural desert (see below, Ch. 7 §11). It is no wonder that the Seleucids and the Attalids strove to confine the Galatian invaders, whom they represented as the archetypal enemies of Greek civilization and culture (Ch. 2 §III), in the centre of Anatolia around Ancyra.

[9] L. Robert, *A travers l'Asie Mineure* (1980), 51–2, 67–76, 176–86, and index s.v. forêts.
[10] L. Robert, *BCH* 102 (1978), 443–52 = *Documents*, 139–48.
[11] Russell Meiggs, *Trees and Timber in the Ancient Mediterranean World* (1982), 392–4. He too emphasizes that most of the deforestation of Anatolia has occurred during the last 100 years.
[12] Two handbooks on the geography of Turkey may be treated as standard: *Geographical Handbook Series: Turkey*, Naval Intelligence Division, 2 vols. (1942–3); W.-D. Hütteroth, *Die Türkei* (1982). It is worth recalling an emblematic paragraph of W. M. Ramsay: 'If geography be regarded as the study of the influence which the physical features and situation of a country exert on the people who live in it, then in no country can geography be studied better than in Asia Minor. The

physical features of the country are strongly marked; its situation is peculiar and unique; its history can be observed over a long series of centuries; and, amid its infinite variety there is always a strongly marked unity, with certain clear principles of evolution, standing in obvious relation to the geographical surroundings', in 'Asia Minor: the Country and its Religion', *Luke the Physician and other studies in the History of Religion* (1908), 105.
[13] S. Mitchell, 'The Hellenization of Pisidia', *Mediterranean Archaeology* (Sydney), 4 (1991), 1–41, and a revised version of this study, 'Hellenismus in Pisidien', *Asia-Minor-Studien* (Münster), 5 (1992), 1–27.

Fig. 5. Pontus. The valley of the Lycus (Yeşil Irmak = Green River) looking east from the acropolis of Amaseia.

Fig. 6. The Milyas. A view of the Bozova, north of modern Korkuteli, which was part of the territory of the Milyadeis. The villages at the foot of the hills which surround the valley, today ringed with trees (especially poplar), preserve the names of the small ancient cities of Sibidunda (Zivint), Andeda (Andya), and Pogla (Fuğla). The Roman colonists of Comama and wealthy inhabitants of the Pamphylian cities owned parts of this fertile land in Antiquity.

Landscapes in Pontus and the Milyas

The character of Anatolia under Roman rule, and the consequences of integrating the region into the Roman empire, are not best studied by limiting oneself to a single province, even to one which covered as broad an area as Galatia-Cappadocia in the time of Trajan. In Part II, therefore, I have largely ignored Roman provincial boundaries and have extended coverage to any area of the interior where evidence survives to illustrate important themes in the region's development between the principate of Augustus and the third century AD. The early stages of urbanization can be followed clearly in Galatia, Lycaonia, and Pontus, where towns were virtually unknown before the introduction of Roman rule, and where it was essential to create a network of cities with dependent territories in order that the existing machinery of Roman administration could function at all (Ch. 7). The imperial cult, whose overall significance in the development of Roman Asia Minor has been the subject of an outstanding recent study,[14] had a key role to play as a vehicle for urbanization in these previously uncivilized regions (Ch. 8). On the other hand the later development of a provincial urban culture in Anatolia can only be studied in cities where inscriptions, coins, and monumental remains are more abundant, and it is necessary to look to Bithynia, Phrygia, and to the mountainous zones of the south, to form a sharper impression of city life during the heyday of the second and third centuries AD (Ch. 12).

The foundation of cities, which flourished only for a relatively brief period in the long evolution of Anatolian history, modified but did not supersede the indigenous pattern of settlement which has, in many respects, persisted until the present day. Asia Minor as a whole, and in particular the interior, remained a land of villages, many of which belonged to large landed estates. The core of any general investigation of Asia Minor must be a study of the countryside. Since there have been virtually no archaeological surveys or excavations devoted to rural settlements between the Hellenistic and Byzantine periods, attention must be focused on the country regions which have produced large numbers of gravestones, votive steles, and other inscriptions; notably Phrygia, a huge area which spanned the provincial boundary dividing Asia from Galatia; and Lydia (Ch. 11). The evidence for landed estates, their proprietors and administrative personnel, which were another key feature of Roman domination, may be well studied in the central Anatolian plateau. The results of this investigation can be controlled, and interesting differences observed, by surveying the

plentiful evidence which also exists in Phrygia, Bithynia, and northern Lydia (Ch. 10).

Roman rule was enforced, where necessary, by a military presence. In the reign of Augustus this was concentrated in and around the Pisidian section of the Taurus, whose tribesmen and cities had successfully resisted all attempts by Hellenistic kings to control them, and who therefore offered a constant threat not only to neighbouring regions, but also to the land routes running between western Asia Minor, the south coast, and Syria. The pacification of the Taurus was essential if Anatolia was to be integrated successfully into the empire. Military activity, the foundation of a network of colonies of veteran soldiers, and the construction of a major highway, the *via Sebaste*, offer a paradigm example of Roman methods of subduing mountainous zones (Ch. 6). Thereafter the focus of military attention moved to the upper Euphrates frontier, where permanent garrisons were stationed from the early years of Vespasian. The history of this fortified frontier lies beyond the scope of this study, but its impact on the remainder of the Anatolian hinterland was profound. Roads, regular movements of supplies and troops, military contingents stationed at key points in the communications network, recruitment for legions and for auxiliary contingents, and the resettlement of veterans, not in colonies but *viritim* in their former communities or near the post where they had served, were important ways in which the military presence on the Euphrates directly affected the inhabitants of central Asia Minor. The military influence is naturally most pronounced in areas which lay on the direct routes to the frontier but it is necessary to cast the net wide to take in the evidence for smaller military units, which were stationed elsewhere in Anatolia, especially in mountain regions (Ch. 9).

Asia Minor in the later first and second centuries AD was not primarily controlled by demonstrations of military force, and soldiers were rarely to be seen in most of the cities of the interior and in the countryside off the main roads. This state of affairs altered drastically at the beginning of the third century, when military movements and the consequences of military deployment made a much wider impact on civilian life. In order to understand the changes of this period it is necessary to range over the whole peninsula, taking in the external threats from Goths in the north and north-east, and from the Sassanians in the south-east, which prompted not only very intensive troop movements along the main military axis which linked the Balkans with Syria, but also self-defence measures in cities across the whole of Asia Minor (Ch. 13).

In assessing the impact of Roman rule on Anatolia the focus has to move from one area to another according to the subject and period under scrutiny. The

---

[14] S. R. F. Price, *Rituals and Power: The Roman Imperial Cult in Asia Minor* (1984).

same remains true in tracing the rise of Christianity and the gradual recession of traditional forms of pagan worship. The Acts of the Apostles and Paul's Epistle to the Galatians throw an intense spotlight on a very restricted area at a narrowly defined period, the south Galatian communities, above all Pisidian Antioch, where Paul preached in the middle of the first century AD (Vol. II, Ch. 15). Christianity did not establish a firm hold on large numbers of the population before the third century AD. The distribution of evidence requires that attention is transferred to Lydia and Phrygia, whose inscriptions give the best picture of an intelligible pattern of pagan worship, and to Phrygia alone for the emergence of powerful Jewish and Christian communities, which were well established by AD 250 both in the cities and also in many villages of this predominantly rural environment. Anatolian pagan beliefs, which were accompanied by a severe moral code, provided soil where Judaism and Christianity readily took root (Ch. 16).

From the fourth century onwards, attention again shifts eastwards, above all to Cappadocia, where the enormous literature produced by the three great Fathers of the Cappadocian Church makes it possible to study in detail what the conversion of a whole Anatolian region to Christianity meant for the structure, organization, and practices of society. The picture of a new Orthodox Christian world in Cappadocia invites comparison with contemporary developments in Galatia, where paganism was more deeply entrenched, particularly among intellectual circles at Ancyra; and in Phrygia and Lycaonia, where the traditional morality of the rural population provided a solid foundation for the development of the rigorist Novatian Church (Ch. 17).

After the fourth century the evidence becomes too fragmented for these regional differences to be properly observed. The growth of monasticism and ascetic practices appears to have had an important part to play in the transformation of Christian society in the fifth and sixth centuries, but it is easier to form hypotheses about these developments than to test their general validity (Ch. 18). The most revealing fifth-century source for the beliefs and behaviour of a Christian ascetic community, the *Life and Miracles of St Thecla*, illuminates the world of the southern city of Seleuceia on the Calycadnus and its neighbourhood, a region which looked more to Syria and to the East than to Anatolia north of the Taurus.[15] The balance cannot be

redressed until the late sixth and early seventh century, when the *Life of Theodore of Sykeon* draws attention once more to the north-west corner of the central Anatolian plateau, an area of Galatia which enjoyed close relations with Nicomedia in Bithynia and with the capital Constantinople (Ch. 19).

The decision to range widely across the landscape of Anatolia in the second and third parts of this book, therefore, has been determined in large part by the survival of evidence which can throw light on the dominant themes of Anatolian history in the first seven centuries AD. I hope that what has been lost in rejecting a precise geographical definition is compensated by the wider overall view that this approach entails.

As those who have worked on the study of Asia Minor well know, the historical material, in the form of literary texts, inscriptions, locally minted coins, and archaeological remains, is extraordinarily abundant but often not easily accessible. The dispersion of the evidence has discouraged attempts at historical synthesis. It need hardly be said that much of the published work on Asia Minor is of extraordinarily high interest and quality, but it has concentrated on the elucidation of specific topics, and especially on explaining the significance of particular inscriptions and other documents. It is difficult for those not already familiar with this detailed evidence to make headway in a world of highly specialized study. In this book, I have cited a very wide range of evidence, drawn from this specialized work, in order to throw light on the broader problems of Anatolia's history. Sometimes this accumulation of material makes clarity of exposition difficult to attain, but I have generally preferred to retain rather than excise material for two reasons. Firstly, direct citation or summary allusion to the particulars of the evidence provides far more immediate access to the world of ancient Anatolia than a more hypothetical reconstruction of social and historical developments. Secondly, I have been conscious of the need to provide those interested in the subject with a map to this historical terrain, on which they will be able to identify as many landmarks as possible. I anticipate that readers may be interested not only in the overall exposition of the subject matter, but also in the abundant brief allusions to items in the historical record, to which they may attach a particular significance. The footnotes at these points draw attention to published discussions which take the investigation further than is possible in a general study. Since the geographical range of the work is so wide, and the topography both of ancient Anatolia and of modern Turkey is unfamiliar to many, I have also used maps as generously as possible to make the subject more accessible and intelligible.

---

[15] G. Dagron, *Vie et miracles de Sainte Thècle, Subs. Hag.* 62 (1978), esp. 109–12.

I

The Celts in Anatolia

Qui sint Galatae, vel quo et unde transierint. Utrum indigenas eos fuderit, an advenas quam nunc incolunt terra susceperit; et utrum linguam connubio perdiderint, an et novam didicerint et non amiserint suam.

Jerome, *Comm. in ep. ad Galatas* II.1 (*PL* 26. 379)

1. *Invasion*

In 280 BC[1] a mass of migrating Celtic peoples invaded Macedonia. By arrangement between the leaders, one group led by Kerethrios made for the Thracians and the Triballi in the east; a second under Brennos and Akichorios invaded Paeonia; and a third under Bolgios picked the Macedonians and Illyrians, attacking and indeed killing Ptolemy, called Keraunos, who had recently acquired the kingship of Macedon.[2] This was not the first direct contact between Celts and the Greek world of the eastern Mediterranean; Celtic mercenaries had been seen in Greece in 369/8 BC when they were sent by Dionysius I of Syracuse to help his Spartan allies in the Peloponnese;[3] and Illyrian Celts had sent embassies to Alexander the Great, on the banks of the Danube and even at Babylon on the Euphrates.[4] But Alexander's own Macedonian kingdom, while still strong, served as a buffer against the migrating hordes which had been pushing eastwards from their homelands in the upper Rhine and Danube basins for more than a century, and kept them away from the Aegean.[5] When the defences were lowered they took full advantage of a moment of weakness: in 281 BC Seleucus I had defeated Lysimachus the master of Macedon at the battle of Kurupedion in Lydia, only

to be murdered himself within a year by Ptolemy Keraunos. Macedon itself was disorganized, the cities of Greece were enfeebled by the wars of Alexander's successors,[6] and neither could put up an effective defence against the invaders.

Whatever the misfortunes and disasters which the Greek world certainly suffered from the enemy in their midst, the invasions produced at least one favourable outcome for the historian. Now, for the first time, the Celtic movements were documented in a literate tradition which throws an immense amount of light not only on the immediate confrontation, but on the character of the Celtic migrations as a whole. Within ten years the Celts left an indelible mark, both in the history of Macedonia, Greece, and Asia Minor, and in the local legends and traditions of the cities and communities which lay in their path.

The most famous of their exploits, which left extensive traces in the literary record but which had the least long-term effect, was the invasion of Greece, led by the chieftain Brennos, and the unsuccessful attack on the sanctuary of Apollo at Delphi.[7] Reputedly no Celt escaped alive from the attempt,[8] but others had been posted as a rearguard to hold Macedonia,[9] or had broken away from Brennos' leadership and were operating independently.[10] The group led by Bolgios into eastern Thrace eventually suffered defeat at the hands of Antigonus Gonatas at Lysimacheia in the Thracian Chersonese,[11] a victory which signalled the return of a strong ruler to Macedonia and drove

---

[1] For the date see F. W. Walbank, *Commentary on Polybius* (1957), i. 49–50 on Polybius 1. 4. 5; Nachtergael, *Galates*, 129–37 argues that the death of Ptolemy Keraunos belongs in February 279, as does H. Heinen, *Untersuchungen zur hellenistischen Geschichte des 3. Jht. v. Chr.* (1972), 55.

[2] Pausanias, 10. 19. 4.

[3] Xenophon, *Hell.* 7. 1. 20–3, 28–31; Diodorus, 15. 70. 1.

[4] Arrian, 1. 4. 6–8; 7. 15. 4.

[5] For this Celtic expansion see H. Hubert, *Les Celtes dans l'époque de la Tène et la civilisation celtique*[2] (1950), 1–170, esp. 40–81; Nachtergael, *Galates*, 3–14 with ample bibliography. Compare the observation made by Quintus Flamininus to the Aetolians, that Macedonia was the shield of Greece, Polybius, 18. 37. 9; Livy, 33. 12. 10. For a very speculative reconstruction of an earlier Celtic presence in Anatolia, see B. Sergent, 'Les Premiers Celtes d'Anatolie', *REA* 90 (1988), 329–58. The arguments are based almost entirely on onomastic evidence, and find no support in the archaeological or historical record.

[6] Pausanias, 1. 4. 1–2.

[7] Nachtergael, *Galates*, *passim*.

[8] Pausanias, 10. 23. 8; Justin, *Epit.* 25. 1–2. Diodorus, 22. 9 says that the survivors of Brennos' expedition rallied in Macedonia, eventually to suffer defeat at the battle of Lysimacheia. These may simply have been the men left behind by Brennos. Pausanias, 1. 4. 5 implies that the survivors of the attack on Delphi crossed to Asia, but no store can be placed by this telescoped account.

[9] Justin, *Epit.* 25. 1–2.

[10] Livy, 38. 16. 2.

[11] Pompeius Trogus, *Prol.* 25; Justin, *Epit.* 25. 1–2; Diogenes Laertius, 2. 141–2; *SIG*[3] 401 (Athens). For the site see Robert, *Hellenica* x, 268 n. 2.

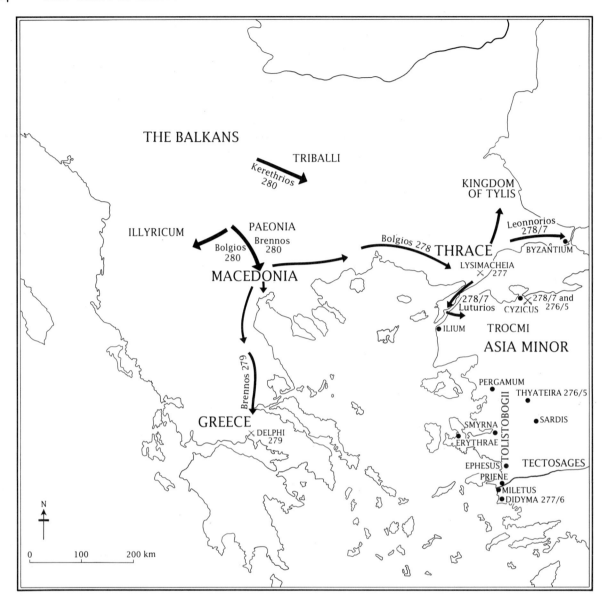

Map 2. The Galatian invasions of Greece and Asia Minor

the Celts northwards, where under the leadership of Kommontorios they formed the kingdom of Tylis on the west shore of the Black Sea north of Byzantium.[12]

The detailed sequence of events in Greece, Thrace, and Macedonia between 280 and 278 is extremely difficult to unravel: the Celts' own movements could be wayward and unpredictable, and certainly hard for an observer to assess at the time or in retrospect; their

Greek opponents had every reason to exaggerate their successes and distort the record of what had taken place; but the overall impression given by the more reliable sources is not likely to be seriously misleading. They imply a huge number of migrating peoples, even as many as 300,000 in the first instance,[13] and a total of 150,000 still poised on the northern frontiers of Greece.[14] These figures are high but not necessarily far

[12] Pompeius Trogus, *Prol.* 25; Polybius, 4. 46; 8. 22. For the location of the kingdom see G. Mihailov, *Athenaeum*, 49 (1961), 33 ff., esp. 39–41. It is not clear that the Celts under Kommontorios were the survivors of Lysimacheia, and it is likely, in any case, that they included other Celtic groups now excluded by Antigonus from Macedonia.

[13] Justin, *Epit.* 24. 4. 1–7 (the beginning of the migration); Suda s.v. Galatia.
[14] Pausanias 10. 19. 6 specifies 152,000 infantry and 20,400 cavalry, but since two mounted grooms accompanied each horseman this last figure should be reckoned at 61,200; Justin, *Epit.* 25. 1 gives 150,000 infantry and 15,000 cavalry;

from the truth if they are taken as an assessment of the total Celtic manpower. The actual numbers connected with specific battles or exploits, representing their effective fighting forces, are much lower: 15,000 infantry and 3,000 cavalry left behind by Brennos in Macedonia, 20,000 men transported to Asia Minor by Nicomedes of Bithynia,[15] and a force of 9,000 Celts hired by Antigonus Gonatas after Lysimacheia to secure victory over the Macedonian incumbent Antipater Etesias.[16] The Greek world was clearly facing a whole nation on the move. According to Diodorus, the Celts were accompanied by 2,000 baggage waggons, a host of provisioners, and many merchants; and an anecdote told by Polyaenus about Antigonus' mercenaries reveals them claiming pay not simply for the warriors but for the unarmed men and their wives and children as well.[17] The Gauls who crossed into Asia Minor included 10,000 non-combatants and sixty years later, when Attalus I imported a further tribe of Celtic mercenaries over the Hellespont, they too were accompanied by their families and a baggage train.[18]

Their leaders were aristocratic chieftains, united in a loose federation, Kambaules, Kerethrios, Akichorios, Bolgios,[19] Kiderios,[20] Kommontorios,[21] Leonnorios, and Luturios,[22] who co-operated with one another only when it was in their obvious interest to do so. Their aims were various. Land on which to settle may have been the ultimate goal but was not necessarily a priority; money or booty was a more immediate enticement,[23] and could be acquired in various ways—by hiring out their services as mercenaries,[24] by demanding protection money from rulers or cities whose land they were in a position to ravage,[25] by attacking wealthy settlements or sanctuaries,[26] and simply by plundering the countryside.[27]

The record of the Celtic invasion of Greece anticipates their more widespread activities in Asia Minor. Since our authorities for the crossing into Asia view the event from an Anatolian point of view, it is not simple to dovetail their accounts into the record of Celtic activity in Europe. Justin places it after the battle of Lysimacheia,[28] but this cannot be squared with the more detailed versions. According to Livy, two bands of Celts under Leonnorios and Luturios had made their way into Thrace, conducting themselves in familiar fashion by fighting those who resisted and by selling protection to those who were prepared to pay. They occupied the shore of the Propontis, captured Lysimacheia by a trick, and were stationed in force in the Thracian Chersonese. Here they negotiated with Antipater, decribed as being in charge of the coast, about crossing to Asia. When a dispute arose between the two chieftains, Leonnorios turned eastwards to Byzantium, while Luturios eventually managed to cross the Hellespont in five small boats obtained by a ruse from the Macedonian garrison.[29] Since it is unlikely that any company of Celts would have been able to impose themselves on the area in this way after Antigonus' victory, it is reasonable to place the crossing before the battle of Lysimacheia, presumably in the winter months of 278/7, which, according to Pausanias, was the year of the Celtic arrival in Asia Minor.[30] Their arrival and its consequences were heralded in the oracular verses of Phaenno of Epirus, fortuitously preserved by the Byzantine historian Zosimus, who warned Nicomedes of the danger of admitting the lion, Leonnorios, and the wolf, Luturios, into his rich but vulnerable possessions.[31]

While Luturios' men slipped over the Hellespont, the larger band under Leonnorios came to an agreement with Nicomedes I of Bithynia and crossed the Bosporus at Byzantium, where the two groups linked up again. Byzantium had hitherto resisted intense pressure from

---

Diodorus, 22. 9. 1 150,000 infantry, 10,000 cavalry καὶ ἑτέρου ἀγοραίου ὄχλου καὶ ἐμπόρων πλείστων καὶ ἁμαξῶν δισχιλίων. No doubt fear and self-congratulation have inflated these figures, which the Greeks were in no position to assess accurately.

[15] see above, nn. 9–10.

[16] Polyaenus, 4. 6. 17. The figure is implied not stated in the account.

[17] This was usual among Celts and Germans (Strabo, 4. 4. 2, 196). Celtic society on the move, as in Caesar's Gaul, was steeply stratified, and by no means all adult men would have been armed warriors.

[18] See below, n. 108.

[19] Pausanias, 10. 19. 4.

[20] Polyaenus, 4. 6. 17, perhaps identical to Kerethrios; both are attested in Thrace.

[21] See above, n. 12.

[22] The leaders of the *diabasis* to Asia, both named by Livy, 38. 16. 2 (Lonorios and Lutarios), and Memnon (*FGrH* IIIB 434), 11; Strabo 12. 5. 1, 566 and a restored inscription (*I. Erythrai* no. 24. 14–15) name Leonnorios alone.

[23] Livy, 38. 16. 1 'magna hominum vis, seu inopia agri seu praedae spe, nullam gentem, per quas ituri essent parem armis rati...'.

[24] Polyaenus, 4. 6. 17; Diodorus, 22. 5; see Launey, *Recherches* i. 491.

[25] As from Ptolemy Keraunos, Justin, *Epit.* 24. 5. 1, cf. 24. 4. 7, and Livy, 38. 16. 3.

[26] Apart from the attack on Delphi, there is the assault on Antigonus' camp at Lysimacheia, Justin, *Epit.* 25. 1–2.

[27] Diodorus 22. 4; Justin, *Epit.* 24. 6. 1–2; Pausanias, 1. 4. 5 (Asia).

[28] *Epit.* 25. 2. 7 ff.; see P. Moraux, *Ist. Mitt.* 7 (1957), 66 n. 27 and Nachtergael, *Galates*, 167–8 n. 191, against M. Launey, *REA* 66 (1944), 217 ff.

[29] Livy, 38. 16. 6.

[30] Pausanias, 10. 23. 14, when Demokles was archon at Athens.

[31] Zosimus, 2. 37. 1, with the long note in the edn. by F. Paschoud (Paris, 1971), 109–10; 237–41.

the Celts to allow them to cross into Asia, and had not unnaturally been helped by her allies in Bithynia,[32] but Nicomedes was in need of military support against his brother Zipoetas and succumbed to the temptation of enlisting Celtic aid. Memnon of Heracleia preserves a version of the treaty struck on this occasion[33] which, while clearly derived from a literary source, perhaps from Nymphis the third-century historian of Heracleia,[34] has the look of authenticity. The Celts agreed to become allies of Nicomedes and his descendants; to make no treaties with others who approached them without Nicomedes' consent; to share the same friends and enemies with him; and to become allies of the main Bithynian cities, Byzantium, Tium, Heracleia, Chalcedon, and Cius. They were allies, not hirelings; but Nicomedes paid a high price for their help, by providing them with weapons, ceding them all the spoil in the ensuing campaign, and not least by admitting them to the rich plunder to be had in Asia.[35] It is certain that his true intention was to use them not merely against his brother but against the Seleucid kingdom of Antiochus I, who was supporting Zipoetas and who aimed to bring the whole of Asia Minor under his control.[36]

In effect, once the campaign against Zipoetas was successfully completed in 277,[37] the Celts were free to raid the rest of Anatolia (apart from Bithynia) at will. According to Livy the three tribes, here mentioned for the first time, divided Asia into raiding areas; the Trocmi were given the Hellespontine coast, the Tolistobogii Aeolis and Ionia, the Tectosages the hinterland of Asia.[38] The nature and extent of these raids is well illustrated by contemporary documents. The earliest of these is a relief from Cyzicus dedicated by the generals and phylarchs of the city to Heracles,

who is shown clubbing a Galatian warrior wearing breeches and a sheath, and armed with a short sword and the characteristic large oval shield, or *thureus*.[39] The relief is dated to the hipparchate of Phoenix, whose name occurs on another inscription listing benefactions made to Cyzicus by Philetaerus of Pergamum over a number of years.[40] These can be dated with confidence to the period 281/0 to 276/5, with Phoenix' year of office falling in 278/7, the exact year of the *diabasis*.[41] The dedication to Heracles is evidently an *ex voto* offering of thanksgiving for deliverance from the enemy, during a year when the list of benefactions refers to the expense of protecting the countryside. The documents together should refer to the passage of Luturios' Celts from the Hellespont to join Leonnorios in Bithynia, and the unspecified defence expenditure may well have included money to buy the enemy off.[42] Two years later, in 276/5, when the Galatians were free to raid as they wished, Philetaerus again helped the city with gifts of wheat and barley during the war with the Galatians, and there is other evidence for fighting in north-west Asia Minor. According to Hegesianax, the Galatians (presumably the Trocmi) considered using Ilium as a base for operations, but rejected it as unfortified;[43] and a passage in a letter of Antiochus I to Meleager, his commander in the Hellespont, allowing the local population to take refuge in a fortified place called Petra, has been referred to the same circumstances.[44]

The raids on the coastal regions of Ionia are also well illustrated by inscriptions. Didyma, perhaps the richest shrine of western Asia Minor, was a natural target, attacked in the first year, 277/6.[45] From Miletus

[32] Memnon, 2. 1.

[33] 11. 2; H. H. Schmitt, *Die Staatsverträge des Altertums*, iii (1969), 111–12 no. 469.

[34] The Gauls are described as βάρβαροι which would not be possible in the original document to which they were a party, and the treaty is abbreviated, lacking introductory and closing clauses. For the source see Jacoby's discussion of this passage, Laqueur, *RE* xvii (1936), 1608–23 s.v. Nymphis, and Moraux, *Ist. Mitt.* 7 (1957), 67–8 with n. 34.

[35] Memnon, 2. 3.

[36] Pompeius Trogus, *Prol.* 25; Moraux, *Ist. Mitt.* 7 (1957), 66–72; M. Wörrle, *Chiron*, 5 (1975), 59 ff.; C. Habicht, *RE* suppl. x (1972), 453 ff.

[37] Habicht, *RE* suppl. x. 456 ff.

[38] Livy, 38. 16. 11–12; described as 'eine regulierte Räuberwirtschaft' by Mommsen, *Hermes*, 19 (1884), 321 n. 1. Compare the division of the Balkans into three raiding areas by the Celts in the winter of 280/79 (n. 2 above). According to Moraux, *Ist. Mitt.* 7 (1957) the Tectosages obtained the least fruitful raiding area because they arrived later than the other two tribes. There is no authority for this and it is contradicted by the suggestion in Livy that the areas were divided by lot (*sortiti sunt*).

[39] Mendel, *Cat. Mus. Imp.* no. 858, interpreted by M. Launey, *REA* 66 (1944), 217 ff.

[40] *OGIS* 748; the implications of this document for relations between Cyzicus and Philetaerus are discussed by K. M. T. Atkinson, *Antichthon*, 2 (1968), 44–8 although she was unaware of Launey's study. A metrical dedication inscribed at Delos records that Philetaerus won a victory over the Galatians. It should perhaps be placed in this context. See *IG* xi. 4. 1105 (F. Durrbach, *Choix d'inscriptions de Délos* (1922), no. 31, with R. E. Allen, *The Attalid Kingdom: A Constitutional History* (1983), 31 n. 8, and 136–7).

[41] The arguments are presented by Dittenberger in his notes on *OGIS* 748, and reinforced against the doubts of M. Segre by Launey (*REA* 66 (1944)). M. Wörrle, *Chiron*, 5 (1975), 64 suggests that the hipparchs need not have held office in consecutive years, but this scepticism is unwarranted.

[42] See Launey, *REA* 66 (1944). J. and L. Robert, *Bull. ép.* (1946/7), 347 no. 177 criticize Launey's inference that no actual battle was involved.

[43] Hegesianax (*FGrH* I no. 45) fr. 3 *apud* Strabo, 13. 1. 27, 594. There is a problem with the walls of Ilium, for which see Magie, *RR* ii. 923 and the literature cited there.

[44] Welles, *Royal Correspondence*, 62 ff. on no. 11, ll. 22 ff.

[45] *I. Didyma*, 426 l. 7 with Rehm's commentary on pp. 257 ff.; W. Otto, *Beiträge zur Seleukidengeschichte der 3 Jh. v. Chr.*,

itself, which controlled the shrine of Didyma, there is the romantic story, told by Parthenius following Aristodemus of Nysa, about a group of women captured by a band of Gauls while they were celebrating the Thesmophoria outside the city. Most were ransomed, but one was taken by her abductor Cavarus back to Gaul. Her husband, one of the nobility of Miletus, followed her by way of Italy to Massilia.[46] The moralizing sequel and end to the story, which ensured its survival, is no doubt fictitious. Another tale with a Milesian setting concerns three girls who preferred death to another fate at the hands of their Galatian captors.[47] The plausibility of these anecdotes is emphasized by an inscription from Priene, clearly belonging to the 270s, which honours a certain Sotas for measures he had taken to protect his city.[48] The text is not complete, but it shows that the Galatians had invaded the territory of Priene, taken prisoner citizens living in the countryside, and treated them with characteristic savagery;[49] they had desecrated temples and shrines,[50] and on their retreat had set fire to farms and homesteads, killing many of the inhabitants. Sotas had organized the defence, paying citizens to fight as infantry or cavalry, and had driven them off. He had brought all the country-dwellers, men, women, and children, inside the city walls; meanwhile seizing strong points in the country from which resistance could successfully be carried out.

While Sotas energetically organized his fellow citizens at Priene, Erythrae seems to have preferred to buy off trouble. Two inscriptions of the 270s refer to the Galatians.[51] The earlier apparently is a decree of thanks, proposed by Polycritus on behalf of the generals

during the first four months of an unspecified year, for having taken on the defence and armament of the city, and for maintaining the peace at no slight personal expense. They had preserved Erythrae unscathed by collecting money and sending it to the barbarians under Leonnorios.[52] To guarantee receipt of this protection money, the Gauls would take hostages, and these along with other prisoners, were retrieved by Polycritus himself, who was honoured by a second decree, after he had led an embassy to the barbarians to achieve this.[53]

A comparable picture emerges from the inland cities of Asia, in the raiding area of the Tectosages. In a dedication to Apollo found at Thyateira, firmly dated to the late summer of 275, a father thanked the god for the safe rescue of his son who had been captured by the Galatians.[54] Another text, dated to January 267, was set up by two villages on what was later to be the territory of Laodicea on the Lycus, but at the time formed part of the private property of Achaeus, given to him by Antiochus I. It thanks two of Achaeus' agents for their services in the Galatian war, and in particular for ransoming prisoners.[55] If the editor of this inscription is right to argue that these services were rendered only shortly before it was inscribed, and that the nomadic ways of the Gauls prevented their holding prisoners for long periods, it is clear that they were still an active threat as late as 269 or 268. Perhaps other anecdotal evidence for their activities in the region of the Maeander valley should belong to the same period. Pausanias has stories of divine intervention saving the inhabitants of Themisonium and Apamea-Celaenae.[56] Themisonium was not in fact founded until 251,[57] but the legend could have passed from the existing local community to the later city. There is also some obscurity about the date of a Galatian attack on Lycia averted by Neoptolemus, who is known to have held a priesthood at Alexandria in 252/1, and was probably the Ptolemaic *strategos* in Lycia before that date. An epigram preserved by Stephanus of Byzantium claims that he defended the city of Tlos against Pisidians, Paeonians,

Abh. Ak. München, phil. Hist. Klasse, xxxiv. 1 (1928), 22 ff. The barbarians of the inscription are assumed to be Gauls; M. Wörrle, *Chiron* 5 (1975), 66–7 effectively argues against these authors' interpretation of *I. Didyma*, 428 ll. 8 ff.

[46] Parthenius, 8; see B. Haussoullier, *Études sur l'histoire de Milet* (1902), 64 ff.; Stähelin, *Galater*, 8 ff. The story is discussed with considerable finesse in an interesting article by M.-P. Loicq-Berger, *Les Études classiques*, 52 (1984), 39–52.

[47] *Anth. Pal.* 7. 492, attributed to Antonius Thallus of Miletus (*PIR²* i. 170: A no. 880) by M. Boas, *Rh. Mus.* 62 (1907), 64–5. There is a very similar story in Hieronymus, *adv. Iovinianum*, 1. 41, and another, but less credible, moralizing tale about Ephesus in Plutarch, *Mor.* 309 (after Clitophon). Compare also Pausanias, 10. 22. 2.

[48] *OGIS* 765, improved in *I. Priene*, 17. See W. Günther, *Das Orakel von Didyma in hellenistischer Zeit* (1971), 41 ff.

[49] ὠμότης, cf. *SIG³* 226 l. 107 referring to Gauls at Olbia in south Russia; Pausanias, 10. 22. 2; Diodorus, 22. 5. 2.

[50] Another Galatian characteristic. Compare the stories about the invasion of Greece and the *asebeia* of Brennos, Pausanias, 10. 22. 3, and Justin, *Epit.* 24. 6. 4.

[51] For the most recent comprehensive discussion, see W. Orth, *Königlicher Machtanspruch und Städtische Freiheit* (1977), 77 ff.

[52] *SIG³* i. 410, *I. Erythrai*, 24. For similar payments see n. 25, and those made by Byzantium to the Celtic kingdom of Tylis, Polybius, 4. 45. 9 ff.

[53] *I. Erythrai*, 28.

[54] *KP²* 14 no. 19 = *TAM* v. 2, 881, dated to the month Hyperberetaios in the 37th year of Antiochus I and his co-regent Seleucus II. See Otto, *Seleukidengeschicte*, 46 n. 5.

[55] M. Wörrle, *Chiron*, 5 (1975), 59–87, dated to the month Peritios in the forty-fifth year of Antiochus and Seleucus.

[56] Pausanias, 10. 32. 4 (cf. *BMC Phrygia* (1906), civ) and 30. 9. For the site of Themisonium, see Robert, *Villes²*, 112 n. 4. Stähelin, *Galater*, 9 and Magie, *RR* ii. 731 date these raids to the reign of Eumenes II (cf. Robert, *Noms indigènes*, 338), which is also possible.

[57] W. Ruge, *RE* va (1934), 1638–41.

Agrianians, and Galatians. The text gives a tantalizing glimpse of the complex and confused conditions in third-century Asia Minor. The invaders from Europe included not only Celtic but also Thracian tribes, who combined with the *montagnards* of Pisidia to ravage the rich valley communities of western Lycia. Galatian raids may even have extended to Limyra on the south coast, where an imposing circular temple on a high podium base was built in the 270s BC to celebrate the cult of Ptolemy II and Arsinoe. A panel from the balustrade between the columns of the tholos displays a Celtic shield carved in relief, anticipating the sculptural display of Galatian armour on the victory monuments of Pergamon.[58]

The inscriptions relating to the Galatians in Asia Minor during the 270s are among the more secure items of evidence in an extremely obscure decade.[59] The invasion had come at a time when rival kings were in contention for control of Asia, so much so that they had little energy to intervene to save the cities from the Galatian threat. Antiochus I, after disputing the domination of Syria and western Asia with Ptolemy II, had sent armies into Anatolia to fight both Antigonus Gonatas and Zipoetes I of Bithynia for control of the north-west. In 279 or 278 he had concluded a peace treaty with Antigonus, whose own attention was claimed by the Gauls in the Chersonese, coming north for the purpose in person. It was probably at this time that the city of Ilium had decreed cultic and other honours to him, for securing the peace of the cities, and for establishing his own affairs and kingdom on a firmer and more splendid footing.[60] The celebrations were premature, since the calm was at once shattered by the arrival of the Gauls, and it will have been their presence, as well as the precarious hold which he retained over Asia, that kept Antiochus in Sardis between 276 and 274.[61] At some date he won an

important victory over the Galatians, which earned him the title *Sōtēr*, and this is commonly ascribed to the years around 275.[62] However, the fact that the Gauls were still dangerous as late as 269 undermines the case for this early date, and it is likely that, when the first Syrian war took Antiochus away from Sardis to the Syrian part of his kingdom in 274, the Galatian menace remained.[63] The date of the first appearance of the title *Sōtēr* cannot be established, but his cult is attested by an inscription of the Ionian League belonging to 268–261,[64] and the word *Sōtēr* appears on an inscription of Bargylia dated to 270–261, perhaps towards the end of that period.[65] These indications would fit well with a late date around 269 or 268 for the major battle in which he defeated the Gauls. The victory itself naturally offered a suitable subject for poetic description and embellishment; Simonides, an epic poet of the third century from Magnesia ad Sipylum, wrote an account,[66] which may have formed the basis for the surviving description in Lucian's *Zeuxis*.[67] Other fragments of poetry may refer to the event,[68] and the most memorable feature of the battle, Antiochus' use of elephants to overwhelm the enemy, was an inspiration to the terracotta workshops of western Asia Minor. Figurines, the first of which was discovered in the necropolis of Myrina in Aeolis, depict an elephant trampling a Galatian warrior to death.[69]

Antiochus' victory was probably as decisive for the security of Asia as the battle of Lysimacheia was for Thrace and Macedonia. Perhaps in the aftermath of the battle Antiochus wrote to the city of Erythrae, in response to an embassy to grant them autonomy and freedom from various imposts, particularly that due

---

[58] Stephanus Byz. s.v. Ἀγρίαι, interpreted by A. Wilhelm, *Praktika*, 6 (1931), 319 ff. See further L. Robert, *JSav.* (1983), 241–58. For the monument at Limyra see *JHS Arch. Reports* 1989/90, 118. The excavator, J. Borchhardt, suggests a connection with a Celtic belt-buckle found nearby at Finike. The Galatian invasion and settlement receive a careful and interesting treatment from K. Strobel, 'Die Galater im hellenistischen Kleinasien: historische Aspekte einer keltischen Staatenbildung', in J. Seibert (ed.), *Hellenistische Studien, Gedenkschrift H. Bengtson* (1991), 101–34, which is to be developed in a forthcoming monograph.

[59] For what follows I rely heavily on a surer guide than most, E. Will, *Histoire politique*, i. 88 ff., 117 ff.

[60] OGIS 219, I. Ilion 32; for the date, which is conjectural and controversial, see Orth, *Königlicher Machtanspruch*, 64; Wörrle, *Chiron*, 5 (1975), 67 ff.; Otto, *Seleukidengeschichte*, 21 n. 3, and *Philologus*, 86 (1931), 410 f.

[61] Wörrle, *Chiron*, 5 (1975), 67 citing the Babylonian cuneiform tablet BM 62689, trans. S. Smith, *Babylonian Historical Texts* (1924), 154 ff.

[62] Appian, *Syr.* 65 for the title and its occasion. In a strictly comparable gesture Antigonus Gonatas was first recognized as king of Macedonia after defeating the Gauls at Lysimacheia.

[63] Wörrle, *Chiron*, 5 (1975), 68 ff.

[64] OGIS 222, I. Erythrai, 504; Habicht, *Gottmenschentum*[2], 91 f.

[65] SIG[3] i. 426, ll. 20 ff.; Habicht, *Gottmenschentum*[2], 103.

[66] Suda s.v. Simonides. See B. Bar-Kochva, *PCPS* 199 (1973), 1–8.

[67] Lucian, *Zeuxis*, 9–11, a description which is clearly largely fantastic.

[68] J. U. Powell, *Collectanea Alexandrina* (1925), 131–2, as interpreted by Bar-Kochva, *PCPS* 199 (1973), 7–8; but there is nothing specific in this 3rd-cent. fragment to connect it with the elephant victory. See now the new edition and commentary of H. Lloyd-Jones and P. Parsons, *Supplementum Hellenisticum* (1983), 459–60 no. 958, who suggest, cogently, that it should relate to the victory of Ptolemy II over his mutinous Galatian mercenaries in Alexandria, c.274–272 BC.

[69] S. Reinach, *BCH* 9 (1885), 484–93; id., *La Nécropole de Myrina* (1887), 318 and pl. 10; P. Bienkowski, *Les Celtes dans les arts mineurs gréco-romains* (1928), 141–50.

'for Galatian matters'.[70] This levy has been variously interpreted as a war fund,[71] or, less plausibly, as the money (*stipendium*) paid to the Gauls by Seleucid kings;[72] in either case it points towards the lifting of a threat.

II. *Settlement in Central Anatolia*

Probably as a direct result of the battle the Celts were driven away from the rich and populous areas of the west into the thinly settled hinterland of Anatolia. The ancient writers contradict one another about when, and in what circumstances, they occupied the area of eastern Phrygia around Ancyra, which from now on was to be called Galatia. Justin, epitomizing Pompeius Trogus, says that they divided the kingdom which they had won back for Nicomedes;[73] Strabo, and by implication Pausanias, states that the Gauls were nomads for a long period before they were eventually confined to Galatia as a result of Attalus I's victories;[74] Livy, with slightly different emphasis, says that they imposed a *stipendium* on the whole of cis-Tauric Asia and that they chose their area of settlement for themselves;[75] while only Appian clearly states that Antiochus drove the Gauls from Asia by his elephant victory.[76] Here we are at the mercy of the sources:[77] Strabo and Pausanias may reflect Attalid boasts about the extent of their victories; Livy may emphasize the former independence of the Gauls in order to highlight the achievement of Manlius Vulso in 189; Appian may simply have inferred the effect of Antiochus' victory from the title which he received. However, his claim accords well not only with Antiochus' subsequent reputation, but with such information as we have about Galatian history between 270 and c.230, which shows them active not in western Anatolia, but in Bithynia and Pontus, as well as engaged in a great battle near Ancyra against Seleucus II. It is reasonable to assume that the Gauls had found their Anatolian home by the end of the 260s.

The numbers of the Gauls raise further problems. Livy's version of the *diabasis* states that Nicomedes of Bithynia enlisted the support of 10,000 fighting men, and 10,000 others. The first figure is roughly in line with the numbers of Celtic mercenaries enlisted on other occasions at this period,[78] but if the Gauls were indeed imported as a whole nation we would expect the second figure for non-combatant men, women, and children to be higher than it is. Even allowing for this, the total seems small. Growth in the Galatian population is attributed to their fecundity, on which both Livy and Justin remark,[79] but it should not be forgotten that in the early years, while they still menaced Asia, the Gauls were well placed to put pressure on the cities of the Bosporus and Propontis to allow reinforcements to cross over and join them, and on the European side of the straits the Byzantines, at least, were in no position to refuse demands of this sort.[80]

During the middle years of the third century the Gauls are linked chiefly with Bithynia and Pontus to the north and east. When Nicomedes I of Bithynia died, probably about 255–253 BC, he left his kingdom to Zipoetas, his son by a second marriage. The legacy was disputed by Ziaelas, son by a previous marriage and now living in exile in Armenia, who enlisted the help of the Tolistobogii to reclaim his kingdom. The people of Heracleia Pontica eventually succeeded in mediating between the brothers, bringing a damaging civil war to an end. The Galatians, deprived of the profits that they will have hoped to gain, turned on Heracleia, and invaded its territory as far as the river Calles, returning home laden with booty.[81]

The Gauls also became embroiled with the kingdoms of Cappadocia and Pontus. An isolated fragment of the *Karika* of Apollonius of Aphrodisias records how, soon after their arrival in Asia, they fought alongside Mithridates of Pontus and Ariobarzanes of Cappadocia to repel a Ptolemaic force in the Black Sea. They

[70] OGIS 223, Welles, *Royal Correspondence*, 15, I. Erythrai, 31. There are fragments of a second similar inscription, I. Erythrai, 30.
[71] Wörrle, *Chiron*, 5 (1975), 70.
[72] Welles, *Royal Correspondence*, pp. 78 ff. Livy 38. 16. 13 states that Seleucid kings paid a *stipendium* to the Gauls up to the time of Attalus' victories in the late 240s or 230s, but this probably only refers to the period after the 'Brothers' war', see below, n. 92.
[73] *Epit.* 25. 2. 11.
[74] 12. 5. 1, 566, confirmed by Pausanias, 1. 4. 5.
[75] 38. 16. 13.
[76] *Syr.* 65.
[77] There is a full discussion in Moraux, *Ist. Mitt.* 7 (1957), 56 ff.

[78] 9,000 hired by Antigonus after Lysimacheia, drawn from a total tribal strength of 30,000, see above, nn. 16 and 24.
[79] Livy, 38. 16. 13 'multitudine etiam magna subole aucta'; Justin, *Epit.* 25. 2. 8–9 'quamquam Gallorum ea tempestate tantae fecunditatis iuventus fuit, ut Asiam omnem velut examen aliquod implerunt. Denique neque reges Orientis sine mercennario Gallorum exercitu ulla bella gesserunt, neque pulsi regno ad alios quam ad Gallos confugerunt.' Their use as mercenaries is amply confirmed by Launey, *Recherches*, i. 490–534. For Celtic fertility, in Gaul, see Strabo, 4. 1. 2, 178; 4. 4. 3, 196.
[80] Polybius, 4. 45. 9 ff. K. Strobel, 'Die Galater im hellenistischen Kleinasien', makes the important point that Galatian numbers were evidently increased by a 'Keltisierung' of the native population of central Anatolia.
[81] Memnon, 14; C. Habicht, *RE* suppl. x (1972), 387–91.

captured the anchors of the enemy ships, received the country around Ancyra as a reward for their success, and named their capital after these trophies.[82] The second half of this story, with its aetiological myth, is fanciful and inexact; Ancyra did not become a Galatian capital before the creation of the Roman province; but something may be salvaged to the credit of the reference to a battle with Ptolemaic forces in the Euxine. There is a confused tradition suggesting that Ptolemy II helped Byzantium, Heracleia, Sinope, and other Pontic cities with corn, cash, and military support, for which he received cult honours at least at Byzantium.[83] The raid on the Pontic coast should be placed after this initiative, perhaps as an attempt to re-establish Ptolemaic influence, but before the death of Mithridates I Ktistes in 266 BC. If it is to be believed that Mithridates helped the Gauls to settle in Galatia, the episode may have taken place in the early 260s, after the battle of the elephants.[84] However, the friendship between them and the Pontic royal house seems to have expired on the death of Mithridates' successor Ariobarzanes, since they took advantage of the accession of his son Mithridates II, who was still a child, to plunder his kingdom. The people of Heraclea again stepped in to supply grain to a beleaguered Amisus, but only succeeded in attracting an expedition against themselves. The city was forced to come to terms and an embassy to the Gauls, led by the historian Nymphis, who is presumably the source of the information, agreed to buy them off at a cost of 2,000 gold pieces for the army, and a further 200 for each chieftain.[85]

The Seleucid empire had been untroubled since the early 260s. For this it could thank Antiochus I's victory, but also an active policy of defence by which the Seleucids founded a string of military colonies at strategic points in the headwaters of the valleys that led from central Anatolia to the west coast, and marked the possible routes of invasion. In the valley of the Caicus there were foundations of Antiochus I at Thyateira, Nacrasus, and Acrasus;[86] there was a Seleucid settlement of 'Macedonians' in Phrygia Epictetus, guarding the upper Hermus valley;[87] and in the upper Maeander and Phrygia Paroreius there were foundations at Apamea, Apollonia, Seleuceia Sidera, and Pisidian Antioch; as well as at Pelta, Blaundus, Hierapolis, and Laodicea.[88]

A division in the Seleucid ranks could, however, be exploited. Seleucus II, the successor of Antiochus II, had made over his Anatolian territories to his brother Antiochus Hierax during the third Syrian war with Ptolemy III. After making peace with Ptolemy, Seleucus turned against his brother who had aspirations beyond mere co-regency, and attempted to take back his Asian territory. After initial successes in the west, he marched against his brother's ally, Mithridates II of Pontus, but was resoundingly defeated by an alliance of Antiochus, Mithridates, and Galatian mercenaries near Ancyra.[89] The battle was fatal to Seleucus' position, but hardly less so for Antiochus, who had no authority over his Celtic hirelings. These now saw an opportunity to oust the Seleucids from Anatolia altogether, allowing a profitable state of anarchy to prevail.[90] Under pressure Antiochus agreed to treat them not merely as mercenaries but as allies.[91] Presumably this concession involved recognizing their right to independence, and probably ceding part of the war spoils and tribute which he was exacting from the cities of Asia. When Livy refers to the fact that no Syrian king had dared refuse to pay a levy to the Gauls, he probably refers to the aftermath of this 'Brothers' war', rather than to the whole period since the Celtic invasion of Asia Minor.[92] The agreement with Antiochus Hierax marked the high point of Galatian success against the Seleucids, reversing the situation achieved by Antiochus I after the battle of the elephants. They apparently underlined this superiority by posing a direct threat to Antiochus' life, which he could avoid only by fleeing for refuge in Magnesia.[93] The part played by the Gauls in this war is entirely typical of their role throughout the third century. Their guiding interest was their own profit and advantage, for which they would change any allegiance or break any pact. While fighting for Antiochus Hierax they had clearly made up their earlier quarrel with Mithridates II; after the battle of Ancyra they took full advantage of their military strength to force him to become their ally in circumstances damaging to him but advantageous to themselves.

[82] Stephanus Byz. s.v. Ἄγκυρα. (FGrH 740 F 14).

[83] Habicht, Gottmenschentum,² 116–21 combines the sources in a brilliantly argued if conjectural reconstruction. B. Niese, Gesch. der gr. und mak. Staaten, i (1889), 129 n. 9 transplanted the whole episode to Caria.

[84] For Galatian relations with Pontus, see E. Meyer, Geschichte des Königreichs Pontos (1879), 43 ff.

[85] Memnon, 16.

[86] G. Cohen, The Seleucid Colonies: Studies in Founding Administration and Organization (1978), 15; TAM v. 2, p. 309; also below, Ch. 11 § II at n. 142.

[87] C. Habicht, JRS 65 (1975), 71 ff.; the settlement was not at Cadi, as previously believed, but in the same area.

[88] Cohen, The Seleucid Colonies, 15.

[89] The sources for this war are Eusebius, Chron. 1. 251; Justin, Epit. 27. 2; 41. 4. 7; Pompeius Trogus, Prol. 27; Phylarchus apud Athenaeus, 13. 593e; Polyaenus, 4. 9. 6; Plutarch, Mor. 489a–b.

[90] Justin, Epit. 27. 2. 12 'Galli arbitrantes Seleucum in proelio cecidisse in ipsum Antiochum arma vertere, liberius depopulaturi Asiam si omnem stirpem regiam extinxissent.'

[91] Ibid. 'quod ubi sensit Antiochus, velut a praedonibus auro se redemit societatemque cum mercenariis suis iunxit.'

[92] 38. 16. 13.

[93] Eusebius, Chron. 1. 251.

III. *The Galatians, Pergamum, and Rome*

This resurgence of Galatian power led to renewed pressure on western Asia Minor, and especially on the Attalid kingdom of Pergamum, which had become a major power during the reigns of Philetaerus and Eumenes I. It seems that they, like the other inhabitants of western Anatolia, paid a tribute to the Gauls to save themselves from pillage; by refusing payment they provoked a decisive war.[94] The Pergamene successes over the Gauls are well known, thanks above all to the monuments which Attalus I had erected to commemorate them. He represented his victories as among the great triumphs of the Greeks over the barbarians, to be compared with the Athenian victories over the Persians in 490 and 480 BC, or the legendary struggles of the gods with the giants and the Athenians with the Amazons, all of which formed the subject of dedicatory reliefs set up on the south wall of the Athenian acropolis.[95] These have not survived, but the monuments set up at Pergamum itself are well known, at least in Roman copies of the age of Trajan, and depict his enemies in heroic guise: a Gaul dying from his wounds, and naked except for a torque round the neck, supporting himself on his great round body shield, and distinguished by his long curved trumpet and short, broad-bladed sword; another warrior is shown committing suicide with his wife. These statues, originally in bronze but copied in marble, were the work of the sculptor Epigonus, and not only set the fashion for a new style of lifelike Hellenistic sculpture, but fixed, once and for all, the pictorial image of the Celt for classical observers, influencing all later portraits and written descriptions.[96] The original sculptures were set up on a great plinth in the temple of Athena on the acropolis of Pergamum, which carried a series of inscriptions giving details of the king's victories. These and other separate inscriptions are the principal source of information on the actual campaigns. The separate texts, which themselves form part of two grandiose bases erected in or by the same temple, consist of a dedication to Athena after a battle with the Tolistoagii near the sources of the river Caicus (*OGIS* 269), and a dedication to Zeus and Athena for a victory over Antiochus Hierax beside the river Harpasus in Caria (*OGIS* 271). The main monument carries seven inscriptions: the first a thank-offering to Athena (*OGIS* 273); the remainder (*OGIS* 274–9) providing details of the two battles already mentioned, and a further four victories, over Antiochus in the Hellespont and at Coloe in Lydia, over Antiochus and the two Galatian tribes of the Tectosages and the Tolistoagii beside the temple of Aphrodite, and over Lysias and the generals of Seleucus III. Yet another base, carrying a statue of Attalus himself, was set up by the generals and soldiers after the battles with Antiochus and the Galatians as a votive to Zeus and Athena (*OGIS* 280).

The wars with the Gauls, then, must be seen as part of a wider pattern, Attalus' attempt to carve out a strong and independent kingdom for himself at the expense, chiefly, of the Seleucids. The Galatians took part in two battles; one involved the Tolistoagii, the Tectosages, and Antiochus Hierax (their ally from the 'Brothers' war') in a defeat at the temple of Aphrodite which lay close to Pergamum itself;[97] the other was the defeat of the Tolistoagii alone at the sources of the Caicus.[98] There is no certainty either about the date of the battles or even of the order in which they were fought.[99] According to Polybius, Attalus received the title 'king' only after his Galatian victory,[100] and when he died in 197 he had reigned for forty-four years.[101] This should place the victory in 241/0, and we could take this to have been a battle against the Tolistoagii on their own, before the 'Brothers' war' and the Galatian alliance with Antiochus Hierax. But doubts arise since the victory could have been that over the combined forces of Antiochus and the Galatians at the temple of Aphrodite, with the latter emphasized in the victory propaganda.

[94] Livy, 38. 16. 14 'primus Asiam incolentium abnuit Attalus, pater regis Eumenis, audacique incepto praeter opinionem omnium affuit fortuna, et signis collatis superior fuit.'

[95] Pausanias, 1. 25. 2; for discussion see A. Stewart, *Attika: Studies in Athenian Sculpture of the Hellenistic Age* (1979), 19–25. The comparison between the Gauls and the mythological enemies of civilization, in this case the Titans, was made by Callimachus, *Hymn to Delos*, 171 ff. For the Attalids and Athens see C. Habicht, *Hesperia*, 59 (1990), 561–77.

[96] The most recent discussions of these famous sculptures are E. Künzl, *Die Kelten des Epigonos von Pergamon* (1971), reviewed by C. Havelock, *Gnomon* (1974), 823–6; R. Wenning, *Die Galateranatheme Attalos I, Perg. Forsch.* 4 (1978); and Radt, *Pergamon*, 182–7. It is easy to trace the influence of these artistic representations on descriptions of Celtic appearance, such as Diodorus 5. 28. 1–3. The Gauls were given a heroic appearance to magnify the achievement of their conquerors, cf. M. Launey, *REA* 66 (1944), 222–6.

[97] *OGIS* 278 with Dittenberger's n. 8; cf. Polybius, 18. 2. 2; 6. 4 for the sanctuary. Pompeius Trogus, *Prol.* 27 *Galli Pergamo victi ab Attalo* may refer to this battle rather than to the defeat at the sources of the Caicus, but we should not expect too much precision from the epitomator.

[98] Pausanias, 1. 25. 2 καὶ Γαλατῶν τὴν ἐν Μυσίᾳ φθορὰν ἀνέθηκεν Ἄτταλος. The sources of the Caicus were in Mysia, Strabo, 12. 8. 3, 572; 13. 1. 70, 616.

[99] See Stähelin, *Galater*, 23 for a range of suggestions between 241 and 230. See now the discussion by Allen, *The Attalid Kingdom*, 195–9.

[100] Polybius, 18. 41. 7 (Livy, 33. 21. 3); cf. Strabo, 13. 4. 2, 624.

[101] Dittenberger, *OGIS* 268 n. 2; 269 n. 1. Walbank on Polybius 18. 41. 7.

Furthermore, Polybius' forty-four years might refer to the whole period of Attalus' hegemony, not simply to the period when he had the title of king.[102] Other sources help little. Eusebius dates the victory over Antiochus at Coloe in Lydia to 229/8, followed within a year by Antiochus' death in Thrace.[103] So his battle with Galatian allies belongs to an earlier date, sometime in the 230s when he was still on the offensive against Pergamum.

Uncertainty then persists about the sequence of events in the first war between Pergamum and the Gauls, but not about its cause, Attalus' decision to refuse to pay their *stipendium*, or about its result, a victory as decisive as Antiochus I's in the battle of the elephants. It brought a Galatian agreement not to attack the Pergamene kingdom,[104] and relative peace for a generation. But it would be a mistake to over-emphasize the importance of these victories. Attalus secured his own kingdom but offered less reassurance to the rest of Anatolia. The Galatians had been defeated on campaign but their territory remained intact; they were forced to relinquish none of the spoils they had accumulated over the previous two generations, and the terror they inspired remained unalloyed until the expedition of Manlius Vulso in 189.[105]

Within a few years the gilt of Pergamene success was badly tarnished by a resurgence of Seleucid power under Antiochus III, who succeeded Seleucus III in 223, and his uncle Achaeus. Within a year of the king's accession Achaeus had deprived Attalus of all the territory he had recently gained, and restored Seleucid rule over much of Anatolia.[106] In 220 he declared himself king in his own right of the newly regained territories at Laodicea on the Lycus.[107] These unexpected setbacks drove Attalus to the same course taken by Nicomedes sixty years before; he invited a tribe of Celts, the Aegosages, across the Hellespont to act as mercenaries on his behalf.[108] The aim of Attalus' campaign was to persuade the cities of Aeolis, which had been intimidated into revolt by Achaeus, to come

into line again, and the expedition was initially successful. Most communities rejoined Attalus without resistance, and only a few needed to be encouraged by a show of force. Opposition, organized by one of Achaeus' generals, Themistocles, was slight and ineffective. However, at the river Megistus[109] an eclipse of the moon, datable to 1 September 218, caused the Celtic mercenaries, who had been disgruntled throughout the campaign, to mutiny. Their grievance may be traced to physical circumstances. The tribe had joined Attalus in its entirety, accompanied by the traditional slow-moving baggage train with wives, children, and possessions.[110] They were not equipped for the wide-ranging and rapid marches which they were called upon to perform,[111] and the military action, when it occurred, was uncongenial. There was little fighting, and correspondingly little booty, especially as Attalus was merely winning back the area into his own dominion, and had no wish to see it plundered and ruthlessly intimidated. Where there had been resistance it had been conducted from behind protective walls, and had been overcome by siege and blockade, a form of warfare to which the Gauls were ill adapted.

The king was seriously embarrassed by the mutiny, as Antiochus Hierax had been at the end of the 'Brothers' war'. His mercenaries could not readily be abandoned where they were, repatriated to Thrace, or overcome by force of arms. He chose to settle them in a military colony in the Hellespontine region towards the Troad;[112] and the cities of Lampsacus, Alexandria Troas, and Ilium were charged to keep an eye on them. There was immediate and predictable trouble when, in 217/16, the Gauls actually laid siege to Ilium, before they were driven off to Arisbe near Abydus by a force of 4,000 men raised from Alexandria Troas. Prusias I of Bithynia, no less alert to the danger, was on hand to inflict a final defeat, killing all the fighting men on the battlefield, the women and children in the camp.[113]

During the rest of the third century BC nothing directly is heard of the Galatians, perhaps still recovering from their defeat by Attalus. In 197/6 the people of Lampsacus wrote to their kinsmen at Massilia, another Phocaean colony, asking for letters of introduction to the Tolistobogii. The purpose of the request is unclear although the context appears to rule out the possibility that the Gauls were directly threatening Lampsacus. The most interesting implication of the episode is the assumption that the people of Massilia, the Greek city most closely linked to the

[102] So Stähelin, *Galater*, 23 against Dittenberger.

[103] *Chron.* 1. 253 'Attamen CXXXVII olompiadis anno quarto bellum in Lidiorum terra bis aggressus, debellatus est, et e regione Koloae cum Attalo praelium commitebat, et anno primo centesimae tricesimae octavae olompiadis in Thrakiam fugere ab Attalo coactus post praelium in Karia factum, moritur.'

[104] Livy, 38. 16. 13.

[105] Note Livy, 38. 47. 11 ff. (Manlius' speech) and esp. 38. 37. 1–4.

[106] Will, *Histoire politique*, ii. 10–12.

[107] Polybius, 4. 46. 4; 5. 27–8; Will, *Histoire politique*, ii. 18–21.

[108] Polybius, 5. 77. 2 ff.; Holleaux, *Études*, ii. 17 ff. The Gauls may have been refugees from the kingdom of Tylis which had collapsed in 218, Polybius, 4. 46. 4 with Will, *Histoire politique*, ii. 39.

[109] Certainly the Macestus, see Robert, *Ét. anat.* 185 ff.

[110] See above, n. 18.

[111] For the topography, see Robert, *Ét. anat.* 185 ff.

[112] Polybius, 5. 78. 5.

[113] Polybius, 5. 111.

Celtic world in the west, would have influence with their eastern cousins.[114]

Perhaps also at this time[115] the Galatians again turned their attention to Heracleia Pontica. In search of an outlet to the sea, perhaps in order to establish direct contact with Celtic tribes settled on the lower Danube, they attacked the city again, but without success, losing some two-thirds of their force.[116] Only the fortunate survival of the works of a local historian, Memnon of Heracleia, has preserved this and further stories of Galatian confrontations with his home city. It is probably fair to assume similar contacts between the Gauls and the other cities of Bithynia, Paphlagonia, and western Pontus,[117] and there may be a trace of this in Strabo's reference to a district of Paphlagonia known as the country of Gaezatorix.[118] The only known Galatian of that name was a noble, attested as a chieftain in 180.[119] If the territory was his, it confirms that the Gauls exercised some influence in northern Anatolia in the early part of the second century, perhaps before 189 when their power was so thoroughly shattered by Manlius Vulso.

The Romans were drawn into the affairs of Asia Minor for the first time during the reign of Antiochus III, and their involvement culminated in the battle of Magnesia in 190; Scipio Africanus, fighting on behalf of the consul of the year L. Cornelius, inflicted a major defeat there on the Seleucid king, ending any hopes the latter entertained of maintaining his kingdom in Asia Minor. The consul of the following year, Cn. Manlius Vulso, assumed command of the Roman forces, and made plans for an extensive military expedition to pacify Asia Minor, and especially the Galatians, once and for all. The purpose of Manlius' expedition was a matter for question, both then and now; beside the laudatory aim to crush Antiochus' erstwhile allies and to rid the cities of Asia of an ever-present threat, there were rumours, not without foundation, that Manlius and his army were mainly concerned to milk cis-Tauric Asia of plunder and booty, and it was said that with their return Rome was flooded for the first time by all the debilitating luxury of the East—fancy clothing,

elaborate furniture, and professional cooks.[120] While admitting that there was much to be deplored in the conduct of Manlius and his troops, the whole campaign does reveal an overall Roman strategy for Asia. Antiochus was to be confined to Cilicia, Syria, and the eastern parts of the Seleucid empire. By the treaty of Apamea of 189/8 he was forbidden to intervene north of the Taurus and west of the river Tanais; Anatolia west of the Halys was now to be in the sphere of influence of the kings of Pergamum and other monarchs friendly to Rome.[121] Manlius' march up country, along the Maeander valley, through eastern Caria into Pisidia as far as the border of Pamphylia, then north again through eastern Phrygia and into Galatia, was a bold and successful attempt to impress cis-Tauric Asia with the seriousness of Roman intentions.

The Galatian campaign itself is beset with problems of detail, above all in the topography which is impenetrably obscure. According to Livy's account, taken directly from Polybius who himself relied on a highly detailed source, Manlius reached the border of Galatian territory at Abbassium, north of Emirdağ and south of Pessinus,[122] where he entered negotiations with Eposognatus, a dissident chieftain of the Tolistobogii.[123] While Eposognatus tried unsuccessfully to arrange the peaceful submission of his tribe, Manlius took his army on a five-day march into the *Axylon*, or treeless country, before bridging the Sangarius and marching to Gordium, the one fixed

---

[114] SIG³ 591; M. Holleaux, REA 18 (1916), 1 ff. = Études, v. 141–55.

[115] Memnon gives the date as οὔπω τῶν Ῥωμαίων εἰς τὴν Ἀσίαν διαβεβηκότων. This may indicate a time very shortly before the arrival of Scipio's force in 190.

[116] Memnon, 20.

[117] For links of various kinds with these areas, see below, Ch. 4 § VI nn. 129–32.

[118] 12. 3. 41, 562. For the location of this district, the upper valley of the Girmir Çay, see the note of F. Lasserre in the Budé Strabo, vol. ix (bk. XII, 1981), 212.

[119] Polybius, 24. 14. 6, with Walbank's n. See below, n. 144.

[120] The professed motive, Livy, 38. 12. 2 ff., but Manlius, who was prosecuted on his return to Rome, was accused of conducting a 'privatum latrocinium' (38. 45. 8). The luxuries, Livy, 39. 6. 7–9.

[121] This geographical conception of the treaty of Apamea is essentially that of Holleaux. The crucial clause in Livy's text has been much discussed: 'excedito urbibus agris vicis castellis cis Taurum montem usque ad Tanaim amnem et ea valle Tauri usque ad iuga quae in Lycaoniam vergit, ne qua (praeter) arma efferto ex iis oppidis agris castellisque quibus excedit.' Most modern editors emend ad Tanaim to ad Halyn (Livy, 38. 38. 4–5; Holleaux, Études, v. 2, 208 ff.). This interpretation seems to be confirmed by Strabo, 6. 4. 3, 287 τῆς Ἀσίας οἱ ἐντὸς Ἅλυος καὶ τοῦ Ταύρου, and Appian, Mith. 62 where Sulla says that the Romans expelled Antiochus καὶ τὸν Ἅλυν καὶ Ταῦρον αὐτῷ θέμενος τῆς ἀρχῆς ὅρον. However, in an elegant and convincing article A. Giovannini has argued that the received text of Livy should be retained; the boundaries of Antiochus' territory were indeed to be the Tanais, and the Taurus which crossed Asia Minor from Trapezus to Lycia. The vallis picked out for special mention was the pass through the Cilician Gates (Athenaeum, 60 (1982), 224–36). But the passages from Strabo and Appian show that, in Asia Minor at least, Rome did not hope to exercise control beyond the Halys.

[122] For a possible site, at Göme, see A. Körte, Ath. Mitt. 22 (1897), 9.

[123] Tectosagan, according to Livy, 38. 18. 3, but this is a slip, as Polybius, 21. 37 shows.

point which can be established for this stage of the march or for any of the Galatian episode.[124] Here he received the final report from Eposognatus that the Gauls remained intransigent. Joined by the fighting men of the Trocmi and led by Ortiagon, the Tolistobogii collected their full force (including women and children) on Mount Olympus, a day's march from Gordium and two days from Ancyra but otherwise unlocalized, which they defended with ditches and ramparts as a hill fort. Manlius' forces, divided into three assault groups, stormed the defensive *vallum* thrown up to protect the southern approach, and the Gauls were overwhelmed,[125] losing heavy casualties in the battle and subsequent pursuit, and as many as 40,000 captives, doubtless destined for slavery.[126]

Meanwhile the Tectosages and the remaining Trocmi established a similar defensive position on Mount Magaba, about ten miles east of Ancyra, where they were joined by a Paphlagonian chieftain Morzius of Gangra,[127] and Ariarathes of Cappadocia.[128] After failing to lure Manlius himself into an ambush at a parley, they too collapsed under a direct assault. 8,000 men were reputed to have fallen in the battle, while the rest managed to escape eastwards, across the Halys. Manlius was unable to restrain his troops as they looted the Galatian camp of the booty accumulated during ninety years of raiding and extortion inflicted on the cities of Asia. Galatian spokesmen sued for peace, and as winter closed in Manlius marched westwards off the plateau to winter quarters near Ephesus.[129]

The settlement of Asia during the winter 189/8 was arranged at Apamea, to the permanent detriment of the Seleucids, and to the advantage of Eumenes II of Pergamum, and of Rhodes. Manlius did not concern himself with the Gauls until he had sailed from Ephesus to the Propontis, where he met their representatives at Lampsacus, chosen perhaps because of Galatian connections there. He laid down terms by which they should keep the peace with Eumenes; they were to stop their habitual raiding and vagrancy, and keep to their own territory.[130] The fact that he required no indemnity to be paid can doubtless be explained by the fact that the Gauls had already been stripped of most of their wealth. Manlius had consulted Eumenes before he imposed these terms,[131] and it is clear that from now on the responsibility for containing the Galatians lay above all with Pergamum, which was to dominate the next two generations of Galatian history.

Livy singles out four chieftains during the war with Manlius: Ortiagon of the Tolistobogii, Comboiomarus, Gaudotus, and Eposognatus.[132] Ortiagon emerged as the dominating figure in the difficult years that followed. Polybius provides a character sketch of a man of intelligence and humanity, as well as martial prowess,[133] and similarly civilized qualities were attributed to his wife Chiomara, who had spent some time in captivity in Sardis;[134] both were symptomatic of a growing level of sophistication and Hellenization among the Celtic aristocracy in the second century BC. Ortiagon apparently succeeded in uniting the shattered pieces of the Galatian commonwealth under his sole rule, and played a significant part in the wars of the 180s, when the various kings and dynasts who had lost territory at the expense of the Attalids attempted to win them back. The most important of these was Prusias I of Bithynia who had been forced to give ground in Phrygia Epictetus.[135] Little is known about this war, since the detailed narrative of Polybius is all but lost,[136] but Pompeius Trogus states that one of Prusias' leading allies was Ortiagon,[137] and an inscription from Telmessus in Lycia celebrates Eumenes' victories over Prusias and Ortiagon at the end of 184,[138] for which he received

---

124 For the topography see Perrot, *Exploration*, 149 ff., followed by Magie, *RR* i. 1307, favouring a detour into the Eskişehir plain, which would then be the *Axylon*; A. Körte, *Ath. Mitt.* 22 (1897), 1 ff., supported, though not in detail, by K. Bittel, *Kleinasiatische Studien* (1942), 2–6, suggested a march to the east, towards the Haymana district and the central plateau.

125 Livy's account is the most detailed surviving description of a battle with the Gauls.

126 40,000 according to Claudius Antipater; 10,000 according to the usually generous Valerius Antias, but Livy stresses the difficulty in computing the number of casualties. Prisoners could be more easily reckoned.

127 Cf. Strabo, 13. 3. 41, 562.

128 Livy, 38. 26. 3.

129 Polybius, 21. 43.

130 Livy, 38. 40. 1–2.

131 Livy, 38. 37. 6; Polybius, 21. 41. 7.

132 38. 19. 2. For the emendation from Gaulotus to Gaudotus, see Robert, *Hellenica*, xiii. 261–4; Comboiomarus is an emendation of Combolomarus *vel. sim.* in the MSS. Ortiagon, guaranteed by other sources including an inscription (n. 138 below), is rendered as Orgiago.

133 Polybius, 22. 21.

134 Polybius, 21. 38. 1 ff. (= Plutarch, *Mor.* 258c–f); Livy, 38. 24. 2 ff. with Walbank's notes.

135 C. Habicht, *Hermes*, 84 (1956), 90–110; Will, *Histoire politique*, ii. 241; B. M. Levick and S. Mitchell in *MAMA* ix, pp. xl–xli.

136 Polybius, 3. 3. 6; 22. 8. 5; 23. 1. 4; Livy, 39. 46. 9, 51; Memnon, 19.

137 Justin, *Epit.* 32. 4. 2–8; Pompeius Trogus, *Prol.* 32 (mentioning only Ortiagon).

138 M. Segre, *Riv. fil.* 10 (1932), 446 ff.; L. Robert, *Rev. phil.* 8 (1934), 285 n. 1 (= *OMS* ii. 1184 n. 1); for the date see Habicht, *Hermes* (1956), 99. The battle was fought at Mount Lypedron, an unknown site in Bithynia, *OGIS* 298 (Eumenes' victory dedication), with Magie, *RR* ii. 1194, 1196 for the site. A bronze statue group at Delos celebrated the victory, Stähelin, *Galater*, 62; Rostovtzeff, *SEHHW* 1450 ff.; Durrbach, *Choix d'inscriptions de Délos*, no. 31; *IG* xi. 4. 1105.

the now familiar title of *Sōtēr*.[139] Significantly the Telmessus inscription places the Gauls on an equal footing with the Bithynian king, thereby implying that they fought as allies not as mercenaries. In the following year, 183, a Roman delegation led by T. Quinctius Flamininus intervened to make peace and confirm Eumenes' control over the regions awarded to him by the treaty of Apamea.[140]

As soon as this war was over Eumenes faced a further threat from Pharnaces I of Pontus who, by organizing an eastern Anatolian coalition consisting of some Galatian chieftains and Mithridates II of Armenia,[141] with designs both on the Black Sea and on western Asia Minor, sketched out the outline of an aggressive policy which was to be filled in a century later by Mithridates VI. He attacked and captured Sinope, an obvious target and the most important commercial centre on the Euxine.[142] The events of the following year are obscure, but it is known that Eumenes twice sent his brother Attalus to Rome to ask for help against Pharnaces,[143] and on the second occasion received an assurance that mediators would be sent out to resolve the situation. In 180 Pharnaces sent his general Leocritus to ravage Galatia, while he himself attacked Ariarathes III in Cappadocia. Eumenes, in alarm, sent Attalus into Galatia with a force which failed to overtake Leocritus; Cassignatus and Gaezatorix, two Galatian leaders who had previously supported Pharnaces, now offered their services to Attalus but were refused. Then, on the borders of Cappadocia at Parnassus, Attalus joined forces with Ariarathes, crossed the Halys and advanced east into Camisene. At this moment ambassadors from Rome, sent on from Ephesus by Eumenes to persuade Pharnaces to come to terms on the spot and accompanied by a second Pergamene force equal in size to the one already in the field, arrived to settle the dispute. Negotiations followed and the participants were summoned to further discussions at Ephesus, but when these too foundered, the war continued.[144] The events of this year reveal a number of points about the state of Galatia. The loyalties of its chieftains were divided, some supporting and some resisting Pharnaces, while others, like Cassignatus and Gaezatorix, were all too ready to change sides. Furthermore Galatia, while not perhaps technically subject to Pergamum, was

directly in its sphere of influence, as had been intended by the terms dictated by Manlius Vulso in 188.[145] In 179 Eumenes campaigned with a still stronger force which defeated Pharnaces and compelled him to make peace with Pergamum, with Prusias II of Bithynia who was now friendly to Eumenes, and with the king of Cappadocia. The agreements he had made with the Gauls were to be void, he was forbidden to enter Galatia for any reason, and compelled to withdraw from Paphlagonia, removing the troops which he had settled there and vacating any territory which he had occupied illegally.[146] Faithful to Pergamum's own interests, as well as to Rome's intentions, Eumenes had again imposed peace on Asia west of the Halys, and conclusively brought the Gauls under Attalid control.[147]

For the next decade there is another hiatus in Galatian history, if we discount the fleeting reappearance of Cassignatus as commander of Eumenes' mercenary cavalry against Perseus in Macedonia;[148] but in 168, while Eumenes' attention was distracted by the third Macedonian war, the Gauls mounted another sudden uprising, inflicted a serious defeat, and actually threatened Eumenes' person, compelling him once again to send Attalus to Rome to ask for help.[149] Eumenes himself was mistrusted by the senate, and his brother, although in favour, failed to win more than a promise of a diplomatic mission.[150] While Eumenes himself mustered a large force at Sardis,[151] P. Licinius, the consul of 171, was sent out to mediate, and met the Gauls at Synnada, to which they had advanced in the spring of 167.[152] The substance of what Licinius said to the Gauls was not known to Polybius, but its effect was apparently to encourage rather than discourage their warlike intentions. At about the same time Prusias II of Bithynia, now once again at odds with Eumenes, came to Rome to make a claim to territory occupied by Galatians; a request which they politely refused.[153] He was followed by Eumenes himself, looking once again for support against the Gauls; but the senate, embarrassed at the prospect of having to make a firm decision for or against him, preferred to

[139] Magie, *RR* ii. 764, following L. Robert, *Rev. phil.* 8 (1934), 284 n. 1 (= *OMS* ii. 1183 n. 1).
[140] Livy, 39. 51. 1.
[141] Polybius, 24. 14. 6; 25. 2. 3; with Memnon, 19.
[142] Polybius, 23. 9. 1–3; Livy, 40. 2. 6; Strabo, 12. 3. 11, 545, cf. Polybius, 4. 56 and Livy, 38. 18. 12.
[143] Polybius, 24. 9. 1–3; Livy, 40. 20. 1–4.
[144] Polybius, 24. 14–15 with Walbank's notes, especially on the topography.

[145] See above, n. 131.
[146] Polybius, 25. 2.
[147] Diodorus, 31. 14.
[148] Livy, 42. 57. 7–9; Launey, *Recherches*, 521.
[149] Polybius, 29. 22; 30. 1. 1 ff.; Livy, 45. 19. 3 *Gallici tumultus acceptaeque clades,* cf. 19. 12 and 20. 1. Polyaenus, 4. 8. 1 may belong here.
[150] Livy, 44. 20. 7; Velleius, 1. 9. 2; cf. Livy, 42. 42. 6.
[151] Polybius, 30. 3. 7–9; 19. 12; Livy, 45. 34. 10–14; E. Badian, *Foreign Clientelae* (1958), 104 ff.
[152] Unpublished epigraphic evidence appears to show that Eumenes' headquarters were at Apamea, well placed to oppose the Gauls in Synnada, T. Drew Bear, *HSCP* 79 (1975), 357.
[153] Polybius, 30. 30. 2 ff., cf. 28; Livy, 45. 44. 11 ff.

defer the problem by introducing a law forbidding the presence of foreign kings at Rome.[154]

Eumenes was thus left to his own devices against the Galatians, whose influence was felt as far afield as Amblada in eastern Pisidia.[155] Mounting a major effort he and Attalus raised an army and defeated them at a battle in Phrygia, doubtless near Synnada,[156] which was again the cause for great jubilation among the Greek cities. Statues were set up in Eumenes' honour, and the inhabitants of Sardis instituted a five-yearly festival in celebration.[157] The Galatians themselves, encouraged by Licinius' earlier equivocation, approached Rome in 165 to appeal against the treatment they were receiving, but the senate, not inclined to intervene in the complexities of Asian politics, merely underwrote their autonomy but instructed them to remain within their traditional homeland.[158] This was, effectively, a return to the situation of 188 BC, regulated in favour of the Attalids; not, as has been suggested, tacit support for the Galatians and a negation of Eumenes' efforts in the recent fighting.[159] A year later in 164 Prusias again accused Eumenes of interfering in Galatian affairs, but the senate would do little except once again reaffirm Galatian autonomy.[160] The same complaints were repeated, also unavailingly, a few years later.[161]

The Gauls continued to disrupt eastern Anatolia. In 163 the Trocmi had attempted but failed to annex territory from their neighbour Ariarathes V of Cappadocia. The Gauls again appealed to the senate at Rome, which instructed two successive delegations, the first under M. Iunius, the second under Cn. Octavius and Sp. Lucretius, to settle the differences. They found in favour of Ariarathes to whom they had been well disposed for some years.[162]

If any consistent policy can be discovered behind these manœuvres, it is a desire by Rome to maintain the *status quo* of 188, tempered by a certain mistrust of Eumenes. Eumenes himself was anxious to increase his protectorate over Galatia by any reasonable means of war or diplomacy, as emerges clearly from a series of seven private, and indeed secret, letters written by him and by his successor Attalus II to the Attis (or high priest) of the temple state at Pessinus, which were later inscribed for public display in the late first century BC or in the early empire. They date to 163–156 BC and reveal a conspiratorial preoccupation with political control over the region. There are references to the possible capture of a place called Pessongi by treachery,[163] to the Attis' brother Aioiorix, clearly a Celt, who is said to have insulted the priests of the sanctuary,[164] enquiries into the state of the inhabitants of 'the upper districts',[165] and councils of war, presumably aimed at the Galatians, held at Apamea.[166] In the last letter we gather that Attalus II, who had succeeded to the throne in 158, was dissuaded from taking military action by an adviser who warned him of Roman power and possible displeasure. The correspondence is too allusive for its full implications to be appreciated, but it surely represents continuing Pergamene efforts to exercise influence over central Anatolia and the Galatians by acting through their supporters in Pessinus, where they had vigorously patronized the shrine of Cybele and financed the construction of its important temple.[167]

[154] Polybius, 30. 18–19; Livy, *Per.* 46; Justin, *Epit.* 38. 6. 3 ff.

[155] OGIS 751, Welles, *Royal Correspondence*, 54; Swoboda, *Denkmäler*, 74 iii, ll. 15 ff. A silver Pisidian coin, allegedly dating to about 100 BC, carries the legend Σολοέττου, perhaps to be identified with the Solovettius who was in charge of the Galatian forces at Synnada in 167 (Livy, 44. 34. 12). See Regling, *RE* iiiA (1927), 935.

[156] Diodorus, 31. 14; *I. Pergamon* 165 + *Ath. Mitt.* 27 (1902), 90 no. 74.

[157] OGIS 763, Welles, *Royal Correspondence*, 52; OGIS 305.

[158] Polybius, 31. 2 τοῖς παρὰ τῶν ἐκ τῆς Ἀσίας Γαλατῶν πρεσβευταῖς συνεχώρησαν τὴν αὐτονομίαν μένουσιν ἐν ταῖς ἰδίαις κατοικίαις καὶ μὴ στρατευομένοις ἐκτὸς τῶν ἰδίων ὅρων.

[159] Cf. n. 130, against Will, *Histoire politique*, ii. 246 and Walbank on Polybius 30. 28.

[160] Polybius 30. 30.

[161] Polybius 31. 32 (Prusias in 161) and 32. 2 (Galatians in 160).

[162] Polybius, 31. 8; cf. Livy, 42. 29. 4; A. N. Sherwin-White, *JRS* 67 (1977), 63.

[163] Welles, *Royal Correspondence*, 55 ll. 6 ff. The correspondence has been republished by B. Virgilio, *Il Tempio-stato di Pessinunte fra Pergamo e Rome nel II–I secolo a. C.* (1981).

[164] Ibid. no. 56.

[165] Ibid. no. 60, ll. 11 ff.

[166] Ibid. no. 61.

[167] Magie, *RR* ii. 776.

3   The Allies of Rome

1. Tribal Organization and Political Structure

Strabo, in book 12, provides an account of the Galatian constitution which, although brief, is probably the most complete description of Celtic political organization in any part of the ancient world:

The three tribes used the same language and differed from one another in no other respect; they were divided each into four sections, and called them tetrarchies, each having its own tetrarch, one judge and one military commander, subordinate to the tetrarch, and two junior commanders. The council of the twelve tetrarchs consisted of three hundred men, and they assembled at the so-called *Drynemetos*. The council decided murder cases, the tetrarchs and the judges all others. This, therefore, was the constitution in the old days, but during my time power has passed to three, then to two and then to a single ruler, namely Deiotarus, and then to Amyntas who succeeded him.

(12. 5. 1, 567 (Loeb translation, adapted))

When the Gauls first invaded Asia Minor they had seventeen separate chieftains, and authority among them, then and afterwards, was often divided between a large number of individuals. It is clear, therefore, that the formal and carefully balanced constitution under twelve tetrarchs that Strabo depicts, cannot, as it stands, date back to the period of the Celtic invasions or to any time in the third century BC. Nothing that is known of their social and political structure at that period would lead one to expect such organization and discipline. Even in the second century, when Manlius Vulso invaded Galatia, there is no mention of this tetrarchic rule, and the sources refer to four chieftains: two from the Tolistobogii and one from each of the other tribes—a system that does not correspond to Strabo's account (although it is not necessarily inconsistent with it).[1] It is probable that the office of tetrarch, and the constitution described by Strabo, developed during the second century BC, as the tribes increasingly

came under the civilizing influence of Pergamum and the other kingdoms of Asia Minor.[2] The specialization implied by the division of responsibility among the subsidiary officers is doubtless another product of increasing sophistication, but at base the whole system was decidedly Celtic. The fourfold division of the tribes is paralleled in the west, for instance in the four cantons of the Helvetii in the western Alps, or the four kings of the Cantii in south-east Britain;[3] and the tribal gathering of elders at a central meeting place to decide capital cases and other matters of moment was a feature of all Celtic societies.[4] The word *Drynemetos* is Celtic, meaning a sacred grove of oak trees, and points to the use of religious sanction to confirm the political and judicial activities of the tribes.[5]

The development of Galatian tribal organization from the raiding bands of the 270s to this incipient state constitution, which drew a widely scattered population together into a politically united body, matches a similar development among the Celtic tribes of the west. There, between the third and first centuries BC, increasing contact both with the Roman world and with the Greek city states of southern Gaul and Spain, above all Massilia, gradually effected a transformation from loosely structured, unstable tribal groupings under a warrior aristocracy to a more formal and centralized oligarchic form of government.[6] One result of this development, both in the west and in the east, was the emergence of dominant dynastic families in Celtic political life, to replace warrior chieftains whose chief claim to authority was their personal prowess. It has already been noted that for much of the Hellenistic period there is no sign of continuity within a single

---

[1] Livy, 38. 18. 1; 19. 2. Schwahn, *RE* vA (1934), 1093 s.v. *tetrarch* treats the four chieftains as tetrarchs of the Tolistobogii; Stähelin, *RE* vi (1937), s.v. Tolistobogioi argues convincingly for the view adopted here.

[2] See Ch. 2 §1.

[3] Caesar, *BG* 1. 5; 5. 22; both adduced by Mommsen, *Hermes*, 19 (1884), 316–21.

[4] See Ch. 4 n. 180 for the comparable gathering of the Gallic tribes in the territory of the Carnutes.

[5] See Holder, ii. 708–13 for the countless examples of *nemeton* in the toponymy of Celtic areas.

[6] See the remarks of D. Nash, *Num. Chron.* 15 (1975), 204–18 and *Britannia*, 7 (1976), 11–26.

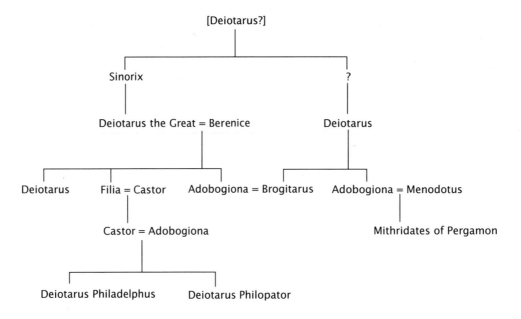

Stemma: The family of Deiotarus.

family among the Galatian leaders. The first indication of a change comes at the end of the second century BC, when Sinorix, a dominating figure in his own day, saw his authority inherited by his son Deiotarus, the central figure of Galatian history in the first century BC.[7]

During the first century the dynastic principle of succession prevailed, bringing Galatian practice into line with that of the other aristocracies of Asia Minor and the Levant, a point that may be illustrated in detail, at the cost of some anticipation of the story to come. The key figure is Deiotarus, son of Sinorix and tetrarch of the Tolistobogii. His son by his wife Berenice,[8] also called Deiotarus, was appointed to succeed him and made his co-regent, but predeceased his father.[9] The old king had allegedly put his other sons to death to ensure a peaceful succession, a ploy not unparalleled in the behaviour of other potentates,[10] but he had other kin to follow him, notably his grandson Castor, the son of the tetrarch of the Tectosages, also called Castor, who had married Deiotarus' daughter but been put to death by his father-in-law in or soon after 43 BC.[11] The younger Castor himself

died or was deposed to make way for a member of a different family, Amyntas, in 36, but his own line was continued by his son Deiotarus Philadelphus, who became king of Paphlagonia.[12] Deiotarus' family was allied to that of Brogitarus the ruler of the Trocmi, who was married to Adobogiona, a daughter of the great Deiotarus.[13] But Brogitarus' own father was also called Deiotarus, presumably a member of a Trocmian branch of his father-in-law's family, and they may both have owed their name to a common grandfather.[14] A second Adobogiona was the sister of Brogitarus and married Menodotus, a wealthy Pergamene, evidence for relations between Galatia and Pergamum that had begun with the early interest of the Attalid house in the sanctuary at Pessinus, and can be detected long into the Roman imperial period.[15] The son of Menodotus and Adobogiona was Mithridates of Pergamum, a friend and ally of Julius Caesar who became Trocmian tetrarch in 47 BC, *iure gentis et cognationis*.[16] Yet another Adobogiona appears to have been married to Castor of the Tectosages, and may have acted as regent for her son, Deiotarus Philadelphus of Paphlagonia. She could

[7] See below, § III.

[8] *RECAM* ii no. 188; Plutarch, *Adv. Coloten*, 1109b; in Plutarch, *De mul. virt.* 258c she is called Stratonike, but this is probably a slip.

[9] For the younger Deiotarus as *rex* see *RECAM* ii no. 188; Cicero, *Att.* 5. 17. 3; *Deiot.* 25, 36, 41. Last mentioned alive in Feb. 43 BC, Cicero, *Phil.* 11. 31.

[10] Plutarch, *De Stoic. repugn.* 1049c. The practice of the Ottoman sultans springs most readily to mind.

[11] Strabo, 12. 5. 3, 568.

[12] Strabo, 12. 3. 41, 562; Magie, *RR* ii. 1283–4.

[13] A. Ippel, *Ath. Mitt.* 37 (1912), 294–6 (*IGR* iv no. 1683); *IGR* iv no. 3; Cicero, *Har. resp.* 29.

[14] Stähelin, *Galater*, 113 and stemma.

[15] Strabo, 13. 4. 3, 625. The most notable Galatian noble of the 2nd cent. AD, C. Iulius Severus, claimed descent from Attalus of Pergamum (Bosch, *Ankara* nos. 105–6). Cf. Th. Reinach, *Rev. celt.* 22 (1901), 1–8 and Dittenberger on *OGIS* no. 544. See below, Ch. 10 § III at n. 102 and following.

[16] [Caesar], *Bell. Alex.* 78.

have been a daughter of Mithridates of Pergamum.[17] The complexities of the family relationships appear more clearly on the stemma, which demonstrates graphically the transformation which had come over the Galatian ruling class.

At a certain point, according to Strabo, power passed from twelve tetrarchs to three rulers. He states that this was in his own time, which should be after his birth between 70 and 64 BC,[18] but this should not be taken literally. In 86 BC Mithridates of Pontus had summoned the sixty leading men of Galatia to Pergamum, and had all but three put to death.[19] Strabo's description implies a total of sixty magistrates in the old Galatian constitution, reduced to three, and it is economical and probably correct to infer that Mithridates' massacre was the immediate cause of the transformation of the Galatian leadership.[20] The old system was not reinstated as the nobility recovered its strength, partly no doubt because of the ambitions of the surviving chieftains, who preferred to retain the eminence which they had fortuitously acquired; but also because Rome, now more seriously involved in Anatolian politics than ever before, had a vested interest in a strong and coherent leadership. The old title of tetrarch survived to denote not one of twelve rulers, but the chief of each of the three Galatian tribes, or any important member of one of the ruling families. From now on the principle appears to be established that a Galatian chieftain was tetrarch of his own tribe; if he received the title king, it was by virtue of a kingdom, conferred by Rome, elsewhere in Asia Minor.[21]

II. *Rome in Asia Minor, 133–63 BC*

After the middle of the second century BC there is no detailed record of Galatian activity for almost a century. Although in physical presence the Gauls had not declined and their political system had become more sophisticated, their power was for a long time eclipsed by that of the neighbouring kingdoms, Pergamum, Bithynia, Pontus, and Cappadocia. When they did become prominent again, definitively after 63 BC, two fundamental developments had brought about a deep-seated transformation in the social, political, and economic circumstances of Asia Minor. The first of these was the bequest of the Attalid kingdom to Rome in 133 BC, the beginning of a gradual and almost reluctant process by which Asia, now a Roman prov-

ince, became enmeshed into a system of empire which had a profound influence on the province itself, and increasingly important implications for neighbouring territories. The second was the rise of the power of Pontus under Mithridates VI, as a direct challenge to Roman control of Asia, and the conflict between the two powers, involving all the territories and peoples between the Euphrates and the Aegean, not least the Galatians.

Direct Roman control in Asia Minor developed only slowly. Events since 189 had shown that Rome was reluctant to intervene directly, preferring to leave control of affairs in the hands of her allies. Between the expedition of Manlius Vulso and 131 BC no Roman force set foot in Anatolia, and it was rare for her even to be represented by official delegations in the area.[22] This pattern did not change substantially after the unexpected bequest by Attalus III of his kingdom to Rome in 133. Rome was driven to intervene in force by the widespread revolt of the pretender Aristonicus, but after his resistance was broken in 129, no further troops were sent to the area. Furthermore, much of the Pergamene kingdom was voluntarily relinquished, Great Phrygia being given to Mithridates V of Pontus, and Lycaonia to Ariarathes of Cappadocia,[23] and many of the important cities of Asia, autonomous under Pergamene rule, remained free in the Roman province.[24] Apart from a command against the pirates in 102 BC, no Roman legions were sent to Anatolia until 87, when Sulla began the offensive against Mithridates VI. Instead, when force was needed, Rome relied on levies of native troops, or on the support of allied kings.[25]

If the senate was reluctant to become too deeply involved in Asiatic affairs, this was clearly not true of other sections of Roman society. In 123 BC a law of the tribune C. Gracchus had awarded the right to

[17] Th. Reinach, *L'Histoire par les monnaies* (1902), 151, 162 ff.
[18] E. Honigmann, *RE* viA (1931), 76–7.
[19] Plutarch, *De mul virt.* 259; Appian, *Mith.* 46.
[20] P. Stadter, *Plutarch's Historical Methods: An Analysis of the Mulierum Virtutes* (1965), 110 ff.; Hoben, *Kleinasiatische Dynasten*, 59.
[21] F. E. Adcock, *JRS* 27 (1937), 12–17.

[22] See Ch. 2 § III n. 143 (180 BC, mediation between Eumenes II and Pharnaces I of Pontus); nn. 150–2 (168 BC, mediations between Eumenes and the Galatians); n. 162 (163 BC, mediation between the Trocmi and Ariarathes V of Cappadocia). In more detail, A. N. Sherwin-White, *JRS* 67 (1977), 62–75.
[23] Justin, *Epit.*, 37. 1. 2; 38. 5. 3; Appian, *Mith.* 11, 12, 15, 56, 57. Great Phrygia certainly excluded the Maeander valley, which the milestones of M'. Aquillius show to have been part of the province, but probably included most of N. and E. Phrygia, see Magie, *RR* ii. 1042 n. 26; T. Drew Bear, *Historia*, 21 (1971), 80–7. Both areas reverted to Roman rule before long; Phrygia soon after 120; Lycaonia perhaps a decade or so later, after the death of Ariarathes VI of Cappadocia. See C. Nicolet, *et al.*, *Rome et la conquête du monde méditerranéenne*, ii, *Genèse d'un empire* (1978), 777.
[24] Sherwin-White, *JRS* 67 (1977), 68–9.
[25] Appian, *Mith.* 11, 17, 19 (90/89 BC, Phrygians and Galatians); Memnon, 22. 7; Justin, *Epit.* 38. 3. 8; Plutarch, *Sulla*, 5. 7.

collect the Asian taxes to members of the Roman equestrian order, who acquired a genuine political identity at precisely this time. Now, as holders of public contracts to farm the Asian taxes, they must have moved swiftly to make the most of their opportunity. There is little direct evidence for their activities during the first forty years of the province's existence, but in the mid-90s BC, the propraetor Mucius Scaevola was forced to take measures to protect the native communities from their depredations,[26] and in 88 Mithridates, having conquered Asia, ordered the slaughter of all Romans or Italians in the province, regardless of their age or status. The sources give very high figures for the number of victims, 80,000 or even 150,000 persons, and while these are certainly exaggerated they do give an impression of the perceived scale of Roman penetration of Asia.[27] After Sulla's reconquest, and his new settlement in 85, the old pattern of government was brought back, but imposed with more rigour, and the pace of exploitation was increased.

The right to collect the various Asian taxes was certainly exploited to the full by profiteers. Should the Asian communities be unable to produce the sums demanded of them, they might be compelled to borrow, often at punitive rates of interest, from Roman bankers and moneylenders. Their chief security was certainly land, with the result that individual Romans from the start began to acquire property in Asia, either in default of debt payments, or by direct purchase from landowners, unable to raise the capital to pay Roman levies by other means.[28] The need to pay taxes also forced the cities of Asia to sell other assets, primarily to Roman buyers, notably works of art, manufactured goods in increasing quantities, and slaves.[29]

The intimate relationship between taxation and the vigorous economic exploitation of the province by Roman entrepreneurs explains why the latter operated much more rarely beyond Roman provincial boundaries. There is clear evidence, cited later, to show that the activities of Roman moneylenders and businessmen took them outside Asia into Galatia and elsewhere in eastern Anatolia, but they did not acquire property or establish permanent bases there before it became provincial territory during the reign of Augustus. It is likely that Galatia, under these conditions, remained a source of slave labour, as it had been in the second century,[30] although probably not on the large scale attested in Bithynia, where Nicomedes IV complained that his kingdom had been virtually depopulated by slave-trading, a traffic that he was probably forced to encourage in order to maintain the country's liquidity and its ability to pay Roman dues.[31]

Before the 50s BC Galatia may have escaped relatively unscathed from the economic exploitation of Asia Minor by Rome. By contrast it was profoundly affected by the long wars between Rome and Mithridates from 89 to 63 BC. Its geographical position ensured its political and military importance in any war with Pontus. In 99–98 BC C. Marius had paid an extended visit to Galatia and Cappadocia, ostensibly for religious reasons, but possibly with an eye to securing a major military command against Mithridates.[32] When Rome voluntarily gave up Great Phrygia to Mithridates V of Pontus in 129 BC she must have surrendered effective control over Galatia as well, since it lay directly between Phrygia and Pontus. Although Phrygia was taken back within a decade,[33] Mithridates VI, who succeeded in 120, probably continued to exercise a protectorate over Galatia until about 96, when he lost the allegiance of Nicomedes of Bithynia and was obliged to give up his sovereignty in Paphlagonia and Cappadocia. Since these territories stood on either side of Galatia, his grip must have been loosened there also.[34]

The Gauls were predictably divided in their allegiances with their neighbours. When the Romans intervened in strength in Anatolia in 89, their three armies, under M'. Aquillius, P. Cassius, and Q. Oppius, consisted largely of Phrygian and Galatian levies.[35] Two years later, when Mithridates sent his general Archelaus to invade Greece, his army too contained a substantial number of Gauls.[36] Their behaviour is

[26] Magie, RR i. 173–4.

[27] Ibid. i. 216 ff.; ii. 1103 ff.; 80,000 Valerius Maximus, 9. 2. ext. 3 and Memnon, 31, 4; 150,000, Plutarch, Sulla, 24, 4. The figures are exaggerated, perhaps drastically, see P. A. Brunt, Italian Manpower (1971), 224–7.

[28] Cf. H. Zehnacker, REL 57 (1979), 165–86.

[29] M. H. Crawford, Ec. Hist. Rev. 30 (1977), 42–52.

[30] See below, Chs. 4 § III, and 14 § VI at n. 87.

[31] Diodorus, 36. 3. 1. See Crawford, Ec. Hist. Rev. 30 (1977) 49 n. 5. Bithynia, rich only in slaves, makes a point of the joke in Catullus 10.

[32] Plutarch, Marius, 31 and other sources and literature cited by R. D. Sullivan, ANRW ii. 7. 2 (1980), 1129 n. 19; for possible reasons, see E. Badian, Athenaeum, 37 (1959), 279 ff. = Studies in Greek and Roman History (1964), 56 ff.; T. J. Luce, Historia, 19 (1970), 162 ff.; Sherwin-White, JRS 67 (1977), 74 n. 87 is sceptical.

[33] See n. 23.

[34] Justin, Epit. 38. 5. 6; Th. Reinach, Mithridate Eupator (1890), 100; Sherwin-White, JRS 67 (1977) 70 ff.

[35] Appian, Mith. 11–19; other sources in Sherwin-White, JRS 67 (1977), 72 n. 74. He rightly emphasizes the new departure in Roman policy initiated by these hostilities.

[36] Appian, Mith. 41; Justin, Epit., 38. 4. 9 ff. Note that Q. Oppius was short of troops when he was besieged in Laodiceia on the Lycus, J. M. Reynolds, Aphrodisias and Rome (1982), 14 with Appian, Mith. 20. His native levies had deserted.

precisely what one would expect from a small state between two great powers. Their allegiance passed decisively to Rome after 86, when Mithridates, suspicious of their intentions after Sulla's victory in Greece, summoned the tetrarchs to Pergamum and had them treacherously put to death.[37] He sent envoys to Galatia to complete the task by murdering those nobles who had not accepted his summons, but three escaped the slaughter and evicted the satrap Eumachus who had been sent to take over their territory.[38] The episode conclusively turned the Gauls against Mithridates, leaving him with nothing except the money and possessions which he had sequestered from his victims, and a legacy of hatred which was to be fully exploited by Rome. Individual Gauls remained in his pay, notably Konnakorix commander of 4,000 troops stationed in Heraclea Pontica,[39] and Bituitus, another Celtic leader who was on hand to assist Mithridates to suicide in 63,[40] but their services were far outweighed by those offered to Rome by the most conspicuous survivor of the massacre, Deiotarus.

In speeches delivered in 44 and 43 BC Cicero sang the praises of Deiotarus as the ally and helper of almost every Roman commander who had operated in Anatolia since 90 BC—Sulla, Murena, Servilius, Lucullus, and Pompey[41]—assistance which had been rendered in virtually every theatre of war.[42] Until the final defeat of Mithridates in 63 his contributions are only sporadically recorded. There is no other record of the help given to Sulla, but it is clear that the aggressive campaigns of Licinius Murena into Pontic territory between 84 and 82 must have been launched from Galatia.[43] Servilius' activities in southern Anatolia between 78 and 75 made him the first Roman general to cross the Taurus, and he campaigned widely in Isauria, Pisidia, and Phrygia Paroreius, where Galatian assistance would have been invaluable.[44] Their services to Lucullus were important and various. As the Roman forces tried desperately and ultimately successfully to relieve Mithridates' siege of Cyzicus in 73, Eumachus,

the former short-lived satrap of Galatia, made inroads into Pisidia, Isauria, and Cilicia, killing many Roman citizens, until Deiotarus pursued him back to Pontus.[45] Then, when Lucullus took the offensive in 72, he used a huge supply train of 30,000 Galatian porters to carry grain for his five legions as they advanced from Bithynia into the territory of Amisus in Pontus.[46] In the following year he used Galatian cavalry in the fighting at Cabeira, and in 69 they accompanied him to Tigranocerta.[47] Indeed, had they not paused to loot a pack-mule laden with gold and silver, a posse of Galatian horseman might have captured Mithridates himself as he fled into Armenia in the face of Lucullus' advance. No doubt, although the sources do not record it, the same cavalry and other assistance was available to Pompeius when he received the command of Lucullus' troops, precisely at Posdala, a fortress of the Trocmi in east Galatia.[48]

III. *The Settlement of Pompey*

Galatian services rendered during the Mithridatic wars were richly rewarded in Pompey's arrangements for the east, drawn up at Amisus in 63, and finally ratified by the *Lex Vatinia*, four years later. These arrangements need to be seen as a whole, since they involved a completely new plan for the defence and administration of the whole of eastern Anatolia, to say nothing of the rest of the Levant. The key factor was the decision to turn the whole Pontic heartland of Mithridates' kingdom into a province, to be attached to Bithynia.[49] This province was divided into the territories of eleven cities, but various adjacent regions were handed over to native rulers who had supported Pompey during the war. The identification of the eleven cities has been a matter for dispute,[50] but the essentials of the strategy are clear. The new province contained three long-standing Greek colonial foundations on the Black Sea coast, Amastris, Sinope, and Amisus. The others, in all probability, comprised Mithridates' former royal capital at Amaseia, called a *polis* by Memnon in 70 BC and evidently one of the most thriving communities of Pontus;[51] and several other inland cities either founded

[37] Appian, *Mith.* 46, 58; Plutarch, *De mul. virt.* 259a–d.
[38] Appian, *Mith.* 46. For Mithridatic satraps, cf. Welles, *Royal Correspondence*, 297.
[39] Memnon, 29–36.
[40] Appian, *Mith.* 111; Livy, *Per.* 102.
[41] Cicero, *Phil.* 11. 33–4; cf. *Deiot.* 26.
[42] Cicero, *Deiot.* 37: Asia, Cappadocia, Pontus, Cilicia, and Syria.
[43] Geyer, *RE* xv (1932), 2178 s.v. Mithridates 12; Appian, *Mith.* 85.
[44] For these campaigns see H. Ormerod, *JRS* 12 (1922), 35 ff.; Robert, *Hellenica*, vi. 46 n. 1 (bibliography); Magie, *RR* i. 287–90; ii. 1167–74; S. Mitchell, *Tenth Congress*, 311–18 for the territory of the Orondeis and part of Phrygia Paroreius, well to the north of the Taurus. See below, Ch. 6 at n. 31.

[45] Appian, *Mith.* 75.
[46] Plutarch, *Lucullus*, 14. 1; Appian, *Mith.* 78.
[47] Memnon, 44; Plutarch, *Lucullus*, 28. 2.
[48] Plutarch, *Lucullus*, 36; *Pompeius*, 31; Cassius Dio, 36. 46; Strabo, 12. 5. 2, 567. The place-name is uncertain for the MSS of Strabo are unreliable at this point. See the edn. of F. Lasserre (Budé ix (1981), 233–4), who suggests, without much conviction, that the site lay west of the Halys, perhaps near Aspona.
[49] See *Note* at the end of this chapter.
[50] Magie, *RR* ii. 1232–4 provides all the essentials of the problem and cites earlier discussions.
[51] Memnon, 38. 9; Strabo, 12. 3. 39, 561.

or completed by Pompey himself: Magnopolis built on the site of Mithridates' half-finished capital Eupatoria; Megalopolis, almost certainly to be identified with the later Sebasteia; Neapolis in the territory of the Phazimonitae in eastern Paphlagonia; Pompeiopolis on the river Amnias in northern Paphlagonia; Diospolis at Cabeira, which already had the nucleus of a city thanks to Mithridates' own building there; the former temple state of Zela, now for the first time made a self-governing city; and Nicopolis in the western part of Armenia Minor, settled with Pompey's veterans.[52] One enclave of independent territory was set aside in the centre of Pontus—the temple state of Comana, which was entrusted to Archelaus, a high priest whose family had connections with the Roman aristocracy.[53]

Most of the inland cities lay on the main routes of Pontic territory, which had become familiar to the Romans during the campaigns of the Mithridatic wars. The valleys here run mainly from west to east, not north to south, and the lines of communication follow them. Advancing from the west, Pompeiopolis, Neapolis, Magnopolis, Diospolis, and Nicopolis all lay along the northern route which was the main artery of Pontus,[54] and was later followed by the Roman military road to Satala.[55] Megalopolis was on the southern route connecting Nicopolis and Armenia Minor with Galatia; while Amaseia and Zela, in the basin of the river Iris, were both sited in the fertile areas of central Pontus between the two routes.

If the new foundations were to achieve their purpose successfully, Pompey had to ensure firstly that they could effectively control the whole territory of Pontus, and secondly that they could govern themselves. For the first he had to arrange for the cities' authority to cover the whole area of the province; this he did by adding substantially to the territories of the existing centres and by giving very large grants of land to the new cities, so that their boundaries were contiguous.[56] The second condition was harder to satisfy. Autonomous city life was new to Mithridates' kingdom, although Greek influence was becoming increasingly deeply rooted during his reign and as a result of his

encouragement.[57] Some attempt had been made to develop *poleis*, for instance at Amaseia, Cabeira, and Eupatoria, but this last had been cut off before it had become properly established.[58] Coins bearing the names of several Pontic cities were issued, but they are of a standard type and reflect the initiative of a central authority, not that of the cities acting independently.[59] In two cases, Nicopolis and Eupatoria-Magnopolis, Pompey introduced settlers from outside. At Nicopolis there was a mixture of the local inhabitants and his own veterans, the latter earning the place the status of an 'Italian colony';[60] at Magnopolis, Strabo's claim that he added territory and settlers to the place does not exclude the possibility that this was simply a synoecism of the surrounding communities, but again is more reasonably taken to show the addition of colonists from outside.[61] In addition, in a way familiar from other new provinces of the empire, a stream of *mercatores* and *negotiatores* moved into Pontus, who were to suffer badly in the invasion of Pharnaces in 47 BC.[62]

The creation of the new province did not account by any means for all of Anatolia east of Asia and Bithynia. The south-east was placed in the care of one of Rome's staunchest allies, Ariobarzanes I of Cappadocia, who, in addition to his traditional kingdom, received control of Sophene, east of the Euphrates, and the eastern part of Lycaonia, around Cybistra, commanding the Cilician gates.[63] The small kingdom controlled by Antipater of Derbe, including the towns of Derbe and Laranda, apparently adjoined this on the west. Antipater, the son of Perilaus, was probably of Macedonian origin; the only survivor of a number of petty Macedonian chiefdoms which had been established around the margins of the central Anatolian plateau.[64]

Inland Paphlagonia and Galatia, which separated Asia and Bithynia from Pontus, had hitherto been

[52] For this list cf. Magie, loc cit. Magnopolis: Strabo, 12. 3. 30, 556; Megalopolis: 12. 3. 37, 560, and Jones, *CERP*² 426–7; Neapolis: 12. 3. 38, 560, and Cumont, *SP* ii. 125 ff.; Pompeiopolis: 12. 3. 40, 562; Cabeira/Diospolis: 12. 3. 31, 556–7, and Cumont, *SP* ii. 259 ff.; Zela: 11. 8. 4, 512; 12. 3. 37, 559, and Cumont *SP* ii. 189 ff.; Nicopolis: 12. 3. 28, 555; Appian, *Mith.* 115; Cassius Dio, 36. 50. 3.

[53] Strabo, 12. 3. 32–6, 558–9.

[54] Magie *RR* ii. 1083–6; D. Winfield, *AS* 27 (1977), 151–66.

[55] Cf. T. B. Mitford, *ANRW* ii. 7. 2 (1980), 1183–6. See below, Ch. 9 § 11 at n. 69.

[56] See Strabo's remarks on Magnopolis, Megalopolis, Zela, and Neapolis; W. G. Fletcher, *TAPA* 70 (1939), 21–3; Jones, *CERP*² 159.

[57] E. Olshausen, *Anc. Soc.* 5 (1974), 153–70.

[58] Appian, *Mith.* 115, cf. 78. Note a fragmentary inscription from Amisus, which mentions a descendant of kings and tetrarchs, *IGR* iii no. 1435.

[59] Head, *HN*² 502.

[60] Cassius Dio, 36. 50. 3; *AE* (1909), 19.

[61] Strabo, 12. 3. 30, 556 προσθεὶς χώραν καὶ οἰκήτορας.

[62] [Caesar], *Bell. Alex* 41, 70; Appian, *BC* ii. 91; *Mith.* 120; Cassius Dio, 42. 46. 3; Plutarch, *Caesar* 50. 1.

[63] Magie, *RR* i. 374–5; soon to be succeeded by his son, Ariobarzanes II, R. D. Sullivan, *ANRW* ii. 7. 2 (1980), 1135–6.

[64] Cicero, *Fam.* 13. 73. 2; Philomelos and his son Lysias at Philomelium and Lysias respectively, Magie, *RR* ii. 1313; A. Wilhelm, *Neue Beiträge*, i, *Sb. Ak. Wien*, 166 (1910), 48–54; Holleaux, *Études*, iii. 357 ff.; Robert, *Villes*², 155–7; and at Docimeium, founded by the Macedonian Dokimos from Synnada, L. Robert, *A travers l'Asie Mineure* (1980), 240–4.

governed by a multiplicity of local rulers.[65] Paphlagonia, apart from the city territories of Pompeiopolis and Neapolis which belonged to the province of Pontus, was divided between two dynasts, descendants of Pylaemenes, called Pylaemenes and Attalus;[66] Galatia, meanwhile, was assigned to its surviving tetrarchs,[67] Deiotarus of the Tolistobogii, Brogitarus of the Trocmi, and an unknown ruler of the Tectosages.

Deiotarus was now a man of mature, if not advanced years.[68] His power was clearly based on his ancestral leadership of the Tolistobogii where he held the strongholds of Blucium (his palace), and Peium (his treasury). Both were fortified positions, the latter certainly built with the help of Greek architectural experts and equipped to a sufficient standard of comfort to afford suitable lodging for Julius Caesar returning from Pontus in 47.[69] Pompey not only confirmed this hegemony in Galatia, but also gave Deiotarus control over more distant parts of Asia Minor; namely part of the Gazelonitis, a particularly fertile area on the east bank of the Halys on the Black sea coast, dividing the territories of Amisus and Sinope; and also the territory of Pharnaceia and Trapezus as far east as Colchis and south to Armenia Minor.[70] We know from Appian that Colchis was in the hands of another dynast called Aristarchus,[71] so Strabo's 'as far as' should be taken in an exclusive sense. However, Strabo may well have been mistaken about Armenia Minor which Deiotarus certainly controlled by 47 and which, according to one source, he received from Pompey.[72] In virtue of these territorial additions Deiotarus was given the title king, which was ratified by the senate in 59.[73]

Brogitarus, the tetrarch of the Trocmi, received similar, though less-generous treatment. He was given a section of Mithridates' old kingdom, including the fortress Mithridateion, which probably amounted to an eastward extension of his Galatian possessions, and it was probably because of this that he too received the title of king.[74]

The first consideration in all these arrangements was to provide military protection for Roman-dominated territory, both against enemies beyond the new provinces to the east, and in the wilder parts of the Anatolian hinterland; and all the rulers installed by Pompey were men who had proved their worth by providing military aid in the past, or who were to do so in the future. As the events of the previous hundred years had made clear, Rome was extremely reluctant to commit herself to providing a permanent garrison for her Anatolian provinces, and the cities of the provinces themselves were incapable of providing for their own defence even before the advent of Roman rule. It became almost a cliché of Roman administrative practice that wilder and more unruly territory was best controlled by client kings, while direct provincial administration was confined to the more civilized areas.[75] Strabo makes this point precisely in the context of the Black Sea area,

[65] The twelve Galatian tetrarchs before 86 BC have already been discussed; Paphlagonia: Strabo, 12. 3. 41, 562, μικρὸν μὲν πρὸ ἡμῶν ἦρχον πλείους.

[66] Appian, *Mith.* 114 (Attalus alone); Eutropius, 6. 14. 1 (Attalus and Pylaemenes); Magie, *RR* ii. 1234–5.

[67] Cf. Strabo, 12. 3. 1, 541 cited in the *note* at the end of this chapter.

[68] Cf. Plutarch, *Cato Minor*, 15, which implies that Deiotarus was advanced years when Cato visited Asia Minor either in 67 or in 62 BC (cf. R. Flacelière and E. Chambry, *Plutarque Vies tome X* (1976), 60–1). He was old enough to have a daughter of marriageable age c.70 BC, since his grandson Castor fought with Cicero in 51 (*Deiot.* 28). He was reckoned an old man by Crassus, himself over 60, in 54 BC (Plutarch, *Crassus*, 17. 2), and had to be lifted into the saddle at Pharsalus, seven years later (*Deiot.* 28). Cassius Dio remarked on his age after 44 BC, 47. 24. 3. See Hoben, *Kleinasiatische Dynasten* 67.

[69] R. O. Arık, *TTAED* 2 (1934), 133 ff., and *JHS Arch. Reports* (1989/90), 130 (Blucium); S. Mitchell, *AS* 24 (1974), 61–75 (Peium); Cicero, *Deiot.* 17 ff.

[70] Strabo, 12. 3. 13, 547: ταύτης δὲ τῆς χώρας [the Gazelonitis], τὴν μὲν ἔχουσιν Ἀμισηνοί, τὴν δ' ἔδωκε Δηιοτάρῳ Πομπήιος, καθάπερ καὶ τὰ περὶ Φαρνακίαν καὶ τὴν Τραπεζουσίαν μέχρι Κολχίδος καὶ τῆς μικρᾶς Ἀρμενίας. καὶ τούτων ἀπέδειξεν αὐτὸν βασιλέα ἔχοντα καὶ τὴν πατρῴαν τετραρχίαν τῶν Γαλατῶν τοὺς Τολιστοβωγίους. Cf. Robert, *A travers l'Asie Mineure*, 20.

[71] Appian, *Mith.* 114; cf. Eutropius 6. 14. 1; and coins, Head, *HN²* 496.

[72] Eutropius 6. 14. 1, presumably from Livy.

[73] The problem of Deiotarus' territory has been much discussed. See especially Magie, *RR* ii. 1237–8; T. Liebmann-Frankfort, *La Frontière orientale*, 280–1; Hoben, *Kleinasiatische Dynasten*, 69–73. Adcock, *JRS* 27 (1937), 11–16 argued that Armenia Minor was originally given to Brogitarus in 63, and passed to Deiotarus when Brogitarus died in the late 50s, but there is no evidence for this. Strabo's μέχρι Κολχίδος καὶ τῆς μικρᾶς Ἀρμενίας should certainly be taken in an exclusive sense, as is shown by Appian on Aristarchus of Colchis (see Anderson, *ASBuckler*, 4 ff.). However, the old conjecture made by Unger to read μέχρι Κολχίδος καὶ τὴν μικρὰν Ἀρμενίαν (*Philologus* 55 (1896), 250), is worth considering. For the award of the title king, see Cicero, *Har. Resp.* 29; *Deiot.* 10; *Phil.* 11. 94; *Div.* 11. 79; [Caesar], *Bell. Alex.* 67. His possessions may have included the Caranitis south of Zela, which lay outside the Pompeian province of Pontus.

[74] Strabo, 12. 5. 1, 567. For conjectures about Mithridateion, identified with the huge hill fort at Kerkenes Kale east of Yozgat, see Anderson, *SP* i. 25 ff.; Cumont, *SP* iii. 226; K. Bittel, *Kleinasiatische Studien* (1942), 54 ff., but observe the doubts of Magie, *RR* ii. 1094 and Ruge, *RE* xv (1932), 2215 ff. Brogitarus could apparently thank Clodius for the title king (Cicero, *Har. Resp.* 28–9 discussed below). It is attested by silver coins, perhaps minted at Tavium, bearing the legend ΒΑΣΙΛΕΩΣ ΒΡΟΓΙΤΑΡΟΥ ΦΙΛΟΡΩΜΑΙΟΥ (*BMC Galatia*, xvii), but on the inscriptions *OGIS* no. 349 = *IGR* iv no. 1328 = *I. Kyme*, no. 15; *IGR* iv no. 1683; and *I. Didyma*, 475. 36 he is called *tetrarches*. See Th. Reinach, *L'Histoire par les monnaies* (1902), 155.

[75] Strabo, 14. 5. 6, 641.

in his detailed account of the tribe known as the Heniochi. Settled at the east end of the Euxine beyond Colchis, they practised piracy and raiding against merchant ships, coastal areas, and even cities, selling their loot to the communities of the Crimea with the connivance of the Bosporan kings, or ransoming captives back to their families. Areas ruled by dynasts (and here Strabo may be thinking of the area around Pharnaceia and Trapezus under Deiotarus) could gain redress against them since their rulers were prepared to retaliate, but help was far less forthcoming in the Roman provinces because of the negligent attitude of their governors.[76]

The military role of the Galatians is confirmed by the size and organization of their forces. In 51 BC Cicero, to his relief, could count on 12,000 infantry divided into thirty cohorts and equipped in Roman fashion, and 2,000 cavalry led by Deiotarus, to pit against the Parthian threat.[77] By 47 BC these troops were organized as two legions, which fought alongside Cn. Domitius at Nicopolis against Pharnaces.[78] The main strength clearly lay in the infantry, and the tyrannicides were supported by a strong contingent of foot soldiers, as well as by 5,000 cavalry at Philippi in 42.[79] Normally, however, when Galatian help was summoned outside Anatolia during the battles of the civil wars, they supplied cavalry. At Pharsalus 600 horsemen under Deiotarus and 300 Tectosagans fought for their patron Pompey;[80] and at Actium, fighting for Antony, they again sent cavalry only.[81] The presence of Galatian troops in such numbers, organized, equipped, and presumably trained to Roman standards, serves as a useful reminder that Rome had to rely on two legions to defend Anatolia over 120 years before Vespasian stationed the legions *XVI Flavia Firma* and *XII Fulminata* along the Cappadocian *limes*.

IV. *Galatia during the Civil Wars*

After 63 Asia Minor saw a dozen and more years of relative quiet and stability. The power of Pontus had been broken, and the challenge of the Parthians had not yet been posed. Pompey's *acta* were finally confirmed by a plebiscite in 59, and in the same year, or at any rate by 58, P. Clodius Pulcher had measures passed through the senate giving the title of king to Brogitarus

and Deiotarus.[82] Cicero's attacks on Clodius in 56 bring to light his various dealings with Brogitarus, who had apparently obtained from Clodius the privilege of nominating the high priest of Pessinus and thus gained control of the shrine—something which must usually have been in the power of the Tolistobogii to grant or withhold.[83] Money, or promises of money, had been exchanged between Clodius and Brogitarus—it was rumoured that the latter had subvented the construction of the temple of Castor at Rome—and it was this financial angle which persisted in 55 BC, when Clodius attempted to obtain permission from the senate to conduct a *libera legatio* to Brogitarus. Cicero's comment was succinct: 'plena res nummorum'.[84] No doubt Clodius' original intervention on behalf of Brogitarus had been in response to a promised bribe, which was never fully paid when the ploy came to nothing.[85] Deiotarus had, in fact, taken matters into his own hands and had evicted his son-in-law from Pessinus, reclaiming it for himself.

The personal connections between Rome and Galatia, implied by this episode, are a feature of the period which becomes increasingly noticeable. Deiotarus himself had already established by his military services personal ties with a long succession of Roman generals active in the east, and we learn of contacts with other leading politicians, notably Cato and Brutus.[86] Cicero's correspondence from Cilicia in 51–50 shows him in a number of roles, which can only have strengthened his ties with the Roman aristocracy. Cicero himself was on terms of close personal friendship; the two men apparently passed much of their time together in camp on the borders of Cappadocia, or elsewhere on Cicero's tour as governor, discussing divination and augury, in which the king was an expert and devotee;[87] and Cicero entrusted his two young children to Deiotarus' protection in Galatia, rather than take them on campaign into the Taurus.[88] Businessmen also sought refuge and assistance in his

[76] Strabo, 11. 2. 12, 496.
[77] Cicero, *Att.* 6. 1 (SB 115), 14.
[78] [Caesar], *Bell. Alex.* 34. Note the implication of Cicero, *Deiot.* 24 that Deiotarus was forbidden to use slaves in his army; further evidence for a Roman organizational hand behind it.
[79] Appian, *BC* 4. 88.
[80] Caesar, *BC* 3. 4. 5.
[81] Horace, *Epod.* 9. 17–18; cf. Plutarch, *Antonius*, 63; Velleius, 2. 84. 1; Cassius Dio, 50. 13. 8.

[82] Magie, *RR* ii. 1237–8; Cicero, *Har. Resp.* 28–9 (*Sest.* 56; *Dom.* 129).
[83] Inferred from geographical realities, as much as from *Har. Resp.* 28–9. Plutarch, *Cato Minor*, 15 may be taken to show that Deiotarus controlled Pessinus during the 60s BC. He minted coins there in the mid-1st cent. BC, see J. Devreker, *Pessinus I* (1984), 17.
[84] Cicero, *ad Q. Fr.* 2. 7. 2.
[85] Magie, *RR* ii. 1236; E. Rawson, *Historia*, 23 (1973), 236–7.
[86] See Hoben, *Kleinasiatische Dynasten*, 87 n. 158; 112–13 n. 280. For Cato see Plutarch, *Cato Minor*, 12, 15 (the latter passage implies that the family contact had begun in an earlier generation), and Cicero, *Fam.* 15. 4 (SB 110), 15; Brutus: Cicero, *Att.* 6. 1 (SB 115), 4; 14. 1 (SB 355), 2; Brutus: 21; Plutarch, *Brutus* 16. 5 ff.; Tacitus, *Dial.* 21.
[87] See below, Ch. 4 § IV at n. 57.
[88] Cicero, *Att.* 5. 18 (SB 111), 4.

kingdom, and were even subvented by him.[89] A certain Pinarius, whom Atticus had recommended to Cicero, had been taken ill and was recovering under the king's care; he had a Greek doctor.[90] Another obscure figure, P. Valerius, in debt both to Atticus and to the state treasury at Rome, seems to have relied on Deiotarus' protection; the latter told Cicero that Valerius had no money to his name and was reliant on Deiotarus' own charity.[91] Brutus, whose financial interests in the East were notorious,[92] was as ready to use client kings as he was to use provincial governors such as Cicero to put pressure on men who owed him money, and he found a willing partner in Deiotarus who was asked to help recover debts from Ariobarzanes of Cappadocia.[93] The favour was naturally returned, for Brutus spoke up with notable forcefulness on the king's behalf when he faced a hostile Julius Caesar at Nicaea in 47 BC.[94]

So, alongside military service, Rome's financial involvement in Anatolia was beginning to bring links at a personal level. There are other glimpses of this more intimate contact between individuals. In 50 BC Cicero makes a fleeting reference to a visit paid by Diogenes, a Greek associate, and Philo, a freedman of M. Caelius, to Adiatorix at Pessinus. Adiatorix is probably the man later picked by Mark Antony to rule Heracleia Pontica. Cicero's letter leaves no question that the objectives of the visit were financial.[95] Another possible contact with Pessinus may reasonably be inferred from the names of a Pessinuntine high priest of the imperial cult in the reign of Tiberius, Q. Gallius Pulcher.[96] The names should be a guide to some Roman patron who had passed them into a Pessinuntine family. Pulcher inevitably recalls Clodius, whose links with the place have already been discussed, but more interestingly the *praenomen* and *nomen* seem to derive from a Q. Gallius who was quaestor of Cilicia in *c.*47/6 BC.[97] Cicero's surviving letters addressed to him, asked him to help two Romans, L. Oppius and the knight and money-lender L. Egnatius Rufus, who had business interests at Philomelium, no great distance from Pessinus.[98]

Increasing contact between Rome and the central Anatolian aristocracy presupposes a certain minimum level of common cultural interests. It is clear that by the middle of the first century BC the Galatian aristocracy was Hellenized to a large degree. Deiotarus had connections with Athens, where his statue was put up probably during the 50s BC, as well as with other cities of the Greek East, such as Nicaea, Laodicea, and Ephesus.[99] Brogitarus was honoured by an unknown community of western Asia Minor, in the valley of the Hermus,[100] and his sister, Adobogiona, was similarly honoured on an inscription found in eastern Lesbos, but probably carried there from a site on the Aeolic mainland.[101] Her portrait head has been discovered at Pergamum, where she had married a prominent citizen Menodotus; their son, Mithridates, a loyal follower of Caesar in the war with Pompeius, was to be rewarded with the grant of the Trocmian tetrarchy.[102] Deiotarus himself was certainly not uncultured. He quoted a Greek verse on being told of the death of Cn. Domitius Calvinus in a shipwreck; and he received from a Bithynian friend Diophanes a six-book abridgement of the Greek translation of the agricultural treatise by Mago the Carthaginian.[103] The Galatian aristocracy, in short, had become enmeshed in the aristocratic Hellenistic culture of the eastern Mediterranean under Roman rule.

By the late 50s Brogitarus was probably dead; and it is virtually certain that Deiotarus took the opportunity to annex his Trocmian tetrarchy, thus concentrating power in Galatia in the hands of two chieftains, as Strabo says.[104] At about the same time Deiotarus was

---

89 Cf. Cicero, *Deiot.* 26 *ad fin.*
90 *Att.* 6. 1 (SB 115), 23; cf. *Deiot.* 17, 'Phidippum medicum, servum regium'.
91 *Att.* 5. 21 (SB 114), 14, with *Fam.* 5. 20 (SB 128), 3.
92 Magie, *RR* i. 394–6.
93 *Att.* 6. 1 (SB 115), 2.
94 *Att.* 14. 1 (SB 355), 2; cf. Cicero, *Brutus*, 21; Tacitus, *Dial.* 21.
95 *Fam.* 2. 12 (SB 95), 2. For Adiatorix, see below, n. 159.
96 Bosch, *Ankara*, no. 51, l. 72.
97 Cicero, *Fam.* 13. 43 and 44 (SB 268, 270). R. Syme, *ASBuckler*, 315 argues for the reading Q. Gallius against Q. Gallus (which would be confirmed if the conjecture made in the text is right), and identified him with the *praetor* of 43 who was implicated in a plot against Octavian in that year (Appian, *BC* 3. 95; Suetonius, *Augustus*, 27. 4).

98 For Egnatius see *Att.* 4. 12 (SB 81), 1; 7. 18 (SB 142), 4; 10. 15 (SB 207), 4; *Fam.* 13. 43–5; 73–4 (SB 268–73). Another Italian *gens*, no doubt with business interests at Philomelium, the Dindii, appears on an inscription, M. Christol and T. Drew Bear, *Tyche*, 1 (1986), 41–3; Waelkens, *Türsteine* no. 671.
99 *IG* ii². 3429; Cicero, *Deiot.* 25.
100 *OGIS* 349 = *IGR* iv. 1328.
101 *OGIS* 348 = *IG* xii. 2. 516 = *IGR* iv. 3.
102 Strabo, 12. 4. 3, 625; [Caesar], *Bell. Alex.* 78; cf. n. 114.
103 Cicero, *Deiot.* 25; Varro, *RR* 1. 1. 10. One may compare the Hellenization of the Galatian aristocracy in the 1st cent. BC with that 100 years earlier of the Cappadocian royal dynasty, especially Ariarathes V, who had made generous gifts to Greek cities and sanctuaries, paid for buildings, acted as agonothete for the Panathenaic games, and as patron to the guild of Dionysiac artists; see Robert, *Noms indigènes*, 494–6 with further references, and cf. below, Ch. 7 §II nn. 13–15.
104 12. 5. 1, 567 quoted at the beginning of this chapter. Brogitarus was certainly dead by 47, [Caesar], *Bell. Alex.* 67, but coins dated to his 6th regnal year show that he survived at least until 53, *BMC Galatia*, xvii; Reinach, *L'Histoire par les monnaies*, 155; Adcock, *JRS* 27 (1937), 12–17.

also involved in dynastic politics outside Galatia, when his son was betrothed to and may have married the daughter of Artavasdes V, king of Armenia. Deiotarus was already king of Armenia Minor, and his commitment to the area in shown by the fact that one and possibly two fortresses in the area are said to be Galatian foundations.[105]

Predictably both Deiotarus and the two leaders of the Tectosages, Castor Tarcondarius and Domnilaus, took the Pompeian side at Pharsalus in 47, although their contributions to the battle were small: Caesar, who arrived at Ephesus soon after his victory, made no attempt to dispossess them of their territory, but simply imposed a heavy fine.[106] Any further measures which he might have been planning were forestalled by Pharnaces, the son of Mithridates VI, who invaded Armenia Minor. A story was current that the invasion had been invited by some of Pompey's defeated followers;[107] but Deiotarus quickly rallied to help Caesar's legate in Asia, Cn. Domitius Calvinus, and threw his two legions into the campaign to defend what was, after all, his own kingdom.[108] Battle was joined at Nicopolis, close to the border between Armenia Minor and Pontus, and resulted in the total defeat of the pro-Roman forces,[109] leaving Pontus as the prize for Pharnaces' advancing army. The weakness of Pompey's arrangements was now exposed for the first time; without protection from the armies of client kings, whose attentions had been claimed by the civil war, the Pontic cities were an easy prey. Some, such as Sinope and particularly Amisus, are said to have put up stout resistance; others, by implication, capitulated more readily.

Caesar himself took the situation in hand. After successfully completing the Alexandrian war, he marched through Syria to Tarsus, and then crossed the Taurus to Mazaca in Cappadocia. Close to the borders of Pontus and Galatia he was met by a suitably contrite Deiotarus, conscious of the fact not only that he had supported the wrong man in the civil war, and even

accompanied Pompey in his flight, but that he had also failed in his duty to protect Pontus against invasion from the east.[110] Taking the Galatian king and the remains of his army Caesar advanced into Pontus and won the celebrated victory at Zela, in the summer of 47. After the battle he passed through Galatia and stayed at Deiotarus' two fortresses Blucium and Peium, before making new arrangements for the administration of Anatolia at Nicaea in Bithynia.[111] In addition to his failure in Armenia Minor, Deiotarus faced criticism from his fellow tetrarchs for encroaching on their territory,[112] and owed the comparatively gentle treatment he received from Caesar to the stout support of his friend Brutus. Half of Armenia Minor was taken away from him and given to Ariobarzanes III of Cappadocia, a decision dictated by prudence in the light of recent events;[113] more seriously, the tetrarchy of the Trocmi was handed over to Mithridates of Pergamum, Brogitarus' nephew and in all probability his nearest surviving male relative and natural heir.[114] Mithridates had earned this reward from Caesar for conspicuous services rendered during the Alexandrian war.

In a surprisingly emphatic passage Cassius Dio underlines the fact that Caesar's redistribution of responsibilities was no great setback for Deiotarus,[115] and the point is well made. At a purely personal level the two men were far from friendly; something which may have given initial plausibility to the charge laid against Deiotarus by his grandson Castor, that he had intended to murder Caesar during his passage through Galatia after Zela; and which led Cicero, in a highly rhetorical passage, to say that no two men were ever less well-disposed towards one another.[116] Yet, despite this Deiotarus remained the most powerful dynast in Anatolia, and an indispensable agent in Roman plans for Asia Minor.

Caesar did not alter Pompey's arrangements for Pontus, which remained a Roman province, although a stiffening of Roman colonists was admitted to Sinope

[105] *Att.* 5. 21 (SB 114), 2; for the fortresses of Sintoion and Sinoria, see Honigmann, *RE* iiiA (1927), 259 and 253. Appian, *Mith.* 101 refers to the latter as Σηνόρηγα φρούριον, suggesting a connection with Deiotarus' father Sinorix. However, the passage raises a problem since it dates to a period before 63 BC, when Deiotarus is not known to have any stake in Armenia Minor.

[106] See n. 80; cf. Appian, *BC* 2. 71; Florus, 2. 13 (41. 2) 5; [Caesar], *Bell. Alex.* 34; Cicero, *Phil.* 2. 94. The scale of the fine is shown by the fact that Deiotarus had to conduct three auctions to raise the money, Cicero, *Deiot.* 14.

[107] Appian, *BC* 2. 87 ff.

[108] [Caesar], *Bell. Alex.* 34; Cassius Dio, 42. 45; Cicero, *Deiot.* 14.

[109] [Caesar], *Bell. Alex.*, 41, 70; Appian, *BC* 2. 91; *Mith.* 120; Cassius Dio 42. 46. 2; Magie, *RR* i. 408–9; ii. 1262–3.

[110] Magie, *RR* i. 411; ii. 1263–5; [Caesar], *Bell. Alex.* 67; Cicero, *Deiot.* 8, 14, 24; Cassius Dio, 41. 63. 1.

[111] See above, n. 69 for the fortresses; Magie, *RR* ii. 1266–7; [Caesar], *Bell. Alex.* 78; Cassius Dio, 42. 49. 1.

[112] *Bell. Alex.* 67 reveals the complaints of other Galatians even before Zela that Deiotarus 'tum quidem tetrarches Gallograeciae paene totius' was encroaching on their territory.

[113] Cassius Dio, 41. 63. 3; cf. 42. 48. 3. H.-W. Ritter, *Historia*, 19 (1970), 124–7.

[114] [Caesar], *Bell. Alex.* 78. 2; Cicero, *Div.* 1. 27; 2. 79; *Phil.* 2. 94; Strabo, 13. 4. 3, 625; Appian, *Mith.* 121; Cassius Dio, 42. 48. 4.

[115] 41. 63. 3, perhaps owing something to Cicero, *Deiot.* 35.

[116] *Phil.* 2. 94, contradicting the tenor of the *Deiot.*, a speech which Cicero did not rate highly: *Fam.* 9. 12 (SB 263).

and Heracleia, which both appear to have become double communities,[117] and to Amisus, where Roman settlers were integrated into the constitution of the Greek city.[118]

Deiotarus swiftly recouped some of the losses of 47. Before a year had passed Mithridates of Pergamum was dead, killed in the Cimmerian Bosporus on an expedition encouraged but not supported by Rome,[119] and Deiotarus reoccupied Trocmian territory *suo Marte*.[120] He soon renewed pressure on the Tectosages, goading Castor (son of their tetrarch Castor Tarcondarius) to accuse him of Caesar's attempted murder, which led to Cicero's successful defence *pro rege Deiotaro*, delivered *in domo Caesaris* in the autumn of 45.[121] Soon afterwards Deiotarus turned on the Tectosages openly, putting to death Castor Tarcondarius and his wife—his own daughter—at their fortress of Gorbeous.[122] The date of the assassination probably fell after the death of Deiotarus' own son, in or after 43 BC,[123] since the latter's funerary inscription refers to both father and son as tetrarchs of the Tolistobogii and Trocmi alone, not of the Tectosages as well.[124] It was only with the murder of Castor Tarcondarius that Galatia came under the rule of one man for the first time.

After the death of Julius Caesar relations with Antony were not good. In April 44 Deiotarus had been required to pay ten million sesterces for the Trocmian tetrarchy which he had already recovered by his own efforts.[125] On the other hand in the confusing political picture of 44 and 43, the king was not ready to declare himself openly for any of the contending politicians. He helped L. Tillius Cimber, one of the tyrannicides who had already been appointed to govern Bithynia, to inflict a defeat of Cornelius Dolabella the governor of Syria, after the latter had murdered the proconsul of Asia in the spring of 43.[126] As the lines of conflict, between Brutus and Cassius on the one hand and

Antony and Octavian on the other, began to emerge with more clarity, Deiotarus at first refused to help Cassius, but allowed himself to be prevailed upon by his old friend Brutus.[127] He sent a large force of foot soldiers and cavalry to Philippi under the command of his secretary Amyntas, but it is no surprise that these defected to Antonius during the course of the battle.[128] Deiotarus clearly approved of the initiative, for soon afterwards he issued coins to commemorate the victory, depicting Antony and Octavian in the guise of the Dioscuri on the obverse, and a portrait of Fulvia, in the guise of *Nike*, on the reverse.[129]

In or around 40 BC Deiotarus died, as did another of Pompey's long-standing nominees, Attalus in Paphlagonia, and their joint kingdoms were given to Deiotarus' old accuser Castor.[130] The deaths in succession of Brogitarus, Mithridates of Pergamum, Deiotarus the younger, Castor Tarcondarius, and finally Deiotarus himself had left him the natural heir to the three Galatian tribes.

Mark Antony had passed through Asia Minor in the winter of 42/1 after the victory at Philippi. In the wake of his triumphant arrival at Ephesus, where he was hailed as a new Dionysus, he proceeded to extort nine years of taxation from the cities of Asia to be paid within two years. Asia was already enfeebled by the levies imposed by Brutus and Cassius, and it was still worse off when Antony departed for Egypt.[131] Illusions were swiftly shattered; in 40 Q. Labienus, who had been sent by the tyrannicides to seek support from the Parthian king Orodes, returned with the Parthian prince Pacorus and a cavalry force which simply advanced unopposed up the main highway from Syria to Asia. The province of Cilicia which was designed to protect this route had ceased to exist in the late 40s BC, and nothing had taken its place. Labienus was able to achieve what the Parthians had failed to do in 51/50, when they were opposed by Cicero, with his own and his allies' forces.[132] Now neither Castor, if he had already succeeded Deiotarus, nor the king of Cappadocia[133] provided the necessary protection, and the Parthians slipped through the gap in the defences.

[117] Magie, *RR* ii. 1267; S. Mitchell, *Historia*, 28 (1979), 417.

[118] *IGR* iv no. 314, cf. Bowersock, *Augustus and the Greek World*, 64; for these *sympoliteuomenoi Romaioi*, see T. R. S. Broughton, *TAPA* 66 (1935), 20 ff.; *Roman Asia Minor*, 582; Mitchell, *Tenth Congress*, 311–18.

[119] Strabo, 13. 4. 3, 625.

[120] Cicero, *Att.* 14. 12 (SB 366); *Phil.* 2. 95; Magie, *RR* ii. 1275.

[121] *Deiot. passim*; for the place see ibid., 5.

[122] Strabo, 12. 5. 3, 568; Suda s.v. Castor Rhodius; the site of Gorbeous is fixed near Oğulbey, south of Ankara, French, *Pilgrim's Road*, 25, 29. For Tarcondarius Castor, cf. Reinach, *L'Histoire par les monnaies*, 156–7.

[123] Cicero, *Phil.* 11. 31 is the last mention of him alive.

[124] *RECAM* ii no. 188; cf. Hoben, *Kleinasiatische Dynasten*, 106–7.

[125] See above, n. 120.

[126] Cicero, *ad Brut.* 1. 6 (SB 12), 3 (19 May 43); Cicero, *Phil.* 11. 9, 15, 29.

[127] Cassius Dio, 47. 24. 3.

[128] Cassius Dio, 47. 48. 2; Appian, *BC* 4. 88.

[129] *BMC Galatia*, xvii; A. von Sallet, *ZfN* 12 (1885), 371.

[130] Cassius Dio, 48. 33. 5, *pace* Strabo, 12. 5. 1, 567 who forgets Castor's brief reign. Castor had fought under Cicero in 51/50, Cicero, *Deiot.* 28.

[131] Cassius Dio, 48. 24. 1; Plutarch, *Antonius*, 24; Appian, *BC* 5. 4 ff.; Magie, *RR* i. 427 ff.; ii. 1278 ff.

[132] Magie, *RR* i. 430 ff.; ii. 1280 ff.; for Cilicia, see Syme, *ASBuckler*, 299–306 = *RP* i. 120–6.

[133] Where there had been some dispute over the kingdom, see Magie, *RR* ii. 1286; Hoben, *Kleinasiatische Dynasten*, 175 n. 116, and 175–9; R. D. Sullivan, *ANRW* ii. 7. 2 (1980), 1147–9.

Resistance was organized here and there, by individuals and individual cities; the brigand chieftain Cleon of Gordiucome (later Juliopolis in south-east Bithynia) struck back at them; and some of the cities of Asia resisted with success, among them Laodicea on the Lycus, where the defence was organized by the orator Zeno and his son Polemo, the latter marked out for an important role in the future.[134] Among the dynasts who connived with the invaders may have been Antipater of Derbe.[135]

The Parthian threat was not, in the long term, a very serious one. The invading force was soon driven back and defeated at the Amanus gates by P. Ventidius, the consul of 43 BC. Antony then took the necessary steps to secure the invasion route. In 39, Polemo, the son of Zeno of Laodicea, was brought into the front line and given a kingdom consisting of Cilicia and parts of Lycaonia, including Iconium which became his capital.[136] Meanwhile Amyntas, Deiotarus' former right-hand-man, was given Pisidia and Phrygia Paroreius, including Antioch and Apollonia.[137] These two new kingdoms covered the whole span between Cilicia Pedias and the eastern border of Asia. Polemo evidently held the area from Iconium eastwards, including the Lycaonian plain and the passes through the Taurus, especially the Cilician gates. He may also have controlled the western route along the Calycadnus valley from Seleuceia to Laranda, which Augustus was later to garrison with a veteran colony.[138] However, the north end of this route lay within the domain of Antipater of Derbe, and it is uncertain whether he was displaced to make way for Polemo or not. After Polemo's departure for Pontus in 37/6 he was certainly in charge of his old possessions, since at some time in the late 30s or early 20s Amyntas found it necessary to evict him.[139]

Amyntas' own territory in 39 was of equally crucial strategic importance, a fact again underlined by the later foundation of Roman military colonies there. Phrygia Paroreius, between Antioch and Apollonia, was one of the main military routes of western Anatolia; if it could be held, any invading force was compelled to make a long detour north of Sultan Dağ to avoid it.

Amyntas was the first Galatian leader of any consequence who did not bear a Celtic name. There is, however, no real reason to doubt his Celtic origins, even though he clearly did not belong to the same dynastic network as the tetrarchs of the previous generation. C. Iulius Severus of Ancyra in the early second century AD numbered among his ancestors two tetrarchs called Amyntas, the sons respectively of Dyitalus and Brigatus, both clearly Celts.[140] A new inscription confirms that the great Amyntas was the son of the former. It is notable, however, that Amyntas had much stronger associations with southern Anatolia than other tetrarchs. Much of his personal wealth was derived from the 300 flocks of sheep which grazed the central plateau area west and south of lake Tatta; he is particular associated with military operations along the whole length of the Taurus, from rugged Cilicia to Pisidia and Phrygia Paroreius, and he built himself a royal residence at Isaura.[141] Coins bearing his name were minted at Side in Pamphylia and at Cremna in central Pisidia.[142] The centre of gravity of his kingdom and the focus of his activities lay well to the south of those of Deiotarus.

Also in 39 Antony made new arrangements in Pontus, by appointing Darius the son of Pharnaces and grandson of Mithridates VI to the kingship.[143] This was an important new departure from previous policy, since hitherto Pontus had been a Roman province, albeit one over which control was not always cer-

[134] Strabo, 12. 8. 9, 574; Cassius Dio, 48. 26–7; Magie, *RR* ii. 1280–1.

[135] Syme, *ASBuckler*, 328. There were similar suspicions about Commagene and Cappadocia.

[136] Appian, *BC* 5. 75; Strabo, 12. 6. 1, 567; 12. 8. 16, 578.

[137] Appian, loc. cit.; Strabo, 12. 6. 4, 569 τὴν γὰρ Ἀντιοχείαν ἔχων τὴν πρὸς τῇ Πισιδίᾳ μεχρὶ Ἀπολλωνιάδος τῆς πρὸς Ἀπαμείᾳ τῇ Κιβωτῷ καὶ τῆς Παρωρείου τινὰ καὶ τὴν Λυκαονίαν. The text reads awkwardly and since Apollonia lay in the Paroreius there is much to be said for the reading, suggested to me by Mr E. W. Gray, τὴν γὰρ Ἀντιοχείαν ἔχων τὴν πρὸς τῇ Πισιδίᾳ καὶ τῆς Παρωρείου τινὰ μεχρὶ Ἀπολλωνιάδος κτλ.

[138] Ninica: for this and the strategic implications, see Mitchell, *Historia*, 28 (1979), 431. See further R. Syme, *AS* 36 (1986), 159–64 = *RP* v. 661–8.

[139] Strabo, 12. 6. 3, 569. The status of Antipater is unclear. He had been in control round Derbe at the time of Cicero's proconsulship in 51/50 (*Fam.* 13. 73 (SB 273), 2; Syme, *ASBuckler*, 309), and had fallen foul of Q. Philippus, proconsul of Cilicia in 47/6 (Syme, op. cit. 306) possibly because, like Deiotarus, he had supported Pompey in the civil

war. Polemo's kingdom in Lycaonia and Cilicia, as interpreted here in the text, leaves no room for him in his old kingdom in 39. Syme suggested that his Pompeian sympathies led him to favour Q. Labienus in 40 (op. cit. 328), which makes it likely that he was deposed to make way for Polemo, although Syme also suggests that 'Polemo left him alone, as did Amyntas, at first', which is an alternative solution.

[140] *OGIS* 544; Bosch, *Ankara*, no. 105.

[141] Strabo, 12. 5. 4; 6. 1; 6. 4; 8. 14.

[142] Cremna: see Aulock, *Pisidien*, ii, nos. 911–1047. These bronze issues bear the regnal years 2–7. If the latest issues date to 25 BC the series should have begun in 31 BC. Cremna had fallen to Amyntas by that date; see Aulock, *Pisidien*, ii. 38–9. Side: S. Atlan, *Belleten*, 39 (1975), 595–611, a plentiful series of silver tetradrachms (6 obverse and 33 reverse types in thirteen years) with Nike bearing a garlanded sword or staff as the commonest reverse design. Doubtless pay for Amyntas' troops.

[143] Appian, *BC* v. 75.

tain.[144] It is intriguing to speculate about the reasons that may have led Antony to favour the grandson of Rome's principal adversary in Asia Minor, but in the total absence of further evidence such speculation must remain purely hypothetical.

In the winter of 37/6 more radical and extensive changes were made. Polemo was moved from Cilicia to Pontus, in place of Darius who had either died or been superseded.[145] The exact extent of his kingdom, apart from the Phazemonitis which he explicitly controlled,[146] is quite uncertain; but the fact that other rulers were installed in Zela, Comana, the Caranitis, Amaseia, Amisus, and Heracleia Pontica indicates that it was much less extensive than the former Roman province. Presumably it was largely restricted to eastern Pontus, including the territories of Trapezus, Pharnaceia, Cabeira/Diospolis, and Magnopolis, all of which belonged to the district of Pontus Polemoniacus, which became part of the empire again in AD 64/5.[147] The date of Polemo's appointment can be fixed with some assurance. The *terminus post quem* is the appointment to Cilicia in 39; the *terminus ante* is Antony's Parthian campaign of 36, which Polemo accompanied as king of Pontus.[148] In 38 Antony had campaigned in Commagene and settled some minor business in Syria, before returning to Athens. There is no place in the narrative of these events for any activity in Asia Minor.[149] In 37 Antony travelled west to the meeting at Tarentum, and his return from the confrontation with Octavian there makes the most suitable opportunity for him to make new arrangements in Asia Minor, during the winter of 37/6.

At much the same time, Amyntas was made king of Galatia, along with Lycaonia and a part of Pamphylia.[150] He evidently succeeded Castor in Galatia (although the latter's family was not out of favour, since his son Deiotarus Philadelphus was given the Paphlagonian part of his father's kingdom, with Gangra the royal residence as his capital).[151] Dio puts the event at the end of 36, after the Parthian expedition, and this is confirmed by Appian who refers to Amyntas as king of Galatia in early 35.[152] However, it is again likely that the appointment was in fact made late in 37 or early in 36 before the Parthian expedition, and Dio has listed the miscellaneous events of the year at the end of 36. The southern part of Amyntas' new kingdom (notably Lycaonia) overlapped with Polemo's former territory, and if the two appointments of Amyntas and Polemo were simultaneous an uncomfortable *interregnum* is avoided.[153] At all events by this decision Amyntas became the ruler of an enormous tract of Anatolia—stretching from the Pamphylian coast to the border of Paphlagonia, and from the border with Asia at Apollonia to the frontiers of Cappadocia and Pontus—essentially the dimensions of the Augustan province of Galatia.

In between the two major kingdoms of Amyntas and Polemo, other new nominees were installed by Antony. Most of the Caranitis, which lay to the east of the Trocmian tetrarchy and was part of the territory of Megalopolis, was given to a Galatian tetrarch called Ateporix;[154] while the rest of the Caranitis was divided between the priest kingdoms of Zela, now resuscitated by Antony, and Comana, left independent in Pompey's original settlement and now ruled by Lycomedes.[155] Amaseia, according to Strabo, was also given to kings. This vague expression could refer to Polemo of Pontus, but this is unlikely since Amaseia was incorporated into the province of Galatia in 3/2 BC, long before Polemonian Pontus in AD 64/5, and it is logical to assume that they were under different regimes. The city was probably controlled by some local dynast.[156] Amaseia was Strabo's birthplace, and personal hostility on his part may have caused him to suppress the name of a man whom he considered unworthy of the task. It may be possible to supply it: the list of high priests of the imperial cult at Ancyra during the reign of Tiberius includes the son of a king Brigatus, a Galatian ruler for whom no kingdom is specified.[157] Amaseia would not be inappropriate.

Amisus is a similar case except that, far from being a relatively new civic foundation, it was one of the old Milesian colonies of the Black sea, and had a community of Roman citizens settled there by Julius Caesar, who had declared the place a free city. Antony gave it to kings, and it was badly governed by the

[144] Hoben, *Kleinasiatische Dynasten*, 34–9; for Darius' brother Arsaces seizing power in the Phazemonitis without Roman permission, see Strabo, 12. 3. 38, 560.

[145] Appian, *BC* v. 75.

[146] Strabo, 12. 3. 41, 562.

[147] See Vol. II, App. 1 at nn. 42–5.

[148] Cassius Dio, 49. 25. 4; Plutarch, *Autonius*, 25. 4.

[149] Cassius Dio, 49. 20. 5; 22. 1–2; Magie, *RR* i. 432; ii. 1281–2.

[150] Cassius Dio, 49. 32. 3; 53. 26. 3; Strabo, 12. 5. 1, 567; Plutarch, *Antonius*, 61. 3.

[151] Strabo, 12. 3. 41, 562; Reinach, *L'Histoire par les monnaies*, 151–65.

[152] Appian, *BC* 5. 137.

[153] A coin of Amyntas, bearing the regnal year 12, and minted at Side in Pamphylia, may support this interpretation (*BMC Galatia*, 2 nos. 3 and 4; cf. S. Atlan, art. cit. (n. 142)). See below, Ch. 5 n. 1, and S. Mitchell, 'Termessos, King Amyntas, and the War with the Sandaliotai', in D. H. French (ed.), *Studies in the History and Topography of Lycia and Pisidia* (1994), 95–105.

[154] Strabo, 12. 3. 37, 560.

[155] Strabo, 12. 3. 35, 558.

[156] Strabo, 12. 3. 39, 561. Polemo was suggested by Magie, *RR* ii. 1284–5; a local dynast by Jones, *CERP*[2] 427.

[157] Bosch, *Ankara*, no. 51 l. 7. Bosch's restoration [Ταρκοδάριος Κάσ]τω[ρ] βασίλε[ω]ς Βριγάτ[ου υἱός] is not permitted by the traces on the stone.

tyrant Strato.[158] The man is otherwise unknown, but the name recurs in the family of the Tarcondimotids, dynasts of Hierapolis-Castabala in Cilicia Pedias, which would be a suitable recruiting ground for a petty client ruler. A fourth appointment to a Pontic city was that of the Galatian tetrarch Adiatorix, son of Domnecleius, to Heracleia Pontica sometime before 30 BC. Domnecleius is generally taken to be identical to Domnilaus, the Tectosagan tetrarch present at Pharsalus, and Adiatorix may be the man mentioned by Cicero in 50 BC.[159] Heracleia, like Amisus, was another city with a long history which had recently received a settlement of Roman colonists; these may have retained their autonomy when the rest of the city was handed over to dynastic control.

As an addition to Antony's arrangements in eastern Anatolia, and his patronage above all of the Galatian nobility, it is worth noting the appearance at Phrygian Eumeneia of a magistrate with the Celtic name Zmertorix son of Philonides, sometime in the decade between 40 and 30 BC when the city was renamed after Antony's wife Fulvia.[160] Neither geographically nor politically is the situation comparable to the Pontic appointments, and Zmertorix may have been a member of a Celtic family long established in Eumeneia, but the fact should not be overlooked as another item attesting Galatian prominence in the 30s BC.

The new arrangement amounted to a complete reversal of Pompey's solution for Pontus; a province was handed back to native rulers. No doubt Antony himself, based in Alexandria and surrounded by most of the trappings of a Hellenistic monarch, viewed such

a system with more sympathy than his predecessor, but he would not have found it difficult to justify what he had done by appealing to military need. In 36 he launched an expedition through Armenia into Parthia, using not only his own legions but also 30,000 troops recruited from his eastern allies, among them Polemo.[161] From a military point of view the effectiveness of dynastic rule was widely recognized both for defence and offence, and the new rulers of Galatia and Pontus could be relied upon both to provide troops for the campaign and to hold the area firm against any threat. A parallel may be drawn with the plans for the invasion of Armenia in AD 55 when Nero levied troops from the adjoining provinces, instructed client kings to furnish soldiers, and allocated the vital territories of Armenia Minor and Sophene to new rulers.[162]

When Antony's policy is viewed in this context, the old question, whether or not Pompey's attempts to foster city life in Pontus had failed, seems to be the wrong one. Circumstances had changed between 63 and 37, and solutions valid for one occasion were inappropriate for another. However, certain similarities between the two settlements should not be overlooked. Perhaps the most striking feature of 37 was the prominence, in positions of responsibility, of Galatian chieftains. Apart from Polemo in eastern Pontus, the temple states of Comana Pontica and Zela, and the mysterious Strato at Amisus, virtually the whole of central and north-eastern Anatolia was ruled by Gauls, and it is they who provide the essential element of continuity between Pompey and Antony. Amyntas, Deiotarus Philadelphus, Adiatorix, Ateporix, and 'King Brigatus' inherited the same responsibilities, if in changed circumstances, as those formerly held by Deiotarus, Brogitarus, and Castor.

After the failure of the Parthian expedition, these rulers were left in control of their kingdoms and cities. Indeed Polemo took over Armenia Minor as an eastern extension of his territory.[163] The events of 47, when Pharnaces had overrun Pontus, were not to be repeated. After Actium, Octavian was forced to make certain adjustments, but for the most part existing arrangements were allowed to stand. Cleopatra's territory in Cilicia Tracheia was added to Amyntas' kingdom,[164] and Adiatorix, who had put to death the Roman colonists at Heracleia, was deposed and executed, along with his second son. He pleaded Antony's orders, not implausibly since the Romans in Heracleia will hardly have shown favour to Antony, who had imposed a native ruler on them. However,

[158] Strabo, 12. 3. 14, 547; for interpretations of the passage see Magie, *RR* ii, 1284–5 and Jones, *CERP*² 427. Bowersock, *Augustus and the Greek World*, 44 suggests the connection with the Tarcondimotids. Tarcondimotus I was the son of a Strato (*OGIS* 752), and a Iulius Strato, son of king Tarcondimotus, was duumvir at Pisidian Antioch (W. M. Calder, *JRS* 2 (1912), 105–9). For the dynasty see Hoben, *Kleinasiatische Dynasten*, 210–11, and (G. Dagron and) D. Feissel, *Inscriptions de Cilicie* (1987), 67–71.
[159] Strabo, 12. 3. 6, 543; 12. 3. 35, 558; cf. Bowersock, *Hermes*, 98 (1964), 255 ff. Since Niese, *Rh. Mus.* 38 (1883), 590 n. 1 the identity of Domnecleius with the Domnilaus of Caesar, *BC* 3. 4. 5 has been generally accepted. Adiatorix may be the Adiatorix of Cicero, *Fam.* 2. 12 (SB 95), 2. See above, n. 95. An inscription of Ephesus, dated by letter forms to the late 1st cent. AD mentions a Galatian]ατοριγος (gen.), restored as ['Αδι]ατόριγος by the editors, but other restorations are possible (e.g. ['Επ]ατόριγος), and in any case the inscription appears to be too late for Adiatorix of Heracleia (*GIBM* iii. 2, 558; *OGIS* 534; J. H. Oliver, *The Sacred Gerusia* (1941), no. 15; *I. Eph.* no. 1558).
[160] *BMC Phrygia*, lxi. It appears that coins of Deiotarus with a portrait of Fulvia in the guise of Victory were minted at Eumeneia; see A. Sallet, *Num. Zeitschr.* 12 (1888), 371, and A. Zwintscher, *De Galatarum tetrarchis et Amynta rege quaestiones* (Leipzig, 1892), 29–30.
[161] Plutarch, *Antonius*, 37. 3; 38. 6; Cassius Dio, 49. 25. 4.
[162] Tacitus, *Ann.* 13. 7.
[163] Cassius Dio, 49. 33. 2; 44. 3.
[164] Strabo, 14. 5. 6, 671.

the elder son Dyteutus was spared and so impressed Octavian with his qualities that he was soon appointed ruler of Comana Pontica, after a brief and unsuccessful experiment there with the former brigand chieftain of Gordiucome, Cleon.[165] Amisus too was freed from its tyrant, for which it may have had to thank its resident population of Roman colonists.[166] This intricate concatenation of *ad hoc* arrangements served Rome well, it seems, until the central link was knocked away. Amyntas was murdered *c*.25 BC while campaigning in the Taurus. His son Pylaemenes was clearly too young to succeed him. Rome was driven to annex his kingdom and a new chapter in the story of Roman rule in central Anatolia was begun.

[165] See above, n. 159.
[166] Strabo, 12. 3. 14, 547.

Note

Strabo, 12. 3. 1, 541. The passage needs to be discussed at some length. Mithridates had controlled the whole Euxine coast from Heracleia Pontica to Colchis and lesser Armenia, which he had added to Pontus; καὶ δὴ καὶ Πομπήιος καταλύσας ἐκεῖνον ἐν τούτοις τοῖς ὅροις οὖσαν τὴν χώραν ταύτην παρέλαβε· τὰ μὲν πρὸς Ἀρμενίαν καὶ τὰ περὶ τὴν Κολχίδα τοῖς συναγωνισαμένοις δυνάσταις κατένειμε, τὰ δὲ λοιπὰ εἰς ἕνδεκα πολιτείας διεῖλε καὶ τῇ Βιθυνίᾳ προσέθηκεν, ὥστ' ἐξ ἀμφοῖν ἐπαρχίαν γενέσθαι μίαν. μεταξὺ δὲ τῶν Παφλαγόνων τῶν μεσογαίων τινὰς βασιλεύεσθαι παρέδωκε τοῖς ἀπὸ Πυλαιμένους, καθάπερ καὶ τοὺς Γαλάτας τοῖς ἀπὸ γένους τετράρχαις. Cf. Appian, *Mith.* 114 for the client rulers, and compare too Livy, *Per.* 102; Velleius, 2. 38. 6. The view of Pompey's settlement offered above is essentially an orthodox one, along the lines of Magie's judicious discussion, especially his long note in *RR* ii. 1232–4. K. Wellesley, *Rh. Mus.* 96 (1953), 293 ff. argues that Pompey's province of Pontus extended no further east than the Halys, except to include an enclave around Amisus and Sinope on the Black Sea coast, that Deiotarus ruled a continuous stretch of territory from western Galatia to the border of Colchis and Armenia Minor, and that Brogitarus held another uninterrupted strip of territory from eastern Galatia to Armenia Minor (see his sketch map on p. 307). Since this view has been mentioned with approval recently (for instance by E. Olshausen, *ANRW* ii. 7. 2 (1980), 906 n. 9; W. Ameling, *Epig. Anat.* 3 (1984), 19 n. 1), it needs to be refuted in detail. Firstly, an unprejudiced reading of Strabo makes it quite clear that Deiotarus' kingdom was fragmented, since at the very least his Tolistobogian tetrarchy must have been separated from the Gazelonitis by free Paphlagonia (under Attalus and Pylaemenes), and by the northern part of the Tectosagan tetrarchy which he did not control until the late 40s. Secondly, Brogitarus' control of Armenia Minor is entirely a matter for conjecture (see below); even if it should be accepted nothing in the sources suggests that he held the huge expanse of Pontic territory which linked it to eastern Galatia. Thirdly, and most crucially, Wellesley's central arguments for a reduced province of Pontus, based on his interpretation of Strabo, 12. 3. 1, 540–1, rest on several misapprehensions. Regarding the east of Mithridates' kingdom Strabo says that he held the territory μέχρι Κολχίδος καὶ τῆς μικρᾶς Ἀρμενίας; which indeed he added to Pontus. Pompey after his victory took over the whole area within these boundaries. He assigned τὰ μὲν πρὸς Ἀρμενίαν καὶ τὰ περὶ τὴν Κολχίδα to dynasts who had supported him, and divided the rest into eleven *politeiai* which were attached to Bithynia. Wellesley argues that the area called τὰ πρὸς Ἀρμενίαν is the central Pontic region of the valleys of the Lycus and Iris. This is a possible although improbable interpretation of the phrase τὰ πρὸς μικρὰν Ἀρμενίαν but it cannot stand as an interpretation of the words of Strabo's text, which must refer to Armenia proper. τὰ πρὸς Ἀρμενίαν is a natural and reasonable way of describing Armenia Minor, and this is clearly what is meant here, since the expression picks up the earlier reference to μέχρι τῆς μικρᾶς Ἀρμενίας. Even if this were not clear from the context, it would be quite extraordinary for Strabo to refer to his own homeland, the Lycus and Iris basins, with such noteworthy centres as his own birthplace Amaseia, the burial place of the kings of Pontus, and the great shrines at Comana and Zela as τὰ πρὸς Ἀρμενίαν. This area had never been known by any other name but Pontus. So, τὰ πρὸς Ἀρμενίαν (Armenia Minor) was handed over to dynasts, while τὰ λοιπά was divided into city states and attached to Bithynia. Already it appears probable that this area comprised inland Pontus, the basins of the Lycus, the Iris, and the upper Halys. This is confirmed by the words which follow: μεταξὺ δὲ τῶν Παφλαγόνων τῶν μεσογαίων τινὰς βασιλεύεσθαι παρέδωκε. Wellesley refers μεταξύ to the area between τὰ πρὸς Ἀρμενίαν καὶ τὰ περὶ τὴν Κολχίδα on the one hand, and Bithynia on the other. But the word should refer to the last two geographical areas that have been mentioned in the text, namely τὰ λοιπά (see above) and Bithynia. Inland Paphlagonia does indeed divide the Lycus/Iris basin from Bithynia. See now, at length, C. Marek, *Stadt, Ära und Territorium in Pontus-Bithynia und Nord-Galatia* (1993).

4 Ethnography and Settlement of the Anatolian Celts

1. *Tribes and Leaders*

The history of the Gauls for a century and a half after the invasion of Asia Minor is not an inspiring one, nor does it contribute a major topic to Hellenistic history. 'Commandés souvent dans leur propre langue, par des officiers qui sont des leurs, munis de leurs armes traditionelles, il ne semble pas que ces hommes qui traversaient en tout sens les pays grecs qu'ils pillaient aient apporté grande chose à la civilisation hellénistique.'[1] The remarks are just; the Galatians lived on the margin of civilized life, plundering temples, sacking cities, and inspiring fear, well-merited, among the defenceless population of the Asian countryside. The damage they caused far outweighed the contribution they provided: an unceasing supply of mercenary soldiers; and a series of assassins responsible for the murder of several Hellenistic kings.[2] The central theme of the history of this period is the Greek city, a society, culture, and form of political life whose complexity and richness reflected centuries of development from more primitive types of settlement and social organization. Central Europe, more than half a millennium behind the Mediterranean in political evolution, was still controlled by tribal groups whose corporate values and way of life were closer to those of the epic poems of Homer than to the Greek world of Alexander's successors.

Greece and Asia Minor had been invaded by a loose federation of tribal groups, led by warrior chieftains. At the time they were a nation on the move, travelling in carts, on horseback, and on foot; with no fixed home, their eyes set on plunder not lands for settlement. This was no novelty for the Celtic people; in the West too migration was the rule and not the exception[3] for a race, many of whose tribes buried their dead not in tombs resembling permanent homes[4] but on wagons or chariots, and which supplied the Mediterranean world not only with a sophisticated and varied technology of wheeled vehicles but also with a whole vocabulary to describe it.[5]

These vagrant habits had important social consequences, as they had for the German peoples at a slightly later date.[6] Land, if held, was only a temporary possession, and might be reallocated to different cultivators from one year to the next.[7] The investment and accumulation of wealth, therefore, was difficult, and a regime of relative equality would persist between members of a tribe. Since there were only restricted opportunities to concentrate wealth and increase power in one place, the aristocracy would often choose a leader from among themselves one year, and replace him the next.[8] Further, the constant movement of peoples—in search of better land or richer spoils, or simply under pressure from powerful neighbours—favoured the development of small and flexible groupings, loosely connected with one another, not large, monolithic, centrally controlled tribes.

More than half a dozen separate chieftains are linked with the events in the Balkans and northern Greece between 280 and 278,[9] along with one tribe, the Prausi, to which Brennos belonged.[10] Of the Gauls

---

[1] C. Préaux, *Le Monde hellénistique*, i (1978), 317–18, of barbarians in general.

[2] Centoarates, murderer of Antiochus Hierax, Pliny, *NH* 8. 158; Solinus, 45. 13; Aelian, *NA* 6. 44; Apaturius who killed Seleucus III, Polybius, 4. 48. 8 and other references in Launey, *Recherches*, i. 508 n. 1; Ziaelas of Bithynia, Phylarchus, *FGrH* 81 F 50; cf. Launey, *Recherches*, i. 506 n. 7; Bituitus, who assisted the suicide of Mithridates VI (Appian, *Mith.* 111; Livy, *Per.* 102).

[3] Nachtergael, *Galates*, 3–14 with notes; Strabo, 4. 4. 2, 196.

[4] M. Waelkens, *Antike Welt*, 11. 4 (1980), 3–12.

[5] P. Vigneron, *Le Cheval dans l'antiquité gréco-romaine*, i (1968), 150–3.

[6] The point is made by Strabo, 4. 4. 2, 196; cf. E. A. Thompson, *The Early Germans* (1965), 1–28.

[7] Cf., for the Germans, Caesar, *BG* 6. 22, with 4. 1. 7.

[8] Strabo, 4. 4. 3, 197 (Gaul); Caesar, *BG* 6. 23 (Germans).

[9] See Ch. 2 nn. 19–22.

[10] Strabo 4. 1. 13, 187; Nachtergael, *Galates*, 138 n. 52. Note Strabo's remark that 'probably no trace is left of (the Trocmi and the Tolistobogii) because of their mass migrations, as happens with numerous other peoples. For example the second Brennos, the man who led the attack on Delphi, is said by some to have been a Prausan, but I am unable to say of the Prausans where on earth they lived before.'

who crossed to Asia Minor the sources refer to two leaders by name, Leonnorios and Luturios, but Memnon speaks of a total of seventeen chieftains.[11] This proliferation is not at all surprising. Moreover, the tribes in Asia were also numerous. Most of the sources refer to the Tolistobogii, Tectosages, and Trocmi, which formed the three component tribes of Galatia when it became a Roman province in 25 BC. But the developed constitution of the late second and early first centuries BC described above[12] implies that these tribes were split into four sections, each with its own leader; and the predominance of the three tribes has not excluded the names of other groupings. Pliny mentions the Voturi and Ambitouti, associated with the Tolistobogii, and the Toutobodiaci alongside the Tectosages;[13] while Plutarch refers to a tetrarch of the Tosiopae, otherwise unknown, in the early first century BC.[14] The accounts of the Galatians written in the imperial period by Livy, Memnon of Heracleia, and others, certainly simplify these divisions, mentioning only the groupings which prevailed in their day.

In western European Celtic society prowess in war and personal prestige, rather than hereditary influence, determined tribal leadership,[15] and the strictly Galatian evidence tends to conform with this. There is no evidence before the first century BC for elaborate genealogies, indeed even the parentage of most Galatian chieftains is unrecorded. The exception to this rule is a revealing one. Ortiagon—the *regulus* of the Tolistobogii in the war with Manlius Vulso, who was singled out by Polybius for the typical civic virtues of munificence, magnanimity, charm, and intelligence—and his wife Chiomara—a woman of sensibility and perceptiveness[16]—are the earliest aristocratic couple to produce a son whose name is known and who held a position of influence in Galatian society, Paidopolites, a tribal dicast.[17] This name itself, 'Son-citizen', reveals a feeling for Greek culture and city life, which matched the increasing sophistication of Galatian social and political structure in the mid-second century BC.[18] Two

generations after this, the evidence is clear that the Gauls had sufficiently absorbed the values and behaviour of more advanced and settled aristocracies to behave as hereditary dynasts, like their *confrères* elsewhere in Asia Minor. The contrast with their earlier habits is significant for the whole development of Galatian society.

The behaviour of Celtic chieftains in the company of their peers, clients, and retainers is well known from written accounts of Gallic tribes in the West. Ideally, it was a world of heroic action and Homeric extravagance, of feasting and competition, of lavish gifts and largesse, of hospitality and warfare. The most revealing descriptions are those quoted by Athenaeus from Posidonius, who made his observations in Gaul in about 90 BC. 'When a large number dine together they sit around in a circle with the most influential man in the centre, like the leader of the chorus, whether he surpasses the others in warlike skill, or nobility of family, or wealth. Beside him sits the host and next on either side the others in order of distinction. Their shieldsmen stand behind them while their spearsmen are seated in a circle on the opposite side and feast in common like their lords. The servers bear around the drink in terracotta or silver jars like spouted cups...'. 'The Celts sometimes engage in single combat at dinner. Assembling in arms they engage in mock battle-drill, and mutual thrust and parry, but sometimes wounds are inflicted, and the irritation caused by this may lead even to the slaying of the opponent unless the by-standers hold them back.' 'In former times, when hindquarters were served up, the bravest hero took the thigh piece, and if another man claimed it they stood up and fought in single combat to the death.' 'The Celts have in their company, even in war (as well as in peace), companions whom they call parasites. These men pronounce their praises before the whole company and before each of the chieftains in turn as they listen. Their entertainers are called bards. These are the poets who deliver eulogies in song.' 'Louernius son of Bituitus, who was dethroned by the Romans (in 122 BC), says that in an attempt to win popular favour he rode in a chariot over the plains, distributing gold and silver to the tens of thousands of Celts who followed him; moreover, he made a square enclosure one and a half miles each way, within which he filled vats with expensive liquor and prepared so large a quantity of food that for many days all who wished could enter and enjoy the feast prepared, being served without a break by the attendants. And when at length he fixed a day for the ending of the feast, a Celtic poet who arrived too late met Louernius and composed a song magnifying his greatness and lamenting his own late arrival. Louernius was delighted and asked for a bag of gold and threw it to the poet who ran beside his

[11] See above, Ch. 2 §1.
[12] Ch. 3 §1.
[13] Pliny, *NH* 5. 146; Polybius, 5. 55. 3 mentions a tribe of Rigosages, otherwise unattested, fighting as mercenaries in the Seleucid army in 221 BC. Note too the Σκορπίοι, a group of people living near Ancyra, Steph. Byz. s.v. Ἀγκύρα.
[14] *Mor.* 259a–c.
[15] Cf. Athenaeus, 4. 151.
[16] For Ortiagon see Plutarch, *Mor.* 258c–d = Polybius, 21. 38. 1; Suda s.v. = Polybius, 22. 21. 1; Pompeius Trogus, *Prol.* 32; Livy (after Polybius), 38. 19. 2; 24. 9. For Chiomara, see Plutarch, *Mor.* 258d–f = Polybius, 21. 38; Livy, 38. 24.
[17] Suda s.v. Paidopolites. For dicasts in the Galatian constitution, see Strabo, 12. 5. 1, 567 cited at the beginning of Ch. 3.
[18] See above, Ch. 2 §III at n. 134; Ch. 3 §1.

chariot. The poet picked it up and sang another song saying that the very tracks made by his chariot on the earth gave gold and largesse to mankind.'[19] While his accounts are neither so lengthy nor so detailed the third-century Athenian historian Phylarchus provides very comparable descriptions of Celtic behaviour in the East, either in Thrace or in Galatia; as of a chieftain Ariamnes, who promised to provide a feast for all his fellow Gauls for a year and set up marquees along the roads for the entertainment of 400 and more people at a time. Invited from nearby cities and villages were not only visiting Celts but any guests who came to participate; wine, bread, and all types of meat in abundance were served from great bronze cauldrons.[20] A shorter passage mentions Celtic feasting, and especially the priority which was given to the king in the company.[21] The memory of Galatian feasting lies behind an illuminating anecdote recorded in the mid-seventh century AD by the biographer of St Theodore of Sykeon. The Saint and two companions, returning from the arduous journey to Jerusalem, lodged incognito at a monastery in south Galatia, near the Salt Lake. After eating well as guests of the monastery, Theodore twice observed, 'Truly, my children, we have eaten like Galatians', thereby giving a clue to his identity which soon became known to all.[22] The value of the story in this context is first to confirm that feasting was something for which the eastern Celts were as famous as their western cousins, and second to show that their reputation in this respect survived, at least in the recollection, until the end of Antiquity.

In fact the parallels between the brief but explicit description of Phylarchus, and the more extended observations of Posidonius are close enough to need no underlining. The competitive ethos of the potlatch sustained the lavish feasting, and may even have acted as a significant stimulus to higher production and economic growth. It often led to blows and fighting among the participants,[23] for the Celts were a warlike people and warfare is a theme that runs through all their activities.

II. *Warfare*

Fighting among the Galatians was clearly not so much a predilection as a necessity.[24] When the tribes were not attacking cities, temples, and farmsteads or looting and taking prisoners for future ransom, they hired themselves as mercenaries to fight for others. There was not a Hellenistic ruler of any importance who did not, at one time or another, have Celts to fight for him.[25] The fear that the Gauls inspired among their opponents is well known;[26] attributable at least in part to their notorious cruelty including, it is assumed, the sacrificial slaughter of captives.[27] As enemies in battle they were formidable, above all for the sheer impact of their physical presence: 'procera corpora, promissae et rutilatae comae, vasta scuta, praelongi gladii; ad hoc cantus inchoantium proelium et ululatus et tripudia, et quatientium scuta in patrium quendam modum horrendos armorum crepitus, omnia de industria composita ad terrorem.'[28] They relied on the initial effect of their terrifying appearance; if the impetus and enthusiasm failed, their morale and resistance could easily collapse.[29] The fighting force was both mounted and unmounted; the latter doubtless largely consisted of the dependants of the aristocrats who invariably accompanied them both in peace and in war.[30] Pausanias says that the 20,400 Gaulish cavalrymen in Brennos' invading army of 279 BC were each accompanied by two mounted attendants, forming a *trimarkisia*.[31] The word and the institution are authentic, although Pausanias' figures are exaggerated, and other sources suggest that these battle companions fought on foot.[32] The nobles could be mounted on

---

[19] These four well-known passages of Athenaeus are quoted directly from Posidonius, 4. 36. 151e–2d; 40. 154a–c; 6. 49. 246c–d; 4. 37. 152d–f. They are cited in the translation of J. J. Tierney, *Proc. Royal Irish Academy*, 60 (1959/60), who conveniently quotes the relevant sections *in extenso*, and discusses them in the context of a reconstruction of Posidonius' Celtic ethnography. But the remarks of D. Nash, *Britannia*, 8 (1976), 111–26, criticizing Tierney's attempt to attribute not only the Athenaeus passages but also most of the Gallic ethnography of Strabo, Diodorus, and even Caesar to Posidonius, are entirely just.

[20] *FGrH* 81 F 2 (quoted by Athenaeus 4. 34. 150d–f), cited by Rostovtzeff, *SEHHW* i. 584.

[21] Fr. 9.

[22] *Vita S. Theodori*, 64.

[23] Athenaeus, 4. 40. 154a–c; Diodorus, 5. 28. 5.

[24] Cf. Caesar, *BG* 6. 15. 1 for Gaul.

[25] Launey, *Recherches*, i, ch. 8, an exemplary account which makes it unnecessary to rehearse the abundant evidence again.

[26] Livy, 38. 16. 13; 17. 1; cf. Diodorus, 5. 32. 2; *I. Erythrai*, 1 no. 24 πολλῶν δὲ φόβων καὶ κινδύνων περιστάντων; C. Jullian, *Histoire de la Gaule*, i (1920), 333–8.

[27] For cruelty, see Ch. 2 n. 49; for sacrifice of captives in the West, Diodorus, 5. 31. 3; 32. 6; Strabo, 4. 4. 5, 198; in Galatia, see below, nn. 59 and 61.

[28] Livy, 38. 17. 3–5.

[29] Ibid. 17. 7, cf. 21. 7–8. But this is a topos, which can be traced back at least as far as Thucydides 4. 126. 5.

[30] Diodorus, 5. 29 (charioteers and shield-bearers); Athenaeus 4. 36. 151e–2d mentions shield and spear bearers in attendance on their lords, and 6. 49. 246c–d calls them παρασίτοι; Caesar, *BG* 6. 15 mentions the dependants and clients of the *equites*.

[31] 10. 19. 11.

[32] Livy, 44. 26. 3; Plutarch, Aem. 12. 2; the clearest description of the fighting technique is provided by Caesar, describing Ariovistus' Germans, in *BG* 1. 48. 5–7.

horses or on chariots. The latter are attested, unreliably, in Lucian's version of the Battle of the Elephants;[33] they were absent from the battles fought with Manlius Vulso, where the terrain was clearly unsuitable. But reliefs found at Pergamum, commemorating Attalus I's victories, show the wheels of carts or chariots taken as trophies, and they had a part to play in battles fought on level ground.[34] However, as in the Homeric descriptions, chariots were often only used as transport, delivering warriors to the field of battle where they engaged the enemy in single combat.[35] The Gauls in general were renowned horsemen, and Galatians serving as mercenaries were frequently mounted.[36] Livy shows that they also fought on horseback on their own behalf, at Cuballum in the *Axylon* when they attacked Manlius' forces, and at Mount Olympus and Mount Magaba where the Tectosages and the Trocmi numbered 1,500 infantry and 10,000 cavalry, who abandoned their mounts to fight on foot in the broken terrain.[37] The readiness to dismount and fight on foot is again apparent, and the most characteristic image of the Galatian at war, reinforced above all by the famous Pergamene sculptures, is of a warrior carrying the great oval shield called the *thureus* and armed with long, broad-bladed swords, daggers, and spears.[38] They would sometimes wear defensive body armour and helmets but more often fought naked, or virtually so, as part of the ritual of primitive war to inspire courage in themselves and terror in the enemy, advancing into battle amid the din of trumpets, shouts, and rhythmic chanting.[39]

The unorthodoxy of Celtic fighting was their main weapon in battle with more sophisticated opponents.[40] At first sight their success seems unexpected. The Hellenistic art of war, modelled on and developed from the revolutionary innovations of Philip and Alexander, was highly sophisticated. Soldiers were becoming increasingly professional, often being mercenaries or residents of military colonies with obligations to fight on behalf of the rulers who had settled them there. They formed the phalanxes of the large Hellenistic armies, and Strabo remarked that against a well-armed phalanx in battle order a tribe of barbarians was utterly weak and exposed.[41] Against this, the Galatians had two advantages denied to their opponents. One was psychological, their enormous and exaggerated reputation for physical courage and brutality, and the terror which this inspired; all of which was manifested by their outlandish appearance, great stature, long hair, and unfamiliar weapons. Their second advantage was, quite simply, that they did not fight in the same way as other Hellenistic armies; they did not follow or respect the rules of Greek warfare. Their strength was their *thumos*, the enthusiasm which swept all before it, and the element of the unexpected in their fighting which consisted of sudden and unpredictable attacks.[42] Their tactics were adapted to rough country, rapid skirmishes, and swift evasive action. The limitations of the Greek phalanx under such difficult conditions are clearly stated by Polybius, comparing it to the Roman legion. It needed a clear flat field of battle, unimpeded by ditches, stream beds, crags, or ravines.[43] Given these limitations of the Hellenistic armies Galatian successes become more intelligible, but their impact can best be understood by considering the type of campaign which they conducted and the opposition which they faced. Their attacks were usually aimed at individual cities and their territories, which were often undefended. The field armies of the Hellenistic kings could not garrison the cities of Asia Minor, and when a force was organized locally to resist the Gauls, as at Priene, it was the result of a private initiative. More often, the cities were completely vulnerable, and it was their success in these unequal confrontations which gave the Galatians their reputation. On the occasions in the third century when they did face substantial armies in the field—at Lysimacheia, in the Battle of the

[33] Lucian, *Zeuxis*, 9; 240 chariots, 80 with scythes (plainly fictional).
[34] Discussed by P. Couissin, *Rev. arch* (1927) ii. 66–72; note the chariot in the story of Kamma and Sinorix, Plutarch, *Mor.* 257e–f; 768b–f.
[35] Diodorus, 5. 29. 1–2. Cf. Caesar, *BG* 4. 33 and 5. 16 on Celtic chariot tactics in Britain.
[36] Launey, *Recherches*, i. 520–2.
[37] Livy, 38. 19. 5; 20. 3; 26. 3. Mommsen thought that Polybius was actually present at these battles; if so he would have been very young. It is better to suppose (with Walbank, *Commentary*, i. 1 n. 1, and iii. 140) that he derived his account from a detailed eyewitness source, perhaps, as C. Habicht suggests to me, Chiomara.
[38] For their armour and weapons see M. Launey, *REA* 46 (1944), 222 with notes, on the bas-relief from Cyzicus (Ch. 2 n. 39); and also *Recherches*, i. 528 ff.; P. Couissin, 'Les Armes gauloises figurées dans les monuments grecs, étrusques et romains', *Rev. arch.* (1927), i. 138–176; 301–25; ii. 43–79. Livy, 38. 21. 4 gives the best written account of their armoury: huge shields, long swords, and such stones as came to hand.
[39] For nudity see Livy, 38. 21. 9; 26. 7; cf. Polybius, 2. 28. 8; Diodorus, 5. 29. 2; 30. 3. The famous Pergamene sculptures obviously confirm this. The Dying Gaul is entirely typical, wearing only a twisted torc round his neck to give magical protection, carrying a broad bladed slashing sword, and

collapsing on to his body shield, the oval *thureus*, on which rests his war trumpet or *carnyx* (cf. Diodorus, 5. 30. 3). For the significance of nudity in warfare, see the very interesting study of P. Couissin, 'La Nudité guerrière des Gaulois', *Ann. de la fac. des lettres d'Aix* (1928/9), 65–89.
[40] Polybius, 2. 35.
[41] Strabo, 7. 3. 17, 306.
[42] Polybius, 2. 35.
[43] Polybius, 18. 28–32, esp. 31.

Fig. 7. The Dying Gaul. 'The Gauls are tall of body, with rippling muscles . . . their hair is naturally fair, but they accentuate the natural blond colour by artificial means. They continually wash their hair in lime-water and pull it back from the forehead to the top of the head and back to the nape of the neck, so that they resemble Satyrs or pans; the hair is thickened by the treatment and is just like a horse's mane . . . The nobles shave their cheeks but let the moustache grow until it covers the mouth. . . . Around their wrists and arms they wear bracelets and around their necks heavy gold necklaces . . . For armour they use long shields as high as a man . . . Their trumpets are of a peculiar nature and give forth a hoarse sound, appropriate to the tumult of war. Some of them have iron cuirasses, but others are satisfied with the armour which nature has given them and go into battle naked' (extracts from Diodorus Siculus v. 27–30). The hair-style, the torque, the oval shield on which the wounded warrior rests, and the curved war-trumpet (*carnyx*) make the figure unmistakeable. This idealization of one of the barbarian enemies overcome by Attalus I is a magnificent marble copy of a bronze original by the Pergamene artist Epigonus. Together with other statues of the defeated Galatians it was displayed on a victory monument which was erected in the sanctuary of Athena at Pergamum around 230 BC (see Ch. 2 § III nn. 95–6).

Elephants, and against Attalus I at the sources of the Caicus—they were heavily defeated. The measure of Manlius Vulso's achievement in 189 is that he sought them out in well-defended positions of their own choosing, and broke their morale with a successful initial assault and barrage. Here, once the Celtic spirit was broken, their effective resistance was at an end.

III. *Clients and Slaves*

As one would expect there is far less evidence for Galatian society in peacetime. Accounts of the Celts in the West make it clear that the institution of battle companions standing by their nobles had its counterpart in peaceful contexts, notably at banquets and public gatherings;[44] and further, that below this class the main body of the population served their masters in a form of clientage whose precise nature cannot be legalistically defined, but which evidently involved the rendering of goods and services by the weak in return for patronage and protection by the strong. These clients appear to have been a relatively fickle category whose allegiance could be won by extravagant displays of generosity by rich and powerful leaders, who com-

[44] See the passages from Athenaeus cited above (n. 19).

peted with one another to secure the widest support.[45] Of this there is no trace in Galatia, perhaps due to the lack of evidence, except for the unrevealing observation that the nobility possessed slaves.[46] Until archaeological excavation has provided us with a reasonable conspectus of occupation sites and burials at all levels of society, which is very far from being the case at present, there is no prospect that this defect in the evidence will be remedied.

It is quite possible, however, that the place of the humbler clients in Galatia was taken for the most part by the indigenous Phrygian population, which was certainly not wiped out by the arrival of the Celts. Documents of the Hellenistic period found in other parts of the Greek world—notably at Athens, Delphi, and Rhodes—mention Galatians, usually of slave status, rarely if ever with Celtic names. Delphic manumission inscriptions, for instance, reveal an Agathon, Athenais a craftswoman, Artemon, Eutychus, Maiphatas, Sosandrus, Sosius a cobbler, and Sosos.[47] The craftsmen can hardly have been Gauls by race,[48] and the name Maiphatas is particularly revealing. It is found elsewhere in Asia Minor in Pontus, Cappadocia, and south-east Phrygia and is of Iranian origin, bearing witness to the Iranian strain in the population of central and eastern Anatolia.[49] It is clear that these Galatian slaves at Delphi were part of the pre-Celtic indigenous population, and had either been captured in the several Galatian wars of the second century BC, or sold in the slave markets of the Aegean, perhaps by their Celtic masters. Galatia, like Phrygia of which it originally formed a part, was an important reservoir of slaves throughout Antiquity.[50]

IV. *Religion*

Religious practices and beliefs are better attested than social structure, although to form a coherent picture it is necessary to draw on material from a wide chronological range. At the start of his campaign in Greece,

which was directed at the sanctuary at Delphi, Brennos (along with the rest of the Celtic race) is branded for his impiety by Pausanias, who gibed that he had no Greek prophet and did not use native priests, if indeed there was any such thing as a Celtic science of prophecy.[51] However, other authors, after more careful study, recognized not only their piety but also their particular attachment to the divination which Brennos had supposedly ignored.[52] In his account of the same events Diodorus puts on record Brennos' contempt for the stone or wooden idols of their anthropomorphic gods which the Greeks erected in their temples;[53] but the natural implication of this passage is not that the Celts were unbelievers, but that they did not envisage their gods in the same form as the Greeks.[54] Although it is true that the image of Brennos as an almost legendary sacker and plunderer of sanctuaries put him beyond redemption to Greek observers, this did not prevent them from seeing the Celts as a whole as a superstitious and god-fearing race.[55] Those few aspects of religious life which emerge from the Galatian evidence bear out the more balanced and objective view.

Celtic forms of divination usually took forms familiar to the Graeco-Roman world: augury, the drawing of lots, the interpretation of dreams and natural phenomena, and the study of the entrails of victims.[56] Two at least of these practices are found in Asia Minor. The most famous example is the penchant of King Deiotarus for augury, recorded at length by Cicero. The proconsul seems to have spent some considerable time in Cilicia exchanging stories with the Galatian king on the subject, and he was surprised at the differences between Galatian and Roman practice.[57] In view of the evidence from other sources that this was a Gallic preoccupation, it is at least as likely that Deiotarus' type of augury was Celtic as that it was Greek or Asiatic, although there is no means of being certain.[58] The examination of entrails is also attested among the eastern Celts. Before the battle with

[45] Athenaeus, 154a–c and 152d–f shows how Celtic leaders won support by distributing gifts; Caesar, *BG* 6. 11. 4 gives as the reason for the institutions of clientage 'that no common man should lack aid against one more powerful. The leaders do not allow their clients to be oppressed and defrauded; otherwise they lose their influence with them.'

[46] Livy, 38. 24. 6; in the mid-1st cent. BC Deiotarus, like other Hellenistic monarchs, had a Greek slave doctor (Cicero, *Deiot.* 17).

[47] See the index of slaves in H. Collitz, *Sammlung der gr. Dialektinschriften* iv. 1 (1886), 311–17.

[48] W. M. Ramsay, *CR* 12 (1895), 341–3; *Galatians*, 81–5.

[49] Robert, *Noms indigènes*, 516–18; S. Mitchell, *ANRW* 11. 7. 2 (1980), 1065–6; J. Strubbe, *Mnemosyne*, 34 (1981), 125 n. 83.

[50] See below, Ch. 14 § VI at n. 87.

[51] Pausanias, 10. 21. 2, cf. 21. 6.

[52] C. Jullian, *Histoire de la Gaule* i (1920), 356 n. 7. See esp. Justin, *Epit.* 24. 4. 3 'augurandi studio Galli praeter ceteros excellunt'.

[53] Diodorus, 22. 9. 4.

[54] Jullian, *Histoire* 357; E. Benoit, *Art et dieux de la Gaule* (1969), 54–5.

[55] Jullian, *Histoire*, 356–7; *I. Priene*, 17, ll. 10 and 17 remarks on their *asebeia* in Asia Minor, but they had sacked sanctuaries there too.

[56] Jullian, *Histoire*, 358.

[57] Cicero, *Div.* 1. 26–7; 2. 20, 76–9.

[58] Cicero, *Leg.* 2. 33, with *Div.* 1. 2, 25, 92, 94, 105, and 2. 80, shows that divination from the flight of birds was also an Asiatic skill, practised in Cilicia, Pamphylia, Pisidia, Lycia, and Phrygia; and Ramsay, *Galatians*, 92 argued that the Galatian form of augury was not Celtic but had been learned after their arrival in Anatolia.

Antigonus Gonatas at Lysimacheia in 277, the Gauls studied the entrails of slaughtered victims, presumably animal.[59] However, they were also notorious for human sacrifice, which was described in Gaul itself by Julius Caesar. 'Of all races the Gauls are most devoted to religious practices, and for this reason all those who are afflicted with the more serious diseases, and those who are engaged in battles make a vow either that they will sacrifice victims on their behalf, or themselves, and they use the Druids to attend to these sacrifices'.[60] A very similar practice is found in Galatia. In about 166 BC the Galatian chieftain responsible for a victory over Eumenes II gathered together his prisoners from the battle, and had the most handsome among them garlanded and sacrificed. The religious implications of this act are shown up by the fact that the rest of the captives were simply put to the sword without ceremony.[61] In Gaul religious practice and divination was controlled by the Druids, a privileged class which passed on its knowledge and its power to aristocratic youths, by a prolonged course of oral instruction. No Druids are known in Galatia, but the documentation is very inadequate, and it is at least possible that a similar priestly caste preserved and passed on the religious lore of the country.

Against the evidence which appears to show specific similarities between the religion and superstitious practices of the Galatians and those of the western Celts, there was a prevalent trend by which the Gauls assimilated the native religion of Anatolia. Direct testimony to this does not appear until the second century BC. In 189 the representatives of the priests of Cybele who met the army of Manlius Vulso at the Sangarius, on the edge of Pessinuntine territory, were apparently Phrygian and hostile to the Galatians.[62] However, by the late 160s the brother of the Attis, or high priest (involved incidentally in a dispute with him), was named Aioiorix and was certainly a Celt; proof that by then the Galatians had a place in the organization of the temple state.[63] Although we do have some information about the priesthood at the end of the second century, when the Battakes of Pessinus (the companion priest to the Attis) came to Rome to prophesy victory to Marius in his war with the Teutones,[64] we learn no more about Galatian involve-

ment in the cult until the middle of the first century BC, when a dispute over the high priesthood broke out between Deiotarus and Brogitarus and spread to the senate at Rome.[65] The latest evidence for Galatian involvement comes from the late first century AD when the Attabokaoi, rather shadowy members of the temple hierarchy, honoured as priests of the cult Tiberius Claudius Heras and his son Tiberius Claudius Deiotarus, respectively tenth and ninth after the high-priest, and fifth and fourth of the Galatians.[66]

It is certainly not possible to reconstruct the whole history of Galatian relations with the temple state from this evidence, and the testimony is not all consistent. The priests who sent representatives to meet Manlius Vulso were called Attis and Battakes, the letters of Eumenes II were addressed to an Attis, and the priests in the time of Marius were still known as Attis and Battakes. However, by the middle of the first century BC there was no trace of this dual leadership, implying either that the organization had changed or that one priest, the Battakes, had been completely subordinated to the other. Later, in the first century AD, we are confronted for the first time by a college of ten priests, with the Galatians in an apparently subordinate position, under a high-priest. We are not in a position to say whether these variations represent a genuine historical development or the vagaries of very different sources, but it is clear that in all instances the office or offices were of considerable political importance, and except in the last instance under the Roman empire, their holders were the effective rulers of the temple state.[67] Galatian chieftains were certainly primarily interested in the political importance of the priesthood, and it is reasonable to assume that their earliest appearance as holders of the office coincided with or succeeded the development which brought to an end the ancient practice of castrating the high priests.[68] These may have been factors which contributed to the decline in the religious importance of the shrine noted by Strabo,[69] but there is no question that the Gauls could have taken a part in the priestly administration if they did not in any way subscribe to the beliefs and practices of the cult. At all periods the shrine retained some religious importance, and the priests were its spokesmen in this respect as in others. If the religious

[59] Justin, *Epit.* 26. 2. 2, with an allusion also to human sacrifice, seen nn. 27 and 61.

[60] Caesar, *BG* 6. 16, with Benoit, *Art et dieux*, 62–4.

[61] Diodorus, 31. 13, see above, nn. 27 and 59.

[62] Polybius, 21. 37. 4; Livy, 38. 18. 9.

[63] Welles, *Royal Correspondence*, 242–3 no. 56.

[64] Diodorus, 36. 13. 1; Plutarch, *Marius*, 17. 9–11. The main purpose of the visit, however, was to protest at and seek redress for trouble caused at Pessinus by Asian tax-farmers, at a time when Bithynia was suffering from similar tribulations; see D. G. Glew, *Klio*, 69 (1987), 122–37.

[65] See above, Ch. 3 § III at nn. 83–5.

[66] *IGR* iii no. 225 = *OGIS* no. 541; *IGR* iii no. 230 = *OGIS* no. 540.

[67] Cf. Strabo, 12. 5. 3, 567.

[68] J. Carcopino, *Aspectes mystiques de la Rome païenne* (1942), 76 ff. suggests that eunuchism among the high priests only ceased with the reform of the cult by Claudius. This seems unlikely, at least for those priests who were also political figures.

[69] Strabo, 12. 5. 3, 567.

and political aspects of the temple administration at Pessinus had not been inextricably linked, there is little likelihood that the shrine would have survived as an independent concern at all. The appearance of Celts in the temple organization by the mid-second century BC is certain proof that they had adopted the indigenous cult of Cybele, and her consort Attis.

Confirmation comes from the story of Kamma, the wife of the Galatian tetrarch Sinatos,[70] who was killed by Sinorix, the most powerful of the Galatians, because he had fallen in love with her.[71] Kamma herself was a notable figure, all the more so because she was the hereditary priestess of Artemis, 'the goddess whom the Galatians revere most'.[72] The cult described by Plutarch, with its altar, temple, and statue of the goddess, bears no resemblance to any known Celtic religious institution, but is clearly completely Hellenized.[73] However, it was almost certainly not Greek in origin. There is virtually no later evidence from inscriptions or coins of the imperial period for the cult of a Greek Artemis in Galatia,[74] and her cult could by no means be described as widespread or popular. On the other hand, the major cult of a goddess was that of the Great Mother, Cybele, and it is very probable that the Artemis of the Kamma story is simply a Hellenized version of an Anatolian goddess.[75]

Much later evidence that the Galatians had adopted the indigenous cults of Anatolia can be found in the fact that Dyteutus, son of the Galatian tetrarch

Adiatorix who had been ruler of Heraclea Pontica in the 30s BC, was made high priest of the goddess Ma at Comana Pontica by Augustus, and continued to rule the temple state, probably until AD 34/5. Since the previous incumbent of the office Cleon of Gordiucome had died suddenly, supposedly struck down for ignoring a religious taboo against eating pork in the place, it is unlikely that Dyteutus himself was completely without religious scruple.[76]

It would not be true to say that the Galatians entirely forgot or chose to neglect their Celtic religious practices when they adopted indigenous Anatolian cults.[77] There was nothing to prevent the two subsisting alongside one another, and it is surely correct to assume that the meetings of the three Galatian tribes at the sacred oak grove known as the *Drynemetos*, retained religious, as well as political and judicial features.[78] Strabo's description of the composition and function of this assembly, cited at the beginning of Ch. 3, shows that it consisted of 300 men who advised the twelve tetrarchs, and had to be consulted in cases of murder.[79] There is a parallel for this in Caesar's description of Gaul in the 50s BC which, if at all apt, implies that at least some of the ritual of Celtic religion will have survived in Galatian institutions as it did in Gaul itself: 'The Druids, at a fixed time in the year, assemble at a consecrated place on the border of the territory of the Carnutes, a region which is considered to be at the very centre of all Gaul. Here everyone involved in disputes comes together from every direction, and they obey their decrees and judgements.'[80] Caesar's and Strabo's descriptions do not match one another exactly. The former describes a religious assembly (of the Druids), the latter a secular one (a part of the tetrarchal constitution of Galatia). But the term *Drynemetos* used by Strabo, explicitly a sacred grove,[81] is a clear indication of the religious background of the Galatian assembly. The division between politics and religion, especially in a Celtic cultural milieu, will have been a very fine one, if any valuable distinction could be made at all. So long as the assembly of the Galatians at the *Drynemetos* continued, the religious apparatus which surrounded it must have survived also. The Galatians had rapidly taken over the beliefs and cults of their new homeland,

[70] Plutarch, *Mor.* 257e–f; 768b–f.
[71] For Sinorix, see above, Ch. 3 §1 n. 7.
[72] Plutarch, *Mor.* 257e ἐπιφανεστέραν δ' ἑαυτὴν ἐποίει καὶ τὸ τῆς Ἀρτέμιδος ἱέρειαν εἶναι ἣν μάλιστα Γαλάται σέβουσι περί τε πομπὰς ἀεὶ καὶ θυσίας κεκοσμημένην ὁρᾶθαι μεγαλοπρεπῶς. After her husband's death ἦν δὲ τῇ Κάμμῃ καταφυγὴ καὶ παραμυθία τοῦ πάθους ἱερωσύνη πατρὸς Ἀρτέμιδος (*Mor.* 768c).
[73] S. Reinach, *Rev. celt.* (1895), 261–7 = *Cultes, mythes et religions*, i (1905), 272–8; Ramsay, *Galatians*, 89–90. Reinach also refuted a suggestion made by H. Usener, *Rh. Mus.* (1895), 195 that the Galatians worshipped an Artemis who was identical with an Artemis found among the Aedui of Gaul, and who was also the same as a 'mid-day demon' called Artemis, exorcised in a rural district of Galatia by St Theodore of Sykeon (*Vita S. Theodori*, 16).
[74] Coins of Ancyra, Pessinus, and Tavium do carry reverse types of Artemis the huntress. Ancyra: *SNG von Aulock* 6184 (Caracalla); *Coll. Wadd.* 6517 (Commodus) and 6642 (Valerian); Pessinus: *BMC Galatia*, no. 5 (Ant. Pius); Tavium: *SNG von Aulock*, 6241 (Septimius Severus). For Artemis in the territory of Gangra Germanicopolis, in Paphlagonia, see I. Kaygusuz, *ZPE* 49 (1982), 177ff. no. 1. See further J. G. C. Anderson, *JHS* 19 (1899), 306 no. 246, A. Wilhelm, *Sb. Berl.* 1931, 802–3, L. Robert, *BCH* 108 (1984), 492 n. 27.
[75] An excellent parallel for identification of a native goddess with Artemis is the *thea Perasia* of Hierapolis-Castabala, equated with Artemis by Strabo, xii. 2. 7, 537. See L. Robert and A. Dupont-Sommer, *La Déesse de Hiérapolis-Castabala* (1959).

[76] Strabo xii. 3. 35, 558; xii. 8. 9, 574–5. For Anatolian taboos against pork, see S. Mitchell, *Aşvan Kale* (1980), 46.
[77] So T. Mommsen, *Provinces of the Roman Empire*, i (Eng. trans. 1905), 339; J. G. C. Anderson, *JHS* 19 (1899), 313, 316; 30 (1910), 161ff.; S. Reinach, *Cultes, mythes et religions*, i. 272.
[78] Ramsay, *Galatians*, 72–3.
[79] Strabo, 12. 5. 1, 567.
[80] Caesar, *BG* 6. 13, adduced by T. Mommsen, *Hermes*, 19 (1884), 321 n. 2.
[81] Holder, ii. 712 s.v. nemeton.

but retained those parts of their old religion which were indivisably linked to their peculiar social and communal life.

v. *Language*

Celtic culture as it survives today on the western fringes of modern Europe has been defined by one attribute above all—language; and the struggle to preserve a distinctive Celtic consciousness has become, in effect, a fight for the survival of the Celtic languages. The Celtic of Galatia was evidently as liable to be overwhelmed by the common tongue (Greek) as Welsh or Gaelic are vulnerable to the insidious inroads of English speaking; for the political history of its leaders, especially in the second and first centuries BC, shows them to have acquired many of the trappings of Hellenistic culture, including the language. Deiotarus, after all, was lettered enough to be able to quote from Euripides, and to receive the dedication of a weighty Greek treatise on agriculture.[82] But champions of Celtic languages in the modern world may take comfort from the fact that Celtic remained widely spoken in Galatia, especially no doubt in the country districts, until late Antiquity.[83] A much discussed passage from St Jerome's commentary on Paul's Epistle to the Galatians reads 'Galatas, excepto sermone Graeco, quo omnis oriens loquitur, propriam linguam paene habere quam Treviros'; and this remark should relate to Jerome's own time, the fourth century AD, whether or not it is derived from his personal observation.[84] The statement finds some confirmation for the second century AD from Pausanias, who tells us that in the native language of the Galatians of Asia Minor the holm oak, an important local resource, was called *hys*,[85] and from the story in Lucian's *Alexander*, that the false prophet of Abonuteichos had to wait for interpreters before he could understand and reply to questions from inhabitants of Galatia and Syria.[86] This testimony may have the additional value of suggesting

that the Galatians, who presumably spoke Celtic, and Syrians who spoke Aramaic, were ignorant of Greek, which was not the case in Jerome's day. In the mid-sixth century the story is told of a Galatian monk who was possessed by the devil and unable to speak. He was cured of his dumbness by a posthumous miracle of St Euthymius, but on recovery spoke at first only in his native language Galatian.[87] These casual observations in the literary record must bear the burden of proof for the use and survival of Celtic in Galatia through the Roman period until the fourth century and beyond.

The remaining evidence, suggestive as it may be, is too malleable to lead to irrefutable conclusions. A handful of native Galatian words is recorded in the ancient sources,[88] but Celtic names for places and persons are much more plentiful. Inscriptions and authors have preserved about twenty Celtic toponyms, distributed about the area settled by the Gauls and representing a sizeable proportion of the total number of place names known there.[89] In one case, at least, a Celtic form Vindia or Vinda demonstrably displaced an existing Anatolian place name—none other than that of the old Phrygian capital Gordium.[90] Celtic personal names are not uncommon throughout central Anatolia, and occur also, as a reflection of the Celtic diaspora in the Hellenistic period, in the cities of the west and the north.[91] They tend to be most frequent in the country areas, where Greek and Roman influence had penetrated less than in the cities, but are by no means used to the exclusion of native Phrygian, or Graeco-Roman names, and in no way derive from a 'pure' and isolated ethnic strain in the population. Indeed one inscription from the Haymana district, outside the original area of Celtic settlement and in the *Proseilemmene*, contains the Celtic name Bodoris but ends with a neo-Phrygian curse formula, suggesting that some Gaulish groups might have acquired the language of the country which they occupied.[92] It cannot be denied that the anthroponymy of Galatia, as revealed by inscriptions, was

---

[82] See above, Ch. 3 § IV at n. 103.

[83] For a general account of the survival of native languages in Roman and late Roman Anatolia, see K. Holl, *Hermes*, 43 (1908), 240–54; see further Ch. 11 § II.

[84] *Comm. in ep. ad Galatas* 2. 3; see J. Sofer, 'Das Hieronymuszeugnis über die Sprachen der Galater und Treverer', *Wiener Studien*, 55 (1937), 148–58. H. Müller, *Hermes*, 74 (1939), 68–73 suggests that the information may have come from Lactantius, whose *Epistulae ad Probum* avowedly provided Jerome with much of the ethnographic material on the Galatians with which he prefaced the second book of his commentary.

[85] Pausanias, 10. 36. 1. Red dye from the holm oak, *coccus*, was a characteristic Galatian product; see below, Ch. 10 § 1 at n. 22.

[86] *Alexander*, 51.

[87] See A. H. M. Jones, *CERP*² 121; *LRE* ii. 993; iii. 332 n. 20; the story is to be found in Cyril of Scythopolis, *Vita S. Euthymii*, 55 (ed. E. Schwartz (1939), p. 77). It should be dated not merely after the death of Euthymius in AD 487, but to the time of Cyril's stay in the monastery of St Euthymius, that is after AD 543 (cf. Schwartz, 410 ff.).

[88] They are collected by L. Weissgerber, 'Galatische Sprachreste', *Natalicium Johannes Geffcken zum 70 Geburtstag* (Heidelberg, 1931), 151–75.

[89] See *ANRW* ii. 7. 2, 1058–9 with nn. 24–8. Add the .νοβαντηνοί (*RECAM* ii no. 75); the χωρίον Κονκαρζιτιακωτόν or Κονκαρζτιακιτόν (*RECAM* ii nos. 207–8); and the cults of Ζεὺς Σουωλιββρογηνός (*RECAM* ii no. 191) and Βουσσουρίγιος (*RECAM* ii nos. 203–4).

[90] See the note on *RECAM* ii no. 191.

[91] See below, nn. 133–5.

[92] *MAMA* vii no. 214 from Sinanlı. For the *Proseilemmene* see below, n. 116.

highly susceptible to outside influence, and a sceptic who chose wilfully to ignore the remarks of Jerome and Lucian might use them to reach pessimistic conclusions about the survival of Celtic. But any attempt to argue from the epigraphic evidence that the language was dying or dead is doomed to fail by the fact that the inscriptions themselves are the products of a Hellenized tradition. There is no evidence that Galatian Celtic was ever written down; it was a language which existed in a cultural milieu whose modes of communication were almost exclusively oral. A people whose traditions were dominated by an age of migration, and whose lore, in the West at least, was preserved by bards and Druids who did not confide their wisdom to written records,[93] will not have swiftly adopted the habit of carving their epitaphs on immovable stones.[94]

VI. *The Settlement of Galatia*

The geographical limits of the Galatian occupation of central Anatolia are not firmly established, although there is no doubt about the general area of their settlement. Given their nomadic habits, it would be reasonable to suppose that they were not firmly fixed and constant throughout the Hellenistic period, but the sources give no clear impression of the expansion and contraction of Celtic dominated territory. The easternmost tribe the Trocmi occupied the country adjoining Pontus and Cappadocia where, by the middle of the first century BC, they had three fortified strong points, Tavium, Mithridatium, and Posdala.[95] The site of

Tavium, at Büyük Nefes Köy, west of Yozgat, is not in doubt, and the wild and largely trackless hills between Tavium and the Halys to the west correspond well with Strabo's description of Trocmian territory as the strongest, that is the roughest and most difficult, region in Galatia. In the Roman period the river Halys marked the western boundary of the city territory of Tavium, and this is also indicated by Livy's account of Manlius Vulso's campaign, in which the Trocmi operated at all times outside their own region, joining the Tolistobogii at Mount Olympus in west Galatia, but placing their women and children for safe keeping on Mount Magaba, in Tectosagan territory east of Ancyra but west of the Halys.[96] Their population, like that of the other tribes, grew rapidly despite battle losses, and before the middle of the second century they tried but failed to annex land from their southern neighbour, Ariarathes of Cappadocia.[97] Tavium remains the only identified Trocmian site whose name we know, and both the archaeological and literary evidence show that it was not by origin a Celtic foundation. According to Strabo, in his day it possessed a monumental bronze statue of Zeus and a shrine with the right of asylum, and it was the trading centre for the area. Archaeology shows that the two mounds there had been continuously occupied since prehistoric times, and they have produced a good quantity of high quality Hellenistic pottery, a fair indication of its prosperity. It had clearly assumed, at least in part, the role of the great Hittite site of Boğazköy, which lay about twenty miles to the north, and it must have functioned like a number of other central Anatolian sites as an important centre for commercial traffic crossing the country both from west to east and from north to south.[98] Tavium has also been suggested as the centre of production for a very distinctive genre of pottery, which occurs during the last two centuries BC at a number of sites in east Galatia and north-west Cappadocia.[99] Attempts to show that there are stylistic affinities between this ware and the late La Tène style

---

[93] Caesar, *BG* 6. 14. Caesar observes that apart from the special case of the Druids the Celts of Gaul did use writing for public and private purposes. Strabo, 4. 1. 5, 181 shows that the aristocracy learnt their letters, and more, at Massilia, but literacy even in Gaul only extended to the most civilized tribes, such as the Helvetii (cf. Caesar, *BG* 1. 29).

[94] It is striking to contrast the abundance in which humdrum funerary and votive texts occur in the Haymana district, the southern part of Ancyran and the northern part of Laodicean territory, with their sparseness in most of north Galatia. In the former districts, which lie outside the original area of Celtic settlement, inscriptions occur in almost every village, usually in quantity (see the maps attached to *MAMA* i and vii and the inscriptions collected there to illustrate the point). In Galatia itself inscriptions are much rarer, less numerous at individual sites, and absent from some areas altogether. The map attached to *RECAM* ii shows this, but may mislead unless account is taken of the fact that the numbered dots representing the find spots of inscriptions in many cases only stand for a single text (see the key ibid. pp. 10–12), while the villages marked on the *MAMA* maps are usually the source of several texts at a time. I would argue tentatively that the area where inscriptions are sparse corresponds to the region where Celtic was still regularly spoken in the Roman period.

[95] Strabo, 12. 5. 1, 567. Pliny, *NH* 5. 146 says of the Trocmi that they held 'Maeoniae et Paphlagoniae regionem . . . Praetenditur Cappadocia a septentrione et solis ortu, cuius uberiorem

partem occupavere Tectosages ac Toutobodiaci.' The Trocmi could be said to have taken over a part of Paphlagonia, which lay to the north-west of their territory, but the reference to Maeonia in Lydia means nothing unless it has its origin in a tradition that the Trocmi settled there before they reached central Anatolia; moreover the location of the Tectosages, as described here, does not correspond with the indications of more reliable sources. At best, Tectosagan territory adjoined Cappadocia on the south-east.

[96] Livy, 38. 19. 1; 26. 3.

[97] See above, Ch. 2 § III n. 162.

[98] See K. Bittel, *Kleinasiatische Studien* (1942), 6–35; *Halil Edhem hâtira Kitabi*, TTKY 7: 5 (Ankara, 1947), 171–9; S. Mitchell, *Princeton Encyclopedia of Classical Sites* (1976), 887.

[99] K. Bittel, *Mélanges Mansel*, TTKY 7: 60 i (1974), 227–37.

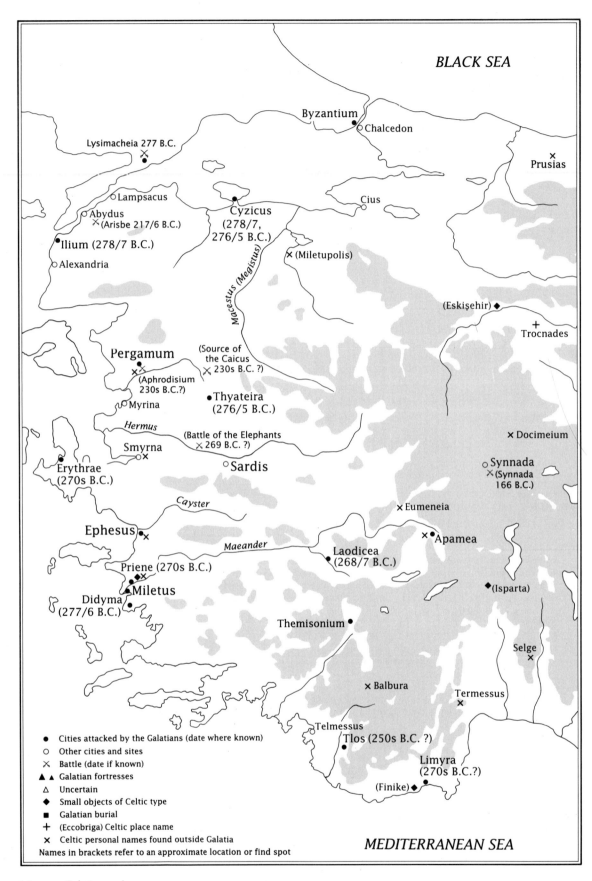

BLACK SEA

Byzantium
Chalcedon
× Prusias

Lysimacheia 277 B.C.
×

Lampsacus
Abydus
× (Arisbe 217/6 B.C.)
Ilium (278/7 B.C.)
Alexandria

Cius

Cyzicus
(278/7,
276/5 B.C.)

× (Miletupolis)

Macestus (Megistus)

(Eskişehir) ◆

+ Trocnades

Pergamum
× ×
(Aphrodisium
230s B.C.?)
Myrina

(Source of
the Caicus
× 230s B.C. ?)

Thyateira
(276/5 B.C.)

× Docimeium

Hermus

(Battle of the Elephants
× 269 B.C. ?)

Smyrna
×

Erythrae
(270s B.C.)

Sardis

○ Synnada
× (Synnada
166 B.C.)

Cayster

× Eumeneia

Ephesus
× ×

Maeander

× ● Apamea

Priene (270s B.C.)
◆ ×
Miletus
Didyma
(277/6 B.C.)

Laodicea
(268/7 B.C.)

◆ (Isparta)

Themisonium ●

Selge
×

× Balbura

Termessus
×

Telmessus
Tlos (250s B.C. ?)

Limyra
(270s B.C.?)

(Finike) ◆ ●

MEDITERRANEAN SEA

● Cities attacked by the Galatians (date where known)
○ Other cities and sites
× Battle (date if known)
▲ ▲ Galatian fortresses
△ Uncertain
◆ Small objects of Celtic type
■ Galatian burial
+ (Eccobriga) Celtic place name
× Celtic personal names found outside Galatia
Names in brackets refer to an approximate location or find spot

Map 4a. Galatian settlements

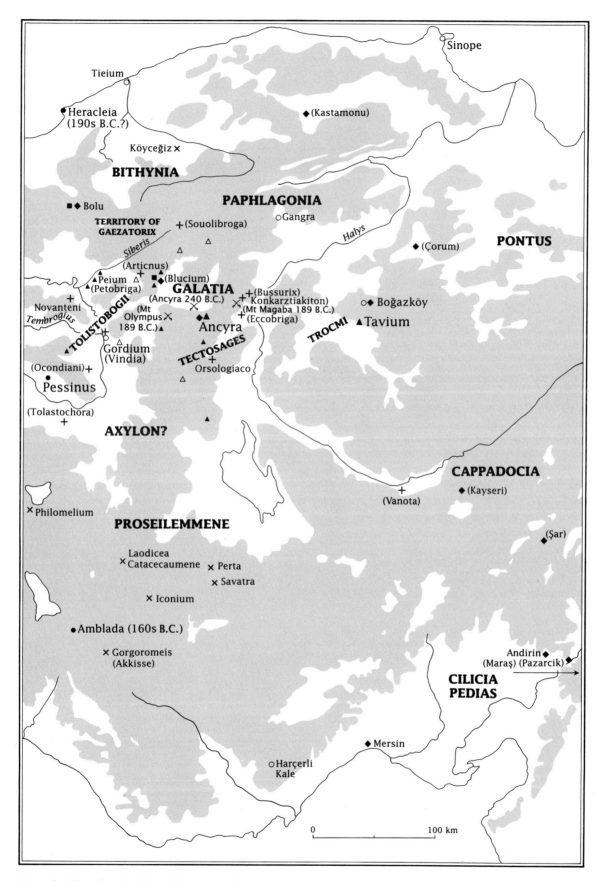

Sinope

Tieium

◆ Heracleia
(190s B.C.?)

Köyceğiz ✕

(Kastamonu) ◆

BITHYNIA

PAPHLAGONIA

○ Gangra

■◆ Bolu

**TERRITORY OF
GAEZATORIX**

+ (Souolibroga)

Siberis

△   △

Halys

(Çorum) ◆

PONTUS

+
(Articnus)

▲ Peium   △
(Petobriga)

■◆ (Blucium)

GALATIA

(Ancyra 240 B.C.)

+ (Bussurix)
Konkarztiakiton)
✕ (Mt Magaba 189 B.C.)
(Eccobriga)

○◆ Boğazköy

Novanteni

Tembrogius

+

(Mt
Olympus ✕
189 B.C.) ▲

✕

◆▲ ▲

Ancyra

▲ Tavium

TROCMI

TOLISTOBOGII

△

▲   Gordium
(Vindia)

TECTOSAGES

+
Orsologiaco

(Ocondiani) +

● Pessinus

△

(Tolastochora)
+

AXYLON?

▲

CAPPADOCIA

(Kayseri) ◆

+
(Vanota)

✕ Philomelium

PROSEILEMMENE

(Şar) ◆

Laodicea
✕ Catacecaumene   ✕ Perta

✕ Savatra

✕ Iconium

● Amblada (160s B.C.)

Andirin ◆
(Maraş) (Pazarcik) →

✕ Gorgoromeis
(Akkisse)

**CILICIA
PEDIAS**

◆ Mersin

○ Harçerli
Kale

0   100 km

Map 4*b*. The archaeological and historical evidence

found on European sites fall short of proof,[100] and it seems more likely that this pottery is the product of a local rather than a strictly Galatian workshop. Observed or excavated Hellenistic sites in Trocmian territory also yield few clues about the nature of their occupants. A number of settlements in the valley north of Boğazköy have produced sherds of the east Galatian pottery, but none could be called a *phrourion*, the only distinctively Galatian type of site. A number of cist graves and child burials in jars have been found at Boğazköy itself, belonging to the Hellenistic period. Two iron and one bronze fibula, and an iron sword from the cist graves may be Galatian;[101] the fibulae are certainly of a Celtic type, and similar pieces have occurred at Trocmian sites near Çorum,[102] at Kayseri in Cappadocia, and in a notable cluster in the eastern Taurus and Cilicia Pedias, between Maraş and Mersin.[103] The same cemetery at Boğazköy has also produced a locally made silver coin, which resembles the Celtic imitations of Macedonian silver found in Thrace and the West.[104] There is, therefore, clear if limited evidence for elements of a Celtic material culture in this late settlement at Boğazköy, in at least two other sites in Trocmian territory, and, less predictably, in Cappadocia and the Cilician plain. The spread to the south-east is confirmed by a Hellenistic fortification tower in the hills of Rugged Cilicia near Olba, where a Celtic shield is depicted among other weapons above the door-lintel.[105]

The Tectosages, according to Strabo, occupied the area adjoining Great Phrygia around Pessinus and the Orcaorci, and their fortified stronghold was Ancyra.[106] Pessinus, the temple state which was intermittently but increasingly dominated by the Gauls, lay within the bend of the Sangarius at Balıhisar; the Orcaorci, a people not mentioned outside Strabo, evidently occupied the plateau region south and east of the Sangarius.[107] This suggests that the Tectosages extended from the Halys to the Sangarius along the southern border of Galatia. Their main centres appear to have been in the east of this territory: at Ancyra itself, where no remains attributable to the Gauls or to the Hellenistic period have been securely identified; at Mount Magaba, also known as Mordiacus, little more than ten miles east of Ancyra where the tribe gathered for their final stand against Manlius Vulso;[108] and at the fortress called Gorbeous, about twenty-one miles south of Ancyra, where the Tectosagan tetrarch Castor and his wife were murdered in the late 40s BC.[109] There are a number of other fortress sites which may have belonged to Tectosagan chieftains. Livy mentions a *castellum* called Cuballum, which might be located somewhere in the region of Haymana, if Manlius' march did indeed involve a detour into the *Axylon* east and south of the Sangarius.[110] Other fortified strongpoints have been identified at Assarlıkaya Hissar, Basrı, and Çanakçı; all south-west of Ancyra but east of the Sangarius, and none of any pretension or elaboration. The only site in this area which has been excavated is the old Phrygian capital of Gordium at Yassıhüyük. Livy describes it in terms that recall Strabo's account of Tavium; 'haud magnum quidem oppidum est, sed plus quam mediterraneum celebre et frequens emporium.' It was roughly equidistant from three seas, and stood on the borders of several important nations, whose commercial needs brought them together at Gordium.[111] No coherent picture of Hellenistic Gordium has yet emerged from the excavations there, although there are

[100] F. Maier, *JdI* 78 (1963), 218–55. A. Müller-Karpe, *Ist. Mitt.* 38 (1988), 189–99, at 198 fig. 4 stresses the similarity between La Tène types from Bavaria and handleless jars found at Hacıbektaş and argues for a common Celtic ceramic tradition. It remains problematic that none of this so-called Galatian pottery has been found outside the territory of the Trocmi.

[101] H. Kühne in K. Bittel, *Boğazköy*, iv, *Funde aus den Grabungen 1967 und 1968* (1969), 35–45; K. Bittel, ibid. 45–9, 121 (cist graves). K. Bittel and R. Naumann, *Boğazköy-Hattusa*, i (1953), 120–1; K. Bittel, *Boğazköy* iv. 36–7 (jar burials). Iron fibula of middle La Tène type, *Boğazköy* iv pl. 24d and fig. 10a; a second similar example in R. M. Boehmer, *Die Kleinfunde von Boğazköy 1931–9, 1952–60* (1972), 139 nos. 1264 and 1264a, pl. XLIV. Bronze fibula, *Boğazköy* iv fig. 36a; sword, fig. 36b.

[102] H. Z. Koşay, *TAD* 15. 1 (1966), 90 ff.

[103] See the distribution maps and references in *Boğazköy* iv. 48; H. Polenz, *BJb.* 178 (1978), 181–216 (middle La Tène fibula from Kayseri); and A. Müller-Karpe, *Ist. Mitt.* 38 (1988), 189–95 (no. 1, near Çorum; no. 2, near Kayseri; nos. 3–7 from Şar. Andırın, Maraş, and Pazarlık in the south-east).

[104] *Boğazköy* iv. 48–9 with fig. 12. Also K. Bittel, 'Die Galater in Kleinasien archäologisch gesehen', in D. M. Pippidi (ed.), *Assimilation et résistance à la culture grèce-romaine dans le monde ancien, travaux du VIe congrès international d'études classiques* (1976), 241–9 esp. 248–9.

[105] See *JHS Arch. Reports* (1989/90), 131.

[106] Strabo, 12. 5. 1, 567. Livy, 38. 24. 1 calls Ancyra 'nobilem in illis locis urbem', expanding Polybius, 21. 39. 1, περὶ τὴν Ἄγκυραν πόλιν. But Polybius' use of the term *polis* merely indicates that it was a substantial settlement, and Livy's addition of the adjective *nobilis* reflects its new status in the Augustan period.

[107] W. Ruge, *RE* xviii (1942), 1089–90.

[108] Livy, 38. 19. 1; Sextus Rufus, *Breviarium*, 11, 'in Magabam montem qui nunc Mordiacus appellatur'. The second name recalls the dynast of Cappadocia, who fought alongside the Galatians in this battle, and the Phrygio-Pisidian city of Mordiaion, later Apollonia; cf. Robert, *Noms indigènes*, 348 n. 7.

[109] See Ch. 3, n. 122.

[110] Livy, 38. 18. 5; for the topography of the march see the studies cited in Ch. 2, n. 124.

[111] 38. 18. 11; Polybius, 21. 37. 8, where the excerptor has left out the detailed description.

impressive chamber tombs of the period,[112] and a considerable quantity of coins and contemporary pottery from the site, one of them carrying a graffito inscription of a Galatian name, Καντυιξ.[113] A heavy destruction level on the site can be dated precisely to the occasion of the invasion by Manlius Vulso and thereafter the site never recovered its former importance. By Strabo's day it was little more than a village, and the evidence of the Roman itineraries suggests that by the second century AD it had lost its old name, and received a new one, the Celtic form Vindia.[114]

There is a possibility that the Tectosages, like the Trocmi, attempted and actually succeeded in extending their territory during the second century BC. According to Pliny, a large part of Lycaonia was given as a tetrarchy to Galatia,[115] and Ptolemy refers to an area west of the Salt Lake called the *Proseilemmene*, 'the added land', which should probably be identical with this tetrarchy.[116] Lycaonia and, by implication, the area immediately to the north of it had been given to Eumenes I in 189, after Manlius' expedition, but was not part of the Attalid kingdom bequeathed to Rome in 133.[117] Hence the acquisition of much of this central area by the Gauls could well fall within these limits. Their presence during the wars of this period at Synnada, at Amblada, and possibly other parts of Pisidia shows that they were capable of expanding into this thinly populated area; the presence of Celtic names in inscriptions of the imperial period from the central plateau, and from cities as far south as Laodicea Catacecaumene, Perta, and Savatra, could be a reflection of this southern colonization. Although the Galatians were not notably strong politically during the second century, there would have been few contesting claims for this barren region. It was not of great strategic importance since few routes ran across it, but it was, as its history under the Roman empire shows, capable of supporting a large population. It could, therefore, have absorbed the Tectosages without

causing serious disquiet among the neighbouring communities and kingdoms.[118]

The Tolistobogii, the most prominent tribe during the Hellenistic period, appear to have settled chiefly in north-west Galatia, adjoining Bithynia and Phrygia Epictetus, whose easternmost city was Midaeum, in the Tembris valley east of Dorylaeum.[119] Blucium and Peium, the two fortresses of their tetrarch Deiotarus, can be located with reasonable certainty at Karalar, overlooking the valley of the Ova Çay, and at Tabanlıoğlu Kale, commanding a gorge of the Girmir Çay, both north-west of Ancyra in the direction Bithynia.[120] Other Tolistobogian forts in this area have been noted at Crentius close to Karalar, at Dikmen a few miles south of Peium, and at Tahirler, which overlooks the crossing of the Girmir Çay at Sykeon.[121] The tribe's territory certainly extended west of the Sangarius into the region on either side of the lower Tembris, north of Pessinus. Here too there is a fortified site of Hellenistic date at Soman Hisar, and there is onomastic evidence of the Roman period for Galatian settlement.[122] The evidence for substantial native sites occupied both immediately before and during the Hellenistic period is much slighter than that at Tavium, Ancyra, and Gordium; but a prominent mound at Tolgeri Hüyük on the Ankara Çay, about fifteen miles east of its junction with the Sangarius, has every appearance of continuous occupation from the third millennium BC to the Hellenistic period, and has produced good quality Hellenistic pottery.

Deiotarus' palace Blucium at Karalar is the only Tolistobogian site to have been excavated.[123] The settlement itself is notable for a rock-cut shaft leading down to a water source within the walls of the fortress which were built of substantial dressed masonry, but otherwise produced few distinctive remains. However, on a hillside which overlooks the fortress on the south, three chamber tombs were excavated, including one belonging to Deiotarus' son and namesake. One has a

[112] R. Young, *AJA* 60 (1956), 250–2; G. R. Edwards, *Expedition*, 5 (1963), 47–8. F. A. Winter, *Source. Notes in the History of Art*, 7 (1988), 60–71 summarizes the evidence for Hellenistic occupation and stresses the continuity with the native Anatolian tradition; for recent work see *JHS Arch. Reports* (1989/90), 129.

[113] For the Hellenistic epigraphy of Gordium see L. E. Roller, *AS* 37 (1987), 103–33; p. 129 no. 56 has the Celtic name Καντυιξ.

[114] Strabo, 12. 5. 3, 568; Vindia or Vinda is the name given in the Peutinger table and the Antonine itinerary to a staging post which ought to have been precisely at the site of Gordium, where there are minor remains of the Roman period.

[115] *NH* 5. 75.

[116] Ptolemy, 5. 4. 10.

[117] Livy, 38. 39. 16.

[118] For this theory see Ramsay, *Galatians*, 64–5. If it be rejected, the most likely date for the addition of a 'Lycaonian' tetrarchy to Galatia is the middle of the 1st cent. BC, under Deiotarus or Amyntas.

[119] Strabo, 12. 5. 2, 567; for Phrygia Epictetus, see 12. 8. 12, 576. W. Ruge, *RE* xv (1932), 1254–6 reviews the evidence for the location of Midaeum, which is not exactly known.

[120] S. Mitchell, *AS* 24 (1974), 61–75.

[121] For details of these and other Galatian forts, see the gazeteer appended to *RECAM* ii, pp. 25–8. The site at Tahirler was identified during a visit to the area around Sykeon in June 1990.

[122] There are clearly Celtic names in *RECAM* ii nos. 19, 28, 29, 41, 83, 103, and 105 from this area.

[123] R. O. Arık, *TTAED* 2 (1934), 102–67; *Rev. arch.* (1935) ii. 133–40; for recent work, showing Roman occupation also, see *JHS Arch. Reports* (1989/90), 130.

Fig. 8. Peium. A view of the treasury of King Deiotarus from the south. High-quality late Hellenistic masonry can be recognized beneath the late Roman and Byzantine work of the fortifications which were built at the east end of the castle; it was protected on the other sides by a great loop of the valley of the river Siberis (Girmir Çay). For further details see S. Mitchell, *AS* 24 (1974), 61–75.

Fig. 9. Blucium. The site of Deiotarus' palace at Karalar. His son was buried in a chamber tomb on a nearby hillside. The andesite ashlar blocks and the rock-cut foundation courses in the background may belong to a large public terrace, and not to the fortification wall. Bibliography at Ch. 4 § VI n. 123.

The Galatian strongholds of Deiotarus

distinctive corbelled roof, which can be paralleled at Gordium and at a number of other sites in north-west Anatolia;[124] the second has a square barrel-vaulted chamber approached by a *dromos*, closely comparable to an example excavated at Küyücek in Bithynia;[125] and the third, belonging to the younger Deiotarus, has a peaked roof for which the parallels again are to be found to the north-west in Bithynia.[126] The architecture of these Galatian tombs, then, belongs to a north-west Anatolian tradition, and owes nothing to the Celtic West. It is not to be expected that nomadic tribesmen should have brought with them designs and architects for stone-built tombs. Celtic funerals, however, were lavish affairs,[127] and the graves at Karalar, even after plundering, still contained the remnants of expensive grave goods. The corbelled tomb yielded fragments of a gold torc, set with precious stones; the barrel-vaulted chamber, perhaps a woman's grave, a golden necklace set with stones, a gold floral diadem, and a bronze fibula; the tomb of Deiotarus itself included a porphyry offering table, a glass vase with gold ornament, and pieces of purple cloth, as well as the remains of a sculptured lion and trophy outside. The Celtic torc confirms that this royal cemetery was genuinely Galatian.[128]

Grave goods found in a tumulus south of Bolu (including two gold torcs, gold bracelets with animal-head terminals, a bronze horse bit, and a gold belt buckle depicting the bearded and moustached face of a Celt) help to identify it too as a Galatian tomb, and point towards an extension of Galatian, presumably Tolistobogian influence northwards into Bithynia.[129] This is not the only evidence for Celtic influence north and west of Galatia as it is generally defined. The area of western Paphlagonia, named after and presumably belonging to the Galatian noble Gaezatorix, has already been noted,[130] and the cult of Zeus Souolibrogenos, a Celtic epithet, is attested by an inscription from the district of Kizilcahamam.[131] Ever since the *diabasis*, relations between the Gauls and Bithynia had been close, if often uneasy, and their territorial ambitions in the north are clear from the history of their attempts to gain control of Heracleia Pontica; so the presence of a Celtic tomb at Bolu is not at all surprising.[132] The finds from the tomb cannot be accurately dated, but it may well be the case that the pressure on Bithynia was increasing during the first half of the second century BC, at the same period as Trocmian attempts to annex part of Cappadocia and the Tectosagan extension into the central plateau, with rapid population growth being the root cause behind all these territorial ambitions. If so, the heavy defeats suffered in 189 and 183 BC cannot have seriously impaired Galatian manpower; war losses, as so often, were rapidly made up by a fertile population.

Individual Celts were not confined to their central Anatolian territories. Celtic names occur at a number of city sites in Asia Minor during the Hellenistic and Roman periods, including the Asian cities of Priene, Smyrna, Ephesus, Pergamum, the country district of inland Mysia, Nicaea, Prusias ad Mare, and Prusias ad Hypium in Bithynia, and, in the Phrygian hinterland, at Eumeneia, Philomelium, Docimeum, and Apamea.[133] Service in the armies of Hellenistic kings was almost certainly the most important way by which Celts became dispersed throughout Hellenistic Asia Minor and elsewhere in the eastern Mediterranean. The Ptolemies had created a virtual colony of Galatians in Egypt near Alexandria, using them as mercenaries;[134] and the epigram of a certain Brikkon, son of Ateuristos, found at Maroneia in Thrace, shows him to have been a citizen of Apamea but leader of a force of Galatians.

---

[124] Karalar tomb C. Compare examples at Gordium, *AJA* 60 (1956), 250–2; Iğdir, nr. Eskişehir, *TAD* 23 (1975), 151–3; Tepecik, nr. Izmit, N. Fıratlı, *IAMY* 15–16 (1969); Gemlik, Kepsut, Milas, and Belevi, A. M. Mansel, *Belleten*, 38 (1974), 181–9; Mudanya, *Belleten*, 10 (1946), 1–12; Pamukkale, E. Schneider Equini, *La necropoli di Hierapolis di Frigia* (1972), 127–31. See in general, M. Waelkens, 'Hausähnliche Gräber in Anatolien vom 3. Jht. v. Chr. bis in die Römerzeit', *Palast und Hütte: Beiträge zum Bauen und Wohnen im Altertum* (1982), 421–45 at 431.

[125] Karalar tomb A. Küyücek, N. Fıratlı, *Belleten*, 17 (1953), 22–5.

[126] Karalar tomb B. Gordium, *Expedition* 5 (1963), 47–8; Bolu, N. Fıratlı, *AJA* 69 (1965), 365–7; Beşevler, W. Hoepfner, *Ath. Mitt.* 86 (1971), 125–39.

[127] Diodorus, 5. 32. 6. Caesar, *BG* 6. 19. 4. But the Galatian tombs clearly do not reflect these spectacular and barbaric funerary practices.

[128] For the finds, see Arık, *TTAED* 2 (1934), 102–67.

[129] N. Fıratlı, *AJA* 69 (1965), 365–7; cf. Bittel, 'Die Galater in Kleinasien archäologisch gesehen' (above, n. 104). For possible representations of Galatians on pottery and terracottas at Gordium, see F. Winter, *Source*, 7 (1988), 64.

[130] See above, Ch. 2 nn. 118–19.

[131] *RECAM* ii no. 191.

[132] It is worth mentioning a passage from the Byzantine author Leo the Deacon, who described a serious earthquake at Claudiupolis (Bolu), which is called τὸ εὐδαιμονέστατον χωρίον Γαλατῶν (*PG* 117, 761). An inscription probably of the 6th cent. AD appears to imply that parts of Paphlagonia around Gangra were then regarded as Galatian, or that there was a Galatian population there, D. Feissel, *Riv. arch. christ.* 58 (1982), 375–6.

[133] The evidence is usefully assembled by Y. Grandjean, *BCH* 95 (1971), 294 n. 52, and O. Masson, *Ét. celt.* 19 (1982), 129–35. For a Celt called Andaev . . . , in charge of a marble workshop at Docimeum, see M. Christol and T. Drew Bear, *Tyche*, 1 (1986), 71 (compare the name Αντεσεικομπος in Galatia, *RECAM* ii nos. 115, 170).

[134] Launey, *Recherches*, i. 530 ff.; for the Galatian name Δαδωριγου (gen.) on a Hellenistic vase at Alexandria, see Masson, *Ét. celt.* (1982), 133–4.

Service in the pay of a Hellenistic king, possibly Antiochus III, will surely have been the avenue by which he acquired full citizenship of a Greek *polis*.[135]

In general, it may be concluded that, while a minority of Celts settled in established Greek cities and became assimilated into the prevailing culture of the cities of Asia Minor, the vast majority settled in an area which was little touched by Hellenistic civilization. They moved into the vacuum caused by the collapse of the kingdom of Phrygia, bringing with them their own distinctive style of political and social organization, elements of their own material culture, and in particular their own language.[136] These were all to survive until the end of the Hellenistic period, and the Celtic language was still spoken in late Antiquity. While the predominant culture was obviously Celtic, and they apparently maintained contacts with their kin in the West,[137] they were naturally not immune to local influences. These are most marked in their religion; the Galatians, without losing touch with all of their native religious traditions, rapidly adopted the beliefs of the native population. In their burial practices also, to judge from the architecture of their tombs, they must have conformed to Anatolian customs. Their settlements too seem to adhere more closely to an Anatolian than to a European pattern. The most distinctive type of Galatian site, attested both by the literary sources and by archaeological discoveries, was the small fortified stronghold, or *phrourion*, usually placed in a well-defended situation remote from the main lines of communication. These were clearly retreats which housed a chieftain's family and his immediate entourage of followers and clients. They point towards a society whose leaders lived in mutual fear and rivalry, a picture broadly confirmed by the literary evidence. It was only on rare occasions, such as the invasion by the Romans under Manlius Vulso, that the Galatians combined to seek refuge in huge hill forts, capable of accommodating whole tribes, and the two fortified enclosures, still unlocated, on Mounts Olympus and Magaba, play no other part in Galatian history. The Celts in Asia Minor never produced great *oppida* as did the tribes of central Europe, Gaul, and southern Britain after about 200 BC, a fact which reflects an important difference in their social and political evolution. The tribes of central and eastern Gaul which began to build large hill forts and establish the beginnings of an urbanized culture in the late second and first centuries BC were simultaneously evolving systems of government which suggest not tribal society but archaic or primitive states.[138] The absence of any such settlements in Galatia strongly suggests that they retained their fissionable tribal organization up to the moment when they entered the Roman protectorate.

---

[135] Grandjean, *BCH* 95 (1971), 283–94; Moretti, *Iscrizioni storiche ellenistiche*, ii no. 115. No doubt mercenary service abetted the Galatian diaspora and explains the presence of Celtic names in Thessaly and Macedonia, Masson, *Ét. celt.* (1982), 129–31.

[136] See above, nn. 83–7.

[137] The inscription from Lampsacus (*SIG*³ 591) presumes an affinity, and possible contact between the Tolistobogii and the Celts of Gaul. The Tectosages were believed to be a branch of the Volcae Tectosages of Gaul, Strabo, 4. 1. 13. Less reliable anecdotal evidence also assumes that links were maintained, see Ch. 2 n. 46. None of this amounts to proof that actual contacts between the two areas were kept up on a regular basis.

[138] D. Nash, 'The Growth of Urban Society in France' in B. Cunliffe and T. Rowley (eds.), *Oppida: The Beginnings of Urbanisation in Barbarian Europe* (1976), 95–133.

II

The Impact of Roman Rule

χωρὶς τῆς Ῥωμαίων ἡγεμονίας οὐδὲ ζῆν προαιρούμεθα

(Decree of Plarasa/Aphrodisias, 88 BC; J. M. Reynolds, *Aphrodisias and Rome* (1982), document 2)

Simul et illud Asia cogitet, nullam ab se neque belli externi neque domesticarum discordiarum calamitatem afuturam fuisse, si hoc imperio non teneretur; id autem imperium cum retineri sine vectigalibus nullo modo possit, aequo animo parte aliqua suorum fructuum pacem sibi sempiternam redimat atque otium.

(Cicero, *ad Q. Fr.* 1. 1. 11, 34, 59 BC)

Mountainous, colourless, lifeless, unsubdued by a people whose thoughts travel no further than to the next furrow, who live and die and leave no mark on the great plains and the barren hills—such is central Asia, of which this country is a true part. And that is why the Roman roads make so deep an impression on one's mind. They impressed the country itself, they implied a great domination, they tell of a people that overcame the universal stagnation.

(*The Letters of Gertrude Bell* (1930 edn.), 198–9; written near Lake Beyşehir, 7 May 1907)

In formam provinciae redacta

Annexation and the Framework of Roman Administration

In 25 BC the possessions of Amyntas were annexed to the Roman empire, and the province of Galatia was created.[1] During the preceding two centuries Rome had acquired new territory in a host of different circumstances. There were wide vicissitudes in the forms of provincial administration, and the term *provincia* itself could convey a broad spectrum of meanings in different contexts, ranging from the purview and responsibilities of a Roman magistrate, devoid of any geographical connotation, to the precise topical definition of the area where those responsibilities were undertaken, that is a province in the modern sense of the word.[2] But by the reign of Augustus Rome's relationship with her non-Italian subjects had begun to harden, through habit and custom, into a more or less formalized system of government. In January 27 BC Augustus' 'New Deal', which gave legal form to a power structure that had essentially been established by twenty years of extra-legal revolutionary activity and which was to be reinforced throughout his principate, entailed a reappraisal of provincial administration which further defined the nature and status of the various provinces according to the type of governor

sent to administer them. Dio and Strabo, our sources for this transaction, both clearly drawing at first or second hand on a decision of the senate, distinguished one group of provinces governed by proconsuls drawn by lot from the senate, from a second group governed by *legati* of the emperor. These were also senators, but were specially appointed by the emperor himself and operated, in a formal sense at least, as his agents rather than as independent commanders.[3] The significance of this decision is by no means unambiguous, and it is certainly not true that thereafter one portion of the empire was controlled by the senate through its proconsuls, and another by the emperor through his legates,[4] but the enactment of the division in a law that was crucial, at least in the short term, to the settlement of Rome's current political problems, went far to establishing what a province actually was, simply by defining the official status of its governors. When Galatia was annexed, some two years later, it was assigned to the group of major provinces administered by the emperor through his legates. We know the name of the first governor, Marcus Lollius, a praetorian senator who was to hold the consulship in 21 BC, presumably soon after his return from the newly created command.[5]

The only hint of the legal mode by which the transfer of power was effected from Amyntas to Rome, or to Augustus, comes from the observation in Strabo that a group of persons responsible for reallocating the temple possessions of Mēn Askaēnos in the plain of Pisidian Antioch, had been sent out to deal with the *kleronomia*, the bequest, of Amyntas.[6] Perhaps in this

---

[1] The date is provided by Dio, 53. 26. 2; B. M. Levick, *CQ* 1971, 483 n. 4 has suggested that Amyntas might have been killed in 26 or even 27 BC. The issue would be resolved if we could establish that the coins minted by Amyntas in Side and dated to his twelfth regnal year, reckoned those years from the winter of 37/6 BC when he acquired most of his kingdom including Pamphylia, or from 39 when he was given his first 'command' by Antony (see above, Ch. 3 n. 153). The former possibility entails a date of 25/4 or even later for annexation. The era of the three north Galatia cities may not have begun until 23–21 BC, but this need have no bearing on the date of Amyntas' death (see below, Ch. 7 § III n. 78 and Ch. 8 n. 29). H. Halfmann, *Chiron*, 16 (1986), 35–40 argues that an interval probably fell between Amyntas' unexpected death and the decision to annex his kingdom, which might have been taken by Agrippa after his arrival on Lesbos in the second half of 23 BC.

[2] Th. Mommsen, *Staatsrecht*, i³. 52; J. Marquardt, *Römische Staatsverwaltung*, i (2nd edn. 1881), 497–502; G. Wesenberg, *RE* xxiii. 1 (1957), 995–1029 with bibliography. In the Anatolian context, cf. Syme, *ASBuckler*, 299–302 = *RP* i. 120–3.

[3] Dio, 53. 12 ff.; Strabo, 17. 3. 25, 840. See the brief but useful remarks of R. Syme, *RP* iii. 870–1.

[4] Fergus Millar, 'The Emperor, the Senate and the Provinces', *JRS* 56 (1966), 56–66.

[5] For M. Lollius see *PIR*² v. 1 (1970), 83: L. no. 311; Sherk, i. 19; ii. 963–4.

[6] Strabo, 13. 8. 14, 577: ἦν δ' ἐνταῦθα καὶ ἱερωσύνη τις Μηνὸς Ἀρκαίου, πλῆθος ἔχουσα ἱεροδούλων καὶ χωρίων ἱερῶν· κατελύθη δὲ μετὰ τὴν Ἀμύντου τελευτὴν ὑπὸ τῶν πεμφθέντων ἐπὶ τὴν ἐκείνου κληρονομίαν. These persons were certainly not the members of a senatorial commission but, in all probability, military surveyors like the *evocatus Augusti* who conducted a land allocation for

connection, it appears that a number of royal slaves passed into the imperial household.[7] Territory had passed to Rome by this means before, and was to do so again in the future. Five Hellenistic monarchs, between Ptolemy VIII Euergetes in 155 BC and Nicomedes IV of Bithynia in 74 BC had left their kingdoms to Rome.[8] Only in the earliest instance, where an inscription appears to preserve a summary of the principal terms of the bequest, are we at all well informed about the transaction.[9] Then, the king stated that his kingdom was to pass to the Romans if he died without leaving heirs. The absence of heirs is a common factor evident in all these cases, and certainly one motive behind the bequests was to avoid an unseemly scramble for power where no clear-cut succession could be discerned. Bequeathing one's possessions to Rome was also a useful insurance policy, designed to deter assassination attempts by jealous rivals and relatives. The initiative for making the wills generally emanated from the kings, not from Rome, and this is particularly clear in the case of the kingdom of Pergamum, left to Rome by Attalus III; the new masters of the Attalid domain were caught unawares, with no clear plan of action to handle the windfall of extensive new possessions in Asia Minor.[10] That is not so certain in the later case of Bithynia, which was left to them by Nicomedes IV in 74 BC. The shadow of Mithridates VI hung over the succession there, and it is at least possible that Rome had prompted the king to make his bequest in order to prevent his possessions falling into the hands of their rival.[11]

The transfer of power from one monarch to another has always been a notoriously hazardous transaction. For this reason Rome, either of its own volition or upon request, often assumed guardianship over kingdoms which lay within its sphere of interest; and this *tutela* (as Romans might term it) could also be conferred by will, as was particularly appropriate or timely in cases where a king's heirs were too young to assume full responsibility, or lacked the ability to defend themselves against determined rivals.[12]

But the situation in Galatia fits neither the first case, when a king without heirs might hand over his domains to Rome, nor the second, where Rome would be asked to guarantee the rule of a minor. On the one hand there was an heir, Pylaemenes, although he was clearly too young to assume full responsibility;[13] on the other, Rome did not merely assume *tutela* of Amyntas' kingdom, but annexed it into the empire. The closest parallels, although neither is exact, can be found in Thrace and in Britain. In 42 BC the Thracian ruler Sadalas II left his kingdom to the Romans; Dio mistakenly suggests that he was childless, but this is disproved both by a passage in Appian and by an inscription from Bizye, which mention that he had a son, at the time still only a boy, by his wife Polemocratia.[14] Thus far, the comparison with Amyntas and Pylaemenes is close, but in this case the bequest was not taken up, for Sadalas' kingdom remained under dynastic control. Not so in Britain in AD 60, where the Icenian king Prasutagus had made a will making the reigning emperor and his daughters heirs to his kingdom, in preference most notably to his consort Boudicca.[15] The daughters, like Pylaemenes, were overlooked, and Icenian territory was unceremoniously annexed.

The will of Prasutagus, making provision for his own family, may largely have been the king's own design, and we should by no means assume that Rome had dictated the terms of Amyntas' bequest. The king's son would have been conspicuously vulnerable to the forces which had eventually put an end to Amyntas himself,

---

veterans in Pannonia under Trajan. See Hyginus Gromaticus *De cond. agr.*, Lachmann 121; C. Thulin, *Corpus Agrimensorum Latinorum*, i (1913), 84; with R. K. Sherk, 'Roman Geographical Exploration and Military Maps', *ANRW* ii. 1 (1974), 55–6. Magie, *RR* ii. 1304 n. 3 follows Dessau and Anderson in doubting that Amyntas' kingdom was literally bequeathed to Rome; this is hypercritical in view of the numerous parallels for the procedure.

[7] Several freedmen in the imperial household bear the *cognomen* Amyntianus (*CIL* vi. 4035, 4175, 8738, 8894, 10395) but in themselves they provide no confirmation that Amyntas had bequeathed his whole kingdom to Rome, or the emperor. They merely show that the emperor was one of his legatees. Cf. D. C. Braund, 'Royal Wills and Rome', *PBSR* 38 (1983), 42 n. 112.

[8] For recent discussion, see Th. Liebmann-Frankfort, 'Valeur juridique et signification politique des testaments faits par les rois hellénistiques en faveur des Romains', *Rev. int. des droits ant.* 3: 13 (1966), 73–94; Braund, *PBSR* 38 (1983), 16–57.

[9] *SEG* ix. 7; see E. Bickermann, *Gnomon* (1932), 425–30.

[10] A. N. Sherwin-White, *JRS* 67 (1977), 66 ff., with discussion of the will of Attalus.

[11] Argued by Liebmann-Frankfort, *Rev. int. des droits ant.* 3: 13 (1966), 73–94.

[12] See Braund, *PBSR* 38 (1983) 30–5, 44–8. *Tutela* by bequest is only clear in one of the cases which he discusses, that of Ptolemy XII Auletes, 51 BC, see Caesar, *BC* ii. 108; Cassius Dio, 42. 35. 4. For the general principle, see Cicero, *Sest.* 64; Suetonius, *Aug.* 48. For individual cases where *tutela* was assumed, see that of Hiero II in 263 BC, Polybius, i. 16. 10; Ethiopia in 30 BC, *ILS* 8995; Cappadocia in 167 BC, Livy 43. 19. 4; in 51 BC, Cicero, *Fam.* 15. 2 (SB 105). 4; *Att.* 6. 1 (SB 115). 3; and under Augustus, Cassius Dio, 57. 17. 5.

[13] See below, Ch. 8 at n. 50

[14] Cassius Dio, 47. 25. 1–2; Appian, *BC* 4. 75; *IGR* i. 775; discussed by R. D. Sullivan, *ANRW* ii. 7. 1 (1979), 191–2.

[15] Tacitus, *Ann.* 14. 31: 'Rex Icenorum Prasutagus, longa opulentia clarus, Caesarem heredem duasque filias scripserat, tali obsequio ratus regnumque et domum suam procul iniuria fore.' H. F. Pelham, in Furneaux's commentary ad loc., suggests that the will only concerned the king's private possessions, not his kingdom; but the context, and the conjunction of *regnum* with *domum suam* contradicts this.

and in the absence of eligible and trustworthy associates, Amyntas may well have decided that making over his kingdom to Rome was the only reasonable way to ensure that the gains which he had made during twelve years of campaigning in the Taurus did not slip immediately from his grasp.[16] On the other hand Rome was in no way unprepared to take over the burden; there is no sign of embarrassment or reluctance to take control, and a complex policy of military intervention and colonial settlement was soon brought to bear in the regions which Amyntas had set out to pacify.

The conversion of Amyntas' kingdom into a province provided a model for the annexation of a large part of the rest of Anatolia over the following century. The province was simply enlarged as existing dynasts died and their territories became available for annexation. Paphlagonia was added first in 6/5 BC, followed by Pontus Galaticus in 3/2 BC, the temple-state of Comana Pontica in AD 34/5, and Pontus Polemoniacus in AD 64/5 (see Vol. II, App. 1 for details). Much of this area had already been under direct Roman rule in the late republic, as the eastern part of Pontus and Bithynia. Cappadocia to the south, however, had always been ruled by kings and lacked even a rudimentary civic structure. When Archelaus died in AD 17, amid allegations of disloyalty to Rome, Tiberius and the senate annexed his kingdom but appointed only an equestrian procurator to administer it.[17] The new governor's main responsibility was patently to divert the flow of revenue, which had formerly been extracted by the king, to the Roman treasury. Tiberius announced that the income from Cappadocia enabled him to defer raising other taxes.[18] Little attention need have been paid to jurisdiction, since the few cities ran by their own laws (see below, Ch. 7 § 11 at n. 29), and the only soldiers employed were native auxiliaries.[19] Events of the 50s and 60s AD showed that these measures were inadequate if Rome were to maintain firm control over all Asia Minor west of the Euphrates. Under Nero, both Domitius Corbulo and Caesennius Paetus controlled Cappadocia as consular legates; and under Vespasian, Cappadocia, together with Armenia Minor, was joined with the remaining parts of Galatia to make a giant, garrisoned province (see Vol. II, App. 1).

Writers of the early imperial period, from Velleius to Suetonius, used the expression *in formam provinciae redacta* to describe provincial annexation, and it proved so convenient a shorthand way of referring to a complex, but increasingly familiar transaction, that it

almost became a technical term.[20] The phrase was actually used on the texts of the Trajanic milestones of Arabia, one of Rome's last major acquisitions, which became part of the Empire in AD 106, and the crisp formulae found on milestones elsewhere, such as this example from Galatia of 6 BC, may usefully summarize the steps taken by Rome to impose direct rule in a new province: 'Imp. Caesar divi f. pont. maxim. cos. XI, des. XII, imp. XV, tr. pot. XIXX, viam Sebasten, curante Cornuto Aquila leg. suo pro praetore, fecit' (CIL iii. 6974). The text simply demonstrates imperial authority, the presence of his agent as provincial governor, and the existence of a Roman road which was at the same time a visible symbol of Roman dominion and an essential requirement of the military presence which could enforce it. At a basic level this spells out what it meant for a region to become a province.

From the arrival of M. Lollius in 25 BC until the later third century AD Galatia was governed by *legati Augusti pro praetore*, of consular or, more often, of praetorian rank. Under Augustus their status varied; most, like Lollius were ex-praetors, others had already been consuls.[21] The presence of praetorians as well as consulars in the early sequence of governors is not evidence that the province was held to be variously more or less important at different times, but simply reflects a system of administration that was still fluid, and, above all, the fact that competent and reliable ex-consuls were not as numerous as they were to become even by the later years of Augustus' reign.[22] Thereafter, in the province's history, the choice between praetorian or consular governor seems largely to have been determined by Galatia's importance, and above all its strategic importance, as it was viewed from Rome. The Augustan legionary garrison was withdrawn by AD 7,[23] and from then until the middle of the first century the legates were all, to the best of our knowledge, praetorian. In Nero's principate Galatia was joined with Cappadocia to form a vast eastern command for Domitius Corbulo, the most important military and political figure of the age barring the emperor himself, and it passed in turn to another consular P. Caesennius

---

[16] See below, Ch. 6.

[17] Strabo, 12. 1. 4, 534; R. D. Sullivan, ANRW ii. 7. 2, 1159–61.

[18] Tacitus, Ann. 2. 42. 6.

[19] Tacitus, Ann. 2. 49. 2; 13. 8. 2; 15. 6.

[20] For the usage see TLL vi. 1, 1076 s.v. forma B. I. c: Livy, Per. 45, 102, 134, but not in Livy himself; Velleius, 2. 97. 4, cf. 2. 44, 109. 1; Tacitus, Agr. 14; Ann. 2. 56; cf. Hist. 3. 47; Suetonius, Rhet. 30; Iul. 25. 1; Aug. 18. 2; Tib. 73. 4; Gaius, 1. 2; Nero, 18; Vesp. 8. 4; CIL iii. 14149, 14150 (Trajanic).

[21] Sherk, i. 19–26; ii. 963–70. The certain consular legates are L. Calpurnius Piso (for whom see Syme, 'The Titulus Tiburtinus', RP iii. 869–84), P. Sulpicius Quirinius, and M. Plautius Silvanus.

[22] Cf. R. Syme, The Roman Revolution (1939), 389 ff., esp. 394. The regular institution of suffect consulships, after 5 BC, greatly increased the supply of consular candidates.

[23] See below, Ch. 6 n. 41.

Paetus. These arrangements foreshadowed the organization of central and eastern Anatolia under the Flavians, Nerva, and Trajan, when a huge multiple province was governed by senior men in the Roman governing class, usually, but not necessarily in every case, ex-consuls.[24] The demands of administering so large an area were too much for one man, and it is certain that a series of *legati Augusti*, without the additional title *pro praetore*, served alongside the full governor. There is no warrant for calling these men *legati iuridici*, and their powers would certainly not have been confined to judicial matters,[25] but it is probable enough that they undertook some of the heavy judicial duties of the governor, thus releasing him, to some extent, to concentrate on the military aspects of his command. After Trajan's Parthian war, the eastern frontier area of the combined province was removed to a separate administration with consular legates, while Galatia and the rest of central Anatolia was governed by praetorians. This pattern remained unchanged until the radical adjustments of the middle and later third century.[26]

It is no doubt misleading to attempt to classify a governor's duties, since his *imperium*, his right to command, by its very nature allowed him to intervene and expect compliance in virtually every aspect of provincial life. It is, however, at least convenient to place the multifarious activities of Roman provincial governors into two broad categories, namely the administration of justice, and the maintenance of security in the face of internal dissent or external threats, if necessary by force. The military responsibilities of the governor of Galatia were concentrated initially in the mountain regions of Pisidia and Isauria, where several campaigns are attested;[27] later, when Cappadocia was added to the command, attention moved to the eastern part of the province and the Euphrates where a fortified *limes* was created. Two uniquely valuable texts show one governor of Cappadocia, the writer Flavius Arrianus, inspecting, organising, and drawing up battle lines along the

frontier system in the reign of Hadrian.[28] However, year by year, military action was the exception not the rule and the garrisons were more often engaged in peaceful than wartime pursuits; the governors' military role may be more truly reflected by their activities as road builders in the provincial hinterland, a long-term preoccupation which will have made an important impact on the local population, than by fighting in frontier areas.[29] Far more administrative time in any event would have been consumed in judicial business. At least at certain periods and in certain places it is possible to assess the pattern of this juridical and judicial activity in some detail. Cicero's letters from Cilicia, written in 51 and 50 BC, show that as he advanced from the borders of Asia into his province, and moved along the main highway which ran east to the Amanus Gates, he regularly held judicial assizes at the principal towns, Laodicea, Synnada, Philomelium, and Iconium, staying long enough in each for litigants, petitioners, and others to bring their cases and complaints before him for assessment and judgement.[30] In fact Cicero's term of office, beginning in this fashion and ending with a campaign in the Amanus mountains and with diplomatic and military activity to protect the province from Parthian incursions, precisely illustrates the two most important functions of a Roman governor. More than a century and a half later the younger Pliny adopted a similar administrative style in Pontus and Bithynia, moving around the province from city to city, certainly holding court in the major centres where assizes were held, as well as carrying out the special duties for which he had been appointed.[31] The most detailed evidence for the assize system under the empire comes from the province of Asia. Since the time

---

[24] Sherk, ii. 991–1023. It is only a presumption that all the Flavio-Trajanic governors had already held the consulship. There is no independent evidence for the consular status of Cn. Pompeius Collega, M. Hirrius Fronto Neratius Pansa, A. Caesennius Paetus, P. Valerius Patruinus (?), or Q. Orfitasius Aufidius Umber. In an important discussion of Flavian policy on the upper Euphrates frontier, H. Halfmann suggests that Pompeius Collega was probably only a praetorian (*Epigr. Anat.* 8 (1986), at p. 47).

[25] The term is used by Sherk, ii. 998, and by G. Iacopi, *Dizionario epigrafico*, iv. 542–3 s.v. *legatus iuridicus*, discussing the earlier literature.

[26] For the administrative changes which took place at this period see Vol. II, App. 2.

[27] Below, Ch. 6.

[28] Below, Ch. 9 § I. For Arrian see A. B. Bosworth, *HSCP* 81 (1977), 217 ff.

[29] Below, Ch. 9 § II.

[30] L. W. Hunter, 'Cicero's Journey to the Province of Cilicia', *JRS* 3 (1913), 73–97; A. J. Marshall, 'Governors on the Move', *Phoenix*, 20 (1966), 231–46.

[31] For Pliny's movements during his eighteen months in office, see U. Wilcken, *Hermes*, 49 (1914), 120 ff.; L. Vidman, *Étude sur la correspondance de Pline le jeune avec Trajan* (Prague, 1960), 61 ff.; A. N. Sherwin-White, *Commentary on the Letters of Pliny* (1965), 529–33. His travels took him to Prusa, Nicomedia, Nicaea, Claudiopolis, Nicomedia, Nicaea, Byzantium, Apamea, Nicomedia, Prusa, Sapanca göl, Nicaea, Juliopolis, Nicaea, Sinope, Amisus, and Amastris. There is little information about the assize centres of the province. Nicomedia and Nicaea are assumed to be certain candidates (Broughton, *Roman Asia Minor* 709, endorsed by C. P. Jones, *The Roman World of Dio Chrysostom* (1978), 86). Dio of Prusa won the status of assize centre for his native city, *Or.* 40. 33; 45. 6, 10; 48. 11, with Jones, op. cit. 52, 108; Pliny, *Ep.* 10. 58. 1; Sherwin-White, ad loc., suggests that Nicomedia, Prusa, Amastris, Sinope, and, when it was not a free city, Byzantium were the most likely assize centres.

of Sulla it had been divided into twelve or thirteen districts (*conventus*, διοικήσεις), named after the most important cities where assizes were held. In each of these the proconsul of Asia, or one of his legates, would, at a specified time, attend to the cases and problems raised by his subjects living in that region.[32] There is no doubt that the governors of Galatia carried out similar duties in a broadly similar fashion. As early as the reign of Augustus, when military problems were a paramount concern, Strabo remarks that a reason for handing over remote and inaccessible parts of the Taurus to local rulers was that these were better able to keep the peace and engage in military action than the provincial governors who travelled round the province on judicial business.[33] A governor who attended to his duties conscientiously would be constantly on the move. As such he might impose a considerable burden on the local population which was required to provide hospitality, transport, and in some notorious cases much more besides for governors and their staff.[34] The edict of the Tiberian governor Sex. Sotidius Strabo Libuscidianus,[35] found on the territory of Sagalassus, which was designed to protect the local population from abusive requisitioning and illegal impositions, is welcome confirmation that conditions in early imperial Galatia conformed to a pattern that can be observed across the empire.[36]

It is convenient to describe a governor's judicial and military functions in this fashion, but it does not exhaust an account of his role. In the provinces of the empire where there is extensive information from literary sources it is clear that a governor's relationship with the local aristocracies was of paramount importance. It could hardly be otherwise for an official sent for a year as proconsul—or for several years as a legate—to a more or less remote province, with no more than a modest entourage of staff and friends.[37] The unavoidable travelling would bring him as a guest, perhaps for weeks at a time, to the homes of local civic leaders, even if there were permanent governors'

residences in some of the main cities.[38] The legate of Galatia, or of other provinces would not only be the arbiter of men's lives, but for three years the leading figure in provincial society, whose contacts outside the province and above all with Rome itself, could provide a stepping-stone for the advancement of the local nobility.

Relations between civic leaders in the eastern provinces and provincial governors could thus be very significant for both. At the beginning of the second century AD Plutarch and Dio of Prusa took pains to point out to local politicians that they were not rulers of independent cities, but subject to Roman governors. If they were to retain any freedom of action they must act cautiously and within strict limits.[39] We obtain some impression of relations between local aristocrats and Roman governors in Asia Minor from three sources of this period. Pliny's letters recall the trials of Iulius Bassus and Varenus Rufus, two Bithynian governors who were arraigned for maladministration before the Roman senate. Both had become embroiled in local political arguments and had made enemies among the leading figures of the province, who were strong enough to pursue them in court in Rome.[40] Pliny's own correspondence from the province gives sparing glimpses of this same world, but it is best explored through the speeches of two participants: Dio, whose difficulties in his home city of Prusa came to Pliny's attention;[41] and Aelius Aristides, who recorded in some detail his dealings with proconsuls of Asia and their legates in the early 150s, when he wriggled to avoid undertaking liturgies and magistracies in his home town of Hadriani and at Smyrna. In all such cases personal ties between leading provincials and Roman governors had a material bearing on the latters' conduct of their duties. The affairs of Dio and

[32] C. Habicht, *JRS* 65 (1975), 64–91 for the development of the system and its geographical organization, and G. P. Burton, ibid. 92–106 for its operation. See further W. Ameling, *Epigr. Anat.* 12 (1988), 9–24.
[33] Strabo 14. 5. 6, 671: ἐδόκει βασιλεύεσθαι μᾶλλον τοὺς τόπους ἢ ὑπὸ τοῖς Ῥωμαίοις ἡγέμοσιν εἶναι τοῖς ἐπὶ τὰς κρίσεις πεμπομένοις.
[34] See S. Mitchell, 'Requisitioned Transport in the Roman Empire', *JRS* 66 (1976), 106ff., esp. 130–1; and W. Eck, *Chiron*, 7 (1977), 365–83.
[35] Mitchell, loc. cit.; *SEG* xxvi (1976–7) no. 1392; *AE* (1976), no. 653.
[36] See further, W. Langhammer, *Die rechtliche und soziale Stellung der Magistratus Municipales und der Decuriones* (1973), 128–38 on *vehiculatio*, and the *munus hospitalitatis*.
[37] We are ill-informed about the staff and associates of governors and procurators in Galatia. For the surviving evidence see below, n. 46 and Ch. 9 §II nn. 117–20.

[38] The question of where a governor stayed on his travels, or even at provincial centres, remains obscure, especially in the early empire. Certainly there were some official residences, known as *palatia* or *praetoria* in the provinces (see R. MacMullen, *Athenaeum*, 54 (1976), 26–36; Th. Mommsen, *Ges. Schr.* vi, 128–33; S. Mitchell, *AS* 28 (1978), 95); an inscription of the late empire mentions a *palatium* at Ancyra (Bosch, *Ankara*, no. 306), and a *praetorium* occurs in a fourth century Saint's life (see S. Mitchell, *AS* 32 (1982), 105). On the other hand, governors are known to have taken up residence in private houses, as welcome or unwelcome guests (cf. Cicero, *Verr.* II. 1. 63–70 and Philostratus *VS* I. 25 (ii. 44 Kayser), both famous passages).
[39] Plutarch, *Praec. reip. ger*, 813e; Dio, *Or.* 48 passim, esp. 10ff.
[40] Pliny, *Ep.* 4. 9; 5. 20; 6. 5 and 13; 7. 6; 9. 13.
[41] Pliny, *Ep.* 10. 81. See Jones, *The Roman World of Dio Chrysostom*, on the politics of Dio's world. Note R. MacMullen, *Corruption and the Decline of Rome* (1988), 121, 'It is the web of favours given or owed that enables an imperial administration of only a few hundred really to rule an empire.'

of Aristides are known to us by chance. For the most part the documentary sources are completely silent on a subject that must have had important implications for governors and governed alike. Such dealings were not commemorated by public advertisement.[42]

Inscriptions, however, do depict the governor in a range of activities that do not fall within a narrow definition of his duties. He was the most important and most influential figure in the province; his intervention, unprompted or surely much more often solicited, could secure benefits and advantages for cities and individuals, who would reciprocate by erecting statues and inscriptions in his honour, often specifically identifying him as their patron and benefactor.[43] Such ties could last for many years. L. Fabius Cilo, who had governed Galatia in the early 190s, was honoured by Ancyra as its champion (prostates) a dozen or more years later when he was praefectus urbi.[44] In one case only from Galatia the inscription provides the reason for the honour conferred: L. Antistius Rusticus, who had issued an edict to alleviate the effects of famine, was hailed at Antioch as patron of the colony, 'quod industrie prospexit annon(ae)'.[45] Those closest to a governor were best placed to receive his favours, and it is natural that apart from cities, or whole communities, the individuals who were most commonly responsible for setting up inscriptions of this sort were members of a governor's own household, or his staff.[46]

Nothing prevented a legate from becoming closely involved in the public life of provincial cities, even on an official basis. In the Augustan age one if not two imperial legates were made honorary duumvirs at Pisidian Antioch, although the actual duties of office were assumed by a praefectus in their stead.[47] It is assumed that such titles were purely honorific, for otherwise clashes of interest between the governor acting ex officio and simultaneously representing the interests of Antioch would scarcely have been avoidable. Priesthoods were no doubt less problematical, and could be held by a governor to enhance both his own reputation and that of the cult, as in the case of T. Licinnius Mucianus, priest of a cult of Sarapis and his associated gods at Ancyra in AD 178.[48] Characteristically his term as priest was used as an occasion for vows made on behalf of the imperial household.

Governors would take the initiative in some activities, above all in making gestures of homage and loyalty to the emperor or his family, by erecting dedications in their honour, or making offerings for their safety and prosperity.[49] In many cases no great significance can be attached to these inscriptions, but there are instances where the circumstances in which they were erected appear to lend more importance to the dedication. T. Axius, legate under Gaius or early in the reign of Claudius, dedicated a monumental structure at Ancyra. The inscription adds one further precision after his title leg. pro pr., a priesthood; Axius was a fetialis, and this priestly office held in Rome would add special point to a religious dedication made in the province.[50] Another, clearer, instance is the monumental Latin text erected for Claudius by his legate M. Annius Afrinus on the south shore of Suğla Göl, in the heart of Isaurian country. Afrinus was the most energetic governor of the Julio-Claudian period, to judge from the numerous appearances which he makes on coins and inscriptions through the province;

[42] C. A. Behr, Aelius Aristides and the Sacred Tales (1968), 61–90.
[43] M. Plautius Silvanus, patron and benefactor at Attaleia (SEG vi. 646); Cn. Pompeius Collega, patron at Pisidian Antioch (CIL iii. 6817); M. Hirrius Fronto Neratius Pansa, patron(?) at Comana Cappadociae (IGR iii. 125; R. P. Harper, AS 18 (1968), 94 no. 1); P. Calvisius Ruso Iulius Frontinus, patron of the colony at Antioch (AE 1914, 267); (?Q.Vi)bius Gallus at Antioch (CIL iii. 6813, with W. Eck, Chiron, 12 (1982), 354 n. 292); C. Iulius Scapula at Ancyra (Bosch, Ankara, nos. 135–7, honoured by a tribe and by an individual); L. Fulvius Rusticus Aemilianus, benefactor at Ancyra (Bosch, Ankara, no. 159); Iulius Saturninus at Ancyra (Bosch, Ankara, no. 132); an acephalous inscription for a governor at Ancyra, honouring him as raro et sanctissimo (Bosch, Ankara, no. 169).
[44] L. Fabius Cilo was honoured by Ancyra as its champion (prostates) in an inscription set up at Rome after he had become prefect of the city in AD 204 (Bosch, Ankara, no. 219; G. Moretti, Insc. Gr. Urbis Romae, i no. 68 with commentary). He was also honoured by Pisidian Antioch, W. M. Ramsay, JRS 14 (1924), 185. He will have represented Ancyra's interests at Rome, presumably to the emperor. For the significance of the term προστάτης, roughly equivalent to patronus, cf. Habicht, Alt. v. Perg. viii. 3, pp. 72–3.
[45] AE (1925), 126; see below, Ch. 10 §1 n. 16.
[46] Ti. Iulius Candidus Marius Celsus, honoured at Ancyra by Iulius N..., perhaps a libertus (Bosch, Ankara, no. 71); P. Caesennius Sospes, honoured by his libertus, Thiasus, at Antioch (CIL iii. 6818); P. Pomponius Secundianus, honoured at Ancyra by Q. Aelius Macedo (Bosch, Ankara, no. 138); L.

Saevinius Proculus, honoured at Ancyra by his cornicularii (Bosch, Ankara, no. 197; for further literature see Sherk iii. 170 no. 13); L. Petronius Verus, also honoured at Ancyra by his corniculari (CIL iii. 6754; Bosch, Ankara, no. 218).
[47] ILS 9502 and 9503, both at Pisidian Antioch. For other honorary duumviri at Antioch, represented by praefecti, see the list compiled by S. Demougin, ZPE 43 (1981), 108. For the practice elsewhere, see W. Liebenam, Römische Städteverwaltung (1900), 261–3; W. Langhammer, Die Stellung der Magistratus und Decuriones, 36, 62–4, 213.
[48] Bosch, Ankara, no. 184.
[49] M. Annius Afrinus at Lystra for Claudius (MAMA viii no. 53); (?) L. Nonius Calpurnius Asprenas at Antioch for Vespasian (B. M. Levick, AS 17 (1967), 102–3); Valerius Antoninus(?) at Ancyra for Caracalla (CIL iii. 243); L. Egnatius Victor Lollianus at Ancyra for Elagabalus (Bosch, Ankara, no. 273).
[50] CIL iii. 248; Bosch, Ankara, no. 54. For the date and identification see W. Eck, ZPE 42 (1981), 252–4.

Claudius, through city foundations, left a more conspicuous mark on the province than any of the other early emperors except Augustus; and the Isaurians had been Rome's toughest opponents. This was clearly no routine dedication, but a palpable symbol of Roman power, which expressed in itself all of Rome's successful efforts to bring order to this recalcitrant mountain country, and which had surely been set up, with much ceremony, by the governor in person.[51]

In the imperial provinces most matters involving finance, compulsory services, and the collection and disbursement of revenue were the ultimate responsibility of the provincial procurator, and from the early empire the activities of these equestrian agents, appointed by the emperor, form an essential complement to the activities of the governors themselves. The system was an innovation of Augustus' principate, and was certainly established in Galatia by the early Tiberian period, for the edict of Sotidius from Sagalassus laid down rules concerning transport requisitioning by the procurator and his staff, in the same way as it provided for the governor himself.[52] Thereafter, the records for procuratorial activity in the province are far more patchy than they are for governors. At the end of Claudius' reign L. Pupius Praesens collaborated with Q. Petronius Umber, probably a legate of Lycia and Pamphylia rather than Galatia, in enforcing a boundary decision regulating the adjacent territory of Sagalassus and an imperial estate at Tymbrianassus in Pisidia. The procurator may have been directly involved since the decision affected an imperial estate, for which he would have had particular responsibilities. On the other hand his concern for the allocation of taxes and demands for services to all communities meant that he would have had a direct interest in territorial decisions of any type.[53] The same man is also known from an inscription at Iconium which honours him as benefactor and founder.[54] The last term need mean no more than that he played a part in erecting buildings, an appropriate activity in a city which had recently been created.[55]

Very little can be read into the later inscriptions which bear witness to procurators at work. The recently founded cities of Savatra and Kinna set up statues in honour of T. Flavius Titianus and T. Furius Victorinus, procurators it seems under Hadrian and Antoninus Pius respectively.[56] This might reflect the fact that procurators would be heavily involved in supervising the assessment of communities for the provision of taxes and services, especially in the case of recently founded cities; but it is in any case a clear reminder that procurators with these duties would be as well placed as governors to render services to cities and to receive recognition for doing so. An official in control of revenue had ample opportunities for corrupt behaviour, and it is not therefore surprising that qualities such as fairness and justice should be an occasion for comment on inscriptions, whether or not they were truly deserved.[57]

The edict of Sotidius, which allowed a procurator to obtain almost as many mounts and wagons from the local population as the governor,[58] implies that in rank and prestige there was no wide gulf between them. Notoriously, through the Imperial period procurators began to encroach on the governors' monopoly of jurisdiction; and they might in exceptional circumstances even take the governor's place, as occurred in the case of C. Iulius Senecio around the middle of the third century AD.[59] But, as with governors, a large part of the actual business of procurators remains unnoticed by the sources, certainly by those that have a direct bearing on Galatia and the rest of central Anatolia. This silence covers not only their unofficial activities or

---

[51] CIL iii. 6799; see below, Ch. 6 at nn. 92–7. This brief enquiry into the epigraphic evidence for the activities of governors in Galatia may be compared with the comparably scanty results deduced for Pontus and Bithynia by B. Rémy, Epigr. Anat. 6 (1985), 43–53, and for Galatia itself in Rev. arch. 92 (1990), 85–108.

[52] Mitchell, JRS 66 (1976), 124; for discussion see also G. Alföldy, Chiron, 11 (1981), 201 n. 163, who argues that the clause giving transport privileges not only to the procurator but also to his son should be allowed to stand. For a procurator aided by his son see B. Isaac, 'The Decapolis in Syria, a neglected inscription', ZPE 44 (1981), 68.

[53] G. E. Bean, AS 9 (1959), 84–8 no. 30. Three copies of the text are known, see Sherk, ii. 977. For Petronius Umber, see Vol. II, App. 1 at n. 62.

[54] IGR iii. 263.

[55] For the early history of Iconium see S. Mitchell, Historia 28 (1979), 411 ff. Its early Julio-Claudian buildings included a theatre, which may have been started under Augustus (IGR iii. 262; H. S. Cronin, JHS 22 (1902), 119 no. 44; the restoration of the name and titles of Augustus is almost certain), and it was apparently provided or refurbished with seats some time between the reigns of Claudius and Hadrian (Cronin, JHS 1902, 123 no. 55; G. Mendel, BCH 26 (1902), 211 no. 2, cf. Mitchell, Historia 28 (1979), 414 n. 40).

[56] The inscription, in Latin for Flavius Titianus from Savatra, was copied by Mr M. H. Ballance, but remains unpublished. For T. Furius Victorinus, see RECAM ii no. 397; the two procurators are discussed by Pflaum, CP i. 231 no. 99 and 326 no. 129.

[57] Standard terms are ἄγνος and δίκαιος. See Bosch, Ankara, nos. 222 (Aufidius Iulianus), 65 (C. Iulius Senecio, cf. no. 64 praeposito incomparabili); MAMA iv no. 150 (Aur. Apollonius at Apollonia). Cf. Robert, Stud. clas. 16 (1974), 71 n. 8 for discussion of the vocabulary.

[58] Above, n. 34.

[59] See Vol. II, App. 2 at nn. 7–10. For procuratorial jurisdiction, see P. A. Brunt, Latomus, 25 (1966), 460–89 = Roman Imperial Themes, 163–87.

their relationships with the provincial élite, but also the central core of their responsibilities, to raise revenue. The impact of Roman tax demands on the provincial communities can be shown, time and again, to have been crucially significant for their history and development.[60] It is entirely characteristic of the nature of our evidence that it tells us nothing about the presumed role of the procurators in imposing and organizing this taxation.

Indeed the multiple forms of provincial taxation are only marginally attested in the evidence from Anatolia, and it is hazardous to presume that taxes, or methods of raising revenue known elsewhere in the empire, would also have been applied there.[61] In the communities of the empire censuses, periodically brought up to date, must have been the foundation of the direct taxation imposed on persons (tributum capitis) and property (tributum soli) in the provinces. Officials with specifically censorial functions, are sporadically attested in the Asia Minor provinces.[62] The principal forms of indirect taxation were those imposed on the manumission of slaves, the making of wills, and the import and export of goods between provinces or from outside the empire altogether. Equestrian officials concerned with supervising the vicesima libertatis and the vicesima hereditatium are known from the Asian provinces, including Galatia,[63] but only the last, the portoria, are directly attested there. Two inscriptions imply the existence of a customs post at Apollonia, the last city of Galatia before the Asian boundary at Apamea,[64] and a text from Amorium indicates that this was another regular point of entry between Galatia and Asia where customs dues were collected.[65]

The administrative responsibilities of procurators were, for the most part, quite separate from those of the legates, and it is striking that at least until the reign of Hadrian the geographical region within which they exercised their authority was not coterminous with the provincia of the governor. C. Cassius Salmallas was procurator of Lycia, Pamphylia, and Galatia between 98 and 102, covering two provinces,[66] while a near-contemporary was in charge of Galatia and Paphlagonia;[67] their successor under Hadrian, Valerius Eudaemon, was procurator not only in Lycia, Pamphylia, and Galatia, but also in Pisidia, Pontus, Paphlagonia, and Lycaonia, thus spanning the boundaries of three provinces;[68] another successor, L. Valerius Proculus, held office in Cappadocia, Paphlagonia, and Galatia, a different combination again.[69] Similar variations can be noted in the procuratorial administration of Cappadocia, Cilicia, Pamphylia, and Lycia. Rather than look for overall guiding principles to explain these changes, it seems better to interpret them simply as examples of a very flexible administrative structure.[70] In the late second and third centuries the procurators of Galatia, with one exception,[71] are simply called by that title, but even at this period it is risky simply to assume that they exercised their authority within precisely the same geographical limits as the governors.

Roman military, administrative, juridical, and financial control over Galatia was thus maintained by the governors, legati Augusti pro praetore, aided in the Flavio-Trajanic period by subordinate legati Augusti, and by equestrian procurators, whose powers to intervene in public life were virtually unlimited. Moreover, the consequences of introducing major changes in these central areas of provincial life were crucial to the development of the province as a whole, and all its communities. For all that, any account of the history of Roman Anatolia, in a broad sense, has to be written without reference to the individual actions of its administrators, since these are so infrequently attested. This is in part due to the nature of the evidence. Detailed written memoirs, if they existed, would doubtless reveal many individual initiatives or actions of governors and procurators which made a real

---

[60] The most thought-provoking modern discussion is by Keith Hopkins, JRS 70 (1980), 101–25. See below, Ch. 14 §§ III–VI.

[61] For the diversity and variety of Roman taxes, see A. H. M. Jones, 'Taxation in Antiquity', in The Roman Economy, ed. P. A. Brunt (1974), 151–85; Brunt, JRS 71 (1981), 161–72, reviewing L. Neesen, Untersuchungen zu den direkten Staatsgaben der röm. Kaiserzeit (1980); R. MacMullen, The Roman Government's Response to a Crisis (1976), 129–52; and below, Ch. 14 § VI.

[62] AE (1924), 82, P. Gavius Balbus (Hadrian-Ant. Pius, Pflaum, CP i. 343–5); ILS 1039, an anonymous Trajanic governor of Galatia, who held the post ad census Paphlag.; note the bilingual fragment from Ancyra for a census official, a libellis et censibus, CIL iii. 259, Bosch, Ankara, no. 204. T. D. Barnes, The New Empire of Diocletian and Constantine (1982), 226–30 argues against the conventional view, and holds that censuses may have been a regular occurrence in the provinces, perhaps held every five years. See also Brunt, JRS (1981), 163–6, suggesting that censuses were 'universal and regular', if not on so fixed a pattern as Barnes argues.

[63] Q. Cosconius Fronto, responsible for the vicesima hereditatium, ILS 1359; cf. Pflaum, CP ii. 706–8.

[64] H.-G. Pflaum, 'Le Bureau de la quadragesima portuum Asiae à Apollonia de Pisidie', ZPE 18 (1975), 13–14.

[65] Copied by M. H. Ballance and now published by R. M. Harrison, AS 38 (1988), 180–1 no. 1.

[66] Sherk, i. 96.

[67] AE (1965), 48; with Pflaum, CP supplément (1982), 29–31 no. 88a.

[68] IGR iii no. 1077; ILS 1449.

[69] ILS 1341.

[70] Against Pflaum, CP i. 233–5.

[71] C. Iulius Senecio. See below, Vol. II, App. 2 at n. 7.

impact on the life of the cities and their inhabitants. But even the most active governors within such a system could not expect to introduce radical and deep-rooted innovations effective across the whole region. For one thing, the number of governors and administrators, in proportion to the size of the area and population for which they were responsible, was minute. Two senior senatorial officials had ultimate responsibility for the whole of central Asia Minor from the eastern boundary of Asia to the Euphrates, and even for military posts beyond it. The non-military staff available to assist them amounted to no more than a handful of *beneficiarii*, *cornicularii*, *tabularii*, and *commentarienses* who appear to have been attached to the central office at Ancyra.[72] No doubt a governor might often be accompanied by friends and *comites* of his own choosing, who would assist in his duties, provide the core of a *consilium* to advise him, or simply act as an insulating barrier from the local inhabitants.[73] But these could not act independently of the governor, and could hardly operate without his presence.[74] The administrative cadre was simply too

small to be able to introduce all-embracing reforms, still less enforce them. Further, if it is true that a great proportion of a governor's time was consumed by judicial hearings, his role was essentially a passive one, hearing litigants and adjudicating disputes; handling problems as they were presented to him, not seeking them out spontaneously. The province was thus governed in a determinedly *ad hoc* manner. Even in the rare cases where it is possible to discern a deliberate pattern of provincial policy, it is impossible to attribute it with any certainty to the initiative of the governor on the one hand, or to the central administration at Rome on the other. Roman officials in the provinces were judges or generals, but not politicians or administrators, still less reformers.

It is, therefore, not a cause for despair that the surviving sources tell us so little about the substance of what they did. Roman rule brought immense changes to newly annexed areas, but the instruments of these changes were not, for the most part, the governors, but the new social, economic and political conditions entailed by annexation to the empire. Apart from clearly defined military decisions, which imposed roads, fortresses, and garrison armies, it was the intangible impact of universal factors such as the development of a monetarized economy, the growth of urban settlements, and new forms of exploitation of provincial land which had a deep and lasting effect on the structure of provincial life. An analysis of the administrative framework within which these changes occurred hardly even supplies a skeleton round which to shape an account of a Roman province. For a full appreciation of what annexation to the empire meant for any region, the net must be cast much wider.

[72] It is significant that none of these junior administrative staff appears in other cities of the province. They clearly maintained the governor's establishment in the principal city.

[73] One Galatian text refers to a *comes*, Bosch, *Ankara*, no. 364 for L. Tuccio L. f. Pom. Secundo comiti M. Valeri Itali leg. Aug. On the evidence, or rather absence of evidence for the composition of governors' councils, see MacMullen, *The Roman Government's Response to a Crisis*, 238 n. 32.

[74] The implications of the inscription from Samothrace which show a governor and his full *comitatus* visiting a shrine are significant in this respect, J. H. Oliver, *AJPhil.* 77 (1976), 75–80.

6 The Pacification of the Taurus

Rome's new Anatolian possessions, the province of Galatia, required military intervention from the outset. The final subjugation of the intransigent tribal peoples of the Taurus—Cilicians, Isaurians, and Pisidians—remained incomplete and, formidable as the achievements of Amyntas had already been, a generation was to pass before their mountainous homelands were finally subdued and secured. These were among the unsung wars of the Augustan age. No narrative account survives from any ancient source, and the course of the campaigns has to be recovered from hints in the ancient writers, inferences deduced from the careers of the Roman commanders who conducted them, and epigraphical evidence for the disposition of military units and veteran settlements through the area in the early principate.

However its boundaries are finally defined,[1] the southern part of the province of Galatia was a land of mountains. A relief map of Turkey shows a great wedge of highland country thrusting northwards from Lycia in the west and from Cilicia in the east towards an apex north of Pisidian Antioch, the mountainous range of Sultan Dağ.[2] Only one practicable route ran through this country from west to east, from Apamea through Apollonia to Pisidian Antioch, and then south-east towards Iconium and the Lycaonian plain. This was the line followed for most of its course by the Augustan *via Sebaste*.[3] From south to north there was a wider, although still restricted range of possibilities.

The great barrier was the steep ring of mountains which encloses the Pamphylian plain. The main route today crosses the Çubuk Boğazı, north-west of Attaleia, but in Antiquity the main road ran a short way to the east. Inspection has revealed a major highway running north of the village of Döşemealtı to the plain round the town to Dağ, on the territory of ancient Ariassos, and then on to the site of the Roman colony of Comama. The 140th milestone of the *via Sebaste*, measured from the *caput viae* Pisidian Antioch, still stands *in situ* in the pass. Thus Perge, Attaleia, and the other cities of the coast were linked to the highlands by Augustus' new road. The remains show that this was a broad paved highway intended for the use of wheeled traffic; not one of the narrow, often stepped, stone tracks designed for pedestrians and pack-animals, which are typical of Hellenistic and Roman road building in most of the Anatolian highlands. The *via Sebaste* was clearly the major line of communication from the south coast to the interior; there can be little doubt that this was the route along which St Paul travelled from Perge to Pisidian Antioch on his first missionary journey.[4] A second route ran through central Pisidia, along or close to the valley of the Cestrus (Aksu), leading past Cremna to Sagalassus, or following a branch through Adada to Lake Eğridir, and thence to northern Pisidia. A third route, which may already have been used by P. Servilius in his Isaurian campaign, ran north-north-east from Side, through the mountains to the basin of Lake Beyşehir, and from there to the Lycaonian plain and to Iconium.[5] Two observations may be added. Firstly, even these important, long-distance routes could be difficult to traverse in unfavourable conditions and were easily defensible. Secondly, travel would not have been restricted to them alone. Pisidia was a region of cities, which already in the Hellenistic period were connected with one another by paved roads and smaller tracks,

---

[1] See Vol. II, App. 1.

[2] See Fig. 5 (based on the Turkish 1:500,000 sheets), and Levick, *Roman Colonies*, map 2 at end. For more detailed accounts of the geography see Levick, *Roman Colonies*, 7–20, and X. de Planhol. *De la plaine pamphylienne aux lacs pisidiens* (1958), chs. 1, 11, and 12.

[3] For a map of its course as far as Comama, see D. H. French and S. Mitchell, *TAD* 24 (1977). The southern section linking Comama with the coastal plain and dated by Augustan milestones, has been identified by David French, *VIII Araş*, 233–5 with Figs. 7–12, *AS* 41 (1991), 10–11. He also reports the even more remarkable discovery near Side of the 331st milestone from Pergamum belonging to the Asian road built by M'. Aquillius between 129 and 126 BC (*Epig. Anat.* 17 (1991), 53–4).

[4] Acts 13: 9; see below, Vol. II, Ch. 15.

[5] Magie, *RR* ii. 1140 n. 18; Levick, *Roman Colonies*, 15; G. E. Bean and T. B. Mitford, *Journeys in Rough Cilicia 1964–68* (1970), 23 with map A.

which may still be traced today, cutting across the grain of the hills in this rugged territory.[6]

The highland region itself was by no means uniform. On the north side Pisidia is enclosed by a series of upland plains and lakes, which may be traced from Elmalı and Korkuteli in the west, through the basins of lakes Burdur, Eğridir, and Beyşehir, into Lycaonia around Iconium. The land has various aspects: the Bozova north of Korkuteli is rich and fertile;[7] the surroundings of Lake Burdur are largely bare and denuded; and there is impenetrable mountain country on the west sides of both Lake Eğridir and Lake Beyşehir. But taken as a whole the plain-land in this crescent-shaped belt of country is extensive, and its landscapes often recall the long vistas of the central plateau rather than the broken horizons of the Taurus.[8] Most of the Augustan colonial foundations belong in this territory. They enclosed the highland region proper, where massive mountain ranges alternate with deep river valleys of the Cestrus, the Eurymedon, and the Melas. These valleys themselves vary between fertile plains, as for instance the territory of Cremna in the middle and upper reaches of the Cestrus and the Yılanlı Ova south of Lake Eğridir, which belonged to ancient Tymbriada; and deep gorges, like those of the Eurymedon east of Selge.[9]

It has been commonplace to regard the Pisidians themselves as a truculent and independent, semi-barbarian people, who lived in a difficult and fragmented mountain region and posed a continual menace to the more stable areas of central and southern Anatolia. This characterization misrepresents the cultural development of the highlands and under-estimates their significance. Not all mountain populations were primitive and sparse in numbers, living on the margins of subsistence from bare and unproductive land.[10] Pisidia was a region with considerable natural resources and a substantial reservoir of population.[11] Its chief cities, Selge, Termessus,[12] and Sagalassus, were advanced and well-organized communities as early as the fourth century BC.[13] They had large and productive territories,[14] which produced considerable wealth.[15] The cities' military potential can be judged by their ability to put large forces in the field: the Selgians could field an army of 20,000, and allegedly lost half that number during the war with Achaeus in 218 BC;[16] Termessus had 6,000 fighting men in 319 BC;[17] the less well-known city of the Etenneis mustered 8,000 hoplites in the late third century;[18] and the Homonadeis, the most ferocious opponents of Amyntas and of the Romans, lost 4,000 men taken into captivity when they were finally subdued, doubtless after suffering heavy casualties earlier in prolonged fighting.[19] Outside Pisidia itself the Isaurians were reckoned to be a great community with a large population of fighting men in the time of Alexander the Great,[20] and it is worth comparing the figures for another highland city, Cibyra, which had an army of 30,000 infantry and 2,000 cavalry.[21] Although Cibyra itself had belonged to the province of Asia since 85 BC,[22] its neighbours in the Cibyratis, including Oenoanda and Balbura, whose populations included a large Pisidian component, may in fact have fallen under the jurisdiction of the governor of Galatia during the Augustan period, when

---

[6] Very few observations have been published on the Hellenistic and Roman roads of Pisidia. Archaeologists from the Antalya Museum have noted traces of two to three metre wide paved tracks in the mountains, especially in the territory of Selge; similar roadways linked Cremna with Sagalassus and Comama, Adada with Perge, and Ariassus with Termessus. For a typical section of this last road, see *AS* 41 (1991), pl. XXXIIc. See now D. H. French, *Asia-Minor-Studien*, 6 (1992), 167–75 with maps.

[7] S. Mitchell, *JRS* 64 (1974), 34 with pl. II.

[8] De Planhol, *De la plaine pamphylienne*, 408 ff.

[9] Ibid. 426–8 describing the valley of the Aksu, with the observation that 'la prospérité des villes antiques (i.e. Adada and Cremna) de cette haute région ne peut guère se comprendre qu'en admettant leur main-mise sur une partie de la plaine basse, où, au pieds des grandes falaises calcaires et dans les premières vallées, se distinguent encore les alignements géométriques des olivettes antiques'. For the valley of the Köprü Su (the Eurymedon) see pp. 430–2; also D. Kaya, *AS* 35 (1985), 39–55; T. Drew Bear, *Kadmos*, 26 (1987), 122–8. For Selge's territory see J. Nolle, *I. Selge*, pp. 17–19.

[10] F. Braudel, *The Mediterranean in the Age of Philip II*, i (1966, Eng. trans. 1973), 30.

[11] Note the comments of Strabo, 12. 6. 5, 569 and 7, 3, 570; and, at a much later date, Justinian, *Novellae*, 24, κῶμαι μέγισται . . . καὶ πολυάνθρωποι.

[12] Arrian, *Anab*, 1. 28. For Hellenistic Pisidia, see S. Mitchell. *Mediterranean Archaeology*, 4 (1991), 119–45, and *Asia-Minor-Studien*, 5 (1992), 1–27.

[13] Sagalassus: Livy, 38. 15. 9; for its territory see S. Mitchell, *JRS* 66 (1976), 118–19 with map; Selge: Strabo, 12. 7. 1–3, 570 (cf. Pliny, *NH* 15. 31, 24. 95). It is described as σφόδρα εὔκαρπος, confirmed by the discussion of Nollé, *I. Selge*, 23–6.

[14] Livy, 38. 15. 9, again for Sagalassus.

[15] Note the size of the indemnities exacted by Manlius Vulso in 189 BC: Cibyra, 100 talents and 100,000 medimni of wheat (Polybius, 21. 34. 13, Livy, 38. 14. 4); Sagalassus, 50 talents and 20,000 medimni each of wheat and barley (Livy, 38. 15. 9); Termessus, 50 talents (Polybius, 21. 35. 4).

[16] Strabo, 12. 7. 3, 570; Polybius, 5. 73. 4.

[17] Diodorus, 18. 45. 5.

[18] Polybius, 5. 73. 3; for the site of Etenna see G. E. Bean, *Klio*, 52 (1970), 13–16; J. Nollé, *Epigr. Anat*. 3 (1984), 143–56, with map and photographs; *Asia-Minor-Studien*, 6 (1992), 61–141.

[19] Strabo, 12. 6. 5, 569.

[20] Diodorus, 17. 22. 2.

[21] Strabo, 13. 4. 17, 631.

[22] Strabo, loc. cit., with Liebmann-Frankfort, *La frontière orientale*, 197–200; A. Balland, *Xanthos*, vii (1981), 26 n. 101.

Roman military action was planned in the mountain regions.[23]

The warlike reputation of the Pisidians is noted by all writers who refer to them,[24] and is reflected in the fact that none of the major cities, or indeed their lesser neighbours, paid more than token respect to any Hellenistic king. Strabo tells us that Selge was always at odds with the kings over the hegemony of Pamphylia and territory within the Taurus, and the city fought wars with the Attalids in the mid-second century BC.[25] Archaeological testimony to Pisidian military prowess is ubiquitous: the circular embossed shields, helmets, and infantry weapons with which they decorated their burial chests (ostothecae) and their public buildings;[26] and the large and sophisticated fortification walls which surrounded their cities.[27]

It is not easy to assess the extent to which any of the cities and tribes of Pisidia had been subject to foreign control, and in particular to Roman rule before the age of Augustus.[28] It is certain that the province of Asia, created by M'. Aquillius between 129 and 126 BC, extended as far as Pamphylia. Pisidia thus nominally should have been under direct Roman control. A Roman quaestor had dealings with Prostanna, a city at the south-west corner of Lake Eğridir, as early as 113 BC,[29] and Termessus was subject to a Roman law,

promulgated probably in 70 BC, which defined its status as a free city, at least as the term was understood by Rome; it is possible to trace the subject relationship of Termessus to Rome between the late 90s and this date.[30] But it is unlikely that Roman control extended far beyond the line of the road which Aquillius had built linking Pamphylia with the Maeander valley. Even if other cities such as Selge, Sagalassus, and Cremna acknowledged Roman hegemony during the time of the Mithridatic wars, the disturbed conditions of the middle and later first century BC evidently allowed them to reassert their independence. The campaigns of Servilius Isauricus in the early 70s mark the earliest Roman military intervention in and north of the Taurus, but his conquests seem to have been confined to Isauria, to the territory of the Orondians, and to the region around Neapolis in the basin of Lake Beyşehir; he did not reach the main part of Pisidia.[31] That was the task which awaited Amyntas after 39 BC, and it is a measure of his achievement that, by force or diplomacy, he gained control of such powerful potential enemies as Sagalassus and Cremna in Pisidia itself, that he had evicted Antipater from his princedom around Derbe, and that he had occupied the formidable site of Isaura and fortified it as his southern capital with a massive defensive system, which remained incomplete at his death.[32] However, there was unfinished business in Pisidia and elsewhere. The native stronghold of Sandalium still held out between Sagalassus and Cremna,[33] and the Homonadeis were

---

[23] See below, n. 81.

[24] See, among others, Arrian, 1. 28; Strabo, 12. 7. 3, 570; Pliny, NH 5. 74; Diodorus, 18. 45. 5.

[25] Strabo, 12. 7. 3, 576; Pompeius Trogus, Prol. 34; I. Perg. i no. 25 (restored).

[26] The material has not been systematically collected. See e.g. the note to the index of the inscriptions of Termessus, TAM iii. 1, p. 357 clipeus simplex passim.

[27] These have been largely neglected in general surveys of Hellenistic fortifications. Apart from numerous small fortified positions, major Hellenistic circuits can be traced at Adada, Termessus (Lanckoroński, Städte Pamphyliens und Pisidiens, ii. 22–5, 28) Selge (Machatschek and Schwarz, Bauforschungen in Selge (1981), 36–46), Sagalassus (largely dismantled in the Roman period), Pednelissus (G. Moretti, Ann. della scuola archeologica di Atene e delle missioni italiane in Oriente, iii (1921), 84–105), Etenna, Ariassus (AS 41 (1991), 159–60), and Cremna (S. Mitchell, in D. H. French and C. S. Lightfoot (eds.), The Eastern Frontier of the Roman Empire, i (1989), 315). For further discussion of these and several smaller fortified sites in the region, see the works cited in n. 12. The only Pisidian fortification to have received detailed study in print is the defensive system in the valley below Termessus, which controlled the pass from the Pamphylian plain: F. E. Winter, AJA 70 (1966), 127–37, and also G. E. Bean, Turkey's Southern Shore, 136 for the view that it was built by the Termessians themselves. Its date and purpose need to be reconsidered in the light of the discovery that a Roman road probably ran through this pass in 129–126 BC (cf. n. 3).

[28] See A. N. Sherwin-White, JRS 66 (1976), 1–14 for what follows; for Attalid interest see p. 3 n. 8.

[29] I. Delos, iv. 1. 1603, cf. Robert, Hellenica, xiii. 83 n. 1. For the site of Prostanna, see M. H. Ballance. AS 9 (1959), 125–9.

[30] ILS 38, discussed by Sherwin-White, JAS (1976) 11–14 and J.-L. Ferrary, Athenaeum, 63 (1985), 419–57.

[31] For Servilius' campaigns see H. A. Ormerod, JRS 12 (1922), 35 ff., Magie, RR ii. 1169–76; other bibliography in Robert, Hellenica, vi. 41 n. 1. For the Orondians see Robert, Hellenica, xiii. 74–87 and for the probable conquest of the territory of Neapolis, see Mitchell. Tenth Congress, 313 ff.

[32] Strabo, 12. 6. 3, 569; for the fortifications, see Swoboda, Denkmäler, 119 ff. and F. E. Winter, Greek Fortifications (1971), index s.v. Isaura. A. S. Hall established that Isaura Palaea was at or near the modern town of Bozkir, and that Zengibar Kale is the site of Isaura Nea, Amyntas' capital, known in imperial inscriptions simply as Isaura (Akten des VI. Int. Kongress für griech. und lat. Epigraphik (1973), 568–71).

[33] Strabo, 12. 6. 4, 569 and S. Mitchell, 'Termessos, King Amyntas, and the War with the Sandaliotai', forthcoming. G. Hirschfeld, M.-Ber. Preuss. Ak. Wiss. (1897), 307 suggested that the fortified site called Kapılıtaş, south-east of Sagalassus, might be Sandalium. The true site has now been fixed on the west side of the upper valley of the Aksu above the village of Harmancık, at a ruin field still known locally as Sandal Asar, N. Mersich, J.öst.Byz. 36 (1986), 194. It lay near the city of Ceraitae, which itself has recently been located at Belören, 8 km. NW of Cremna, K. Dörtlük, TAD 23 (1976), 17–13 and 27 (1988), 69–71; cf. Bull. ép. (1978), 501 and Aulock, Pisidien, ii. 33–4; the site was described but not correctly identified by B. Pace and P. Romanelli, Mon. ant. 23 (1914), 251 ff.

palpably unconquered. Moreover, it was more than possible that Amyntas' early successes would prove illusory in the face of a determined native insurrection: an Isaurian war was to flare up again in AD 6,[34] and the mountain people of Rugged Cilicia further east were a thorn in Roman flesh throughout the Julio-Claudian period.[35] Amyntas' death at the hands of the Homonadeis precipitated a crisis for Rome which required firm and decisive intervention.

The foundation of the so-called Pisidian colonies, advertised in the *Res Gestae*,[36] has been interpreted as Augustus' initial solution to the problem of Pisidia.[37] However, it was not his only, or even perhaps his principal response to the situation. Augustan Galatia has usually been regarded as an *inermis provincia*, that is a province with no more than a modest auxiliary garrison to defend it. In fact early imperial inscriptions demonstrate the presence of serving soldiers of *legio VII* at Pisidian Antioch and on the territory of Apollonia;[38] veterans occur at Iconium, Cormasa, and Cestrus in Rugged Cilicia,[39] and a centurion of the legion was honoured for some activity, probably military in nature, by a Lydian community in AD 11/12.[40] The most economical interpretation of this evidence is to suppose that the seventh legion, which had fought for Octavian at Mutina, Philippi, and in the Perusine War, and also against Sextus Pompeius in Sicily, was transferred to Galatia when the province was created. One of the veterans from Iconium was called M. Lollius M. f., and he appears to have acquired his name, his Roman citizenship, and a fictitious patronymic when he was recruited by the first governor of Galatia, Marcus Lollius, soon after 25 BC.[41] He is typical of many of his fellow soldiers: not only was the legion stationed in south Galatia, but it recruited locally on a large scale, often enough from the highland communities already renowned for their fighting qualities (see below, Ch. 9 § III). Twenty-five years of

service as a legionary was a sure method of integrating such recruits into habits of loyalty to Rome.[42]

As well as the distribution of the inscriptions, common sense suggests that the legion would have been stationed in or close to the southern highlands. Three arguments speak for Pisidian Antioch or its immediate neighbourhood. Firstly, a legion here would have been ideally placed to advance south-east into Isauria, or south-west into Pisidia itself, and yet it remained far enough from the real centres of trouble to serve as a safe and secure base; secondly, Antioch was singled out to receive the most important veteran colony in southern Asia Minor, and represented the natural focus of Roman interest in the region; thirdly, the city and its territory continued to serve as the base for auxiliary units after the legion had left Asia Minor altogether.

Alongside the men of *legio VII*, auxiliary soldiers were present in some numbers. A *cohors Apula*, originally recruited from the inhabitants of Apulia in Italy, was based somewhere in Anatolia in the early principate. A serving soldier, L. Salvius L. f. Serg., was buried at Side,[43] and a colonial magistrate of Alexandria Troas in Asia, C. Fabricius C. f. Ani. Tuscus, was prefect of the cohort and in charge of construction work which it carried out in the colony on the orders of Augustus, before he became military tribune of *legio III Cyrenaica* and supervised an emergency levy in Rome in AD 6 or AD 9.[44] The Side inscription could well date to the Augustan period, and it is as likely that the cohort was regularly based in Pamphylia as in the Troad.[45] Side had probably been the base from which Servilius marched into Isauria; Amyntas had struck coins there, presumably to pay his

[34] Below, n. 82.
[35] Tacitus, *Ann.* 6. 41; 12, 55; cf. 2. 42, 78, and 80, with A. Wilhelm, *AEMÖ* 17 (1894), 1 ff. Note also the campaigns of Q. Veranius between AD 43 and 48 against the .. acheotarum, perhaps the Cilicum Tracheotarum, A. E. Gordon, *Q. Veranius, Consul 49 A.D.* (1952) (*AE* (1953), 251).
[36] *Res Gestae*, 28.
[37] Levick, *Roman Colonies*, 33 ff.
[38] *CIL* iii. 6827; *MAMA* iv. 237, an early gravestone for an *eques*, C. Paenius Numisius found at Yaztören, which was later in the territory of Tymandus but which belonged to Apollonia in the early empire.
[39] *CIL* iii. 1476; G. E. Bean, *AS* 9 (1959), 93; Bean and Mitford, *Journeys in Rough Cilicia 1946–68*, 163 no. 169, which is best interpreted as a dedication set up by a former cavalryman of *legio VII*, who had retired to his home town.
[40] *TAM* v. 1, 425.
[41] S. Mitchell, 'Legio VII and the Garrison of Augustan Galatia', *CQ* 26 (1976), 298–308.
[42] My reconstruction of this evidence has been questioned by Sherk, ii, 1047. His substantive argument is that a province with a legionary garrison would have required a consular governor, but several of Galatia's early governors were praetorian. I would concede that my tentative suggestion that *legio V* was part of the Augustan garrison should be abandoned, both for Sherk's reason and because there is no evidence at this early date either for Asiatic recruits into the legion or for the presence of soldiers and veterans in the Asiatic provinces. But the detailed case for *legio VII* still stands, and the distinction drawn by Cassius Dio, 53. 15 between consular and praetorian provinces suggests that consular governors were only a requirement when the garrison was larger than one legion. For the pattern of recruitment, see below, Ch 9 § III at nn. 150–7.
[43] *AE* (1966), 478 (bilingual).
[44] G. E. Bean in J. M. Cook, *The Troad* (1973), 412 no. 50 (*AE* 1973, 501), a text which has been discussed at length by P. A. Brunt, *ZPE* 13 (1974), 161–85.
[45] Suggested by M. Speidel, *TAPA* 106 (1976), 339–41 (= *Roman Army Papers*, i (1984), 91–3), who first drew attention to the interest of these texts for the history of the *cohors Apula*.

troops; and its military importance re-emerged with particular clarity during the troubles of the later third century. As the terminus of the Roman road from Asia, with a fine harbour, it was ideally situated to serve as a base for campaigning in east Pisidia, Isauria, or Cilicia.[46]

Pisidian Antioch itself has produced several inscriptions mentioning auxiliary units. One is the cavalry regiment known as the *ala Augusta Germaniciana*, which twice set up inscriptions to honour citizens of the colony, one certainly in the Flavian period.[47] Two other stones from the colony refer apparently to one of its commanders, L. Calpurnius L. f. Serg. Frugi, who was *duumvir, pontifex, praefectus fabrum*, and *praefectus alae Aug. Germanicianae*.[48] Another prefect of the same unit, M. Sempronius Albanus, set up a statue in the early Flavian period at Perge or Attaleia in Pamphylia, to honour his friend, the Roman senator from Perge, M. Plancius Varus.[49] These texts make it clear that the regiment was stationed in southern Asia Minor, most probably at Antioch itself.[50] A third unit which certainly operated in Pisidia was the *cohors I Hispanorum*. A cavalryman from the unit, M. Iunius Rusticus, set up the gravestone of a fellow soldier at Olbasa, the westernmost of the Augustan colonies in Pisidia, and both men are likely to have seen active service in the region in the early imperial period.[51]

Auxiliary soldiers, like legionaries, were also locally recruited from the province. Two cavalry regiments, the *ala Antiochiensium* and the *ala I Augusta Colonorum* were in all likelihood levied from the Augustan settlements in south Galatia; the former, to judge from its name, from Antioch itself, the latter from the other communities. The *ala Antiochensium* appears twice, once in an inscription of Pisidian Antioch which honoured one of the regiment's prefects in the late Augustan or early Tiberian period,[52] and again in AD 75, when it was associated with other legionary and auxiliary troops building a canal to the east of Antioch in Syria.[53] We may reasonably deduce that the unit served in Galatia, before it was transferred to Syria, perhaps under Nero during Corbulo's campaigns. The *ala I Augusta Colonorum* is mentioned on one inscription from Perge and two from the territory of Iconium. M. Claudius Rutilius Varus of Perge was an equestrian prefect of the unit,[54] and both the Iconian texts relate to members of the *gens* Aponia, a family which probably belonged among the original colonists of Iconium, who themselves came from one or more equestrian units. It was perfectly natural that the colony should continue to be used as a recruiting ground for cavalry.[55]

In the early principate, therefore, the southern half of Galatia possessed a garrison which amounted to at least one legion, two cohorts, and three *alae*, a strength on paper not far removed from the two legions which Deiotarus had commanded in 50 BC.[56]

Did the colonies themselves have military obligations? Certainly they contributed to the strength of two auxiliary regiments; were they also expected in themselves to make a positive contribution towards the pacification of Pisidia? Evidence to suggest that the inhabitants of Roman colonies might have obligations to military service can be inferred from observations made by Roman writers about the nature of the settle-

---

[46] Amyntas and Side, see Ch. 3 n. 153 and Ch. 5 n. 1. For Servilius' route see Magie, *RR* ii. 1171 n. 23 and my study cited in n. 33.

[47] *CIL* iii. 6822; W. M. Calder, *JRS* 2 (1912), 99 no. 31 (*AE* (1914), 128), for C. Iulius C. f. Serg. Proculus, whose full name appears on an inscription of Side, *AE* (1966), 472. He was procurator of Cappadocia and Cilicia under Nero, and the Antioch stone was apparently set up under Vespasian, Pflaum, *CP supplément* 11 no. 25.

[48] *CIL* iii. 6831 and 6821, the latter acephalous but set up by one of his freedmen.

[49] *AE* (1973), 539. The inscription has traditionally been attributed to Attaleia, where it was found, but C. P. Jones, *HSCP* 80 (1976), 234 has suggested that it might have been brought from Perge.

[50] Elsewhere it appears only on an inscription from Ephesus, *I. Eph.* iii no. 837, which gives the incomplete career of one of its *praefecti*. The fact that the *ala* set up inscriptions at Antioch is a clear sign that it was stationed there, despite the doubts of M. Speidel, *Armies and Frontiers*, 32 n. 58 (= *Roman Army Papers* i. 286).

[51] G. E. Bean, *AS* 9 (1959), 98 no. 51 with Speidel, *Armies and Frontiers*, 15. P. A. Holder, *Studies in the Auxilia of the Roman Army* (1980), 159 suggests that the inscription is Claudian, but it could readily be earlier.

[52] *AE* (1926), 82. The restoration of the whole text is controversial, but the reading *ala Antiochiana* now seems assured; cf. L. Keppie, *PBSR* 41 (1973), 13 ff.; S. Demougin, *ZPE* 45 (1981), 97 ff.; Pflaum, *CP supplément*, 9 no. 7a; Speidel, *Armies and Frontiers*, 32 n. 58.

[53] D. van Berchem, *Mus. Helv.* 40 (1983), 185–96.

[54] *IGR* iii. 797 = *Epigr. Anat.* 11 (1988), 127 no. 48, M. Cl. Rutilius Varus, ἔπαρχος ἱππέων εἴλης α' κολωνῶν. A branch of the *gens Rutilia* is known at the colony of Cremna, and this helps to explain why they were assigned to a regiment recruited principally from colonists.

[55] *MAMA* viii. 94 and 327; compare *JHS* 22 (1902), 367 no. 142 mentioning another member of the same family. For the equestrian component in the original colonial settlement at Iconium, see *Historia* 29 (1980), 414 and Speidel, *Armies and Frontiers*, 32 n. 58, who first drew attention to the connection between the *ala colonorum* and the south Galatian colonies. L. Keppie, however, suggests to me that the letters EQ on the coins from Iconium might better refer to veterans from *legio X Equestris*, later *X Gemina*.

[56] R. Syme, *RP* iii, 871 points out that *XXII Deiotariana* ought to have been formed after *XXI Rapax*, in about 15 BC. He therefore suggests that native Galatian troops may have stayed in the province after Amyntas' death, without being formally incorporated into a Roman unit. The hypothesis, which goes back to Ritterling, *RE* xii. 1224, is not necessary.

Fig. 10. Latin honorific inscription set up for C. Caristanius C. f. Ser. Caesianus Iulius, one of the early colonists of Pisidian Antioch who had acted as prefect when P. Sulpicius Quirinius, the victor of the Homonadensian war, had been honorary duumvir in the colony. Caristanius was the first person to be voted a statue by Antioch's decurions. Now in Yalvaç Museum. See G. L. Cheeseman, *JRS* 3 (1913), 258 no. 3, and Levick, *Roman Colonies*, 111.

Fig. 11. Latin inscription for St. Pescennius L. f. Ser., perhaps of Campanian origin, who had acted as prefect when Drusus, brother of the emperor Tiberius, was honorary duumvir of the colony. Now in Yalvaç Museum. *CIL* iii. 6843 = *ILS* 7201.

Fig. 12. *CIL* iii. 6852. The influence of the leading colonial families of Antioch is most easily traced through the freedmen who took their names and continued to work in their service, sometimes as estate managers. This inscription lists eight freedmen of the Caristanii. It was found south of Antioch at the village of Özgüney, whose former name Gemen (= γῆ Mηνός) shows that the area belonged to the sanctuary of Men Askaenos which occupies the mountain between the modern village and the site of Antioch itself.

Leading colonial families of Pisidian Antioch

ments themselves, and from the analogous duties of the inhabitants of colonies elsewhere in the empire. Cicero, in a speech of 63 BC, recalled that in former times colonies had been founded in suitable sites, 'contra suspicionem periculi ... ut esse non oppida Italiae sed propugnacula imperii';[57] and he used similar language to describe Narbo Martius, founded in 118 BC, as a 'colonia nostrorum civium, specula populi Romani ac propugnaculum, illis ipsis nationibus oppositum et obiectum'.[58] The same conception of a colony can be found in the remark of Siculus Flaccus, that colonies were often founded 'vel ad ipsos priores municipiorum populos coercendos, vel ad hostium incursus repellendos'.[59] Indeed the internal organization of colonies, which preserved much of the hierarchy of the legions from which the settlers were drawn, argues at least that they retained military ideals, if not military functions.[60] In addition, the surviving municipal law of Urso has a clause which made it the responsibility of the duumviri to muster and arm their fellow citizens to protect the colony in times of danger.[61] However, the military activities which Cicero and the *agrimensores* envisage for frontier colonists seem to have been primarily defensive, and this suits the context of the Urso law. The citizens of a municipium took up arms in unusual circumstances, to defend themselves. Veteran military colonists in frontier areas might expect to do so more often than settlers in peaceful areas, but they too were not designed as an aggressive strike force. If the Pisidian colonies were designed to play an active military role, and to take the battle to the unruly peoples of the highlands, then the argument must be constructed, if at all, on the basis of the dates at which they were founded, and their geographical locations.

Firm evidence for the foundation dates of the Pisidian colonies is disappointingly thin. The best information comes from Antioch, where commissioners were sent out immediately after Amyntas' death to administer his inheritance. One of their tasks was to break up the possessions of Men Askaenos, that is presumably the land which lay in the broad plain overlooked by the temple itself on top of Karakuyu.[62] If the purpose of this action was to make land available for new settlers, we should expect the colony to have been founded very soon after Amyntas' death. Coins,

issued by Antioch in AD 76, by Cremna and Lystra under Marcus Aurelius between AD 161 and 180, and by Cremna under Aurelian between AD 270 and 275, all with legends and types recalling their foundation by Augustus, have been interpreted as centennial issues, reckoned from an original date of 25 BC.[63] But the theory encounters too many objections to be convincing, not least the fact that a comparable issue from Cremna dates to the reign of Valerian (AD 253–60) and cannot possibly commemorate the colony's centenary.[64] It has also been suggested that since Antioch was described as the sister city (ἀδελφή) of Lystra and Tavium, all three should have shared a common foundation date, between 23 and 21 BC, which can be established with reasonable certainty at least for Tavium.[65] But terms of kinship such as this were a standard way by which cities indicated or claimed mutual relationships, and they convey no precise chronological implications. Moreover, not all sisters are twin sisters.[66]

We can deduce a late terminus for the foundation of the more important colonies from the building of the *via Sebaste* in 6 BC, during the governorship of Cornutus Arruntius Aquila.[67] However, it seems implausible that a twenty-year interval separated the annexation of the province from the foundation of the colonies. Whatever their precise strategic role, the colonies indicate Rome's determination to bring new territory firmly under control. It has been remarked of Cremna that it would be unthinkable to allow so strong a position to slip back into enemy hands.[68] The same may be said, *mutatis mutandis*, of the other sites. It is probable, but by no means certain, that most of the colonies were founded within a few years of 25 BC.

[57] *Agr.* 2. 73.
[58] *Pro Fonteio*, 3.
[59] Siculus Flaccus, *De condicionibus agrorum*, ed. Thulin, *Corpus Agrimensorum Romanorum*, 99 (135 Lachmann).
[60] Hyginus Gromaticus, 141 (Thulin; 176 Lachmann): 'cum signis et aquila et primis ordinibus ac tribunis, modus agri pro portione dabatur.'
[61] *ILS* 6087, ciii: 'colon(iae) fin(ium) defendendorum causa'; cf. lxvi on 'vacatio militiae'.
[62] Strabo, 12. 8. 14, 577; see above, Ch. 5 at n. 6.

[63] Levick, *Roman Colonies*, 73; 34–6 for the numismatic argument. The coins are A. Kryszanowska, *Monnaies coloniales d'Antioche de Pisidie* (1970), 136; Cremna: Aulock, *Pisidien*, ii no. 1091 (M. Aurelius), 1697–1709 (Aurelian); Lystra: von Aulock, *Chiron*, 2 (1972), 515 (Augustus) and 517 (M. Aurelius).
[64] Aulock, *Pisidien*, ii nos. 1518–20. The difficulties were acknowledged by Levick, and by E. L. Bowie, *JRS* 60 (1970), 204.
[65] Sterrett, *WE* no. 352; W. M. Calder, *JRS* 2 (1912), 84 no. 3; for the era of Tavium see below, Ch. 7 § III. The argument was adduced by Bowie, loc. cit.
[66] L. Robert, *Stud. clas.* 16 (1974), 68–9 (= *OMS* vi. 290–1) for a review of the more important kinship terms, as they occur in Greek inscriptions. It may, however, be relevant that the three cities of Antioch, Lystra, and Tavium were all Augustan foundations. Compare Strabo, 16. 2. 4, 749 on the four cities of the Seleucids in Syria, Antioch, Seleuceia, Apamea, and Laodicea, ἅπερ καὶ ἐλέγοντο ἀλλήλων ἀδελφαὶ διὰ τὴν ὁμονοίαν, Σελεύκου τοῦ Νικάτορος κτίσματα.
[67] Levick, *Roman Colonies*, 39, and references to several unpublished texts by French, *ANRW* ii. 7. 2 (1980), 727 table 2 nos. 2–10. See also n. 3 above.
[68] Levick, *Roman Colonies*, 37.

The geographical distribution of the sites reveals something of their strategic importance. It is now established that there were at least thirteen Augustan foundations in Galatia, twelve in the south of the province. There were full *coloniae* at Antioch, Cremna, Parlais, Olbasa, Comama, Lystra, Iconium, and Ninica, and settlements of *coloni* within existing communities at Apollonia, Neapolis, Isaura, and Attaleia.[69] The territories of these settlements lay mostly in the upland plains which encircle central Pisidia, running from Olbasa and Comama in the west to Lystra and Iconium in the east, areas of good agricultural land, which readily lent itself for division into colonial allotments.[70] These colonies were linked with one another and to the Pamphylian plain by the *via Sebaste*. This new road was not only the essential symbol of Roman political control (see above, Ch. 5 n. 20), but fitted exactly into the communication system which had been created under the republic. It joined the main southern highway across Anatolia at Iconium, and Aquillius' road from Asia to Pamphylia north of Comama.[71] Ninica in the Calycadnus valley, which controlled the direct route south from Iconium to Seleuceia on the Calycadnus, extended the system south-east into Rugged Cilicia. It is not impossible that an Augustan road was built along this route also.[72] Only two of the Augustan colonies were situated in the heart of the mountainous district: at Cremna, between Sagalassus and Selge, newly conquered itself and adjacent to the still un-subdued stronghold of Sandalium; and at Isaura, the strongest castle of the northern Taurus south of Lystra. Both had been important centres of Amyntas' kingdom.[73] With the possible exception of the last two, the colonies cannot be seen as offensive bases in themselves. The other settlements were founded in areas which were already reasonably secure from the Pisidian threat. They may have embodied a negative strategy, not to allow these fertile areas to slip from Roman control, but they did not in themselves con-tribute to any Roman plan to dominate the highlands. In so far as we can make any deductions about the military purpose of the colonies from their geographical positions, they tend to conform to the defensive role implied by the brief remarks of Cicero and Siculus Flaccus.

Augustus had deployed substantial numbers of troops for the pacification of south Galatia, but there is little to show for the actual campaigns, which ex-tinguished the danger or major *montagnard* uprisings until the later third century.[74] It is clear that there was one major war, the campaign against the Homonadeis conducted by P. Sulpicius Quirinius, perhaps be-tween 6 BC and AD 4, which brought the *ornamenta triumphalia* to the commander, and annihilation to his enemies.[75] The Homonadeis were a tribe with a large territory covering the basin of Lake Trogitis (Suğla Göl) and the remote mountain valleys to the south and east, in the borderland between east Pisidia and Isauria.[76] The sources for the campaign mention the painstaking destruction, one after another, of forty-four *castella*, including the capital Omana; four thou-sand men who survived the battles and the blockades were taken into captivity and then resettled in the neighbouring cities; thereafter the Homonadeis as a tribe, and as a name, ceased to exist.[77] Under the empire their place was taken by smaller tribal groups, the Sedaseis, the Gorgoromeis, the Pedaieis, and the Psekaleis, who were perhaps originally their subor-dinates. The whole area was kept under strict military surveillance. The Roman road which ran west of Lake Beyşehir, south to Suğla Göl, and thence to Isaura, was patrolled by *stationarii* and by small cavalry detach-ments.[78] The large number of Roman names attested in

---

[69] Levick discusses only the first six in detail. For Iconium and Ninica, see *Historia*, 28 (1979), 409 ff.; for the 'non-colonial *coloni*', see *Tenth Congress*, 311–18. The list above in the text omits Germa in north Galatia. Further Augustan settlements may yet be identified in and around Pisidia. Late inscriptions refer to colonies at Trebenna, south of Termessus (*Mon. ant.* 23 (1914), 214 no. 152 = *AE* (1915), 53), and at Balbura, one of the members of the Cibyran tetrapolis (*IGR* iii. 479, now C. Naour, *Tyriaion en Cabalide* (1980), 38 no. 8). Both might date back to Augustus, although alternative theories are possible (for instance, on Balbura, *CR* 32 (1982), 114).

[70] See above, Ch. 5. For the colonial territories, see Levick, *Roman Colonies*, 42–53.

[71] See above, n. 3.

[72] On the position of Ninica, see *Historia*, 28 (1979), 426–30 and R. Syme, *AS* 36 (1986), 162–3 = *RP* v. 661–7.

[73] See above, nn. 32–3.

[74] Below, Ch. 13 § III, and see also Ch. 11 § VI. The important general study of this phenomenon by B. D. Shaw, 'Bandit Highlands and Lowland Peace: The Mountains of Isauria–Cilicia', in *Journal of the Economic and Social History of the Orient*, 33 (1990), 199–233 and 237–69, neglects to consider the specific ways in which the Highlands were controlled under the Romans.

[75] Levick, *Roman Colonies*, app. V gives a full account with detailed citation of the sources.

[76] Apart from Levick, see Magie, *RR* ii. 303–4; A. S. Hall, *AS* 21 (1971), 157 ff.; and Bean and Mitford, *Journeys in Rough Cilicia 1964–68*, 29–30 on the territory of the Homonadeis.

[77] Pliny, *NH* 5. 94; Strabo, 12. 6. 5, 569.

[78] For the later tribal groups, see Hall, loc. cit. On the *stationarii* in general see Robert, *Hellenica*, xiii, 80. At Artanada in Isauria note the *stationarius* in *IGR* iii. 812; other inscriptions from this site mention a στρατιώτης (*IGR* iii. 815), a soldier of *I Parthica* (*IGR* iii. 814), a standard-bearer (*IGR* iii. 813), and probably another *stationarius* (unpublished). Among the Gorgoromeis there is a centurion and two *stationarii*, Hall, *AS* 21 (1971), 125, 129 no. 1 and 130 no. 2; moving north to Vasada, we meet a κῆρυξ ἱππεὺς σινγλάριος στατιωνάριος, Swoboda, *Denkmäler*, no. 34; there is a *stationarius* on the imperial estate around Kireli, Robert, *Hellenica*, 80 on

the district may be directly attributed to this strong military presence. There is no evidence for civic organization in any of these tribes, and it is natural to assume that the local military commanders played a large part in administering the area.[79]

One of the most remarkable facts about the Homonadensian war is the long gap that separated the death of Amyntas from the final defeat of the tribesmen. It has been well observed that Augustus, as Amyntas' heir, owed a debt of vengeance on his behalf, which would normally have been paid in short order.[80] We must assume that the problems of controlling not only the Homonadeis but the whole mountain region were judged to be so formidable that a policy of extreme caution and thoroughness was adopted: firstly, land that was already under Roman control was secured by founding colonies; next, communications around and through the mountains were assured by building the *via Sebaste*; finally, a war of conquest crushed remaining resistance. Pisidia was garrisoned throughout this period. The soldiers cannot have been idle before Sulpicius' campaigns, but their role will have been the unglamorous, although not unobtrusive one of imposing a tight grip on the native population. The length of time that this occupied may be attributed both to the difficulty of the task, and to the huge area which the operation covered. It is possible that operations in the Taurus directed between 15 and 13 BC by one of the early governors of Galatia, L. Calpurnius Piso, extended from Oenoanda in the west to the Cilician city of Hierapolis-Castabala in the east, a distance even as the crow flies of more than 500 kilometres, and of course far longer by any practicable route.[81] Furthermore, even the Homonadensian war did not mark an end to hostilities. As so often in the history of Roman expansion, initial conquest was followed by native rebellion. Dio mentions an Isaurian uprising in AD 6, and it appears to have taken the legate M. Plautius Silvanus a full season of campaign-

ing to bring this under control before he was able, belatedly, to march his troops out of Asia Minor to Moesia, to confront the far more serious disturbances in Pannonia.[82]

Rome was to be thankful for the thoroughness with which the pacification of southern Galatia had been carried out. The disasters on the Danube and the Rhine in the last years of Augustus' principate never allowed legionary garrisons to return to the Taurus. It was fortunate that the Isaurians, the Pisidians, and the Homonadeis could find no further reserves of strength with which to rise up themselves.

To appreciate the nature of the Augustan achievement, it is helpful to glance briefly ahead over the rest of the Julio-Claudian period, at the risk of anticipating the story to come. The military presence was thinned, no doubt to the relief of the native population, but the imprint of Roman rule was no less marked, above all by the foundation or refoundation of cities, which took their names from members of the ruling dynasty. With the Tiberian foundations of Germanicopolis at Ermenek west of Ninica, and at Pappa-Tiberiopolis, and the new Claudian cities at Claudiopolis alongside the colony of Ninica itself, Claudioderbe, Claudiconium, Claudiolaodicea, Claudiocaesareia Mistea, and Claudioseleuceia, the whole of south Galatia was integrated into a single administrative system which held the province together and consolidated the Roman grip on the Taurus (see below, Ch. 7 § v).

The urban titles are not the only indications of this process. The great programmes of public building which took place in the cities of north Galatia and at Pisidian Antioch, and the development of the imperial cult (see below, Ch. 8) were matched throughout the cities of the south by the erection of statues and other monuments dedicated to the early emperors. Sagalassus, the greatest city of northern Pisidia, emerged as the major provincial centre; arches and monumental entrances were added to both its Hellenistic agoras under Tiberius and Claudius, and the sanctuary and temple of Apollo Clarius is probably of Augustan origin. Other important early imperial monuments confirm that the culture and prosperity of a sophisticated Hellenistic city continued unbroken under the first emperors.[83] Imperial dedications to Augustus are found both in the colonies of Antioch,[84] Lystra,[85] and Olbasa,[86] and in other cities such as Seleuceia Sidera,[87]

MAMA viii no. 340, and a ἱππ(εὺς) κῆρυξ at Fakılar in the territory of Neapolis, Robert, *Hellenica*, xiii. 105 on *MAMA* viii no. 370. For the militarization of this region see further below, Ch. 9 §1 at nn. 33–8, and G. Laminger-Pascher, 'Römische Soldaten in Isaurien', *Festchrift für Artur Betz* (1985), 381–92.

[79] As suggested by Hall, *AS* 21 (1971), 155 ff. Anyone who has witnessed the power wielded by commanders of the Jandarma in the small communities of modern Turkey will appreciate what such military control might amount to.

[80] W. M. Ramsay, *JRS* 12 (1922), 148, cited by Hall, *AS* 21 (1971), 158.

[81] This claim rests on an unpublished inscription from Oenoanda and on Keil and Wilhelm, *JÖAI* 18 (1915), 51 ff. from Hierapolis, both of which honour Piso, *legatus Augusti pro praetore*, as benefactor and patron. If both refer to the same man in the same command, the geographical scope is breathtaking.

[82] Cassius Dio, 55, 28, 2–3; Syme, *Klio*, 27 (1934), 140–3; Mitchell, *CQ* 26 (1976), 298–300.

[83] M. Waelkens, *AS* 38 (1988), 62–4; 39 (1989), 66 with Fig. 2; *Asia-Minor-Studien* 6 (1992), 43–60; *JHS Arch. Reports* (1989/90), 122 with Fig. 53.

[84] *JRS* 14 (1924), 177 no. 22.

[85] *CIL* iii. 6786; *MAMA* viii no. 5 (*divum Augustum*).

[86] G. E. Bean, *AS* 9 (1959), 101 no. 59; however the style and the lettering appear to be later than the Augustan period.

[87] *CIL* iii. 6869.

and Casae in Rugged Cilicia.[88] A high priest of Tiberius is attested at Iconium,[89] but the Claudian evidence is particularly telling. Seleuceia Sidera hailed Claudius as a god manifest,[90] while Olbasa and Sagalassus both set up inscriptions soon after his accession. These may be connected with the new administrative arrangements of AD 43 which led to the creation of the province of Lycia and Pamphylia, probably also incorporating Pisidia as far north as Sagalassus.[91] However, the most striking inscription has already been cited in another context, the Latin dedication set up for Claudius by his legate M. Annius Afrinus at Yalı Hüyük on the south shore of Lake Trogitis, in former Homonadensian territory.[92] Annius Afrinus was probably the first governor to visit this area since the campaigns of Sulpicius Quirinius,[93] and the traces which he left behind him amount to the clearest possible indication of the change that had overtaken the whole region.

During his term of office between AD 49 and 54 he played a more active role than any of his predecessors in stamping Roman authority across the province. His name and portrait occur on coins of Iconium and Pessinus, and his name alone on other issues of Pessinus and of the Galatian *koinon*.[94] He set up another inscription for Claudius at Lystra,[95] and his own name passed into Galatian nomenclature.[96] He appears to have been one of only two Galatian legates between the death of Augustus and the accession of Nero who reached the consulship.[97] His activities set the seal on a process of pacification which had begun three-quarters of a century earlier. Henceforward the western Taurus was not only secure from insurrection but was firmly integrated into the rest of the province. The history of its cities, at least as reflected by their inscriptions, buildings, and coins, is one of peaceful and prosperous development.

[88] Bean and Mitford, *Journeys in Rough Cilicia 1964–68*, 49–50 no. 27.

[89] *IGR* iii. 1473.

[90] *IGR* iii. 328.

[91] *CIL* iii. 6889 (AD 42–3); 6871 = *IGR* iii. 344 (AD 43). Cf. Balland, *Xanthos* vii. 25–8 on Claudius and Lycia at this date, and a dedication to Claudius from Cremna, to be published by S. Mitchell and G. H. R. Horsley.

[92] *CIL* iii. 6799.

[93] Observed by Ramsay, *JRS* 12 (1922), 159.

[94] Iconium: Aulock, *Lykaonien*, nos. 253–62; Pessinus: *SNG von Aulock*, 6208–9, and *BMC Galatia*, Pessinus no. 3; for the portrait see M. Grant, *Num. Chron.* 10 (1950), 45 n. 23; Koinon: E. Babelon, *Rev. num.* 5 (1887), 109–18. In general *PIR*² i. 106: A no. 630.

[95] *MAMA* viii no. 53.

[96] *RECAM* ii no. 124, in the territory of Pessinus.

[97] In AD 67, cf. Sherk, ii. 976–7. The other eventual consul was T. Axius, see *Chiron*, 16 (1986), 37.

I. The Graeco-Roman City

When were there ever so many cities both inland and on the coast, or when have they ever been so beautifully equipped with everything? Did ever a man who lived then travel across country as we do, counting the cities by days, and sometimes riding on the same day through two or even three cities, as if he was passing through one only? ... Now all the Greek cities rise up under your leadership, and the monuments which are dedicated in them and all their embellishments and comforts redound to your honour like beautiful suburbs. The coasts and interior have been filled with cities, some newly founded, others increased under and by you.[1]

These familiar passages from Aelius Aristides' encomium of Rome and Roman power, delivered around the middle of the second century AD, focus on the most striking and the most enduring material legacy of Roman rule, the cities and their resplendent public buildings and monuments, which had by that time emerged in almost every corner of the empire. A famous paragraph of Pausanias, written about a generation after Aristides' speech, helps to define what the word city meant to a contemporary. His description of northern Greece reaches the city of Panopeus in Phokis, 'if you can call it a city when it has no state buildings, no gymnasium, no theatre and no agora, when it has no running water at a fountain and the inhabitants live on the edge of a torrent in hovels like mountain huts.'[2] The emphasis on monumental public buildings is important and distinctive, for Greek and above all Graeco-Roman cities, to a much greater degree than urban centres in other cultures, were marked out as such by the nature of their public architecture. By the second century AD a city was expected to be endowed with a whole series of major buildings and structures, which would include fortifications (wall, gates, and towers); religious structures (temples, sanctuaries, and altars); political meeting places, notably bouleuteria or basilicas to house the city council, but also including large areas for public assembly; places where well-defined forms of cultural or educational activity, themselves a distinguishing mark of urban civilization, could take place (gymnasia, odeia, theatres, libraries); civic amenities, especially connected with the water supply (aqueducts, nymphaea, and bath-houses); and decorative monuments of every shape and size, which were not merely designed as ornaments, but were intended to enhance the prestige of the rich and powerful, including of course the emperors (triumphal arches, statues, monumental inscriptions, heroes' tombs). Simply to list these building types will be enough to evoke an image of a city of the Roman empire which should be instantly recognizable, and nowhere in the Roman world is the image more apt than in Asia Minor, a land of 500 cities,[3] sometimes so densely packed that they literally bear out Aristides' claim than a man might ride through three in a single day, yet be under the impression that he was passing through a single one.

Central and eastern Asia Minor were not in Aristides' mind when he wrote those lines; the regions with which he was most familiar were the densely populated and heavily urbanized parts of the province of Asia, whose civic life becomes the object of praise in many other of his orations,[4] not the vast expanses of the central Anatolian plateau. Yet here too the provinces were made up of a patchwork of cities and their territories, each adjacent to its neighbours. The creation of these constitutes the single most remarkable difference that can be perceived between central Anatolia before it came under Roman rule, and the Asian provinces of the high empire.

The search for the origins of Roman cities in the preceding Hellenistic period is not always straightforward. For one thing, the origins of any phenomenon will be something less well developed and less immediately recognizable than its fully fledged successor.

---

[1] Aelius Aristides, *To Rome* (*The Roman Oration*), 93–4; trans. Oliver.

[2] Pausanias, 10. 3. 4, trans. P. Levi.

[3] Josephus, *BJ* 2. 16. 4 (366); in fact an exaggeration.

[4] Aelius Aristides (ed. Keil), *Orr.* 17–22 (Smyrna); 23 (on the concord of Smyrna, Pergamum, and Ephesus); 27 (Cyzicus); 53 (Pergamum). See A. Boulanger, *Aelius Aristide: La Sophistique dans la province d'Asie au IIe siècle de notre ère* (1923).

Moreover, in the case of Graeco-Roman cities there is another key factor to be taken into account—the changing nature of the institution itself. In the classical and Hellenistic periods, for reasons that were as much cultural as economic, few communities could lay claim to the range of public buildings that were characteristic of cities under the Roman empire. Indeed, the most significant defining characteristic of a *polis* was a negative one, namely that it was not politically dependent on any other community. Autonomy was the key to civic status. Pausanias effectively alludes to this when he reveals that Panopeus, for all its miserable appearance, was yet a city because it still sent its own delegate to the Phocian assembly. Between the fourth century BC and the first century AD the change in emphasis on what a city really was came about gradually, through complex historical processes, as well as through changing expectations, but the diminishing importance of cities in international affairs was surely crucial. Under the Hellenistic kingdoms and during the rise of Roman imperialism effective power—at least in inter-state and inter-city relations—slipped away from the cities to kings, commanders, and emperors. The prized and vaunted freedom or autonomy of classical times was set in the course of decline which led to the so-called freedom of the late Hellenistic and imperial period; a time when a small city in Asia, which was jealously to protect this very freedom for more than three further centuries, could acknowledge in a public document of 88 BC that 'without the rule of the Romans we do not choose even to live'.[5] The shift from political autonomy to other criteria, in particular public building, as an index of city status, ran parallel with these broader political developments. The end of the process, notoriously, occurred in the most prosperous period of the Roman empire, when public buildings remained one of the few forms of independent political expression open to the cities, with the result that they too had to be restricted, in the interests of preventing wasteful expenditure and unhealthy inter-city rivalry.

II. *Central Anatolia before Augustus*

The only coherent guide to the urbanization of central Anatolia before Augustus is Strabo's book 12, which was probably completed in AD 18 or 19, but which draws heavily on sources of the first century BC, and pays little attention to developments that had occurred under Augustus when most of the area was annexed to the empire.[6] The canvas is virtually blank. In the whole of Cappadocia, he claims that there were only two cities: Tyana, towards the Cilician gates, which was called Eusebeia next to the Taurus; and the metropolis of Cappadocia, Mazaca, renamed Eusebeia by Mount Argaeus. Both had been founded in the middle of the second century BC by Ariarathes V.[7] In Pontus to the north-east there were Greek colonial foundations along the coast of the Black Sea—Heracleia, Sinope (the most important), Amisus, and Trapezus (the last called a *polis Hellenis* to mark the contrast with the un-Hellenized settlements of eastern Anatolia).[8] In the hinterland the picture had been recently modified by a series of new cities founded by Pompey, when he had created the province of Pontus and Bithynia in 63 BC, but these had enjoyed mixed fortunes after most of Pontus had been returned by Antony and Augustus to dynastic rule.[9] In Galatia there was nothing. Ancyra was no more than a fortress, and the old centres of Phrygian power had dwindled away, preserving no trace that they had once been cities; even Gordium was a village hardly larger than its neighbours.[10] The picture in the southern part of the central plateau is the same, and it is not until one reaches its western fringes, that cities begin to appear in Strabo's account.

Strabo does not ignore the fact that there were other settlements in these areas, and that some of these could be substantial centres of population and power. The most important of these were temple states, ruled by priests and inhabited by sacred slaves or serfs. The ruling priests of Comana and Venasa in Cappadocia ranked second and third in importance after the Cappadocian king, and controlled respectively 6,000

[5] J. Reynolds, *Aphrodisias and Rome* (1982), 12 doc. 2.

[6] See F. Lasserre, *Strabon Géographie livre XII* (Budé edn. ix, 1981), 6–10 pointing to 12. 1. 4, 534 (concerning the death of Archelaus of Cappadocia in AD 17), 12. 3. 29, 556 (on the elevation of Zenon, son of Pythodoris, to the throne of Armenia in AD 18), and 12. 8. 18, 578 (on Tiberius' restoration of Sardis after the great earthquake of AD 17). For Strabo's sources in this book, see Lasserre, 12–32.

[7] Strabo, 12. 2. 7, 537; note also 12. 2. 6, 537 with the clear statement that there were no cities in Cataonia or in Melitene. He does, however, ignore Ariaratheia and Hanisa, discussed below, and elsewhere states that Cappadocian Comana was a πόλις ἀξιόλογος (12. 2. 3, 535). Here he is not using the word *polis* in a technical sense, but simply as a term to describe a large settlement presumably well endowed with public buildings (cf. L. Robert, *A travers l'Asie Mineure* (1980), 241 on his similar use of the word κωμή).

[8] Strabo, 12. 3. 2–4, 542; 3. 11, 545–6; 3. 14–16, 547–8; 3. 17, 548.

[9] For Pompey's cities in Pontus, see Strabo, 12. 3. 1, 541. See above, Ch. 3 § III. The best discussion of them in Magie, *RR* ii. 1232–4. These foundations were preceded by another Roman city, Licineia, founded by Licinius Murena as a bulwark against Mithridates in 81 BC perhaps in eastern Bithynia, Memnon, 25.

[10] Strabo, 12. 5. 3, 568: ἐπὶ δὲ τούτῳ τὰ παλαιὰ τῶν Φρυγῶν οἰκητήρια Μίδου καὶ ἔτι πρότερον Γορδίου καὶ ἄλλων τινῶν, οὐδ' ἴχνη σώζοντα πόλεων ἀλλὰ κῶμαι μικρῷ μείζους τῶν ἄλλων, οἷον ἐστι τὸ Γόρδιον καὶ Γορβεοῦς.

and 3,000 hierodouloi.[11] There were similar large temple states in Pontus, based on the sanctuaries of Men Pharnakou at Cabeira, of Ma at Comana Pontica, and of Anaitis at Zela, and in western Galatia based on the shrine of Cybele at Pessinus.[12] The status of the population, the nature of the administrative structure, and the character of the cult in these cases made them readily distinguishable from Greek cities—Strabo remarks of Zela that before his time it was administered by the kings of Pontus not as a city but as a sanctuary of the Persian gods—but they could be transformed into cities, or at least acquire the trappings of Hellenism. Pompey made Cabeira into Diospolis, one of his eleven Pontic cities, and Strabo himself refers loosely to Cappadocian Comana as a noteworthy city on account of its large population and the fine temple dedicated to Ma. The patronage of the Pergamene kings had given Pessinus a temple of white marble, doubtless built to a Greek design, by the mid-second century BC, an important step in the Hellenization of the community.

Royal patronage was a crucial factor elsewhere, for the Hellenization of Anatolia worked from the top downwards. The two cities of Cappadocia had been founded by the vigorously philhellenic Ariarathes V, who was versed in Greek culture and proved his credentials by promoting Greek games, both in Cappadocia itself and at Athens.[13] His father had been responsible for founding another city—ignored by Strabo—Ariaratheia, one of whose citizens appears to have been the sculptor of a statue erected as early as 100 BC in the agora of Samos.[14] It is noteworthy that another Cappadocian settlement, Cadena in the district of Sargarausene, whose site has not been localized, should be described by Strabo as a royal residence which had the trappings of a city; aristocratic preferences naturally tended to promote Hellenism.[15]

The same story can be told of Pontus, where the impetus towards Hellenization was largely due to one man, Mithridates VI Eupator. Mithridates had taken numerous steps to improve the condition of many settlements, in many cases probably paving the way for the grants of civic status by Pompey. Amaseia, the burial place of the Pontic king, could be called a city in 70 BC.[16] He had half-built Eupatoria before his defeat; Pompey was to complete the job, pointedly renaming the place Magnopolis.[17] At Cabeira, the site of one of his palaces, he had created a water-mill, a zoological park, hunting grounds, and mines; again Pompey was to turn this into the city of Diospolis.[18] Several of the Pontic communities which he founded or enhanced issued a Greek-style bronze coinage,[19] and he himself chose the Greek city of Sinope as his principal residence.[20] The Greek experts of all kinds who surrounded him—commanders and administrators, writers and doctors—were only to be expected.[21]

Inter-regional and local trade was clearly another important spur to the growth and development of the central Anatolian communities, although it did not necessarily lead to or entail Hellenization. Pontic Comana, the main centre for trade with Armenia, is the outstanding example. Its commerce, and the throng of prostitutes who were readily available from the temple slaves, earned it the reputation of a lesser Corinth.[22] Much of the trade of central and eastern Anatolia passed through Sinope, the best harbour on the south shore of the Black Sea. Cappadocian red ochre which was exported through it took the name Sinopic, and it was surely an important outlet for many other products of the region—semi-precious stones such as onyx or alabaster, metals from the Pontic mines, wool, hides, and slaves.[23] In Galatia Tavium, which also had

---

[11] Strabo, 12. 2. 3, 535 (Comana); 2. 6, 537 (Venasa). Note 12. 2. 5, 537 on a third smaller temple of Zeus Dacieos(?). Diodorus Siculus, 31. 34 mentions another Cappadocian sanctuary on a mountain called Ariadne, and imperial coins and gems of Caesareia show a mountain-top shrine on Argaeus, or indeed depict the whole mountain as a holy place (P. Weiss, *JNG* 35 (1985), 21–48).

[12] Strabo, 12. 3. 31, 556 (Cabeira); 3. 32–6, 557–9 (Comana Pontica); 3. 37, 559 (Zela); 5. 3, 567 (Pessinus).

[13] Robert, *Noms indigènes*, 494–7, citing the evidence that he was *agonothetes* at the Panathenaic games, and was honoured by the Dionysiac artists with a cult, and with annual and monthly festivals. He founded games which took his name in Cappadocia, which are attested by a victor's inscription from Delos, *I. Delos*, 1957; L. Moretti, *Iscrizioni agonistiche greche*, no. 51.

[14] Robert, *Noms indigènes*, 497; *Hellenica*, ii, 84–5. The Samian inscription was published by W. R. Paton, *CR* 13 (1899), 78–9.

[15] Strabo, 12. 2. 6, 537. Again, however, the word *polis* is not

intended to convey more than that the place had fine, presumably Hellenized public buildings.

[16] Memnon, 38. 9.; Strabo, 12. 3. 39, 561. It is characteristic, however, that the leading official in the place was the phrourarch, *OGIS* 365; *SP* iii no. 278, see below nn. 32–42.

[17] Strabo, 12. 3. 30, 556; Appian, *Mith.* 78; Pliny, *NH* 6. 2. 7; Memnon, 45.

[18] Strabo, ibid. Memnon (*FGrH* IIIB no. 434), 45 alludes to both Cabeira and Eupatoria as *poleis* in 71 BC and implies that both were walled.

[19] Head, *NH*² 503, Jones, *CERP*² 157.

[20] Strabo, 12. 3. 11, 545. Note too that Mithridates built a temple at Amisus, Appian, *Mith.* 112.

[21] Th. Reinach, *Mithridates Eupator* (German edn., trans. A. Goetz, 1895), 272–95; E. Olshausen, *Anc. Soc.* 5 (1974), 153–70.

[22] Strabo, 12. 3. 36, 559.

[23] For the red ochre see Strabo 12. 2. 10, 540 with the comments of Magie, *RR* ii. 1077: ἐν δὲ τῇ Καππαδοκίᾳ γίνεται καὶ ἡ λεγομένη Σινωπικὴ μίλτος, ἀρίστη τῶν πασῶν... ὠνομάσθη δὲ Σινωπική, διότι κατάγειν ἐκεῖσε εἰώθεσαν οἱ ἔμποροι πρὶν ἢ τὸ τῶν Ἐφεσίων ἐμπόριον μέχρι τῶν ἐνθάδε ἀνθρώπων διῖχθαι. Red ochre was waterproof and so vital for ship building. The same passage continues

an important sanctuary of Zeus, was the emporium of the Trocmi; it issued a very sparse silver coinage in the late Hellenistic period, and may possibly have been the principal centre of manufacture of the attractive so-called East Galatian pottery, which occurs at second and first century BC sites east of the Halys bend.[24] Pessinus likewise became the largest emporium in western Galatia, and was probably the entrepôt for the products of sheep-rearing and stock-raising in the central plateau.[25] It may have become more important after 189 BC when Manlius Vulso and his Roman force had sacked the old Phrygian capital of Gordium.[26] Livy (following Polybius) tells us that at that time Gordium, although no longer a great city, was the most notable market of central Anatolia.[27]

The most striking example of a city which derived its importance from trade was unknown to or unremarked by Strabo or any other ancient author, and comes from a bronze tablet, now in Berlin. This carries the text of a civic decree, passed by the council and people of the Hanisenoi, in recognition of the services rendered to them by a certain Apollonius, son of Abbas, who had represented the city in a legal dispute about the possession of an estate before the authorities in the neighbouring city of Eusebeia/Mazaca.[28] The law in question was Greek and had presumably been imported when Mazaca was founded, for Strabo remarks that it used the archaic code of Charondas, devised in the seventh century BC for the South Italian colonies of Zancle and Rhegium, which was expounded by a specially appointed *nomodes*.[29] The inscription was

found precisely at Kültepe, twenty kilometres north of Mazaca, the modern Kayseri, site of the Assyrian trading colony of Kanes, whose affairs are documented by cuneiform tablets of the early second millenium BC which have been excavated there by the thousand. Thus it appears that Kanes/Hanisa, the chief commercial entrepôt between central and eastern Anatolia and Upper Mesopotamia in the middle and late Bronze Ages, survived as a substantial community until the late Hellenistic period. There is no reason to doubt that the commerce, chiefly in metals, which had sustained the Assyrian colony, continued to guarantee the prosperity of Kanes/Hanisa as a town through the third century BC, when it minted coins under the supervision of a local dynast,[30] until the late Hellenistic period when it was apparently subsumed and absorbed into the neighbouring royal capital. The character of the city can be deduced from the inscription. The personal names of the magistrates and other persons named in the decree show that the population was indigenous, with Pontic, Cappadocian, Phrygian, and Iranian affiliations. The formula prescribing the publication of the decree shows that the principal cult of the community was that of Assyrian Astarte, surely introduced by the colonists two millenia before; but the language of the decree, the principal festivals of the city in honour of Zeus Soter and Heracles, and its constitution are purely Greek.[31] This single document serves better than any other item of evidence to illustrate the complexity of urban development and cultural influence in this remote area of the Hellenistic world.

Thus substantial centres of population had grown up during the Hellenistic period in central and eastern Asia Minor around the principal centres of local and regional trade, and around several major sanctuaries. Moreover, the kings of Pontus and Cappadocia, at least those with the means and the will to do so, had actively promoted the Hellenization of their countries,

---

with mention of slabs of crystal, an onyx-like stone mined for Archelaus near the Galatian border, a white, ivory-like stone used for sword pommels, and a transparent stone used for lenses or windows. For other products of Cappadocia and Pontus, R. Teja, Kappadokien, *ANRW* ii. 7. 2, 1093–102; *TIB* ii. 64–5; Olshausen, *RE Suppl.* xv (1978), 460–91.

[24] Strabo, 12. 5. 2, 567. Coins: *BMC Galatia*, 24 nos. 1–2; pottery, see above, Ch. 4 n. 99.

[25] Strabo, 12. 5. 3, 567.

[26] The American excavators of Gordium have noted widespread evidence for a Hellenistic destruction level, after which finds are very sparse. They reasonably attribute this to the passage of Manlius Vulso's forces. Livy writes 'Id tum desertum fuga incolarum oppidum, refertum idem copia rerum omnium invenerunt. Ibi stative habentibus...' (38. 18. 13–14). See Ch. 4 n. 112.

[27] Livy 38. 18. 10–12: 'Id haud magnum quidem oppidum est, sed plus quam mediterraneum celebre et frequens emporium. Tria maria pari ferme distantia intervallo habet, Hellespontum, ad Sinopem, et alterius orae litora, qua Cilices maritimi colunt; multarum magnarumque praeterea gentium finis contingit, quarum commercium in eum maxime locum mutui usus contraxere.'

[28] Michel, *Recueil*, no. 546; re-edited with a full discussion by Robert, *Noms indigènes*, 457–523.

[29] Strabo, 12. 2. 9, 539. The case involved the estate of Sindenos,

a citizen of Hanisa who had died intestate and without heirs. Apollonius, chief magistrate of Hanisa, had successfully upheld the city's claim to the estate in the face of a counterclaim by some of his fellow citizens. Judgement was given by two royal appointees in Mazaca, the head of the financial administration and the governor of the city. In view of Strabo's comment about the laws in force at Mazaca, we cannot assume that this particular procedure for intestate succession to a man without heirs was normal in Cappadocia, or in the Seleucid empire, as has been suggested or assumed.

[30] K. Regling, 'Dynasten und Münzen von Tyana, Morima und Anisa in Kappadokien', *ZfN* 42 (1932), 1–23; Robert, *Noms indigènes*, 484–6.

[31] Robert, *Noms indigènes*, 499–501 is inclined to think that 'Zeus' and 'Heracles' at Hanisa were Hellenized forms of local gods. But it is evident that they had Greek-style cults and festivals in their honour, and it is easier to suppose that they were Greek gods themselves. If not, they had been very thoroughly Hellenized.

and had converted some of these centres, and certain settlements into Greek cities, by introducing at least some of the features by which Greek civic life could be defined: a constitution based on meetings of the council and people, Greek civic cults and festivals, and the training of the gymnasium.

However, only a small minority of the settlements in Anatolia fell into these categories. Strabo's description indicates that a large part of the country was controlled by castles (*phrouria*). At the eastern boundary of Cappadocia stood the castle of Tomisa, which guarded the crossing of the Euphrates into Sophene;[32] there were strong mountain castles at Azamora and Dastarcon, which seem to have controlled the route over the Taurus south from Mazaca to the Cilician plain;[33] and at Argos and Nora or Neroassus which guarded the western edge of Cappadocia and looked over Lycaonia.[34] The security of the capital Mazaca, which was not fortified, was dependent on the defence of a large number of castles, some belonging to the king others to his friends.[35] The north-west boundary between Cappadocia and the Pontic regions was marked by another fortress at Dasmenda.[36] In Pontus itself Mithridates Eupator had created many new strongholds in addition to those that existed already. On his eastern flank he is said to have built seventy-five castles where he kept his treasure, including Hydara, Basgoedariza, Sinoria, and Dasteira, which was his last refuge before he was driven into Colchis and the Cimmerian Bosporus by Pompey.[37] Pompey then took it upon himself to raze most of Mithridates' Pontic forts. The most important of these was at Kainon Chorion near Cabeira, which was a major and heavily fortified treasury;[38] the fortress of Camisa in Camisene was incorporated into the territory of Megalopolis;[39] in the Phazimonitis there was a mountain castle at Sagylium which was destroyed on Pompey's orders so that it should not become a refuge for bandits, and

another at Ikizari(?), associated with a royal palace near Lake Stiphani, which was in ruins by Strabo's own day.[40] To the south there were several other ruined forts of Mithridates in the territory of Amaseia, and another at Pimolisa, a royal stronghold west of the Halys on the boundary with Paphlagonia.[41] In Paphlagonia itself Mithridates V Ctistes had built a fortress at Cimiata, which had been strengthened by Mithridates Eupator. This too seems to have ceased to exist by Strabo's time, in contrast to the capital of the Paphlagonian dynasts at Gangra, which served as a royal palace until the regions was annexed to the province of Galatia in 6/5 BC.[42]

Strabo names several forts in Galatia, including the two strongholds of Deiotarus at Blucium and Peium, the Tectosagan castles of Ancyra and Gorbeous, and three fortified positions among the Trocmi: Tavium, Posdala(?), and Mithridateium. Archaeological exploration has predictably revealed several other forts in the region.[43] South central Anatolia, with its great open plains, is a less suitable terrain for building small strongly defended *phrouria*, but here too there were fortified settlements. The village-city (komopolis) of Garsauira, the later Archelais, in western Cappadocia, and its neighbour the Lycaonian village of Coropassus, are both described as *phrouria*,[44] facing one another across the east Lycaonian steppe. In a contrasting landscape there was a well-constructed late Hellenistic fortification at Baş Dağ, in the highlands of Karadağ between Iconium and Laranda.[45] Strabo provides no detailed information about most of the communities in this area. Iconium was well-populated with a wealthy territory, and had been since the fourth century BC when Xenophon passed through on the march to Mesopotamia.[46] It minted coins in the first century BC as did Soatra, the later Savatra, south-west of Tuz Göl.[47] Both places, like Laranda (which existed at least

[32] Strabo, 12. 2. 1, 535; cf. T. Frankfort, *Latomus*, 22 (1963), 181–7; S. Mitchell, *Aşvan Kale* (1980), 8 with n. 23.

[33] Strabo, 12. 2. 5, 537. These dominated the valley of the Zamanti Su (Yenice Irmak). See Lasserre, *Strabo*, ix. 204–5; and for the Byzantine successors of these forts, *TIB* ii. 257–8 s.v. Phalakrukastron.

[34] Strabo, 12. 2. 5, 537. See Lasserre, *Strabo*, ix. 187 and 226 for suggested localizations. Neroassus has been identified with the fortress at Gelin Tepe, 34 km. ESE of Aksaray, where there is a Hellenistic tower, a Roman vaulted building using the *opus reticulatum* technique, and Byzantine fortifications, *TIB* ii. 245–6.

[35] Strabo, 12. 2. 7, 538; 2. 9, 539.

[36] Strabo, 12. 2. 10, 540.

[37] Strabo, 12. 3. 28, 555.

[38] Strabo, 12. 3. 31, 556. See G. de Jerphanion, *Mél de l'Univ. St. Joseph*, 5 (1911), 135–41 who puts the site at Mahalle Kalesi (Ahret Hisar).

[39] Strabo, 12. 3. 37, 560.

[40] Sagylium: Strabo, 12. 3. 38, 560; it has been located at Kele Tepe, 20 km. N. of Merzifon, by J. Biller and E. Olshausen, *Festschrift Dörner*, i. 168–72. Ikizari (the reading is uncertain): Strabo, ibid.; Lasserre, *Strabo*, ix. 215.

[41] Territory of Amaseia: Strabo, 12. 3. 40, 561; Pimolisa (modern Osmancık), 3. 40, 562 with J. G. C. Anderson, *SP* i. 100–2. For these and other Pontic *phrouria* (Taulara, a treasury, Appian, *Mith.* 115; Dadasa, Dio, 26. 12. 2), see Magie, *RR* ii. 1070. D. H. French, *AS* 41 (1991), 8 identifies a Mithridatic fort near Çukurhan, which controlled the route between Boyabat and Sinope.

[42] Strabo, 12. 3. 41, 562 for Cimiata see F. Lasserre, *Strabo*, ix. 200; for Gangra, Robert, *A travers l'Asie Mineure*, 203–19.

[43] See above, Ch. 4 § VI.

[44] Strabo, 12. 5. 6, 568; 6. 1, 569.

[45] K. Belke and M. Restle, *JÖAI* 52 (1978–80), Beiblatt 1–30.

[46] Strabo, 12. 6. 1, 568. Xenophon, *Anab.* 1. 2 (the last city in Phrygia); see S. Mitchell, *Historia*, 28 (1979), 411–12.

[47] Strabo, 12. 6. 1, 568. For the coin see Aulock, *Lykaonien*, 49 (one specimen).

as early as the time of Alexander the Great) and Derbe in southern Lycaonia, were to emerge as cities under the Roman empire.[48] In the Taurus beyond Lycaonia both Isauras are described as villages, but they controlled many others and they were certainly places of some importance. The Isaurians were numerous and well organized as early as the time of Alexander, and the new centre at Zengibar Kalesi had received a massive Hellenistic fortification wall from Amyntas in the 30s BC.[49]

It is only at the western edge of the central plateau that cities reappear in Strabo's account. He mentions Philomelium, Pisidian Antioch, and Synnada respectively on the east, west, and north of the fertile slopes of Sultan Dağ, as well as the village of Docimiun, which lay close to the last of these. An inscription suggests that it too may have been a *polis*, although clearly a modest one.[50] Epigraphic and other evidence exists to confirm that these cities of Phrygia Paroreius were indeed Hellenized,[51] and that the area included other important settlements like Tyraion, the Seleucid city of Laodicea Catacecaumene, and Neapolis in the Cillanian plain.[52] The historical origins of some of these communities around the southern and western fringes of the central Anatolian plateau can be traced back to Macedonian military settlements. Philomelium and its northern neighbour Lysias took their names from a Macedonian dynastic family which had no doubt been responsible for their foundation in the third century BC.[53] Docimium minted coins under the Roman empire in the name of the 'Macedonians of Docimium', and second- and third-century-AD inscrip-

tions refer to a founder Docimus, a Macedonian officer of Antigonus and Lysimachus who had been given control of nearby Synnada in 319 BC.[54] The one Hellenistic inscription of Docimium contains the name Pleistarchus, regularly used by Macedonians, underlining the origin of the settlers;[55] and the distinctive Macedonian name and patronymic of the last ruler of Derbe—Antipater son of Perilaus—show that there too there must have been a small Macedonian colony, which probably dated back to the period of the diadochi.[56]

The western confines of the central plateau mark a clear political and cultural boundary in Hellenistic Asia Minor. From here to the Aegean the influence of the Seleucid and Attalid monarchies becomes increasingly evident in city foundations and other signs of Hellenization. Important areas of western and southern Asia Minor with distinctive and complex native cultural and political traditions (such as Lycia, Caria, and even supposedly barbarous Pisidia) had adopted Greek culture readily and enthusiastically from the fourth century BC or even earlier. The contrast with central and eastern Anatolia is stark. Here cities were the exception not the rule. Not only were Greek cities few and far between, but other forms of settlement (such as the temple states or the royal palaces) offered an alternative to civic life and civic organization, which not only enjoyed a traditional primacy but may often have appeared to be politically and culturally more attractive to the inhabitants than Greek cities would have been.

The presence—or rather absence—of cities is not the only criterion by which the Hellenization of central and eastern Anatolia may be assessed. The defining characteristics of Greek culture and Greek settlement are also largely absent. Archaeologically the region is little known (there have been no notable excavations anywhere which relate to the Graeco-Roman period), and there are surely more exceptions to be found; but it remains a striking fact that, to return to the criterion of public building with which this chapter began, the only surviving constructions which can be defined stylistically, rather than chronologically, as Hellenistic are the first-century-BC fortifications at Peium in Galatia, on Baş Dağ in Lycaonia, and at Isaura.[57]

The epigraphic habit, of carving inscriptions to record and display information whether in the private

[48] Strabo, 12. 6. 3, 569. For Laranda, cf. Diodorus Siculus, 17. 22.

[49] Strabo, 12. 6. 3, 569. Old Isaura was at or near Bozkir; New Isaura, or simply Isaura was at Zengibar Kalesi. On Isauria, see R. Syme, in E. Frézouls (ed.), *Sociétés urbaines, sociétés rurales dans l'Asie Mineure et la Syrie hellénistiques et romaines* (1987), 131–47. Also above, Ch. 6 nn. 20 and 32.

[50] Strabo, 12. 8. 14, 576–7; the inscription implying that Docimium was an autonomous civic community was found in Smyrna, Kaibel *Epigrammata Graeca* no. 797; Robert, *A travers l'Asie Mineure*, 242–3.

[51] See S. Mitchell and M. Waelkens, *Pisidian Antioch: The Site and its Monuments* (forthcoming), ch. 1.

[52] For Tyraion see Xenophon, *Anab.* 1. 12. 14; Waelkens, *Türsteine*, 267–8 argues against Calder, *AJA* 36 (1932), 456; and *MAMA* vii. xvii that it retained civic status through the Hellenistic and imperial periods. The evidence is inconclusive. Laodicea Catacecaumene is only mentioned by Strabo as an intermediate point on the trade route from Ephesus to the East, whose description he takes from Artemidorus (14. 4. 29, 563). For further bibliography see Waelkens, *Türsteine*, 254. For Neapolis see n. 109.

[53] For Philomelium and its Macedonian founders, see A. Wilhelm, *Neue Beiträge Sb. Ak. Wien* (1910), 48–54; Holleaux, *Études*, iii. 357–63; Robert, *Villes*, 155–7; *Noms indigènes*, 40–41, 333–4.

[54] Robert, *A travers l'Asie Mineure*, 240–3; *Rev. phil.* (1934), 267–8 (*OMS* ii. 1167–8). *J Sav.* (1961), 90–1 nn. 10–12.

[55] See above, n. 50.

[56] Robert, *A travers l'Asie Mineure*, 243–4.

[57] It is obvious from the non-archaeological sources cited above that Hellenistic public buildings are waiting to be discovered in the more important settlements of Pontus and Cappadocia, especially the places which had enjoyed royal patronage.

domain of the cemetery or in the public areas of a city, is a centrally important feature of Greek civic culture; inscriptions from the region tell the same story as buildings. It is possible to list and describe the entire epigraphic harvest of pre-Roman Galatia, Cappadocia, and Pontus, excluding the south coastal cities of the Black Sea, in a single paragraph: the epitaph of Deiotarus' son found at Blucium (Karalar) in Galatia;[58] a text of the early second century BC from Amaseia in Pontus, set up for the Pontic king Pharnaces I by a phourarch, and another inscription from the same place which stated that only those with the phrourach's permission could enter the acropolis;[59] a Graeco-Aramaic bilingual inscription of the third century BC from north-eastern Cappadocia recording the activities of two Iranian satraps;[60] a Mithraic text perhaps of the same period, from southern Cappadocia;[61] and finally three inscriptions from genuinely Hellenized Cappadocian contexts: the decree of the Hanisenoi, perhaps of the late second century BC,[62] a dedication of the same period to Hermes and Heracles from the gymnasium of Eusebeia-Tyana,[63] and an honorific inscription, also from Tyana, for certain associates of Ariobarzanes III, set up between 52 and 42 BC.[64] Despite the illumination that some of these texts throw on the introduction of Hellenization to the area,[65] and despite the likelihood that renewed exploration will produce many additions to this tiny list, the most important remark that can be made about them is that they are extremely rare finds.

Coinage is another important mark of Hellenization. The only pre-Roman issues consist of coins, usually silver tetradrachms or drachms, issued by the kings of Cappadocia and Pontus;[66] bronze issues from a handful of Cappadocian communities, including Hanisa, Tyana, and Morimene in the third, and Eusebeia-Caesareia in the late first century BC;[67] a series of homogeneous bronze coins which were issued in the name of about a dozen communities of Paphlagonia and Pontus under Mithridates VI, but certainly at royal instigation;[68] occasional silver mintings by the last Galatian rulers, Deiotarus and Amyntas;[69] and the very rare and sporadic minting of silver by assorted central Anatolian communities in the late Hellenistic period: at Tavium, Pessinus, Soatra, and Iconium.[70] The wealth that was stored by Mithridates or Deiotarus in their various treasuries was doubtless gold or silver bullion, or precious objects, not coin.[71]

Galatia, Cappadocia, and Pontus on the eve of Roman rule presented a rich and diverse cultural mixture. In the western parts of central Anatolia Isaurians and Pisidians gave way to the peoples of the plateau—Lycaonians, Phrygians, and Celts; further east, and to the north, these were replaced by other strains from Paphlagonia, Pontus, and Cappadocia, whose cults and nomenclature show that the most powerful external influence came from further east, from Persia.[72] These races spoke a bewildering diversity of local languages, mostly completely unknown to us; an anecdote suggested that Mithridates Eupator himself was a master of all the twenty-two tongues that his subjects spoke.[73] To all this, Hellenism was a late and superficial addition.

III. Augustan City Foundations

The most appropriate place to start in assessing the development of urbanization under Roman rule is in north Galatia, the heartland of the Celtic tribes. Three new cities were created in a region where none had existed before, at Pessinus, Ancyra, and Tavium. All three date to the Augustan period, more precisely to the years immediately following the annexation of the province of Galatia c.25 BC. Tavium issued coins between AD 196 and 198 which carry an era date of 218, implying that the city was founded between 22 and 20 BC.[74] Pessinus used an era date both on coins and on inscriptions; the latter are not independently dated and so are unhelpful, but the coins, dating to the forty-third and fiftieth year of the city, both belong to the reign of

---

[58] *RECAM* ii no. 188.

[59] *OGIS* no. 365; *SP* iii no. 278.

[60] E. Lipiński, 'The Greek-Aramaic Inscription from Ağaca Kale', *Tenth Congress*, 267–72 (*SEG* xxix (1979), 1531).

[61] H. Gregoire, *CRAI* (1908), 437–47; for the date cf. *SEG* xxix (1979), 1532.

[62] See above, n. 28; for the date cf. Robert, *Noms indigènes*, 481; at least before 12–9 BC, when Mazaca-Eusebeia was renamed Caesareia.

[63] E. Preuner, *Ath. Mitt.* 46 (1921), 25 no. 42 (*SEG* i. 466; Robert, *Noms indigènes*, 492).

[64] H. Rott, *Kleinasiatische Denkmäler*, 370 no. 78.

[65] Exploited to the full by Robert, *Noms indigènes*, esp. 476 ff.

[66] Summary details in Head, *HN*² 499–502, 749–52.

[67] See above, n. 30; for the issues of Eusebeia/Caesareia, see Head, *HN*² 752. An obol issued by Laranda in the 4th cent. BC is discussed by P. Weiss, *Asia-Minor-Studien* 6 (1992), 145–6 n. 12.

[68] Head, *HN*² 502 ff. Imhoof-Blumer, *Num Zeitschr.* 45 (1912), 169–92.

[69] For coins of Deiotarus issued at Pessinus, see J. Devreker, *Fouilles de Pessinonte*, i. 17, 173–4 (Ch. 2 n. 83); for coins of Amyntas issued at Side and Cremna, see above, Ch. 3 n. 142.

[70] For Iconium, see Aulock, *Lykaonien*, nos. 190–244 (although these may be Augustan); Savatra, ibid., no. 154; Pessinus, Devreker, *Fouilles de Pessinonte*, i. 173–4; Tavium, *BMC Galatia* etc., 24 nos. 1–2.

[71] Cf. Strabo, 12. 3. 28, 555; 3. 31, 556; 5. 2, 567.

[72] Robert, *Noms indigènes, passim*, but esp. 503 ff.

[73] Sources cited by Reinach, *Mithridates Eupator*, 279 n. 1. The story was variously told, and the number of languages ranges from seventeen to fifty.

[74] Details in S. Mitchell, *Chiron*, 16 (1986), 20–1.

Tiberius. The latest possible date for the foundation of Pessinus can thus be established by subtracting fifty years from the date of Tiberius' death in AD 37, and the earliest by subtracting forty-three from the date of his accession in AD 14, giving a range between 29 and 13 BC.[75] The era of Ancyra is found on several inscriptions of the city and its territory.[76] None is independently dated, but none is inconsistent with a foundation in the early Augustan period. It is possible to argue that these three civic eras began at different dates, with Ancyra and perhaps Pessinus being founded *c.*25 BC when Galatia was annexed, and Tavium a few years later;[77] but it is preferable to assume that all three were founded simultaneously, in 22 or perhaps 21 BC.[78] Not only do they share names and titles that were derived from the same model, but their creation from the three Galatian tribes of the Tolistobogil, Tectosages, and Trocmi involved a redefinition of territorial boundaries that was surely synchronic. This conclusion allows the inference that the process of establishing Roman rule, including the regulation of city constitutions and city territories, had taken three or four years since Amyntas, the last pre-Roman ruler, died.[79]

The three communities were called, respectively, the Sebasteni Tolistobogii Pessinuntii,[80] the Sebasteni Tectosages Ancyrani,[81] and the Sebasteni Trocmi Taviani,[82] and the first element in each title underlines that it was an Augustan foundation. The titles are revealing in another way. They show that the population of the three Galatian tribes was considered to be identical with that of the three cities. Indeed, one Ancyran inscription describes its governing body as the council and people of the Sebasteni Tectosages.[83] It is not the case, however, that the tribal territories of the first century BC were simply transformed into city territories of the imperial period, for important changes were carried out which affected the relative importance of the communities. The Tolistobogii, who had hitherto been the strongest of the three tribes, suffered the most: their territory around Pessinus was confined to the area west of Mount Dindymus, reaching as far as the Sangarius, probably to its source.[84] The fertile land east of the mountain, well watered by springs and streams, and the lower part of the Tembris valley to the north were taken away to become the territory of the Augustan colony of Germa.[85] This isolated Pessinus from the northern parts of Tolistobogian country, where Deiotarus' strongholds had lain,[86] all of which was now assigned to Ancyra. Strabo remarks that the

---

[75] Inscriptions: A Domaszewski, *AEMÖ* 7 (1883), 182–3 no. 47 (J. Strubbe, *I. Pessinus*, no. 69). J. Mordtmann, *S.-Ber. München* (1860), 196 no. 14 (*I. Pessinus*, no. 94). Coins: M. Grant, *Num. Chron.* 6: 10 (1950), 43 no. 1 (year 43, in the governorship of Priscus), 2–3. (cf. Devreker, *Fouilles de Pessinonte*, i. 190–1 nos. 1–3); *SNG von Aulock*, 5020 is an example of the second type, misattributed to Etenna in Pisidia. The authors of *Index Aulock*, ii reassigned it to Galatia (presumably to the *koinon*), but not precisely to Pessinus.

[76] *RECAM* ii, p. 400, index for the list of inscriptions using era dates (where no. 156 is included in error). For Ancyra itself see Bosch, *Ankara*, nos. 133, 188, and 211 (all imperial period), and Byzantine texts collected by H. Grégoire, *Byzantion*, 4 (1927/8), 453 ff. *RECAM* ii no. 197 of the year 485 is a further example of the era being used at a late date.

[77] Levick, *Roman Colonies*, 193–4; I was agnostic in *RECAM* ii. 29–30.

[78] The view of E. Bosch, *Anadolu Araştırmaları*, i (1955), 68–74, who very reasonably wrote that 'Es ist sicher richtig, dass die drei Aeren miteinander korrespondierten, denn unmöglich konnen die galatischen städte, die in engen Beziehungen miteinander standen, verschiedene Zeitrechnungen gehabt haben.' See *Chiron*, 16 (1986), 21–2 for the complicated argument which leads me to prefer 22 BC over 21 BC. New arguments for the alternative view, however, have been put forward by W. Leschhorn, 'Die Anfänge der Provinz Galatia', in *Chiron*, 22 (1992); I am very grateful to him for showing me a copy of this in advance of publication.

[79] See also Ch. 5 n. 1 on the annexation date of Galatia.

[80] See coins of Ant. Pius and L. Verus, *SNG von Aulock*, 6210–11, 6217, 8725, and inscriptions, see J. Strubbe, *Fouilles de Pessinonte*, i. 217 n. 14.

[81] Pseudo-autonomous coins of the 1st cent. AD, *SNG von Aulock*, 6129, and Titus and Domitian, ibid. 6132–4; 2nd cent. inscriptions, Bosch, *Ankara*, nos. 92, 225.

[82] Coins from the pseudo-autonomous 1st-cent. AD issues (*BMC Galatia* etc., Tavium nos. 3 and 5) through Vespasian and Titus (ibid. nos. 1–2) to the Severan period (*SNG von Aulock*, 6240 ff.).

[83] Bosch, *Ankara*, no. 92; the inscription listing the Tiberian priests of Rome and Augustus at Ancyra (*Ankara*, no. 51, cf. *Chiron*, 16 (1986) 17–23) regularly uses the term ἔθνη to denote the tribes; however, the word πόλις refers to Ancyra in l. 27. It is, of course, probable that many inhabitants of the rural regions were not given full citizenship in the new cities. Elsewhere in Asia Minor rural inhabitants could be less privileged than their urban counterparts, for instance at Heracleia Pontica (Strabo, 12. 3. 4, 542), Prusias ad Hypium (*IGR* iii. 1427 = *I. Prusias*, no. 29; *IGR* iii. 69 = 1419 = *I. Prusias*, no. 17, with Ameling's commentary). But these country dwellers (τὴν ἀγροικίαν κατοικοῦντες) would still be juridically dependent on the cities. See below, Ch. 11 § III.

[84] See *RECAM* ii. 20–1, and J. Strubbe, in *Fouilles de Pessinonte*, i. 217. A coin of the time of Ant. Pius (*SNG von Aulock*, 6211 = *BMC Galatia* etc., Pessinus, no. 9), which depicts a reclining river god with an overturned water jar and reeds, shows that Pessinus' territory included the sources of the Sangarius near Çifteler. Compare Strabo, 12. 5. 3, 567, and especially 12. 3. 7, 543 (of the Sangarius) ἔχει δὲ τὰς πηγὰς κατὰ Σαγγίαν κώμην ἀφ' ἑκατὸν καὶ πεντήκοντα που σταδίων οὗτος Πεσσινοῦντος.

[85] For the territory of Germa see Waelkens, *Byzantion*, 49 (1979), 447–64, and *Die Kleinasiatische Türsteine*, 280–1; but note also K. Belke, *TIB* iv. 163, 166–8, 247; and *Festschrift für H. Hunger* (1984), 1–11; the discussion and below in Vol. II, Ch. 19 n. 48.

[86] See above, Ch. 4 n. 120.

influence of the priests at Pessinus was much reduced in his day, and this may be an allusion not only to the declining fortunes of the temple of Cybele and the growth of the secular power of the city, but also to the severe truncation of Tolistobogian territory which had taken place under Augustus.[87] The territory of Ancyra and the Tectosages was correspondingly increased. It certainly occupied the whole area between the Sangarius and the Halys; the northern boundary is ill determined but probably extended to the middle reaches of the Girmir Çay in the east, where Galatia gave way to Paphlagonia; in the south the territory was very extensive, for its nearest civic neighbours in this direction were Laodicea Catacecaumene and Iconium. It is likely, however, that some of the great estates of central Anatolia, which extend all over the region south of Ancyra, were outside civic jurisdiction.[88] The southern part of Ancyran territory may be a legacy from the activities of the independent Tectosages. If indeed the Tectosages had gained control of a large part of the Proseilemmene in the second century BC,[89] they appear to have retained it in their new guise under the empire. The territory of the Trocmi around Tavium remained substantially unaltered. In the west it reached the Halys, in the north-east it adjoined the territory of Amaseia, and in the south it stretched to the border of Cappadocia.[90]

It is clear from this that the Augustan arrangements for north Galatia involved a series of rulings about the territorial extent of each tribe, which were designed firstly to accommodate the new colony of Germa, and secondly to ensure that the boundaries of the city states were contiguous. Presumably by design Ancyra, henceforward to be the seat of the governor and the most important city of the province, was given a very large territory, while that of Pessinus was reduced. The obvious parallel for this series of administrative decisions is to be found in the arrangements whereby Pompey had divided the newly created province of Pontus into eleven *politeiai*, and assigned coterminous territories to them.[91] In that case, as in Galatia, the

initiative for creating the cities came not from the local population but from Rome.

Pompey's arrangements for Pontus were certainly incorporated in the *lex Pompeia*, whose other provisions, as far as they are known (principally from Pliny's letters to Trajan) concerned the internal organization of the cities of Pontus and Bithynia. As Cassius Dio says, it was concerned with constitutional and public law: it laid down regulations governing the age at which public office could be held; sought to control the size and composition of the city councils; and specified rules for the admission of new citizens to civic bodies.[92] Like its counterparts—the municipal and colonial laws of the Roman West—it also indicated the types of magistracy that a city should possess, especially in the case of newly founded cities. The influence of these hypothetical clauses in the *lex Pompeia* can be seen in the highly standardized groups of magistracies which are attested in the cities of Pompey's newly created province. The chief magistrates of each city were the *archontes*, an annually elected college of between three and five officers headed by a 'first archon' (*protos archon*). To distinguish them from lesser positions, these archonships were sometimes called the greatest or principal magistracies. The full terminology of these official positions can be deduced from the splendid and homogeneous group of late second- or early third-century-AD public inscriptions that have been preserved in the late Roman walls of Prusias ad Hypium, but the system is attested in many other Bithynian, Pontic, and Paphlagonian cities: Nicomedia, Nicaea, Prusa, Cius, Claudiopolis, Abonuteichus, Amastris, Amisus, Apamea, and Pompeiopolis.[93] The constitutions of these cities show a very Roman preoccupation with the duties of censors, whose responsibilities included the task of enforcing the terms of the *lex Pompeia* as far as it concerned the citizen bodies, governing councils, and magistracies of the cities.[94] *Timetai* are attested at Prusias ad Hypium, Nicaea, Heracleia Pontica, and Prusa, and *kosmetai* at Nicaea and Cius;[95] *politographoi* occur at Prusias and *boulographoi* at

[87] Strabo, 12. 5. 3, 567: οἱ δ' ἱερεῖς τὸ παλαῖον μὲν δυνάσται τινες ἦσαν, ἱερωσύνην καρπούμενοι μεγάλην. νυνὶ δὲ τούτων μὲν αἱ τιμαὶ πολὺ μεμείωνται, τὸ δ' ἐμπόριον συμμένει.

[88] A. Schulten, *Die römischen Grundherrschaften* (1896), esp. 9 ff.

[89] See above, Ch. 4 nn. 115–18.

[90] *RECAM* ii. 19; Robert, *A travers l'Asie Mineure* (1980), 99 for the western boundary at the Halys. A milestone of Hadrian found at Güngörmez, east of Çorum and according to the inscription 42 Roman miles from Amaseia, carries the formula *at* (= *ad*) *fines Galatorum*, and marks the NE corner of Tavian territory (D. French, *AS* 34 (1984), 11; *II Araş* (1984 pub. 1985), 123, 126 fig. 2). A second milestone with a similar text has been found at Bağlıca nearby, *III Araş* (1985 pub. 1986), 144.

[91] See above, Ch. 3 nn. 49–55.

[92] See A. N. Sherwin-White's commentary on Pliny, *Ep.* 10. 79–80, 112–15; A. J. Marshall, *JRS* 58 (1968), 103–9; Millar, *ERW* (1977), 397; de Ste Croix, *Class Struggle*, 529; S. Mitchell, *Eighth Congress*, 123.

[93] Briefly indicated by Mitchell, *Eighth Congress*, 123–4; the full case, with documentation, W. Ameling, *Epigr. Anat.* 3 (1984), 19–31.

[94] Ameling, op. cit. 27 with nn. 64–7; they are also mentioned by Pliny, *Ep.* 10. 72 and 79.

[95] For Nicaea see *ILS* 8867 (where the word is restored by Dessau), cf. *I. Iznik*, i. no. 56; Cius: *I. Kios* no. 16 (*IGR* iii. 24), l. 12. They appear to have been connected with the training of ephebes in the gymnasium.

Nicaea.[96] These offices occur only rarely outside Bithynia,[97] and they should surely be connected with the careful provisions of Pompey's law about the composition of the citizen body (the task of the *politographos*), and the composition and qualifications of the governing council (the task of the *boulographos* or *timetes*). The lesser civic magistracies also fall into a regular pattern, although they are much less extensively attested than the archonship. It seems safe to assume that each city had a secretary (*grammateus*), an *agoranomos* to control market prices, and treasurers (*tamiai*, *argyrotamiai*) to oversee the collection and above all the spending of public revenues. In some instances from Prusias ad Hypium a distinction was drawn between those who were responsible for money used to buy grain, and those concerned with buying oil. Most of the cities of Bithynia and Pontus were divided into tribes. Each of the twelve at Prusias ad Hypium was headed by a pair of phylarchs, representing a middle rank in the governing class of the city whose membership does not overlap with those eligible for the greatest magistracies but who, nevertheless, to judge from the frequency with which they erected honorific inscriptions, played a conspicuous part in public life.[98]

It is striking that the constitutions of Ancyra and Pessinus closely resembled this Bithynian pattern. In each there were 'first archons', archons, *agoranomoi*, secretaries, tribes, and phylarchs.[99] Neither constitution contained any unusual or distinctive magistracy apart from *boulographoi* and *politographoi* which both occur at Ancyra and point to a connection with

Bithynia.[100] The simplest explanation of these links and similarities is to suppose that when the cities of north Galatia were founded, the terms of the *lex Pompeia* served as a model, *mutatis mutandis*, to be applied in Galatia. Moreover, the aim of these arrangements would have been the same as it had been in Pontus and Bithynia, to ensure that the cities survived as viable self-governing units, and that their authority extended over the whole of provincial territory.

The simultaneous creation of cities at Pessinus, Ancyra, and Tavium, by a deliberate act of Roman policy soon after the annexation of Galatia, marked an important step towards the urbanization of the province. They were matched by an even more extensive series of foundations, namely the Roman colonies or colonial settlements, whose foundation dates and strategic significance have already been discussed. Apart from Germa in north Galatia[101] they were situated in and around the Tauric highlands, and even more clearly than the cities of north Galatia they reflect a deliberate act of policy.

Colonies had constitutions which were laid down by Roman laws; we possess one specimen, the *lex Coloniae Genetivae Iuliae* of the Caesarian period (*ILS* 6087), but all no doubt adhered closely to a standard format which is reflected in the stereotyped range of magistracies which are attested by the coins and inscriptions of the Galatian communities and of colonies elsewhere. Detailed study of the constitution of Antioch and five other Pisidian colonies shows them to have possessed *duoviri* and *duoviri quinquennales* in the highest offices, as well as aediles and quaestors in junior positions, and the same magistracies can be found in several of the other Augustan foundations. A duovir, aediles, and a quaestor are found at Germa, a duovir at Iconium, and duoviri and a quaestor at the Claudian colony of Archelais.[102] There is no doubt at all that these eastern colonies had a broadly similar formal structure to colonies in the West and they introduced a distinctively Roman form of political organization to the Greek world. The evidence from Antioch and elsewhere shows that they were not

---

[96] *I. Prusias* nos. 3, 4, 10, and 17 (the last with Ameling's commentary). *I. Iznik*, ii. 1 no. 726, following the restoration of L. Robert, *BCH* 52 (1928), 410–11 (*OMS* ii. 1278). The stone is attributed to Cius by Corsten, *I. Kios*, no. 7.

[97] See L. Robert, *OMS* ii. 1278 n. 8 on *kosmetai*, and 882 on *timetai*, which are rarely attested elsewhere in the Greek East (Aphrodisias, Pergamum, Cyprus). *Politographoi* are known from the Hellenistic period, where the office-holders on record were involved in increasing the citizen body (cf. Kiessling, *RE* xxi. 1403 citing *SIG*³ 472 l. 41 (Ephesus, 85 BC); 633 l. 63 (Miletus and Heraclea ad Latmum, *c*.180 BC); 543 l. 26 (Larisa in Thessaly, 214 BC); 426 l. 30 (Bargylia, 270–261 BC)). In these instances it appears that the πολιτογραφηθέντες had lower status than full citizens. The office is also found at Nacolea in Phrygia in the imperial period, where the recorded task of the magistrate was to restrict the numbers of those eligible for a corn dole (*CIL* iii. 6998 with note; republished as *MAMA* v no. 202). *I. Prusias*, no. 17 shows the *politographes* enlarging the citizen body by enrolling rural inhabitants.

[98] See Ameling, *Epigr. Anat.* 3 (1984), 26–7, and the long list of inscriptions from Prusias set up by phylarchs, *I. Prusias*, nos. 1–16.

[99] See below, ch. 12 § II.

[100] T. Flavius Gaianus held the office of *politographos* at Ancyra under Caracalla (*Ankara*, nos. 249–53, *AS* 27 (1977), 73 no. 7), and Cl. Caecilius Hermianus *c.* mid-3rd cent. (*Ankara*, nos. 287–8; a squeeze of no. 287 in the Kleinasiatische Kommission in Vienna shows that the reading in line 4 is not ι′ but γ′, indicating that Caecilius Hermianus, who had been *boulographos* twice, held the office not ten but three times).

[101] For Germa as an Augustan foundation, see S. Mitchell, *JRS* 64 (1974), 29; note the corrections of M. Waelkens, *Byzantion*, 49 (1979), 462–4.

[102] Germa: *RECAM* ii no. 91 (aedile); Iconium; *ILS* 9414 (IIvir, eirenarch, sebastophant); Archelais: D. H. French, *TAD* 23 (1976), 52; *ZPE* 27 (1977), 247–9.

immune to local influences since inscriptions frequently mention Greek magistracies in the colonies, including gymnasiarchs, *grammateis*, *agonothetai*, and *agoranomoi*.[103] Colonial charters could readily be modified as circumstances changed.

When the colonies were founded Augustus was by no means a totally free agent. After the battle of Actium he was faced with the daunting task of finding land not only for his own veterans but also for the armies of his enemies, Antony and Lepidus, which were now under his command. He claims in the *Res Gestae* to have settled 300,000 out of the 500,000 men who served under him between 30 and 2 BC, at a personal cost of 1260 million sesterces.[104] It was an urgent priority both to find land to accommodate such large numbers, and to find economical ways in which to appropriate it. The colonial settlements in Galatia reflect both constraints. Firstly, they do not all correspond to a single format but demonstrate a flexible approach to the question of choosing sites which enabled Augustus to maximize the opportunities offered in southern Asia Minor. Seven of the foundations were colonies pure and simple, either set up where there had been no previous settlement of any consequence as at Germa; or supplanting the existing community once and for all, as at Antioch, Comama, Olbasa, Cremna, Parlais, and Lystra. The same approach was adopted at Ninica and Iconium, but there in the course of time, the native towns were allowed to develop as autonomous units, and during the reign of Claudius both became double communities, consisting of a *polis* side by side with a colony. At Iconium the colony seems to have absorbed the *polis* in the time of Hadrian; at Ninica, by a reverse process, all trace of the small and isolated colony eventually disappeared, leaving simply the city of Claudiopolis.[105] Attaleia, Isaura, Apollonia, and Neapolis make up a third group of communities where the existing population was too large or too influential to be absorbed into the colony, and here the Roman veterans were introduced into the constitution of the city, in the first two cases as *sympoliteuomenoi Romaioi* (Romans who belonged to the polis), and in the last two as *coloni*.[106] Another consideration which clearly influenced the choice of colonial sites was the availability of land. It is highly probable that land for the colonists of Antioch was originally part of the territory owned by the temple of

Men Askaenus, which was bought or confiscated by the commissioners who were sent to administer the inheritance of Amyntas in 25 BC.[107] We are not told what hardship this caused the local inhabitants, or how much it cost the emperor. So far as we know the people of Antioch had been supporters of Amyntas (and therefore of Rome) in the years before 25 BC, and had done nothing to merit punishment.

To the south, however, it appears that a good deal of the land between Neapolis and Isaura had been confiscated to become Roman *ager publicus* after the campaigns of Servilius Isauricus. The evidence is clearest in the case of Orondian territory; Cicero tells us that Servilius' successes led Rome to acquire public land known as the *ager Orondicus*, and this should be identical to a *tractus Oronticus* mentioned by the elder Pliny.[108] In the same context Pliny also refers to a *tractus Cillanicus*, which clearly comprised all or part of the Cillanian plain in which Neapolis lay. It is plausible and economical to conjecture that it had shared the same history as the *tractus Oronticus*, had become *ager publicus* in the late republic, and was used to provide land for the veterans whom Augustus certainly settled there.[109] The *tractus Oronticus* itself appears not to have received colonists but under the empire became an imperial estate;[110] nor do we know the fate or status of a tract of public land near Amblada in the valley between Lake Beyşehir and Lake Suğla,[111] but there should surely have been much public land in the territory of Isaura itself, and it was probably this that passed to Amyntas when he is said to have taken over Isaura 'from the Romans'.[112] In the same passage in which he refers to the *ager Orondicus*, Cicero mentions two other unidentified tracts of public land acquired by Servilius, the *ager Gedusanus* and the *ager Agerensis*; neither has been identified, and editors have suspected that the names may have been corrupted in the transmission of the text. If they are right, the simplest way to emend the second name is to

---

[103] Cf. Levick, *Roman Colonies* 74 ff; note, however, that ἀγοράνομος could reproduce *aedilis* (*RECAM* ii no. 91).
[104] Implied by *Res Gestae* 3 and 16 (600,000 HS for Italian land, 260,000 HS for provincial land; 400,000 HS for *praemia militiae* between 7 and 2 BC).
[105] See *Historia*, 28 (1979), 411–35.
[106] S. Mitchell, *Tenth Congress*, 311–18; cf. J. and L. Robert, *Bull. ép.* (1980), no. 387.

[107] Strabo 12. 8. 14, 577, elucidated by Jones, *CERP*² 134 and Levick, *Roman Colonies*, 219–20.
[108] Cicero, *Agr.* 2. 50 (cf. 11. 50); Pliny, *NH* 5. 147.
[109] For the *coloni* at Neapolis, see Mitchell, *Tenth Congress*, 317–18. The site of Neapolis has been localized not, as formerly supposed, at Şarkıkaraağaç, but to the south at a place called İznebolu (that is εἰς Νεάπολιν) near the village of Kiyakdede, at the NE corner of Lake Beyşehir, a little N of Kireli (which was the centre of the Orondian imperial state). See D. H. French *AS* 34 (1984), 11 and *II Araş.* (1984 publ. 1985), 124 and 128 fig. 6, a dedication set up by Νεαπολειτῶν [ἡ] πόλις. Cf. H. S. Cronin, *JHS* 22 (1902), 108; W. Ruge, *RE* xvi (1935), 2126–7.
[110] See below, Ch. 10 § III n. 135.
[111] A. S. Hall, *AS* 18 (1968), 77–8 no. 24.
[112] Strabo, 12. 6. 3, 569.

suppose that Cicero originally wrote *ager Isaurensis* which was corrupted into *Agerensis* by simple ditto-graphy.[113] Cicero also tells us that Servilius acquired public land on the coast at Attaleia, Olympus, and Phaselis, confiscated no doubt from communities or individuals who had aided the pirates. Once again, it is reasonable to suppose that the *ager publicus* at Attaleia formed the basis for the colonial allotments there.[114] There is nothing surprising in all this. Siculus Flaccus, writing in the reign of Nero, indicates that *ager publicus* was highly favoured as a source of land for colonists, since it could be acquired at little or no cost.[115] Augustus will gladly have seized the opportunity made available by Servilius' conquests to keep his own expenses to a minimum level.

There is only one other item of evidence which reveals a possible source of land for the Pisidian colonists. A fragmentary inscription of Apollonia, known only from a single copy and variously restored since, appears to record the reallocation to the city of territory which had previously been assigned to Tymbriada by an unnamed king. The most convincing interpretation of the text suggests that it should be dated to the founda-tion of the province of Galatia and that the king should be identified as Amyntas.[116] The theory is not susceptible of proof, but if it is correct it is tempting to go one step further and suppose that the reallocation was made to accommodate Apollonia's new colonists. Here too the cost to Augustus would have been modest for it is not likely that Tymbriada reveived compensa-tion for the land which it lost.

The creation of colonies over so much of the new province did not simply help solve Augustus' problems with surplus military manpower after the civil wars, or ensure the security of newly pacified territory, im-portant as these two achievements were; it also marked a massive advance in the urbanization of the new province.

IV. *City Foundations from Tiberius to Hadrian: The North*

Before the creation of Roman provinces in northern Anatolia, Paphlagonia and Pontus, like much of the rest of central and eastern Anatolia, were divided into rural districts whose names usually end in the suffix -ene

or -itis. Northern and eastern Paphlagonia comprised the districts of Blaene and Domanitis, which adjoined the territory of Sinope in the valley of the river Amnias, and were incorporated into the territory of Pompeiopolis; and Pimolisene to the south, which straddled the river Halys.[117] Towards Bithynia in western Paphlagonia lay the domain of Gaezatorix and the districts of Timonitis, Marmolitis, Sanisene, Potamia, and Climiatene; the last covering the western slopes of Mount Olgassys.[118] Pontus was similarly divided. Strabo's account of the creation of the city of Zela shows how these rural districts were related to Pompey's city foundations. Pompey, he says, attached several *eparchiai* to the existing temple state at Zela and called it a city; he also united the regions of Culupene and Camisene to form the territory of Megalopolis. Moreover the district of Caranitis, which has been ruled by the Galatian dynast Ateporix, was also called an *eparchia*.[119] These passages appear to give the technical term by which these rural districts were known. However, *eparchia* is the familiar and common Greek word normally used by Strabo for all or part of a Roman province, not for a modest rural district, and there is much to be said for the suggestion that what Strabo actually wrote in these cases was *hyparchia*, less well-attested but familiar as a term used to describe a subdivision of a satrapy in the Seleucid and, by implication, the Persian empire.[120] In any case, Pompey, in order to create new cities, had brought together the *eparchiai* or *hyparchiai* into which the country had been divided to make up larger units, his new *poleis* with their huge territories. He did not of

[117] Strabo, 12. 3. 40, 562.

[118] Strabo, 12. 3. 41, 562.

[119] Strabo, 12. 3. 37, 560: Πομπήιος δὲ πολλὰς ἐπαρχίας προσώρισε τῷ τόπῳ (Zela) καὶ πόλιν ὠνόμασε καὶ ταύτην καὶ τὴν Μεγαλόπολιν, συνθεὶς ταύτην τε εἰς ἓν τήν τε Κουλουπηνὴν καὶ τὴν Καμισηνὴν, . . . οἱ δὲ μετὰ ταῦτα ἡγέμονες τῶν Ῥωμαίων τῶν δυεῖν πολιτευμάτων τούτων τὰ μὲν τοῖς Κομάνων ἱερεῦσι προσένειμαν, τὰ δὲ τῷ Ζήλων ἱερεῖ, τὰ δ' Ἀτεπόριγι . . . τελευτήσαντος δ' ἐκείνου, ταύτην μὲν τὴν μερίδα, οὐ πολλὴν οὖσαν, ὑπὸ Ῥωμαίοις εἶναι συμβαίνει καλουμένην ἐπαρχίαν, καὶ ἔστι σύστημα καθ' αὑτὸ τὸ πολίχνιον συνοικίσαντων ⟨αὐτῶν⟩ τὰ Κάρανα, ἀφ' οὗ ἡ χώρα Καρανῖτις λέγεται (text of Lasserre).

[120] The proposal was made by F. Cumont, *REG* 14 (1901), 39 n. 1 precisely in connection with the restoration of line 37 of the Gangra oath. It has not been heeded by editors of Strabo, but Cumont drew attention to the fact that the families of words beginning ὑπαρχ- and ἐπαρχ- are often confused in Strabo's manuscripts. So, A. Meinecke, *Vindiciarum Straboniarum liber* (1852), 130 on 9. 394 (ὑπάρξαντας in the MSS where ἐπάρξαντας should be read). In 4. 1. 3, 142 and 1. 9, 184 the MSS have ὑπαρχίας but all editors since Coraes have emended to ἐπαρχίας. For hyparchies as subdivisions of the Seleucid empire, see B. Hausoullier, *Rev. phil.* (1901). 24; E. H. Minns, *JHS* 25 (1915), 22 ff. esp. p. 43 (Parthia); Dittenberger's notes on *OGIS* 225. 36 and 238. 1 (this is the clearest reference of all, to οἱ ἐν τῆι περὶ Ἔριζαν ὑπαρχίαι φυλακῖται; Welles, *RC*, 371). For the term *eparchia*, see now T. Drew Bear, *ANRW* II. 18. 3, 1974–7.

---

[113] None of the other emendations that have been suggested at this point is at all convincing. See H. A. Ormerod, *JRS* 12 (1922), 47 as well as the standard editions of the speech.

[114] Mitchell, *Tenth Congress*, 312–14.

[115] Siculus Flaccus, *De cond. agr.* p. 100 (Thulin).

[116] Mitchell, *Tenth Congress*, 316–17; discussing Sterrett, *WE* no. 548 (rival restorations are set out by Ramsay, *JHS* 38 (1918), 139–50). Note, however, the justifiable caution of Levick, *Roman Colonies*, 45 n. 1.

course abolish the old districts, for inscriptions of the imperial period and other later sources often refer to rural districts and village territories by the traditional names. So there were districts called Zeitene, Karzene, and Kimistene in Paphlagonia,[121] and Kalmizene, Lagantine, and Mnizene in Galatia.[122] A series of texts discovered at the sanctuary of Zeus Stratios in the territory of Amaseia records dedications made to the god by delegates from the whole Pontic area; illustrated example mention communities from Pimolisene and the Babanomitis, both familiar from Strabo's description, thereby showing that the regional divisions of the first century BC survived long after they had ceased to operate as the primary administrative units.[123]

The urbanization of the Paphlagonian kingdom of Deiotarus Philadelphus, which had passed to Rome in 6/5 BC, should be seen against this background. The key document from the early empire is the oath of allegiance sworn to Augustus in 3 BC, whose text was found at Vezirköprü, east of the Kızıl Irmak on the main highway through northern Anatolia.[124] Broadly speaking it confirms that Paphlagonia was little if at all urbanized at this date, but the details are not all clear. Initially the oath was administered in Gangra, the old royal palace, to the inhabitants (katoikountes) of Paphlagonia and Romans who were doing business among them. The wording of the text specified a place or building at Gangra where this was to take place, but damage to the stone has obscured what this was.[125] Gangra itself does not seem to have been a city and the term katoikountes, commonly used in other contexts to describe rural inhabitants of Anatolia in contrast to city dwellers, is also an indication of the status of the Paphlagonian population and settlements.[126] The oath was then taken by the people of the region at large. The restored text indicates that this was done by the inhabitants of the countryside (chora) at the Sebasteia in the hyparchies. This would confirm that, as one would expect, the rural areas of Paphlagonia were still divided up into the districts described by Strabo three

years after annexation by Rome. Unfortunately this cannot be claimed beyond doubt since the words chora and hyparchiai have both been restored to the inscription and do not survive on the stone.[127] The final clause of the text relates to the taking of the oath by the community which erected the inscription, namely the Phazimonitai who now live in the place called Neapolis. This phraseology closely echoes Strabo's description of this people, and he also states that Neapolis had been founded by Pompey.[128] However, the fact that the Phazimonitai seem to be subsumed within the rural dwellers of Paphlagonia, and the use in an official document of their local name in a preferred position to that of the new city, suggests that urban life had not taken root here. In confirmation it appears that Neapolis did not survive under the empire but gave way to a new foundation, Neoclaudiopolis.[129]

The Paphlagonian section of the province of Galatia certainly extended beyond the bounds of ethnic Paphlagonia. In the west lay a district adjoining Bithynia inhabited in the first century AD by a people called the Caisareis Proseilemmenitae, later to become the city of Caesareia Hadrianopolis.[130] This was apparently a part of Bithynia that became attached to Galatia under Augustus. A number of inscriptions found in the communities of Kimistene and Karzene, which belonged to Hadrianopolis, use an era which is presumed by their editor to have begun in 6/5 BC like that of the rest of Paphlagonia, giving a series ranging

---

[121] I. Kaygusuz, ZPE 49 (1982), 177 no. 1 for Xeitene; for Zeus Karzenos (BCH 21 (1897), 98 no. 12) and Zeus Kimistenos (BCH 25 (1901), 24 no. 161), see Kaygusuz, Epigr. Anat. 4 (1984), 63–8 and 69–72 (also TAD 26. 2 (1983), 111–45).

[122] RECAM ii, 22.

[123] D. H. French, AS 35 (1985), 9–10, photographs in III Araş. (1984; pub. 1985), 149 figs. 5–6. Note also a boundary stone recorded at Kale Köy, SE of Amaseia, reading Δακοπηνῆς Γαλαλῶν, H. Grégoire, BCH 23 (1909), 21 no. 7.

[124] F. Cumont, REG 14 (1901), 27; SP iii. 75 no. 66; (ILS 8781; IGR iii. 137; OGIS 532; P. Herrmann, Der Romische Kaiserreid (1968), 123–4 no. 4).

[125] [K]α[ισαρείωι] is perhaps the most favoured reading, but for alternatives see Herrmann, Der Romische Kaiserreid, 97 n. 26.

[126] See especially the evidence collected by W. Ameling in his commentary on I. Prusias, no. 17.

[127] Cumont reported reading YI in l. 37, the crucial point for the restoration of ὑπ[αρχίας]. No one has offered a plausible alternative.

[128] Strabo, 12. 3. 38, 560: ἡ Φαζιμωνῖτις . . . ἦν Πομπήιος Νεα-πολῖ⟨τι⟩ν ὠνόμασε, κατὰ Φαζημῶνα κώμην ⟨. . . πόλιν⟩ ἀπο-δείξας τὴν κατοικίαν καὶ προσαγορεύσας Νεάπολιν.

[129] There is a topographical problem concerned with the site of Neapolis. The town of Vezirköprü is the find spot of the Gangra oath inscription, and also of a dedication of AD 282 set up for the emperor Carinus by the city of Neoclaudiopolis (JHS 20 (1900), 152; SP iii no. 67; IGR iii. 139). Ruge, RE xvi. 2 (1935), 2394–6 argued that the site of Phazimon-Neapolis should be clearly distinguished from that of Andrapa-Neoclaudiopolis (the old village name of Andrapa is preserved alongside that of Neoclaudiopolis by Ptolemy and reasserted itself in the late empire); he suggested, with Jerphanion, Mél. Univ. St. Joseph, 5 (1911), that the text with the Gangra oath had been carried from the plain of Merzifon to the south, which contained the true site of Phazimon-Neapolis. Against this, see Magie, RR ii. 1067–8, who stresses the point that the plain round Merzifon was always, as far as we know, part of the territory of Amaseia. If Neapolis had been situated at or near Merzifon, its territory would have had to be transferred to Amaseia between the date of the Gangra oath and AD 17/18 when Strabo completed book 12, which includes an account of Amaseian territory which certainly takes in this area. Magie's solution seems preferable, despite F. Lasserre, Budé Strabo, ix. 230.

[130] R. Leonhardt, Paphlagonia (1915), 244 ff.; G. Mendel, BCH 25 (1901), 5–10; OGIS 539, a statue for Nerva.

from AD 204/5 to 262/3.[131] However, although on this dating only one inscription out of six dates before AD 212, none of the persons named in them was an Aurelius. For this reason, one should prefer an earlier era, most probably the Pompeian era for Pontus and Bithynia beginning in 63 BC, which gives a series running much more plausibly from AD 147/8 to 205/6. If this argument is valid, it suggests that the district had been part of Pompey's province. The title of the inhabitants, Caisareis Proseilemmenitae, is evidence that they had been added on to something else, almost certainly under Augustus; moreover we know that by the time of Hadrian they were under the authority of the governor of Galatia.[132] It is plausible, therefore, to suggest that they were added to the province of Galatia in the early imperial period, either on the occasion of the death of Deiotarus Philadelphus in 6/5 BC, or at some other time. The district, as has been seen, remained without a city until the time of Hadrian.

Paphlagonian territory also extended further to the east than the traditional regional boundaries, for, whatever the exact location of Neapolis may have been, the Phazimonitis included a large tract of fertile land east of the Halys which was explicitly described as part of Pontus by Strabo.[133] Cities took the place of the hyparchies here and in central Paphlagonia in the time of Tiberius and Claudius. The community round the old fortress and palace at Gangra was refounded as a city called Germanicopolis, either under Tiberius, when it may reflect the activities of Germanicus himself in the east in AD 17–18,[134] or under the latter's son Claudius,[135] who was obviously responsible for creating the new centre of the Phazimonitis, Neoclaudiopolis, which certainly lay at or near Vezirköprü.[136] The third Paphlagonian city was Pompeiopolis, which lay at Taşköprü in the valley of the Amnias north of Mount Olgassys. Since Strabo treats it as a city, and since it retained its original name throughout the empire, it is fair to assume that unlike Neapolis it did not decline

to the point where reformation was necessary.[137] Its position on the main military route through northern Anatolia made it a place of considerable and growing importance, and coins and inscriptions of the second century show that it became the metropolis of Paphlagonia, while Gangra, which had evidently been regarded as the centre in 3 BC, had to console itself with titles which commemorated its antiquity and its mythological pre-eminence.[138] It is quite possible that the change in status had come in the early years of the province, as it had in Galatia when Tectosagan Ancyra was given precedence and territorial advantages at the expense of Pessinus, but there can be no certainty without fresh evidence. It is clear, however, that by the reign of Claudius the territories of the three cities of Gangra-Germanicopolis, Pompeiopolis, and Neoclaudiopolis occupied a huge swathe of central and eastern Paphlagonia between the territories of Ancyra, Tavium, and Pessinus in the south and that of Sinope on the Pontic coastline to the north.[139]

In Pontus we can reconstruct a similar picture, although the process is complicated by the several stages in which the Romans took over the client kingdoms and dynasties. It seems reasonably clear that in 3 BC the disposition of cities and territories was as follows: Amaseia belonged to kings, possibly, as suggested above (Ch. 3 nn. 156–7), to the Galatian king Brigatus. To the east, Comana was ruled by another Galatian Dyteutus, and his territory was surrounded by that of Pythodoris of Tralles, the queen of Pontus, who had succeeded her husband, Polemo I, around 8 BC.[140] This comprised the Phanaroea (with Magnopolis), the Zelitis, and the Megalopolitis. She also held Cabeira/Diospolis which she renamed Sebaste and made her capital.[141] Part of the old territory of Megalopolis or Zela, known as the Caranitis, was in the hands of a Galatian dynast, Ateporix.[142] In the east, Armenia Minor belonged to Archelaus of Cappadocia, whose kingdom thus stretched from Cilicia Tracheia almost to the Euxine, while Trapezus,

131 I. Kaygusuz, *Epigr. Anat.* 4 (1984), 64 no. 3; 66 no. 8; 67 and no. 10 (Karzene); 71 nos. 8 and 10; 72 no. 14 (Kimistene).

132 Namely C. Iulius Scapula, AD 136–8, attested as governor here (and also at Ancyra), *IGR* iii. 151 (cf. Vol. II, App 1. n. 39). See now C. Marek, *Stadt, Ara und Territorium in Pontus-Bithynia und Nord-Galatia* (1993), 116–22 for a better interpretation.

133 xii. 3. 38, 560.

134 For Germanicus' activities in Asia Minor, where his principal achievement (or at least that of his deputy Q. Veranius) was to organize the province of Cappadocia; see W. Orth, *Die Provinzialpolitik des Tiberius* (1970), 94 ff.; Lasserre, *Strabo*, ix. 8–9. For the retention of the name Gangra to denote the old citadel, see Robert, *A travers l'Asie Mineure*, 205 with n. 29.

135 Robert, *A travers l'Asie Mineure*, 217 believes that the transformation of Gangra into a city took place 'sans doute sous Claude'. Not, however, 'sans aucun doute'!

136 See above, n. 129.

137 Strabo, 12. 3. 40, 562. The only problem with this is the apparent absence of any reference to Pompeiopolis in the terms for administering the Gangra oath.

138 See Robert, *A travers l'Asie Mineure*, 217–19. There is no evidence, however, to support his more precise suggestion that 'le nom dynastique de Germanicopolis avec ce qu'il supposait d'avantages materiels, ne fut…octroyé à la ville en compensation du titre de metropole donné a Pompeiopolis' (217 n. 76).

139 For the territories of the three cities, see F. Cumont, *REG* 14 (1901), 33–7; Robert, *A travers l'Asie Mineure*, 208 ff.

140 See above, Ch. 3 §IV for the circumstances of these dynastic appointments. For Amaseia, see Strabo, 12. 3. 39, 561; Comana: 3. 35, 558; Pythodoris: ἡ νῦν βασιλεύουσα ἐν τῷ Πόντῳ (14. 1. 42, 649), Strabo, 12. 3. 37, 539.

141 Strabo, 12. 3. 31, 557.

142 Strabo, 12. 3. 37, 560.

Pharnaceia, and the tribes in their hinterland belonged again to Pythodoris.[143] Some time after Polemo's death Pythodoris married Archelaus, and between them, with the exception of the Galatian enclaves and the kingdom of the Tarcondimotids in Cilicia Pedias, they controlled the whole of non-Roman Asia Minor west of the Euphrates.

In 3 BC Ateporix died and his kingdom, lying east of the Trocmian part of Galatia, passed to Rome. A city, Sebastopolis, was founded at its centre which used 3 BC for its era date.[144] Directly adjacent to the Caranitis in the south and to Paphlagonia in the west, Amaseia followed in 3/2 BC, and the area became known as Pontus Galaticus with Amaseia as the chief city.[145]

Dyteutus died in 34/5 AD and Comana became part of Pontus Galaticus. Archelaus' Cappadocian possessions were annexed and placed under a procurator in AD 17, when he was brought to trial at Rome.[146] Armenia Minor probably passed to Pythodoris. The date of her death is unknown, but in 38/9 AD all her possessions were given by Gaius to her grandson Polemo II.[147] Thus they remained until AD 64 when the Pontic cities were annexed to make up Pontus Polemoniacus. The metropolis of the area was Pythodoris' old capital Cabeira/Diospolis/Sebaste, which took the name Neocaesareia, possessed to this day by the Turkish town of Niksar. The same era, beginning in AD 64/5, was used by Cerasus, Zela, Trapezus, and Megalopolis-Sebasteia.[148] Throughout this period, Pompey's policy of administering Pontus by organizing cities under the rule of Rome was gradually being re-enacted. There is absolutely no documentary evidence to show in detail how this process was taking place, but it is safe to assume that the arrangements for the cities made by Pompey in 63 BC, where they had fallen into abeyance under dynastic rule, were simply brought into operation again. Zela and Amaseia retained the names that they had always used; Neoclaudiopolis, Neocaesareia, and Sebasteia replaced the Pompeian foundations of Neapolis, Diospolis, and Megalopolis; Eupatoria-Magnopolis

must have been swallowed up by Neoclaudiopolis or Neocaesareia, its neighbours to west and east, for there seems to have been no imperial city there; the district around Carana and the sacred territory of Comana were organized into the *poleis* of Sebastopolis and Comana respectively, presumably on the same model as the others. The final Pompeian city in north-east Anatolia was Nicopolis, in Armenia Minor. The district remained under dynasts until about AD 71; once it was annexed to the Galatian Cappadocian complex Nicopolis simply resumed its position as the only city in the region.[149] The boundaries between these cities doubtless corresponded more or less to the boundaries described or implied in Strabo's description of Pontus. On the ground they seem to have been marked by long raised banks, which are still to be seen in places.[150] The urbanization of Pontus, or at least the division of the region into contiguous city territories, was therefore complete by the beginning of the Flavian period. Genuine urban development, above all the construction of public buildings, may not have occurred until the second century AD.[151]

v. *City Foundations from Tiberius to Hadrian: The South*

The reigns of Tiberius and Claudius were also crucial in the development of the southern parts of Galatia. In this period cities were founded in the whole of the northern Taurus, and the southern half of the central plateau, from Olba of the Cennatae in the east to Seleuceia Sidera in the west, thus filling in the gaps between the territories of the Roman colonies.

In the hinterland of Rugged Cilicia above Seleuceia on the Calycadnus, in the small kingdom ruled by M. Antonius Polemo,[152] the old tribal capital of the Cennatae, Olba, yielded priority to its neighbour Diocaesareia, which honoured Tiberius in an inscription as its saviour and founder,[153] clearly signifying an

[143] Dio, 54. 9. 2; Strabo, 12. 3. 39, 555–6.
[144] H. Dessau, *ZfN* (1906), 339 (Head, *HN*² 499); Magie, *RR* ii. 1285. There are two dated inscriptions, *IGR* iii. 111 (= *ILS* 8801) and 114.
[145] For the era see Babelon, *Recueil général*, 140.
[146] Tacitus, *Ann.* 2. 42; Suetonius, *Tib.* 37. 4; Cassius Dio, 57. 17. 3; Strabo, 12. 1. 4, 534.
[147] Magie, *RR* ii. 1368; R. D. Sullivan, *ANRW* ii. 7. 2 (1980), 921.
[148] For the annexation of this region, the kingdom of Polemo II, son of Pythodoris, see Vol. II, App. 1 nn. 42–3. W. Wieser, *Schw. Num. Rundsch.* 68 (1989), 58–61 shows that Megalopolis-Sebasteia used the same era as the other cities of Pontus Polemniacus, not beginning in 2 BC–AD 2, as supposed by Babelon, *Recueil général*, 140.

[149] For civic inscriptions of Nicopolis see *IGR* iii. 132; *BCH* 33 (1909), 35 no. 13 = *AE* (1909), 19 calling it an Ἰταλικὴ κολωνία in the time of Gordian III. The identification of Megalopolis with Sebasteia, and hence with modern Sivas, is not proved beyond doubt. Megalopolis was the only name known to Strabo; Pliny, *NH* 6. 8 indicates that Sebasteia and Sebastopolis were the two cities of Culupene. The imperial names were probably conferred at the time of annexation.
[150] D. H. French, *AS* 33 (1983), 10 for walls at Altınyayla in the province of Sivas which may mark the territorial boundaries between Sebasteia, Melitene, and Caesareia; *AS* 35 (1985), 10 for a boundary wall in the Çamlıbel pass between Sebasteia and Sebastopolis.
[151] See below, Ch. 12.
[152] R. D. Sullivan, *Num. Chron.* 7: 19 (1979), 6–20.
[153] The inscription published by A.-M. Verilhac and G. Dagron, *REA* 78 (1974), 237–42 shows Olba to have been the centre of the Kannatai in the 1st cent. BC. For the creation of a new

advance in Diocaesareia's status. Another Cilician city, Germanicopolis, which lay to the west of the Calycadnus, appears to have been founded in the same period.[154] Germanicopolis was one of the communities of the Lalasseis, a tribe which had minted in conjunction with the Cennatae, and whose chief centre was at Ninica, the site of one of Augustus' colonies. It may have been emulation of its neighbour that led the native community at Ninica to seek the status of a *polis*. At all events before long there was a double community in the valley of the Calycadnus, at the point where the road from Seleuceia begins to climb steeply up into the mountains and over into the Lycaonian plain, Ninica Claudiopolis, consisting of a Greek city side by side with the Roman colony.[155]

There is a similar pattern to the urbanization of the Orondian tribe, which occupied the hilly territory west of Iconium as far as Lake Beyşehir. The Orondeis had originally been conquered by Servilius Isauricus, who had declared their territory to be *ager publicus*. By the imperial period the picture had become more complex. It is evident that an important tract of Orondian land around Kıreli on the west side of Lake Beyşehir had become an imperial estate, administered by a procurator at least until the fourth century AD.[156] The Orondians themselves were organized into a *koinon*, whose members probably comprised not only the inhabitants of the estate but also those of the two known Orondian communities; Pappa which lay close to the line of the via Sebaste between Iconium and Antioch; and Mistea, at the south-east corner of Lake Beyşehir.[157] The former appears to have become a *polis*

under Tiberius and was renamed Pappa Tiberiopolis,[158] while Mistea, soon after, became Claudiocaesareia Mistea.[159] The nomenclature of both cities preserves a reference to the Orondians who, we may presume, had rehabilitated themselves since their conquest by Servilius, as the Homonadeis never did.

The imprint of Claudius is marked over the whole of south Galatia. Apart from Ninica and Mistea, Iconium, which had been an important centre as early as the fourth century BC and had minted under Augustus, advanced its position (at least in name) to become Claudiconium, another example of a Greek city existing alongside a full Roman colony.[160] Its neighbour in the north, the Seleucid city of Laodicea Catacecaumene, became Claudiolaodicea,[161] and in Lycaonia to the south Antipater's old capital was renamed Claudioderbe.[162] On the east side of the central plateau, within the province of Cappadocia but close to the border with Galatia, Claudius founded a colony at Archelais, an isolated tailpiece to the great Augustan programme,[163] while in the west in northern Pisidia the old Seleucid foundation of Seleuceia Sidera became Claudioseleuceia.[164]

The new civic titles do not imply that each city had reached an identical level of development or that each received the same treatment. Some of these communities, such as Germanicopolis, Ninica, and Pappa have no earlier history known to us; Mistea is called a *polis* in an Attalid royal letter of the mid-second century BC, further evidence for the organization of Pisidia in the Hellenistic period;[165] Iconium had clearly long been an important community and had presumably acted as a political and economic centre for south east Phrygia, as Isaura had for Isauria, in the fourth century BC and throughout the Hellenistic period;[166] Laodicea and Seleuceia Sidera had probably fulfilled a military role alongside the other Seleucid foundations of Apollonia and Neapolis, protecting and securing the

capital at Diocaesaria, see E. Kirsten, *Anz. Wien*, 110 (1973), 347–63, taking as the principal document the inscription published by R. Heberdey and A. Wilhelm, *D. Ak. Wien*, 44 (1986), 84 no. 160; cf. S. Mitchell, *Historia*, 28 (1979), 432.

[154] Jones, *CERP²* 440 n. 36. R. Syme, *AS* 36 (1986), 162 (= *RP* v. 666) conjectures that the native name of Germanicopolis may have been Clibanus.

[155] G. F. Hill, *Num. Chron.* 3: 19 (1899), 181–207; Magie, *RR* ii. 1354–5; cf. A. Wilhelm, *AEMÖ* 17 (1894), 1–6; Mitchell, *Historia*, 28 (1979), 426–34.

[156] *MAMA* viii no. 341, with Robert, *Hellenica*, xiii. 80 ff.; R. Paribeni, *Not. Scav.* (1925), 410–11 no. 6, a tombstone set up at Rome by an imperial freedman who had been *vestitor* and *proc. Orondici*.

[157] For the *koinon* see MAMA viii. 333 and, in one possible restoration, A. S. Hall, *AS* 18 (1968), 63 no. 1. Both texts are from Pappa which was the metropolis of the tribe. Robert, *Hellenica*, xiii, 76 suggests tentatively that the *koinon* only comprised the inhabitants of the imperial estate. But both Pappa and Mistea explicitly called themselves Orondian cities, and Robert's hypothesis requires that we understand the term Orondian in two senses, both to denote the inhabitants of the estate, and to denote any inhabitant of Orondian territory. This is awkward and implausible.

[158] The city is named in *MAMA* viii. 331 (AD 244–9), 332; *IGR* iii. 1469 (Trajanic) and 309 (from Pisidian Antioch); Hall, *AS* 18 (1968), 63 no. 1 (Severus Alexander).

[159] A. S. Hall, *AS* 9 (1959), 119–24.

[160] Mitchell, *Historia*, 28 (1979), 411–25.

[161] W. M. Calder, *Klio*, 10 (1910), 234 ff. nos. 2 and 4; Magie, *RR* ii. 1405; Aulock, *Lykaonien*, nos. 141–53.

[162] Aulock, *Lykaonien*, nos. 77–82; M. H. Ballance, *AS* 7 (1957), 147–51; Magie, *RR* ii. 1406.

[163] Pliny, *NH* 6. 8.

[164] Lanckoronski, *Städte Pamphyliens und Pisidiens*, ii. 225 no. 194; Aulock, *Pisidien*, ii nos. 1875–2105 (issues from Hadrian to Claudius II).

[165] Swoboda, *Denkmäler*, 33–5 nos. 74–5. Neighbouring Amblada is shown by the same document to have been ruled by *gerontes*.

[166] Xenophon, *Anab.* 1. 2. 19; for Isaura, see Diodorus, 17. 22.

same belt of territory as the Augustan colonies;[167] Archelais was known to Strabo by its old name Garsaoura and described as a village city (κωμόπολις) or small town (πολίχνιον). Although it was a regional centre in Augustan times it is unlikely that it had a developed city constitution even after it acquired the name Archelais from the last Cappadocian monarch.[168] Derbe has become better known not because it was Antipater's capital but because it was visited by St Paul,[169] but there is no trace of the institutions of a *polis* there before the reign of Claudius.[170]

The scanty sources do not indicate whether these new cities in south Galatia were created on the initiative of the local inhabitants or at the behest of Rome. It is possible that inter-communal rivalry and emulation of successful neighbours may have led Ninica and Mistea to seek city status from Claudius, but it strains belief that all the Claudian foundations should have sought and gained promotion in a frantic period of petitioning for the indulgence of the *princeps*. These foundations do not have the appearance of a haphazard response to local initiative, but should reflect a consistent official policy, and Rome's conscious intention to urbanize the province. It is at least possible that the very considerable task of organizing these new cities and adjudicating on their territorial boundaries lay with the energetic governor of Claudius' last years, M. Annius Afrinus.[171]

The Julio-Claudian programme for creating cities in Galatia left one area very sparsely covered, the central plateau between Ancyra and Iconium. For most of its history nomad encampments or modest villages have been the normal mode of settlement in this region,[172] and it is a revealing comment on the pressures towards urban development under the Roman empire that four small cities were created there by the second century AD, which are not even matched today, in a country with a higher level of population than existed in the Roman period, by comparable modern settlements. The northernmost of these was Kinna, north-west of

Tuz Göl at the modern village of Karahamzılı.[173] The city is known to have existed for certain in the third century, when its magistrates, council, and people set up a statue of the emperor Gordian,[174] but an inscription from the site erected in honour of an Antonine procurator of Galatia, T. Furius Victorinus,[175] makes it virtually certain that the polis had been founded by that date.[176] Perta, Savatra, and Kana, the remaining cities in this group, all lie on the north-east slopes of Boz Dağ, east of Iconium and south-west of the Salt Lake. The northernmost, Perta, at the modern village of Giymir,[177] had also been founded by the reign of Hadrian, since three fragments of an inscribed architrave, apparently part of an imperial temple, carry a text dedicated to Hadrian's well-being.[178] Savatra appears to have been a place of more consequence.[179] It was mentioned by Strabo,[180] and even minted autonomous coins in the first century BC with the legend ΣΟΑΤΡΕΙΣ.[181] The earliest dateable inscriptions which imply the existence of a polis belong to the second century AD. One is a Latin text set up by the *civitas* of Savatra for the mid-second-century procurator T. Flavius Titianus;[182] and the other an honorific inscription for Ancharene, daughter of Sacerdos, wife of Flavius Marcellus, who had presumably received the citizenship from one of the Flavian emperors. Both husband and wife held high priesthoods of the imperial cult, and the husband was also priest of the *theoi patrooi* at Savatra, Ares and the Areiai.[183] Moreover, the city minted under Trajan

---

167 See G. Cohen, *The Seleucid Colonies*, 15; the positive evidence for this, however, is scanty. See Mitchell and Waelkens, *Pisidian Antioch*, ch. 1.

168 Strabo, xii. 2. 5, 537; 6. 1, 568; 14. 2. 29, 663; Magie, *RR* ii. 1353–4.

169 Acts 14: 6, 20: 4.

170 Derbe is called a λίμην καὶ φρούριον Ἰσαυρίας by Stephanus of Byzantium s.v., and Ramsay took this to mean that it functioned as a frontier station between Galatia and the kingdom of Antiochus in Rugged Cilicia (*Galatians*, 231 n. 3; *Cities of Saint Paul* (1905), 399 n. 19). For the meaning of λίμην see Rostovtzeff, *AEMÖ* 19 (1896), 127 ff., and *YCS* 3 (1932), 79–81; S. J. de Laet, *Portorium* (1949), 273 ff.; and G. W. Bowersock, *Class. Phil.* 82 (1987), 178–81.

171 See above, Ch. 6 nn. 93–7.

172 See below, Ch. 10 § 11 and Ch. 14 § 111.

173 For the site see *RECAM* ii. 21–2.

174 *RECAM* ii. 396.

175 *RECAM* ii. 397. The man who set up the inscription was called Aelius Procillianus Menodorus, and had presumably been enfranchised by Hadrian.

176 *RECAM* ii. 398 mentions a T. Flavius Valentio, which is evidence that the place was attracting interest in the late 1st cent. AD.

177 W. Ruge, *RE* xix (1937), 1058–9; *MAMA* viii. pp. xiii–xiv; Robert, *Hellenica*, xiii. 57 ff.

178 Fragments *b* and *c* of the text were assembled by Robert, *Hellenica*, xiii. 63–4; fragment *a* was copied by M. H. Ballance but remains unpublished. The whole text may run:

$$\qquad a \qquad\qquad\qquad b \qquad\qquad\qquad c$$
[ὑπὲρ τῆς τοῦ Αὐ]τοκράτορ[ος Καίσαρ]ος Τραια[νοῦ] Ἀδριανοῦ
αἰ[ωνίου διαμονῆς]
[. . . . . . ?Δι]οκλῆς Σε[. . . . ἱ]ερεὺς Διὸ[ς καὶ] πρόβουλο[ς . . . .]
[. . . . . . .]εἰς κατασ[κευὴν] τοῦ τε ν[αοῦ καὶ τοῦ ἀγάλματος τοῦ
Σεβαστοῦ?]

179 See Robert, *Hellenica*, x. 72 ff.; xiii. 42–4.

180 Strabo, 12. 6. 1., 568, following the text of F. Lasserre, . . . καθάπερ ἐν Σοάτροις, ὅπου καὶ πιπράσκεται τὸ ὕδωρ (ἔστι δὲ κωμόπολις Γαρσαούρων πλησίον), which rightly connects the rare term κωμόπολις with Garsaura, not with Savatra.

181 Aulock, *Lykaonien*, no. 154.

182 An unpublished text copied by M. H. Ballance.

183 H. S. Cronin, *JHS* 22 (1902), 371 no. 144; (*IGR* iii. 1481); cf. Robert, *Hellenica*, x. 76–7.

and again under Antoninus Pius.[184] Much less is known about Kana, whose name survives at the modern village of Gene, south of Savatra. However, virtually the only public inscription which has been recorded on the site records the erection by the council and people of a temple and statue for Trajan in AD 105, during the governorship of P. Calvisius Ruso Iulius Frontinus.[185] Again, then, the existence of the city by the early second century is not in doubt.

These four cities had much in common. All were situated in the same geographical region, which has seemed at other periods to have been hostile to urban development; in contrast to the earlier Galatian foundations each of them was simply known by its native name and did not take an imperial title; in all cases the evidence suggests a foundation date in the late first or early second century AD. Once again it is economical to suppose that the decision to found all four cities was taken more or less at the same time, and reflects a deliberate policy to encourage urban development in the central plateau. It is even suggestive that two of the four cities chose to honour provincial procurators soon after their foundation. If one of the chief purposes of these Roman city foundations was to facilitate the collection of revenue and the provision of services by the provincial communities, as argued above (Ch. 5 n. 56), then the procurator, whose responsibilities lay precisely in these areas of Roman administration, will have had much business to do in the cities in the period immediately after their foundation.[186]

There is virtually no evidence for the civic offices and constitution of any of the group, but the inscription from the temple at Perta shows that the man responsible for its construction was not only priest of Zeus (presumably the city's chief god) but also a *proboulos*. This office is not found elsewhere in Galatia, but is widely attested in Pisidia and elsewhere in southern Anatolia.[187] The provisions of a *lex provinciae* drafted over a hundred years before would not be the only guiding factor to be taken into account when new cities were created in the second century AD.

VI. *Cappadocia: The Exception*

There remains Cappadocia. Under its last king Archelaus II it had been a virtual protectorate of Rome.[188] When the king was confronted by charges and complaints from his subjects in the 20s BC he was summoned to Rome for trial like any provincial governor, and although he was acquitted, he returned to his kingdom accompanied by an imperial procurator.[189] When he died, after coming to Rome to face further accusations in AD 17, his kingdom was annexed and made into a province administered by a Roman knight, an equestrian praesidial procurator.[190] As has been seen, Strabo completed his description of central and eastern Asia Minor at precisely this time, and he is accordingly no guide to conditions in the new province. Hellenistic Cappadocia with Greek cities at Tyana, Caesareia, and Hanisa had been if anything more developed than Galatia, Lycaonia, or Pontus; but this position was not maintained. The elder Pliny, writing in the 70s AD, gives a list of Cappadocian towns (*oppida*) which, beside the Claudian colony at Archelais, comprises Diocaesarea, Tyana, Castabala in the Cilican Taurus, and Melita towards the Euphrates.[191] Pliny is a highly unreliable source for the geography of eastern Asia Minor; the information he provides is neither exhaustive nor comprehensive and he certainly does not pretend to identify the places which had the status of a *polis*; Melita (Melitene) for instance, did not become an independent city until Trajan's day, a generation after a legionary fortress had been established there.[192] However, given the extraordinary but revealing absence of epigraphic material from the province, Pliny's information is the best that is available. We may infer that some attempt was made during the Julio-Claudian period to create cities in the western areas, where apart from Caesareia, Tyana, and Archelais the 'insignificant city' of Diocaesarea was founded at a site about seventy kilometres east of Archelais. Gregory of Nazianzus in the late fourth century recalled that it has been created by kings, but it is not known to which of the early emperors it should be attributed.[193] Nothing whatever is known of its history before the fourth century. Only one community seems to have achieved the status of a city in central Cappadocia under the empire, the flourishing temple

---

[184] Aulock, *Lykaonien*, nos. 155, 156–88. Also 189 under L. Verus.

[185] *MAMA* viii. 211. The date is disputed since the reading of the numeral after Trajan's tribunician power on the inscription is unclear. The editors suggested *IE* or *IΘ*, both impossible. Now a coin bearing the name of the processor from Cybistra in Cappadocia, dating to 104/5 (*SNG von Aulock*, 6535) makes it highly probable that the true reading was *Θ*, i.e. precisely AD 104/5. See W. Eck, *Chiron*, 12 (1982), 340 n. 242 and P. R. Franke, *Chiron*, 9 (1979), 379 ff., against Sherk, *ANRW* ii. 7. 2 (1980), 1018–19, who preferred *IΓ*, 108–9. G. di Vita Évrard, *MEFRA* 99 (1987), 305–6 also pleads for *Θ* or *I*, AD 104/5 or 105/6.

[186] For the duties of procurators, see, very briefly, S. Mitchell, *JRS* 66 (1976), 124.

[187] Robert, *Hellenica*, xiii. 63–4.

[188] See T. Liebmann-Frankfort, 'Les Étapes de l'integration de la Cappadoce dans l'empire romain', *Le Monde grecque: Hommages à C. Préaux* (1975), 416–26.

[189] Dio, 57. 17. 5.

[190] For sources see R. Teja, 'Kappadokien in der Prinzipätzeit', *ANRW* ii. 7. 2. (1980), 1085 n. 1.

[191] Pliny, *NH* 6. 8.

[192] Procopius, *Aed.* 2. 4. 15–20. See Ch. 9 n. 3.

[193] For Diocaesarea see *TIB* ii. 171; Greg. Naz. *Car.* 2. 1. 19, 25 ff.; and *ep.* 141.

state at Comana, which was known by the reign of Vespasian as the city of Hierapolis.[194] Even Ariaratheia sank into obscurity until it re-emerged to form part of the ecclesiastical organization of the fourth century.

So Cappadocia was not covered by a network of city territories, like its neighbours to the north and west, and the principal reason for this seems to have been that most of its land, which had formerly been owned by the kings and provided the basis of their revenue, passed directly into the possession of the Roman emperor or the Roman people. The decision that it should be governed by an equestrian procurator, whose traditional duties were mainly with the collection and disbursement of revenue, is probably significant; it is also revealing that Tiberius, at the moment of annexation, declared that the income from the former kingdom would enable him to cut other taxes which were used to maintain the military treasury.[195] Cappadocia, like Egypt, was administered through domains and estates, not cities.[196]

If the above analysis is broadly correct, by the end of the Julio-Claudian period most of Pontus, Paphlagonia, north Galatia, Galatian Phrygia, Lycaonia, and Pisidia was divided up between contiguous city territories; only Cappadocia was left outside this pattern of settlement, and remained largely without cities. These developments which occurred during the first century of Roman rule, above all under Augustus and Claudius, completely transformed the political geography of central and eastern Anatolia. Moreover, as with Pompey's city foundations and the organization of Pontus and Bithynia, the main pressures and impetus

towards urbanization came from above, not from below.

There were, perhaps, two main driving forces behind the process. Firstly, the emperors in the eastern part of the empire certainly saw themselves as heirs to a Hellenistic tradition of kingship, and one of the most characteristic actions of a king was to found cities, which were usually named after himself or a close relative. The Sebasteias and Caesareias of the early empire are a natural sequel to the Alexandrias and Antiochs of the Hellenistic period. The urge to found cities was not simply fuelled by sentiment or by public expectation of what an emperor should do, but was certainly seen as part of a programme, which would hardly have been consciously articulated, to civilize and improve the non-Roman or non-Greek world. A province without cities, in a sense, was one that had no place in the Roman empire; and indeed Roman reluctance to annex remote and underdeveloped regions of Asia Minor and other parts of the world known to them may owe as much to the fact that the possibilities of establishing city life were very restricted, as to the belief that client rulers would be better able to control their unruly inhabitants than Roman governors.[197] Secondly, and crucially, the task of regulating provincial life in all its facets far outstripped the capacity of governors or other Roman officials, and it was essential to devolve much of the burden of administration on to the local communities. The dues and services that the provincial communities rendered to Rome, including taxation and the provision of supplies and transport to armies and officials, were all organized at a local civic level, since otherwise the demands made on strictly Roman personnel would have been overwhelming. It is difficult to resist the conclusion that whatever other factors lay behind the foundation of cities, the interests of Rome herself will have been paramount.

---

[194] See R. P. Harper, *AS* 18 (1968), 93–147; 19 (1969), 27–40; 22 (1972), 225–39.
[195] Tacitus, *Ann.* 2. 42.
[196] A. H. M. Jones, *CERP*² 182–3; Teja, 'Kappadokien in der Prinzipätzeit', 1109–18.

[197] See above, Ch. 3 § III at nn. 75–6.

Note on Map 6 (opposite)
Cities printed in bold type trace their origins to Pompey, the Hellenistic period or earlier; cities underlined are Augustan foundations or refoundations; cities with broken underlining are Tiberian or Claudian foundations; cities printed in *italic type* were probably founded between Vespasian and Hadrian; the foundation date of cities in normal type with no underlining is uncertain. The provincial boundaries of AD 150 are indicated by the continuous lines. The smaller broken lines are an attempt to show the possible boundaries of city territories in Pontus and Bithynia, Galatia, and the Lycaonian section of the Tres Eparchiae. This has not been attempted for Isauria and Cilicia, where not all the cities themselves are indicated, or for Cappadocia, where the proportion of imperial property outside civic jurisdiction was probably very large. Scale 1:3,000,000.

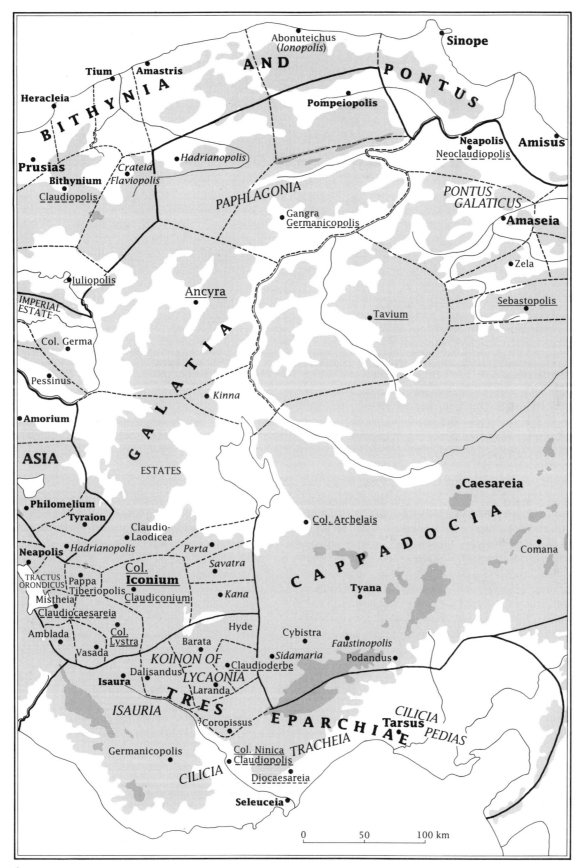

Map 6. The cities of central Anatolia from Augustus to Hadrian

8 The Imperial Cult

Only three Roman cities in central Anatolia outside the province of Asia have yet been excavated on a substantial scale: Ancyra, Pessinus, and Pisidian Antioch. In each case the central feature of these excavations has been a temple dedicated to the imperial cult, built in the time of Augustus or Tiberius. Emperor worship was from the first an institution of great importance to the provincial communities, and one that had, quite literally, a central role to play in the development of the new cities.[1]

The diffusion of the cult of Augustus and of other members of his family in Asia Minor and throughout the Greek East from the beginning of the principate was rapid, indeed almost instantaneous. In 29 BC Octavian gave authority to the inhabitants of Asia and Bithynia to set up sanctuaries in their leading cities, Ephesus and Nicaea, dedicated to the cult of Roma and his deified father Julius Caesar, where resident Roman citizens could worship. At the same time he allowed the Greek inhabitants to establish cult centres for himself at Pergamum and Nicomedia.[2] Perhaps during the same year the organization or *koinon* of the Greeks in Asia, the body which was to be responsible for emperor worship at a provincial level, announced a competition to reward the person who could devise the greatest honour for the new god.[3] In 27 BC Octavian took the name Augustus, *Sebastos* in Greek, redolent with religious associations, and Nicolaus of Damascus, a contemporary writer from the eastern part of the empire, suggests that this led directly to the swift dissemination of further cults: 'Because men call him by

this name as a mark of esteem for his honour, they revere him with temples and sacrifices, organized by islands and continents, and as cities and provinces they match the greatness of his virtue and the scale of his benefactions towards them.'[4] Indeed, within a year of Augustus receiving his new name, randomly preserved epigraphic evidence has produced records of the man responsible for erecting a statue of the *Sebastos* and the consecration of his *temenos* at Ephesus and a priest of Rome and Augustus at Philadelphia in Lydia.[5] By 9 BC (and surely already much earlier) the Asian *koinon* which had instituted the competition in Augustus' honour, and which concluded it by awarding the prize to a provincial governor who proposed that the New Year should henceforth begin on 23 September (Augustus' birthday), passed a decree which took for granted the fact that every major city possessed a 'Caesareum' (an imperial sanctuary), where the decision could be proclaimed and inscribed.[6] In fact, priests of Augustus are attested in thirty-four cities in Asia Minor, mostly in the province of Asia, and this is doubtless only a fraction of the original total.[7] A selective survey of the evidence, which comes almost exclusively from inscriptions, shows local civic cults of Rome and Augustus at Pergamum before 1 BC,[8] at Mytilene soon after 27 BC,[9] at Mylasa, where a temple was dedicated between 12 BC and AD 2,[10] at Samos probably by 21 BC,[11] at Erythrae,[12] at Ios between 27

---

[1] Three recent books have placed the study of the imperial cult on a new footing and have made this chapter immeasurably easier to write: R. Mellor, *ΘΕΑ ΡΩΜΗ: The Worship of the Goddess Rome in the Greek World* (1975); C. Fayer, *Il culto della dea Roma: Origine e diffusione nell' Impero* (1976); and above all S. R. F. Price, *Rituals and Power: The Roman Imperial Cult in Asia Minor* (1984). My debt to these often extends beyond what is indicated in the footnotes.

[2] Cassius Dio, 51. 20. 5–7.

[3] Sherk, *RDGE* no. 65 (re-edited by U. Laffi, *Studi clasici e orientali* 16 (1967), 5–98), ll. 42–3; cf. Price, *Rituals and Power*, 54.

[4] *FGrH* 90 F. 125, 1.

[5] Ephesus: *SEG* xxvi (1976/7), 1243 (cf. F. Millar, in Millar and E. Segal, *Caesar Augustus*, 37 (1984), 37); Philadelphia: R. Meriç and J. Nollé, *Epigr. Anat.* 5 (1985), 24–5 no. 2 (*SEG* xxxv (1985), 1169). Both from 27/6 BC.

[6] Sherk, *RDGE* no. 65D, l. 61.

[7] Price, *Rituals and Power*, 58, misquoted as 43 by Millar, *Caesar Augustus*, 37. Compare the findings of H. Hänlein-Schäfer, *Veneratio Augusti. Eine Studie zu den Tempeln des ersten römischen Kaisers* (1985), quoted by Price, *JRS* 76 (1986), 300, that 56 municipal temples of Augustus are known, at least 50 of which date to his lifetime.

[8] Fayer, *Dea Roma*, 135–7.

[9] Ibid. 137.

[10] Ibid. 138; Price, *Rituals and Power*, 262; *I. Mylasa*, no. 31.

[11] Fayer, *Dea Roma*, 138–40.

[12] Ibid. 140.

Fig. 13. The temple of Augustus and Rome at Ancyra. The view shows the south wall of the cella, which would originally have been masked by the fifteen columns of the peripteros. A tendril frieze ran along the top of the wall between Corinthian pilaster capitals at either end. Above the orthostat course (half-hidden by the modern fence) the lowest three courses of masonry were smoothed flat to receive the Greek text of the *Res Gestae*. The windows probably date to the fifth century AD, when the temple was converted into a church.

Fig. 14. The imperial temple at Pisidian Antioch. This view from the south-west shows the rock foundations of the Roman podium temple surrounded by fallen white limestone blocks from the superstructure. The temple was framed by a semi-circular portico, also cut into the rock. The beam holes visible in the rock face at the right mark the height of its first storey.

The imperial temples of Ancyra and Antioch

and 13 BC,[13] at Thyateira before 2 BC,[14] at Priene,[15] and at Alabanda.[16]

The foundation of provincial centres of emperor worship in Asia and Bithynia in 29 BC acted according to Cassius Dio as a model for other provinces to follow all over the empire, and it also prompted the spread of civic or locally organized cults. Macedonia, for instance, had a cult of Augustus in 27 BC, where its high priest also served as agonothete for imperial games.[17] In Asia Minor the process is particularly clear in Paphlagonia where by 3 BC, only three years after it had been annexed to the existing province of Galatia, the oath of loyalty to Augustus and his family could be administered in *Sebasteia* throughout the rural sub-divisions of the region.[18] The spread of emperor worship therefore seems to have been as rapid in remote Paphlagonia as it had been in the more familiar territory of Asia. This speed is matched even in Cappadocia. In AD 20, three years after Cappadocia was annexed, an inscription shows that a provincial organization or *koinon* had been created and was sponsoring games. Since all the other provincial *koina* of Asia Minor were responsible in the first instance for maintaining the provincial cult, and the games which they mounted were invariably imperial festivals, it is clear that Cappadocia also enjoyed organized emperor worship virtually from the moment that it came under direct Roman rule.[19] Lycia became a province in AD 43. Between January and May of that year the emperor Claudius himself took responsibility for dedicating a building in one of the porticos of the sanctuary of Leto at Xanthos, which has been identified as the Caesareum of the province.[20] Not only the early date

but also the active role played by the emperor in erecting the cult building are worth emphasis.

One of the best illustrations to show the same pattern occurring elsewhere in the empire comes from Britain, in the far west, where a huge imperial temple, designed on a classical model, was under construction at the colony of Camulodunum only six years after the Claudian conquest of the island in AD 43. It was built and maintained with contributions, evidently often unwilling ones, from the local nobility, and the pressures which this brought to bear are cited as one of the causes of the great revolt against Rome led by Boudicca in AD 60.[21] The parallel is geographically distant but not inappropriate to the circumstances surrounding the introduction of emperor worship to Galatia. Britain and Galatia were both dominated by a Celtic ruling class; both received Roman colonial settlements when they became part of the empire; neither had an independent civic tradition; and in each case the creation of imperial temples gave them their first flavour of urban building in the grandest Graeco-Roman tradition.

Much the most detailed evidence for the spread of emperor worship in the central Anatolian provinces comes from Galatia. Explicit testimony of the earliest stages in the cult's development is sparse, but this is likely to be no more than an accident in the survival of documents; after all our knowledge of the cult in Paphlagonia and Cappadocia is confined to a single inscription in each case. The parallel evidence from the other regions and provinces of Asia Minor makes it overwhelmingly probable that the imperial cult was established in Galatia, both at a provincial and at a civic level, soon after it was annexed.

Within the boundaries of Augustan Galatia the inhabitants of Attaleia in Pamphylia set up a cult for the goddess Rome *archegetis*, an adjective which is characteristically attached to founders of colonies and reflects the fact that the city had received a colony of Roman citizens under Augustus.[22] The unparalleled description of the goddess Rome as *archegetis*, implying that she was acknowledged as a founding leader as Apollo was regularly worshipped in Greek colonies, is surely proof that the cult was initiated by the Roman element in the population, and this is confirmed by the names of its early priests which show that they came from the immigrant group: Caecilia Tertulla, priestess

[13] Fayer, *Dea Roma*, 140–1.
[14] Ibid. 141–2, 169–70; *TAM* v. 2. 902–3.
[15] Fayer, *Dea Roma*, 145.
[16] Ibid. 145–6.
[17] C. Edson, *HSCP* 51 (1940), 132 ff.; for the early dissemination of the imperial cult under Augustus, see now D. Kienast, *Augustus. Prinzeps und Monarch* (1982), 202–14.
[18] OGIS 532, discussed above in Ch. 7 §IV at nn. 124–9. I do not agree with Price, *Rituals and Power*, 79 and 267 that the oath would only have been taken in the regional centres of Neapolis, Pompeiopolis, and Caesarea, where cities existed or were founded at a later date. The hyparchies of Paphlagonia were to be subdivisions of city territories (above, Ch. 7 §IV nn. 119–20). Price's judgement is coloured by his view that the imperial cult in Asia Minor was always, and in essence, an urban phenomenon, or the product of 'organized communities'. The point is overemphasized and the argument tends to circularity. Often the only substantial evidence that a particular community was 'organized' is the presence of some manifestation of emperor worship.
[19] L. Moretti, *Iscrizioni agonistiche greche* no. 62; See Deininger, *Provinziallandtage*, 16 ff., 36 ff., and 82 on the evidence from Cappadocia.
[20] A. Balland, *Xanthos*, vii (1981), 25 ff. no. 11.

[21] Tacitus, *ann.* 14. 31; see D. Fishwick, *Phoenix*, 15 (1961), 161 ff.; *Britannia*, 3 (1972), 164–81.
[22] B. Pace, *Ann. Sc. It.* 3 (1916–20) (*SEG* ii. 696; *AE* (1922), 2); E. Bosch, *Belleten*, 11 (1947), 94 no. 10, cf. J. and L. Robert, *Bull. ép.* (1948), pp. 199–200; G. E. Bean, *Belleten*, 22 (1958), 26 no. 11.

of Iulia Augusta and Rome,[23] and Sextus Paccius Valerianus Flaccus, *sacerdos* of Rome, agonothete, and gymnasiarch.[24] Another doubtless early official was priest of *Roma Archegetis* and of Tiberius' son Drusus.[25] These cults, held by the leading Roman inhabitants of Attaleia, were surely one of the principal means by which the new settlers established their corporate identity, and underlined their Roman origins in a predominantly Greek environment. As is perfectly clear from the Asian evidence, emperor worship was as much a matter for Romans as for Greeks or other native inhabitants of the provinces.

The cult is attested in Galatia simultaneously in a very different context, but with revealing similarities. In 5/4 BC the people of the Milyas who were tribal kinsfolk of the Pisidians, in concert with the Romans who did business among them and Thracian inhabitants of the region, erected a large altar to Rome and the divine Augustus at a site on the west bank of the river Lysis in western Pisidia, close to the line of the Augustan *via Sebaste* (which is dated by milestones to the previous year) and within sight of the provincial boundary between Galatia and Asia. Here too it seems safe to conjecture that the Roman element in the population, which in any case is likely to have been socially and economically dominant, was largely responsible for the initiative.[26] Emperor worship was not a political subterfuge, designed to elicit the loyalty of untutored provincials, but was one of the ways in which Romans themselves and provincials alongside them defined their own relationship with a new political phenomenon, an emperor whose powers and charisma were so transcendent that he appeared to them as both man and god.

No doubt locally organized cults of Rome, Augustus, or other members of the imperial household made an early appearance in other parts of central Anatolia.

Meanwhile the centrally regulated provincial cult was established in the chief city, Ancyra, under the auspices of the Galatian *koinon*. Documentary evidence is not available before the reign of Tiberius, but the most notable building of all Galatia—the temple of Rome and Augustus at Ancyra—was already under construction by the middle years of Augustus' reign. This large Ionic temple, whose imposing peripteros, eight pillars by fifteen, stood on a high podium of seven steps, belongs to a Hellenistic architectural tradition that can be traced back to the temple of Athena Polias at Priene. Indeed the ground plan is so reminiscent of Hermogenian temples that the most detailed existing study assigns it to the mid-second century BC.[27] Closer examination of the decorative mouldings shows that this is impossible. One of the earliest parts of the temple superstructure to be completed, the socle moulding of the cella walls, has a finely carved palmette and lotus anthemia design which recalls late Hellenistic work, but other parts of the decorated order, notably the lintel and frame of the cella door, probably belong between 10 BC and AD 10,[28] and the temple may not finally have been dedicated before the early years of Tiberius, perhaps in AD 19/20, which is probably the year in which the earliest priest in the list inscribed on the anta of the pronaos held office.[29]

A second temple almost certainly dedicated to the provincial cult was built at Pessinus not long afterwards. This is the hexastyle Corinthian temple associated with a theatre-like building which occupies a conspicuous position at the southern end of the city. A series of coins minted at Pessinus under the governor of Galatia T. Helvius Basila, whose term of office probably ran from about AD 35 into the reign of Gaius, depicts a temple with six columns across the front which should be identified with the excavated building (cf. Fig. 18c). Moreover, twice towards the end of Tiberius' principate citizens of Pessinus held the chief priesthood of the provincial cult: M. Lollius (?) in AD

[23] She was the mother of M. Calpurnius Rufus, a Roman senator who was a *legatus Augusti* under Claudius; for the family see W. Eck, ZPE 86 (1991), 97–106.

[24] Bosch, *Belleten*, 11 (1947), 97 no. 14 = Bean, *Belleten*, 22 (1958), 32 no. 20 (SEG xvii. 577); Bean, ibid. 32 no. 19 (SEG xvii. 578). For the family estates in central Anatolia, see below, Ch. 10 § III nn. 85–6.

[25] Bosch, *Belleten*, 11 (1947), 99 no. 16 = Bean, *Belleten*, 22 (1958), 34 no. 24 (SEG xvii. 582). For further discussion of the Attaleia evidence see Fayer, *Dea Roma* 172–3.

[26] A. S. Hall, AS 36 (1986), 137–58, who (153) aptly compares the inscription set up by οἱ Μιλυαδεῖς καὶ οἱ πραγματευόμενοι παρ' αὐτοῖς Ῥωμαῖοι καὶ Θρᾷκες οἱ κατοικοῦντες παρ' αὐτοῖς with the terminology of the almost contemporary Gangra oath, which was taken ὑπὸ τῶν κατοικούντων Παφλαγονίαν καὶ πραγματευομένων παρ' αὐτοῖς Ῥωμαίων. The resident Romans presumably had a major part to play in that initiative also. I am doubtful, however, whether the cult of Rome among the Milyadeis should be traced back to the second century BC (cf. Hall, op. cit. 156), for which there is no positive evidence.

[27] M. Krencker and M. Schede, *Der Tempel in Ankara* (1936).

[28] For the architectural evidence for an Augustan date see E. Weigand, *Gnomon*, 13 (1937), 418 ff.; and the recent appraisals of K. Fittschen, *Arch. Anz.* 1985, 314–15; and M. Waelkens, *Epigr. Anat.* 7 (1986), 48 ff.

[29] For this date see the independent conclusions of S. Mitchell, *Chiron*, 16 (1986), 17–33 and H. Halfmann, *Chiron*, 16 (1986), 35–42. Halfman conjectures that there may have been an earlier priest list than the one which survives on the temple, and this would allow for an earlier dedication of the building. This is possible but unnecessary; temples were consecrated at their completion: G. Wissowa, *Religion und Kultus der Römer*[2] (1912), 472 ff. In what follows I have assumed the correctness of this chronology without further argument. W. Leischhorn's arguments concerning the Galatian era (see *Chiron*, 22 (1992)) do not substantially affect the chronology of the priest list on the Ancyra temple.

31/2, and Q. Gallius Pulcher in AD 35/6. The former dedicated a divine statue at Pessinus, perhaps marking the formal introduction of the provincial cult, while the latter probably presided over the inauguration of the temple under Basila's governorship.[30]

The third major Julio-Claudian temple found in Galatia is the Corinthian podium temple at Pisidian Antioch. In contrast to the basic Greek types of the Ancyra and Pessinus buildings, but appropriately for a Roman colony, this followed a typically Roman or western design. There was no peripteros, but the cella was approached by a massive staircase leading up to four frontal columns. The Corinthian pilaster capitals from the cella wall are probably middle to late Augustan, and the one surviving Corinthian capital from the prostyle colonnade is perhaps a little later. The gable ends of the roof would have been finished last of all, and the arrow-like darts in the ovolo mouldings of a mock door-frame in the east pediment can be dated to the 30s AD, and anticipate stylistic developments of the mid-first century.[31] As at Ancyra therefore there is good evidence from the style of the moulded decoration that construction was drawn out over a long period, perhaps from the later years of Augustus until the final years of his successor. It is not known whether the Antioch temple served the provincial or a local civic cult, but the dedication to Augustus seems beyond question. The design not only of the temple but of the whole sanctuary in which it stands is almost entirely Roman or western. In fact it is an outstanding example of early imperial civic planning. The propylon which led into the sanctuary was decorated with reliefs which depicted Augustus' victories over the Pisidians, and included his birth sign, the capricorn. A copy of the Res Gestae adorned the area around the propylon, and since the other exempla of the text come from the Galatian imperial sanctuaries of Ancyra and Apollonia, this further strengthens the case identifying the imperial cult here at Antioch. It should be obvious from the parallel evidence at Attaleia, as well as from many other places in the Greek East, that there was no incongruity in a Roman citizen population energetically promoting the cult of Augustus who was, after all, the founder of their colony.[32]

The cult developed elsewhere under Tiberius. There was a priest of Tiberius in the colony at Iconium,[33] and an imperial sanctuary at the mixed community of Apollonia, whose centrepiece was a large pedestal which carried the text of the Res Gestae and supported statues of the divine Augustus, Iulia Augusta, Tiberius, Germanicus, and Drusus, all set up between AD 14 and 19; in addition equestrian statues of the last three were dedicated by Apollonius son of Olympichus, a member of a leading local family who had undertaken an embassy to Germanicus, doubtless in AD 18–19 when he was in the East. Both Apollonius and his brother Demetrius, who had been involved in two embassies to Augustus himself at Rome, held priesthoods of Rome, and there is every likelihood that the embassies in each case were connected with the establishment or development of the cult. The nature of the evidence surely demonstrates that some fusion of the cult of Rome, which may have had a republican origin, and the worship of Augustus' family had taken place.[34]

The temples at Ancyra, Pessinus, and Antioch were not isolated buildings but were linked both topographically and functionally with other structures in the centre of the new Augustan cities. The architectural context of the Ancyra temple is least clear since most of the Roman city lies hidden by modern Ankara. There are traces of foundations for an altar in front of the temple, and it stood in a *temenos*.[35] The inscription listing the Tiberian priests of the cult shows that

---

[30] See *Chiron*, 16 (1986), 31–2. *IGR* iii. 230 (*I. Pessinus*, no. 17) proves the existence of a provincial Imperial temple at Pessinus. The excavated building has been studied in detail by M. Waelkens, *Epigr. Anat.* 7 (1986), 37–73. The coin evidence has been discussed by M. Grant, *Num. Chron.* 6: 10 (1950), 44–5 nos. 4–8. Nos. 4–6 depict the temple, 7 a lion facing right, 8 Cybele betwen two lions. Grant argued that these and other issues were part of an official Roman coinage in Galatia; perhaps rather they were minted by the *koinon*. The hexastyle temple is also shown on a number of other Galatian issues which he cites: an unattributed coin with the legend *ΕΠΙ ΑΦΡΕΙΝΟΥ* (Devreker, *Fouilles de Pessinonte* i. 191 no. 11, referring to M. Annius Afrinus, governor of Galatia from AD 49 to 54); a Neronian type of the *koinon* inscribed [*ΤΟ*] *ΚΟΙΝΟΝ ΓΑΛΑΤΩΝ* (where *ΤΟ* should be expanded to *ΤΟΛΙΣΤΟΒΟΓΙΩΝ* or -*ΟΙΣ*, Coll. *Wadd.* 6593); another *koinon* issue, obv. [*ΚΟΙΝΟΝ*] *ΓΑΛΑ[ΤΩΝ*], bust of Mēn facing right; rev. *ΣΕΒΑΣΤΩΝ*, hexastyle temple (Coll. *Wadd.* 6591; Imhoof-Blümer, *Griechische Münzen*, 226 no. 746). In this case the reverse legend seems to imply that the temple was dedicated to the emperors. Grant also reports a small coin of Tiberius or Claudius with the obverse legend *ΤΙΒΕΡΙΟΣ*, bare head facing right; rev. *ΣΕΒΑΣΤ....*, hexastyle temple.

[31] Waelkens, in S. Mitchell and M. Waelkens, *Pisidian Antioch: The Site and its Monuments* (forthcoming), gives a full account of this building and argues against the suggestion of K. Tuchelt, *Beiträge zur Altertumskunde Kleinasiens. Festschrift für K. Bittel* (1983), 301–24 that it was probably dedicated to Mēn and Cybele.

[32] *Pisidian Antioch*, forthcoming.

[33] *IGR* iii. 1473.

[34] *MAMA* iv. 142 (cf. Ramsay, *JHS* 38 (1918), 178 no. xvii); *MAMA* iv. 143. Discussion in *Chiron* 16 (1986), 30–1. Coins of M. Aurelius show an imperial temple with a cuirassed imperial statue (Price, *Rituals and Power* 270). For another embassy about expenditure on the imperial cult from nearby Apamea, see L. Robert, *CRAI* (1968), 580–2.

[35] Price, *Rituals and Power*, 267–8 citing Krencker and Schede, *Der Tempel in Ankara*, 30.

Pylaemenes son of Amyntas, the fourth office holder, had donated land where the *Sebasteion* itself could be built, and where a *panegyris* (the commercial gathering associated with a religious festival) and a horse race could take place. The phrasing of the text leaves it uncertain whether these were also buildings or simply places where these events could be held, but it is certain that they were physically proximate to the temple. Activities related to the imperial cult will therefore have occupied much of the central area of the city.[36] The temple stood on a prominent hill on the west side of the Ankara Çay, a perennial stream which ran through the Roman city. To the east, beyond the stream and on the lower slopes of the rocky acropolis that became Ancyra's Byzantine citadel, there was a theatre probably also of Augustan date;[37] while other civic buildings, notably the huge third-century bath–gymnasium complex, lay to the west. Even without the information that modern urban archaeology might provide, it is obvious that the Ankara temple was a focal point of the ancient city.

At Pessinus the plan of the imperial temple can be more exactly defined in relation to associated buildings and the overall city plan. Civic layout was to a large extent determined by the local topography, in particular the course of the river Gallus which runs through the site from north-north-east to south-south-west, virtually dry in summer but a torrent after heavy rains and a stream for much of the year.[38] In the imperial period from the time of Augustus the river bed was paved, and served, according to the seasons, as a street with colonnades on either side, or as a canal to carry away flood water. In either case it was the principal axis of the city. All the pre-Roman remains of Pessinus which have been identified to date lie on its east bank, and Pessinus' most important building, the Attalid temple of Cybele, should probably be sought here, perhaps under the mosque of the modern village.[39] This lies about midway along the length of the street/canal, and the Tiberian imperial temple was in a matching position on a low hill further south, overlooking the point where the street/canal turns sharply away to the west. The excavations show that it was built over Phrygian levels of the fifth and fourth centuries BC, with no Hellenistic strata intervening, and so it must have represented an extension of the urban centre to a part of the settlement which was then unoccupied. It was centrally placed in a rectangular temple enclosure, which was open only on the west. Here a theatre-like structure led down to a colonnaded square some eleven and a half metres below the floor level of the temple. This theatre consisted of a central block of thirty steps, centrally aligned with and running parallel to the short axis of the temple, flanked on either side by curved banks of twelve seats resting on a high podium above an area which served as the orchestra. This unique building was clearly designed as an integral part of the temple complex and was contemporary with it. The flight of steps in the centre provided a majestic monumental approach and was surely used for grand processional rituals; the seats on either side were intended to accommodate spectators and it is likely that the staircase too could be adapted for this purpose when necessary. Although temples and theatres were often linked in Greek civic architecture, the thoroughly integrated design of the Pessinus buildings certainly derives from temple-theatre complexes in late republican Italy, and the overall conception of the sanctuary is as western, or Roman, as that at Pisidian Antioch.[40] These archaeological and architectural details strengthen the case for identifying it as an imperial sanctuary. It cannot be the temple of Cybele for there are no Hellenistic remains beneath the Roman building; the western origin for the plan of the whole sanctuary is particularly appropriate for a Roman cult: and above all the design of the theatre, with its high podium separating the lowest row of seats from the spectacle below, strongly suggests that it was designed to accommodate gladiatorial shows and wild-beast fights (*venationes*) which were regularly associated with emperor worship at Pessinus as elsewhere. The large colonnaded square that lay beyond the theatre to the west was apparently first constructed under Claudius, and doubtless represents the next stage of civic development.[41]

At Antioch the setting of the temple is even clearer. The tetrastyle prostyle podium temple that dominates the city centre was visible from miles away to every traveller approaching the colony from the west. It was integrated into an axially aligned central building complex. Behind it was a two-storey colonnade which formed a semicircle half excavated from the rock of the hillside, half free-standing. The lower storey had Doric and the upper Ionic columns; these combined and contrasted with the Corinthian order of the temple itself in a characteristic example of Roman imperial symbolism, uniting the three main architectural orders of the Greek world within a single design. In front was a broad open square, apparently rectangular, but whose sides in

---

[36] *Chiron*, 16 (1986), 29.

[37] S. Mitchell, *JHS Arch. Reports* (1984/5), 98; (1989/90), 129–30.

[38] M. Waelkens, *Byzantion*, 41 (1971), 349–73. For the archaeological remains of the street/canal see Waelkens in J. Devreker and M. Waelkens, *Fouilles de Pessinonte*, i (1984), 77–141.

[39] Information from M. Waelkens.

[40] Waelkens, *Epigr. Anat.* 7 (1986), 37–73.

[41] Ibid. 59.

Fig. 15. Block from the garland and bull's head frieze of the imperial temple at Pisidian Antioch. Tiberian.

Fig. 16. Corinthian capital from the prostylos of the imperial temple at Pisidian Antioch. Tiberian.

Fig. 17. Fragment of a limestone block with an acanthus tendril frieze found at Tavium. Tiberian? The quality of the work suggests that like the other cities of north Galatia Tavium may have benefited from an ambitious building programme, probably in connection with the imperial cult, in the Julio-Claudian period.

Imperial architecture from Julio-Claudian Galatia

fact tapered slightly as they neared the temple, thus enhancing the imposing perspective. The entrance to the sanctuary on the west of the square was marked by the triple-arched propylon dedicated to Claudius in AD 50, probably the last element of the central buildings to be completed, which stood at the top of a flight of twelve steps leading down to the colonnaded avenue of Tiberius. This massive and symmetrical design provides one of the most notable examples of the transformation of civic space, whereby imperial buildings literally took over and dominated the urban landscape, thus symbolizing unequivocally the central position that emperor worship occupied in city life, and the overwhelming manner in which the emperor dominated the world view of his subjects.[42] In so exuberant an atmosphere it is no surprise that the Roman citizens of Antioch should have defied Roman 'custom' by establishing cults of the emperors Vespasian and Antoninus Pius there during their lifetimes.[43]

These buildings are the best evidence for the purely physical impact that emperor worship had on provincial cities; they also evoke patterns of public life and religious activity which are more fully defined by documentary evidence. Inscriptions associated with the imperial cult show the changes which it brought to society.

The key document for Galatia is the list of priests of Tiberian date from Ancyra. Tacitus remarks of emperor worship in Britain that the men who had been picked for priestly office poured out their entire fortunes under the guise of maintaining the cult.[44] In another Celtic province, Gallia Comata, former friends and enemies alike served the provincial cult at Lugdunum, which had been set up by Drusus in 9 BC. The first priest of Augustus and Rome was C. Iulius Vercondaridubnus, an Aeduan whose tribe had been Rome's earliest ally in Gaul.[45] One of his successors within a few years was C. Lucterius Leo of the Cadurci, patently a descendant of one of Julius Caesar's bitterest enemies in the great uprising of Vercingetorix.[46] In Galatia the priests of the cult under Tiberius are in many cases demonstrably descended from Rome's

friends and allies of the late Republican period. To aid discussion and understanding the main contents of this priest list are set out in tabular form (overleaf).

The first name that can be restored with any confidence is that of Castor, son of King Brigatus, who was surely connected with Tarcondarius Castor the last known tetrarch of the Tectosages (murdered by Deiotarus c.41 BC), and Tarcondarius' son (also Castor), who briefly ruled all three tribes between the death of Deiotarus and the accession of Amyntas in 37/6.[47] The name Brigatus also recurs among the tetrarchs, and his title shows him to have been one of the Galatian leaders who controlled territory outside the tribal areas in the period of independence.[48] His kingdom is not known from the scanty surviving literary sources, but he may have ruled Amaseia, immediately adjoining Trocmian territory, before it was annexed to the province in 3 BC.[49] The doubt that may remain about the identity and connections of Castor and Brigatus is replaced by certainty in the case of the fourth priest, Pylaemenes son of King Amyntas. His liberalities during his two terms of office are on a larger scale than any others in the list, as would be expected of the son of the most powerful Anatolian dynast of the late republic. The dating of the inscription itself explains why he had not succeeded his father as ruler of an independent kingdom: he held priesthoods in AD 22/3 and 30/1, the latter fifty-five years after Amyntas' death in 25 BC; he can hardly have been of an age then to inherit the huge responsibilities which his father had sustained. On the other hand he must surely have contributed to the stability of the province between the annexation of Galatia and the middle years of Tiberius' reign, and in fact he is encountered once: an epigram of the contemporary poet Antipater of Thessalonica depicts him presenting a helmet to L. Calpurnius Piso, legate of the province between 15 and 13 BC.[50] The friendly relationship between tribal chieftain and governor and the martial overtones of the gift are both evocative of political realities in Galatia under Augustus. One other priest held office twice. Albiorix son of Ateporix, whose own son Aristocles was also

[42] S. Mitchell, *JHS Arch. reports* (1984/5), 99; *AS* 33 (1983), 9–11; 34 (1984), 8–10. Full publication by Waelkens (*Pisidian Antioch*, forthcoming). There is no doubt, despite Price, *Rituals and Power*, 270, that it dates to the Julio-Claudian period.

[43] *CIL* iii. 6820 (Antoninus Pius): *JRS* 2 (1912), 102 no. 34 (*sacerdos Imp. Caesaris Vespasiani*); see Levick, *Roman Colonies*, 88: Price, *Rituals and Power*, 89.

[44] Tacitus, *Ann.* 14. 31: 'delectique sacerdotes specie religionis omnis fortunas effundebant.'

[45] Livy, *Per.* 139.

[46] *CIL* xiii. 1541 (*ILS* 7041); *Inscriptions latines des Trois Gaules* 223 (*AE* (1955), 212). For Lucterius of the Cadurci, see Caesar, *BG* 7. 5. 1.

[47] The text in l. 8. of the inscription reads *ΤΩ. ΒΑΣΙΛΕΩΣ ΒΡΙΓΑΤΟ[Υ]*. Bosch restored [*Ταρκοδάριος Κάσ*]/*τωρ* but the traces in l. 7 cannot be reconciled with this (see the photo in Krencker and Schede, pl. 44*a*); ll. 6–7 should belong to the entry for the first priest in the sequence. But [*Κάσ*]*τω*[*ρ*] is a plausible restoration in l. 8 if we assume that the name was offset to the left like the others lower down in the column.

[48] C. Iulius Severus claimed descent from the tetrarch Amyntas son of Brigatus (and from the more famous Amyntas, son of Dyitalos), Bosch, *Ankara*, no. 105.

[49] See above, Ch 3 § iv n. 157.

[50] *Anth. Pal.* 6. 241 (A. S. F. Gow, *The Greek Anthology*, i (1968), 38–9 no. xliii; interpreted by C. Cichorius, *Römische Studien* (1922), 328–30.

Table 8.1. Galatian Priests of the Divine Augustus and the Goddess Rome

19/20	1. (Name of first priest missing)	
20/21	2. ?Castor s. of King Brigatus	Public banquet; olive oil for 4 months; gladiatorial spectacles with 30 pairs of gladiators; bull hunts and wild-beast hunts.
21/22	3. Rufus	Public banquet; gladiatorial spectacles; a hunt.

In the Governorship of Metilius (arrived ?spring/summer AD 22)

22/23	4. Pylaemenes s. of King Amyntas	Two public banquets; two gladiatorial spectacles; competitions for athletes; chariots, and horse races; bull fighting; a hunt; olive oil for the city; provided the places where the *Sebasteion* stands, and where the *panegyris* and horse race take place.
23/24	5. Albiorix s. of Ateporix	Public banquet; set up statues of (Tiberius) Caesar and Iulia Augusta.
24/25	6. Amyntas s. of Gaezatodiastes	Two public banquets; a hecatomb; gladiatorial spectacles; a grain distribution at the rate of 5 *modii* to each person.
25/26	7. . . . eias s. of Diognetos	
26/27	8. Albiorix s. of Ateporix	Public banquet.

In the Governorship of Fronto (arrived ?spring/summer AD 27)

27/28	9. Metrodorus s. of Menemachus	Public banquet; olive oil for 4 months.
28/29	10. Musanus s. of Artiknos	Public banquet.
29/30	11. . . . s. of Seleucus	Public banquet; olive oil for 4 months.
30/31	12. Pylaemenes s. of King Amyntas	Public banquet for the 3 tribes; a hecatomb for the tribe in Ancyra; gladiatorial spectacles; sacred procession; bull fighting; bull wrestling; 50 pairs of gladiators; oil for the whole year for the 3 tribes; wild-beast fight.

In the Governorship of Silvanus (arrived ?spring/summer 31)

31/32	13. ?M. Lollius	Public banquet in Pessinus; 25 pairs of gladiators and 10 pairs in Pessinus; olive oil for the 2 tribes for the whole year; erected a divine statue in Pessinus.
32/33	14. Seleucus s. of Philodamus	Public banquets.
33/34	15. Iulius Ponticus	Public banquet; hecatomb; olive oil for the whole year.
34/35	16. Aristocles s. of Albiorix	Public banquet; olive oil for the whole year.

In the Governorship of Basila (arrived ?spring/summer 35)

| 35/36 | 17. Q. Gallius Pulcher | Two public banquets; hecatomb in Pessinus; olive oil for the 2 tribes for the whole year. |
| 36/37 | 18. . . . ides s. of Philon | Public banquet; 2 hecatombs; olive oil for the whole year. |

Half a block uninscribed, followed by several fragmentary lines which end with references to benefactions and to the dedication of an altar.

| ? | 19. Pylaemenes s. of Menas | Public banquet for the 2 tribes; hecatomb; 30 pairs of gladiators; olive oil for the 2 tribes for the whole year. |
| ? | 20. ?Iulius Aquila | Public banquet for the 2 tribes; olive oil for the whole year; gladiatorial spectacles; (text damaged and incomplete). |

priest in AD 34/5. Ateporix is known from Strabo to have ruled the Caranitis in southern Pontus until his presumed death in 3/2 BC.[51] The family, to judge from its benefactions, had less disposable wealth than Pylaemenes. Another figure also has origins that may be traced to the first century BC: Q. Gallius Pulcher of Pessinus who served in AD 35/6 appears to be a member of a family that owed its Roman citizenship to the influence or patronage of a Roman quaestor, Q. Gallius, known to have been active in Cilicia in 47 BC; and, perhaps, to a connection with P. Clodius Pulcher, whose interest in the sanctuary at Pessinus in the mid-50s BC had been notorious.[52] Roman citizenship was a rare commodity in Anatolia in the mid-first century BC, and one can presume that the family had provided a long history of service to Rome.

Since the heading of the list designates the office holders as Galatians it is fair to assume that most if not all of the priests were Celts or had strong Celtic connections. Celtic names, not only in the dynastic families, but in the cases of Amyntas son of Gaizatodiastes and Musanus son of Articnus, confirm the point. Some of the aristocracy had been Hellenized to the extent of taking Greek names, like ... eias son of Diognetus, Metrodorus son of Menemachus, Seleucus son of Seleucus, or ... ides son of Philo: others had obtained Roman citizenship, like ?M. Lollius, probably a member of a family known from an Augustan gravestone found at Pessinus;[53] the names of Iulius Ponticus and ?Iulius Aquila suggest possible links with Pontus, which would be perfectly normal in the Galatian aristocracy,[54] just as the name Pylaemenes evokes contacts with Paphlagonia.[55]

The Celtic origins of the Galatian provincial community continued to be emphasized by its title, the *koinon* of Galatia or of the Galatians, in contrast to the other well-known provincial *koina* in Asia Minor, which were associations of the Greeks in Asia and Bithynia respectively. There the cult was organized in a civic context by Greeks, who distinguished themselves both from the non-Hellenized rural populations and from resident Romans.[56] It is tempting therefore to look for elements of Celtic tradition in the behaviour and benefactions of the Galatian priests while in office, for which the Ancyra inscription provides such explicit and detailed evidence.

In a small number of cases the benefactions took the form of permanent buildings or constructions connected with the cult, such as the site of the temple, the *panegyris*, and the horse race provided by Pylaemenes, the statues of Tiberius and Iulia Augusta which came from Albiorix, or the divine statue erected at Pessinus by M. Lollius. More often the gifts were ephemeral, and they fall into five categories: the provision of oil for use in the gymnasium; the multiple sacrifice of animal victims (*hecatombai*); the holding of public feasts (*demothoiniai*); the organization of gladiatorial shows, *venationes*, and related forms of public entertainment; and, on one occasion only, the distribution of grain. The nature of these liberalities in fact reveals a mixture of Greek, Roman, and Celtic traditions which was presumably characteristic of the behaviour of the Galatian aristocracy taken as a whole at this period.

The provision of oil was a normal and regular feature of Greek euergetism. The gymnasium where the oil would have been put to use was a central, almost a defining institution of a Greek city, and it is one of the remarkable aspects of the spread of Greek city life from its Mediterranean origins that olive oil, a foreign luxury in Galatia as in all of the remoter upland areas of the Hellenized world, was transported at the expense of the cities, or their wealthy inhabitants, to maintain the character of their Greek institutions.[57]

The multiple sacrifice of animals, although not necessarily a hundred at a time as the word hecatomb might suggest,[58] can be paralleled in Greek, Roman, and indeed Celtic contexts,[59] and it is hardly possible to decide which influence, if any, was decisive in leading to its adoption as a standard feature of the imperial cult in Galatia. Only six of the priests are said to have offered hecatombs among their generosities, and they appear to have been among the wealthiest of the series. The word *hecatombe* does not appear commonly in Greek inscriptions, and was hardly a regular form of cult offering at most temples and

---

[51] Strabo, 12. 3. 37, 560. See above Ch. 3 §IV n. 154.

[52] See above, Ch. 3 §IV nn. 82–5 and 97–8. Cicero's predecessor as governor of Cilicia, Appius Claudius Pulcher, is another possible source for the cognomen.

[53] Waelkens, *Türsteine*, no. 723 (*I. Pessinus* no. 78).

[54] Cf. the Neronian procurator of Pontus and Bithynia, C. Iulius Aquila, generally assumed to be of local origin, *PIR*[2] iv. 144: i no. 166; Magie, *RR* ii. 1405. Conceivably the Galatian priest and the procurator might be the same man. Remember too Aquila of Pontus in Acts 18: 2.

[55] Justin, 37. 4. 8, 'Paphlagonum regum nomen'; Magie, *RR* ii. 1093.

[56] See Deininger, *Provinziallandtage*, 36 ff. (Asia); 60 ff. (Bithynia); 66 ff. (Galatia); Price, *Rituals and Power*, 87 ff.

[57] Two much-discussed passages in Strabo suggest that olives were grown on the Anatolian plateau at Melitene (12. 2. 1, 535) and at Phrygian Synnada (12. 8. 14, 577). L. Robert, *JSav.* (1961), 141 ff. (*OMS* vii. 1 ff.), examines the question at length and suggests that Strabo's claim might result from confusion between the olive and the jujube (*elaeagnus*, Turkish *iğde ağaç*).

[58] *RE* vii (1912), 2786–7 s.v. ἑκατόμβη (Stengel); cf. F. Sokolowski, *Lois sacrées d'Asie Mineure* (1955), no. 50 l. 19: ἡ πόλις δίδοι ἑκατόνβην τρία ἱερῆια τέλεια (Didyma).

[59] For Celtic sacrifices see above, Ch. 4 §IV.

shrines, at least in the Roman period,[60] but the evidence does not allow us to claim that the Ancyran examples show a Celtic tradition akin to that attested in accounts of vast sacrifices in the Celtic West.

Demothoiniai were a common feature of Greek civic generosity, often associated with the imperial cult, or with the worship of the principal gods of a city. For instance, the priests of Zeus at Panamara in Caria regularly entertained the citizens of Stratonicaea and its neighbourhood to public banquets, as did the eponymous archons on the island of Syros, the latter in connection with prayers and sacrifices for the emperors' health and safety.[61] *Demothoiniai* as such are attested in the imperial period at Argos[62] and at Callatis.[63] But the giving of public feasts could be described in other ways, as is clear from the most explicit epigraphic evidence, the decrees set up by Acraephia in Boeotia in the middle of the first century AD to honour their citizen Epaminondas.[64] On the other hand *demothoiniai* were not a regular accompaniment to emperor worship and they are not widely attested in the cities of Asia. Their prominence in the Ancyra inscription is worth emphasizing. The word usually appears in the singular or plural without further qualification, but Pylaemenes son of Amyntas, who could afford the gesture, offered a banquet in his second term for all three tribes; his namesake Pylaemenes, son of Menas, and (?)Iulius Aquila did so for the two tribes (that is the Tolistobogii and the Tectosages); while M. Lollius specifically provided for his compatriots at Pessinus. Although it is inconceivable that banquets were laid on for all tribal members, and the most likely recipients of the benefaction were the delegates and other representatives of the tribes who came together at Ancyra for the festivals and ceremonies of the imperial cult, it is difficult to resist the conclusion that these feasts perpetuated the well-attested traditions of the Celtic nobility, for whom public banquets offered to the whole tribe were a central part of their culture. The ethnographic sources which describe Celts both in Gaul and in the eastern Mediterranean make it clear that an important part of a leader's prestige and status depended on his ability to offer unstinting hospitality to his own kinsmen and even to all comers. The public feasts of the Galatian *koinon* fulfilled a comparable function and it would be surprising if they did

not preserve some elements of this distinctive Celtic tradition.[65]

Gladiatorial competitions and shows, or fights involving wild animals (*venationes*), were by origin a Roman institution, originally introduced as part of lavish aristocratic funerals. In the later republic however they were commonly sponsored by office holders (or those seeking public office), and they thus acquired a central position in Roman public life. In the mid-second century BC the exaggeratedly philo-Roman Antiochus IV Epiphanes mounted gladiatorial games when he returned to Syrian Antioch. Although this was an isolated forerunner of the widespread dissemination of gladiatorial shows through the Greek East under the empire, Livy's comment on the local reaction to the spectacle is revealing and interesting: 'he presented a display of gladiators in the Roman fashion, which at first inspired more terror than pleasure among men who were unused to such spectacles. Afterwards, as he put on shows rather frequently, he made it a spectacle that was both familiar and pleasing to onlookers and fired many young men with the desire to take up armed combat themselves.'[66] In the late Roman republic the giving of a gladiatorial show became a *munus*, an obligation on would-be magistrates, and it was in this form that it was exported to the western provinces, where high priests of the provincial cult of the emperors sponsored competitions as part of their official duties.[67] The emperors themselves exercised some control over their activities, for an imperially sponsored *senatus consultum* of AD 177, known from a copy published at Italica in Baetica, attempted to regulate the expenditure of high priests in Italy, Gaul, and by implication the Spanish provinces.[68] It is clear that gladiatorial games reached the eastern provinces by the same route. The vast majority of gladiatorial inscriptions are linked with the imperial cult, and in most cases the responsibility for mounting gladiatorial fights lay with the high priest.[69] Indeed part of a copy of the *senatus consultum* of AD 177 has been found in Asia at Sardis,[70] demonstrating that its terms were as applicable in the East as they were in the West.

The Galatian evidence not only conforms to this overall picture but reinforces it strongly. Half the priests on the Ancyra list provided gladiatorial games

[60] Note the association of hecatombs with *demothoiniai* at Argos, *IG* iv. 602, 606.
[61] Stratonicaea: A. Laumonier, *Les Cultes indigènes en Carie* (1958), 319–20; Syros: *IG* xii. 5. 659–68. On public feasts at Aeolian Cyme and elsewhere, see also *Bull. ép.* (1983), 323 pp. 123–8.
[62] *IG* iv. 602. cf. 597.
[63] *SEG* xvi. 428.
[64] *IG* vii. 2712; cf. J. H. Oliver, *GRBS* 17 (1971), 221–37.
[65] For Celtic banquets, see above, Ch. 4 §1. For banquets in Greek cities, note the observations of Robert, *Gladiateurs*, 246 n. 3; *Hermes* 65 (1930), 115; *BCH* 59 (1935), 422 ff.
[66] Livy, 41. 20. For gladiators in the eastern provinces, see Robert, *Gladiateurs, passim*.
[67] G. Ville, *Les Gladiateurs en Occident* (1981).
[68] J. H. Oliver and R. E. A. Palmer, *Hesperia*, 24 (1955), 320 ff.; for contemporary attempts to restrain expenditure on Greek *agones* see *JRS* 90 (1990), 190, and Ch. 12 §v n. 160.
[69] Robert, *Gladiateurs*, 270–80.
[70] W. H. Buckler, *Sardis* vii. 1 no. 16.

or *venationes* during their term of office. Even more significantly the 'theatre' at Pessinus, which was designed and built at the same time as the imperial temple to which it is linked, was apparently intended from the outset to accommodate these dangerous spectacles. The connection between gladiators and emperor worship was not merely contingent, but there was an essential link between them.

It is noteworthy that gladiatorial games, directly derived from a Roman institution, are far more prominent in the Tiberian list than any reference to Greek games or *agones*. There is a hint of these in the benefactions of Pylaemenes son of Amyntas, who provided competitions for athletes and chariot- and horse-racing during his first term. But the last of these was in fact again more typical of Roman than Greek competitive spectacles, and it is worth noting that the *panegyris* and the *hippodromos*, which Pylaemenes provided to accommodate these events, occur also in the description which Dio gives of the games mounted by Augustus at Rome in 28 BC to celebrate the victory at Actium.[71] This event could easily have provided a model for provincials to copy, and the wide dissemination of victory celebrations would naturally have been encouraged by the emperor and his legates. Galatian public life did not become distinctively Hellenized until late in the first century AD.

Another trace of Roman influence probably lies behind the one instance of grain distribution, by Amyntas son of Gaizatodiastes in AD 25/6. The distribution of grain at no cost, or at a low price, was common in Greek cities, although by no means as widespread as the subsidized provision of oil.[72] The means by which grain might be provided and its cost underwritten varied from period to period and from city to city, although it was naturally common for the financial burden to be borne by city magistrates or other wealthy liturgists. However, the evidence taken as a whole does not show that the equal division of a fixed ration of grain, the method implied by the phrase found in the Ancyra inscription, *sitometria ana pente modious*, was a common occurrence in Greek cities. The model for this method being used at Ancyra is much more likely to have been the distribution of free grain to the *plebs* at Rome. It is significant that the inscription uses the Latin word *modii* rather than the Greek *medimni* to describe the grain measures, and it is equally telling that the amount involved, five *modii*, was precisely the monthly total allocated to members of the *plebs frumentaria* at Rome in the late Republic,[73] a ration that corresponded closely to an adult's daily caloric requirements.[74] It thus appears that, for one year at least, a Galatian magnate, presumably the owner of extensive grain lands,[75] chose to imitate the Roman corn dole in his native city. Perhaps the daunting organizational problems, as well as the expense involved, were a reason why the experiment was not repeated. More than a century later there is evidence that comparable schemes for distributing free corn were inaugurated in Lycia. An inscription from Xanthos, which catalogues the benefactions of Opramoas or of some other unknown benefactor, includes an expression which is strongly reminiscent of the Ancyra text: 'to all citizens of Xanthos, individually, he gave grain at a ration of ten *modii*'; in several Lycian cities during the second century these beneficiaries were described as *tois sitometroumenois*, 'those who received the corn measure'. The verbal similarities and the absence of comparable evidence from elsewhere in the Greek world strongly support the view that both the Lycian and the Ancyran schemes were based on Roman not Greek models.[76]

---

[71] Cassius Dio, 53. 1. 4: καὶ τὴν πανήγυριν τὴν ἐπὶ τῇ νίκῃ τῇ πρὸς τῷ Ἀκτίῳ γενομένῃ ψηφισθεῖσαν ἤγαγε μετὰ τοῦ Ἀγρίππου, καὶ ἐν αὐτῇ τὴν ἱπποδρομίαν διά τε τῶν παίδων καὶ διὰ τῶν ἀνδρῶν τῶν εὐγενῶν ἐποίησε. καὶ αὕτη μὲν διὰ πέντε ἀεὶ ἐτῶν μέχρι που ἐγίγνετο. In the 3rd cent. AD games known as the *Megala Augusteia Actia* were celebrated at Ancyra (Bosch, *Ankara* nos. 286–7; cf. Robert, *Hellenica*, xi/xii. 366 ff.); in the mid-3rd cent. Nicomedia also staged Augustus' Actian games (Αὐγούστου Ἄκτια) and Αὐγουστεῖα Ἄκτια are also attested at Tarsus in AD 255/6 (Ziegler, 25–6, 117–18). In the last instance the games were newly founded in the mid-3rd cent. in connection with the imperial cult in Cilicia and the increasing presence of Roman troops and emperors in the region at that period, and it appears that the Actian games of Ancyra and Nicomedia were also introduced or reintroduced in the 3rd cent. since there is no other epigraphic or numismatic evidence for them at an earlier date (Ziegler, 116 n. 314, and below, Ch. 12 § v n. 184).

[72] Since the gymnasium was a central public institution of Greek cities it was quite natural for benefactors to endow the provision of oil. The provision of grain, for private use, was never so institutionalized. In general see H. Francotte, 'Le Pain à bon marché et le pain gratuit dans les cités grecques', *Mélanges Nicole* (1905), 143–54 = *Mélanges du droit public grec* (1910), 291–302; L. Robert, *BCH* 1928, 426–32

(= *OMS* i. 108–14); A. Wilhelm, *Mélanges Glotz*, ii (1932), 899–908; P. Veyne, *Le Pain et le cirque* (1976), 222–3 with nn. 120–1.

[73] M. Rostovtzeff, *RE* vii. 1 (1910), 172 ff. s.v. frumentum.

[74] R. D. Duncan-Jones, *The Economy of the Roman Empire: Quantitative Studies* (1973), 146–7.

[75] Compare Ch. 10 § III for many examples.

[76] A. Balland, *Xanthos*, vii. 214 ff. on inscription no. 67 l. 23. The attribution of the benefaction to Opromoas is disputed by J. J. Coulton, *JHS* 108 (1988), 171–8. The evidence for *sitometria* and its recipients, the *sitometroumenoi*, in Lycia has been further discussed by Wörrle, *Stadt und Fest*, 123–31, and N. Milner, *AS* 38 (1988), 138–9. The former calls into question the Roman influence behind the Lycian institution, but Balland's hypothesis of strong Roman influence remains attractive. Balland, op. cit. 214 n. 318 asserts without argument that the Tiberian *sitometria* at Ancyra follows a Greek pattern of munificence, but this takes no account of the detail

The priest list from Ancyra taken as a whole shows that the most lavish displays of civic or communal generosity in Galatia were provided by the priests of the imperial cult. Rivalry between successive holders of the post, as well as their intrinsic wealth, was certainly a potent factor in maintaining the level of donations, as it would have been in a strictly Celtic tribal milieu; the effects of competition may have left their mark in the fact that the provision of oil for four months, which had been standard between AD 20/1 and 29/30, was increased to provision for the whole year after Pylaemenes son of Amyntas set this new level.

The liberality and public generosity of the wealthy, designed in the first place to confirm the prestige of the donor and to secure in the widest sense his political authority, was as much a characteristic of the Greek city or of Roman public life as it was of tribal society, the three elements that played a part in shaping the character of Ancyra's priests.[77] These patterns of aristocratic behaviour were confirmed, but also modified, by the later history of the Galatian communities. In the late first and second centuries the high priest (archiereus) of the koinon was the most prominent official at Ancyra or Pessinus. The post was held by the leading men in public life, usually once only,[78] but sometimes on two or three occasions.[79] When an inscription singles out the liberality of an honorand it is usually in connection with this position: so Ti. Claudius Bocchus of Ancyra is said to have served as high priest of the Galatian koinon, to have provided oil with magnificent generosity, and to have made many distributions in his native city.[80] C. Iulius Severus, the most distinguished man in the province in the first half of the second century, brought his civic career to a climax as archiereus, when he excelled all those who had previously obtained that honour in his

distributions and his other distinctions.[81] Not long afterwards under Hadrian, Latinius Alexander was high priest twice and 'sebastophant', and provided oil at his own expense more splendidly than his predecessors throughout the whole year, during the period when the emperor and his sacred armies passed through the city.[82] The forms of benefaction familiar from the Tiberian inscription persisted, but with certain changes. The provision of oil was still a regular duty; explicit references to demothoiniai disappeared, perhaps eclipsed as the aristocracy became more Hellenized; the tradition may have persisted in less convivial mode in the form of epidoseis or dianomai, hand-outs or distributions. Gladiatorial games were still a regular occurrence in second and third century Ancyra, and were doubtless still sponsored by high priests of the imperial cult,[83] but they were now rivalled by Greek agones. Games of the Galatian koinon, held on a four-yearly cycle, are known both at Ancyra and Tavium from as early as the reign of Nero,[84] and the post of agonothetes was regularly associated with the high-priesthood on civic career inscriptions.[85]

The Ancyra inscription shows beyond question that the koinon and its officials played a decisive part in setting the tone for civic and provincial life in north Galatia. While the institutions of the new cities were still in their infancy, it seems to have been proportionately more important than it was to be later. It minted coins through much of the first century AD; the so-called official Galatian coinage of the Tiberian period was probably struck for the koinon,[86] and issues which explicitly name it run from Nero to Trajan.[87] Some time in the first half of the first century it set up an

---

that grain was to be distributed in quantities of five *modii*. A later Ancyran text, Bosch, *Ankara*, no. 101 honours a man σειτομετρήσαντα, ἀγορανομήσαντα τὸ δ', μονομαχίας κὲ θηρομαχίας κὲ θεωρίας δεδωκότα ἡμέραις να'.

[77] H. Bolkestein, *Wohltätigkeit und Armenpflege im vorchristlichen Altertum* (1939); A. R. Hands, *Charities and Social Aids in Greece and Rome* (1968); P. Veyne, *Le Pain et le cirque* (1976); A. Balland, *Xanthos*, vii. 173–224.

[78] Ancyra: C. Iulius Severus, Bosch, *Ankara*, nos. 105–6; Q. Aelius Macedo, ibid. no. 139; L. Papirius Alexander, ibid. no. 140; Tertullus Varus, ibid. no. 287. Pessinus: Ti. Cl. Deiotarus, *IGR* iii. 225 (*I. Pessinus*, no. 18); M. Lydianus... Claudius(?), *IGR* iii. 232 (*I. Pessinus*, no. 14); M. Cocceius ...Seleucus, *I. Pessinus*, no. 12.

[79] Ancyra (apart from the Tiberian list): Latinius Alexander, Bosch, *Ankara*, no. 117; and Ti. Cl. Bocchus, ibid. no. 142 (both twice); Ti. Iulius Iustus Iunianus, ibid. nos. 255–8 and *AS* 27 (1977), 72–3 no. 6 (*SEG* xxvii (1977), 842) (three times).

[80] Bosch, *Ankara*, no. 100 ll. 8–11.

[81] Ibid. no. 105 ll. 15–17.

[82] Ibid. no. 117 ll. 6–12.

[83] Robert, *Gladiateurs*, nos. 87–90; *Hellenica*, viii. 40; Bosch, *Ankara*, nos. 101, 149–51, and 152, the last not included in Robert's collection.

[84] Moretti, *Iscrizioni agonistiche greche*, no. 65 (*SEG* xiv. 663) from Syrian Antioch. For the Actian games of Ancyra see above, n. 71.

[85] Both Q. Aelius Macedo (Bosch, *Ankara*, no. 139) and T. Flavius Gaianus (ibid. nos. 249–53 and *AS* 27 (1977), 73–5 no. 7 = *SEG* xxvii (1977), 844) were specifically *agonothetai* of the games of the Galatian koinon. In other inscriptions *agonothesia* is mentioned immediately after the high priesthood and was presumably associated with it (*IGR* iii. 230, 232).

[86] The analysis by minting authority of coin issues from Roman Asia Minor published by P. R. Franke *et al.*, *Index Aulock* (i.e. the composite index to *SNG Deutschland*, von Aulock collection), reports an unpublished Augustan issue of the Galatian koinon in the collection of the American Numismatic Society. When I inspected this, by kind permission of the late Dr Nancy Waggoner, it proved to be a Claudian issue, with the legend *EΠI AΦPEINOY* (see n. 30 above).

[87] See *Index Aulock*.

inscription for Q. Iulius Q. f., who must have been one of the first Ancyrans to receive the Roman citizenship,[88] and it is also known to have erected an honorific inscription at Phrygian Acmonia in the first century AD.[89] In the inscription for Q. Iulius Q. f. the organization carries its full title, the *koinon tōn Sebastēnōn Galatōn*, and this emphasizes the fact that it was made up from the three Celtic tribes, each of which was also described by the adjective *Sebastenos* through the imperial period.[90] Also during the first century, the tribes themselves minted without specifically mentioning the urban centres of Pessinus, Ancyra, and Tavium around which they revolved.[91] It would be a mistake to build too large a distinction between city and tribe,[92] but these coin legends suggest that in the first century tribal feeling and loyalty remained strong, and the prominence of the *koinon* as an institution reflects this. It is probably no coincidence that after the reign of Trajan the *koinon* ceased to mint coins or erect statues for prominent local citizens. The cities by then had confidently assumed the role that they were designed to play, as the primary institutions of local government in the province.

An outline of the history of the imperial cult may be traced without difficulty at least until the Severan period, when the relationship between the emperors and the cities of the eastern part of the empire began to undergo significant changes (see below, Ch. 12 § v at n. 192). Although the evidence from Galatia and the rest of central and eastern Asia Minor on its own is sporadic and incomplete, and does not provide a satisfactory basis for detailed analysis or discussion of the cult's wider significance, the information from the well-documented cities of western Asia Minor shows that emperor worship was arguably the most significant way in which provincial subjects were made aware of and came to terms with imperial power within the framework of their communities.[93] Religious activity in the cities of the empire was, with rare exceptions, explicit and public, often involving the whole community in unified celebration of the gods. Its significance lay in rituals which all could observe and in

which many citizens participated. These range from prayer, sacrifice, solemn ceremony, and religious processions to feasts, games, and festivals.[94] Emperor worship in essence conformed to this familiar pattern, but imperial festivals and rituals in provincial cities frequently outnumbered and outweighed those of the other gods. Details of how emperors were worshipped varied from city to city, and show some significant deviations from the forms of worship of the traditional gods,[95] but no other cults had so widespread a distribution. They were to be found in every city and in many other organized communities. It is hardly surprising that when the Roman authorities sought a means by which men could profess their attachment to paganism and renounce Christianity, oaths and sacrifices to or on behalf of emperors were the element common to almost all instances of the enforcement of paganism, although in such contexts important distinctions between emperors and gods were carefully maintained.[96]

Roman provincial officials and the local populations were bound together by their relations with the emperor. A governor marked significant imperial anniversaries by sending letters of congratulation to the emperor, while provincial cities took these as occasions for prayer and public rejoicing; both parties, as has been seen, helped to establish the detailed local framework of the cult.[97] New Year's Day in the province of Asia, and certainly in other provinces also, began on Augustus' birthday, 23 September; months and days took imperial names; and so the whole organization of time, at least in urban contexts, reflected this imperial takeover of the calendar, both sacred and secular.[98] The great temples of the Asian cities, dedicated to the traditional civic gods, made room for emperors and members of their families. They were matched by new temples dedicated to the emperors alone, and in new cities and communities the imperial sanctuary was typically the centrepiece of the civic layout. This pattern, which is so clear in the chief cities of Julio-Claudian Galatia continued in the later first and second centuries. The minor cities of Cana and Perta on the northern boundary of Lycaonia acquired imperial temples by the reigns of Trajan and Hadrian respectively.[99] Marcus Aurelius transformed the

---

[88] Bosch, *Ankara*, no. 56.

[89] *MAMA* vi. 255 simply reading τὸ κοινὸν Γαλατῶν. The rest of the text must have been on another stone; it may have commemorated a member of the connected families of the Iulii Severi and the Servenii, who were prominent both at Acmonia and Ancyra in the early empire. See Halfmann, *Senatoren*, 102–3.

[90] See above, Ch. 7 § III nn. 80–2.

[91] e.g. *SNG von Aulock*, 6120 and *BMC Galatia* etc., 8 nos. 1–2 (Ancyra); *SNG von Aulock* 6208–9, and *BMC Galatia* etc., 18 no. 3 (Pessinus); *SNG von Aulock* 6237–8, and *BMC Galatia* etc., 24 nos. 3–7 (Tavium).

[92] See above, Ch. 7 § III.

[93] Price, *Rituals and Power*, ch. 9.

[94] Ibid., esp. chs 5, 7, 8.

[95] Ibid., ch. 7, 8.

[96] Ibid. 220–2; F. Millar, 'The Imperial Cult and the Persecutions'. in W. den Boer (ed.), *Le Culte des souverains dans l'empire romain* (1973), 145–65.

[97] Price, *Rituals and Power*, 101 ff.

[98] Ibid. 106.

[99] Kana: *MAMA* viii. 211, for the date see Ch. 7 § v n. 185 above; Perta: *MAMA* viii. 259 with M. H. Ballance, 'An Archaeological Reassessment of the Classical Period in Central

Cappadocian village of Halala in the northern foothills of the Taurus into a Roman colony Faustinopolis in memory of his wife who had died there, and built a temple in her honour.[100] In each case the imperial temples are the only public buildings known to have existed in these modest settlements. Likewise the civic space of Pisidian Adada was dominated by no less than four temples, each dedicated jointly to one of the traditional gods and to the emperors, which are also the only clear examples of religious architecture on a well-preserved site.[101] In rural north Galatia an imperial freedman procurator of an imperial estate was responsible for building a temple there between AD 177 and 180; surely an isolated public building in a community whose inhabitants lived scattered between seven villages.[102]

The epigraphic evidence, with the focus on local office-holding, tells a similar story. At Ancyra and Pessinus the careers of the leading citizens were crowned by posts connected with the cult. The hierarchy of the provincial koinon included the offices of archiereus, 'sebastophant', 'hierophant', and 'galatarch'. By the later first century AD the priests of the Tiberian list had become high priests (archiereis). In the second century the inscriptions of C. Iulius Severus, Q. Aelius Macedo, and L. Papirius Alexander all place the high priesthood at the head of their locally held offices,[103] as does Cl. Caecilius Hermianus in the mid-third century.[104] Only the latter's contemporary Tertullus Varus relegated the post behind other priesthoods, of Men and Asclepius.[105] The position could be held twice, as by Latinius Alexander and Ti. Claudius Bocchus in the first half of the second century,[106] or three times by Ti. Iulius Iustus Iunianus in the time of Caracalla.[107] His inscrip-

---

Asia Minor,' unpub. Ph.D. thesis (Edinburgh, 1960), 207 no. 190; the text is reconstructed above, Ch. 7 n. 178.

[100] Script. Hist. Aug. M. Aurelius, 26; Carcalla, 11.

[101] IGR iii. 364–6; Price, Rituals and Power, 269. Note in particular the coin of Valerian and Gallienus which depicts a hexastyle temple labelled as the Traianeion, Aulock, Pisidien, i. no. 114.

[102] RECAM ii. 34–6; for the seven villages see RECAM ii. 37.

[103] Bosch, Ankara, nos. 105, 139, 140.

[104] Ibid. no. 287.

[105] Ibid. no. 280; for this person see JRS 64 (1974), 30.

[106] Bosch, Ankara, nos. 117, 142.

[107] Ibid. nos. 255–8 and AS 27 (1977), 72–3 no. 6.

Fig. 18a. Lystra. Obv. Head of Augustus; rev. Priest with two oxen ploughing, COL IUL FEL GEM LVSTRA. The type characteristically commemorated the foundation of a Roman colony. It was also highly appropriate for this small agricultural town. H. von Aulock, Chiron, 2 (1972), 509–18 at 515. Düsseldorf Gips-Sammlung 11889. The reference numbers at the end of the coin descriptions in Figs. 18, 35, 36, and 38 are all to this collection.

(b) Ninica Claudiopolis. Obv. Portrait of Maximus Caesar, C. IUL. VER. MAXIMUS CAES; rev. Wolf with the twins Romulus and Remus under a fig tree. COL N[INI]C CLAUΔ. This obscure colony emphasized its Roman connections. Ziegler, Münzen Kilikiens, nos. 354–7. 7146.

(c) Pessinus. Obv. Head of Claudius, ΚΑΙΣΑΡ; rev. Front of temple with six columns, ΕΠΙ ΑΦΡΙΝΟΥ. The type depicts the Tiberian imperial temple at Pessinus and was minted when M. Annius Afrinus was the governor of Galatia, AD 49–54 (see Ch. 6 at n. 94; 8 at n. 30). SNG von Aulock, 6208. 1971.

(d) Sardis. Obv. Bust of Elagabalus; rev. Four temples. Above left an imperial temple with an imperial statue; above right the temple of Artemis with cult statue; below two further imperial temples, ΣΑΡΔΙΑΝΩΝ ΤΡΙΣ ΝΕΩΚΟΡΩΝ ΕΠ ΕΡΜΟΦΙΛΟΥ ΑΡ Α ΤΟ Β. Sardis was entitled to three imperial temples; this issue challenged Asia's leading city, Ephesus, which by a dispensation of the emperor Elagabalus could claim a fourth neocorate for its temple of Artemis. Compare BMC Lydia, 265 no. 171 (a similar but not the same type). 10446.

(e) Pergamum. Obv. Four-columned temple with crown in gable, containing a seated Zeus and an armed imperial statue, ΦΙΛΙΟΣ ΖΕΥΣ ΑΥΤ ΤΡΑΙΑΝΟ ΣΕ[Β ΠΕΡ]; rev. Four-columned temple containing statues of Augustus and Roma, ΘΕΑ ΡΩΜΗ ΚΑΙ ΘΕΩ ΣΕΒΑΣΤΩ. The reverse shows the imperial temple authorized in 29 BC (Ch. 8 at n. 2), the obverse the Traianeum built under Trajan and Hadrian (see Radt, Pergamon, 239–50). H. Stiller, Alt. von Perg. v. 2, 53. 5691.

(f) Neocaesareia. Obv. Bust of Severus Alexander; rev. Two temples with four columns, each with a prize crown above the gable, ΜΗΤΡ ΝΕΟΚΕΣΑΡΙΑΣ ΣΑ ΔΙΣ ΝΕΩΚΟΡ ΕΤ Ρ[Ο]Α (AD 234/5). Neocaesareia, the metropolis of Pontus, received a second neocory under Severus Alexander, which gave it the right to a second temple and (as the crown shows) a second series of sacred games. Recueil général des monnaies grecques d'Asie Mineure i², 125 no. 40. 6002.

(g) Tarsus. Bust of Gallienus with radiate crown; rev. ΤΑΡΣΟΥ ΜΗΤΡΟΠΟΛΕΩΣ ΑΜΚ Γ Γ. Victory, with foot resting on a globe, carrying a shield which is inscribed ΕΙΣ ΑΙΩΝΑ ΤΟΥΣ ΚΥΡΙΟΥΣ. The acclamation formula signals the actual presence of an emperor (probably Valerian in AD 255/6) in the city. SNG von Aulock, 6080; cf. Ziegler, 118 n. 319. 10472.

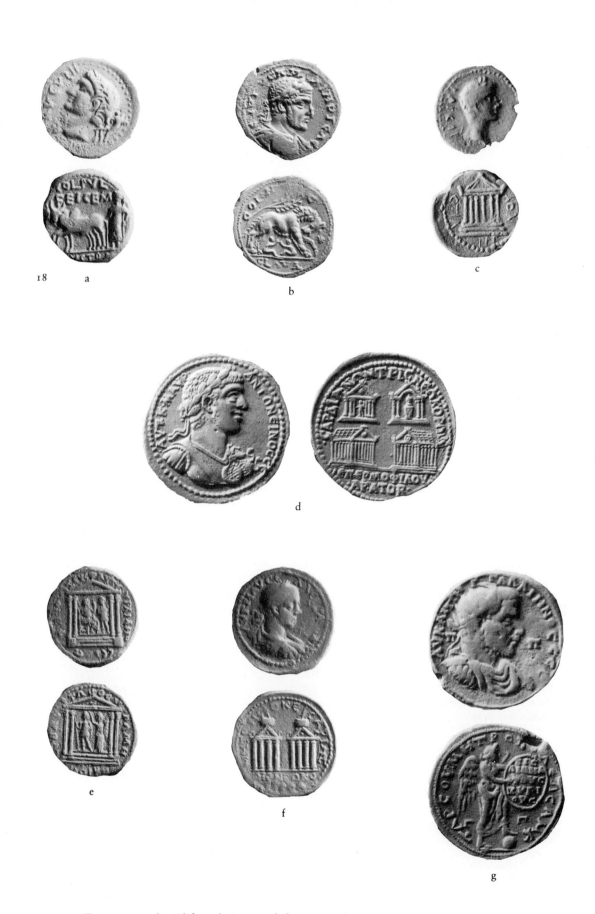

18

a

b

c

d

e

f

g

Coin-types illustrating colonial foundations and the Imperial Cult

tions mention only the three high priesthoods among his official positions, along with the honorific titles 'founder of the metropolis' (he had built Ancyra's great bathing complex), and 'lover of his country'.

Outside Ancyra high priests of the *koinon* are known only from Pessinus, and it seems likely that the provincial Galatian cult was not established outside Ancyra except here and at Tavium where games of the *koinon* were held.[108] The Pessinuntine office holders were Ti. Claudius Heras, his son Ti. Claudius Theodotus, M. Lydius . . . Claudius, and M. Cocceius Seleucus, the last of whom should be identified with the Cocceius Seleucus who headed the second, perhaps Trajanic list of high priests on the right hand *anta* of the temple at Ancyra.[109] Ti. Claudius Heras' inscription is particularly informative and shows that he had been six times high priest of the emperors, high priest and agonothete of the *koinon*, and sebastophant of the temple in Pessinus. The first post was clearly attached to the civic cult of Pessinus; no Galatian is known to have held the provincial high-priesthood itself more than the three times of Ti. Iulius Iustus Iunianus, and Heras held that position, with its attendant responsibility for presiding over the provincial games, only once. The office of sebastophant of the temple in Pessinus is reminiscent of the many inscriptions from Asia which describe officials of the imperial cult as having held office at the temple of one of the five cities which had been allowed to build provincial temples, and it confirms that the temple excavated there was indeed a building of the provincial not the civic cult.[110]

The lesser positions of sebastophant and hierophant were held by men of the same background as the high priests, even when they did not serve as stepping stones on the way to the top position.[111] The title of galatarch is more puzzling. The comparable word asiarch in Asia was apparently used by persons who had been high priests but no longer held office. This will not explain all the instances where the word galatarch appears in inscriptions of Ancyra and Pessinus. Some honorands are described as having held both positions,[112] while in other cases the post of galatarch was held by young men who might reasonably have been expected to reach the high priesthood in due course, like Ti.

Claudius Procillianus, son of the high priest Ti. Claudius Bocchus, who was described as the 'new hope of his country'. Perhaps galatarchs achieved this status by virtue of family connections; children of high priests may have taken the title by right, just as the wives of high priests seem to have been automatically dignified with the title of high priestess.[113]

No other city or area of the province is so richly documented by public inscriptions as Ancyra and the evidence for the offices of the imperial cult elsewhere is correspondingly much more patchy. Pontus had its own *koinon* as well as civic cults.[114] The most explicit civic inscription comes from Sebastopolis and was erected for M. Antonius Rufus, who was pontarch in the Pontic metropolis Neocaesarea, but also along with his wife Antonia Stratonice lifelong high priest of the emperor Hadrian; and it was in this capacity that he had provided wild-beast shows and gladiatorial games, as well as taking care of annual processions and public feasts, apparently by endowing a lifelong foundation.[115] The main features of emperor worship recorded here need no further comment in the light of the previous discussion of the Ancyra evidence. In Armenia Minor, the single civic inscription of Nicopolis honours a certain Iulius Patroeinus as first of the Hellenes, a title particularly associated with the *koinon* organization,[116] and first Armeniarch.[117] Pompeiopolis, the metropolis of Paphlagonia, was the home city of the Claudii Severi, several of whom entered the Roman senate.[118] An inscription set up for one of them gives a senatorial career, and two local offices: high priest of the emperors and, apparently, Paphlagoniarch.[119]

The same picture emerges from the communities of Lycaonia and Isauria. The imperial high priesthood was the most prominent public position at Iconium,[120]

[108] See above, n. 84.

[109] See above, n. 78. For M. Cocceius . . . Seleucus see *AS* 27 (1977), 74 n. 48.

[110] For Asia see Deininger, *Provinziallandtage*, 38–9.

[111] Ti. Cl. Heras, M. Lydianus . . . Claudius(?), and M. Cocceius . . . Seleucus were all sebastophants at Pessinus. Ancyra: Ti. Cl. Bocchus, Cl. Balbina the younger, C. Iulius Severus, Latinius Alexander, and Q. Aelius Macedo (Bosch, *Ankara*, nos. 100, 98, 105, 117, 139). The two hierophants at Ancyra, Q. Aelius Macedo and I. Aelius Iulianus (ibid. nos. 139 and 98) both held office for life.

[112] Q. Aelius Macedo, T. Flavius Gaianus, and Tertullus Varus.

[113] Bosch, *Ankara*, no. 142. For the post of *archiereia* see Deininger, *Provinziallandtage*, 41, 154. However, R. Kearsley, *GRBS* 27 (1986), 183–92 argues that some *archiereiai*, of Asia at least, held office in their own right and did not simply acquire the title by virtue of their husbands' office-holding. For the post in Galatia see Bosch, *Ankara*, nos. 107–8 (Cl. Aquillia, wife of C. Iulius Severus, cf. ibid. no. 105 ll. 27–8, καὶ τὴν γυναῖκα καταστήσαντα ἀρχιέρειαν καὶ αὐτὴν ὑπερβαλοῦσαν ἐπιδόσεσιν).

[114] See Deininger, *Provinziallandtage*, 64–6 contesting the older view that there were two Pontic *koina* in Asia Minor: one for the Pontic cities in Pontus and Bithynia and one for those that belonged to Galatia and Cappadocia.

[115] *IGR* iii. 115; commentary by J. G. C. Anderson, *JHS* 20 (1900), 153.

[116] See W. Ameling, *I. Prusias*, 31 n. 28.

[117] *IGR* iii. 132.

[118] Halfmann, *Senatoren*, 135–6.

[119] *IGR* iii. 134.

[120] H. S. Cronin, *JHS* 22 (1902), 119 nos. 54–6 (*IGR* iii. 1474); cf. *ILS* 9414.

Isaura,[121] Savatra,[122] Vasada,[123] Pappa-Tiberiopolis,[124] and in the territory of the Gorgoromeis.[125] The pattern of discovery elsewhere surely leads one to expect that further exploration or excavation of these ill-documented cities would only confirm the dominance of emperor worship in local public life.

There are many strands that can be unravelled in pursuing the understanding of the imperial cult, which like any complex institutional phenomenon was not only materially diverse but also meant different things to different participants and observers. In the context of the newly annexed and largely non-urbanized regions of Roman central Anatolia it is appropriate to emphasize the ways in which it helped to create and perpetuate new traditions and patterns of civic life. In one sense the actual buildings connected with the cult regularly provided both the earliest and the most splendid examples of the public architecture which was a crucial defining characteristic of city life in the period. Beyond this, it is plausible to argue that the specific benefits provided by the local aristocracy for their communities, above all in the context of office-holding for the cult, add up to the essential difference between urban and non-urban living. What the cities had to offer their inhabitants were precisely the distributions of corn and oil, the feasts and banquets that accompanied public sacrifices, games, festivals, and gladiatorial shows. The imperial cult, in its broadest sense, made all this possible and thus gave tremendous impetus to civic life and urban growth. The benefactions and liturgies which accompanied performance of the cult were of central importance not simply for the recipients of philanthropy; or for the humble spectators of shows and games; but, more crucially, for the rich themselves. For the institutions gave them a context, even a language, in which they could express their ambitions, impress their communities, and achieve positions of power and authority. The immediate purpose of high priests and other office holders in behaving as they did was not to further economic activity, still less to offer charity to their less fortunate fellow citizens, but to achieve social and political prestige as a result of service to the emperor.

It is commonly held that the overriding object of the imperial cult was to capture and channel the loyalty of the emperors' subjects, and thus to assure the stability of the principate as an institution. This reductionist and strictly functional view, with its fatally restrictive conceptual limitations, does not do justice to the far-reaching and intricate symbolic significance of the cult. But alongside the message that the cult conveyed about the nature of imperial rule, and the relationship between ruler and subject, it brought radical changes to the material conditions and patterns of behaviour which henceforth were to dominate provincial life. Without the imperial cult there might have been little substance to civic life over much of the empire; and the cities themselves, the bed-rock of the empire, could hardly have flourished as they did. This was the most critical contribution that emperor worship made to provincial life.

[121] Sterrett, *WE* nos. 180, 181, 184, 193 (*IGR* iii. 280, 292, 293); Swoboda, *Denkmäler*, no. 152.
[122] Cronin, *JHS* 22 (1902), 371 no. 144 (*IGR* iii. 1481).
[123] Swoboda, *Denkmäler*, no. 39.
[124] *MAMA* iii. 332, 337.
[125] Sterrett, *WE* no. 280, cf. A. S. Hall, *AS* 21 (1971), 125.

9 The Euphrates Frontier and the Impact of the Roman Armies

Garrisons, Roads, and Recruitment

1. *Garrisons*

At an uncertain date in the 90s BC L. Cornelius Sulla, then governor of Cilicia, reached the river Euphrates in the company of a modest force of Asiatic levies and the new king of Cappadocia, Ariobarzanes.[1] He was met by Orobazus, an ambassador from the Parthian king Arsaces, and, at an encounter whose significance was not lost on observers, presided over an agreement between Parthia and Rome which set the Euphrates as the limit of their respective spheres of influence.[2] Over a century and a half later the emperor Vespasian fully realized the implications of that early parley, when he planned and constructed a system of frontier defences stretching from the Black Sea and the upper Euphrates, across the Taurus to the Syrian and Arabian deserts. The creation of this *limes* was crucial to the development of Roman Asia Minor.

The only explicit allusion in a literary text to the new frontier policy in Anatolia comes in a single sentence of Suetonius' *Life of Vespasian*, 'Cappadociae propter adsiduos babarorum incursus legiones addidit consularemque rectorem imposuit' (*Vesp.* 8. 4). This testimony is confirmed and amplified by inscriptions and other indirect allusions to the new military situation. After the destruction of Jerusalem in September AD 70 *legio XII Fulminata*, which had suffered defeat by insurgents early in the Jewish war, was transferred from Raphaneae in Syria to Melitene in eastern Cappadocia, a strategic position which controlled the approaches to the Euphrates' crossing at Tomisa.[3] The legion was said to have been demoralized, and the transfer to new quarters in upland Anatolia probably imposed a vastly more disciplined regime than the one which it had enjoyed in Syria, although the unit was no stranger to the Cappadocian frontier and had served there under Corbulo.[4]

The northern part of the Anatolian frontier, guarding the routes into Pontus, was probably reinforced a few years later. In AD 72/3 the client kingdom of Armenia Minor, which had been ruled since 54 by Nero's appointee Aristobulus,[5] was annexed to the empire,[6] and sometime thereafter a legion was stationed east of Nicopolis at Satala. An inscription found there mentions a soldier and a standard-bearer of *legio XVI Flavia Firma*, which had been recruited in Syria as recently as AD 70,[7] and it is reasonable to suggest that this unit had been sent to Cappadocia under the Flavians.[8] However, the move came later than that of *legio XII*, for another inscription found near Syrian Antioch shows that at least part of the legion was occupied in digging a canal there in AD 75. The decision to fortify and garrison Satala was not precipitate. An impressive dossier of circumstantial evidence exists to suggest that AD 75/6 was a crucial year. Threats from the Alani, north of the Caucasus, led Vespasian to

---

[1] C. Nicolet *et al.*, *Rome et la conquête du monde méditerranéen, ii, Genèse d'un empire* (1978), 796–9.

[2] Plutarch, *Sulla*, 5; Appian, *Mith* 10, 57; Livy, *Per.* 70.

[3] Josephus, *BJ* 8. 1. 3, 18; T. B. Mitford, *JRS* 64 (1974), 166 and *ANRW* ii. 7. 2 (1980), 1186 thinks it unlikely that the troops arrived before 71, but abrupt dispatch at an unseasonable time might represent punishment for their earlier failure. E. Dabrowa, *Latomus*, 41 (1982), 619 n. 30 contrasts the immediate redeployment of *legio XII* with the slower dispersion of the other legions which had taken part in the siege of Jerusalem.

[4] Cf. Tacitus, *Ann.* 13. 35 on the effect of transferring troops from Syria to Cappadocia and Armenia under Domitius Corbulo. Mitford, *ANRW* ii. 7. 2, 1186 points out that *XII Fulminata* had wintered in Cappadocia in 61/2.

[5] He is attested there in 70/1 by coins of his 17th regnal year, Th. Reinach, *REA* 16 (1914), 144 ff., corrected as to the date by A. B. Bosworth, *Antichthon*, 10 (1976), 66 n. 22.

[6] Reinach, *REA* 16 (1914), 133, 149–53 for coins of Nicopolis (dated 113/14) and of the Armenian *koinon* (of 114/15), which belonged to the 42nd and 43rd years of the local era; annexation, therefore, in 72/3, cf. Bosworth, *Antichthon*, 10 (1976), 66 n. 24.

[7] T. B. Mitford, *JRS* 64 (1974), 165 no. 3 (*AE* 1975, 817). For the recruitment of the legion see Dabrowa, *Latomus*, 41 (1982), 614–19. For C. S. Lightfoot's new survey of Satala, see *AS* 40 (1990), 13–16; *VIII Araş*, 299–309; and *AS* 41 (1991), 15–17.

[8] The three gravestones of centurions of *XVI Flavia Firma* found at Ancyra (Bosch, *Ankara*, nos. 110–12) presumably belong to the period before Trajan's Parthian war. Connections between Ancyra and Satala were naturally close (see below, nn. 112–13). Samosata would have been reached from Syrian Antioch.

authorize major military action in Armenia and Iberia under the command of M. Hirrius Fronto Neratius Pansa, who led an expedition into the region, helped to construct the fortifications of Harmozica in Iberia, and may also have built the legionary fortress at Satala itself.[9]

The southern section of the Anatolian Euphrates frontier had been fortified a little earlier. In AD 72/3, Vespasian's fourth year, the governor of Syria L. Caesennius Paetus sent letters to the emperor, in which he alleged that Antiochus IV of Commagene was involved in a conspiracy with the Parthians, and invaded his kingdom, accompanied by the very Aristobulus who had lately been displaced from Armenia Minor.[10] The main target of the campaign was the fortress of Samosata, which commanded one of the important crossings of the Euphrates.[11] The legion which accompanied the governor was the *VI Ferrata*, but an inscription dated to the second quarter of 73 shows that *legio III Gallica* was responsible for building a hydraulic device at Aynı, on the river bank south of Samosata, and it was probably already in place as the garrison legion there by this date.[12] The disposition of legionary garrisons on the upper and middle Euphrates was completed by *legio IV Scythica*, which had guarded the crossing at Zeugma in north Syria since the early 60s, and remained in station there until the third century AD.[13]

So by a gradual process through the 70s AD a system of frontier defence based on legionary fortresses was established on the left bank of the Euphrates: Zeugma and Samosata belonged to the province of Syria, while Melitene and Satala were in the newly constituted composite province of Galatia-Cappadocia. The legions were complemented by auxiliary units. There were probably six smaller forts along the river between Satala and Melitene, and four between Melitene and Samosata.[14] Not all the sites and the garrisons have been firmly identified, but work carried out in recent years shows that this *limes*, for all its remoteness, was as elaborately organized as the better-known frontier systems of northern Europe.[15] At least one auxiliary regiment, a *cohors II...*, was stationed at Dascusa, north of Melitene, by the year 82, when it set up a dedication for the governor A. Caesennius Gallus,[16] and it cannot conceivably been an isolated unit. From Arrian's *Extaxis* against the Alani of the 130s we learn that the governor of Cappadocia then commanded twelve cohorts and four *alae* on campaign,[17] while at least five more cohorts remained encamped at Apsarus on the Black Sea, near modern Batoum.[18] The size of the force may be explained by the double task of holding the Euphrates and controlling the approaches to the Caucasus, which still, as in Vespasian's time, were seen as the main source of an enemy threat.[19] Soldiers were probably regularly sent to various destinations beyond the Euphrates, to help create a system of defence in depth. Legionaries in AD 75 helped the king of Iberia to strengthen his fortifications at Harmozica,[20] and a centurion of *legio XII Fulminata*, presumably accompanied by soldiers from the legion, is

[9] D. van Berchem, *Mus. Helv.* 40 (1983), 185–96 (*AE* (1983), 927), cf. *BJb.* 185 (1985), 85 ff. It is true that only part of the legion was involved, but the other troops engaged in the same task were all from the Syrian garrison, so *XVI Flavia Firma* was also certainly stationed in the province at the time (so H. Halfmann, *Epigr. Anat.* 8 (1986), 47). Van Berchem argues that the legion may never have moved to Satala at all, remaining throughout its existence in Syria (cf. Cassius Dio 55. 24. 3), and that the soldiers mentioned in *AE* (1975), 817 at Satala might be explained, for example, by troop movements during Trajan's Parthian war. See against this M. Speidel, *Armies and Frontiers* 8; and T. B. Mitford, *ZPE* 71 (1988), 168 n. 7. Further discoveries should settle the issue. For the reconstruction of events in 75/6, see H. Halfmann, 'Die Alanen und die römische Ostpolitik unter Vespasian', *Epigr. Anat.* 8 (1986), 39–51.

[10] Reinach, *REA* 16 (1914), 141, although the equation of this Aristobulus, now king of the Syrian Chalcidice, with the ruler of Armenia Minor is not absolutely certain.

[11] Josephus, *BJ* 8. 7. 2, 220–5, esp. 225: τὰ γὰρ Σαμόσατα τῆς Κομμαγηνῆς μεγίστη πόλις κεῖται παρὰ τὸν Εὐφράτην, ὥστ᾽ εἶναι τοῖς Πάρθοις, εἴ τι τοιοῦτο διενενόηντο, ῥᾴστην μὲν τὴν διάβασιν, βεβαίαν δὲ ὑποδοχήν.

[12] *IGLS* 66 (*ILS* 8903). They were constructing an *opus cochliae* under the governor of Syria A. Marius Celsus. For the date see T. V. Buttrey, *Documentary Evidence for the Chronology of the Flavian Titulature* (1980), 23 and Syme, *ZPE* 41 (1981), 133 = *RP* iii. 1383. For the circumstances see van Berchem, *Mus. Helv.* 40 (1983), 188–91.

[13] J. Wagner, *Seleukeia am Euphrat/Zeugma* (1976), 135–46,

and *Studien zur Militärgrenzen Roms II. 10 Int. Limes Kongr.* (Cologne, 1977), 517–39; Speidel, *Armies and Frontiers*, 9.

[14] See the map published by D. H. French, *Armies and Frontiers*, 98 fig. 7. 1, which corrects and supplements those of Mitford, *ANRW* ii. 7. 2, 1212 fig. 1, and of French and Crow, *Roman Frontier Studies 1979. 12th Int. Limes Congr.*, iii (1980), 903–12. Map 9 is derived from these.

[15] See above, n. 14: Mitford, op. cit. 1169–211; and French, opp. citt. both citing much further bibliography.

[16] Mitford, *JRS* 64 (1974), 172 no. 8 (*AE* (1975), 809).

[17] On this see E. Ritterling, *Wiener Studien*, 24 (1902), 359–72; A. B. Bosworth, *HSCP* 81 (1977), 217–55; Speidel, *Armies and Frontiers*, 16–17.

[18] Speidel, loc. cit., and *Aegyptus* 62 (1982), 165–72. For an appraisal of the Roman role in Colchis, see D. C. Braund, in D. H. French and C. S. Lightfoot (eds.), *The Eastern Frontier of the Roman Empire*, i (1989), 31–43, esp. 34–5 on Apsarus.

[19] See above all Bosworth, *Antichthon*, 10 (1976), 63–76, and *HSCP* 81 (1977), 217 ff. These studies probe deeper than Dabrowa, *Klio*, 62 (1980), 379–88.

[20] *ILS* 8795 with Bosworth, *Antichthon* (1976), 72–3 and Halfmann, *Epigr. Anat.* 8 (1986), 49.

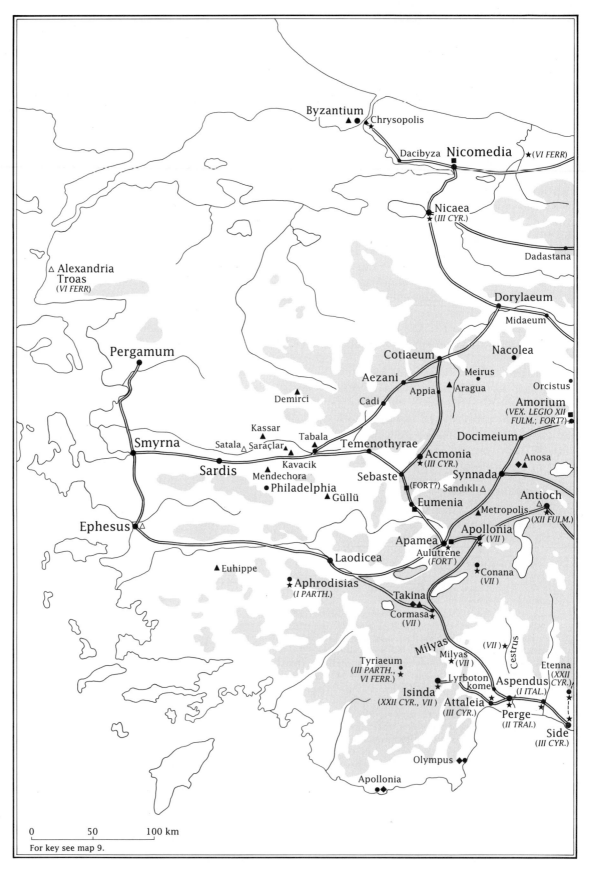

Byzantium ▲● Chrysopolis

Dacibyza **Nicomedia** ★(*VI FERR*)

Nicaea
★(*III CYR.*)

Dadastana

△ **Alexandria Troas**
(*VI FERR*)

Dorylaeum

Midaeum

Pergamum

Nacolea

Cotiaeum

Aezani   Meirus   Orcistus

Demirci   Appia   ▲ Aragua

Cadi   **Amorium**
(*VEX. LEGIO XII FULM.; FORT?*)

Kassar

Tabala   **Docimeium**

Smyrna   Satala △ Saraçlar ▲   **Temenothyrae**   ●Acmonia   ◆▲ Anosa
              ★(*III CYR.*)

Sardis   Kavacik   **Synnada**

Mendechora   **Sebaste**   **Antioch**
                        ■(*FORT?*) Sandıklı △   △
● **Philadelphia**   ★(*XII FULM.*)
      ▲ Güllü   **Eumenia**   ▲ Metropolis

Ephesus △   **Apollonia**
                    Apamea■ ★(*VII*)
                    Aulutrene
                    (*FORT*)

              Laodicea
▲ Euhippe   ★Conana
                                  (*VII*)
        ★**Aphrodisias**
         (*I PARTH.*)   **Takina**★
                        Cormasa★
                          (*VII*)   (*VII*) ★
                                      Milyas
                                  Milyas   (*VII*) ★   Etenna
              Tyriaeum●   ★(*VII*)   (*XXII CYR.*)
              (*III PARTH.,*) Lyrboton
              VI FERR.)●   ●kome **Aspendus**
                        Isinda   (*I ITAL.*)
                    (*XXII CYR., VII*) **Attaleia**
                                  (*III CYR.*) **Perge**
                                          (*II TRAI.*)
                                                  Side
                                                  (*III CYR.*)
              Olympus ◆◆

      Apollonia
              ●◆

0   50   100 km

For key see map 9.

Map 7. The Roman military presence in western Anatolia

known to have been stationed at a strategic fortress overlooking the Caspian Sea.[21]

Garrisons beyond the Euphrates frontier were matched by several units stationed in the hinterland of Asia Minor during the first two centuries AD. Asia is often regarded as a province without a significant military garrison, but this is to ignore the growing dossier of evidence to suggest that the routes that traversed Phrygia between the provinces of Asia and Galatia were well guarded, and that legionary contingents were stationed on either side of the provincial boundary. Legionaries from *legio XII Fulminata* were responsible for building the road between Eumeneia and Apamea in eastern Asia, probably during the first century AD,[22] and a vexillation of the legion is attested at Amorium, where there are traces of what may have been a Roman military camp.[23] The *cohors I Claudia Sugambrorum veterana equitata* was brought from Moesia inferior to Eumeneia in the mid-130s AD.[24] In AD 148 a diploma was issued to an Isaurian veteran of *cohors I Raetorum*, which was stationed in Asia, and three inscriptions from Eumeneia which name members of the unit prove that it was stationed in the vicinity.[25] North of the city, beside the Roman road which led to Phrygian Sebaste, are the ruins of what may well be another Roman fort.[26] East of Apamea, virtually on the provincial frontier between Asia and Galatia, soldiers of *legio XI Claudia* and *I Italica* formed part of a Severan vexillation which manned another *castellum* at Aulutrene near Apamea, a site which controlled the east–west route from the Maeander valley to Phrygia Paroreius, as well as the north–south route between Pisidia and Phrygia (Fig. 19).[27] Other inscriptions found here mention serving legionaries of *legio IV Flavia* and *XI Claudia*, as well as three members of a mounted auxiliary unit of Emesenes in the third or fourth century.[28] A legionary of *IV Flavia* is also attested at Synnada, where he may have had responsibilities for security in the Phrygian marble quarries or been attached to the administrative headquarters there.

Within the province of Galatia, auxiliary units were placed at strategic centres on the routes that ran east from Asia towards the frontiers. The best evidence concerns the *cohors I Augusta Cyrenaica*, a cavalry unit largely recruited from south Galatia itself, several of whose members died while on service in Ancyra. They include two brothers from Savatra, Quintus and Lucius Valerius Valens, who were buried by their wives (Fig. 20); Proclus of Iconium, buried by his foster-daughter and by his brother who was presumably a soldier in the same unit; and a certain Sergianus Longus.[29] The cohort is also mentioned on a fragmentary text from Iconium,[30] but the concentration of inscriptions at Ancyra, and the fact that the soldiers died while on service there, suggest that it was the unit's headquarters.[31] Another Ancyran text, which has been dated to the pre-Flavian period, gives a list of officers (*decuriones*) of the *cohors II Hispanorum*, and this may have preceded the *cohors I Augusta Cyrenaica* as the principal garrison unit of north Galatia.[32]

[21] *AE* (1951), 263; Bosworth, loc. cit. The precise site is indicated on the sketch map published by R. Heidenreich, *ZPE* 52 (1983), 213–14.

[22] T. Drew Bear and W. Eck, *Chiron*, 6 (1976), 294 no. 5 (*AE* (1976), 658).

[23] *CIL* iii. 353, the tombstone of a soldier of *legio XII Fulminata*, set up by a *vexillatio leg. eiusdem*. M. H. Ballance in his unpublished Ph.D. thesis, 'A Reassessment of the Archaeology of Central Asia Minor from Alexander the Great to the Turkish Conquest' (Edinburgh, 1961), reported observing a large rectangular area 'like a military camp' south and west of the citadel of Amorium. On the map of the site published by R. M. Harrison, *AS* 40 (1990), 207 this enclosure appears to the SSE of the citadel.

[24] Buckler, Calder, and Cox, *JRS* 16 (1926), 74–5; E. Ritterling, *JRS* 17 (1927), 30, on the *cohors Sugambrorum*.

[25] B. Overbeck, *Chiron*, 11 (1981), 265–76 for the diploma, now M. M. Roxan, *Roman Military Diplomas* (1985), ii no. 100. For the Eumeneian inscriptions see Ramsay, *CB* i. 2. 379 ff. nos. 211, 215, and 216 (*IGR* iv. 736, 729, 728), which all name the *cohors Raetorum*. Cf. T. Drew Bear, *Nouvelles inscriptions de Phrygie*, 18 for a *cornicularius* of an unnamed cohort.

[26] For the possible fort, which lies beside the Roman road running from Eumeneia to Sebaste, see J. G. C. Anderson, *JHS* 17 (1897), 415, who identified it with Bria; D. H. French, *AS* 41 (1991), 9, and *Epigr. Anat.* 17 (1991), 59–60. A precise date in the Roman or late Roman period cannot be fixed without excavation.

[27] M. Christol and T. Drew Bear, *Un castellum romain près d'Apamée de Phrygie* (1987). For the topography see their discussion pp. 12–27 and 56–8. The main inscription, pp. 34 ff. no. 5, has been revised by M. Speidel, *Epigr. Anat.* 10 (1987), 97–9. The commander of the garrison was a *primipilaris*, Nonius Felix. It seems likely that Iulius Ligys, another *primipilaris* who was honoured at Apamea as the city's benefactor in the time of Antoninus Pius, was an earlier commander of the same fort (*IGR* iv. 786).

[28] *IV Flavia*: Christol and Drew Bear, *Un castellum romain*, 46 no. 6, 53 no. 9 (seen in Apamea), and *CIL* iii. 13663 (veteran at Apamea); *XI Claudia*: Christol and Drew Bear, *Un castellum romain*, 55 no. 10; *numeri Hemesenorum*: ibid. 48 no. 8, with Speidel, *Epigr. Anat.* 10 (1987), 99–100. Note also two centurions of *legio VII Claudia* at Apamea, *CIL* iii. 7055 and 7056 (the latter = *CB* i. 2. 474 no. 329, giving the date AD 170/1).

[29] Bosch, *Ankara*, nos. 113, 114, and 115. The last tombstone mentions no other members of his family. Perhaps it was erected by his companions in the regiment.

[30] W. M. and A. M. Ramsay, *JRS* 18 (1928), 183; W. M. Ramsay in *JRS* 19 (1929), 155 n. 1 recalls a soldier of the unit at Pisidian Antioch. I have been unable to trace the inscription.

[31] See the notes of Bosch, *Ankara*, on no. 113, against Speidel, *Armies and Frontiers* 16.

[32] Bosch, *Ankara*, no. 116, dated by P. Holder, *Studies in the*

Troops were also widely distributed in south central Anatolia, especially in the mountain areas. A serving cavalryman, Flavius Alcibiades, was stationed close to the city of Tyriaeum in Phrygia Paroreius, where he buried his wife;[33] and another serving soldier, P. Aelius Natalis, appears at Kozanlı in the central plateau.[34] In the fourth century the numbers of soldiers in this area increased notably (see below, Vol. II, Ch. 17 § v n. 171). As already noted, the roads which ran south from Iconium and Lake Beyşehir past Lake Suğla into Isauria, were regularly policed by garrisons of mounted *stationarii*, at Neapolis, Kireli, Vasada, Akkisse, Artanada, and perhaps in the neighbourhood of Lystra.[35] Not unexpectedly there were also soldiers at Bozkır, the site of Isaura Palaia, and elsewhere in Isauria.[36] This traditionally troubled area was thoroughly policed during the second and third centuries by regular soldiers, almost always auxiliary cavalrymen who reinforced the armed and mounted *diōgmitai* in the local cities (see below, Ch. 11 § VI). Similar conditions may have existed in parts of Pisidia to the west, and one text shows an *eques singularis*, Iulius Valerius, responsible for burying his father who was a *principalis*, presumably in the same regiment.[37] It is hardly surprising that a second- or third-century inscription from Lyrbōtōn kōmē on the territory of

Perge in Pamphylia shows soldiers passing through the village and presenting formal greetings to the village elders.[38]

The most revealing items of evidence for the routine presence of soldiers on the roads of Asia Minor and elsewhere are a widely distributed group of funerary texts, which prescribed that fines for violating tombs should be paid to *stationarii* or similar military *gendarmes*. At Tium on the Paphlagonian coast fines were due 'to the *stationarius* at the time' (τῷ κατὰ καιρὸν στατιοναρίῳ),[39] at nearby Prusias 'to the soldier on the spot' (τῷ κατὰ τόπον στρατιώτῃ),[40] at Lydian Apollonis to another *stationarius*,[41] and at Olympus in eastern Lycia 'to the soldier at the posting' (τῷ στατίζοντι). At this sheltered enclave on the rocky east coast of Lycia, a pirate haven of the first century BC, there was a permanent military post, commanded at one time by an Isaurian *beneficiarius*.[42] A steep mountain route ran south-west from Olympus to Rhodiapolis, Limyra, and the other cities of southern Lycia, and the soldiers may have had the responsibility of patrolling this road. Strong evidence has also been assembled to suggest that another small garrison operated on the coast road which led from Laertes, the easternmost city of Pamphylia, to Syedra in Rugged Cilicia.[43] The ubiquity of these detached soldiers, as well as the natural tendency for them to take the law into their own

Auxilia of the Roman Army (1980), 312; see too Speidel, *Armies and Frontiers*, 14–16 and 34.

[33] *IGR* iii. 241; J. G. C. Anderson, *JHS* 18 (1898), 124 no. 79.
[34] *IGR* iii. 236.
[35] See above, Ch. 6 n. 78. Note *MAMA* viii. 95 at Karahüyük near Lystra, where [στατιων]άριος is an almost inevitable restoration; *MAMA* viii. 59 from Seçme nearby also mentions another serving soldier, buried by his wife.
[36] *IGR* iii. 284; G. Laminger-Pascher, *Festschrift für A. Betz* (1985), 380–92.
[37] *IGR* iii. 394, erroneously reproduced again as *IGR* iii. 503.

[38] *Epigr. Anat.* 11 (1988), 164 no. 165 = J. Keil, *JÖAI* 33 (1926), *Beiblatt*, 7 no. 4 (*SEG* vi. 675).
[39] Robert, *Ét. anat.* 285.
[40] *I. Prusias*, no. 92, with Ameling's excellent note which collects all the parallels.
[41] *TAM* v. 2. 1219.
[42] *TAM* ii. 3. 953, 987, and in particular 1185, discussed by Robert, *Hellenica*, x. 172.
[43] J. Russell, *AJA* 95 (1991), 469–88.

Fig. 19. Dedication to Iupiter Optimus Maximus and to Juno for the Severan imperial family set up by a *vexillatio* of soldiers from *legio XI Claudia* and *legio I Italica* at Aulutrene, where a *castellum* controlled a strategic road junction east of Phrygian Apamea. The soldiers listed are called *conductores*, perhaps indicating that they played a role in collecting military supplies. T. Drew Bear and M. Christol, *Un castellum romain près d'Apamée de Phrygie* (1987) with M. P. Speidel, *Epigr. Anat.* 10 (1987), 97–9.

Fig. 20. Greek gravestone from Ancyra for Quintus and Lucius Valerius Valens from Savatra, soldiers of the *cohors I Augusta Cyrenaica*, which was presumably stationed in the city. Bosch, *Ankara*, no. 113. Now in the Roman Baths Museum, Ankara.

Fig. 21. Latin gravestone built into the Byzantine castle at Ankara of M. Aebutius M. f. Ulp. Papir. Troiana Victorinus from Poetovio in the province of Pannonia. He died aged 62 after 45 years service as centurion in eight legions. The last unit mentioned, *legio XV Apollinaris*, was based at Satala. *CIL* iii. 260, 6761; Bosch, *Ankara*, no. 187.

Fig. 22. Milestone from the road between Ancyra and Gangra set up in AD 122 by A. Larcius Macedo, governor of Galatia. His name occurs on 28 milestones from north Galatia, and this burst of activity may represent the completion of the road-building programme in central and eastern Anatolia which had begun in the time of Vespasian. S. Mitchell, *ZPE* 21 (1973), 73; D. H. French, *Roman Roads and Milestones of Asia Minor*, 2. 1 (1988), 35 no. 86.

19

20

21

22

The Roman military presence in central Anatolia

hands, is perfectly shown by the injunction found in the Justinianic Code, that if anyone thought that he had suffered injury at another's hands and wished to bring a complaint, he should *not* turn to the *stationarius* but appeal to the praesidial authorities, that is to the provincial governor.[44] It has long been clear that there were substantial military detachments posted on the military highways of eastern Anatolia, as these approached the frontier itself (see below, § 11); the principle of protecting routes with soldiers is no less clear on roads which ran through mountain areas, or crossed potentially sensitive provincial boundaries, throughout the rest of Asia Minor.

11. *Roads and the Impact of Military Traffic*

Inevitably the imposition of this elaborate military structure was accompanied by a massive upgrading of the system of communications. The fortresses of the frontier were joined to one another by paved roads. Two routes linked Samosata with Melitene: a broad highway which ran as directly between the two places as the terrain would allow, and a narrow roadway which followed the river bank and gave direct access to the auxiliary forts.[45] The highway between Melitene and Satala, much of which is well preserved, followed a course much closer to the Euphrates, obviating the need for a supplementary road in the manner of the southern section.[46] The earliest dated milestone from the frontier area was set up by Cn. Pompeius Collega, governor of Galatia-Cappadocia, in AD 75/6, and may have stood on the road from Nicopolis to Satala or on the northern stretch of the frontier road itself.[47] A road also ran from Satala to Trapezus, thereby linking the Euphrates garrisons with the ships of the *classis Pontica*. Vexillations of *XII Fulminata* and *XV Apollinaris* were stationed at Trapezus in the second century AD, and it received its own legion *I Pontica* in the time of Diocletian.[48] The difficult route from the Black Sea to the upper Euphrates had been an essential supply line for Corbulo's armies during the late 50s and 60s AD, when it had been guarded with a chain of forts,[49] and these may have been consolidated in the Flavian period. Unfortunately no milestones or

other inscriptions of any period have been discovered from this part of the frontier to confirm or refute this hypothesis.[50]

The frontier itself was joined to the hinterland of Asia Minor, and ultimately with the Balkans and Europe, by an immense network of major highways. Milestones found in Galatia and Pontus point to three major construction periods within half a century of Vespasian's accession: under A. Caesennius Gallus from AD 80 and 82, under T. Pomponius Bassus between 97 and 100, and under A. Larcius Macedo between 119 and 122. Since the whole Anatolian system was an organic unity, with each individual road functioning as an integral part of a much larger scheme, logic suggests that the whole network was conceived and built (at least in its essentials) as soon as was practicable after the establishment of the frontier itself. This is in some degree confirmed by the milestones of Caesennius Gallus, which state explicitly that he laid roads in the provinces of Galatia, Cappadocia, Pontus, Pisidia, Paphlagonia, Lycaonia, and Armenia Minor[51] and thereby suggest that the whole road system of central and eastern Asia Minor was built under his auspices, leaving only minor additions, restorations and repair work to his successors.[52] There is, however, room for doubt. Flavian activity is not so far attested on a number of important routes, above all on the great highway from Caesareia to Melitene, whose earliest milestones are Severan,[53] and it is legitimate to ask whether so much road construction could have been completed by the end of AD 82. In the province of Arabia the building of the *via Nova Traiana*, a much smaller project, was not complete until AD 114, although work had certainly begun as soon as the province was annexed in AD 106.[54] The practical achievement in Anatolia probably fell some way short of the ideal. However, even if we choose not to believe that the whole network was finished by the early 80s, the combined efforts of the various road builders between the reigns of Vespasian and Hadrian add up to a formidable achievement. No pains were spared in the construction of the highways themselves; as a rule they measure about eight metres wide; each side was stabilized by a row of *margines*, rectangular blocks measuring up to sixty centimetres along the

[44] *CJ* 9. 2. 8.

[45] French, *Armies and Frontiers*, 71–82.

[46] Mitford, *ANRW* ii. 7. 2, 1183–6, with French, *Armies and Frontiers*, 84 ff.; also Mitford, in French and Lightfoot, *The Eastern Frontier of the Roman Empire*, ii. 329–33.

[47] *CIL* iii. 6056 (*ILS* 8904), cf. Mitford, *ANRW* ii. 7. 2, 1183 n. 29. The date coheres with the suggestion (see above, n. 9) that the legionary fortress at Satala itself was built at about this time, perhaps by Hirrius Fronto, Collega's successor.

[48] *Legio XII Fulminata*, *CIL* iii. 6745; *legio XV Apollinaris*, *CIL* iii. 6747 with Mitford, *JRS* 64 (1974), 163 no. 2.

[49] Tacitus, *Ann.* 13. 39, see Vol. II, App. 1 n. 45.

[50] D. H. French, BIAA *Thirty-Fourth Annual Report* (1982), 8–9. The *Antonine Itinerary*, 216. 4 marks the road from Trapezus to Satala.

[51] This is the usual formula, as on *ILS* 268 (= Bosch, *Ankara*, no. 68).

[52] So French, *ANRW* ii. 7. 2, 709–11.

[53] Contrast the map in *ANRW* ii. 7. 2, 710 fig. 3 showing what is at present known to have been built under the Flavians, with the hypothetical complete Flavian system, p. 712 fig. 4.

[54] T. Pekary, *Untersuchungen zu den römischen Reichsstrassen* (1968), 140–1.

Fig. 23. The highway which ran north from Apamea through the Phrygian Pentapolis (Sandıklı Ova).

Fig. 24. A section of the chaussée of the *via Sebaste* west of Lake Beyşehir near Orondian Pappa, linking Pisidian Antioch and Iconium.

'Broad-gauge' Roman highways of central Anatolia

sides, which contained a surface of packed cobbles sloping gently down on either side from a central *spina*; a section of the highway from Pessinus to Ancyra, which has been excavated at Gordium, had an excellent gravelled surface well suited to wheeled traffic.[55] There is no reason to doubt that road surfaces in the rest of Anatolia were maintained to a uniformly high standard. Moreover the milestones provide ample evidence for repairs, in some cases not long after the original construction date.[56]

The cost of the whole undertaking, both in human and in financial terms, must have been gigantic. Road-building on this scale will have made demands on the inhabitants of Anatolia as no other aspect of Roman rule had done before. By a rough calculation the network of major highways shown in Maps 7 and 8 covered about 9,000 kilometres (5,600 Roman miles). Even if the stone from which they were built was readily available and no extensive transport of materials was required, an enormous labour force will have been involved. It was surely beyond the capacity of the Roman troops stationed in Anatolia to have carried out the construction unaided, although their participation may be taken for granted.[57] Local labour was essential, but under normal conditions would have been very expensive. Inscriptions from Roman Italy of the late republican and early imperial periods give costs for road repairs of 66,666, 103,750, 108,958, and 111,500 HS per mile respectively.[58] Certainly repair costs might have been close to the original construction costs, if the road was in very poor condition,[59] but it

is natural to suppose that new road-building would normally be even more expensive.[60] If we assume similar expenses in Asia Minor, the cost will have been ludicrously and prohibitively high. The cost of the road system of Galatia-Cappadocia, calculated merely at the level of road repairs in Italy, would have been close to 600 million HS. The size of the sum may be judged by comparing it with an annual wage bill for the army that garrisoned the Anatolian frontier of about 25 million HS, and an annual empire-wide military wage bill of about 450 million HS.[61] In addition, if the roads were maintained to a high standard, as appears to have been the case, repairs would have been frequent and extensive. Heavy use and the harsh climate would take a considerable toll, and the initial capital outlay would have to be matched with much recurrent expenditure.[62] If Rome paid for all her roads in Anatolia or elsewhere at a rate equal to or approaching the attested costs of road repair in Italy, the price would have comfortably exceeded the cost of paying all her troops.[63] The state would have been bankrupt almost at once by the financial burden.

---

initial task of levelling the ground and preparing foundations would not have to be done again. For an example of a relaid surface on one of the typical Anatolian highways, see *ANRW* ii. 7. 2, 713, diagram 6.

[60] Pekary, loc. cit. suggests that the original construction of a *via publica*, including all the additional features such as bridges, *praetoria, mansiones*, milestones, and so forth, might cost 500,000 HS per mile. This figure appears to be much too high, and in any case, if the arguments about the cost of road construction advanced here are sound, it is misleading to assess such costs in monetary terms at all.

[61] For argument's sake I adopt K. Hopkins' figures, *JRS* 70 (1980), 117–19, 124–5.

[62] Note Procopius, *Aed.* 5. 3. 12 on the damage caused by bad weather and heavy traffic on a road running from Nicaea, perhaps to Dorylaeum. I am grateful to Keith Hopkins for discussing this and other issues concerning road-building with me. He suggests that maintenance costs, if a road was to be kept near to its original condition, might run at 5% per annum, so the original construction cost would be matched over twenty years. Perhaps the time interval between construction and repair in the case cited above in n. 56 reflects these conditions, although one would also expect some repairs to be carried out piecemeal through the lifetime of a road, not in major operations every twenty years or so. W. Eck, in *La Via Appia: Decimo incontro di studio di comitato per l'archeologia laziale* (1990), 34–5, argues that inscriptions which refer to road repairs were usually occasioned by special circumstances, such as landslides, marshy incursions, or damage from floods and earthquakes to bridges. The inference that normal road surfaces suffered little damage from daily wear and tear, however, is not compelling.

[63] One rough estimate sets the total length of roads in the Roman empire at 79,500 kilometres, say 50,000 m.p. (A. Leger, *Les Travaux publics aux temps des Romains* (1875)). Costed at 100,000 HS per mile every twenty years, the price of these roads would amount in monetary terms to 5,000 million HS, or 250 million HS per annum.

---

[55] R. Young, 'Gordion on the Royal Road', *Proc. Am. Philosophical Soc.* 107 (1963), 348–60 at 350 fig. 2, publishes a photograph of this paved section with an excellent, smooth, gravelled surface. Compare the important description of the road surface of the *via Nova Traiana* in Arabia by H. C. Butler, *Princeton Expedition to Syria*, iii A (1914), x–xi, noting 'a top finish of volcanic cinders to a depth of 10 cm. and an upper layer of beaten clay which brings the level of the road to the top of the ridge and the bonding stones, sloping gently from the center' (quoted by D. L. Kennedy, *The Roman Frontier in North-East Jordan* (1982), 145–6).

[56] Note e.g. the stone published by I. W. Macpherson, *AS* 4 (1954), 115 no. 8 from the road between Ancyra and Tavium, which was built by Caesennius Gallus in 81/2 and restored by Pomponius Bassus in 98/9.

[57] For legionaries as building engineers, see in general W. Liebenam, *RE* vi. 2 (1909), 1655–9 s.v. *exercitus*; A. Passerini, *Diz. epigr.* (1950), 619 s.v. *legio*; Eck and Drew Bear, *Chiron* 6 (1976), 294 no. 5 with notes; D. L. Kennedy, *The Roman Frontier in NE Jordan*, 179 inscr. no. 36.

[58] Pekary, *Römische Reichsstrasse*, 93–5 with references and calculations. See too W. Eck, *Die staatliche Organisation Italiens in der hohen Kaiserzeit* (1979), 58.

[59] *ILS* 5875 describes the *via Appia*, one of the restored roads, as *longa vetustate amissam*. Replacing a road surface would require almost as much material and labour as laying one *a novo*, although *margines* could doubtless be reused and the

On the other hand, the figures given above also make it clear that the cost of building roads in central and eastern Anatolia cannot have been supported by the local communities, at least in monetary terms. No Anatolian city had such cash resources at its disposal (see below, Ch. 14 § IV). Nevertheless, there is clear evidence from many parts of the empire, including Asia Minor, that the cities were at least partly responsible for the construction of Roman highways (*viae publicae*) within and sometimes beyond their territories.[64] Since not even wealthy communities could hope to pay for these at rates close to the Italian figures, the conclusion seems inevitable that they discharged their responsibilities by a corvée labour system forced upon their citizens and slaves. Further, since so much of the area was thinly and recently urbanized, it is also fair to assume that the authorities who enforced this system were often not city magistrates but soldiers and officers of the Roman army.[65]

After the decline of the Roman system, parts of which were certainly in use in the early seventh century AD,[66] Anatolia had to wait until the end of the nineteenth century before it acquired new roads on a remotely comparable scale. It is instructive to learn how the later system was built. Late Ottoman roads were designed, like their Roman predecessors, for wheeled traffic as well as for pedestrians and pack-animals, but were built to less rigorous specifications. The surface was usually made from tightly packed stones, which were typically rather smaller than those used by Roman engineers; the roads also lacked the massive *margines* and well-defined central spine. They too, however, were built by corvée manpower; 'The construction of these roads was carried out by forced labour which was imposed on the inhabitants, at a rate of between four and twenty days per year. The state for its part provided the engineers, the tools, and the materials.'[67] In the vilayet of Angora in 1889, a total of 163,429 men out of a total population of 892,901 was registered as being liable to provide corvée labour (18.3 per cent). In Sivas the figures were 252,965 from a population of 1,086,015 (23.3 per cent), and in Trebizond 176,571 out of 806,700 (21.9 per cent). More details are recorded for Erzerum, where 742 kilometres of public highway were built and maintained by forced labour drawn from a pool of 124,925 men, aided by 1,267 skilled engineers, 5,727 wagons, and 4,380 beasts of burden.[68]

It is not always possible to translate these statistics into real terms. We do not know how many of those whose names were inscribed on the lists of 'préstataires' actually gave their labour, or for how many days a year; nor do we know whether their services were called on annually, or only intermittently. For all that the figures serve admirably to give some notion of the manpower needed to build the road system in Anatolia, and underline the point that the Roman achievement would have been inconceivable without the use of forced labour on a huge scale.

There were four major routes in the Anatolian network; Galatia, and especially its main city Ancyra, held a central place in three of them. The northernmost ran from Byzantium and Nicomedia, along the valleys of Paphlagonia and Pontus, through Pompeiopolis, Neoclaudiopolis, Neocaesareia, and Nicopolis, to the legionary headquarters at Satala. This was the route along which Mithridates, Lucullus, and Pompey had marched and countermarched in the first century BC, and it linked the cities which Pompey had founded. It skirted the northern boundary of the province of Galatia, but it is worth noting that from the time of Domitian until the early third century Galatian governors were responsible for the construction and upkeep of the Paphlagonian section of the road between Pompeiopolis and Neoclaudiopolis.[69]

[64] In AD 202, under the guidance of Q. Sicinius Clarus, legate of Thrace, villages in the territory of Alexandrupolis and Traianopolis were required to repair the *via Egnatia*, a mile each (F. Mottas, 'Les Voies de communication antiques de la Thrace égéenne', *Labor Omnibus Unus: Festschrift G. Walser* (1989), 82–104, esp. 101–4). See further Pekáry, *Römischen Reichsstrassen*, 91–171. His is by far the best-documented and most useful discussion of this issue, marred by a tendency to seek a common system for organizing road construction when diversity might be expected, and by the expectation that what was suitable for the roads of republican Italy might readily be applied, *mutatis mutandis*, to the vastly different scale of the empire in the second century AD. It is telling, in this context, to note the remark of Cato, *RR* 2. 4, that road repair or construction could be accommodated on holidays into the normal round of agricultural tasks: 'per ferias potuisse fossas veteres tergeri, viam publicam muniri, vepres recidi, hortum fodiri.' *Tempora mutantur*! For road construction in imperial Italy, see Eck, *Die staatliche Organisation Italiens*, 69–79.

[65] Note the large local labour force which Pliny planned to use to build the proposed canal between Sapanca Göl and the Sangarius in the territory of Nicomedia, *Ep.* 10. 41: 'hoc opus multas manus poscit. At eae porro non desunt. Nam et in agris magna copia est hominum et maxima in civitate, certaque spes omnes libentissime aggressuros opus omnibus fructuosum.'

[66] See below, Vol. II, Ch. 19 § I nn. 10–12 for the evidence in the *Life of St Theodore of Sykeon*.

[67] Quotation from V. Cuinet, *La Turquie d'Asie*, i (1892), 271.

[68] Ibid. i. 271 and iv. 27.

[69] See above, Ch. 3 § III nn. 54–5; Magie, *RR* ii. 1083–6. Note D. H. French, *ZPE* 42 (1981), 150 no. 3 for a milestone of Caesennius Gallus from the region of Sinope, which probably came from the northern route as it ran through the Amnias valley. His p. 149 no. 1, which was erected by a Domitianic procurator of Pontus and Bithynia in the same region, raises a problem. It should belong to a road leading to Sinope (cf. ll. 6–7, *viam … Sinopens.*), perhaps a link to the northern highway. L. Petronius Verus, who was certainly a governor of

Fig. 25. Narrow Roman road in Pamphylia linking Perge and Magydus. Photo by David French.

Fig. 26. Narrow Roman road from the Augustan colony of Comama approaching the west gate of the colony at Cremna.

'Narrow-gauge' Roman roads of Pamphylia and Pisidia

The second major route crossed the centre of Anatolia, starting in the north-west at the Bosporus, or in the eastern part of the province of Asia at Dorylaeum. These roads converged at Ancyra and then ran almost due east to Tavium, Sebastopolis, and Sebasteia, from where there were branches north to Nicopolis or south to Melitene.[70] A third route left the second at Ancyra and ran south-east to Caesareia in Cappadocia, before taking the long and lonely path across Uzun Yayla, through Cocussus, John Chrysostom's place of exile at the end of the fourth century, to Melitene.[71] Finally there was the so-called Pilgrim's Road, which traversed Anatolia from north-west to south-east, leading from Byzantium through Ancyra to the Cilician Gates and into northern Syria.[72]

Other highways, no less imposing in construction, included the roads which linked the two northern routes, bringing the cities of Amaseia, Zela, and Comana Pontica into the system,[73] and those which ran across northern Cappadocia connecting Caesareia with Tavium and Sebasteia.[74] Given their evident ability to press-gang a labour force, thus subsidizing construction costs almost to the point of their elimination, Roman governors could even appear profligate in the number of paved highways they chose to build, and some may have been surplus to strictly military requirements. However, it must be remembered that they were not simply designed to facilitate troop movements, but they also served as the channels of communication by which supplies were moved from civilian producers to consumers along the frontiers. That was only possible thanks to an all-embracing road network (see below, Ch. 14 § III and IV).[75]

Roman military control rested on rapid communications, as well as the ability to move troops and supplies efficiently between provinces and frontiers. The vast overland distances that faced travellers in Anatolia posed a perpetual challenge to ancient rulers. Throughout Antiquity attempts were made to devise an effective messenger system. The relay of couriers by which the Persians linked their western capital Sardis

with Susa evoked a more detailed description from an admiring Herodotus than almost any other aspect of their empire.[76] After the end of our period the Byzantines constructed a series of intervisible mountaintop fortresses, where beacons could be lit to carry urgent, although necessarily very restricted information from the war zone in the south-east, where they faced the Arabs, to Constantinople.[77]

The Romans, as one would predict, devised an elaborate series of networks. In Asia the headquarters was Ephesus, where a college of *tabellarii* was based, and from which routes must have radiated to all the administrative centres of the province.[78] However, the route which can be most readily traced ran from north to south across Anatolia, linking the Balkans and Byzantium with the south coast and ultimately with Syria. Its importance can be illustrated by two travellers of the early modern period. When the English merchant, Arthur Pullinger, went from Aleppo to Constantinople in 1739, he crossed the Taurus at the Cilician Gates, followed the regular caravan trail, well-marked by caravanserais and wells, west to Konya, and then skirted the western edge of the central plateau, passing through Ladik (Laodicea Catcecaumene), Akşehir (Philomelium), Hosrev Paşa Han (on the east side of the Phrygian Highlands), Eskişehir (Dorylaeum), Iznik (Nicaea), and Gebze (Dacibyza).[79] This was a standard itinerary, and the section between Constantinople and Konya was followed exactly by one of the best-known topographers of Asia Minor, Colonel Leake, who crossed Anatolia very rapidly in 1800. South of Konya Leake took the direct route to the south coast, by Karaman, Mut, and the Calycadnus valley to the neighbourhood of Seleuceia.[80] The Roman courier route exactly duplicated the northern section. Probably the first post station out of Byzantium was at Dacibyza, where senior muleteers and soldiers from *ala VI equitata*, who were responsible for manning stations which were concerned with documents and accounts, honoured Lucullus son of Hedys, an imperial slave in charge of the Emperor's *ktene*, evidently the stud and stables.[81] The establishment was

---

Galatia (Bosch, *Ankara* no. 218 was erected by members of his staff at Ancyra) set up a milestone close to Neoclaudiopolis in AD 198 (*CIL* iii. 14184[34]).

[70] Magie, *RR* ii. 1309–10. For roads from Sebasteia to the *limes* and to Melitene, see French, *Armies and Frontiers* 87.

[71] Magie, *RR* ii. 1349–50.

[72] French, *Pilgrim's Road*.

[73] Magie, *RR* ii. 1309–10; D. R. Wilson, *AS* 10 (1960), 133–40.

[74] For the first see French, *AS* 24 (1974), 143–51 with map on p. 145 and K. Bittel, *Kleinasiatische Studien* (1942), 19–28; the second is recorded in *It. Ant.* 178, 6–7.

[75] Eastern Galatia and Pontus between Tavium and Neocaesareia were served by an abundance of routes. See below, Ch. 14 § IV for the supply system.

[76] Herodotus, 5. 52–3.

[77] P. Pattenden, 'The Byzantine Early Warning System', *Byzantion*, 53 (1983), 258–99.

[78] *Forsch. Eph.* iv no. 12 = *I. Eph.* 2200 A, 4112, set up by *decuriones et tabellarii et equites qui sunt ad Lares Dominicos* for the procurator of Asia. Also *TAM* v. 2. 1125 (Thyateira). See also below, Ch. 10 § v n. 209.

[79] T. Drew Bear, C. Naour, and R. Stroud, *Arthur Pullinger: An Early Traveler in Syria and Asia Minor*, Trans. Am. Philosophical Soc., lxxv part 3 (1985), map at p. 47.

[80] See J. M. Wagstaff, *AS* 37 (1987), 23–35, map at p. 25.

[81] Robert, *Hellenica*, x. 46–62 for full discussion: οἱ στρατιῶται σπείρης ἑκτῆς ἱππικῆς οἱ ἐπὶ τῶν στατιωνῶν τῶν ἄκτων καὶ νουμέρων καὶ οἱ μουλίωνες οἱ ἐπέστωτες συνωρίᾳ εὐχαριστοῦσιν Λευκούλλῳ

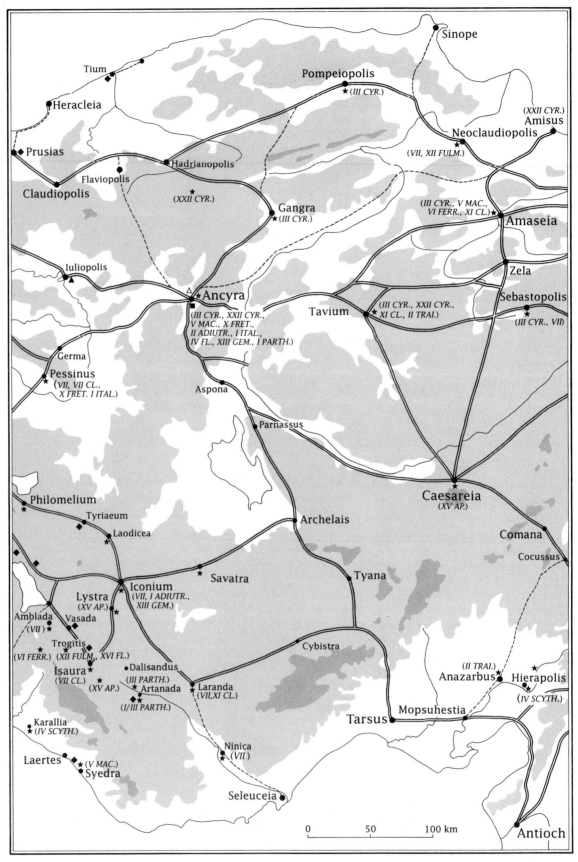

Map 8. Roads, garrisons, and recruitment in central Asia Minor

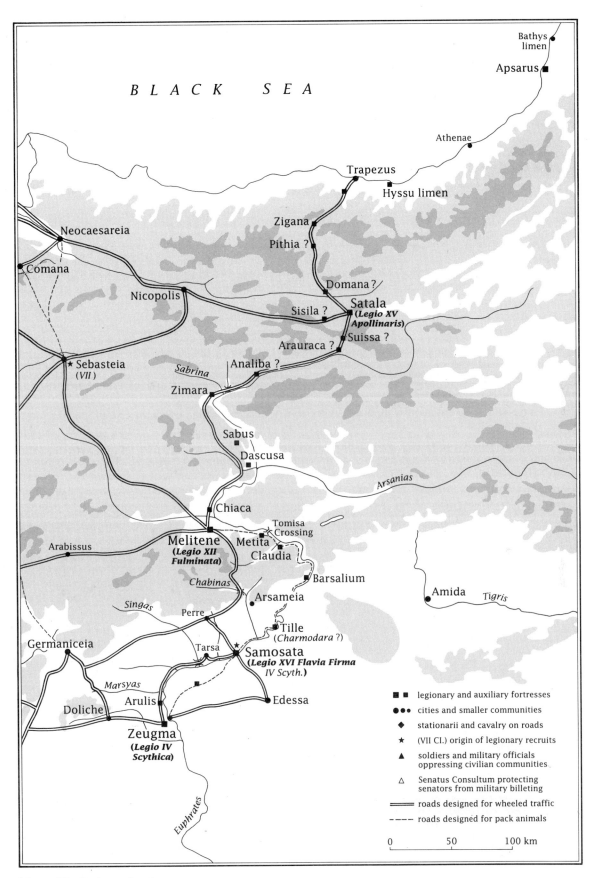

BLACK SEA

Bathys limen

Apsarus

Athenae

Trapezus

Hyssu limen

Zigana

Pithia ?

Neocaesareia

Comana

Nicopolis

Domana ?

Satala
(*Legio XV Apollinaris*)

Sisila ?

Suissa ?

Arauraca ?

Analiba ?

Sebasteia
(*VII*)

Sabrina

Zimara

Sabus

Dascusa

Arsanias

Chiaca

Tomisa Crossing

Melitene
(*Legio XII Fulminata*)

Metita

Claudia

Arabissus

Chabinas

Barsalium

Amida

Tigris

Singas

Arsameia

Perre

Tille
(*Charmodara ?*)

Germaniceia

Tarsa

Samosata
(*Legio XVI Flavia Firma IV Scyth.*)

Marsyas

Doliche

Arulis

Edessa

Zeugma
(*Legio IV Scythica*)

Euphrates

■ ■ legionary and auxiliary fortresses

●●● cities and smaller communities

◆ stationarii and cavalry on roads

★ (VII Cl.) origin of legionary recruits

▲ soldiers and military officials oppressing civilian communities

△ Senatus Consultum protecting senators from military billeting

══ roads designed for wheeled traffic

---- roads designed for pack animals

0   50   100 km

Map 9. The Euphrates frontier

evidently a large one, and it was positioned so as to provide mounts, couriers, and military personnel, who could escort documents, accounts, and perhaps also cash along any of the major routes leading into Anatolia, to the frontier and to Syria. The cross-country courier route itself consisted of relays manned by households of imperial slaves, where the menfolk occupied the post of mounted courier. At Dorylaeum three brothers, all *hippeis*, erected their father's gravestone, which was decorated with a relief showing a wreath and a dagger in a sheath with a baldric.[82] Another gravestone at Dorylaeum was set up for Agathopous, evidently a *nom parlant*, *hippeus* from the establishment at Synnada. It shows a horseman in relief.[83] A further stage is marked by a gravestone from Oinan, north-west of Philomelium. The wife who set up her courier husband's tomb, combined the motifs of the Dorylaeum stones and had it decorated with a figure of a horseman and a round shield with two spears.[84] Next come three gravestones from Laodicea Catacecaumene all set up by or for similar slave messengers.[85] The route thus exactly replicates its Ottoman successor. Just as the Dacibyza text indicates a horse-breeding establishment connected with the station there, it is hard to resist the suggestion that the imperial horse-breeding estates of the Phrygian Highlands were also responsible for providing mounts for the section of the courier route which ran nearby.[86]

Ancyra, Caesareia, Tavium, and Amaseia were key points in the eastern part of the road system. The remains of seven highways can be traced converging on modern Ankara, five on Caesareia, and four each on Tavium and Amaseia, thus confirming that the evidence of the ancient itineraries is no figment of the map-maker's imagination. The traffic which passed along the roads and through the cities can be divided broadly into two categories. The first comprised official, military, and administrative personnel, for whom the roads had been built in the first place. They

will have ranged from whole armies marching to and from the frontier in connection with major campaigns, to individual couriers and messengers of the imperial post; between these extremes fell the provincial legates and procurators, accompanied by their staff, detachments from the frontier garrisons seconded for duties elsewhere, and individuals or groups passing through the province on special business, who had the authority of the emperor to use the same facilities and make the same demands on the local communities as other official users.[87] The second category consisted of unofficial traffic, such as traders, travellers, private citizens making their way from one town to the next or, most numerous of all, from the countryside to the cities.[88] It is impossible to assess the precise volume of road users, but official and especially military traffic was considerable, and left clear traces of its passage in the epigraphic record, above all at Ancyra.

The first major campaign which can be traced in Ancyra's inscriptions is Trajan's Parthian war. Substantial numbers of troops went through the city in the winter of 113/14, when C. Iulius Severus, on the eve of his distinguished senatorial career, 'played host to the armies which overwintered in the city and escorted them as they passed through to take part in the war against the Parthians' (ἀπεδέξατο τὰ στρατεύματα τὰ παραχειμάσαντα ἐν τῇ πόλει καὶ προὐπέμψατο τὰ παροδεύοντα ἐπὶ τὸν πρὸς Πάρθους πόλεμον).[89] Three years later troops returning from the same war, now under Hadrian, also stopped in the city and gave occasion for more munificent spending by a local aristocrat, Latinius Alexander, who provided oil 'from his own funds more splendidly than anyone before him for the whole year when the emperor Hadrian and his sacred armies were passing through' (ἐκ τῶν ἰδίων λαμπρότατα τῶν πρὸ αὐτοῦ δι' ὅλου τοῦ ἔτους ἐπὶ τῇ τοῦ μεγίστου Αὐτοκράτορος Τραιανοῦ Ἀδριανοῦ Σεβαστοῦ παρόδῳ καὶ τῶν ἱερῶν στρατευμάτων).[90] Unlike Iulius Severus he seems not to have supplied the basic needs of the troops, but merely provided for some of the celebrations which attended the arrival and passage of the emperor, who did not winter in the city.[91] A prolonged stay during the winter months was one of

---

Ἤδυος ἐπιμελητῇ κτηνῶν Καίσαρος. Note also another text from the same establishment, *Bull. ép.* (1976), 683.

82 A. Körte, *Gött. Gel. Anz.* (1897), 415 no. 81; (*IGR* iv. 530); L. Robert, *Rev. phil.* (1939), 207–10.

83 *BCH* 28 (1904), 195 no. 12 = Mendel, *BCH* 33 (1909), 301 no. 55, with illustration fig. 8 on p. 264 (*IGR* iv. 531). Synnada itself lay off the courier route discussed here, but was the major administrative centre of eastern Asia. See recently T. Drew Bear, *Nouvelles inscriptions de Phrygie*, 10–12, and *Tyche*, 1 (1986), 55 ff.

84 W. M. Calder, *CR* 1913, 12, who distinguishes the shield from the Pisidian type; *MAMA* iv. 114.

85 *MAMA* i. 27 (*IGR* iii. 253) Κόσμος οὐέρνας ἱππεύς; Calder, *CR* (1913), 12, Ἀγριπεῖνα Κυρίου Καίσαρος δούλη Ἀπρειλίῳ ἱππεῖ καὶ Κοσμᾷ γονεῦσι; *MAMA* i. 30, [ὁ δεῖνα] οὐέρνα ἱππεὺς Ζωητρόφῳ τέκνῳ (another *nom parlant*).

86 W. M. Ramsay, *JHS* 38 (1918), 35–6; cf. J. Strubbe, *Anc. Soc.* 6 (1975), 241–2.

87 That is holders of *diplomata*, see *JRS* 66 (1976), 106–31.

88 For a speculative but suggestive discussion of overland transport, see K. Hopkins, in P. Garnsey and C. R. Whittaker, *Trade and Famine in Classical Antiquity* (1983), 75–83.

89 Bosch, *Ankara*, no. 105. No doubt the tombstone of a *signifer* of *XXX Ulpia Victrix* also dates to the passage of this legion through Ancyra during the same war.

90 Bosch, *Ankara*, no. 117.

91 On 13 Nov. 117 Hadrian dispatched a letter to Pergamum from Iuliopolis, the next city west of Ancyra along the 'Pilgrim's Road', (*SIG*³ 831). A coin of Iuliopolis struck almost a century later commemorates the passage of Elagabalus, accompanying the sacred Black Stone of his native

the heaviest burdens for a provincial community to bear, and prudence, if not necessarily a sense of justice and fair play, led military planners to distribute the burden of support among several provincial communities, and not allow it to fall exclusively on the city where the troops chose to encamp. An inscription from Thyateira in Asia, which is connected either to Trajan's or to Lucius Verus' Parthian campaign, mentions an individual who took charge of the arrangements for the winter provisions of four legions in one of the Asiatic provinces, perhaps Galatia itself.[92] He will have faced practical problems in collecting and distributing supplies, whose complexity is vividly revealed in two long papyrus texts from the end of the third century found at Panopolis in Egypt, which demonstrate in detail and with perfect clarity the nature of the imposition of military demands on civilian communities.[93] Ancyra in AD 114 or 117 will have been little different.

Stresses on the eastern frontier emerged again in the second half of the second century. The legions *I Adiutrix* and *XXII Primigeneia* were both moved from the Rhine and the Danube to accompany Lucius Verus against Parthia between 162 and 167. Gravestones found at Ancyra of a centurion and a *tribunus laticlavius* of *I Adiutrix* and of an *eques singularis* of *XXII Primigeneia* can be dated to this period.[94] Mortality was high, not least because of the great plague which the Roman armies had brought back with them from the East and which afflicted large parts of the empire.[95] A statue base for a young man of senatorial family, M. Cassius Hortensius Paulinus, set up by a *speculator* and a *beneficiarius* of *legio XIV Gemina*, may also be explained by the fact that they were passing through with all or part of the legion during some second century expedition, perhaps the same war.[96]

The Severan age saw unusual military activity on a

large scale in the East, including two major Parthian campaigns and the civil war with Pescennius Niger. A soldier from Pannonia, Ulpius Maximus of *legio X Gemina*, died in Ancyra on 3 September 195, returning from Septimius Severus' first Parthian campaign,[97] and the appearance of a *librarius*, T. Aurelius Firminus, from the corps of *equites singulares Augusti*, which accompanied the emperor on his travels, has been attributed to the same period.[98] The passage of Severus in the company of his sons Caracalla and Geta was heralded by acclamations, faithfully recorded on stone,[99] and Caracalla's reappearance in 215, after overwintering in Bithynia, was marked in the same fashion.[100]

After the Severan period explicit references to the passage of troops and emperors are more sporadic. An *optio* of *legio VII Claudia* was buried in Ancyra by two fellow soldiers, probably in the course of a third-century campaign,[101] and an item of literary evidence, rare for Ancyra before the time of Constantine, shows that the emperor Aurelian advanced through the city in the course of his efforts to recover southern Asia Minor and Syria from the Palmyrenes in 272.[102]

It would, however, be highly misleading to suppose that the randomly preserved epigraphic evidence gives anything like a complete picture of the passage of troops and emperors through Galatia in the second and third centuries. The roads across Anatolia were continually used by armies moving from the northern to the eastern frontier in the course of foreign and civil wars throughout this period. The sources of information for this activity do not need to tell us that the protagonists in these wars used the Anatolian road network; most of them will have had no option but to have done so.[103] Galatia, like Bithynia to the north-west and Cilicia to the south-east, was a natural transit route for military traffic. All three regions suffered or benefited, as the case may be, from this mass of official traffic.

city Emesa (L. Robert, *Rev. num.* 18 (1976), 50 = OMS vi. 162).

[92] J. Guey, *MEFRA* 35 (1939), 56–77 (*AE* 1939, 132, *SEG* xviii. 544; *TAM* v. 2. 1143): πραγματευόμενος ἐν ἐπαρ[χείᾳ ?Γαλατί]ᾳ παραχειμαστικοῖς λεγ[ιωνῶν] for V Mac., VII Cl., IV Scyth., and I Ital. Cilicia or Bithynia could also be restored as the name of the province. The best evidence for the burden imposed by armies and an emperor overwintering in an Anatolian province comes from Cassius Dio's description of Caracalla in Bithynia, 78. 9. 6–7; 18. 3.

[93] T. C. Skeat, *Two Papyri from Panopolis* (1964), briefly evoked by Mitchell, *Armies and Frontiers*, 143–4.

[94] Bosch, *Ankara*, nos. 175–7.

[95] J. F. Gilliam, 'The Plague under Marcus Aurelius', *AJPhil.* 82 (1961), 225 ff. = *Roman Army Papers* (1986), 227–53. Note the dedications to Asclepius from Pessinus, *CIG* iii add. 4082 b (*I. Pessinus*, no. 24), which has been dated to this period by Ruge, *RE* xix. 1 (1937), 1108, and from Aezani, *MAMA* ix. 79.

[96] *AS* 27 (1977), 65–6 no. 3 (*AE* (1977), 811). The inscription for Lucius Verus from Tavium, *RECAM* ii. 412, does not prove that the emperor was there in person.

[97] Bosch, *Ankara*, no. 213.

[98] Bosch, *Ankara*, no. 182, dated to c.200 by M. Speidel, *Die Equites Singulares Augusti* (1965), 32. For another *eques singularis*, but not necessarily from the imperial corps, see Bosch, *Ankara*, no. 367. Bosch misinterprets the ethnic at the end of the text; he was a man from Orondian Pappa, so another cavalry recruit from south Galatia.

[99] Bosch, *Ankara*, nos. 215–17.

[100] Bosch, *Ankara*, nos. 259–61; *AS* 27 (1977), 64–5 no. 1 with comm.

[101] Bosch, *Ankara*, no. 269.

[102] Zosimus, 1. 50. 1–2.

[103] The evidence is exhaustively discussed by E. Gren, *Kleinasien und der Ostbalkan in der wirtschaftlichen Entwicklung der römischen Kaiserzeit* (1941), ch. 4. For 3rd-cent. Bithynia see below, Ch. 13 §11 nn. 27–8 and for official and military traffic in the 6th and 7th cents., Vol. II, Ch. 19 §1 nn. 13–18.

It has been argued that the constant presence and passage of armies through the region acted as a significant stimulus to the local economy, for not only would the military roads open up opportunities for more economical and efficient overland transport and trade, but also the presence of soldiers with money to spend would be a boon to local markets.[104] There are good reasons to doubt this thesis. For one thing the roads themselves would have brought relatively little benefit to private traders, for whom long-distance overland trade always remained prohibitively expensive and impracticable. Apart from the distribution systems which were explicitly created to bring supplies for the armies (see below, Ch. 14 § IV), surplus crops and other low-cost bulky goods were rarely transported more than a short distance between the countryside and the nearest market.[105] The highways which linked the cities were only incidentally useful to peasant producers; in dry summer weather their paved surfaces may even have been a liability for pack-animals, which tended to be more comfortable on the grass verges.[106] On the other hand, the obligations which fell on civilian communities to provide for troops on the march were a distinct economic burden. Provincial cities and their dependent villages had duties to feed, clothe, house, and even to provide armour and equipment for the armies.[107] This *munus*, known as *prosecutio* or παραπομπή ('escort duty'), devolved in the first instance on the municipal authorities. From time to time a public-spirited or ambitious aristocrat took the burden on himself; more often, presumably, the more irksome demands were distributed among the population, especially the peasant inhabitants.[108] The liturgy, like all such civic duties, gave aristocrats the opportunity for self-advertisement, but in general they must have shared Cassius Dio's view, that the system was a severe imposition. Local discomfort was doubtless often aggravated by the typical behaviour of armies at all times, their readiness to seize or extort goods, services, and cash to which they were in no way entitled.[109] It is obvious that their presence in the cities of the empire was normally far from welcome. The increased commercial opportunities which the passage of troops offered to enterprising traders were outweighed by the oppressive demands that were imposed on the community as a whole.[110]

Their heavy demands could only be exacted legitimately if illegal extortion was kept within tolerable bounds. In a famous letter Pliny asked Trajan for a centurion to be sent to Iuliopolis, on the border of Galatia and Bithynia, to keep order in a small town that was especially burdened by military traffic.[111] The same letter reveals that a centurion with a small detachment of soldiers had already been posted for this purpose at Byzantium, and the epigraphic evidence from Ancyra suggests that the same was true there also. Inscriptions mention eight centurions, three from *legio XVI Flavia Firma*, who should belong to the period between AD 76 and Trajan's Parthian expedition, when the legion was moved south from Satala to Samosata,[112] four from *XV Apolliniaris*, which replaced *XVI Flavia Firma* at Satala,[113] and one from *XII Fulminata* at Melitene.[114] These proportions suggest that as a rule Ancyra received detached officers

[104] This is the principal thesis of Gren's book. For discussion, mostly sceptical, see E. W. Gray, *JRS* 37 (1947), 213; MacMullen, *Soldier and Civilian*, 89–98; Mitchell, *Armies and Frontiers*, 131 ff. There are interesting observations on the poor transport and road system, which prevented the vilayet of Angora from exporting its agricultural surplus at the end of the 19th cent. in Cuinet, *La Turquie d'Asie*, i (1892), 644. For the problem in Cilicia and Pamphylia in the 3rd cent., see Ziegler, and J. Nollé, *Chiron*, 17 (1987), 254–64; the latter emphasizes the positive benefits brought to a city by a military and official presence. Further discussion below, Ch. 12 § V, and Ch. 13 § IV n. 75.

[105] See K. Hopkins, 'Models, Ships and Staples', in P. Garnsey and C. R. Whittaker, *Trade and Famine in the Ancient World* (1983), 84–109.

[106] In Antiquity, as in early modern Europe, traffic often used the verges, rather than the road itself. See Pekary, *Römischen Reichsstrassen*, 32–3 esp. n. 128; F. Braudel, *Civilisation and Capitalism 15th–18th Century*, i (Eng. trans. of 2 edn., 1981), 415–16; and especially H. Bender, 'Verkehrs- und Transportwesen in der römischen Kaiserzeit', in *Untersuchungen zu Handel und Verkehr der vor- und frühgeschichtlichen Zeit in Mittel- und Nordeuropa*. Part 5 (Göttingen, 1989), 108–54 at 113–15 (a very valuable study).

[107] See the Panopolis papyri *passim* for details.

[108] Troops and officials were regularly billeted on civilians, and no payment could be exacted for this *hospitium* (cf. *JRS* (1976), 127–8). An imperial letter of AD 204 which refers to an earlier *senatus consultum* was posted, at local initiative, in several cities of Asia Minor and exempted senators from this burdensome duty. See T. Drew Bear, P. Herrmann, and W. Eck, *Chiron*, 7 (1977), 365–83, esp. Eck's commentary, pp. 365 ff., which discusses the issue in depth. Further examples of the text are published by L. Robert, *BCH* 102 (1978), 435–7 and by D. Knibbe and R. Merkelbach, *ZPE* 31 (1978), 229–32. C. P. Jones, has identified further exemplars at Pisidian Antioch and Alexandria Troas, *Chiron*, 14 (1984), 93–9. The Antioch text, and possibly the copy in the Ankara Museum published by Robert, are from Galatia; all the others are from Asia: Paros, Satala in Lydia, Troas, the Phrygian Pentapolis, and Ephesus.

[109] See the erocative account of MacMullen, *Soldier and Civilian* 58–77. For the contrast between literary and epigraphic evidence compare *I. Iznik*, i no. 60 with Cassius Dio, 78. 9. 6–7, and 18. 3.

[110] Mitchell, *Armies and Frontiers*, 139–45; see also W. Ameling, *Epigr. Anat.* 1 (1983), 68–73.

[111] Pliny, *Ep.* 10. 77–8.

[112] Bosch, *Ankara*, nos. 110–12.

[113] Bosch, *Ankara*, nos. 178, 187, and 366.

[114] Bosch, *Ankara*, no. 268. A soldier of *legio XII* was buried at Cappadocian Caesarea by his companion, who was a *strator*

and troops from the northern legionary fortress, but it is worth noting that among the coins of the north Galatian cities which depict military standards, a type which is especially characteristic of Bithynia but common also in Galatia, there is an issue of Ancyra with the legend XII between two legionary eagles, another clear allusion to the Melitene garrison.[115] In any case it seems likely that these detached centurions and the soldiers who will have accompanied them had duties like their colleagues at Byzantium, to protect the city from the excessive demands of passing soldiers, but at the same time no doubt to ensure that their legitimate requirements were met in full. Two legionary tribunes, C. Iulius Pudens of *XII Fulminata* and Ti. Claudius Candidus of *XV Apollonaris* also appear in the inscriptions of Ancyra.[116] They may have had official business there, although the attraction of a substantial city to officers who had been posted to a wild and hazardous frontier area should not be underestimated.

Other officials in permanent residence at Ancyra were the members of the staff of the governors and the provincial procurators. Inscriptions mention *tabularii*, *beneficiarii*, and a *cornicularius* of the procurator,[117] a *beneficiarius*, a *cornicularius*, a *comes*, and a *decurialis lictor* of the governor,[118] and a *scriba*.[119] To these may be added several imperial slaves and freedmen without specified duties.[120] The large number of soldiers and government officials to be found at Ancyra was certainly responsible for the high proportion of Latin inscriptions in the city. Of the surviving pre-Constantinian texts, about 200 are in Greek, fifty in Latin, and six are bilingual. The proportion of Latin to Greek texts (one to four) is exceptionally high for an eastern city which was not a Roman colony. Closer inspection shows that Greek was used for local inscriptions, such as decrees and all but one of the building inscriptions, and for most of the funerary texts and dedications. Latin is found on inscriptions relating to the emperor and to members of the imperial administration, military texts, and on a handful of gravestones where the associations of the dead person are not made clear. There is no question that Latin was ever widely used by the native inhabitants of Ancyra, but there was clearly a substantial Latin-speaking minority in the city. It was

the most important urban centre of central and eastern Anatolia, and attracted a large number of visitors, above all military and administrative personnel.

In at least one respect these Latin speakers had a direct influence on local customs. The grave formula *Dis Manibus*, ubiquitous in the Latin-speaking parts of the empire, was rendered into Greek by the phrase θεοῖς καταχθονίοις or, more rarely, by θεοῖς δαίμοσιν. These expessions, although widely attested, are usually only found on the tombstones of persons who can be shown to have had close associations with Latin speakers, or who were themselves soldiers, members of the imperial administration, or employees on imperial estates.[121] At Ancyra there are twenty-two examples of *Dis Manibus* and eleven of θεοῖς καταχθονίοις. All of the former occur on the graves of soldiers, officials, or members of their families, but this is true of only one of the Greek texts, the gravestone of a gladiator from Pergamum who had been a *summa rudis* at Rome.[122] The remainder are simply the gravestones of Ancyran citizens, otherwise indistinguishable from their fellows.[123] It is clear that the formula became familiar in the city and was adopted even by Ancyrans with no specific Roman associations.

Although Ancyra has produced more evidence for the effect of the Roman military presence than any other central or eastern Anatolian city, its smaller neighbours in Pontus offer a very comparable picture. Amaseia in particular seems to have served as a significant focal point for military activity. In the autumn of AD 62 *legio V Macedonica* was stationed in Pontus, in the rear of the Armenian war zone where disaster shortly awaited the governor of Galatia–Cappadocia, Caesennius Paetus.[124] The tenth cohort of this legion set up what appears to have been a building-inscription in the city, probably at this date.[125] *V Macedonica* also consistently recruited from the region, certainly at

---

on the governor's staff, G. de Jerphanion, *BCH* 23 (1909), 66 no. 45.

[115] T. E. Mionnet, *Descr. des médailles antiques grecques*, suppl. vii (1835), 637 no. 29; in general C. Bosch, *Arch Anz.* (1930), 425–8.

[116] Bosch, *Ankara*, nos. 183 and 365.

[117] Bosch, *Ankara*, nos. 64–5, 198, 222; *AS* 27 (1977), 66 no. 4 (*AE* (1981), 788).

[118] Bosch, *Ankara*, nos. 97, 173, 197, 218, 364; cf. nos. 78, 369.

[119] Bosch, *Ankara*, no. 368.

[120] Bosch, *Ankara*, nos. 50 and 373.

[121] L. Robert, *Laodicée du Lycos: Le Nymphée* (1969), 326–7.

[122] Bosch, *Ankara*, no. 149; Robert, *Gladiateurs*, no. 90; *Hellenica*, viii. 64 ff.

[123] Bosch, *Ankara*, nos. 208, 324, 326, 343, 353, 354; *AS* 22 (1972), 222 no. 2. Note the phrase ἀγαθοῖς τὰ ἀγαθά, a translation of *bonis bene*, in this last text.

[124] Tacitus, *Ann.* 15. 9. 2, 'Parthi . . . spem omnem in Armeniam verterent, ubi Paetus imminentium nescius quintam legionem procul in Ponto habebat.'

[125] D. H. French, *Epigr. Anat.* 15 (1990), 135 suggests that *V Macedonica* consistently recruited from this region. He also publishes a new text from Amaseia, carved in good letters on an altar, *Leg. V | Mac. | Coh. X*, apparently a building inscription (rather than a marker or boundary stone), and perhaps associated with a large Roman structure that was unearthed at the same time. As he suggests, the text implies that at least part of the legion was stationed for a time at Amaseia, but the date is uncertain. I prefer a context during the 60s AD or during Trajan's Parthian campaign in 113/14, to the Parthian expedition of Lucius Verus, which he suggests. See also French, 'The *Legio V Macedonica* in

this period and probably also later, and its veterans returned from service to be buried in their home villages of the Chilokomon.[126] Perhaps during the Parthian expedition of 113/14 the *ala I Flavia Augusta Britannica miliaria c. R.* put up a dedication to Iupiter Optimus Maximus,[127] and in the same years a decurion of the *ala Claudia Nova* died in the city.[128] Further texts mention the freedman of a *primipilaris*,[129] and an individual soldier.[130]

Other cities show a similar pattern. Both Neoclaudiopolis and Cappadocian Comana have produced inscriptions for centurions of *legio XII Fulminata*, who had perhaps been posted to control the passage of troops.[131] At Neoclaudiopolis or on its territory there are gravestones of a centurion of *legio III Augusta*, as well as of a cavalryman and a veteran of unspecified units.[132] Zela has produced tombstones of a decurion of an *ala Moesiaca* and a veteran of *legio XXX Ulpia Victrix*.[133] The prime epigraphic specimen of the Roman military presence in Pontus is now the elaborate and detailed Latin epitaph of M. Caesius Verus, formerly a soldier in the Praetorian Guard, who had been promoted to become a centurion of *V Macedonica* but died on the march to the eastern front in AD 113/14 at a road station west of Comana Pontica, where he was buried by his freedmen.[134]

III. *Legionary Recruitment*

The Roman army made its mark throughout Anatolia by another mechanism, the recruitment of soldiers and officers, above all to the legions. Military prowess was the one quality for which the Galatians had been consistently valued throughout their history. Hellenistic rulers had been willing to use their services as mercenaries time and again, in spite of the patent readiness of the Gauls to turn against the masters who had hired them; Ptolemaic, Seleucid, and Attalid kings all found themselves fighting major wars against their erstwhile helpers.[135] For Rome through the first century BC the benefits of Galatian help were available without such risks, and in course of time their forces were transformed from ill-disciplined native levies into formally constituted cohorts and legions, commanded first by Deiotarus, then by Amyntas. As their kingdoms extended to cover most of central Anatolia, recruitment into these Romanized armies no doubt also encompassed the adjacent territories in the Pontus and the Taurus.[136]

The transition to imperial control was smooth and predictable. Augustus acquired command of Amyntas' troops as he had inherited control of his kingdom. Within a generation of the annexation of Galatia three legions in particular, *III Cyrenaica*, *XXII Deiotariana*, and *VII Macedonica*, showed a heavy preponderance of Anatolian soldiers, recruited for the most part from precisely those regions which Amyntas and other Galatian chieftains had controlled during the late Republic: Pontus, Paphlagonia, Galatia proper, Lycaonia, Isauria, Rugged Cilicia, and Pisidia. Attention has naturally focused on *XXII Deiotariana*, which advertised its close connection with the armies of free Galatia, but one must be wary of drawing over-hasty conclusions from the name alone. Under Augustus the legion usually went without a name, or was occasionally known as *XXII Cyrenaica*, like its Egyptian counterpart *legio III Cyrenaica*. The title *Deiotariana* may not have been conferred before the time of Claudius, as a tribute to its now distant origins.[137]

In fact the documentary evidence from the time of Augustus shows that *III Cyrenaica* was as much a product of Anatolian recruitment as *legio XXII*. A *laterculus militum* found in Egypt contains a list of soldiers inscribed in two columns, one drawn from each of the centuries of two legions, who helped to construct forts and watering posts along the desert road which ran from Coptus to the Red Sea.[138] One of the soldiers in the first column, C. Sossius from Pompeiopolis, is known from his tombstone, which was found at Alexandria, to have belonged to *III Cyrenaica*; the first column accordingly contained the names from *legio III*, and the second, presumably, from *legio XXII*.[139] The recruits for the latter comprise six Ancyrans, one each from Tavium, Paphlagonia, Isinda, and Etenna, four Alexandrians, one each from Cyrene and Berytus, and one born *in castris*. The ethnic composition of *III Cyrenaica*, to judge from the

---

northern Asia Minor', *Congrès International sur la Mer Noire I* (Samsun 1990), 555–61.

[126] *SP* iii. 157b, 169.

[127] *SP* iii. 104. Further on Amaseia as a focus of Roman military influence, see D. H. French, 'Cappadocia and the Eastern Limes: Aspects of Romanisation at Amaseia in Cappadocia', in P. Freeman and D. L. Kennedy (eds.), *The Defence of the Roman and Byzantine East* (1986), 277–85.

[128] *SP* iii. 105.

[129] *SP* iii. 106; *IGR* iii. 102.

[130] *SP* iii. 108.

[131] *IGR* iii. 120 = R. P. Harper, *AS* 18 (1968), 111–12 no. 3; *SP* iii no. 60.

[132] *SP* iii. 49, 69, 90.

[133] *SP* iii. 269. The evidence for Roman soldiers in Pontus has been collected by E. Olshausen, *Epigr. Anat.* 9 (1987), 91–3; several inscriptions have still to be published.

[134] T. B. Mitford, *ZPE* 71 (1988), 176–8 no. 12, interpreted by K. Strobel, *Epigr. Anat.* 12 (1989), 39–42.

[135] Launey, *Recherches*, i. 490–534.

[136] See above, Ch. 2.

[137] J. Lesquier, *L'Armée romaine d'Égypte d'Auguste à Dioclétien* (1918), 49–50.

[138] *CIL* iii. 6627 with Mommsen's commentary which remains fundamental (*ILS* 2483; Bosch, *Ankara*, no. 49).

[139] *CIL* iii. 6591.

available sample, was strictly comparable: four from Ancyra, three from Tavium, one each from Pompeiopolis, Sebastopolis, Gangra, Side, and Nicaea, two from Alexandria, one from Paraetonium in Egypt, and one born *in castris*. Also in *legio III* was the odd man out from the western part of the empire, a recruit from Lugdunum in Gallia Comata. The Anatolian strain goes even deeper than these figures suggest. Eleven of the soldiers of *III Cyrenaica* and fifteen of *legio XXII* belonged to the Pollia, the usual tribe of soldiers born *in castris*, even though all but two of them had distinguishing ethnics. These members of the Pollia should, it is argued, be the children born in the camps of first-generation recruits to the legions. Since they were not the issue of *iustum conubium* they gave, as their origin, the *patria* of their mothers, not of their fathers. In seventeen cases the ethnic is Anatolian, against six from Alexandria, and three from the neighbouring areas of Paraetonium, Cyrene, and Berytus. The implication is that most of the first generation recruits had brought their spouses with them from Asia Minor, while the remainder, a sizeable minority, had formed unions with local women after they were transferred to Egypt.[140] The argument also helps to date the document, not to the 20s BC but to twenty or thirty years later.[141] In the 270s BC Ptolemy II had created a Galatian military settlement at Alexandria, designed to provide him with a constant supply of fighting men; 250 years later Augustus essentially repeated the experiment.[142]

None of the remaining documents fom Augustan Egypt invites such detailed analysis. Individual inscriptions of Julio-Claudian date mention soldiers of *legio III* from Pompeiopolis, Tavium, Gangra, and Amaseia,[143] and of *legio XXII* from Ancyra;[144] one

veteran of *III Cyrenaica* appears at Phrygian Acmonia and another, L. Ancharius L. f. Aem. Capito, was buried in his *patria*, Pamphylian Attaleia.[145] All the soldiers attested in Egypt, except the man from Tavium, belonged to the Pollia and the ethnics should presumably be interpreted in the same way as those of the *laterculus*. On the other hand a papyrus fragment which lists fifteen soldiers by their name, filiation, tribe, and origin, may take us back to the first generation itself. The majority are Anatolians—three from Ancyra, two each from Pessinus and from an unspecified Laodicea, and one from Apamea, Philomelium, and Chrysopolis—against two Africans and two soldiers from Cisalpine Gaul.[146] None, however, belongs to the Pollia, and this should be the earliest military document from Roman Egypt.

The practice of using Anatolian recruits for the Egyptian legions did not persist, and the 'military colony' which Augustus had established either failed to reproduce itself or soon concealed its Asiatic origins. No more soldiers from Asia Minor are recorded until after the middle of the second century, when precisely three of the 136 veterans listed in the *laterculus* of AD 157 found at Nicopolis come from Anatolia.[147] That document, showing a heavy preponderance of recruits from the West, including Italy itself, has been the cause of controversy and is presumed to reflect emergency recruitment in AD 132/3 during the crisis of the Bar-Kochva revolt.[148] A more characteristic Egyptian list of AD 194 restores the expected large majority of local recruits, but still contains only one man from Asia Minor.[149] We can be confident that Egypt was not the usual destination of Anatolian legionary recruits in the second and third centuries.

Most of the early recruits from Anatolia into the army of the Balkans belonged to *legio VII*, sometimes known as *legio VII Macedonica* under Augustus and Tiberius, but to be known as *VII Claudia Pia Fidelis* after its refusal to join the unsuccessful revolt of Scribonianus in Dalmatia in AD 42. The evidence suggests very strongly that it was actually stationed in south Galatia from 25 BC until AD 7, except for an absence in Macedonia between 13 and 11 BC, when it accompanied L. Calpurnius Piso to fight a major war

---

[140] G. A. Harrer, 'The Origin of the Third Cyrenaic Legion', *AJPhil.* 62 (1941), 84–7; his explanation is endorsed by R. O. Fink, *Roman Military Records on Papyrus* (1971), 165.

[141] R. Syme, 'Some Notes on the Legions under Augustus', *JRS* 23 (1933), 31 n. 132 argued for a date after 3 BC on the grounds that C. Helvius from Gangra in Paphlagonia and C. Licinius from Sebastopolis in Pontus Galaticus could not have been enlisted before their cities had become part of the province of Galatia in 6/5 and 3/2 BC respectively. But both men belonged to the Pollia, and if Harrer's argument is sound their fathers must have enlisted at a much earlier date. Perhaps they themselves were of provincial origin but had married women from communities which then lay beyond the provincial boundaries. More probably, early Augustan recruits in Anatolia included men from areas which lay outside provincial territory in the strict sense, but which had traditionally provided manpower for the armies of Deiotarus and Amyntas. Rome would not have ignored a reliable and well-established source of recruits.

[142] Launey, *Recherches* i. 496–9, 511–16.

[143] *CIL* iii. 6591 (Pompeiopolis); 6607 (Gangra and Amaseia); 14136³ (Tavium).

[144] *CIL* iii. 6023 = 6606; Bosch, *Ankara*, no. 59 (Neronian).

[145] *MAMA* vi. 283; Paribeni and Romanelli, *Mon. ant.* 23 (1914), 22 (*AE* (1915), 47).

[146] *Berliner Griechische Urkunden* 1083; Fink, *Roman Military Records on Papyrus*, 165 no. 36.

[147] The most accessible text of this much discussed document is *AE* (1969/70), 663. It names one soldier each from Tavium, Perge, and Anazarbus.

[148] First argued by J. F. Gilliam, *AJPhil.* 77 (1956), 359–75 = *Roman Army Papers*, 145–61, and supported by G. Forni, *ANRW* ii. 1 (1974), 382 n. 116.

[149] *CIL* iii. 6850, re-edited by R. P. Wright, *JRS* 32 (1942), 33–8; the list includes a man from Nicomedia.

against the Thracians, and probably acquired its earlier title. If this is so, the majority of its early recruits, the first of whom will have been enlisted between about 23 and 19 BC, were recruited from the region where the legion was stationed.[150] Forty-four soldiers are known from this early period, including twenty-five from communities in the new province of Galatia, five Macedonians, nine Italians, one born *in castris*, and four of uncertain origin. Most of the Galatians were from the south of the province, and it may not be a coincidence that, apart from four men from Pessinus,[151] there are no north Galatians in the list. Recruits from Ancyra and Tavium, at least, may have been steered towards *III Cyrenaica* and *XXII Cyrenaica* in Egypt.

Once *legio VII* was transferred to the Balkans in AD 7, and took up permanent quarters in Dalmatia in AD 9, the stream of recruitment from Anatolia thinned to a trickle. There were soldiers in *VII Claudia* from Pessinus,[152] Isaura,[153] and perhaps from Pontus,[154] who completed their service between AD 42 and the later years of Claudius or the time of Nero, when the unit was moved north into Moesia Superior. During the second and third centuries, when the legion was stationed at Viminacium, recruitment seems to have been exclusively from the Balkans. The same is true of *legio XI*, later *Claudia Pia Fidelis*, the companion of *legio VII* in Dalmatia. At an early date, before the legion acquired its full titles, there was a soldier from Laranda, T. Cillius T. f. Fab., who served for thirty-eight years, presumably under Augustus and Tiberius.[155] After 42 we hear of soldiers from Amaseia[156] and from Tavium,[157] but they were clearly exceptions to the normal pattern of local enlistment.

Small numbers of Anatolians were to be found in the other Balkan legions. *Legio V Macedonica*, stationed at Oescus until Trajan, and at Troesmis on the lower

Danube thereafter,[158] included four Ancyrans,[159] two Amaseians,[160] and a man from Syedra in Rugged Cilicia.[161] One of the two *duumviri quinquennales* who erected a bath-house at the legionary *canabae* at Troesmis was also of Ancyran origin.[162] One of the Amaseians died aged 25 at Emmaus in Palestine, where the legion was stationed between AD 68 and 70.[163] He should have been recruited in or soon after AD 62, when the legion was posted to Pontus to join the army of Caesennius Paetus in Cappadocia and Armenia, and probably took up station precisely at Amaseia (see above, n. 124). This was naturally a moment when it would have sought to make up its strength by local recruiting before some arduous campaigning.[164]

Legiones I and *II Adiutrix*, which were based in upper Moesia during Domitian's Dacian wars before moving to Aquincum in Pannonia Superior under Trajan, also contained Galatian recruits: two Ancyrans in *II Adiutrix*, and a man from Iconium in *I Adiutrix*. But both legions regularly participated in eastern campaigns,[165] and it is possible that this eastern recruiting took place in the context of these expeditions.[166] There were also Ancyrans in *legio I Italica*, stationed at Novae in Moesia Inferior,[167] and in *IV Flavia*, based at Singidunum from Hadrian's time,[168] as well as an Aspendian in *I Italica*.[169] This legion seems to have left the Balkans only rarely, but two serving soldiers are attested by Asian inscriptions, one offering a dedication to Asclepius Soter at Pergamum,[170] the

---

[150] For most of the known soldiers and veterans of *legio VII*, see *CQ* 26 (1976), 305–6 and above, Ch. 6 nn. 38–41. Demonstrably early recruits include M. Lollius M. f. of Iconium (*IGR* iii. 14/6), enlisted by the first governor of Galatia, and L. Domitius L. f. Ani. Aquila (*CIL* iii. 8487), who was enlisted not before 19 BC, but probably very soon thereafter; cf. *CQ* (1976), 303–4.

[151] The Anatolian origins are as follows: Pessinus (4), Conana (3), Milyas (2), Iconium, Laranda, Amblada, Ninica, Isinda, Clistinna (exact location unknown), Cormasa, Phazimon, Sebaste, Sebastopolis, Cestrus, and Apollonia.

[152] *CIL* iii. 12498 (Küstence, Moesia Inferior); *CIL* iii. 9726 = *ILS* 2253 (Delminium).

[153] *CIL* iii. 14153.

[154] *AE* (1910), 174 (Scupi), a Iulius Ponticus married to a Iulia Pontica.

[155] *CIL* iii. 2818.

[156] *CIL* iii. 971, 13263.

[157] *Diadora* 5 (1970), 97, 2.

[158] Ritterling, *RE* xii (1925), 1574.

[159] *CIL* iii. 6184 (Bosch, *Ankara*, no. 172), 6188 (Bosch, *Ankara*, no. 171); *AE* (1957), 266 (all gravestones of veterans who had settled in Troesmis); Bosch, *Ankara*, no. 270 (a veteran who had returned to Ancyra).

[160] *CIL* iii. 14155[11] (Emmaus); *AE* 1914, 135 (a veteran buried *in patria sua*).

[161] G. E. Bean and T. B. Mitford, *AS* 12 (1962), 192 no. 8, a bilingual text for a returned veteran.

[162] Bosch, *Ankara*, no. 170 (AD 163–4).

[163] Josephus, *BJ* 4. 8. 1; 5. 16. 6; Ritterling, *RE* xii. 1575; Schürer[2] i (1973), 499 n. 70.

[164] For the legion's movements see *RE* xii. 1574; cf. K. Strobel, *Epigr. Anat.* 12 (1989), 41 n. 12.

[165] *CIL* iii. 10497 (Bosch, *Ankara*, no. 153); 10499 (Bosch, *Ankara*, no. 154); 11306. For other members of *I* and *II Adiutrix* in the East, see J. Wagner, *Seleukeia am Euphrat/ Zeugma*, 132 no. 1 and 133 no. 2 with notes; M. Speidel, *BJb*. 176 (1976), 123–63, esp. 129–34 = *Roman Army Papers* i. 9–14.

[166] Ritterling, *RE* xii. 1394–5, 1450–1. There are gravestones at Ancyra of a *tribunus laticlavius* (*CIL* iii. 6755 = Bosch, *Ankara*, no. 175) and of a centurion (*CIL* iii. 265 = Bosch, *Ankara*, no. 176) of *I Adiutrix*.

[167] *AE* (1932), 52; cf. 1966, 353, a centenarian veteran of *I Italica* at Novae.

[168] *AE* (1962), 112.

[169] *CIL* iii. 14491.

[170] *IGR* iv. 278, re-edited by C. Habicht, *Alt. v. Perg.* viii. 3, no. 77.

other burying his 4-year-old son at Temenothyrai-Flaviopolis.[171] *IV Flavia* was also active in the East: part or all of the legion certainly took part in one of the major second-century wars,[172] and a gravestone of a serving soldier found at Synnada in Phrygia, together with inscriptions at Apamea, have been taken to show that a vexillation was stationed in the region at some period.[173] Finally there were Anatolian recruits in *XIII Gemina*, the permanent garrison force in Dacia. Two veterans returned to be buried in their family tomb at Iconium,[174] and another set up a bilingual tombstone at a village in the territory of Ancyra.[175]

This epigraphic material provides too slender a base for firm and far-reaching conclusions about overall patterns of recruitment from the eastern provinces to the armies of the Danube. The common view is that the troops in this region were not only enlisted locally, but were also drawn from the western and eastern parts of the empire.[176] This view finds some support from the remark in Tacitus that levies held in AD 65 in Gallia Narbonensis, Asia, and Africa helped to bring the Danube legions up to strength.[177] But the epigraphic evidence does not really support this isolated remark, as far as eastern recruitment is concerned. The great majority of Anatolian soldiers attested in the Balkans were members of *legio VII*, recruited under Augustus when the unit was stationed in south Galatia, and naturally drew most of its strength from there. Thereafter, eastern recruitment was very sporadic. In one case at least a member of *V Macedonica* was demonstrably enlisted while the legion was posted to the East, and the record of eastern campaigning by most of the Balkan units suggests that this may also explain most of the other cases. It is striking that easterners very rarely occur in *laterculi* from the Danube area which, with their long lists of soldiers, usually give a much better impression of a legion's ethnic composition at a given date than isolated finds. To judge from these, the Balkan garrisons were to an overwhelming degree made up of soldiers of local origin.

There remain the legions of the East itself, stationed in Cappadocia and Syria, which should, if the belief in local recruitment is well founded, have drawn heavily on the manpower of the Anatolian hinterland. The evidence has to be pieced together painstakingly. The northern frontiers of Britain, the Rhine, and the Danube, and indeed the southern boundary of the empire in North Africa, are abundantly documented by military inscriptions of many types. The East, partly because there has been so little excavation in the frontier areas, has produced much less comparable epigraphic material. It is only by sorting through the fragmented documentation of the Anatolian hinterland that a picture begins to emerge. Soldiers of *XVI Flavia Firma* and *XV Apollinaris*, stationed at Satala,[178] are known to have been recruited in Isauria,[179] from the colony at Lystra nearby,[180] from Neoclaudiopolis, and from Cappadocian Caesareia.[181] There were men from Laertes in Rugged Cilicia,[182] from the area of Lake Trogitis,[183] from Pisidian Antioch,[184] and from Neoclaudiopolis in Paphlagonia in *XII Fulminata* at Melitene.[185] In the Severan period *I* and *III Parthica* also drew heavily on eastern communities, including Ancyra,[186] and the mountain townships of Rugged Cilicia, Isauria, and northern Lycia.[187] Galatians from Ancyra and Pessinus are known to have joined the

---

[171] *IGR* iv. 616.

[172] *RE* xii. 1545–6 citing legionary gravestones at Alexandria Troas (*CIL* iii. 387) and at Cyrrhus in Syria (*CIL* iii. 195).

[173] T. Drew Bear and W. Eck, *Chiron*, 6 (1976), 308–9 no. 14; *CIL* iii. 13663.

[174] A. S. Hall, *Armies and Frontiers* 49.

[175] *RECAM* ii no. 289; cf. *MAMA* viii. 175 from the borderland of Lycaonia and Isauria, for a veteran who had served and married in Dacia.

[176] Mommsen's thesis, 'Conscriptionsordnung der römischen Kaiserzeit', *Hermes*, 19 (1884), 1 ff. (*Ges. Schr.* vi. 20 ff.), endorsed with some modifications by G. Forni, *Il reclutamento dei legioni da Augusto a Diocletiano* (1953), 78–84. See also M. Speidel, 'Legionary Recruiting from Asia Minor', *ANRW* ii. 7. 2 (1980), 731–3, 741–3.

[177] Tacitus, *Ann.* 16. 13. 3.

[178] See the evidence published by D. H. French and J. R. Summerly, *AS* 37 (1987), 17–22, and T. B. Mitford, *ZPE* 71 (1988), 167 ff.

[179] Sterrett, *WE* no. 227 (*IGR* iii. 281) from Yalı Hüyük south of Lake Trogitis. G. Laminger-Pascher, *Festschrift für Artur Betz*, 390 cites an unpublished text for a soldier of *XVI Flavia Firma* at Kozvıran. For other veterans from this area, see Buckler, Calder, and Cox, *JRS* 14 (1924), 64 no. 77 (a *palaistratiotes*), 68 no. 97 with note; 69 no. 100 (a cavalryman); 70 no. 103 (two standard bearers); 74 no. 109 (the career of an infantryman from *coh. I T...*, who was promoted to the *equites singulares* and eventually became a *cornicularius*); *MAMA* viii. 172 and 175 (the man who had served in Dacia); Swoboda, *Denkmäler*, 94 no. 226. Many of these men were presumably auxiliary cavalry who had seen service locally, helping to police the area (see above, Ch. 6 nn. 78–9).

[180] *MAMA* viii. 15.

[181] T. B. Mitford, *SP* iii no. 34; *JRS* 64 (1974), 163 no. 2.

[182] J. Russell, *AJA* 95 (1991), 486, a careful and interesting study.

[183] Sterrett, *WE* no. 300 = *CIL* iii. 6800 (*ILS* 2403). Cf. Laminger-Pascher, *Festschrift für Artur Betz*, 381–2 no. 1.

[184] *AE* (1914), 135.

[185] *SP* iii no. 70.

[186] *AS* 27 (1987), 84 no. 18 (*AE* (1981), 784).

[187] *IGR* iii. 814 (Artanada); D. Hereward, *JHS* 78 (1958), 72 no. 18 (*AE* (1959), 153; *SEG* xvii. 669) from Aş. Esenler, a veteran of *III Parthica* who had returned home to become *magister* and *notarius* in his home town. His name should be read as Ναλημις. Bean and Mitford, *Journeys in Rough Cilicia 1962–3* (1965), 30 no. 33; C. Naour, *Tyriaion en Cabalide* (1980), 38 no. 8.

Syrian legion *X Fretensis*, although both had duties that led them to Rome, where they were buried.[188] *IV Scythica*, stationed at Seleuceia/Zeugma on the Euphrates, recruited locally from Samosata and Beroea in Syria, as well as from Hierapolis/Castabala and Colybrassus in Cilicia.[189] Legionaries of *VI Ferrata* are known from the heart of Isauria west of Lake Trogitis,[190] and from the region of Tyriaion on the territory of the Lycian city of Balbura.[191] Another veteran was buried near Amaseia,[192] and an inscription from Adapazarı in Bithynia reveals an early, Augustan recruit to *VI Ferrata*, who returned as a veteran to his native village and erected a dedication to Tiberius.[193]

The Isaurian inscription of the recruit of *VI Ferrata* is particularly revealing. It is a dedication set up for his native Apollo by C. Trollius of Kaklouma(?), who had been enlisted by the procurator Arruntius Aquila, served for twenty-seven years, first under Ti. Claudius Caesar, before honourable discharge under Vespasian. Arruntius Aquila, a native of Lycian Xanthos, is known to have built roads in Pamphylia in AD 50, and his term of office, which probably gave him authority in the Taurus regions and Galatia as well as on the south coast, might have extended for a few years on either side of this date.[194] *Legio VI Ferrata* left Syria for the Balkans in AD 69, accompanying Licinius Mucianus in Vespasian's bid for power, but had returned to campaign in Commagene in AD 72, which should probably be taken as the early terminus for Trollius' discharge. The latest possible date for this is the year of Vespasian's death, AD 79. We may thus infer that he was recruited between 46 and 53. There is a good argument for the latter date. Tacitus remarks that on the eve of his Armenian campaigns in AD 54 Corbulo moved two legions, *VI Ferrata* and *III Gallica*, from Syria to bases in Cappadocia close to Armenia, and held levies *proximas per provincias*.[195] In a later passage which summarizes the events surrounding the

transfer and training of these troops and the replenishment of their numbers, Tacitus specifies that the *dilectus* was conducted in Galatia and Cappadocia, the provinces which Corbulo himself commanded as a base for his offensive operations beyond the Euphrates.[196] It is tempting to suggest that C. Trollius was a product of this recruitment, enlisted, with deliberate planning, a year before Corbulo's arrival in Anatolia and the outset of the campaign. At all events Tacitus' remarks reinforce the impression which can be derived in general from the inscriptions, that it was normal practice to enlist new recruits locally, in order to bring the legions up to strength.

Despite the relative dearth of strictly military documents from Asia Minor, it is clear that the communities of Anatolia, particularly those of the mountainous south, offered the legions of Cappadocia and Syria their main reservoir of fresh manpower. It is significant that to date there is no evidence for any recruit to the Anatolian legions from the Balkans or any other part of the empire. It is also typical of the variety of epigraphic material in the cities of the Greek East that the institutional practices of recruiting are at least briefly mentioned in some documents. The role of Arruntius Aquila, rounding up young men for service, is matched by another fragmentary inscription from the same region, which speaks of στρατολογία, conscription. Considerable official effort was need to ensure that isolated mountain regions such as Isauria sent a steady supply of able-bodied young men to join the frontier legions.[197]

Texts from the more civilized regions of Asia, which produced few actual serving soldiers, show how conscription could be commuted into cash payments to the treasury, or to line private pockets. Military recruits, like taxes in cash or kind, were a provision that Rome expected or required from her subjects. Military enlistment, often enforced, supplied their own manpower requirements and helped to symbolize imperial control. By the third century AD conscription could be treated as formally analogous to taxation, and communities were evidently assessed for a manpower quota, as they were for grain, clothing, or cash. An inscription from Lydia describes this obligation to furnish recruits as συντέλεια τειρώνων, but also shows how it might be commuted to a cash contribution. Under the exceptional circumstances revealed by this inscription a village could be exempted from the charge, as it might be from more familiar forms of taxation. This

188 *CIL* vi. 3614, 3627.
189 J. Wagner, *Seleukeia/Zeugma*, 143–6 (note that Bean and Mitford, *Journeys in Rough Cilicia 1962–3*, 15 no. 15 is from Colybrassus). Another Isaurian veteran of *legio IV*, not otherwise named, should be assigned to *IV Scythica*. The man had no *cognomen*, and the inscription (Sterrett, *WE* no. 25 = Paris and Radet, *BCH* 10 (1886), 508 no. 20) is certainly pre-Flavian, so it cannot relate to *IV Flavia Firma*.
190 Bean and Mitford, *Journeys in Rough Cilicia 1964–68* (1970), 21 no. 4 from Balat in the mountain country W of Lake Trogitis.
191 C. Naour, *Tyriaion en Cabalide*, 89 no. 43.
192 *SP* iii no. 157b.
193 M. Cremer and S. Şahin, *Epigr. Anat.* 1 (1983), 44 no. 1; *I. Prusias*, no. 31.
194 For his origin and career, see A. Balland, *Xanthos*, vii. 157 ff. no. 64.
195 *RE* xii. 1590 for the legion's movements. Tacitus, *Ann.* xiii. 1 for recruitment.
196 Tacitus, *Ann.* 13. 35. 1. Forni, *Il reclutamento dei legioni* 54 is wrong to refer this passage to a second recruiting drive in AD 58. The first half of this chapter is intended to be a summary of all Corbulo's doings since 54.
197 Sterrett, *WE* no. 82, with *Bull. ép.* (1960), 230.

system, which was clearly in place during the Severan period, when government demands were beginning to press down with increasing weight on provincial communities, certainly provided a model for recruiting and cash-collecting procedures in the fourth century, when these methods became standard.[198] There are also occasional glimpses of recruiting practices as they affected Greek cities themselves. One of the liturgical immunities allowed by Hadrian to philosophers and others, was from listing conscripts for the army, εἰς στρατείαν καταλέγεσθαι ἄκοντας,[199] and an inscription on a statue base from Teos says of a benefactor that to comply with the emperor's instruction he persuaded citizens to enlist as volunteers by his own generous spirit, εἰς τε τὴν τοῦ Σεβαστοῦ ἐπιταγὴν πείσαντα διὰ τῆς ἑαυτοῦ μεγαλοφροσύνης πολείτας αὐτομόλους στρατεύεσθαι. Perhaps by having citizens volunteer for service, the city would avoid its liability to the *synteleia tironum*.[200] Like all forms of Roman taxation the system was open to abuse. An inscription from Tabala in eastern Lydia, dated to the early months of 193, shows how soldiers had descended on the small town to extort money. Their precise demands had been for cash in lieu of conscripts, described by the official jargon as *supplementa*. No doubt this was not the only self-appointed press-gang to extract its own recruitment tax.[201]

In a famous passage of his panegyric of Rome, delivered in the middle of the second century, Aelius Aristides declared that the cities of the empire 'are free from garrisons; cohorts and cavalry units are sufficient to guard whole provinces, and not even many of these are quartered through the cities of each province, but they are few, taking into account the size of the population, and scattered through the countryside, so that many provinces do not even know where their garrison is.'[202] The statement amounts to something less than the whole truth as far as Anatolia is concerned. Aristides was concerned to emphasize the peaceful and unmilitarized aspect of the provinces of his day. Certainly the mass of soldiers in Asia Minor was concentrated far to the east, in the frontier areas, and by comparison with Anatolia in the first century BC, or the third century AD, troops were not conspicuous everywhere.[203] However, the rhetoric should

not be allowed to disguise the fact that auxiliary regiments and legionary detachments were stationed for long periods in Phrygia and Galatia, at Ancyra and Pisidian Antioch, at Amorium, Eumeneia, and Apamea,[204] to mention only those places where the evidence is relatively clear. Smaller concentrations of soldiers in *stationes* along the roads were almost ubiquitous, especially in areas where the lines of communication skirted or ran through the mountains. And to the inhabitants of cities on the roads which led directly to the Euphrates frontier itself, Aristides' claim would have seemed laughable.

The military roads gave the provinces of the Anatolian peninsula their articulation, and imposed patterns of communication which remained unchanged until the roads themselves fell out of use; official traffic was heavy and imposed a burden which fell particularly hard upon the cities. It will be argued below (Ch. 14 §§ III and IV) that dues and taxation in kind, to provide the armies with their daily needs, weighed heavily on all the country districts. Military recruitment was an institution that directly affected remote mountainous areas, the main source of new soldiers, and cities, which often commuted their obligations into cash payments. Few communities were not directly affected by the multifarious demands of the Roman army.

Enlistment into auxiliary units, or better still into the legions, offered an opportunity for some to acquire higher status and privileges for themselves and their families, whether in the camps and *canabae* where they served, or when they returned home to their native towns and villages. But not all were volunteers; forced conscription was widespread, perhaps even normal, and M. Arruntius Aquila with his entourage, collecting recruits in the Taurus around AD 50, was presumably as feared and hated a figure as his successors in the later fourth century, whose presence led to violent upheavals in the villages of Pontus.[205]

The *pax Romana* was won at a price, not only to be measured in taxation but also in a military presence that was often unwelcome. The evidence remains insufficient to enable one to offer a full and convincing assessment of the real impact of this military presence on the cities and villages of Anatolia. The handful of literary references, and the randomly preserved inscriptions simply do not allow one to make bold interpretative claims. Certainly perceptions of the significance of the militarization of the provinces will

---

[198] M. I. Rostovtzeff, *JRS* 8 (1918), 26–33.

[199] *Dig.* 27. 1. 6. 8.

[200] *IGR* iv. 1572, which is surely not Augustan (so *I. Teos* no. 128) but belongs to the 2nd or 3rd cent.

[201] H. Malay, *Epigr. Anat.* 12 (1988), 47 ff. ll. 6–7 τοῦ λαμβάνειν τὰ σουπλημέντα; on this inscription see further Ch. 13 § II n. 16.

[202] Aelius Aristides, *To Rome*, 67; translation adapted from C. A. Behr, *P. Aelius Aristides: The Complete Works*, ii. *Orations XVII–LIII* (1981), 87.

[203] See above, Ch. 3 §§ III–IV, and below, Ch. 13 §§ II and IV.

[204] Above, nn. 22–32.

[205] P. A. Brunt, 'Conscription and Volunteering in the Roman Imperial Army', *Scripta Classica Israelica*, 1 (1974), 90–115 (= *Roman Imperial Themes*, 188–214). See Gregory of Nyssa, *PG* 46. 784b-c, and below, Vol. II, Ch. 17 §v nn. 174–6.

have varied from place to place and between individuals. For real progress excavations or other discoveries are necessary which can show military and
civilian life in close and telling juxtaposition.

The early empire was a period when peace prevailed over war. Major upheavals rarely disturbed the
rhythms of provincial life. For Aristides, this was a
tribute to the beneficent ideology of the ruling power.
But if we look beyond the narrow time frame of the
first and second centuries AD, to the disturbed conditions of the Hellenistic age, to signs of conflict and
disaffection in the third and fourth centuries,[206] or to

the problems throughout Anatolian history posed by
the need to control its vast countryside, it becomes
clear that the Roman achievement was accomplished
by more than a sleight of hand, or by the placatory
enticements of peace and prosperity. Force or the
threat of force was an ever-present weapon in the
armoury of imperial control. Aristides' speech continued, 'if some city, through its excessive ambition,
has lost the power of self-control, you have not even
begrudged them persons to oversee and protect them.'
The euphemism thinly disguised an iron hand.

[206] R. MacMullen, *Corruption and the Decline of Rome* (1988),
215–16 cites Zosimus, 5. 13. 2, and 15. 2, Ammianus
Marcellinus, 14. 2. 5, and *Artemii Passio* in Philostorgius,
HE p. 73 (ed. Bidez-Winckelmann) to show that there were
numerous garrisons during the 4th cent. in the cities of Asia
Minor, especially in Isauria and Phrygia. See also below, Vol.
II, Ch. 17 § v nn. 169–73.

10 Estates and the Land

1. *The Physical Setting*

The heart of Galatia, and the heart of Asia Minor, is the high arid steppe which runs from Afyonkarahisar to the Kizil Irmak, and from the mountain ranges of northern Anatolia to the Taurus. There could be no greater contrast between this vast bare landscape and the crisp alternation of mountain and valley in the Aegean regions of the south and west, or the sharply etched terrain of the Tauric and Pontic mountains. The pattern of exploitation and human settlement in this central plateau has not been constant, oscillating between pastoralism and settled agriculture, desertion and prosperity, but its bare, unsmiling nature has impressed observers from Antiquity to modern times. For Livy the northern expanses were known as the treeless country, the *Axylon*, and so they remained in the tenth century AD and up to the present day.[1] In the south Strabo characterized the Lycaonian plain, breeding ground for wild asses,[2] as chill and bare;[3] and the Crusaders, who crossed central Anatolia in 1101, claimed to have seen neither man nor beast during a march of fifteen days.[4] Short of citing and exploring the ample testimony of travellers from William of Rubruck and Bertrandon de la Brocquière in the Middle Ages to the systematic explorers of the eighteenth and nineteenth centuries, there is no better illustration of its qualities than a paragraph written by a modern scholar whose study of this 'mittelanatolische Steppenlandschaft' remains a neglected classic of geographical literature:

Every traveller who has journeyed to the interior from the coasts through the fertile lowlands and valleys with their rich woodland cover, and whose heart has been gladdened by the fine forests of the mountain country, will be overwhelmed by the bleakness and the expanse of the plateau. He cannot understand how men can find the means to live in the towns and villages here. The grey-brown or violet hues of the vegetation hide themselves from view in the dusty haze of the lower atmosphere. An isolated willow, poplar or wild pear tree serves merely to enhance the impression of a dismal wilderness. Only during the rains of early summer is the picture enlivened, when the wheat fields are green and the plants of the steppe are in bud. But this adornment is of short duration. By the middle or end of July, according to the length and amount of the rains, the steppe lies as though dead.[5]

But between the bare earth and the pitiless sky of the days of high summer men have made a living from this land, and from favoured corners even a rich one, in

---

[1] Livy, 38. 18. 4, evidently from Polybius. For the topography see above, Ch. 2 § III at nn. 122–6. The 10th-cent. letters of Leon, bishop of Synnada, imply that central Anatolia was as denuded then as in the Hellenistic and Roman periods. Their implications have been explained in a lengthy study by L. Robert, *Les Kordakia de Nicée, le combustible de Synnada et les poissons-scies. Sur les lettres d'un métropolite de Phrygie au Xe siècle. Philologie et réalités*, published both in *JSav.* (1961) and (1962), and as a separate monograph (now *OMS* vii. 1–140).

[2] See Cicero, *Att.* 6. 1 (SB 115), 25 and R. Syme, *JRS* 51 (1961), 23 = *RP* ii. 518 for Vedius Pollio travelling in these parts with wild asses in train. Galatian mules remained famous and expensive, Plutarch, *Mor.* 524a and Philostratus *VS* 1. 43 (Kayser).

[3] Strabo, 12. 6. 1, 568. Note also, on the bareness of central Anatolia, Cicero, *Flac.* 51 (the Phrygian from Dorylaeum 'who had never seen a tree') and Vitruvius 2. 15 on Phrygian building methods which avoided using wood, 'propter inopiam silvarum'.

[4] Albert of Aix, *Historiae* viii, p. xi, in *Recueil des historiens des Croisades. Historiens occidentaux*, iv (1879), 566: 'Dehinc per quindecim dies continuos viam suam continuantes, amplius in solitudines et loca inhabitabilia et horroris, per montana asperrima incedebant, ubi nichil reperientes, non hominem, non pecudem, gravi fame coeperunt coartari.' The wealthy knights had provisions brought to them from Kastamonu and Nicomedia, 'ceteros gravis inopia frondes, cortices arborum ac radices herborum corrodere, et sic ventrem implere cogebat.'

[5] H. Wenzel, *Die Steppe als Lebensraum: Forschungen in Inneranatolien*, ii (Kiel, 1937), 19. I have drawn heavily on this superb study for an evocation of the natural and cultural features that have shaped the history of this land. The unsavoury associations of the book's title, published as it was in Nazi Germany shortly before the outbreak of World War II, doubtless explain its undeserved neglect. Two more technical studies by the same author are also extremely useful: *Sultandagh und Akschehir Ova: Eine landeskundliche Untersuchung in Inneranatolien* (Kiel, 1932), and *Forschungen in Inneranatolien, i, Aufbau und Formen der lykaonischen Steppe* (Kiel, 1935).

the great days of the Seljuk kingdom or in the early twentieth century after much resettlement and the building of the Anatolian railway. So it was under the Roman empire, when this region's importance is easy to overlook.

The essential elements that made for rural prosperity (or disaster) were the soil and the climate. The soils of central Turkey have been placed in three classes.[6] Best of all is the rich red loam found in narrow strips at the foot of the mountains, especially on the west side of the central plateau, the ancient Phrygia Paroreius below Sultan Dağ. It retains moisture well, and can produce good crops even after a dry winter, and its natural richness is sufficient to allow a rotation pattern of one year fallow against two of cultivation. Another rich soil is the black humus formed from decomposed vegetable matter. It is, however, only to be found in valley bottoms and basins, and when these, as often, are inadequately drained, the land becomes too impregnated with salt and soda to bear crops. The third and most widespread soil type is a grey or grey-brown loam, which covers most of central Anatolia to a depth of a metre or more. Where it has not been overworked its bearing capacity and fertility are good, at least for cereal crops of wheat and barley, cultivated on rotation of one year fallow and one year sown. However, the broken limestone marl from which it is derived makes it far more porous than the red loam, and cropping, or vegetation of any sort, is heavily dependent on the annual rainfall.

The geographical situation of central Turkey, and the configuration of highland and plain are the crucial determinants of its climate and the level of precipitation. Important above all is the ring of mountains which encircles the plateau. Whatever the direction of the prevailing winds, these will catch most of the rain before it reaches the steppe. Falls of rain and winter snow on the mountains feed the springs which emerge in their foothills and make for a well-watered, fertile belt along the northern flanks of the Taurus; but in the heart of the plateau water, either from direct precipitation or from springs and wells, is scarce. The rain that does fall comes in a regular but not rigid seasonal pattern. In winter, the strongest influence on the climate is the high pressure zone of central Asia, tempered here both by distance and by the proximity of the milder climate of the Aegean. Cold winters are the norm; temperatures can drop to −20° for short periods, and long periods of frost are common. In spring the high pressure zone recedes to the east, and the cold but relatively stable winter weather gives way to squally rains in March and April. Daytime temperatures can be high, but the nights are cold, with

frosts frequent until the end of April, and recorded even in May and June. From June onwards the Etesian winds blowing from the north bring a hot dry season which lasts through the late summer and early autumn. Some rain is normal in September and October and temperatures begin to fall, but the fine weather usually persists until November. Thus the high summer season is almost completely dry; modest precipitation is regularly recorded in September and October which serves to soften up the parched land for autumn ploughing, but the winter falls of rain and snow do not begin in earnest before November. Intermittent, unspectacular, but generally predictable, this period is crucial in maintaining the level of ground water in the plateau, and feeding its wells and fountains. The coming of spring is marked by the only clear peak in the annual rainfall cycle, on which the main harvest of spring-sown crops are vitally dependent. Wet weather can last into May, and the ground remains soft and muddy underfoot in early June, but already the fine weather has arrived, and the dry, hot days of summer ideally bring cereals to ripen during July.[7]

In good years this pattern is favourable to cereal farming, but success always hangs in the balance. A lack of rain in the early autumn obstructs and delays the ploughing; dry winters reduce the ground water to a perilously low level; and without heavy spring rainfall the early growth of the grain is stunted. When Basil preached to his congregation in Caesareia during a time of famine in AD 368, he spoke of the failure of the rain in precisely these two last periods: 'Winter did not bring its accustomed wetness with the dry weather, but encased and dried up the moisture in an icy grasp; and the season passed without its share of snow and rain. When spring came again, it displayed one of its two characteristics, warmth, but unaccompanied by moisture' (PG 31, 368c–d).

Overall figures for the region show that there is almost no margin for error: the mountains surrounding the plateau can expect annual precipitation of more than 500 mm., and the areas adjacent to them comfortably more than 300 mm.; but rainfall over much of the interior hovers uncertainly around 200 mm., the minimum level required for reliable cereal harvests, and even in normal years there are large stretches of the steppe, south and east of the Sangarius around Turgut, and south and west of the Salt Lake between Cihanbeyli, Aksaray, and Konya, where even 250 mm. is rarely attained, except in the neighbourhood of the rare hills.[8] Crops can fail in part, or totally, and the

---

[6] Wenzel, Steppe, 17–18.

[7] Ibid. 10–16; Sultandagh, 20–7.
[8] See the map in Steppe opposite page 16. For the unpredictability of rainfall in central Turkey see J. Dewdney, Turkey (1971), 112. Note too W.-D. Hütteroth, Die Türkei (1982),

animals die from lack of water and nourishment
with them. In 1873 the rains failed utterly in central
Anatolia and heralded the worst famine in recent
history. Men abandoned the countryside, or starved in
their villages and encampments, and up to 60 per cent
of the livestock is believed to have perished. The
ecological catastrophe was total:

Most naturally one thinks of them simply as destitute of
bread. It is true that they are so and it is a terrible fact, and
yet this does not cover the case. Were their flocks and herds
left they might recover themselves, but these are almost
totally destroyed... But the people are not only destitute of
food and flocks, they have no growing grain.[9]

The plateau may be divided into three zones, each
with its own predominant modes of exploitation. The
best lands lie at the foot of the mountains, especially
the north and east slopes, mostly around the edge of
the plateau, but also where hilly terrain interrupts the
monotony of the steppe itself. So the eastern slopes of
Günüsü Dağ east of Pessinus, and of Boz Dağ north-
east of Iconium, can be set alongside the more obviously
fertile strip of Phrygia Paroreius beneath Sultan Dağ
as fruitful and favoured habitats. Here the soils were
richer and water more abundant, allowing cultivation
not only of cereals, but of vines, garden crops, and the
opium poppy.[10] Beyond this belt lies an intermediate
region of moderate but generally adequate rainfall,
where cereals will normally succeed. In the late nineteenth and early twentieth centuries, when the central
plateau was extensively resettled by immigrants from
the Balkans, Crimea, and the Caucasus, it was this
zone that was most heavily colonized. The remainder
of the terrain is the true steppe, where the rainfall is
too low for the farmer, and herds of sheep and goats
replace the wheat fields. A sedentary life is impossible,
and the inhabitants, often transhumant groups of
Yürük tribesmen, move their flocks from one grazing
ground to the next in search of the thin pasture.[11]

Cereal agriculture and pastoralism were thus the
twin supports on which rural life could be supported,
and in Antiquity the case was no different. The ancient
evidence for the agricultural produce of Galatia is
scanty, but more than adequate to indicate the main
outlines. According to the *Expositio Totius Mundi*,

written in the fourth century, Galatia was a 'provincia
optima sibi sufficiens', and the *Historia Augusta* says
that it abounded in grain, clearly indicating that the
province could normally supply its own needs in the
basic staple, cereals.[12] Despite this, the line between
success and failure was a narrow one, then as now, and
at all levels of society there was a constant and overriding concern for the harvest. Time and again the
agoranomoi of the cities claim to have provided bread
for their community free or at a good price in hard
times,[13] and on occasion the situation became so
serious that the governor had to intervene to secure
the fair distribution of grain. In 51 BC Cicero, travelling through Asia to his province in Cilicia, had prevailed on wealthy local landowners and Roman
residents to make hoarded grain available to the people
by persuasion alone.[14] Not so in the famine which
occurred at the end of Domitian's reign and affected
much of central and western Anatolia.[15] L. Antistius
Rusticus, the Galatian governor, published a long edict
at Pisidian Antioch probably in AD 93, ordering the
inhabitants of the colony to declare their stocks of
grain, and to sell their surplus to the corn dealers at a
price not exceeding one *denarius* per *modius*, double
the usual level.[16] The effects of the famine were not
merely local. Under Domitian Ancyra, for the first and
only time in its history, issued a coin depicting three
ears of corn on the reverse—surely an allusion to relief
from the crisis, or to the recurrence of good harvests in
the sequel.[17] In western Asia Minor an *agoranomos*

111–12 with fig. 35 for the remarkably dry conditions in
which cereals are grown in central Anatolia.

[9] See the account of events by E. J. Davis, *Anatolica* (1874),
appendix K pp. 364–9. Capt. Fred Burnaby, *On Horseback
through Asia Minor*, i (1877), 133 suggests the figure for the
loss of livestock. The quotation is from a letter of W. A.
Farnsworth, chaplain in Caesareia (Kayseri) printed in the
Levant Herald, 29 July 1874 and quoted by Davis, loc. cit.
[10] Wenzel, *Steppe*, 90–104, cf. *Sultandagh*, 43–53.
[11] Wenzel's map labelled Siedlung und Bevölkerung in *Steppe*
graphically illustrates these points.

[12] *Exp. Tot. Mundi* (ed. G. Lambroso 1903), 307; *Script. Hist.
Aug. Tr. Tyr.* 18. 8. Note Columella 2. 9. 8 and 16 on
Galatian barley, allegedly of excellent quality and able to
endure high spring temperatures. The main advantage of
barley over wheat in upland regions is its shorter growing
cycle, which is crucial when winters are long (cf. L. Robert,
JSav. (1961)). However, in recent times, wheat has
predominated over barley. See Wenzel, *Steppe*, and E. Chaput,
Phrygie, i, *Géologie et géographie physique* (1941), 101 with
n. 4; V. Cuinet, *La Turquie d'Asie*, i (1892), 256 for the
vilayet of Angora. Further on Anatolian cereals in Antiquity
see Ch. 11 §1.
[13] *IGR* iii. 226 (Pessinus); *RECAM* ii. 97 (Germa); *MAMA* i. 11
(Laodicea Catacecaumene).
[14] *Att.* 5. 21 (SB 114), 8.
[15] See the important discussion of S. Reinach, reprinted in his
Cultes, mythes, et réligions, ii (1906), 356 ff., although new
evidence has accrued since he wrote and he was wrong to see
the edict as an attempt to protect Italian wine production.
[16] *AE* (1925), 126. The year depends on the dates when Antistius
Rusticus governed Galatia/Cappadocia. See now R. Syme,
Historia, 32 (1983), 369 (*RP* iv. 289) who places him in the
province from 92 to 93 or 94. The edict is most easily
accommodated in 93. The vine edict of Domitian is dated by
Eusebius, *Chron.* iii. 160 (Schoene) to 91/2 and by the
Chronicon Paschale to 90.
[17] *SNG von Aulock*, 6134: *obv.* Head of Domitian, Αὐτο. Δομιτια.
Καῖσαρ Σεβαστός; *rev.* three ears of corn, Σεβαστηνῶν Τεκτοσάγων.

at Miletus was forced to take drastic measures to maintain the food supply at precisely this time,[18] and the events may well have inspired the prophecies of death by starvation in the Apocalypse of St John.[19] Hunger and famine were threats quite as vivid in the popular imagination as war and violence. Even the famous edict by which Domitian himself ordered an end to the planting of vines in Italy, and their partial uprooting in the provinces to make way for cereal cultivation, may have been provoked by the catastrophe in Asia. Certainly Asia was closely concerned, for it was from there that a delegation headed by Scopelian of Clazomenae came to make the emperor change his mind.[20]

If grain kept the province alive, wool brought it wealth. Wool was the product for which Galatia was most famous. 'Negotiatur vestem plurimum', says the *Expositio Totius Mundi*, and the elder Pliny confirms that Galatian wool stood alongside that of Tarentum, Attica, and Miletus in the first rank.[21] Elsewhere he refers to the red dye cochineal, derived from the *Kermes* oak, which was used to colour the wool; an important reminder of the secondary industries which its production supported.[22] In Ottoman and modern times the finest products came from the Angora goat, whose range is sharply limited to the central Anatolian plateau;[23] there is no proof that the breed, or one akin to it, existed in Antiquity, although it is tempting, and may be correct to suppose that this was so.[24] Strabo tells us that the plains in the south were remarkably productive of sheep, and a source of huge fortunes, above all for Amyntas who owned 300 flocks there.[25] At Pessinus an inscription mentions gifts of woollen garments, *trimita* and *infibulatoria*, which were pre-sented to Trajan by a local dignitary,[26] and another text from the Haymana district singles out green dyed wool as a local product of value.[27] The funerary and votive monuments of many parts of central Anatolia regularly depict the tools, possessions, crops, and livestock of the inhabitants, and serve as a prime source of information on the material culture of the region.[28] Explicit allusions to the primary activities of the industry, the herding and shearing of sheep, are surprisingly rare, but one can hardly mistake the implications of the gravestones of women, which regularly depict a spindle, distaff, and carding comb.[29] The fleeces were converted to yarn in peasant households. No doubt much of it was also woven on the spot, although many cities will also have contained extensive weaving workshops.[30] Vines too could be grown in the better areas, principally for local consumption, but one or two Galatian vintages were reputable enough to earn a mention in the ancient literature. Amblada in east Pisidia between Lake Beyşehir and Lake Suğla produced a wine with notable medicinal qualities, and a subdivision of the citizen body took its name from Ambrosia, the nurse of the

---

[18] C. Habicht, *Gött. Gel. Anz.* 213 (1959), 163 discussing A. Rehm, *Die Inschriften von Didyma*, 179 no. 248.

[19] Apoc. vi. 6; the book was dated to 93 by Harnack, but the issue is controversial.

[20] On the vine edict see B. Levick, *Latomus*, 41 (1982), 66–73 with extensive bibliographical references.

[21] *Exp. Tot. Mundi* 41; Pliny, *NH* 29. 33.

[22] *NH* 9. 41; 22. 3. For the dyeing industry in Ankara from the 16th to the 18th cents. see D. H. French, 'A Sixteenth-Century English Merchant in Ankara?', *AS* 22 (1972), 241 ff. The wool trade in all its complexity dominated the economic life of Ottoman Ankara; for a magisterial survey of the evidence see S. Eyice, 'Ankara'nın eski bir Resmi', *Atatürk Konferansları*, iv (1970), 61–124, a study cast in the form of an extended commentary on an anonymous 17th-cent. Dutch painting of the city, now in Amsterdam.

[23] For the Angora goat, see Eyice, 'Ankara'nın eski bir Resmi', pls. XXXVI–XXXVII, claiming to identify the breed on Assyrian seals.

[24] See the excellent articles in *RE* iiA (1921), 373–99 (Orth), and *RE* xA (1972), 398–433 (W. Richter), on sheep and goats respectively.

[25] Strabo 12. 6. 1, 568.

[26] W. H. Buckler, 'Les lettres impériales de Pessinonte', *Rev. phil.* 3: 11 (1937), 105 ff. (*I. Pessinus* nos. 8–11).

[27] *RECAM* ii. 242.

[28] See the pioneering study by M. Waelkens, 'Phrygian votive monuments and tombstones as sources of the social and economic life in Roman Antiquity', *Anc. Soc.* 8 (1977), 277–315.

[29] Waelkens, op. cit. 286 citing Robert, *Hellenica*, vii. 152–60; x. 31; and *Ant. Class.* 35 (1966), 383 (*OMS* vi. 7). Shepherds, who might typically belong to transhumant groups and certainly came from the poorest stratum of the population, would be less likely to erect monuments in stone than peasant farmers. For all that, large numbers of dedications made by shepherds, who are readily identifiable by their heavy felt cloaks (still worn today), have come from rural sanctuaries of Zeus Petarenos and Zeus Alsenos on Emirdağ in the territory of Phrygian Amorium (cf. Drew Bear, *ANRW* ii. 18. 3, 1915–29), which has always been a major grazing area (see Robert, *OMS* iv. 278). From central Galatia Waelkens, op. cit. n. 151, cites only the sheep shears depicted on a tombstone at Sinanlı (*MAMA* vii. 312). Spindle, distaff, carding combs, and a basket of wool, variously combined, are so common as to be ubiquitous on women's tombstones. See e.g. *RECAM* ii. 30, 51, 85 (NW Galatia); 111, 112, 113 (in the territory of Germa on the east slope of Günüsü Dağ); 241, 254, 265, 310, 314, 330, 334, 336, 341, 343, 344, 362, 364, 366, 370, 373, 374, 375, 379, 388, 390 (all from the southern part of the territory of Ancyra); 398 (Kinna).

[30] For weaving workshops in Anatolian cities, see Broughton, *Roman Asia Minor*, 819–22. Several Anatolian cities had specialized wool industries serving a regional or even an international market; notably Saittai in N. Lydia, and Laodicea and Hierapolis in the Lycus valley of S. Phrygia. See H. W. Pleket, *Epigr. Anat.* 12 (1988), 25–37.

infant Dionysus.[31] The elder Pliny and Galen both mention a wine called *skylites*, attributed to Galatia or to Pamphylia.[32] (There need be no contradiction if Pliny was using a source which dated from the time when Pamphylia was in the same province as Galatia.) These chance remarks convey no impression of the extent of viticulture in the province. Tombstones and votive texts depicting grape-clusters, vines, and pruning hooks are widely distributed, both in the foothills of Sultan Dağ, especially in the territory of Laodicea Catacecaumene, and in the central plateau in the borderland between Laodicean and Ancyran territory. Here the flat land of the true steppe gives way to more broken terrain which extends north to the Haymana district, and the hill slopes around the village settlements were well suited to vine culture.[33] Grapes can also be grown in north Galatia proper. The site of Tavium today is covered with vineyards, although, in a traditional Muslim village, the fruit is used to make a sweet syrup (*pekmez*) not wine. By contrast, wine production has become an important local industry in Ankara since the beginning of the Turkish Republic. Scattered evidence shows that this was true in other northern parts of Ancyran territory in Antiquity. A Saint's Life of the fourth century shows that the village of Malos, overlooking the Halys, was famous for its wine which was marketed in Ancyra; and vines were a notable feature of the fertile territory of the small town of Kalecik in the nineteenth century, with which Malos should be identified.[34] A Byzantine grave stele decorated with vines and bunches of grapes found north-east of Ancyra in the Murtad Ova no doubt indicates that they were a local product there;[35] and much further to the west, in fact in the territory of Iuliopolis, the next city, a dedication was set up in a small rural sanctuary to Dionysus the bringer of fair fruits. It should be no coincidence that an inhabitant of

the local community was called Ambrosia.[36] South of here in the region of Mihalıççik, which was part of the territory of Germa, the pruning hook is a standard item depicted on local gravestones.[37] The evidence shows that wine was produced throughout the whole region wherever climate and soil offered an opportunity, and the community pronounced a need for it.

Another distinctive product of the province was salt, principally from the great Salt Lake south of Ancyra. Ancient references to the salt of Lake Tatta are brief, and merely appraise its quality and characteristics,[38] but in Ottoman times Tuz Göl was the single most important source of salt for the whole of Anatolia. Whole villages were employed in its extraction, and it was transported in bulk by camel, mule, or wagon to communities in every direction; but above all along a well-defined road which ran from the west side of the lake, across the central plateau towards Afyon or Eskişehir, from where it could be sent to the cities of the West or to Constantinople.[39] In Antiquity too the extraction and distribution of salt will have brought a livelihood to one of the least prepossessing tracts of the Galatian countryside.[40]

The abundance of salt at Lake Tatta was a fortuitous bounty owed to immutable factors of hydrology and geology, but it is the exception to the rule. The other products of the land were dependent on the productivity of the soil and above all on the coming of the rains in due season. The earth and the sky controlled the rhythms of rural life, and none knew this more surely than the peasants and shepherds themselves. In every community, with a simple eloquence that needs and receives no elaboration, they offered their prayers to the Mother Goddess of the Earth and to Zeus of the Sky, who brought the spring storms that assured the success of the harvest.[41]

---

[31] Strabo, 12. 7. 2, 570; J. and L. Robert, *Bull. ép.* (1969), 576 on pp. 522 ff.

[32] Pliny, *NH* 14. 80; Galen, *De victu acut.* 98; *De san. tuenda* 5. 5. 16; *De bon. mal. Suc.* 11. 1–2; *In Hippocr. de vict. acut.* 3. 1 (632) [refs. from Broughton, *Roman Asia Minor*, 610].

[33] Waelkens, *Anc. Soc.* 8 (1977), 310–11 nn. 119–20 with references chiefly from *MAMA* i and vii; add *RECAM* ii. 233, 253, 314, 333, 337, and 341. Viticulture made an impression on local nomenclature: Ἀμβροσίη (*RECAM* ii. 231, Byzantine), and Οἰνάνθη (*RECAM* ii. 359). For Encratite abstention from wine at Laodicea Catacecaumene, see below, Vol. II, Ch. 17 § x nn. 411–12.

[34] S. Mitchell, *AS* 32 (1982), 93–113 on the Life of St Theodotus, citing extracts from travellers who have visited Kalecik in modern times.

[35] *RECAM* ii. 109 (Bağören).

[36] *RECAM* ii. 155 (Διονύσῳ Καλλικάρπῳ) and 156, both from Sarıyer. Note too the statuette of Dionysus found at Sobran (*RECAM* ii. 150), also on the territory of Bithynian Iuliopolis.

[37] See *RECAM* ii. 41, 46, 51, 52, 69 and 76. Note also the bunch of grapes illustrated on an altar from Nasrettin Hoca, further south in the territory of Germa.

[38] Strabo, 12. 6. 4, 568; Pliny, *NH* 31. 84; Dioscorides, 5. 109 (ed. Wellmann, 1914).

[39] See V. Cuinet, *La Turquie d'Asie*, i (1892), 263–8 (salt mines near Kırşehir and elsewhere east of the Halys), 815 (Tuz Göl). For the significance of salt in Antiquity, see the interesting article of A. Giovannini, *Athenaeum*, 63 (1985), 373–87.

[40] F. Lasserre in his recent Budé edn. remarks on the lacuna in the text of Strabo, 12. 6. 1, 568 that the words ἥ τε δὴ Τάττα should be followed by an adjective with the sense of ἔρημος.

[41] There is no need for an adjective to remind one of Zeus' principal associations in this region. When he is simply Ζεύς or Ζεὺς Μέγιστος the symbol of an ear of corn or a cluster of

II. *The Pattern of Settlement*

In the Hellenistic period central Anatolia was thinly settled. Apart from communities on the fringes of the plateau, such as Philomelium and Iconium, the Galatians themselves seem to have been the only sizeable population group, and there was no one to oppose them when they acquired control of additional territory, the *Proseilemmene*, to the south of their original settlements, principally to accommodate growing numbers.[42] Their earlier traditions as a migrating nation, the abundance of land, and its overall ecology surely conspired to make their economy a pastoral one. Since the grazing on the plateau is never lush, flocks and their owners will have ranged far and wide in search of sustenance between summer and winter pasture, in the manner of the semi-nomadic groups of more recent times.[43] It is hardly surprising, then, that there are virtually no archaeological traces of substantial settlements in this period, apart from the fortlets of the tribal chieftains.[44] The voice of the village may be almost unheard from classical Antiquity, but the encampment of the nomad is invisible.

The profit to be derived from this pastoral economy no doubt mainly accrued to Galatian chieftains. Amyntas with his 300 flocks grazing the steppe lands of Lycaonia was only one of those who drew the bulk of their wealth from this source.[45] A Greek abridge-

ment in six books of the great treatise on agriculture by Mago the Carthaginian[46] had been presented to his predecessor Deiotarus. Latin versions of the same treatise, which concentrated especially on the capitalist farming of vines and olives and on large-scale ranching but paid little attention to cereals, served as a model and an incentive to the *latifondisti* who transformed the face of Italian agriculture in the late second and first centuries BC.[47] Mago's lessons for Deiotarus will have concerned the management of an intensive pastoral regime.

Under the Roman empire, and especially from the second to the fourth century AD, the picture changes. Inscriptions of this period from the whole area between Ankara and Konya, and over most of the western parts of Galatia and the eastern marches of the province of Asia, in the territories of Philomelium, Amorium, Nacolea, Dorylaeum, Pessinus, and Germa, are abundant and show unequivocally that the plateau was densely populated.[48] The chief form of settlement was the village, the χωρίον or κώμη, and there can be no doubt that the inhabitants enjoyed a much more sedentary existence than their Hellenistic predecessors. The crude but solid gravestones of the plateau are the counterparts of the houses in which their owners lived, and the reliefs on these stones show them to have been first and foremost peasant farmers. Even though sheep-rearing and the cultivation of the vine and other crops occupied them all to a greater or lesser degree, cereal agriculture was their main means of livelihood.[49] The transformation in the economy and in the social profile of the region may best be compared with the change which took place in the last years of Ottoman rule after

---

grapes shows that he was the paramount force for fertility (*MAMA* i. 1 and 3 from Laodicea Catacecaumene, the latter discussed by Waelkens, *Anc. Soc.* 8 (1977), 310 n. 119; an inscription from Cihanbeyli also shows Zeus with corn and grapes, Waelkens, *Anc. Soc.* 8 (1977), 304 n. 76). The specific adjectives for Zeus in these regions refer to him as a storm god (Βρόντων, *RECAM* ii. 13, 74a, 77), Βρόντων καὶ Ἀστράπτων (*MAMA* i. 11, cf. *JHS* 38 (1918), 125 ff.), and Κεραύνιος (*MAMA* vii. 7a; Swoboda, *Denkmäler*, 30 no. 68)), or as the bringer of the harvest (Ἐπικάρπιος (*MAMA* vii. 476); Εὔκαρπος (*MAMA* vii. 453)). Note Zeus of the stable, Ζεὺς Φάτνιος, at Laodicea Catacecaumene, holding a corn stalk and grapes (*MAMA* vii 103). See in general Calder, *MAMA* vii. xxxii–xxxiii, and Drew Bear, *ANRW* ii. 18. 3, 1970–2.

[42] See above, Ch. 4 § VI nn. 115–18.

[43] See Wenzel, *Steppe*, 97–100 on animal husbandry and 105–10 on the *yaylas* of the plateau. All the travellers who have left accounts of the area up to the mid-19th cent. comment on the nomadic or semi-nomadic Turkmen and Kurdish inhabitants. For a clearly observed study see G. Perrot, 'Les Kurdes de l'Haimaneh', *Revue des Deux Mondes* (1863).

[44] See *RECAM* ii pp. 25–8 and Ch. 7 § II above. There is a fortress of the 1st cent. BC on Karadağ in Lycaonia which might have been built by one of the dynasts of that region such as Antipater of Derbe, Polemo, or Amyntas; K. Belke and M. Restle, 'Die Festungsanlage auf dem Baş Dağ (Karadağ): Eine hellenistische Burg in zentralem Kleinasien', *JÖAI* 52 (1978–80), Beiblatt 1–30.

[45] Strabo 12. 6. 1, 568: καίπερ ἄνυδρος οὖσα ἡ χώρα πρόβατα ἐκτρέφει θαυμαστῶς, τραχείας δὲ ἐρέας, καί τινες ἐξ αὐτῶν τούτων μεγίστους πλούτους ἐκτήσαντο. Ἀμύντας δ' ὑπὲρ τριακοσίας ἔσχε ποίμνας ἐν τοῖς τόποις τούτοις.

[46] Varro, *RR* 1. 1. 10.

[47] J. Heurgon, 'L'Agronome carthaginois Magon et ses traducteurs en latin et en grec', *CRAI* 1976, 441–56.

[48] This is the overwhelming impression conveyed by the inscriptions published in *MAMA* i, *MAMA* vii, and *RECAM* ii, which amount if not to a complete corpus at least to a wholly representative sample of the epigraphic remains in the area.

[49] The yoke of oxen and the plough carved on gravestones indicate the importance of cereal agriculture. See Waelkens, *Anc. Soc.* 8 (1977), 284–5 with nn. 119–20 which cite full references. The epigraphic finds imply agricultural villages at Sınanlı, Kerpiç, Atkafası, Beşkavak, Kütükuşağı, Kelhasan, Kuşcalı, Insuyu, Cihanbeyli, and Kuyulu Zebil in the heart of the plateau, as well, of course, as along the foothills of Sultan Dağ. Fashion and local styles had a part to play in determining whether or not certain tools and equipment appeared on gravestones. For instance, in the Lycaonian–Isaurian borderland in the valley of the Çarşamba SW of Konya, bill-hooks, pickaxes, and mattocks are common but ploughing implements rare (cf. *JRS* 14 (1924), note on n. 95). When a plough or oxen were shown attention was called to the fact in the text of the inscription (*MAMA* viii. 58). We cannot, however, conclude that cereal agriculture was exceptional.

several centuries when the steppe had remained the preserve of pastoral nomads. In the seventeenth century, throughout the whole plateau area north and east of the highway which ran from Eskişehir to Konya, virtually the only settlements were the large winter villages of Turkmen and Kurdish tribes; a traveller passing through the region in summer, when the herds were taken to find pasture in the hills, made his way through a deserted landscape.[50] The situation remained broadly similar until the second half of the nineteenth century. The rare explorers who ventured off the main highways or went outside the cities and towns observed Turkmen and Kurds in their encampments, their numberless flocks, and little or no trace of cultivation.[51] But in the last quarter of the nineteenth century there was a swift and radical transformation, as large numbers of immigrants, Circassians, Tartars, Turks from the Balkan countries, and Cossacks from South Russia, were brought in to occupy what had hitherto been empty territory.[52] Their settlements were frequently founded on the sites of existing *yaylas*, the summer pastures of the transhumant groups where an adequate water supply, and perhaps some marginal earlier attempts at cultivation, held out the hope that a living could be made. The pastoral groups who could not be adapted into this pattern of settled life, the Yürüks above all, were squeezed out of their best grazing grounds into areas where cereal agriculture has never been a serious proposition.[53] The process may suggest a model for the colonization of the plateau under the Roman empire. Although the spread of settlements through the Galatian countryside was a product of population growth, not of immigration, the newly occupied sites, indicated by the inscriptions which have been found there, are in most cases identical to the settled villages of the later nineteenth century.[54]

These villages formed distinct communities with their own corporate identities; many of their names are known, and there are occasional signs of collective activity such as the offering of prayers on behalf of the whole settlement for success, safety, or prosperity.[55] But the pattern of village settlement was subsumed into two larger systems. The first was the juridical and administrative structure of the provincial cities. City territories were generally coterminous with one another, and thus every village belonged to one city or another.[56] There was no rural limbo into which the settlements of the countryside could sink, beyond the reach of the urban centres which shaped the pattern and style of life in the Graeco-Roman world. The second system to which the villages and their inhabitants belonged was equally important. Much, if not all of the rural territory of central Anatolia was parcelled out into large estates owned by the local city gentry, wealthy aristocrats from further afield, or by the Roman emperor himself, and the village settlements were naturally part of these estates. The regime of the Hellenistic period, in which local dynasts owned and controlled extensive livestock and their herdsmen, was translated into a new idiom: the control of whole villages, with their inhabitants, crops, and livestock, by a class of persons—the aristocracy of the eastern Roman provinces—whose characteristics and personalities can be described and defined with far more precision than those of the obscure chieftains of the Gauls.

III. *Estates in Galatia*

The evidence with which to identify the men who exploited and profited from the production of rural Galatia is almost exclusively epigraphic. It is incomplete, difficult to date accurately, and not always clear in its implications. Nevertheless it provides an opportunity to trace the relationship between city and

---

[50] J. B. Tavernier, *Les Six Voyages*, in V. de St Martin, *Histoire des découvertes géographiques des nations européennes*, iii, *Asie Mineure* (1845), 19. He crossed the plateau in 1657 from Afyonkarahisar to Tuz Göl. Cf. Wenzel, *Steppe*, 64.

[51] See J. N. Kinneir, *Journeys through Asia Minor, Armenia and Koordistan in 1813 and 1814* (1818), 75 on the Pashalik of Angora and pp. 78–84 describing the region south of Angora, where he remarked on the almost complete absence of cereal agriculture and the numerous flocks; a similar impression is conveyed by W. F. Ainsworth, *Travels and Researches in Asia Minor: Mesopotamia, Chaldaea and Armenia* (1842), 136 ff., and by one of the very rare travellers to have crossed the central plateau in a direct line from Konya to Ankara, Mme la princesse de Belgiojoso, *Asie Mineure et Syrie, souvenirs de voyage* (Paris, 1858), esp. pp. 418–19.

[52] Wenzel, *Steppe*, 87 ff. For an account derived from contemporary observers of the impact of Circassian settlers at this period on a very different area, the forested hills of the Phrygian Highlands, see L. Robert, *A travers l'Asie Mineure* (1980), 276 ff.

[53] See the map in Wenzel, *Steppe*, entitled *Siedlung und Bevölkerung*.

[54] See, for example, the string of settlements on either side of the road which crossed the plateau from Cihanbeyli towards the upper Sangarius, at Sülüklü, Sinanlı, Sarıkaya, Beşkavak, Kelhasan, and Böğrüdelik, all of which were villages in the Roman period.

[55] See below, Vol. II, Ch. 16 §§ I and II.

[56] An exception should probably be made for the very large imperial estates where procurators exercised jurisdiction. Cf. P. A. Brunt, 'Procuratorial Jurisdiction', *Latomus*, 25 (1965), 461–89 esp. 484 n. 3 (*Roman Imperial Themes* (1990), 163–88) citing E. Beaudouin, *Les Grandes Domaines dans l'empire romain* (1899), ch. 1, and esp. A. Schülten, *Die römischen Grundherrschaften* (1896), 3 ff. But, as argued below, most of the imperial estates in the central Anatolian plateau did not exist before the 2nd cent. AD.

country, aristocrat and peasant, land and wealth in more detail and with more confidence than is possible for most other parts of the Roman empire. There are several explicit references to estate owners of various types and their agents, and these in themselves can be pieced together to yield a recognizable pattern. They can be confirmed and amplified by the conclusions which can be drawn from examining the nomenclature of the rural areas. In the country districts of Galatia most inhabitants were known simply by a single name. The combination of *nomen* and *cognomen* which indicates a Roman citizen is rarely found, except in the case of the Aurelii, who owed their names and status to the universal grant of citizenship made by Caracalla in AD 212. The inhabitants of the rural areas who had acquired the citizenship before that date are all figures whose backgrounds can profitably be examined more closely. Apart from obvious outsiders, whose rightful place is clearly in the cities and who themselves provide information about the interests of town-dwellers in the country, they usually belong to one of two groups. The smaller consists of veteran soldiers who had acquired citizen status by serving as legionaries or auxiliaries, and who usually indicate the fact by stating it explicitly. The larger group can be identified as freedmen agents, either of the emperors or of private individuals, and members of their families, and they are revealed by characteristic imperial names (for instance P. Aelii and M. Aurelii) or by the *praenomen* and *cognomen* of private *patroni*, which contrast sharply with the stereotyped repertoire of Greek, Roman, or native individual names which were in general use.

It is useful, in identifying the regions where estates are to be found, to draw a distinction between the countryside which was readily accessible from the cities, their immediate hinterland, and the remoter districts which could only be reached with difficulty. We would expect that cities' immediate needs in cereals and other foodstuffs would be supplied as far as possible from the former area. The cities would provide an utterly reliable and predictable market place for the products of their immediate hinterland, and landowners and farmers there could expect to make a good living in consequence. But certain factors combined to restrict their earning potential. Firstly, when the principal product of this land was food for the city, there were necessary limits to the profits that could be made from its sale. Competition in the market place would tend to keep prices in line, and even when scarcity forced them up there was always a point at which the *agoranomos*, or even the provincial governor, would intervene to ensure that the citizens could somehow feed themselves. The edict from Pisidian Antioch provides a dramatic—although clearly exceptional—illustration of the principle. Secondly, the

land itself tended to be divided into relatively small units. The reasons for this were complex and varied from city to city. In the Roman colonies a pattern of smallholdings, although no doubt modified by property transfers in the passage of time, would reflect the original allotments to settlers. Elsewhere the land around the cities was normally of good quality and well watered, easily divisible into small units, but requiring close supervision if its full potential was to be realized. A modestly prosperous city-dweller could exploit it to good effect, although he might lack the means to administer more distant properties. This was the sort of land which he would wish to acquire, as far as his means allowed. Then, the social ethos of the urban bourgeoisie itself should have been hostile to excessive accumulation of land by a single owner in the immediate neighbourhood of the city. Such a monopoly would be too obviously hostile to the ideology of an oligarchy, which demanded at least a semblance of equality among its members. The curial class of the cities, like the senate at Rome itself, could not survive unless curbs were placed on the ambitions of its individual members. The wealthy men of Asia Minor might control great fiefdoms, but custom and prudence would advise them not to do so before the envious gaze of their nominal peers.

So we would expect to find prosperous but relatively modest estates within easy reach of the cities of the province. The evidence is simply not informative enough to make this clear beyond question, but it can at least be accommodated to fit this picture without any strain. Many of the inhabitants of the valleys around Ancyra, notably the Murtad Ova to the north-west, and the Çubuk Ova to the north, appear either to have been Ancyran citizens of substance, or their agents. An inscription from Şimşit in the Murtad Ova mentions a *pragmateutes* of Flavius Metrophanes, clearly of Ancyra, and two other texts from the same valley mention members of the Ancyran *boule*.[57] A fragment from a substantial family tomb names a woman called Aelia Tecusa and an inscription from Zir, formerly Istanos, yields another group of Aelii. They were presumably free citizens, enfranchised under Hadrian, not imperial freedmen.[58] The pattern in the Çubuk Ova is similar. Texts from Buğdüz, where one of the chief village settlements lay in the Roman period, give details of an Ancyran family which had established itself in the city council over several generations, and of the family of L. Claudius Diogenianus, whose names indicate that they were Roman citizens, not typical village people.[59] Two families of C. Claudii appear

[57] RECAM ii. 182, 178, 181 l. 49.
[58] RECAM ii. 177, 185.
[59] RECAM ii. 194–5.

around Ancyra, one on the road which ran west to Juliopolis, the other near Elmadağ, on the road to Tavium.[60] These too may well have been Ancyran families, but it is interesting to note that, whereas no C. Claudii are known from the inscriptions of Ancyra itself, a C. Claudius Antipater was a prominent figure at Colonia Germa, and the two families found in the neighbourhood of Ancyra may have had connections with him.[61] The likelihood is that these substantial citizens, with their freedmen and agents, owned property on the fertile land within easy reach of Ancyra, and maintained their position in society by the income which it brought them.

The same relationship between the city and its surrounding territory can be observed in other parts of the province. In the Cillanian plain north of Lake Beyşehir, which comprised the territory of Neapolis, small proprietors were represented on their estates by a *pragmateutes* and an *oikonomissa*.[62] The division of the plain of Pisidian Antioch, the former territory of Mēn Askaēnus, into allotments for its colonists would lead one to expect Roman families with farms in the rural areas, and this appears to be borne out by the epigraphic evidence.[63] Conditions around Iconium, also an Augustan colony, should have been comparable. An inscription from a *han* four hours east of the city, mentions a councillor of Iconium,[64] and branches of one of the original colonial families, the Aponii, occur in the country districts; at Kötü Delik han and Doksan Dokuz Merdivenli han, about thirty kilometres east of Konya; and at Karahüyük, near the river Çarşamba, about forty kilometres to the south.[65] Presumably the two Aelii who are attested at Ismil, thirty kilometres south-east of Konya, were also either members of the Iconian gentry or their freedmen.[66] At the other extreme of the province the pattern was similar. Inscriptions from the outlying districts of the territory of Neoclaudiopolis in Paphlagonia mention a legionary veteran who was also a city councillor, members of a senatorial family, and a Roman knight.[67]

In these areas around the cities the evidence is too fragmentary to allow one to trace any chronological development of land-ownership through the period of Roman rule. If most of these holdings were relatively small they could have changed hands often by purchase and sale, by inheritance, or by transfer in the form of dowry. But such transactions would not have affected the basic pattern. The fortunes of one family might be eclipsed by another, but the picture of a curial class, deriving its livelihood from farms and estates close to the cities, should hold good through late Antiquity (for Ancyra, see below, Vol. II, Ch. 18 § 1).

Although it may be dangerous to exaggerate the differences, and clear-cut distinctions may be misleading in individual cases, the more abundant evidence for land-holding in the remoter areas of the province suggests a different pattern of exploitation, one of much larger estates whose owners often had no close connection with the cities on or near whose territories those estates lay. Moreover, in some cases it is possible to construct a broad chronological framework within which this specific pattern of land-ownership developed.

The best attested of these large domains is the estate of the senatorial family of the Sergii Paulli, situated in the region of Vetissus, in the heart of the Central Plateau close to the boundary between the city territories of Ancyra and Laodicea Catacecaumene.[68] The central document is the Latin gravestone of Cn. Cornelius Severinus(?), the *decurialis viator* of a Roman senator Cn. Pinarius Cornelius Severus, suffect consul in AD 112, erected by the senator's wife Sergia L. f. Paullina.[69] In the same area there is the tombstone of the wife of a freedman Sergius Carpus, who was a procurator of Paullus,[70] and another freedman, L. Sergius Corinthus, was responsible for building a temple of Men in AD 86, at a site about forty kilometres to the east.[71] Several other Sergii or Sergiani mentioned on inscriptions of the central plateau were clearly connected with the estate, which was evidently a large one.[72] The centre may have been at Sinanlı, where the wife of Sergius Carpus was buried, but it could have extended some twelve kilometres north-east to Emirler, where one group of dependants was buried, and a possible boundary stone was recorded at Yağcı Oğlu, a similar distance due north, and the find spot of the Latin inscription of Cn. Cornelius Severinus(?).[73] Whatever its exact size, the freedmen working on the estate were local figures of some consequence.

[60] *RECAM* ii. 192, 213.
[61] *RECAM* ii. 97.
[62] Sterrett, *WE* nos. 325, 354.
[63] Levick, *Roman Colonies*, 44, and above, Ch. 5 n. 6.
[64] H. S. Cronin, *JHS* 22 (1902), 374 no. 149.
[65] Cronin, *JHS* 22 (1902), 369 no. 142; *MAMA* viii. 94, 327. For the Aponii see above, Ch. 6 n. 55.
[66] *MAMA* viii. 311.
[67] F. Cumont, *SP* iii (1910), 56 ff. nos. 41, 56, and 92. The last, however, was apparently not a local man, see M. Speidel in *Armies and Frontiers*, 13 with n. 28.

[68] The evidence is well discussed by W. M. Ramsay, *JRS* 16 (1926), 202 ff. and by W. M. Calder, *Klio*, 24 (1930/1), 59 ff.
[69] *MAMA* vii. 319; *RECAM* ii. 355. For the family as a whole see Halfmann, *Senatoren*, 30, 105.
[70] *MAMA* vii. 321.
[71] *MAMA* vii. 486; the date is calculated from 22 BC.
[72] *MAMA* i. 108 and vii. 14 (Laodicea Catacecaumene); *MAMA* vii 330 = *RECAM* ii. 358; *MAMA* vii. 331.
[73] *MAMA* vii. 320 = *RECAM* ii. 357.

So too were their patrons. Sergia Paullina was a member of a senatorial family best known for producing L. Sergius L. f. Paullus, the proconsul of Cyprus at the time of St Paul's visit to the island between AD 46 and 48.[74] Late in life he became, as far as we know, the earliest senator from the eastern provinces to reach the consulship, as suffect in AD 70.[75] The family came from Pisidian Antioch, and a daughter or granddaughter of Sergius Paullus established a link with the other leading family of the colony by marrying C. Caristanius Fronto, who was admitted to the senate by Vespasian and became suffect consul in AD 90.[76] An inscription was also set up at Antioch in honour of L. Sergius L. f. Paullus *filius*, presumably the son of the proconsul of Cyprus, who also entered the senate.[77] The construction of the temple of Mēn at Beşkavak gives a *terminus post quem* for the estate of AD 86, but it is more than likely that the property had first been acquired in the Julio-Claudian period, when the more enterprising colonists of Antioch were looking outside the city territory for ways of adding to their original allotments.

It would be reasonable to suppose that the Caristanii had made similar moves to enhance the family fortune in the early empire. As early as the Augustan period they were in the forefront of the municipal aristocracy,[78] and they surely maintained and improved their position up to the time of Caristanius Fronto's adlection to the senate. A Latin inscription found in the valley north of Sultan Dağ towards Synnada appears to show Caristanius Fronto, named as consul and therefore after AD 90, acting in the area. He might have owned property there, but the text makes it appear that he was acting in an official capacity and the question should be left open.[79]

Both the Sergii and the Caristanii of Antioch were families of Italian stock which had come to Asia Minor as colonists. They may be contrasted with the Plancii of Perge, who appear to have settled in the East on their own initiative, in pursuit of good land and business opportunities—a field that was wide open in the rich and lucrative environment of Anatolia.[80] M. Plancius Varus of Perge had entered the senate under Claudius or Nero, and followed a career that led finally, it seems, to the proconsulate of Bithynia, held for two years under Vespasian.[81] Two freedmen attested at the village of Beyköy between the Tembris and the Sangarius, and an inscription set up in his honour at Colonia Germa indicate that he had interests, presumably in land, in north-west Galatia.[82] Another inscription from this area mentions a Plancia as early as AD 62, showing that the Plancii had acquired the property in the Julio-Claudian period, or even before.[83] They also owned an estate in the Bozova, a fertile upland plain in southern Pisidia, which serves to this day as a *yayla* for the more prosperous residents of Antalya and the Pamphylian coast. As well as freedmen a branch of the family itself is attested in the area, and the estate's boundaries were marked off from those of the small cities that ring the plain.[84] It was not, therefore, an insignificant holding.

Sextus Paccius Valerianus Flaccus of Attaleia, although never a Roman senator, had a similar background. Two inscriptions honouring him have been found in his native city, where he had been twice priest of the goddess Rome, agonothete of the quadrennial games held in the emperor's honour known as the *Caesareia*, and gymnasiarch. The second of these was erected by the people of Attaleia in collaboration with the Roman inhabitants of the city, military colonists settled there by Augustus, and it is likely that he was one of their number.[85] In total contrast to the civic opulence of Attaleia, the bleak plain south-east of Tuz Gölu has produced a crude building inscription, set up by Sextus Paccius Niger, also called Philetaerus, and Titus Paccius Niger among others, who were surely freedmen of the colonists from Attaleia, managing family interests in the grazing country on the border of Lycaonia and Cappadocia.[86] Sex. Paccius Valerianus Flaccus, like M. Plancius Varus, was an Italian of Pamphylia with extensive property on the central Anatolian plateau.

[74] Acts 13: 7; Halfmann, *Senatoren*, 101 nos. 3–4.
[75] See below, Vol. II, Ch. 15 n. 40.
[76] Halfmann, *Senatoren*, 109 no. 13; G. L. Cheeseman, *JRS* 3 (1913), 260 ff.; Levick, *Roman Colonies*, 111–12.
[77] Jacquier, *Rev. biblique* 25 (1916), 246; W. M. Ramsay, *The Bearing of Recent Discoveries on the Trustworthiness of the New Testament* (1915), 151; see E. Groag, *RE* iiA (1923), 1718, and Halfmann, *Senatoren*, 105 no. 9.
[78] Levick, *Roman Colonies*, 111.
[79] J. G. C. Anderson, *JHS* 18 (1898), 345; *CIL* iii. 14192⁴. Halfmann, *Senatoren*, 55 and 109 cites the text as evidence for property in the region, but this is very doubtful.
[80] S. Mitchell, *JRS* 64 (1974), 27–39.

[81] Halfmann, *Senatoren*, 104–5 n. 8 with bibliography; W. Eck, *Chiron*, 13 (1983), 202 n. 571.
[82] *RECAM* ii. 82 (and note the Latin gravestone of a child of a Roman citizen family, *RECAM* ii. 83); *RECAM* ii. 90.
[83] *RECAM* ii. 40.
[84] Mitchell, *JRS* 64 (1974), 31–4. C. P. Jones, *HSCP* 80 (1976), 234 n. 31 points out that M. Plancius M. f. Plato Calpurnianus Proculus and probably M. Plancius Plato of *IGR* iii. 782 were not freedmen but free-born members of the family. This was also presumably true of M. Plancius Cornelianus Gaius at Andeda, *IGR* iii. 417. A branch of the Plancii, and not merely their freedmen had settled in the Bozova, and another branch appears at Pisidian Selge in the 3rd cent. (see J. Nollé, *I. Selge*, pp. 84 ff.).
[85] G. E. Bean, *Belleten*, 22 (1958), 32 nos. 18 and 19 = *SEG* xvii. 577–8.
[86] W. M. CALDER, *A Note on a Classical Map of Asia Minor* (BIAA, 1957).

The leading family of Attaleia in the first century AD was that of the Calpurnii. M. Calpurnius Rufus, the son of Caecilia Tertulla who had held the principal priestly offices in the city connected with the imperial cult under Tiberius, became a senator under Claudius (if not before) when he reached the rank of legatus Augusti pro praetore.[87] His son L. Calpurnius Rufus was also a senator, and he was surely closely related to the M. Calpurnius Rufus who owned property at Alastos, in the south-east corner of the province of Asia.[88] An inscription found here was set up by a freedman *misthotes*, called M. Calpurnius Epinicius, and the link with Attaleia is underlined by the presence there of another closely related freedman, M. Calpurnius Epinicianus.[89] The family probably also had interests in Lycaonia, south of Iconium. At Akören north of the river Çarşamba, a certain Sympheron, M. K. δοῦλος, set up a dedication for the local goddess, Athena of the Mouriseis. The patron was evidently familiar enough in the area to be recognized despite the extreme abbreviation of his name; M. Calpurnius is the most likely resolution.[90] Several other Calpurnii of eastern origin are known to have held senatorial office during the first and second centuries, who may, but need not be related to the Attaleian group.[91] Two of them, P. Calpurnius Proculus Cornelianus and his putative son L. Calpurnius Proculus, had close connections with Ancyra, which was probably their *patria*,[92] and the latter owned property near Laodicea Catacecaumene, where one of his slaves appears, and where freedmen Calpurnii are also on record.[93]

Another important property which was originally owned by a family of Italian origin was known as the *choria Considiana*. It lay in fertile country in north-west Galatia, and apparently originally comprised a group of seven villages. The most important item of evidence relating to it is an inscription recording the erection of a temple and statues dedicated to the imperial cult by Eutyches, oikonomos of Marcus Aurelius

and Commodus between AD 177 and 180.[94] The presence of freedmen in the area with the *praenomen* and *nomen* P. Aelius suggests that it had been imperial property as early as the reign of Hadrian,[95] but its name indicates that its original owner had been a Considius. A number of Considii are recorded in the senatorial and equestrian order at Rome; and two are known to have been condemned for *maiestas* under Tiberius: Considius Aequus an *eques*, and Considius Proculus a praetorian senator.[96] If the Galatian estate had belonged to either of these it could have been transferred to imperial ownership as early as the 30s AD. However, neither man has any other known connection with Anatolia, and none of the other imperial properties on the plateau was acquired before the second century AD, so it is preferable to assume that the estate-owning Considius was another Italian emigrant to the East, resident in one of the Roman colonial or business communities of Anatolia.

It is possible that some of these early *émigré* landowners were not based in Anatolia at all. An inscription from Laodicea Catacecaumene gives the *cursus* of an imperial freedman of the second or third centuries AD, who had been ἐπίτροπος καλενδαρίου Οὐηλιανοῦ, ἐπίτροπος χαρτήρας Ἀλεξανδρείας, and ἐπίτροπος Καππαδοκίας (ILS 9490). The first post involved the administration of property that had once belonged to the Velii, a colonial family from Heliopolis in Syria, some of whose members had reached the Roman senate, but which fell from grace with the execution of D. Velius Rufus Iulianus by Commodus in AD 183. The erection of the inscription at Laodicea may be explained by the fact that they had owned large estates there which, like the *praedia Quadratiana* and the estates of Considius, passed into the imperial patrimony.[97]

Distinctive *nomina* may be a clue to other property owned by Romans or Italians in central Galatia. There was a group of Scribonii settled at or near Vetissus, and further south at Kuyulu Zebil, perhaps the site of Gdanmaa, inscriptions mention a C. Marius Priscus and a P. Crasicius Rufus who may also owe their

[87] Halfmann, *Senatoren*, 101 no. 10; W. Eck, ZPE 86 (1991), 403 ff. offers a warning that there is no proof that he governed his home province.
[88] Ibid. 105–7 no. 10.
[89] IGR iv. 894; SEG xvii. 623.
[90] Swoboda, *Denkmäler*, 101 no. 291 corrected at MAMA viii. 66. For K as an abbreviation for Καλπούρνιος cf. MAMA i. 41 interpreted by Halfmann, *Senatoren*, 198.
[91] The Calpurnii had extensive connections in Galatia and through SW Anatolia, see Halfmann, *Senatoren*, 54 ff. Note also the L. Calpurnius Orestes who was a leading figure at Iconium (IGR iii. 264) and the munificent L. Calpurnius Longus of Pisidian Antioch (JRS 14 (1924), 178 no. 5, cf. 15 (1925), 254; Levick, *Roman Colonies*, 83).
[92] Halfmann, *Senatoren*, 176 no. 98 and 198 no. 131.
[93] MAMA i. 41 cited by Halfmann, *Senatoren*, 55 ff. and 199.
[94] RECAM ii. 34 with 36, a fragment from the temple itself, it seems. No. 37 is a dedication to Zeus Heptakometes, presumably the chief god of the estate (cf. below, Ch. 11 §IV n. 195).
[95] P. Aelius Aug. lib. Fortunatus and his family appear in RECAM ii. 36 and there is a Π. Αἴλιος Μηνᾶς nearby at Kızılbölüklü, RECAM ii. 62; also Aelia Corinthia at Sarıyar to the north, RECAM ii. 153.
[96] Tacitus, Ann. 3. 37, 5. 8, 6. 18; cf. ANRW ii. 7. 2, 1074–5.
[97] ILS 9470 with Halfmann, *Senatoren*, 56 and 189 no. 114. It is not quite certain that the imperial freedman honoured at Laodicea was then acting in his capacity as *procurator calendarii Veliani*. Note that a dedication to Zeus Heliopolitanus was set up in the sanctuary of Mēn Askaēnos at Pisidian Antioch, E. Lane, CMRDM iv. no. 109.

names to Roman patrons.[98] We should also fit into this context the bilingual gravestone of C. Rubrius C. f. Pop., set up by his freedmen, C. Rubrius Optatus, in the territory of Laodicea about the mid-first century AD.[99] He could clearly have been another Italian settler in Asia, following the pattern of the Plancii or the Sergii Paulli.

It is worth laying some stress on this important group of non-Anatolian landowners, and speculating about the circumstances that enabled them to acquire a major interest in an area that had hitherto been the little-regarded domain of local dynasts. The Sergii Paulli and Caristanii of Antioch, the Plancii of Perge and the Paccii and Calpurnii of Attaleia were all families of Italian origin which had settled in Asia Minor in the Augustan period, and carved out major landholdings for themselves which served as a springboard for successful careers within the provincial aristocracy and the Roman senatorial class. One reason for the acquisition of these large properties will have been the tenuous hold on the land of its former pastoral inhabitants. One might presume that this transhumant population had no firm title, and therefore posed no obstacle to the wholesale takeover of large areas by newcomers. But there should also have been a more urgent dynamic built into the situation. It is highly probable that the origin and rapid growth of their estates in Galatia can be traced to the same set of circumstances which had existed in Asia and Bithynia after these were annexed to the empire. There, Roman demands for taxes had forced the local inhabitants to mortgage or sell land to meet their new financial commitments. Roman businessmen, closely allied to the equestrian *publicani* who farmed the taxes, were on hand to provide money in exchange for land, and Roman or Italian property ownership had mushroomed accordingly.[100] It is not difficult to cast the forebears of the earliest senators from the eastern provinces in the same role. The taxation imposed on the newly annexed provincial areas may have provided the lever which demolished the existing local monopoly on land-ownership. Within a short time—certainly before the end of the Julio-Claudian period—large stretches of the remoter countryside were prised away from their original owners and fell into the grasp of a class of entrepreneurs, who had the means to supply the immediate need of the native inhabitants for cash,

and thus acquired the opportunity to lay their hands on the province's most important long-term asset, its land.[101]

Not all property, however, passed to outsiders, and the native aristocracies of the central Anatolian cities retained a strong interest in the area. The most prominent Ancyran citizen of the second century AD was C. Iulius Severus, who could trace his lineage back to the kings of Pergamum, and who was adlected into the senate by Hadrian.[102] Among his ancestors he numbered Deiotarus and two Galatian tetrarchs called Amyntas, one the great Amyntas son of Dyitalos. We would expect, therefore, Iulius Severus to have inherited at least something of his predecessors' extensive property, from which he derived his great wealth.[103] His freedmen and interests are not easy to trace. C. Iulius is the least distinctive combination of *praenomen* and *nomen* in the repertoire, and it is difficult to relate freedmen with these names to a particular patron. However, very few members of central Anatolian families apart from soldiers acquired the Roman citizenship as early as the reign of Augustus, when they would normally take these names, and there is no evidence for Augustus' own freedmen operating in this area. These considerations make it likely that at least some of the C. Iulii found on the plateau are connected with C. Iulius Severus. An inscription from the village of Eski Calış, in the Haymana district, mentions a C. Iulius Moschus and a C. Iulius Moschion; the Haymana district was an estate of the Ottoman Sultans at least until the nineteenth century, and the family of Iulius Severus could very plausibly have had comparable interests there in the early empire.[104] Another pair of C. Iulii, C. Iulius Nestor and C. Iulius Phaulus (?Paulus) occur at Sengen, north of Laodicea Catacecaumene,[105] and there are a C. Iulius Paulus and a Iulia Paula at Laodicea itself.[106] Confirmation that Iulius Severus had interests in the southern half of the plateau is to be found in the fact that two citizens of Savatra were responsible for erecting a statue in his honour at Ancyra towards the end of his distinguished senatorial career.[107]

The inscription which records his earlier, civic career prominently advertises C. Iulius Severus' connections

---

98 *MAMA* vii. 365–6; vii. pp. xxvi(a) and (b).

99 *MAMA* i. 14a, cf. 14b. Ramsay's commentary in *ASBuckler*, 223–4 is fanciful. For the date of the doorstone see Waelkens, *Türsteine* no. 662. Compare C. Rubrius C. l. Hilario Rubella, *negotiator Gallicanus et Asiaticus*, on an inscription from Mevania in Etruria, *CIL* xi. 5068.

100 See above, Ch. 3 § II, and T. R. S. Broughton, *TAPA* 65 (1934), 210–11.

101 For the Sestullii in Phrygia, another example, see below.

102 Halfmann, *Senatoren*, 151–2 no. 62.

103 Bosch, *Ankara*, no. 105; see Ch. 9 § II n. 89.

104 *RECAM* ii. 243; Haci Halfa, *Djihan-Numa*, French trans. by Armain in P. de Tchihatcheff, *Asie Mineure*, i (1853), 703 ff. for the Sultan's estate.

105 *MAMA* i. 374; cf. *MAMA* vii. 365–6 for Iulii at Vetissus.

106 *MAMA* i. 34 and 44. Halfmann, *Senatoren*, 55 and 116 no. 20 connects these with Iulius Paullus, a senator from Pisidian Antioch, which is possible although less likely than the suggestion offered here.

107 Bosch, *Ankara*, no. 157.

with a striking group of Asiatic consular senators. Among them was Iulius Quadratus, who should probably be identified with C. Iulius Quadratus Bassus, Trajan's general and suffect consul in 105.[108] He may be the owner of a group of properties known as the *praedia Quadratiana*, which, like the *choria Considiana* of the Tembris valley, later passed into the patrimony of the emperor but retained their original owner's name.[109] Iulius Severus was also related to C. Claudius Severus, the first governor of the province of Arabia which was annexed in 106, whose family came from Pompeiopolis in Galatian Paphlagonia.[110] The Claudii Severi also had a large stake in central Anatolia; their principal estates lay not in Galatia, but in the territory of the Ormeleis in south-east Asia east of Cibyra.[111] With a handful of others these families make up an élite group from the Anatolian aristocracy, which could trace its ancestry back to the kings and tetrarchs of the Hellenistic period, and whose members often became Roman senators under Domitian or Trajan as part of a second wave of eastern recruits after the initial group of Italian emigrants.

There are hints that other senators claimed slices of this same rich cake. A tombstone from Atlandı, the ancient *chorion* Aralleion, in the central plateau north of Laodicea, was erected by a certain Epaphroditus, slave of Pardalas, for his son Phosporus. The master's *cognomen* Pardalas occurs in two notable Anatolian families, based in Sardis and Pergamum respectively, one or the other of which is likely to have owned property in the area of Atlandı, where *misthotai* are also independently attested.[112] An important senatorial family from Anatolia which flourished in the late second and early third centuries was that of the Valerii Paeti, one of whose members Valerianus Paetus was executed for challenging the authority of the emperor Elagabalus, by issuing medallions bearing his own image in Cappadocia. Dio states that the family came from Galatia, and it appears to have owned property in the Lycaonian–Isaurian borderland of the Çarşamba basin, where a slave of the *senatorius* Paetus is known. Once again, the rare *cognomen* is a clue that the owner

here was a member of the Galatian senatorial family, known well enough locally to be referred to in this abbreviated fashion.[113] Domainal landownership was as typical of the Çarşamba valley as it was of the plateau north of Iconium. In addition to the major landowners, the Calpurnii of Attaleia and the Valerii Paeti, inscriptions mention a *pragmateutes* at Almassun, and an *oikonomos* and an *oikonomissa* at Dorla, large village sites south of the river.[114]

Other private landowners in the central plateau did not aspire to such lofty status. An inscription from Köşe Abdulla (now Yurtbeyci), east of the property of the Sergii Paulli, mentions an *oikonomos* of Appuleia Concordia.[115] The only Appuleii of any importance known in the cities of Galatia occur at Germa, where the colony set up a Latin inscription to honour an Appuleius, and where the civic career of a certain L. Appuleius Quartus is commemorated on a bilingual text.[116] Either or both may have been connected with Appuleia Concordia, although she need not necessarily have belonged to a Galatian city at all. Another estate in the same area belonged to an (Aelius) Faustus, to judge from a dedication for the safety of his master Faustus set up by Aelius Paezon at Kötü Uşak.[117] The owner of the estate may well have been P. Aelius Faustus, an imperial freedman at Laodicea Catacecaumene, who would have been well placed to administer his own property as well as estates belonging to the emperor.[118] The domainal nature of landholding around Kötü Uşak is confirmed by yet another text, simply mentioning a *misthotes*.[119] The village of Sarıkaya, south of the estate of the Sergii Paulli, which should perhaps be identified with Vetissus,[120] also seems to have been a centre for freedmen, administering their patrons' properties. Apart from the Scribonii mentioned above there were Iulii and Ulpii in some numbers, agents of Anatolian families that had received the citizenship in the early Julio-Claudian period or from Trajan.[121] Two other properties whose owners are not known at all are to be sought at or near Atkafası, where an *oikonomos* of the Plommeis attested, and at Cihanbeyli where there is a dedication to

[108] *PIR*² iv. 260: i no. 258; Halfmann, *Senatoren*, 119–20 no. 26. For his career inscription see the detailed commentary by C. Habicht, *Alt. von Perg.* viii. 3 (1969), 43 ff. no. 21.

[109] *MAMA* i. 24; Halfmann, *Senatoren*, 114 connects these estates with Iulius Quadratus Bassus' near contemporary, C. Antius A. Iulius Quadratus, also of Pergamon. This cannot be ruled out and there is a freedman A. Iulius Onesiphorus at Laodicea, *MAMA* i. 47.

[110] Halfmann, *Senatoren*, 135–6 no. 39; 161 no. 72; 181–1 no. 101.

[111] See below, nn. 198–9.

[112] *MAMA* vii. 295. Calder's note shows that he misunderstood the text. For the families of Iulius Pardalas at Sardis and of Claudius Pardalas at Pergamum see *MAMA* ix. 21 n.

[113] Cassius Dio, 80. 4. 7; *MAMA* viii. 70. For the family see E. Groag, *RE* viiiA. 173 nos. 282–4 and A. Stein, *Strena Buliciana* (1928).

[114] *MAMA* viii. 136; A. M. Ramsay, *JHS* 24 (1904), 283 no. 24. Roman names occur in the area.

[115] W. M. Calder, *CR* 22 (1908), 215; *RECAM* ii. 324.

[116] *RECAM* ii. 91, 96.

[117] *MAMA* vii. 476.

[118] W. M. Ramsay, *CR* 19 (1905), 369 and, from an independent copy, *IGR* iii. 259.

[119] *RECAM* ii. 325, dated to AD 250.

[120] Cf. *MAMA* vii. 363, but note pp. xxii–xxv where Vetissus is sited further north at Sülüklü.

[121] For the Ulpii see *MAMA* vii. 367–71; for Iulii see above.

Zeus set up by two *misthotai* who were *archiereis* in the local community.[122]

The large landowners who have left their mark across the whole extent of Central Anatolia are thus a diverse group drawn from the gentry of the cities that ringed the plateau, aristocrats from the major cities of Asia, *émigré* settlers from the colonies and business centres of southern Asia Minor, and even perhaps from Syria. Some may have been able to trace their origins to the Galatian chieftains who had political control of the area before the Roman province was created; others belonged to the ruling class of the Greek cities of Asia Minor; while the most significant and conspicuous group were ultimately of Italian origin, official or unofficial colonists who took advantage of local conditions and the terms imposed by Roman rule to secure huge properties for themselves and their families under Augustus and through the Julio-Claudian period.

Although the origins of their properties may have differed, not too much should be made of the difference between this group and the Graeco-Anatolian landowners. Through the first century AD these groups were intermarrying freely; their common interests were enhanced by sharing the benefits of their different talents and backgrounds. The patchwork nature of Italian and native land-holding in central Anatolia is no more than another reflection of the fusion of the western and oriental aristocracies into the many-faceted governing class of second- and third-century Rome.

The pattern of land-ownership changed significantly in the second century, when the emperors began to acquire property for the first time on the plateau. The chief evidence comes from Laodicea Catacecaumene and its territory, where there is a large group of inscriptions mentioning imperial freedmen procurators and imperial slaves. The most important document has already been noted in another context, a dedication to Iulia Mamaea set up by a certain Glycerinus, *lib. (proc.) praediorum Quadratianorum*.[123] Although the freedman here is not specifically said to be a procurator of the emperor, he certainly was so, as were several other *liberti Augusti* named on comparable texts.[124] None of these inscriptions can be dated before the reign of Hadrian, and a high proportion of the freedmen are Aelii or Aurelii.[125] This makes it likely that Hadrian was the emperor responsible for taking the property over from its original owner or owners. Confiscation, inheritance, or purchase would only have

been the principal modes by which estates could have changed hands in this way, and we have no information about the means by which the emperor came by his property at Laodicea. We may note in passing that C. Iulius Quadratus Bassus was given a public funeral in the early years of Hadrian's reign, perhaps in recognition of the bequest of a valuable property, as well as an honour granted to match the services which he had rendered to Rome during the Dacian and Parthian wars.[126] The number of agents—both freedmen and slaves—that occurs on inscriptions at Laodicea is a sufficient indication of the size and importance of the imperial property there, but it may be misleading to think that these estates were concentrated around Laodicea itself. The city probably acted as the centre for imperial interests scattered over the plateau. To the east Iulianus, a *verna* of the Augusti, buried his wife at Kuyulu Sebil;[127] and a group of inscriptions from Pillitokome (Insuyu) nearby name an *instrumentarius tabulariorum* Aurelius Epagathus, who was a freedman of two Augusti, and his wife Aelia Terpsis, another imperial slave, and a family of Aelii.[128] Taken as a whole these texts clearly indicate another property, located east of Laodicea towards the salt lake, acquired not later than the reign of Hadrian, and under the control of freedmen during the reign of Marcus Aurelius and Lucius Verus, or of Marcus Aurelius and Commodus.

West of Laodicea there were imperial interests in Phrygia Paroreius, on the border of Galatia and Asia.[129] There were properties at least at Tyriaeum, which has produced a dedication to Caracalla or Elagabalus by a freedman, M. Aurelius Eucleides, presumably the local procurator,[130] and at the village of Eldes, south of Ilgın, a dedication to Zeus was put up by Cosmion, an imperial slave and eirenarch.[131]

In north Galatia the only certain imperial holdings were the *choria Considiana*, already mentioned in connection with their putative original owner. The presence of P. Aelii in the area, and the dedication of an imperial temple there by the *oikonomos* between 177 and 180 are reminiscent of the situation at Pillitokome, and there is every reason to suppose that the basic history and organization of the two properties were similar.[132]

122 J. G. C. Anderson, *JHS* 19 (1899), 124 no. 136; W. Ruben, *Belleten*, 12 (1948) 173 ff. fig. ix; *Bull. ép.* (1958), 486. Note also at Cihanbeyli other likely freedman families: Iulia Polla, Egnatius Nero, and Calpurnia Eirene, *MAMA* vii. 296–7.
123 *MAMA* i. 24.
124 *MAMA* i. 21, 22a, 23.
125 *MAMA* i. 21, 22, 22a, 37, 38, 39.
126 Habicht, *Alt. von Perg.* viii. 3. 43 ff. no. 21 note at end.
127 *MAMA* vii. 544.
128 Texts published in *MAMA* i. p. xiv; see also *MAMA* vii. 523–4.
129 *MAMA* vii. pp. xvii–xviii.
130 *MAMA* vii. 107.
131 *MAMA* vii. 135. Drew Bear, *ANRW* ii. 18. 3, 1970–4 establishes that the magistracy was held on the estate, not in one of the neighbouring cities.
132 See above, n. 128.

Given that no imperial estates on the central plateau can be securely dated before the reign of Hadrian, and that virtually all the freedmen employed on them were Aelii or Aurelii, they should be seen as a third stage in the evolution of land-ownership in the region, which had begun with the great dynastic holdings of livestock in the first century BC. The second stage is marked above all by the appearance of Italian estate owners in the first century AD, and it is only from the Hadrianic period that the emperors followed their example and began to amass their own possessions, which came to dominate the southern half of the plateau.

It is worth stressing that a number of peculiar local factors gave rise to this particular pattern and development of land-ownership, which was not necessarily to be found in other areas of the province, or in other parts of Asia Minor altogether. The absence of large centres of population, and of cities at all before the creation of the province of Galatia, favoured the development of large rural holdings. The pastoral basis of the pre-Roman economy, and the social structure of tribal society at this period, had meant that individual claims to land, as such, were not strong. Men's wealth resided in their moveable possessions, principally their livestock, not in the soil itself, which was relatively unprotected and vulnerable to usurpation by newcomers. The imposition of Roman rule and the demand for taxes, as elsewhere in Asia Minor and the rest of the empire, gave Italian outsiders an irresistible opportunity to take over large areas; and it was doubtless under these new, domainal landlords that the actual economic exploitation of the central plateau changed, gradually, from pastoralism to cereal agriculture.

Outside the central area, other factors had affected the development of land tenure. From Iconium westwards to the Pisidian lake district, Roman colonies certainly claimed considerable areas of this land to be divided up between their settlers,[133] which must have restricted, although it did not completely exclude, the growth of larger estates. There are clear traces of domainal land-holding in the Cillanian plain, and in the valley of the Çarşamba river,[134] but the Roman veterans at Isaura, Lystra, and Neapolis certainly provided an obstacle to entrepreneurial Italian acquisitiveness. It is perfectly intelligible that the Sergii Paulli, one of the leading families of Antioch, should have looked far afield to the east side of Sultan Dağ to acquire land, for most of the fertile plain of Antioch itself will surely have been divided up into colonial allotments.

There is a different pattern to imperial holdings in this area too. There were, it seems imperial estates

on Orondian territory, administered by à freedman procurator based at Kıreli,[135] at Çarıksaray on the edge of the Cillanian plain,[136] and perhaps around Bademli,[137] at the west, north, and south sides respectively of Lake Beyşehir. The first two were almost certainly sited on *ager publicus* which had been acquired after Servilius' war of conquest[138] and should have existed already by the reign of Augustus. At Bademli the evidence consists of the gravestone of a *dispensator Augusti*, T. Flavius Diomedianus Diomedes, whose names show him to have been a Flavian freedman. Again, this was clearly an estate by the first century AD. Perhaps it too had its origins in a tract of republican *ager publicus*. There were holdings at both ends of the Burdur lake, in western Pisidia. The governor of Lycia and Pamphylia in AD 54, Q. Petronius Umber, and the procurator, L. Pupius Praesens, were responsible for establishing boundaries between the city of Sagalassus and the village of Tymbrianassus, which was part of an imperial estate.[139] Thus the area at the south-west corner of the lake virtually on the border between the provinces of Asia and Galatia was imperial property by the mid-first century AD. Less explicit chronologically but equally decisive for the existence of imperial estates are the boundary stones found near the north-east end of the lake which read *fines Caesaris n.*[140] We should look for the origin of these properties not, as on the Central Plateau, to a transfer from private to imperial ownership in the second century AD, but to the acquisition of *ager publicus* in and around Pisidia, resulting from the campaigns of P. Servilius, and during the Augustan warfare to pacify Pisidia and the adjacent parts of the Taurus.

This survey is inevitably incomplete. For many parts of the province there is simply no worthwhile information; elsewhere the evidence that survives is palpably defective and not always easy to interpret. Nevertheless it has revealed that the history of land-ownership was as varied as the history of the region itself, and that profound changes were brought about by the introduction of Roman rule. *Ager publicus* in the Pisidian Taurus, the reward for Roman victories, was commandeered on a wide scale for Roman use, to

---

[133] See above Ch. 7 § III for the sources of colonial land.
[134] See above nn. 112–14.
[135] Robert, *Hellenica*, xiii. 74–87, and above, Ch. 7 § III n. 110.
[136] *MAMA* viii. 364.
[137] *CIL* iii. 12143.
[138] See above, Ch. 7 § III at nn. 108–10.
[139] G. E. Bean, *AS* 9 (1959), 84 ff. no. 30. Three examples of the text are known, which clearly states that Tymbrianassus was a *kome*. For the likelihood that Q. Petronius Umber governed Lycia and Pamphylia, not Galatia, see Vol. II, App. I, at nn. 62–4.
[140] *CIL* iii. 6882 dated to the 1st cent. AD by H. Dessau, *Geschichte der Kaiserzeit*, ii. 2. 611.

provide land for colonists or to become the basis of early imperial estates; the modes of provincial administration and government, and tax demands in particular, saw to an even more sweeping transference of land in central Anatolia from native leaders to wealthy Roman entrepreneurs who had settled in Asia Minor in the late republic or early empire; much of this in turn passed on to the emperors in the second century AD, as the emperor exercised an ever tighter grip on every facet of Roman political and economic life. The first century AD had been an age of individual opportunity, the second was one of imperial consolidation.

IV. *Estates in Phrygia, Bithynia, and Lydia*

Political circumstances and economic conditions naturally varied considerably in different parts of Anatolia and the pattern of land-ownership which can be traced in detail for the central plateau cannot simply be superimposed on other regions to produce the same picture. Local conditions might lead to considerable chronological variations, and strong, well-established communities were sometimes able to resist penetration by outsiders who sought to acquire their land. The emergence of large estates under Roman provincial government, often owned by immigrant Roman or Italian settlers, was a common but not universal phenomenon; the growth of imperial estates during the second and third centuries was, however, ubiquitous.

One of the best-documented areas of inland Anatolia is the upper Tembris valley of northern Phrygia. In the late Hellenistic period this fertile area was thinly settled, scarcely Hellenized, and not heavily exploited. The rulers of Pergamum and Bithynia had placed military settlers in this border zone between their two kingdoms, and there is a small group of third-century-BC gravestones indicating the presence of Macedonian adventurers, who surely lived the lives of frontiersmen in a corner of the world which was opening up after Alexander's conquests for the first time since the age of Phrygian domination.[141] The earliest doorstones, the characteristic grave monuments of the region, date to the first century BC, but none at this early stage is inscribed.[142] However, by the mid-first century BC the community at the centre of the upper Tembris basin, Appia, emerged as a city with public buildings which minted its own coinage,[143] and the region probably began to attract the attention of Italian *negotiatores*. A *negotiator* family, the Sestullii of Fundi in Latium, had

by this stage acquired important interests in Acmonia to the south. In the late second century AD descendants of the family, M. Sestullius Severus and his son M. Sestullius Severus Flavianus, both high priests of Asia, owned a large property around Altıntaş, a few miles north-west of Appia; and free-born or freedmen members of the family were present in many of the neighbouring cities, including Aezani, Tiberiopolis, Cidyessus, Prymnessus, Stectorium, and Dorylaeum; their connections extended to Pisidian Antioch, Sinope on the Black Sea, and Smyrna on the Aegean.[144] Cicero's evidence in the *Pro Flacco*, which shows them to have been involved in money-lending and related financial transactions in Phrygia in the 60s BC, surely provides the clue to the means by which they became leading representatives of the new Phrygian propertied class. Roman rule in Asia after Sulla's settlement of 85 BC[145] provided the favourable conditions for entrepreneurial activity and led them to anticipate the exploits of their counterparts in Galatia, such as the Plancii of Perge, by some two generations. It is almost a matter for surprise that to date no Sestullius of the imperial period appears to have held an equestrian office or to have entered the Roman senate. They may have preferred the role of *domi nobiles*.

The same region of northern Phrygia was occupied by other large private estate owners; for instance by the Italian senatorial family of the Ummidii, who acquired possessions in the territory of Cadi to match their better-known and more extensive property on the territory of the Ormeleis towards the southern boundary of Asia.[146] But there is prominent evidence also for imperial land-ownership. Two large and finely carved dedications to Zeus Bennios which were set up at a sanctuary near Appia in AD 79 by an imperial freedman, who was also *eirenophylax* of the region, and his wife, suggest but do not prove that the emperors already owned land here by this date. By the third century AD much of the Tembris valley was administered by imperial freedmen procurators. The property was probably not continuous but comprised several separate tracts, perhaps acquired piecemeal in the

---

[141] *MAMA* ix, pp. xl–xlii; see also *MAMA* x. 220 with n.

[142] Waelkens, *Türsteine*, no. 219; another early example in *MAMA* x. 174.

[143] See Aulock, *Phrygien* i. 48–50.

[144] Since S. Mitchell, *AS* 29 (1979), 13–22 there have been further discussions of the family by E. Badian, *AJPhil.* 101 (1980), 470 ff. and T. Drew Bear, *REA* 82 (1980 pub. 1982), 179–82, and another text published from Aezani, *MAMA* ix. 274. An unpublished imperial letter from Antoninus Pius found at Aezani by Professor U. Laffi mentions a Sestullius. Another new text from the upper Tembris valley is published in *MAMA* x. 70. A coin of Cidyessus in Phrygia dating between AD 178 and 187 carries the legend ἐπὶ Σησ. Σεβηροῦ ἀσιαρχοῦ, apparently Sestullius Severus the father buried in the Upper Tembris Valley, and not a Sestius Severus, as suggested by Aulock, *Phrygien*, i nos. 509–10 and 533.

[145] See E. W. Gray, *Tenth Congress*, iii. 941.

[146] See discussion in *MAMA* x, xxxv.

course of the second and early third centuries.[147] To judge from the famous Aragua petition of the 240s, the behaviour of the freedmen and slaves attached to these estates was as predatory as that of the *negotiatores* of the late republican period, when direct Roman interest in the area was first established.[148]

There is considerable evidence for other large-scale imperial properties south of the Tembris valley around the Phrygian cities of Prymnessus, Synnada, and Docimeium but here the personnel of these estates can scarcely be distinguished from the freedmen and slave managers of the huge imperial quarries of Docimeium, and the subsidiary workings in the upper Tembris valley itself.[149] Few discoveries have conveyed a better idea of the power of the Roman empire and the impact that Roman rule could have on even remote areas than the find and identification of a half-finished colossal statue of a Dacian prisoner in one of the polychrome marble (*pavonazetto*) quarries of the upper Tembris valley. This was either destined to adorn Trajan's new forum in Rome, or, as an even more remarkable example of the spread of the imperial victory ideology, formed part of a provincial set of similar statues, to be erected perhaps at Ephesus.[150] Indeed it is likely that the quarries themselves had been opened here as a subsidiary of the Docimian workings to satisfy the huge demands of Domitian's and Trajan's Roman building projects. The industry as a whole must have occupied an enormous labour force and required a vast organization not merely to quarry and work the stone but above all to transport it to cities throughout Asia Minor and beyond to North Africa, Italy, and above all Rome itself. Detailed analysis of the impact of these activities on the economic development of the region

goes beyond the scope of a study of how the agricultural potential of the Anatolian countryside was exploited under Roman rule, but it can at least be said that few forms of economic activity can have been more important than the marble-quarrying which furnished the Roman world with the raw material used for the most extensive and far-reaching building programmes in the history of Antiquity.[151]

East of Appia and the upper Tembris valley lay the Phrygian highlands and the small cities of Meiros and Metropolis, where there were large imperial land-holdings in the third and fourth centuries,[152] and beyond them Nacolea, whose numerous inscriptions evoke a history of exploitation comparable to that in central Galatia. One of the earliest tombstones was erected for his 5-year-old son by a slave of the Caesar Germanicus, 'consul for a second time', that is Tiberius' adopted son in the last year of his life.[153] The presence of the slave and his young child together suggests that he was not simply present as part of Germanicus' travelling entourage to the East in AD 18–19 but was established in Nacolea permanently, presumably to look after family property. Certainly by the second century there were imperial estates here, whose managers played a prominent role in municipal life. P. Aelius Aug. lib. Onesimus bequeathed a portion of his private fortune to endow a corn-distribution scheme in the city;[154] other texts allude to imperial slaves and freedmen in the city and the region,[155] and the emperor's slave Craterus set up a Latin dedication to Commodus on behalf of the city, while holding the office of *exactor rei publicae Nacolensium*, a post evidently concerned with extracting revenue or agricultural products from the local property and transferring it to the treasury.[156]

The emperor was not the only landowner. Villages here as in the central plateau might have a *misthotes* attached to them to handle an estate owner's interests;[157]

---

[147] The dedications are published by Drew Bear, *ANRW* ii. 18. 3, 1967–81. However, the freedman may have been attached to the imperial quarries, and not certainly to a landed estate. For the latter see 1980 n. 264; J. Strubbe, *Anc. Soc.* 6 (1975), 230–6; *MAMA* x, xxxiii–xxxv.

[148] See below, Ch. 13 §11 at n. 23; the text will be re-edited as *MAMA* x, no. 114.

[149] There has been much recent discussion: see M. Waelkens, 'Carrières de marbre en Phrygie', *Bull. Mus. Ant.* (Brussels), 53: 2 (1982), 33–55; 'Marmi e sarcofagi frigi', *Ann. di Sc. Norm. Sup. di Pisa*, 3: 16 (1986), 661–78; M. Christol and T. Drew Bear, *Tyche*, i (1986), 55–87 and *Anatolia Antiqua* (French Archaeological Institute, Istanbul), i (1987), 83–137.

[150] M. Waelkens, 'From a Phrygian Quarry: The Provenance of the Statues of Dacian Prisoners in Trajan's Forum at Rome', *AJA* 89 (1985), 641–53. R. Schneider, *Röm. Mitt.* 97 (1990), 235–60 at 251–3 suggests that the torso in the Tembris valley quarry was intended for a provincial copy of the series, and identifies another possible provincial example at Ephesus. Cf. R. R. R. Smith, *JRS* 78 (1988), 50–77 for an exact Augustan parallel, whereby the *simulacra gentium* from the Forum Augusti inspired the imperial sculpture programme in the Sebasteion at Aphrodisias.

[151] J. Ward Perkins, 'Nicomedia and the Marble Trade', *PBSR* 48 (1980), 23–68 marks a beginning; see now Hazel Dodge, *JRA* 4 (1991), 28–50. This does not take into account all the recent Asia Minor bibliography, on which see M. Waelkens, *apud* S. Mitchell, 'Archaeology in Asia Minor 1984–89', *JHS Arch. reports* (1989/90), 88–9.

[152] *IGR* iv. 592; Haspels, *The Highlands of Phrygia*, no. 31; note nos. 37 and 41 for *georgoi*; Strubbe, *Anc. Soc.* 6 (1975), 230–6.

[153] *MAMA* v. 201, and see in general pp. xxviii–xxix. It is worth recalling that the imperial exploitation of the Docimian quarries begins under Tiberius.

[154] *MAMA* v. 202.

[155] *IGR* iv. 543 and 544; compare also 546 from the village of the Trocnades, east of Nacolea on the border of Galatia, whose inhabitants honour Aelia Maximina, wife of a procurator.

[156] *MAMA* v. 197.

[157] *MAMA* v. 219.

slaves in one case buried their *patron*;[158] a family of Italian origin, the Calidii, used Latin for a gravestone;[159] and the funerary formula θεοῖς καταχθονίοις, directly translating *Dis Manibus*, appears as another likely trace of Roman influence through estate holding.[160] The most intriguing item in this assorted collection is a dedication to the local god Papas and Heracles(?) set up by Apollonius son of Synesis, slave of Cocceianus. The most famous Cocceianus, which is not a common name, was the sophist Cocceianus Dio of Prusa, Dio Chrysostom. Synesis, Intelligence, is a name that a philosopher might well have conferred on a slave, and the stone suggests the possibility that Dio of Prusa was a landowner in the area of Nacolea as well as in his native city.[161]

North-west of Nacolea lay Phrygian Dorylaeum and beyond it Nicaea, the second if not the first city of Bithynia,[162] whose large and fertile territory had been greatly extended when Pompey created the province of Pontus and Bithynia in 63 BC and divided its land between the cities of the new province.[163] Nicaea flourished under the Roman empire; peace, good communications, and above all a spirit of civic enterprise have been identified as the catalysts which enabled it to realize its full potential and channel the profits of agriculture into the visible symbols of urban prosperity.[164] The chief beneficiaries of this transformation of Nicaea from a Hellenistic backwater into one of the major cities of Asia Minor were large estate owners, many of Italian origin. The bankruptcy of Bithynia when it was bequeathed to Rome by its last king in 75 BC and the relentless Roman demands over the next fifty years, until Augustus settled Asia Minor after Actium, opened the doors to *negotiatores*, scrupulous and unscrupulous.[165] To judge from inscriptions found on Nicaea's territory of the imperial period, few opportunities to acquire land were missed.

A prime example of Italian landownership is the case of the family of the Catilii of Apamea. Catilius Longus, patron of *Colonia Iulia Concordia Apamea*, was one of the élite group of early imperial colonists whose

members took part in Roman public life before the end of the Julio-Claudian period. He was a military tribune of *legio IV Scythica* under Claudius, prefect of a cohort under Nero, and adlected into the senate *inter praetorios* by Vespasian, doubtless as a reward for timely support in the civil war of 69.[166] He was patently closely related to Cn. Catilius Atticus a local property owner known from a Latin gravestone set up by his slave estate-manager,[167] and Atticus in turn was probably the father of L. Catilius Severus Iulianus Claudius Reginus *cos. II ord.* in AD 120.[168] The latter's freedmen appear at Keramet on the north shore of Lake Ascanias (Iznik Göl), on the territorial boundary between Kios and Nicaea, and in villages in the region of Göynük east of Nicaea, where the consul himself was honoured with statues by his dependants.[169]

Large estate-holdings were clearly the norm in the eastern part of Nicaea's territory, which had been wild and unexploited before the imperial period. Many texts name *oikonomoi*, an *oikonomissa*, *pragmateutai*, or untitled slave or freedmen agents of their masters, who are variously labelled *despotai*, *kyrioi*, or *patrones*: Claudius Thallos, *oikonomos* of C. Claudius Calpurnianus, supervised property on the north shore of Lake Ascanias (*I. Nikaia*, i. 205); a Chrestus, perhaps the C. Cassius Chrestus who befriended M. Plancius Varus when he governed Bithynia under Vespasian, lamented the death of his aged *vilicus* Italus, on account of his virtuous life and his industrious service (ἀντ᾽ ἀγάθου δὲ βίου καὶ δουλοσύνης φιλοέργου) (*I. Nikaia*, i. 192); female estate owners included Claudia Gallitte (*I. Nikaia*, i. 196), Claudia Eias (*I. Nikaia*, ii. 1. 1201), and Annia Astilla (*I. Nikaia*, ii. 1. 1062, cf. 1208); among their male counterparts were L. Claudius Pacorianus Eupator (*I. Nikaia*, ii. 1. 1128), P. Postumius Severianus Apollothemis (*I. Nikaia*, ii. 1. 1131), P. Ta... Achaicus (*I. Nikaia*, ii. 1. 1203), and members of the *gens Hostilia*, who not only owned possessions near Geyve in the 60s AD but also had active interests in Rome.[170] Claudia Eias, Annia Astilla, and Pacorianus Eupator all ranked as *clarissimi*. Roman *nomina* such as Annius and Postumius suggest that they were descended from *negotiator* families.

Imperial holdings seem to have been largely excluded

[158] *MAMA* v. 240.
[159] *MAMA* v. 233.
[160] *MAMA* v. 225; see above, Ch. 9 § II n. 121.
[161] *MAMA* v. R. 18. For Dio's Prusan estates see C. P. Jones, *The Roman World of Dio Chrysostom* (1978), 7 citing *Or.* 46. 7–8.
[162] L. Robert, *HSCP* 81 (1977), 1–39 (*OMS* vi. 211–49).
[163] S. Mitchell, *Eighth Congress*, 129 ff.
[164] R. Merkelbach, *Nikaia in der römischen Kaiserzeit* (1987), cf. *CR* 39 (1989), 153.
[165] See above, Ch. 3 § II n. 31, and Ch. 4 § IV n. 64; and briefly on *negotiatores* in Bithynia, B. F. Harris, *ANRW* ii. 7. 2, 870–4.

[166] *AE* (1982), 860 = *I. Apamea*, 2 with nn.; Halfmann, *Senatoren*, 115 no. 18.
[167] *CIL* iii. 337 = *I. Apamea*, 21.
[168] T. Corsten, *Epigr. Anat.* 6 (1985), 127–32; Halfmann, *Senatoren*, 133 no. 38.
[169] *I. Kios*, 105 = *I. Iznik*, ii. 1. 756 (Keramet); 1204, 1205; ii. 2. 1445.
[170] *I. Iznik*, ii. 1. 1161 (C. Hostilius Pollio), cf. i. 34 (C. Hostilius Ascanias). In Rome there was C. Hostilius Agathopous, Moretti, *IGUR* 837; *ILS* 3720. See L. Robert, *CRAI* (1978), 375 ff. and discussion below, Vol. II, Ch. 16 § II n. 155.

by private landowners. The one likely exception to this rule is difficult to interpret. The community of the Charmideanoi at the west end of Lake Ascanias, who probably derived their name from a land-owning Charmides of the Hellenistic period, honoured the imperial freedman Aurelius Diodotus and his wife Cassia Ulpia Fulvia Longina, under Marcus Aurelius and one of his fellow emperors between 161 and 180. A generation earlier in AD 138 a certain Philetus had erected a votive stele for Zeus and Demeter on behalf of the village's *despotai*.[171] Since the last term cannot refer to emperors, at least during the sole rule of Antoninus Pius to which the text belongs, it appears that the village was still part of a private estate, perhaps in direct line of inheritance from Charmides, but had passed to the emperor by the time of the later text.

The evidence from Nicaea makes a greater impression when it is matched against the record from another well-documented area, northern Lydia in the province of Asia, where the pattern is significantly different. Conditions here seem to have been more favourable to smallholders than on the central plateau or in Bithynia. The Attalids and Seleucids had planted outposts of Macedonian settlers throughout the region in the third and second centuries BC which survived as viable communities into the Roman empire.[172] The native population of Mysians, Lydians, and Phrygians was also not only culturally resilient,[173] but kept control over its own land in some degree, for several of the case histories recorded in the confession steles of Maeonia, east of Sardis, record disputes over property, which are only intelligible in the context of small peasant holdings.[174] Although there are traces of Italian families acquiring properties in the late republican period, whose influence may be detected in the first century AD,[175] the penetration was not on a large scale and the newcomers seem to have been well integrated with the indigenous inhabitants. Out of a total of more than 1,400 inscriptions recorded on the territories of about twenty mostly modest cities only a handful imply the existence of large private domains. Imperial property, on the other hand, seems to have been more extensive than at Nicaea, although not on the scale of the huge estates of Phrygia and Galatia.

Three women appear as landowners in their own right: Flavia Menogenis held property round Kula in the Lydian Catacecaumene in the early second century.[176] She seems to have had third-century successors in Curtia Iulia Valentilla, perhaps a native of Philadelphia, and Flavia Pollitta, perhaps from Sardis, both wives of Roman consuls. The former contributed towards the building of a bath-house at Thermai Theseos, a village of the Mocadeni in northern Lydia near the boundary with Phrygia.[177] The latter unquestionably owned property at Apollonis in northwest Lydia where she was represented by a slave *pragmateutes*.[178] The only substantial male landowners to emerge from the documentation for the area seem to have belonged to the Pergamene family of Iulii Quadrati. The *familia servorum* of C. Iulius Quadratus honoured one of their number also at Thermai Theseos in AD 141, and five years later a freedman of C. Iulius Quadratus offered vows to Asclepius for his master's safety and health at Kula.[179] There is a likely connection with another freedman, C. Iulius Anicetus, and his wife Iulia Tyche, who made a dedication to Mēn Axiottenos also at Kula; according to an unpublished inscription now in Uşak Museum the same man, identified specifically as a Pergamene, also erected a statue to the divinity Holy and Just.[180]

This meagre harvest is surpassed by the number of inscriptions which refer to imperial holdings. Lydian Philadelphia served as the centre of a *regio* of imperial estates administered by its own procurator and his assistants.[181] Another *adiutor procuratoris*, perhaps employed in the same bureau, is recorded at Hyrcanis.[182] But he might also have been involved in overseeing imperial land nearer at hand, for imperial freedmen are attested at Lydian Attaleia and Apollonis,[183] and a 'Caesarian slave' appears in the territory of Magnesia and Sipylum.[184] At Thyateira, the largest city of the area, there are two records of *procuratores arcae Livianae*, indicating that Augustus' wife Livia had been the first member of the ruling house to

---

[171] T. Corsten, *I. Kios*, pp. 10–1 on nos. 26–7 = *I. Iznik*, ii. 1. 725, 702; further discussion in Robert, *Ét. anat.* 242 ff.; L. Flam-Zuckermann, *Historia*, 21 (1972), 114 ff.; and S. Şahin, *I. Iznik*, ii. 1. 701 n.

[172] See below, Ch. 11 § III n. 142.

[173] Recent work is summarized by P. Debord, 'La Lydie du Nord-Est', *REA* 87 (1985), 345–59.

[174] *TAM* v. 1. 231; *Epigr. Anat.* 3 (1984), 1 ff. nos. 3, 4, and 10 = *SEG* xxxiv (1984) 1212, 1213, and 1219.

[175] P. Herrmann and Z. K. Polatkan, *Der Testament des Epikrates* (1969) with J. and L. Robert, *Bull. ép.* (1970), 441.

[176] *TAM* v. 1. 257, 274.

[177] *TAM* v. 1. 73, 209, cf. 273 with nn.

[178] *TAM* v. 2. 1213; carefully discussed by C. P. Jones, *Class. Phil.* 84 (1989), 129–36; the case for disassociating her from the pagan Politta mentioned in the *Mart. Pionii* (R. Lane Fox, *Pagans and Christians* (1986), 463–5) is not proven.

[179] *TAM* v. 1. 71, 245.

[180] *TAM* v. 1. 253 with n. Eutychis, a *threpte* of C. Iulius Anicetus, set up a confession stele to Mēn Axiottēnos and to the Mother of Mēn, E. Varınlıoğlu, *Epigr. Anat.* 13 (1989), 40 no. 1.

[181] *IGR* iv. 1651.

[182] *TAM* v. 2. 1319.

[183] *TAM* v. 2. 848, 1210.

[184] *TAM* v. 2. 1407.

acquire land here,[185] and a fragmentary official document, perhaps a governor's edict, may contain provisions for letting imperial land out to tenants.[186] Further to the east the city of Iulia Gordus operated as a centre for collecting and where necessary dispensing imperial revenue, staffed by slave *arcarii* and a *dispensator*.[187]

It is hazardous to offer sweeping explanations of this patchy array of evidence for estate-ownership in central Anatolia, Bithynia, and parts of western Asia, but it is legitimate to suggest some generalizations. In central Anatolia, where there were virtually no cities and few substantial settled communities before the early empire, conditions naturally favoured the creation of large estates. The unsettled times of the first century BC seriously destabilized the existing power structure in the region, and the pressure of Roman demands for war indemnities, taxes, and other levies opened the way for entrepreneurs from outside the region, above all Roman or Italian *negotiatores*, to acquire huge properties. Much land still remained unclaimed or thinly settled and was taken over for the large-scale Augustan colonization programme along the northern fringes of the Taurus and around Pisidia.

Although the kingdom of Bithynia had suffered comparably in the late second and early first century BC, and had also been stripped of its liquid assets by *negotiatores*, Pompey's decision to convert the area into a province preserved its land for the local inhabitants. That decision entailed setting up and maintaining a network of self-governing cities, with an elaborate constitutional machinery designed to preserve their viability and autonomy.[188] The provisions of the *lex Pompeia* might even have contained clauses to prevent land in the new city territories being sold to non-resident landlords; at any rate the existence of the cities themselves during the late republic offered a reasonable place for outside entrepreneurs, again mainly of Italian origin, to settle and thus form the core of an effective local land-owning class. The result, in the territory of Nicaea at least, was a network of large estates chiefly owned by the local aristocracy. One effect of this would have been to depress the status of the indigenous peasantry, who were certainly more numerous in this area than in the desolate countryside of the central plateau, and it may be significant that Bithynia is one of the few parts of Roman Asia Minor where the poor rural inhabitants were officially classified as being of a lower status than urban dwellers under the empire.[189]

Lydia offers another variation. For reasons that remain unclear, the indigenous population was better able to retain a grip on its land and peasant freeholding seems to have been widespread under the empire up to the third century AD. Roman *negotiatores* perhaps insinuated themselves into the resident population by intermarriage rather than by the imperialist asset-stripping which characterizes their activity elsewhere. Large private landowners were unusual. One important consequence of this may have been that the wealth of north Lydia was not concentrated in cities where a rentier aristocracy lived and spent the profits from their land, but remained dispersed. The cities of the region consequently remained small, and in many cases can scarcely be distinguished from the larger villages around them.[190] Land-ownership here as elsewhere may suggest a key to understanding the pattern of urban and rural settlement.

v. *Estate Administration*

An owner of property could choose how best to administer his possessions. Smallholdings close to the city might be worked directly by his family and dependants, but the wealthier the proprietor, and the more extensive his interests, the likelier he would be to use agents on his behalf, like the *pragmateutai* of the Murtad Ova or the Cillanian plain, the *oikonomoi*, or even an *oikonomissa*,[191] who occur in almost all the areas that have been examined. Further afield, in the great estates of central Anatolia, direct administration was a more difficult proposition. Landlords themselves might seldom if ever visit these remote areas, and would turn to other systems of management.

By far the best evidence for the running of large imperial estates comes from four North African inscriptions.[192] Taken together, and with the addition of

[185] *TAM* v. 2. 913, 935; see also the mysterious 1210 B with the note.
[186] *TAM* v. 2. 860.
[187] *TAM* v. 1. 692, 713, 745.
[188] Mitchell, *Eighth Congress*, 122–5.
[189] See below, Ch. 11 § III at nn. 119–22.
[190] See below, Ch. 11 § III at nn. 139–53.
[191] See above, nn. 57, 62–3.
[192] They are (1) *CIL* viii. 25902 = Bruns, *FIRA*² 100 of AD 116/17 from Henchir Mettich; (2) *CIL* viii. 25943 = *FIRA*² 101, Hadrianic from Ain-el-Djemala; (3) *CIL* viii. 25943, Severan but quoting essentially the same text as the previous inscription, from Ain-Ouassel; (4) *CIL* viii. 20570 = *FIRA*² 103, AD 180–3 from Souk-el-Khanis, the *saltus Burunitanus*. The inscriptions have been the subject of a vast literature. Early theories are well described and summarized by R. Clausing, *The Roman Colonate: The Theories of its Origin* (1925), 138–201; the four inscriptions have been re-edited by D. Flach, *Chiron*, 8 (1978), 441–92, and also discussed in *ANRW* ii. 10. 2. For more recent discussion of the sharecropping arrangements of the tenancies and other matters see D. Kehoe, 'Lease Regulations for Imperial Estates in N. Africa', *ZPE* 56 (1984), 193–219, and 59 (1985), 151–72.

other shorter texts, they provide a clear, detailed and largely consistent picture of the framework within which imperial holdings were worked between the late first and early third centuries AD. Overall control of these estates was in the hands of an imperial freedman procurator, or procurators, resident not on the properties themselves, but at the provincial capital, Carthage, which clearly housed the bureau from which the estates were administered.[193] The inhabitants of the estates were known as *coloni*, capable from time to time of collective action, for instance dispatching petitions to the emperor, under the direction of community leaders, such as the *magister* and *defensor* named in one of the inscriptions.[194] Between the procurators and the *coloni* there was a third class, of *conductores*, more or less temporary leaseholders on the properties,[195] responsible to the procurators for the overall condition of the estates, but themselves the recipients of a substantial proportion of the estate's produce.

The terms on which the *coloni* farmed the land were governed by Roman laws: a *lex Manciana* named in the earliest, Trajanic inscription; and a *lex Hadriana* which appears to have supplanted it in certain respects.[196] Both laws required the *coloni* to make contributions, in the form of goods and services, to the *conductores*. Typically, a *colonus* had to work for the *conductor* for between six and twelve days a year, during the spring sowing, the harvest and autumn ploughing seasons, presumably on land which was being directly cultivated by the leaseholder. In addition, he had to hand over a fraction of his own crop to the *conductor*, normally amounting to about one-third of his annual produce.

The remaining produce then became the property of the leaseholder to dispose of as he thought fit, thus realizing enough income to pay for his lease, and to leave him a suitable profit. The procurators, however, retained a strong interest in the administration of the estates. In cases of dispute between the *coloni* and the *conductores* they would be judges in the first instance;[197] they acted as intermediaries to convey new imperial regulations to the inhabitants of the estate: and they were above all responsible for seeing that an adequate income accrued to the imperial *fiscus*. The four inscriptions which are the main source of our information all bear witness to an inherent defect of the system, namely the readiness of the procurators and *conductores* to collude and oppress the *coloni* with demands exceeding the level stipulated by the *leges Manciana* and *Hadriana*. Both had an interest in extracting more from the peasants than the regulations permitted, and the procurators clearly could not be relied on to give impartial, or even tolerable decisions in disputes between the leaseholders and the *coloni*; so, on a number of occasions the latter were driven to appeal over the heads of the procurators for fair treatment. On the other hand the actual terms of the *lex Manciana* were clearly more favourable to *coloni* than other forms of tenancy, since to work land governed by its regulations was regarded as a privilege.

The African inscriptions can be made to yield a much more detailed impression of estate administration than this bare sketch may suggest, but it is fruitless in this context to pursue the nuances further, since the evidence from Asia, with which it can be compared, is adequate only to indicate the outlines. However, where comparisons can be drawn, they seem to be close enough to suggest that large Asian properties were administered along broadly similar lines. Most is known about a large property in the territory of the Ormeleis, a little to the west of the Pisidian colony of Olbasa, in the south-west corner of the province of Asia.[198] This was owned by a single family, that of Annia Cornificia Faustina, the sister of the emperor Marcus Aurelius, from the mid-second century until at least AD 260–70. Although the owners were of western origin, it is notable that in two successive generations they married into the family of the Claudii Severi of Pompeiopolis in Paphlagonia, who certainly shared an interest in the estate.[199] The peasant

[193] See (4) col. iii l. 10 ('litterae procuratorum quae sunt in tabulario tuo tractus Karthagiensis'); col. iv. ll. 10–24, a letter written by the procurator and a colleague at Carthage.
[194] (1) col. i ll. 31–2 on the base; (4) col. iv l. 29.
[195] (4) col. iii ll. 22–3, 'quibus per vices successionis per condicionem conductionis notus est'.
[196] For the *lex Manciana* see (1) col. i ll. 11–12 and 24, col. ii l. 29, col. iv ll. 7 and 9; (2) col. i l. 7, col. iii l. 2. *Culturae Mancianae* lasted until the end of the 5th cent., J. Percival, 'Culturae Mancianae', in B. Levick (ed.), *The Ancient Historian and his Materials* (1975), 213–27. For the *lex Hadriana* see (3) col. i l. 7, col. ii l. 10; (4) col. iii ll. 4–5 and 25.

[197] P. A. Brunt, *Latomus*, 25 (1966), 485 = *Roman Imperial Themes* (1990), 484.
[198] Full bibliography by W. Ruge, *RE* xviii (1939), 1098–105. The main inscriptions are (1) Sterrett, *EJ* no. 52 = Ramsay, *CB* i. 287 no. 124 = *IGR* iv. 887; (2) M. Collignon, *BCH* 2 (1878), 243 ff. no. 7 = Sterrett, *EJ* nos. 44–5 = *CB* i. 290 no. 127 = *IGR* iv. 889; (3) *CIG* 4366w = Collignon, *BCH* 2 (1878), 56 ff. = Sterrett, *EJ* nos. 53–5 = V. Bérard, *BCH* 16 (1892), 418 no. 40 = *CB* i. 291 no. 28 = *IGR* iv. 888; (4) Collignon, *BCH* 2 (1878), 250 ff. no. 9 = Sterrett, *EJ* nos. 41–2 = *CB* i. 329 = *IGR* iv. 890; (5) Collignon, *BCH* 2 (1878), 253 ff. no. 10 = Sterrett, *EJ* no. 43 = *CB* i. 289 no. 126 = *IGR* iv. 891; (6) Sterrett, *EJ* no. 59 = Bérard, *BCH* 16 (1892), 418 no. 42 = *CB* i. 288 = *IGR* iv. 893.
[199] See inscription (2) with Ramsay's notes and stemma. Cn. Claudius Severus, *cos. suff.* AD 167?, married Annia Galeria

inhabitants, the *demos* of Ormeleis were collect-ively as an *ochlos*, and their leaders were called *proagontes*.[200] The intermediary roles, between landowner and peasant, were filled by procurators (*epitropoi*), leaseholders (*misthotai*), and by a third class, not attested in the North African inscriptions, of *pragmateutai*.[201] The method of estate manage-ment should be broadly similar in the two areas. The *misthotai* would obtain a lease to farm the land from the procurators or from the landowners themselves, and extract various dues from the peasants, to dispose of as they saw fit. The procurators would collect and control the rents of the *misthotai*, act in a juridical capacity when disputes arose, and undertake overall supervision of the estate. The *pragmateutai*, unlike the *misthotai*, would act directly in the landowners' interest, either overseeing and collecting dues from peasants on parts of the estate which had not been leased out, or managing land which was not worked by share-cropping peasants, but which perhaps required their corvée labour at crucial periods of the agricultural year. The same combination of methods can be ob-served in the neighbouring estate of M. Calpurnius Longus at Alastus, where one of his freedmen acted as a *misthotes*, presumably on a portion of the estate which he had leased, while one of his slaves was an *oikonomos* (surely equivalent to a *pragmateutes*), seeing to interests that remained directly within the landowner's control.[202] The property at Alastus was evidently smaller than the Ormelian estate, and the presence of a procurator was not necessary.

The value of these Asian inscriptions, if the analogy with North Africa is correctly drawn, is to show that the same methods of property management existed on large private holdings as on imperial estates. In the central Anatolian plateau, the more fragmentary evidence can be made to suggest a similar pattern. The large private landowners were extensively represented by their freedmen. In the case of the Sergii Paulli, one of these was a *procurator*, confirming that the property was very extensive and that the *misthotai* or *prag-mateutai* resident on it required supervision.[203] Other freedmen, like M. Calpurnius Epinicus at Alastus, were

presumably leaseholders, but not all *misthotai* were outsiders. The *misthotai* at Köse Abdulla, where Appuleia Concordia and Aelius Faustus owned prop-erty, at the village of the Aralleis, and at Cihanbeyli all seem to have been local men, who were wealthy enough to afford the rents which the landowners demanded.[204] In the last instance, the fact that the two leaseholders mentioned by the inscription were also high priests confirms their high status in the locality. Direct administration of private properties by *oikonomoi* (*vilici*) was also widespread, perhaps in combination with *misthotai*, as in the Asian estates, but probably more often as the sole method of managing smaller properties. Appuleia Concordia's interests were in the hands of an *oikonomos*, and the term occurs also on inscriptions from Laodicea, presumably referring to the agents of private landowners rather than the emperor.

The leasehold system does not seem to have pre-vailed in the imperial estates of Galatia. The *choria Considiana* in north-west Galatia were compact enough to have been run by an Imperial slave *oikonomos*, without the supervision of a procurator.[205] The cen-tral Galatian estates were surely administered from Laodicea, where we find not only a series of freedmen procurators, but also a whole structure of domainal administration in the hands of freedmen and slaves, including an *adiutor tabulariorum*[206] and an *instru-mentarius tabulariorum*,[207] both freedmen, a *cancell-arius*,[208] mounted couriers (Ch. 9 § II at nn. 81–6),[209] and other slaves with unspecified duties.[210] In the presence of so much other evidence, the absence of *misthotai* who can be linked with these imperial properties with any certainty seems significant and suggests that they were not used. The peasants would have paid over the required portion of their produce directly to the imperial slaves, as they would have done in the *choria Considiana*.

Faustina; their son Ti. Cl. Severus Proculus was the husband of the Annia Faustina mentioned in inscription (2). See Halfmann, *Senatoren*, 180–1 no. 101.

[200] See the προάγων in inscriptions (4) l. 9 and (5) l. 9. For the ὄχλος see Sterrett, *EJ* nos. 47–50, and below, Ch. 11 § IV n. 183.

[201] Inscr. (2) l. 8; (3) l. 4.

[202] The texts are (*a*) Collignon, *BCH* 2 (1878), 173–4 = Sterrett, *EJ* no. 78 = *CB* i. 307 no. 114 = *IGR* iv. 894; (*b*) Sterrett, *EJ* no. 79 = *CB* i. 307 no. 115 = *IGR* iv. 895. Cf. also *CB* i. 308 no. 14 = *IGR* iv. 897 mentioning a μισθωτής in the area as late as AD 255.

[203] See above, n. 70.

[204] See above nn. 112, 119, 122.

[205] See above, n. 94.

[206] *MAMA* i. 31 with Robert, *Hellenica* xi/xii. 388. See T. Drew Bear, *Nouvelles Inscriptions de Phrygie*, 10–11 for a critical examination of the attestations of this post in Asia Minor. The duties of *tabularii* principally involved accounting, see G. Boulvert, *Esclaves et affranchis impériaux*, 420–5 and P. R. C. Weaver, *Familia Caesaris*, 241–3, cited by Drew Bear, loc. cit.

[207] *MAMA* vii. 524.

[208] W. M. Ramsay, *Ath. Mitt.* 13 (1988), 243 no. 24 quoted in *MAMA* i. p. 21.

[209] *MAMA* i. 27 and 30, with L. Robert, *Rev. phil.* 3: 13 (1939), 207–11. See above, Ch. 9 § II nn. 81–6. Note the *tabellarius* or courier attached to a private estate near Vetissus, *MAMA* vii. 322. For bibliography on *tabellarii* see Drew Bear, *Nouvelles Inscriptions* 10 n. 42 and KP² 43 no. 75 with note (*TAM* v. 2. 1125).

[210] *MAMA* i. 25–31.

11 Rural Anatolia

1. *Two Views from the City*

Aelius Aristides resumed his encomium of the Roman empire with a reflection on the safety of travel:

Travel is now easy since the whole world is like one man's home country. The Cilician Gates, the sandy passes from Arabia to Egypt, mountains that can scarcely be crossed, broad rivers and barbarian tribes hold no terrors for the wayfarer.[1]

Behind this confident claim it is not difficult to detect a lurking fear of the countryside and its hazards. When Aristides later delivered a speech at the dedication of the imperial temple at Cyzicus, there is similar apprehension in the paragraph which extolled the richness and variety of the city's territory:

The land is extensive and all extremely productive, so that you might judge it to be a continent from its size. There are many types of countryside, largely distinct from one another but all tending to the best. Mountains here are even less forbidding than plains beside other cities, and the plains themselves are sufficient not merely for a city but for nations. There are rivers, lakes, marshes and woodlands—the good cheer, one might say, of the gods.[2]

City dwellers in the Roman empire, even at the height of its prosperity, routinely feared both the natural and the man-made dangers of the countryside,[3] but Aristides had particular reasons to share the general unease. He had been born in AD 117 in the depths of rural Mysia, on the territory of the future city of Hadriani, whose foundation still lay some fourteen years in the future.[4] This area, settled by the tribal groups who occupied the northern slopes of Mysian Mount Olympus, later to be a famous haunt of monks and ecclesiastical refugees during the iconoclastic period,[5] was as uncivilized as any part of western Asia Minor.[6] The brigands of Mysia were notorious in Xenophon's day, and Cicero, congratulating his brother on his administration of Asia in 57 BC, mentioned them in a paragraph that would sit happily enough in Aristides' *Roman Oration*:

Under your government cities which have been destroyed and almost deserted have been rebuilt by your efforts; there is no sedition and discord in the towns; you have seen that the communities are governed by the counsels of the best people; brigandage has been removed from Mysia; murders have been kept to a minimum and peace established throughout the province, so that robbery has been banished not only

---

[3] R. MacMullen, *Roman Social Relations* (1974), 1 ff.; B. D. Shaw, *Past and Present*, 105 (1984), 9–10.

[4] Philostratus, *VS* 2. 9 (251K); C. A. Behr, *Aelius Aristides and the Sacred Tales* (1968), 1–3; *AJPhil.* 90 (1969), 75 ff. correcting the date of birth. For the foundation of Hadriani see E. Schwertheim, *Epigr. Anat.* 6 (1985), 37 ff. and *I. Hadr.* pp. 156–7. Estates belonging to Aristides have been located in the hilly country between Lake Manyas and Balıkesir (Robert, *Ét. anat.* 207 ff.; Behr, *Aelius Aristides and the Sacred Tales*, 5–7), that is between the cities of Poemanenon and the supposed site of Hadrianutherae. On these grounds Philostratus who records Hadriani as Aristides' birthplace is thought to have made a confusion with Hadrianutherae. For decisive arguments in favour of Philostratus, see E. Schwertheim, *Festschrift für T. Pekary* (1989), 249–57. Even the site of Hadrianutherae remains uncertain, despite Robert, *Villes*², 389 n. 3.

[5] See above all the *Life of St Peter of Atroa*, ed. V. Laurent, *Subs. Hag.* 31 (1956); and the *Vita Retractata in Subs. Hag.* 31 (1958)); and the *Life of St Joannicius* (*AASS* Nov. ii. 311–435). Discussion in Robert, *Villes*², and R. Menthon, *L'Olympe de Bithynie* (1935); and below, Vol. II, Ch. 18 § II at nn. 52–3.

[6] See L. Robert, *BCH* 102 (1978), 437–52.

[1] *Or.* 26K. 100: νῦν γοῦν ἔξεστι καὶ Ἕλληνι καὶ βαρβάρῳ καὶ τὰ αὑτοῦ κομίζοντι καὶ χωρὶς τῶν αὑτοῦ βαδίζειν ὅπου βούλεται ῥᾳδίως, ἀτεχνῶς ὡς ἐκ πατρίδος εἰς πατρίδα ἰόντι· καὶ οὔτε Πύλαι Κιλίκιοι φόβον παρέχουσιν οὔτε στεναὶ καὶ ψαμμώδεις δι' Ἀράβων ἐπ' Αἰγύπτον πάροδοι, οὐκ ὄρη δύσβατα, οὐ ποταμῶν ἄπειρα μεγέθη, οὐ γένη βαρβάρων ἄμικτα, ἀλλ' εἰς ἀσφάλειαν ἐξαρκεῖ ῥωμαῖον εἶναι, μᾶλλον δὲ ἕνα τῶν ὑφ' ὑμῖν.

[2] *Or.* 16K. 9–10: πολλὴ μὲν γῆ πᾶσα καὶ ἄφθονος καὶ ὡς ἄν τις ἀξιώσειεν κατ' ἐπωνυμίαν τὴν ἤπειρον εἶναι τὸ μέγεθος, πολλαὶ δὲ αἱ φύσεις καὶ πλεῖστον ἀλλήλων κεχωρισμέναι καὶ πᾶσαι νενούσαι πρὸς τὸ βέλτιστον, ὄρη τε γὰρ ἐνταῦθα ἡμερώτερα τῶν παρ' ἀλλήλοις πεδίων, πέδια τε ἀποχρῶντα οὐ πόλεως ἀλλ' ἐθνῶν εἶναι, καὶ ποταμοὶ καὶ λίμναι καὶ ἕλη καὶ νάπαι, μακάρων δή τινες εὐθυμίαι. For the occasion see Price, *Rituals and Power*, 155–7, 251–2.

from the roads and the countryside but also from the cities and townships.[7]

In this string of generalities the name of Mysia stands out, and the tradition recurs in later writers. Strabo spoke of the thick forests of Olympus which made an ideal refuge for brigand bands, where local 'tyrants' could hold out against legitimate authority for long periods.[8] Arrian wrote the biography of one such robber chieftain, Tillirobus,[9] and Galen of Pergamum compared the conspiracies and deceits of quack doctors and pseudo-sophists with the brigands of his own country who assisted one another's cause by injuring others but sparing themselves.[10] Inscriptions show that this is no literary topos. A decree of the second or first century BC from Aeolian Temnos mentions three men honoured by the city of Smyrna for rescuing some of its citizens who had been carried off by bandits,[11] and other late Hellenistic texts reveal a man abducted and killed by brigands around Miletupolis,[12] and a citizen of Bithynian Apamea who died in Egypt but who had earned fame for protecting his native Asia from bandits.[13] In the early empire Aristides' native region of Hadriani honoured a local prefect (ἔπαρχος) who died in a brigand ambush.[14] This impressive concentration of evidence for a phenomenon which is under-represented in both the literary and the documentary sources,[15] shows that Mysian banditry posed a significant hazard even during the *pax Romana*. In one episode Aristides was almost driven from one of his properties by a violent posse of peasants mobilized against him. When he tried every trick in the early 150s to avoid being made eirenarch and taking charge of law enforcement in his native town, he would have had more than a merely financial incentive to dodge the burdens of this particular office.[16] His attitudes to the countryside will have been shaped and given focus by his knowledge of the dangerous rural environment into which he had been born.

The intimate and detailed jottings of the *Sacred Tales*, that tangled recollection of dreams and real experiences, open a window on to some of these attitudes. In general, Aristides paid little attention to the rural environment. From time to time, responding to the instructions of the god Asclepius, he made forays off the main roads to rural sanctuaries, or to rivers where winter bathing was prescribed, or once to a stretch of valley near his estate at Laneion where he was to perform a ten-stade run; but the surroundings do not impinge on the narrative.[17] Twice he alludes to healthy country produce, as when, in a dream, his old nurse brought him eggs and apples to eat, or his host at Phocaea brought fresh milk from a ewe that had recently given birth on the remote margins of his estate.[18] But none of these episodes reveals his general loathing of the countryside with the clarity of his travel narratives. In AD 143, early in his career as a budding orator[19] he went to Rome, overland by the *via Egnatia* as far as Dyrrhachium, and thence presumably to Brundisium and along the *via Appia*. It was, as he was to recall later, a miserable excursion.[20] He was in poor health when he set out, in the depths of winter travelling from his family estates to the Hellespont and then along the main Roman road through Thrace and Macedonia to Edessa, where illness forced him to stop. He had been on the road for a hundred days when he reached Rome. The worst of the journey was in Thrace.[21] There was rain, frost, snow, and icy wind; the Hebrus which should have been crossed by boat was frozen over; inns were rare and their roofs leaked. Despite all Aristides pressed on at speed, even outstripping the military couriers and rounding up reluctant barbarians from the roadside to act as guides, if he could before they fled to avoid being pressed into this unwelcome service.[22] The journey thus described led to Rome where he was to deliver the Roman oration, with its resounding paragraph about the ease of travel in the empire. Aristides returned by sea—and was shipwrecked *en route*.[23]

In Asia Aristides repeatedly traversed the axis that cut across the north-west corner of the peninsula from Smyrna (and once from Ephesus) to Cyzicus, with fixed points at Pergamum and at his family estates in Mysia. These domestic journeys have the same frenzied hallmarks as the expedition to Rome. From his estates he frequently went south to Pergamum, on one occasion claiming to have covered the 300 stades (about fifty kilometres) 'at a run'.[24] Another regular excursion was

[7] Xenophon, *Hell.* 3. 5. 26; Cicero, *Q. Fr.* 1. 1. 25; cf. *Hell. Oxyrh.* 16. 1, εἰσὶ γὰρ πολλοὶ τῶν Μυσῶν αὐτόνομοι καὶ βασιλέως οὐκ ὑπακούοντες.

[8] 12. 8. 8, 574 (Cleon of Gordiucome).

[9] Lucian, *Alex.* 2; for the unsuccessful attempts to identify a fragment of this work see Robert, *Ét. anat.* 98 n. 3.

[10] Galen, *de Praecognitione*, 4, 10 (ed. Nutton, *CMG* v. 8. 1, 91–2 = Kühn, xiv. 622).

[11] Robert, *Ét. anat.* 90–5.

[12] Peek, *GV* 1728, re-edited by E. Schwertheim, *Epigr. Anat.* 5 (1985), 80 no. 5.

[13] *SEG* viii. 497; Robert, *Ét. anat.* 95; E. Bérard, *Inscriptions métriques d'Égypte*, no. 10.

[14] Robert, *Ét. anat.* 97; *I. Hadr.* no. 84.

[15] B. D. Shaw, *Past and Present*, 105 (1984), 3–52.

[16] *Sacred Tales*, 4. 63–94.

[17] Ibid. 2. 18–22; 50, 51–3; 3. 20; 5. 49–55.

[18] Ibid. 1. 45; 2. 16.

[19] R. Klein, *Historia*, 30 (1981), 337–50.

[20] *Sacred Tales*, 4. 2 (δυσχερὴς ἔξοδος).

[21] Ibid. 2. 5–7.

[22] Ibid. 2. 60–2.

[23] Ibid. 2. 64–8; 4. 32.

[24] Ibid. 1. 65; 2. 8; 3. 6; 4. 83, 90; 5. 28.

north to the hot springs of the Aesepus valley, probably at the modern Gönen. He speaks of travelling the 240 stades in either direction without stopping in the stifling heat.[25] In AD 165 he left Smyrna in response to a warning and travelled without pause to a favourite shrine, the sanctuary of Zeus which stood near his ancestral estates. Departure was in mid-afternoon and by sunset the party reached a terrible inn at the crossing of the Hermus. Aristides pressed on to Larissa, once a city now a mere village, where the inn was no improvement, and then to Cyme, reached after midnight. Everything was closed down and he rallied his servants to continue; at Myrina they clustered round the door of an inn but could raise none of the occupants; not even Aristides could now cajole his servants to continue and with some difficulty he found a lodging for the rest of the night with an acquaintance. However, he rose from this comfortless rest before dawn, made a detour to the shrine of Gryneian Apollo where he sacrificed, and then reached Pergamum. The party spent some time here before continuing up the plain of the Caicus, where the north wind whipped the dust into their faces, and made straight for the sanctuary, bypassing even Aristides' estate at the end of their journey.[26]

Other journeys were equally rapid. In 152 he left his estate and travelled 160 stades to a farmhouse he owned at the south edge of the Hellespontine plain, sixty of these by night through the mud along a track illuminated only by torchlight.[27] In the late summer of 166 he paid another visit to Cyzicus. A midday start brought him to some hot springs around dusk. There was such a crush of visitors that no lodging was to be found and the party continued. Forty stades further on they reached a village but, as Aristides comments, there was nothing to attract them and they continued by night. The servants finally prevailed on him to stop by the lake (evidently the north-east corner of Lake Manyas) still about 120 stades short of their destination. Aristides was persuaded by the availability of a relatively comfortable inn with a sound roof and a clean mattress. They had already covered 320 stades after a late start, and reached Cyzicus early the next day. On the return journey they covered 400 stades without stopping for food or rest, until they reached Aristides' farm, a little before midnight. The next day they covered the relatively short distance to an estate which Aristides had bought at Laneium, at the edge of the plain of Balıkesir, south of his family home.[28]

If we seek confirmation of Aristides' fear of the countryside, surely it is to be found in these manic forced marches by which he moved from one oasis of safety and civilization to another, between his estate and the cities, sanctuaries, and bathing establishments which provided him with the environment in which he was at home. Aristides' neurosis is emblazoned across the *Sacred Tales*. Travel did nothing to soothe his troubled temperament.

It is reassuring that not all aristocratic city dwellers of the second century viewed the countryside with the blinkered alarm of Aristides, and one contemporary, Galen, saw the same world with very different eyes.[29] Galen's father Aelius Nicon describes himself on an inscription as an architect, and according to his son he was versed in geometry, architecture, mathematical logic, and astronomy.[30] Guided by a dream he made his son study medicine and also gave him a grounding in the subjects that interested himself.[31] He was an enthusiast for farming and retired to the countryside to carry out practical experiments in cultivating cereals and other crops, including nuts, fruits, and green vegetables.[32] Galen assisted in these experiments which not only gave him a considerable knowledge of agriculture, but also an interest in it which emerges in much of his medical writing, notably in his treatises on diet.[33]

The most important of his father's experiments evidently concerned cereals, and Galen's descriptions are detailed and revealing.

My father, when in the prime of his life, became a great enthusiast for farming. He used to sow wheats and barley, carefully picking out seeds of other species which had been mixed in with them in order to find out for certain if grasses or wild wheats were produced by some mutation from the norm or whether their seeds were of a genuinely different

---

[25] Ibid. 2. 6, cf. 4. 42.
[26] Ibid. 5. 1–10.
[27] Ibid. 4. 3–4.
[28] Ibid. 5. 1–18. For the topography, see Schwertheim, *Festschrift Pekary*, 249–57.

[29] Galen's dietary works are to be found in the old edition of Kühn, vol. vi, and in *CMG* v. 4. 2. As an introduction to Galen, J. Ilberg, 'Aus Galens Praxis', *Neue Jahrbuch f. das klass. Altertum*, 8 (1905), 276–312, reprinted in H. Flashar (ed.) *Antike Medizin* (Wege zur Forschung 121, 1971), 361–417, is essential. See too Lynn Thorndike, *A History of Magic and Experimental Science*, i (1923), 117–81; D. Eichholz, *G&R* 20 (1951), 60–71; G. W. Bowersock, *Greek Sophists in the Roman Empire* (1966), 59–75; V. Nutton, 'Galen's Early Career', *CQ* 23 (1973), 158 ff. and his edition of *de Praecognitione*, *CMG* v. 8. 1 (1981). See in particular E. Leiber, 'Galen on contaminated Cereals', *Bull. Hist. Medicine* 1970, 332–45; W. Basler, *Janus*, 2 (1897/8), 116–27, 313–26; J. Klüger, *Die Lebensmittellehre der griechischer Ärzte* (Primitiae Czernovicensis 1911) [the last two not seen by me].
[30] *CMG* v. 4. 2, 392; *PIR*² i. 38: A. 226.
[31] *De Praecognitione*, 2. 12 (ed. Nutton, *CMG* v. 8. 1, 76–7 = Kühn, 14. 608) and Kühn, 10. 609 and 16. 202.
[32] *CMG* v. 4. 2, 261.
[33] *CMG* v. 4. 2, 393.

type ... He discovered that changes and variations of this kind came from different seeds so he instructed the persons who handled the seed to sort out the harmful material when the seed was needed for pure use, and not to be contemptuous of this practice like the millers (σιτοποίοι) in the towns. In a bad year all sorts of darnels grow up among the wheat which are not properly cleaned out by the farmers with the sieves designed for this purpose (because this reduces the total amount of flour they produce) or by the millers for the same reason. The result is that those who eat the bread develop headaches, sores on the skin, and other symptoms of malnutrition.[34]

In another passage Galen describes the various diseases caused by rotten grain or by toxic weeds. These, and especially darnel, were the worst threat to health.[35] Darnel was widely and correctly believed by the ancients to produce illness,[36] and its effects on medieval and modern populations, when it causes symptoms including headaches, delirium, and hysterical euphoria, are widely documented.[37] The weed has the scientific name *Lollium Temulentum*, and infected flour produces 'drunken bread'. Other diseases, as Galen also realized, could be caused by a fungus infection of the wheat which attacked it either while it was growing or in damp storage conditions. Grain storage, therefore, was an important preoccupation for the farmer and Galen records that his father took particular care with another crop, *dolichoi*, a kind of pulse, for precisely this reason: 'They must be thoroughly dried so that they remain sound and unrotted (ἀσηπτοὶ καὶ ἀδιάφθοροί) for the whole winter.'[38] Clearly the main object of the experiments that most interested Galen was to prevent outbreak of disease caused by contamination or infection of the grain.

The experiments themselves, and his wide interest as a natural scientist, naturally brought Galen into contact with the country round his native city and introduced him to a way of life that contrasted sharply with that of Pergamum itself. His discussions of the dietary value of foods in two works, *Concerning*

the Powers of Foods (περὶ τρόφεων δυνάμεως) and *On Digestible and Indigestible Foods* (περὶ εὐχυμίας καὶ κακοχυμίας τρόφεων) abound with distinctions between the rural and urban ways of life, and in particular between rural and urban diet. For example:

Once when I was a boy I ventured into the countryside some distance from the city with two friends of my own age, and we ran into a group of country people who had just eaten a meal. The women were about to bake some bread, for they had none, and one of them threw some wheat into a pot to boil. She seasoned it with salt and offered it to us. Naturally we accepted since we had walked a long way and were hungry. We ate plenty and then felt a sort of heaviness in the stomach, as if mud were lying in it. On the next day we had such bad indigestion and felt so little desire to eat that we could take nothing in at all. We suffered from appalling wind, our heads ached and out eyes watered, but we could pass nothing through our bowels, which is the only remedy for indigestion. I asked the country people how they felt when they ate boiled wheat. They replied that they ate it often, when they had to, as we had done, and that cereal cooked like this was indeed extremely heavy and indigestible—which is clear enough anyway even if one does not try it for onself.[39]

Here is plain evidence, if it is needed, that the country people ate a diet which a city-dweller could hardly stomach, and also that rustics did not opt for this turgid porridge from preference.

Further remarks reiterate the point in connection with a whole range of cereals and vegetable foods. The types of cereal varied from area to area. For instance in Thrace and Macedonia the country people made a particularly malodorous black bread from rye (*briza*).[40] People from the parts of Bithynia which suffered severe winters—Galen mentions Nicaea, Prusa, Crateia, Claudiopolis, and Iuliopolis, as well as Dorylaeum, the last city of Asian Phrygia—regularly grew a crop called *zeopyron*, which was in his view as much superior to *briza* as it fell short of genuine wheat, *pyros*.[41] In Cappadocia the speciality was a crop called naked barley, *krithon gymnon*, which could presumably stand the late frosts, as could another crop called *zeia*, identified with *Triticum Monococcum*, commonly used as an animal feed.[42] In the Mysian countryside with which Galen was most familiar one could find all sorts of wild wheats and barleys (*pampollai tiphai kai olyraï*).[43] In all these cases Galen is describing the low-grade local cereals, used in place of wheat and barley where the land or the climate was unfavourable to

[34] *CMG* v. 4. 2, 261.

[35] περὶ διαφθόρων πυρετῶν I. 4 (Kühn, 7. 285).

[36] Theophrastus (Loeb), 8. 4. 6; Ovid, *Fasti* 1. 691; Pliny, *NH* 18. 156.

[37] Piero Camponesi, *Bread of Dreams: Food and Fantasy in Early Modern Europe* (Eng. trans. 1989); extracts printed in *History Today*, 39 (April 1989), 14–21.

[38] *De alim. fac.* I. 28. 8 (*CMG* v. 4. 2, 256); cf. the epidemic at Massilia in 49 BC, which Caesar, *BC* 2. 22 attributed to the consumption of long-stored millet and stale barley. Grain pits, recorded by Varro, *RR* 1. 57. 1–2, and reported by Pliny in Cappadocia (confirmed by the observations of 19th-cent. travellers), Thrace, Spain, and Africa (*NH* 18. 73, 306) were good for storage provided that air and moisture could be eliminated. Varro, loc. cit. insisted on good ventilation if the grain was stored above ground, as in Italy.

[39] *CMG* v. 4. 2, 227.

[40] *De alim. fac.* I. 13. 8 (*CMG* v. 4. 2, 236–7).

[41] *De alim. fac.* I. 9. 10 (*CMG* v. 4. 2, 237).

[42] *De alim. fac.* I. 13. 22 (*CMG* v. 4. 2, 240); I. 13. 6 (*CMG* v. 4. 2, 236).

[43] *De alim. fac.* I. 13. 18 (*CMG* v. 4. 2, 239).

them. It is revealing that modern distribution maps of cereal production in Turkey show that cereals such as millet are grown more abundantly in these regions, and notably in Mysia, than elsewhere.[44]

The high quality wheat was regularly taken to the cities leaving only inferior products for the country people. This was especially true of the area round Pergamum where the rural inhabitants used always to eat *tiphai* (einkorn) and *olyrai* (emmer) because the wheats were removed.[45] Galen says of oats that they were normally used as animal feed, except when people were driven to make bread from them by extreme starvation, but his comments elsewhere suggest that the country people had to resort to them more often than in times of general famine.[46] The bread produced was obviously not normally fit for city consumption, but Galen remarks that it was particularly good eaten with the country cheese known as *oxygalaktinon*, provided that the cheese was soft and the bread still warm from the oven, when it became a delicacy much sought after even by city dwellers.[47] However, leave it for three or four days and even the rustics could not eat it with any pleasure. Wheat, barley, millet, and crushed chick peas could be boiled in milk or water and the resulting mess was moulded into the form of a cheese, which could be eaten with honey, olive oil, pig's lard, or even salt water. There are several descriptions of such concoctions which were standard fare for 'men living in the countryside and the poorest inhabitants of the city', and an inscription from Aeolian Cyme specifies that a concoction of this sort called χονδρόγαλα was to be distributed to the free-born and slave children of the city.[48]

In a frequently quoted passage from the beginning of *On Digestible and Indigestible Foods* Galen spelled out the implications of this for the health of the country dwellers. The frequent famines which had afflicted the empire in recent years clearly demonstrated the connection between poor diet and disease. After the harvest the city inhabitants would take away all the wheat and barley that they needed for their own annual consumption and a good proportion of the less favoured crops. The country people would have to live on the residue. By the end of the winter supplies would be

exhausted and they would have to rely on wild shoots and roots. The results were abundant signs of malnutrition and serious skin diseases. From the wide variety of skin disorders that Galen lists, it is clear that such conditions were widespread and common.[49]

So much for the cereals. The *agroikoi* did little better with the rest of their diet. While the townspeople ate *ochra* (ladies' fingers) and beans, the country people of Asia, especially of Mysia and Phrygia, generally substituted *lathyrai*, an inferior type of pulse.[50] Vetch, normally a cattle feed, was widely consumed in times of famine, which under the circumstances described could become an almost annual condition.[51] Wild fruits, including blackberries, chestnuts, and strawberries, were a common but unsustaining part of the diet. The country people used to store chestnuts and other wild fruits in ditches as winter feed for pigs. In a time of famine they would have to kill the pigs, and live off the chestnuts themselves—the food, Galen ironically remarks, of Arcadians, when all other Greeks had turned to cultivating cereals.[52] At other times the rustics would eat the green shoots of trees and even a species of lizard, dressed in vinegar or brine.[53] Radishes, which were used as an appetiser in the city, were a staple in the countryside taken with bread and served with other wild vegetables and herbs which the town ignored altogether.[54] Garlic was another standard, and Galen in another work recalls meeting an agricultural labourer who lived on bread and garlic, 'the usual diet of the country people'.[55]

It is not difficult to guess that meat was a rare luxury in the villages, as it is today, except when animals had to be slaughtered for lack of winter feed. Pork was the most favoured meat of the city dwellers, especially recommended for athletes, soldiers, and gladiators.[56] Galen would have had opportunity for the last observation when he had served as surgeon to a gladiatorial troop in Pergamum.[57] Pigs were raised in the country and driven to the towns for slaughter; pig-herding was a common profession for the very poor and for small children.[58] Green beans and cabbage were often cooked

[44] *Admiralty Handbook, Turkey II*, 136.
[45] *De alim. fac.* I. 13. 18 (CMG v. 4. 2, 239) on τίφαι and ὀλύραι which both grow in Asia καὶ μάλιστα κατὰ τὴν παρακειμένην Περγάμου χώραν, ὡς τοὺς ἀγροίκους ἀεὶ χρῆσθαι τοῖς ἐξ αὐτῶν ἄρτοις διὰ τὸ τοὺς πύρους εἰς τὰς πόλεις κατακομίζεσθαι. They should be identified as einkorn and emmer wheat.
[46] *De alim. fac.* I. 14. I (CMG v. 4. 2, 241).
[47] *De alim. fac.* I. 13. 19 (CMG v. 4. 2, 239).
[48] *De alim. fac.* I. 13. 21; 14. 1–2; 15 (CMG v. 4. 2, 240–2); see *Bull. ép.* (1983), 323 p. 134 with discussion and reference to *Noms indigènes*, 348–50.
[49] *De bonis malisque sucis*, I. 1–7 (CMG v. 4. 2, 384–9). quoted by R. MacMullen, *Enemies of the Roman Order* (1967), 253; P. Garnsey and R. Saller, *The Roman Empire: Economy, Society, and Culture* (1987), 97; de Ste Croix, *Class Struggle*, 13–14.
[50] *De alim. fac.* I. 2. 6 (CMG v. 4. 2, 253).
[51] *De alim. fac.* I. 29. 1–2 (CMG v. 4. 2, 257).
[52] *De alim. fac.* 2. 38. 1–4 (CMG v. 4. 2, 304–5).
[53] *De alim. fac.* 2. 39. 1–2; cf. 58. 2 (CMG v. 4. 2, 306, 321).
[54] *De alim. fac.* 2. 68 (CMG v. 4. 2, 328).
[55] Kühn, 10. 865.
[56] *De alim. fac.* 3. 1 (CMG v. 4. 2, 332–7).
[57] Kühn, 13. 599–600; 18b. 567.
[58] e.g. *TAM* v. 1. 317.

with pork, but men in the country had to make do with goat or mutton[59]—if that.

Only in one respect did the country have the advantage—its cheese. 'Of all the cheese in the world', wrote Galen with justified pride 'the best is that which we produce in Pergamum and in the hills of Mysia, known to the natives as *oxygalaktinon*. It has the sweetest taste, does least harm to the stomach, and is the most readily digestible of all cheeses.'[60] In spring, before the sun had burnt up the best pasture, cheese and yoghurt must have been the only things which saved the peasants from starvation when their cereals had been consumed. A diet of yoghurt and cheese, traditional recipe for longevity in modern dietary folk-lore, was thought to have similar properties in the ancient world. Galen reports meeting a centenarian farmer who had spent all his life in the country and lived almost exclusively on goats' milk, bread which he broke in pieces and dunked in it, a little honey, and some thyme. He goes on to say that anyone who ascribed the old man's robust health exclusively to this diet was clearly mistaken, and anyone who tried to

follow it would indubitably come to harm.[61] Galen remained a man of the establishment.

II. *Ethnic Diversity*

These views of the countryside of north-west Anatolia, presented by two highly sophisticated urban observers, point to a vast difference between the life and culture of the cities and of the rural areas in Mysia, a region where the world of upland Anatolia encroached closely on the civilization of the Aegean and Propontic coastal areas.

It is a large and daunting task to make further sense of the multifarious yet seriously inadequate evidence for Anatolian rural life in the Roman period—but an essential one, since villages were, from first to last, the bedrock of communal life in Asia Minor.[62] Ancient writers rarely concerned themselves with rural life, and with few exceptions offer little to fill the gap between

[59] *De alim. fac.* 3 (CMG v. 4. 2).
[60] *De alim. fac.* 3. 16. 3 (CMG v. 4. 2, 354). Note the remark in *de bonis malisque sucis* (CMG v. 4. 2, 398) that goat's milk was commoner than any other at Pergamum.

[61] *De sanitate tuenda*, v. 7. 10–11 (CMG v. 4. 2, 148).
[62] See Broughton, *Roman Asia Minor*, 628: 'the villages were the natural centres of the agricultural people—the native tillers of the soil, the shepherds, and the herdsmen—and are still so in Turkey today. They seem to be almost indestructible and have remained in all regions regardless of racial stock, political organization, vicissitudes of conquest, or degree of culture.'

Fig. 27. Tombstone from Koca (Göce) Köy in the lower Tembris valley on the imperial estate known as the *choria Considiana*. The four panels of the stone illustrate the possessions of a prosperous village couple. Top left: vine, pruning hook, small axe, basket, table, three jugs (for wine?), beaker; top right: mirror, comb, wool-carding comb, spindle and distaff, low stool, locked chest with two scent vessels and a basket; unidentified object; bottom left: sandals, goad with tassel, lamp, plough; unidentified object; bottom right: sandals; sealed writing tablet? Tombstones with similarly exhaustive illustration of the possessions of the deceased are typical of the region of Phrygian Dorylaeum (*MAMA* v, nos. 40–4, 70–3). Photo by I. W. Macpherson.

Fig. 28. Tombstone of a musician and his family from Appia, upper Tembris valley. Now in Afyon Museum (Inv. no. E. 1410, 421). In the pediment two swallows on either side of a distaff and spindle. Male and female bust in the upper panel. The lower panel contains a set of reed pipes. Inscription below, Τατιον Ἀλεξάνδρῳ ἀνδρὶ κὲ ἑαυτῇ ζῶσα κὲ τὰ τέκνα αὐτῶν Ἀλέξανδρος κὲ Ἀσκλας κὲ Ἀλεξανδρεία ἐτείμησαν τοὺς γονεῖς μνήμης χάριν. (By pipes) ἐπιμελησαμένου Διοδώρου κὲ Τρόφιμος γάνβρος.

Fig. 29. Marble tombstone from the upper Tembris valley, now in Ankara Roman Baths Museum. In the arch male and female busts with a wreath, a fruit, and a small altar inscribed ἱερῖς (priests). The inscription in the *tabula ansata* below has been erased. Above the vine-decorated pilasters were a pruning hook to the left and a carding comb, distaff, and spindle to the right. The main panel shows a female bust with a carding comb, basket and fruits, and a naked male figure, carrying a wreath filled with fruits, with a dog to the left and a whip to the right. This may be Hermes who accompanied the dead to the other world. In bottom panel a yoke of oxen with a plough and a dog. Very fine work of about AD 220. F. Miltner, *JÖAI* 30 (1937), *Beibl*, 54–5 no. 59.

Fig. 30. Marble transport near Docimeium. *MAMA* iv, no. 32; Waelkens, *Türsteine*, no. 486 from the region of Afyon, now in Afyon Museum. The object at the top is a stretcher with a marble block on it identified by the inscription λεικτικαρ⟨ι⟩ῳ. In the upper panels of the doorstone are (left) a female figure accompanied by a child with a comb and basket containing distaff and spindle, and (right) a male figure who is identified by the inscription as Ὀνήσιμος Θεοῦ δοῦλος. He was un-doubtedly a Christian, and the three bun-like objects on the table beside him may represent the *panis eucharisticus*; Christians in late Antiquity regularly adopted the formula 'slave of God' on their gravestones. Below is a cart drawn by two oxen carrying two marble blocks and followed by a male and a female figure. This is evidently one of the heavy wagons known as *protela* which are mentioned in the transport dispute inscription from nearby Sülmenli, *JRS* 46 (1956), 55 ff. l. 4. Probably third quarter of the third century AD.

27

28

29

30

Rural gravestones

idealization and contempt. Galen's pages from his dietary treatises are a rare exception and even they see their subject unambiguously from a townsman's perspective. Furthermore there has been scarcely any archaeological excavation of non-urban sites of the Graeco-Roman period,[63] and no regional surveys have yet been sufficiently intensive to provide a reliable picture of the density and nature of rural settlement.[64] There remain, as always, the inscriptions, abundant in the countryside as in the cities. But even here there are inherent and serious limitations. Almost without exception they are Greek texts, and as such provide evidence for a Greek cultural overlay which may obscure some or all of the non-Greek native culture. Most of the more elaborate inscriptions from villages, which illustrate communal organization or activities, have close points of resemblance with the public epigraphy of the cities, and therefore throw light not on typical village organization but on the development of exceptional villages which aspired to higher status and a more sophisticated culture.

The aspect of rural Anatolian culture which is most completely obscured by the use of Greek inscriptions is that of language. By the time of the Roman empire almost the only languages used for inscriptions in Asia Minor were Greek and Latin.[65] In the classical and Hellenistic periods it is possible to point to texts inscribed in Aramaic and even Phoenician,[66] as well as in native languages such as Carian, Lycian, Lydian, and the various Pamphylian dialects.[67] Few traces of these

remained by Roman times. Strabo implies that Carian was still spoken in his own time around Caunos and elsewhere;[68] Lycian and Lydian had been superseded at least as written languages by the second century BC, although Lydian graffiti from Sardis should possibly be dated to the Roman imperial period and the language was still to be heard in the Cibyratis in Strabo's day;[69] none of the Pamphylian dialects attested at Side, Lyrbe, Perge, Sillyon, and Aspendos outlived the Hellenistic period. Strabo again, noting the penetration of Greek in north-west Asia Minor, remarked that most of the inhabitants had cast aside their native languages and their native names.[70] But the interior and the remoter regions of the north and east were much more resilient. Mithridates of Pontus, champion of Anatolia against Roman imperialism in the first century BC, was master of twenty-two languages spoken in his north Anatolian or Pontic kingdom (see above, Ch. 7 § II n. 73). Words belonging to a Pontic language were still in use in late Antiquity although they may be no more than isolated survivals absorbed into the local Greek dialect. In an account of the martyrdom of St Hyacinthus of Amastris, it is recorded that the saint cut down a sacred tree and was tried by a judge who required an interpreter to understand him.[71] In the territory of

---

[63] A village site near Ancyra: B. Tezcan, *Yalıncak*, Middle East Technical University Publication 1971; a late Hellenistic farmstead in eastern Anatolia: S. Mitchell, *Aşvan Kale I. The Hellenistic, Roman and Medieval Site* (1980); for Hellenistic Gordium see above, Ch. 4 § VI at nn. 112–14; later remains have been excavated at many prehistoric sites of central and eastern Anatolia, pointing to modest occupation between the Hellenistic and Byzantine periods, but recording techniques have usually been primitive and negligent.

[64] J. M. Cook, *The Troad* (1973) is a partial exception but makes no claims to have covered the ground with the thoroughness of much recent field-work carried out in Greece. The only comparable field-work in Turkey is W. Radt, *Siedlungen und Bauten auf der Halbinsel von Halikarnassos, Ist. Mitt. Beiheft* 3 (1970).

[65] Among the exceptions there are Hebrew inscriptions produced by the Jewish communities of Akmonia (*MAMA* vi. 334), Smyrna (*CIG* 9897 = *Corpus Inscriptionum Judaicarum*, ii. 739 = *I. Smyrna*, 844a) and Sardis (see G. M. A. Hanfmann, *Sardis from Prehistoric to Roman Times* (1983), 171). See below, Vol. II, Ch. 16 § III.

[66] The Aramaic texts have been collected in H. Donner and W. Röllig, *Kanaanäische und Aramäische Inschriften*, vols. i–iii (1962–4; 2nd edn. 1966–9); Phoenician inscriptions have been noted in the coastal regions of Plain and Rugged Cilicia; see most recently P. G. Mosca and J. Russell, *Epigr. Anat.* 9 (1987), 1–28.

[67] For a general view of the epichoric languages of classical Asia Minor see G. Neumann, in G. Neumann and J. Untermann,

Die Sprachen im römischen Reich der Kaiserzeit (1980), 167–85. Lycian texts: E. Kalinka, *TAM* i; G. Neumann, *Neugefunden Lykische Inschriften* (1979); Carian: O. Masson, *Bulletin du société linguistique de Paris*, 68 (1973), 187–213; Lydian: *Sardis* vi. 1 (1916) and 2 (1924); R. Gusmani, *Lydische Wörtebuch* (1964); *Neue Epichorische Schriftzeugnisse aus Sardis* (1958–71), (1975); Sidetan texts: Cl. Brixhe, *Kadmos*, 8 (1969), 54–84 and 143–61; G. Neumann, *Ann. Scuola normale Superiore di Pisa Lett. e Phil.* ser. 8 (1978), 869–86; Sidetan even seems to have been used for literary purposes, J. Nollé, *Epigr. Anat.* 2 (1983), 86–98; for Sidetan as typical of the non-Greek settlements of eastern Pamphylia, including the site at Şıhlar which should now be identified as Lyrbe, not Seleuceia, see J. Nollé, *VI Araştırma Sonuçları* (1988), 257–9. Whereas Sidetan appears to be a completely epichoric language, inscriptions at Perge (*SGDI* 1265 ff.), Aspendos (G. E. Bean, *Jahrbuch für kleinasiatische Forschung*, 2 (1952/3), 201 ff.; *Belleten*, 22 (1958), 58 ff.), and Sillyum (LW 1377, Paribeni and Romanelli, *Mon. Ant.* 23 (1914), 73 ff.) appear to show a dialect of Greek, much influenced by native languages. This is the situation described by Arrian, *Anab.* 1. 26 (with Bosworth's valuable commentary). See above all Cl. Brixhe, *Le dialecte grec de Pamphylie* (1976).

[68] Strabo, 14. 2. 3, 652, cf. 14. 2. 28, 662.

[69] Gusmani, *Neue Epichorische Schriftzeugnisse*, A. iii. 1 identifies a possible Lydian stamp on a Roman tile, but no other Lydian material can be placed securely after the 3rd cent. BC. See n. 72.

[70] Strabo, 12. 4. 6, 565: τὰς διαλέκτους καὶ τὰ ὀνόματα ἀποβεβλήκασιν οἱ πλεῖστοι.

[71] See G. Neumann, *Die Sprachen...*, 167–85 citing the *Life of Eutychius* (patriarch of Constantinople), *PG* lxxxii. 2. 2333c, which cites the word κωλῶθις meaning unleavened bread, used by a Greek-speaking child of Amaseia. For Hyacinthus, see F.

the Cibyratis on the border of Asia and Lycia, four languages could be heard in the time of Strabo: Pisidian, Solymian, Greek, and (surprisingly) Lydian.[72] As they approached the Roman colony of Lystra Paul and Barnabas were hailed by the native, non-Roman inhabitants in Lycaonian.[73] Galatians, like Syrians, who used the oracle of Glycon at Abonuteichos in Paphlagonia, needed an interpreter for their enquiries; and Celtic was spoken in rural Galatia throughout late Antiquity (see above, Ch. 4 § v). Galen indeed, who was a pedantic stickler for the use of good Greek, attacked those who would without good reason introduce to their discourse three words from Cilicia, four from Syria, five from Galatia, and six—from Athens.[74] The final thrust leaves it unclear whether he had in mind foreign words or dialectal aberrations from 'proper Greek'.

The evidence of Christian writers provides compelling confirmation of the survival of indigenous languages.[75] Bendidianus a Mysian visitor to the monk St Auxentius, who lived at the monastery of Rufinianae on the river Scopas in eastern Bithynia, belied his dignified demeanour with his barbarian language: 'in his speech he was a barbarian originating from Mysia, but in his good judgement he was utterly reverent.'[76] Remarkably a stone found in a remote part of the territory of Aezani in northern Phrygia carries a seven-line text which is thought to be in Mysian. It has been dated no later than the fourth century BC.[77] One of the legends of St Martha of Antioch, mother of Symeon the Thaumastorite, shows that a pilgrim to her tomb from Lycaonia spoke only in his own language (τῇ ἰδίᾳ διαλέκτῳ), for he had no knowledge of Greek.[78] The phraseology proves that the 'dialect' in question was a native language, not barbarized Greek.

It is even possible that the two monasteries of the Lycaonians in Constantinople, named after their sixth-century founders, Modestus and Eutychianus, used the native language for the liturgy, like similar establishments for Latins, Egyptians, Bessians from Thrace, and Syrians.[79] Neighbouring Isauria, whose inhabitants were identified with the Solymi by a church historian,[80] certainly retained its native tongue in its mountain retreats. A builder who had worked as a stonemason in the Isaurian colony of Syrian Antioch was saved from death by Symeon Thaumastorites, a miracle which was acclaimed in their own language by his fellow countrymen when he returned home.[81] It is reasonable to assume that the Pisidians, who appear much less frequently in late sources than the Isaurians, also preserved their language, although the only attestation comes from inscriptions of the imperial period: namely a series of simple gravestones from the territory of Tymbriada, which exhibit Pisidian names with their native, non-Greek morphology; and two lengthy as yet undeciphered texts, which have been found in the territory of Selge.[82]

Further east the linguistic situation in Cappadocia may have been still more complicated. Even sophisticated Cappadocians spoke Greek with a thick accent,[83] but their less privileged fellow countrymen spoke other languages which were known to the fourth-century Fathers of the Cappadocian Church and even supplied an argument for contemporary Christological debate.[84] Further, Cappadocia had long contained pockets of Iranian settlement, and Basil in the 370s provided a detailed description of the fire-worshipping Magusaioi who doubtless still spoke in their own tongue at least

Halkin, *Hagiographica Inedita Decem, Corpus Christianorum ser. Graec.* 21 (1989), Ch. 5 with H. Chadwick, *JTS* 42 (1991), 363–4.

[72] Strabo, 13. 1. 65, 613. Links between Lydia and Caria, if not N. Lycia and the Cibyratis, are well attested, in particular at Sardis. Croesus' mother was a Carian, Herodotus 1. 171, and Carian was used by an emigrant community at Sardis, see G. M. A. Hanfmann and O. Masson, *Kadmos*, 6 (1967), 123–5 and Gusmani, *Neue Epichorische Schriftzeugnisse*, 81–8, 106–11. See in general J. Pedley, *JHS* 94 (1974), 96–9.

[73] Acts 14: 11–12.

[74] Galen 8. 585 (Kühn).

[75] K. Holl, 'Das Fortleben der Volksprachen in Kleinasien in nachchristlichen Zeit', *Hermes*, 43 (1908), 240–54; see also R. MacMullen, *AJPhil.* 87 (1966), 1–17.

[76] *Life of St. Auxentius, PG* cxiv. 1428B: τῇ γλώττῃ μὲν βάρβαρος ὑπῆρχεν ἐκ τῆς Μυσίας ὁρμωμένος, τῇ γνώμῃ δὲ πάνσεμνος.

[77] C. W. M. Cox and A. Cameron, *Klio*, 25 (1932), 34–49; not re-edited in the quasi-corpus of Aezani, but cited as *MAMA* ix. P332.

[78] The story cited from manuscript sources by Holl, *Hermes*, 43 (1908).

[79] Holl cites extensive evidence for the use of native languages by monastic communities in Constantinople, including Armenian, Bessian, Syriac, Coptic, and Latin. The case for Lycaonian, however, is not proven.

[80] Theodoret, *Historia Religiosa*, 10 (*PG* lxxxii. 1392A).

[81] For the MS source, see Holl, loc. cit. Isaurian builders were famous and widely travelled. Holl cites Greg. Nys., *Ep.* 25; the *Life of Martha, AASS Mai* V, 418c, 421a, 422; Theophanes, *Chron.* for the year 6051, 232, 29 (de Boor).

[82] All the texts to date have come from a single find-spot, the village of Sofular, close to the source of the river Eurymedon S. of Lake Eğridir. W. M. Ramsay, *Revue des Universités du Midi*, 1 (1895), 353–62; J. Borchhardt *et al.*, *Kadmos*, 14 (1975), 68–72; Cl. Brixhe and E. Gibson, *Kadmos*, 21 (1982), 130–169; and Cl. Brixhe, T. Drew Bear, and D. Kaya, *Kadmos*, 26 (1987), 122–70 (with an excellent series of illustrations) between them publish all the texts. J. Nollé reports the find of epichoric inscriptions near Selge, *VIII Araş* (1991), 218–20 and *I. Selge*, pp. 17–19.

[83] Philostratus, *VS* 2. 13K.

[84] Greg. Nys. *Contra Eunomium*, 12, *PG* xlv. 1045D (the Cappadocian word for heaven); Basil, *De spiritu sancto*, 29 (ed. Pruche, *Sources chrétiennes* (1945), 252); R. Teja, *Organización social e económica de Capadocia*, 79 ff.

for ritual purposes (see below, Vol. II, Ch. 17 §IV at n. 147).

The fullest evidence survives from Phrygia. Socrates in his Church History mentions the Arian bishop of Cotiaeum Selinos, of mixed Gothic and Phrygian origin, who used both languages (apparently Phrygian and Gothic) for his preaching.[85] Cotiaeum was a city which had produced a sophist, Alexander, one of the teachers of Aelius Aristides, and its inhabitants prided themselves on their 'wisdom'; Hellenism had also penetrated the rural parts of their territory in the upper Tembris valley south of the city, where verse inscriptions and reliefs depicting styluses and writing cases offer ample evidence of literacy among the mixed pagan-Christian population of the second to the fourth centuries AD.[86] For all that, Phrygian was still in use, as is shown not only by the remark of Socrates, but by a neo-Phrygian curse formula added to a gravestone of the early third century.[87]

Epigraphically Phrygian is by far the best attested of the native Anatolian languages in the imperial period. More than seventy tombstones have been found in central and eastern Phrygia, spanning the provincial boundary between Asia and Galatia, mostly but not exclusively from rural sites, which add a Phrygian curse formula to otherwise unremarkable Greek epitaphs of the second or third centuries AD.[88] The use of such curse formulae in itself is characteristic of native non-Hellenized populations in Anatolia (see below); there was perhaps an element of additional menace in using the colloquial language of the vernacular to the routine formality of a Greek gravestone. These 'neo-Phrygian' inscriptions revived a language which had not been written or inscribed for centuries. 'Old Phrygian' is known in the main from monumental inscriptions of between the eighth and sixth centuries BC, that is from the time when the Phrygians were a dominant power in central and north-west Anatolia.[89] Between this early series and the texts of the later imperial period there is only a single Phrygian document, but it is one which perfectly illustrates, although it does not explain, the earliest impact of Hellenization on this native culture.

Docimium had been founded as a Macedonian settlement by Dokimos, one of Alexander's own followers, and its earliest inscribed documents are two early Hellenistic grave steles of the late fourth or early third century BC. One carries an eight-line funerary text in Phrygian, with the Greek names Nikostratos in the nominative and Kleumakhos (Kleomachos) in the dative case. Its counterpart carries a much briefer Greek inscription for Tatis daughter of Nikostratos and wife of Theophilos.[90] This family, which clearly belonged to the local aristocracy, had almost immediately assimilated itself to the new Graeco-Macedonian settlers by adopting their style of funerary monument. The father, Nikostratos, and the other men had taken Greek names, but the inscription which he set up for an older relation was carved in Phrygian; the daughter still bears a Phrygian name, but her epitaph was in Greek. The irresistible lure of Hellenization for native aristocracies which came in contact with the Greek world is patent, but the survival of Phrygian as a living language in rural areas and among the poorer people for nearly a thousand years after this first encounter is equally strong evidence for the tenacity of the native culture.

Of course the Greek language was widely if unevenly adopted in the countryside of Anatolia. This was not simply for the purpose of inscribing gravestones, dedications, and other documents, for the dialect and morphology which rural Greek texts display provide clear evidence that the language was alive on the lips of the peasants as well as carved on their gravestones. A study of the Greek language of Asia Minor inscriptions shows that civic epigraphy consistently offers an orthodox regular language of high culture, barely differing from the language of fourth-century-BC Athenian orators, and reflecting the cultural sophistication of the city-dwelling aristocracy. Meanwhile the inhabitants of the countryside spoke a variegated demotic, where assimilation of cases and tenses to one another, and local pronunciation swiftly deformed the written language into something very different from the inscriptions of the cities. It is common to describe this rural epigraphy as 'barbarous', but it is clear that the cause of the 'barbarization' was not the contamination of Greek by native languages, but the ways in which Greek became the language of rural dwellers, through haphazard processes of learning and assimilation not through the schooling of the gymnasium.[91]

[85] Socrates, HE 5. 23; a more confused version in Sozomen, HE 7. 17.

[86] For culture at Cotiaeum see W. Ruge, RE xi. 1 (1922), 1526 ff. For literacy in the upper Tembris valley see below, Vol. II, Ch. 17 §X at nn. 433–6.

[87] Waelkens, Türsteine, 96 no. 226; (O. Haas, Die Phrygischen Sprachdenkmäler (1968), 127 no. 97).

[88] Collected by Haas, Die Phrygischen Sprachdenkmäler, reviewed by Brixhe, Rev. de Phil. 42 (1968), 306–19, to be updated by recent finds: Kadmos, 20 (1981), 68–75; Verbum, i. 1 (1978), 3–21.

[89] M. Lejeune and Cl. Brixhe, Les Inscriptions paléo-phrygiennes; Cl. Brixhe and T. Drew Bear, Kadmos, 21 (1982), 64–87.

[90] T. Drew Bear, III Araş (1985), 257–9.

[91] Cl. Brixhe, Essai sur le grec anatolien au début de notre ère (1984); cf. id., 'La Langue comme critère d'acculturation: l'exemple du grec d'un district phrygien', Hethitica VIII. Acta Anatolica E. Laroche oblata, ed. R. Lebrun (1987), 45–80: 'dans les cités les classes privilégiées parlent une variété linguistique strictement codifiée et normalisée depuis

From these illustrations of the linguistic complexity of Roman Anatolia, it seems reasonable to conclude that between the few who spoke no Greek at all (perhaps in particular women who had less contact outside the household with commerce, officialdom, or public life) and the larger minority who had been cut off completely from their native cultural and linguistic heritage by absorption into city life, a majority of the inhabitants of Asia Minor were in some measure bilingual in Greek and an indigenous language.

In the absence of substantial direct evidence for the native languages themselves, the nature of the ethnic diversity of Anatolia can most readily be illustrated by identifying and classifying the non-Greek nomenclature, which is particularly striking in the rural areas of the centre and in the Taurus mountains. These native names fall into regional groupings, smaller or larger, which doubtless correspond more or less with tribal or ethnic patterns. Intensive study has led to the definition of sharply localized linguistic and cultural groups; such detailed results tend to be provisional and controversial, but the broad outlines are clear and it is possible to offer a crude but coherent reconstruction of Anatolia's ethnic geography on the basis of the onomastic evidence. The north-west regions of Bithynia and the south shore of the Propontis were, as Strabo remarked, extensively Hellenized, and the percentage of native name-types in Hellenistic and imperial inscriptions is low. However, they include a very distinct group of names with strong Thracian affiliations: Diliporis, Mokaporis, Auloukentos, Kamoles, and others which confirm the information provided by Strabo and earlier writers that the population was of Thracian origin, and that close racial ties linked the European and Asiatic inhabitants of the Propontic area.[92]

The routes from Cyzicus and the Hellespontine plain, and from Bithynia led inland to the upland areas of Mysia and especially Phrygia. As the coastal plains gave way to the broken forested country through which the rivers of the north-west run—the Sangarius, the Rhyndacus, the Macestus, and the Aesepus—and then emerged on to the bare expanses of high plain and plateau, nomenclature and population changed. The Bithyno-Thracian name-types were replaced by simpler

Phrygian forms, Tatas, Appas, Nanas, Manes, Meiros, and many others, which predominate across central Anatolia. Of course there was no clear dividing line between these regions, as may be illustrated by the inscriptions from the territory of Mysian Miletupolis, a remote Greek colony on the fringes of the Hellespontine plain but in an area which was also seen as part of Phrygia. The names include Thracian types—Mokaporis, Dindiporis, Diliporis, Doedalses, and the ethnic Dandaenoi—Phrygian types (including several 'Lallnamen' which, though liable to occur in other cultural contexts are particularly characteristic of Phrygia)—Abbeiktis, Amion, Ammia, Attinas, Baba, Babeis, Manes, Mania, Midas Morkis, Nan(n)ia, Nia, Tados(?), Tatein, and -ineis—and even three Celtic names, as evidence for the Hellenistic Galatian diaspora—Ateporis, Arteinos, and Katomaros.[93]

Once on the plateau the ethnographer is confronted with the huge, ill-defined and culturally ambiguous territory of Phrygia itself, which extended east to the salt lake Tatta, and south to Iconium, the so-called Paroreius around Pisidian Antioch and Apollonia, and the upper reaches of the Maeander valley.[94] Although it is surrounded on every side by 'Übergangsgebiete', where Phrygian names jostle alongside those of their neighbours, there is a sharp difference between this nomenclature and that of the Tauric mountain districts of the south: Rugged Cilicia, Isauria, and Pisidia, including the lowland adjuncts of Lycaonia to the north and Pamphylia to the south. Throughout this southern highland area there is more common ground than regional diversity in the onomastic remains, and it is clear that the Taurus mountains, more than anywhere else, preserved the linguistic culture of late Hittite Anatolia and the Luwian language.[95]

In the north, Galatia provided a distinctive linguistic enclave clearly reflected in local toponymy and nomenclature (see above, Ch. 4 § v) while neighbouring Paphlagonia retained affinities with the population of the north side of the Black Sea, with which there were (and are) long-standing commercial and cultural ties.[96]

---

longtemps. Sa contrepartie écrite est representée par la langue des prosateurs, des textes officiels, mais aussi de certains documents privés. Langue écrite et langue parlée divergent considérablement... mais après tout pas plus qu'aujourdhui le français écrit et le français parlé, tels qu'ils sont enseignés.'

[92] See L. Robert *apud* N. Fıratlı, *Les Stèles funéraires de Byzance* (1964), and S. Mitchell, 'Onomastic Survey of Mysia and the Asiatic shore of the Propontis', *Pulpudeva. Semaines philippopolitaines de l'histoire et de la culture thrace*, ii (1978), 119–27 esp. 120–3.

[93] See the index to E. Schwertheim, *I. Miletupolis*.

[94] For a recent definition of the cultural boundaries of Phrygia, see Waelkens, *Türsteine*, 13–15, 42–4, which is largely in agreement with the excellent article of W. Ruge, *RE* xx. 2 (1941), 791 ff. Attempts that have recently been made, e.g. by C. Naour, *ZPE* 44 (1981), 11–44; *Epigr. Anat.* 2 (1983), 107–41; *Études et travaux en Turquie*, 2 (1984), and *Epigr. Anat.* 5 (1985), 37–76, to treat NE Lydia as part of Phrygia turn a blind eye to the transitional features of the culture of this region. Cf. P. Herrmann, *Anz. Wien*, 122 (1985), 149–59 and the well-known observations of Strabo (n. 98).

[95] H. ten Cate, *The Lycian and Luwian Population Groups* (1961).

[96] Robert, *Noms indigènes*, 449 ff.

In the south-east, and to a much greater extent, Cappadocia looked towards Persia.[97]

These non-Greek peoples of Anatolia belonged to a bewildering diversity of tribal groupings.[98] The subdivisions of Mysia included the Abbaeitans, the Abbrettenoi, and the Olympeni;[99] in Phrygia there were the Epicteteis of the north and north-west, the Moxeanoi, the Hyrgaleis, and the Lycaonians of the interior; to the south there were the mixed peoples of the Paroreius between Phrygia and Pisidia, the Orondians, the Homonadeis, extinguished by Augustus (see above, Ch. 6 nn. 75–7), and a plethora of smaller tribes.[100] In Galatia the Celtic tribes retained their separate identities, as did the possibly Celtic Trocnades to the west (see above, Ch. 4 nn. 12–14). In the south there were Lycaonians, Isaurians, Pisidians, Milyadeis,[101] and the Cilician Cietae,[102] to name only the most prominent. Lydians still identified themselves as Hyrcanians, or Mocadeni, and in the back-country behind Ephesus there were the upper and lower Cilbiani.[103] Among others the Milyadeis, the Orondians, the Hyrgaleis of the middle Maeander valley (*MAMA* iv. 315), and the Lycaonians had a recognized central organization, a *koinon*, to be distinguished from the larger provincial *koina* which formed the basis for the organization of the provincial imperial cult.[104]

When Rome first began to organize its Asian province and establish formal legalized relationships with the communities of western Anatolia, the *senatus consulta* and other official documents refer not only to cities, but to *demoi* and *ethne* as independent communities, often containing groups of Greeks and Roman citizens within them.[105] As cities were founded throughout the late Hellenistic and imperial periods these tribal groupings gradually recede from view as they were reconstituted as *poleis*, but the tribal origins were rarely obscured totally: new cities such as

Temenothyrae, Silandus, and Bagis, on the boundary of Lydia and Phrygia, emerged as the centres of the Mocadeni,[106] or Pappa and Misthia in the Pisido-Phrygian borderland, became the cities of the Orondians.[107] The case of the Mocadeni perfectly illustrates a familiar point, that the geographical lines of distinction between these tribal groupings was notoriously hazy in Roman times. Indeed one of their cities, Temenothyrae, was generally classified as Phrygian, the others as Lydian.[108] The pragmatic Roman decisions to decide provincial and *conventus* boundaries according to different criteria are readily understandable.

III. Villages and Rural Communities

There has been much scholarly discussion about the legal and social status of the rural population of Anatolia in the pre-Roman period. Few rural dwellers were recognized as full citizens of civic communities, even where these were well established on the west coast or in the river valleys that ran up towards the interior, but they are often described as *perioikoi*, *paroikoi*, *katoikoi*, non-citizen *kōmetai*, or simply as the common people, the *laos*.[109] Several texts, notably a letter of Antiochus II announcing the sale of land at Zeleia near Cyzicus complete with its resident rural population, to his former wife Laodice,[110] and the famous inscription from Sardis which gives details of the estate of Menemachus, which included inhabitants, settlements, and all their resources,[111] imply that these country dwellers were effectively serfs, tied to the land with obligations to provide the landowner with labour and produce, although they could not be bought and sold as slaves. It has been acutely observed that this was exactly the condition of the sacred slaves or *hierodouloi* of eastern and south-eastern Anatolia in

[97] *Noms indigènes*, 519; cf. R. Teja, 'Kappadokien in der Prinzipätszeit', *ANRW* ii. 7. 2, 114–15.

[98] For the notoriously hazy boundaries between these groups, see Strabo, 12. 4. 4, 12. 8. 3, 12. 8. 10, 13. 4. 10–11, 13. 4. 12; Broughton, *Roman Asia Minor*, 628.

[99] See now E. Schwertheim, *I. Hadr.*, pp. 133–48.

[100] Such as the Sedaseis, Psekaleis, Gorgoromeis, Pedaieis(?), and others; A. S. Hall, *AS* 21 (1971), 125 ff., esp. 155–8.

[101] See A. S. Hall, *AS* 36 (1986), 137–57.

[102] A. Wilhelm, *AEMÖ* 17 (1894), 1 ff.; Magie, *RR* ii. 1364–5.

[103] Magie, *RR* ii. 784; *I. Eph.* vii. 2, 3701–30; *Bull. ép.* (1982), 311 and 384; L. Robert, *Études Déliennes*, *BCH Suppl.* i (1973), 476–8.

[104] The *commune Milyadum* is mentioned by Cicero, *Verr.* 1. 95, cf. Hall, *AS* 36 (1986), 148–9; for the *koinon* of the Orondians see Robert, *Hellenica*, xiii. 76 ff. and Hall, *AS* 28 (1968), 62–3; and for the Lycaonian *koinon*, Aulock, *Lykaonien*, 24–32 with S. Mitchell, *ANRW* ii. 7. 2, 1064–5.

[105] *OGIS* 427–9; *IGR* iv. 297, T. Drew Bear, *BCH* 96 (1972), 286 ff.

[106] See P. Herrmann, *TAM* v. 1, p. 1.

[107] See n. 104, adding Magie, *RR* ii. 1173–4.

[108] Herrmann, *TAM* v. 1, pp. 1, 12–13 (Bagis), 18–19 (Silandus); T. Drew Bear, *Chiron*, 9 (1975), 275–302 provides a convincing demonstration that the third city of the Mocadeni, Temenothyrae, belonged to Phrygia. For all that a native of Lydia, Pausanias, says that it was Λυδίας τῆς ἄνω πόλις (1. 35. 7).

[109] See Broughton, *Roman Asia Minor*, 629 ff.; Wörrle, *Stadt und Fest*, 141–5 esp. 144 n. 382; *Chiron*, 8 (1978), 236–45; 9 (1979), 83–111; P. Briant, *Journ. Econ. Soc. Hist. of the Orient*, 18 (1975), 165–88; P. Debord, 'Populations rurales de l' Anatolie greco-romaine', *Atti del centro di ricerche e documentazione sull' antichità classica*, vii (1976/7), 43–69; de Ste Croix, *Class Struggle*, 147–58.

[110] Welles, *Royal Correspondence*, no. 18; note τοὺς ὑπάρχοντας αὐτοῖς λαοὺς πανοικίους.

[111] *Sardis* VII no. 1; cf. P. Briant, *Actes du colloque de Besançon sur l'esclavage 1971* (pub. 1972), 93–133; *Index (International Survey of Roman Law)*, 8 (1978/9), 48–98, and op. cit. (at n. 109), 165–8.

the time of Augustus, specifically at Comana Pontica and at the great sanctuary of Antiochus I of Commagene on Nemrud Dağ.[112] This may represent a survival, in these distant and unhellenized areas, of conditions which were widespread in early Hellenistic Asia Minor, and not confined to temple states.

In certain unusual circumstances, rural populations were given full citizen status. This occurred at Pergamum in 133 BC, when the city authorities, in conformity with the will of Attalus III, gave citizen rights to much of the rural population of what was now civic territory.[113] The text is worth citing at some length not because it provides the basis for a general view of the status of the rural Asian population, but for the diverse and complex situation which it reveals:

the people resolved to give citizenship to the undermentioned: to those included on the lists (ἀπογραφαί) of the *paroikoi*, to the soldiers settled in the city and in the countryside, and similarly to the Macedonians and Mysians, to the settlers listed in the garrison and in the old city, and to the Masdyeni and..., and also to the rural guards (παραφυλακῖται) and the other free persons (ἐλεύθεροι) settled in or with rights of property ownership in the city or in the countryside, together with their wives and children. Also the descendants of freedmen and the royal slaves, whether adults or the younger men, should be given the status of *paroikoi*...

The terminology makes it plain that rural settlement was far from uniform, and analogies with better-documented societies suggest that any attempt at a sweeping general classification of the rural dwellers of Asia Minor is likely to mislead.[114] The details also show how the military history of the third and second centuries BC had made a deep impact on the pattern of rural settlement and created new hierarchies of status among the population. A later document from Roman Asia, an Ephesian decree of the mid-80s BC, shows that citizenship was offered to the native rural population precisely to secure their loyalty against Mithridates VI.[115]

The diversity of rural status at this period was also to some degree matched by a diversity of rural settlement types. In the *senatus consultum* of 39 BC, by which Rome conferred privileges on the people of Plarasa and Aphrodisias, their assets are listed, specifically and exhaustively, as 'fields, localities, buildings, villages, estates, strongpoints, mountain pasture, and revenues.[116] Similar lists can be compiled from documents relating to Mytilene, Pisidian Termessos, Carian Stratonicaea,[117] and from the definition of Caria contained in the treaty of Apamea of 188 BC.[118] Although there is no reason to doubt that the bulk of the rural population of Asia Minor lived in villages during this period, the primacy of the village as a unit of social organization was not unchallenged. Estate-ownership and the establishment of military garrisons, whether to defend the interests of dynasts or of cities, provided alternative frameworks of organization to which villages were subordinate. Complicated, ill-defined, and perhaps contradictory patterns of relationship helped to articulate the loose power structure which linked kings, garrisons, cities, villages, estates, serfs, and slave communities in Hellenistic Asia Minor.

By the time of the Roman empire, and certainly by the second century AD, the picture had changed and become simpler. At this period there is relatively little direct evidence for the lower status of rural inhabitants. Strabo describes the servile condition of the native Maryandeni on the territory of Heraclea Pontica as akin to that of the helots of classical Sparta,[119] and an

[112] Strabo, 12. 3. 34, 558; *IGLS* I. 1 = *OGIS* 383, ll. 171–89 with de Ste Croix, *Class Struggle*, 154, who gives further references.

[113] *OGIS* 338 (trans. M. M. Austin, *The Hellenistic World*, no. 211). In l. 18 all the standard editions read ἐ[πικού]ρους instead of ἐ[λευθέ]ρους, which is obviously right, see L. Robert, *BCH* 109 (1985), 481–2 = *Documents*, 535–6. K. Rigsby, *TAPA* 118 (1988), 130–7 has recently suggested that this much-discussed text comes not from Pergamum but from another city in the region, possibly from Stratonicaea in the Indeipedion. This is incorrect: the royal freedmen and slaves make sense at Pergamum as they would not elsewhere, the Masdyenoi clearly come from the same community as οἱ ἀπὸ Μασδύης of Pergamene ephebic lists and Masdye must be a village on Pergamene territory (Robert, *Villes*, 52; *Ét. anat.* 155). The soldiers ἐν [τῆι πόλει τῆι] ἀρχαίαι, which is probably to be distinguished from any part of Pergamum itself, could have been stationed at the settlement founded by Pergamum's legendary founder Teuthras, the nearby hill of Teuthrania. Rigsby also offers no convincing explanation of how a large inscribed block from a site in the upper Caicus valley should have been transported to the theatre at Pergamum. The only significant problem is the dating of the stone by an eponymous priest not by a prytanis, but as Rigsby concedes, this is not without parallel even if it remains unexplained. See also P. Gauthier, *Bull. ép.* (1989), 249; SEG xxxviii (1988), 1266.

[114] For the unclear status of serfs and the diversity of servile conditions in medieval society see the remarks of de Ste Croix, *Class Struggle*, 147 and cf. Wörrle, *Stadt und Fest*, 143–4.

[115] *SIG*³ 748 = *I. Eph.* no. 8.

[116] J. M. Reynolds, *Aphrodisias and Rome*, Doc. 8, 58–59; cf. *CR* 34 (1984), 295.

[117] Sherk, *RDGE* no. 25. 1. 13 (ἄγροι, τόποι, οἰκοδομίοι at Mytilene), *ILS* 38 l. 24 (*res, loci, agri, aedificia* at Termessos); Sherk, *RDGE* no. 18, 98, and 105 (πολιτεῖαι, προσόδοι, χωρία, κωμαί, λιμένες at Stratonicaea).

[118] Livy, 37. 56: *oppida, vici, castella, agri*.

[119] Strabo, 12. 3. 4, 542. For other references to the Mariandyni see Magie, *RR* ii. 1192 n. 24, and Robert, *A travers l'Asie Mineure*, 5–10. In the 3rd cent. BC the Greek colonists of Byzantium 'exercised mastery over the Bithynians as the Spartans over the helots', Phylarchus, *FGrH* 81 F 8, cited by

inscription from neighbouring Prusias ad Hypium distinguishes the citizens, οἱ ἐγκεκριμένοι, from those who lived in the countryside, οἱ τὴν ἀγροικίαν κατοικοῦντες. Both were to benefit from a single act of liberality.[120] There are hints, but no more, in Dio of Prusa and the younger Pliny that rural inhabitants of other Bithynian cities had lower status than full citizens.[121] Such distinctions were rare elsewhere in Roman Asia Minor. *Paroikoi* occur at Sillyon in Pamphylia, and 'those living in the territory' were distinguished from city inhabitants at Pisidian Termessos.[122] An inscription from Pisidian Antioch separates *coloni* from *incolae*, but here the division may not have been between urban and rural, but between full Roman citizen members of the Augustan colony, and natives with lower status.[123]

It would be absurd to use this evidence to argue that Roman administration was intent on and successful in securing a better deal for the rural population of Anatolia. Instead we should deduce that the former gradations of rank and status, which had been produced in some measure by random events in Hellenistic history, had become redundant and supplanted by a new perspective on the urban–rural divide. The realities of village life in Asia Minor, which in themselves will have changed little, now appear in a different light against the changed social and political backdrop of Roman rule.

Throughout the entire peninsula the villages remained the essential elements of rural settlement, variously called *kōmai*, *katoikiai*, *chōria*, *dēmoi*, or simply

identified by a toponym.[124] A small selection of evidence may serve to illustrate the point. A recently published inscription from Oenoanda (Termessos Minor) in northern Lycia, dating to AD 125, is the only source which appears to contain an exhaustive list of rural settlements on a city's territory. Thirty-two named communities, defined as *kōmai*, were required to send sacrificial animals for a quadrennial musical festival run by the city: in one case they were organized into a group of twelve villages for this purpose; in another as a group of three, a *trikōmia*; five times as groups as two, *dikōmiai*; while the rest were liable as single communities. All or most of these groupings also had subordinate isolated farmsteads (*monagriai*) which were to share the burden of contributing to the festival. Village magistrates were either *archidekanoi*, a term which may have a bearing on the policing of the countryside (see below, § VI) and is unusual elsewhere in Asia Minor, or, more neutrally, *demarchoi*. In essence it is clear that the territory of Oenoanda was divided between the thirty-two villages, which were directly responsible to the civic authorities.[125]

A rapid survey of other parts of Asia Minor shows that circumstances were similar elsewhere. According to a Byzantine excerptor Caria south of the Maeander was settled *kōmēdon*, by villages, and Strabo indicates that the league which met at the sanctuary of Zeus Chrysaoreus consisted of villages, and the communities with the largest number of dependent villages, such as Ceramos, had the biggest say in the league's voting procedures.[126] At the opposite side of Anatolia, the modern Merzifon Ovası attached to Amaseia was known in Antiquity as the *Chiliokōmon*, the plain of a thousand villages.[127] Between Caria and Pontus lay ancient Phrygia and Galatia, rural Anatolia *par excellence* and the pattern is unaltered. The pattern of Phrygian settlement appears most clearly in the third-century inscriptions of the cult organization called the *Xenoi Tekmoreioi*, found at their sanctuary in the north-west corner of the territory of Pisidian Antioch. The members come from named communities which stretch from central Pisidia in the south as far north as the area of Synnada and perhaps even to Nacolea. They include the names of some seventeen *poleis* and about 120 villages. A sizeable proportion of the devotees are described as citizens of a *polis* living

de Ste Croix, *Class Struggle*, 149, who also discusses the Mariandyni ad loc.

[120] *I. Prusias*, no. 17. Ameling in his note adduces the provision made for Pontus by Pompey in his *lex provinciae* of 63 BC that children of a Pontic mother should be deemed to be *Ponticus*. This presumably means a full citizen of a Pontic city, and Ameling is surely right to interpret the benefaction as granting Pontic citizen status to the children of citizen mothers and rural inhabitants, as well as to the children of marriages between Pontic women and non-Pontic citizen husbands (for which see S. Mitchell, *Eighth Congress*, 124). He also shrewdly notes that the civic office of *politographos*, which is largely confined to Bithynian cities, should be linked to the fact that under the empire a good proportion of the inhabitants of the province were not yet full citizens of the *poleis*.

[121] Dio Chrysostom, 45. 13; Pliny, *Ep.* 10. 86b on *pagani*. Note also the distinction drawn between urban and rural populations in *Ep.* 10. 39 and 96, although these imply nothing about rural status.

[122] *IGR* iii. 800 (ἀπελεύθεροι and παροίκοι), 801 (the same pairing but also slaves freed *per vindictam*, οὐινδικταρίοι [for this rare term in Asia Minor inscriptions see J. R. Rea, *ZPE* 62 (1986), 81–5 (*SEG* xxxv (1985), 1167), rereading and interpreting C. Naour, *Epigr. Anat.* 5 (1985), 56 no. 14); *TAM* iii. 1. 6.

[123] The edict of L. Antistius Rusticus, see above, Ch. 10 § 1 n. 16.

[124] The best general account is in Broughton, *Roman Asia Minor* 627–48; evidence collected by Swoboda, *RE suppl* iv (1924), 961–76; Magie, *RR* ii. 1022–6; see also Price, *Rituals and Power*, 78–100.

[125] Wörrle, *Stadt und Fest*, 12 ll. 72–83; comm. pp. 135–50.

[126] Photius, *Bibl.* 131; ἔθνος μέγα κωμῆδον οἰκοῦντες; Strabo, 14. 2. 25, 680. For Hellenistic Caria see Magie, *RR* ii. 1028–30 and S. Hornblower, *Mausolus* (1982), 52–67.

[127] Strabo, 12. 3. 39, 561.

in a particular *kōmē*; for example, there are men of Synnada living in Kandrukōmē, Algizia, Hermokōmē, Daoukōmē, Obora, Algounia, Mandre, Kumalettos, and Peliganos, and men of Iulia living in Andia, to cite examples of only the commonest formula.[128] It is relevant to note that there is no formal difference in status between men of Synnada itself and men from villages on its territory. All, by this date, were Roman citizens. The inscriptions of north-east Phrygia are particularly rich in village names: thirty-five are attested by inscriptions found in the area of Altıntaş, the upper Tembris valley, on the territories of Appia and Cotiaeum or belonging to one of the large imperial estates of that region;[129] a similar number is recorded for the territories of Dorylaeum and Nacolea.[130] These high numbers have been produced by intensive epigraphic exploration; there is not the slightest reason to suppose that they reveal an exceptional preponderance of villages in these regions. For Galatia the best evidence comes in late Antiquity with the Life of St Theodore of Sykeon, which provides the names of twenty-four villages which should be located in north-west Galatia around Iuliopolis, Lagania, and Mnizos (see below, Vol. II, Ch. 19 § 1 at nn. 36–8). The importance of these Galatian villages as the cardinal units of social organization in late antiquity is confirmed by the epitaphs of Galatians found outside Asia Minor, principally in Rome and Italy, who, in contrast to the *Xenoi Tekmoreioi* from Synnada recall their home villages without mentioning any city on their gravestones.[131]

The consistent thrust of Roman administration in the early empire had been to create or recognize *poleis* with clearly defined coterminous territories as the basic units into which the provinces were divided. One important consequence of this development was to define the status of a village, simply as a community subordinate to a particular *polis*. When political considerations determined the fate of cities under the Roman empire, this could produce some highly anomalous situations. Long-standing autonomous cities were demoted to village status, and subordinated to a neighbour as punishment for delinquency, most often for supporting the wrong side in a civil war. Thus Byzantium and Syrian Antioch were temporarily demoted to villages in the aftermath of Septimius Severus' victory over Pescennius Niger just as, at a much earlier date, Lucullus had reduced Tigranocerta to a *kōmē*,[132] and, in a different context, the emperor Julian stripped Cappadocian Caesareia of civic status for enthusiastic anti-pagan behaviour (see below, Vol. II, Ch. 17 § VIII at nn. 367–9).

Anomalies more often occurred when larger villages developed of their own accord to a level more appropriate for city status. Examples are not difficult to find in the largely prosperous times of the second and third centuries, but the process is clearest in the well-known instance of Orcistus, which petitioned Constantine and his praetorian prefect Ablabius in the 320s to be freed from the control of Nacolea and to be made an independent city. Constantine acknowledged the justice of this claim in his letter on the subject to Ablabius:

They have demonstrated that their village in the course of an earlier age flourished with the splendour of a town, so that it was adorned with the usual symbols of magisterial office and was notable for its councillors and had a large population of citizens. For the site of the town is deemed to be a favourable one both on account of its natural position and by man's devising.

The comments, in this case, are borne out by other remains from the site which include honorific inscriptions for Roman emperors, a system of local government capable of setting up and administering a charitable foundation for a local festival in the late 230s, and archaeological traces of public buildings compatible with the place's civic aspirations.[133] In modern terminology we should certainly want to call Orcistus a town, as Constantine chose to do when he refers to it as an *urbs* rather than a *vicus* in his Latin letter. The administrative framework of Roman Asia Minor, however, seems to have had no room for such a category, resulting in Orcistus' unwelcome subordination to the city of Nacolea, which was hardly larger than itself.

It is not difficult to find comparable cases elsewhere. Tyriaion in north Lycia was the centre of a group of five villages, a *pentakōmia*, which were all presumably located in the plain south of Lake Cabalitis (Söğüt

[128] See Ramsay, *SERP* 305–77 esp. 361–71, a now unreliable list. Some of Ramsay's observations on the topography have been superseded by more recent discoveries, and others are clearly fanciful. Since there are many homonyms among the village names of Anatolia it is not always the case that a village known and located from other sources should be identified with a village named in the lists. The northernmost village may be the Τυιτηνοί/Τευιτηνοί (*SERP* 323, 325, 327) who may come from the territory of Nacolea where a Ζεὺς Τουιτηνός is attested (*MAMA* v. 208). The name in this case is unusual. See further, Vol. II, Ch. 16 § 1 at nn. 48–51 on the *Xenoi Tekmoreioi*.

[129] See *MAMA* x introd.; Drew Bear, *ANRW* ii. 18. 1, 1963–4 n. 204.

[130] *MAMA* v index collects eighteen village names; eight more are known from other sources, *MAMA* v. p. xxxi. Recent survey in the area has added several more: P. Frei, *I Araş* (1983), 56–7; *TAD* xxv. 2 (1981), 71–85; *Epigr. Anat.* 11 (1988), 26 ff.

[131] See D. Feissel, *Riv. di arch. christiana*, 58 (1982), 371–7.

[132] Strabo, 11. 14. 15, 532; Cassius Dio 75. 14. 3.

[133] *MAMA* vii. 305. Statue of Commodus, *MAMA* i, 416; foundation of AD 237, W. H. Buckler, *JHS* 57 (1937), 1–10.

Göl). Nominally it was part of the territory of Balbura, but that small city lay to the west, separated by a high mountain range, and there must have been some significant pressure for local autonomy. Tyriaion duly emerged as an independent bishopric in late Antiquity.[134] A little to the north-east there may have been a similar situation at Takina, on the boundary of Asia and the Pisidian limb of the province of Galatia, which could boast its own bath house, built with funds provided by an important local family, by the beginning of the third century. The chief benefactor, Tryphon son of Apollonides, had behaved like any civic dignitary in completing all his local offices and liturgies and making long overseas journeys to petition the emperor Commodus for permission to erect the building.[135] Under Caracalla in 213 Takina received a letter from the emperor offering some hope of protection from the by now ubiquitous illegal depredations of his soldiers.[136] Takina, to judge by these inscriptions, still did not possess a city constitution with council and people, and minted no coins, another useful indication of civic status,[137] but in material development it can surely hardly be distinguished from a place like the obscure Carian city of Euhippe in the Maeander valley, which earned a similar promise of protection from Caracalla in exactly the same period.[138]

Two virtually adjacent areas of central Anatolia, north-east Lydia and north-west Phrygia, well illustrate the narrow line that divided cities and villages in regions where independent *poleis* were a novelty of the Roman period, and where villages large and small had been the usual form of settlement no doubt since remotest antiquity. East of a line drawn between Thyateira, founded by Seleucus I in 281, and Philadelphia, which was probably another Seleucid city,[139] the upper Hermus basin contained no cities in the pre-Roman period.[140] The local population clearly lived in villages, like their Mysian neighbours to the north.[141] The Seleucid and Attalid kings in an attempt to establish their claims to the region and to protect it from incursions from the east had established military colonies of Macedonians (and sometimes of Mysians) across the region, of which there are abundant traces in the epigraphy. None of their *katoikiai* developed into a city before the Roman period.[142] Only under Roman rule was the area divided into city territories belonging to the *conventus* of Sardis: Bagis and Silandus (dividing the territory of the Mocadeni with Phrygian Temenothyrae), Tabala, Collyda, Saittae, Maeonia, Satala, Iulia Gordus, Characipolis, and Daldis.[143] Although none of these cities has been excavated, hardly any developed into a genuinely prosperous urban centre with important public buildings and a flourishing urban upper class and civic culture. Only Saittai, which was an important centre for the commercial production of textiles,[144] and Iulia Gordus seem to have emerged as urban centres of any significance; the others are hardly to be distinguished from the larger villages of the same area (see below, § IV): several of these were governed by magistrates, who were often required to pay *summae honorariae* for the privilege of office like their urban counterparts;[145] they had assemblies and councils of elders which took

---

134 C. Naour, *Tyriaion en Cabalide* (1980), esp. 37 ff. no. 7. For Balbura see the survey reports by J. J. Coulton, in *IV–VI Araş* (1987–9), and *AS* 38 (1988) and 39 (1989); *IGR* iii. 479 = Naour no. 8, a gravestone set up by a soldier of *legio I Parthica* who calls himself Βαλβουρεὺς τῆς κολωνίας γειτοσύνης Πύρου ποταμοῦ, may somehow allude to the ancient status of Tyriaion, but cannot be readily explained.

135 *IGR* iv. 881.

136 D. H. French and S. Şahin, *Epigr. Anat.* 10 (1987) 133–45 (*SEG* xxxvii. 1186) provide a provisional text. Note that the various letters are addressed only to the *demos* and *archontes*, not to the *boulē*.

137 For the *boulē* as a distinguishing feature of cities, see (e.g.) A. H. M. Jones, *CERP*² 286–7; de Ste Croix, *Class Struggle*, 222; *Bull. ép.* (1984), 384. Possible exceptions in Asia Minor include Sterrett, *WE* no. 96 (Artanada in Isauria); Bean and Mitford, *Journeys in Rough Cilicia 1964–68* (1970), no. 246.

138 L. Robert, *CRAI* (1952), 592–6 = *OMS* i. 545–55.

139 For Thyateira see Magie, *RR* ii. 973, 977; P. Herrmann, *TAM* v. 2 (1989), p. 309; Philadelphia may be a Seleucid or

an Attalid foundation, but the recent discovery of an inscription showing that Antiochus I and his son Seleucus awarded a parcel of land to Apollo Toumoundos there between 279 and 267 BC (*SEG* xxxv (1985), 1170) favours the former.

140 See P. Debord, 'La Lydie du nord-est', *REA* 87 (1985), 345–58.

141 See Robert, *Ét. anat.* 191–4 on Polybius 5. 77. There were many Mysian communities in northern Lydia, see Debord, *REA* 87 (1985), 345–8.

142 For Mysians see last note and *OGIS* 338 (n. 113). For Macedonians see Magie, *RR* ii. 972–3: the Lydian settlements are at Nacrasos (*IGR* iv. 1160), Acrasos (Robert, *Villes*², 75 ff. with *OGIS* 290), Thyateira (*TAM* v. 2, 901, 1109, 1166), Doidye and .espura on the territory of Apollonis which later absorbed the Macedonian colonists (*TAM* v. 2, 1188, 1190, cf. 1203 and p. 421), Agatheira (*TAM* v. 2, 1307). Hyrcanis where the city by the time of Antoninus Pius was ἡ Μακεδόνων Ὑρκανῶν πόλις (*TAM* v. 2, 1308, cf. Robert, *Hellenica* vi. 16 n. 3), Kobedyle near Philadelphia (*TAM* v. 1, 221). For a probable Macedonian settlement at Adrouta near Philadelphia see *KP*³ 46–7 and Robert, *Hellenica*, vi. 23. Note also Mysomacedones (Pliny, *NH* 5. 120; Ptolemy, 5. 2. 13 with *KP*³ 58), Macedones in Mysia Abbaeitis in the region of but not at Cadi (Habicht, *JRS* 65 (1975)) and in the nearby Phrygian city of Blaundos (*IGR* iv. 717 with Magie, *RR* ii. 1001).

143 See *TAM* v. 1, *passim*, and the remarks of W. Eck, *BJb* 183 (1983), 853–7, emphasizing the low level of Romanization of the region.

144 H. W. Pleket, *Epigr. Anat.* 12 (1988), 32.

145 *KP*³ nos. 109 and 110, discussed by G. M. Harrer, 'Village Administration in Roman Syria', *YCS* 1 (1928), 142 ff.

an active part in local government,[146] passed decrees (*psephismata*),[147] controlled village revenues, took care of the public water supply and erected public buildings on the civic model.[148] Only an arbitrary decision about status, designed for administrative convenience, will have ordained a difference between *katoikiai* like Lyendos, Ariandos, Apateira, and the Teirenōn katoikia and *poleis* like Bagis, Maeonia, Tmolus, and Hypaepa.

The same is true for north-west Phrygia and the borderland with Mysia Abbaeitis, where cities and *katoikiai* were generally at a lower level of development. This area was divided between the territories of seven cities, five of which, Synaus, Cadi, Aezani, Appia, and Cotiaeum, are securely located, while Ancyra Sidera and Tiberiopolis have yet to be identified with certainty. Of these only Aezani, with its great temple of Zeus and many other ambitious public buildings erected in the second century, and less certainly Cotiaeum, whose remains lie buried beneath modern Kütahya, emerged as significant urban centres.[149] None of the other sites has produced comparable material in the form of monumental public architecture, decrees or other public documents, or abundant civic inscriptions showing the local council and people, with their magistrates, honouring the leading members of the community or Roman dignitaries. On the contrary it is striking that the site of a village, the Goloēnoi near Bahtıllı, has produced the only 'civic' inscriptions from the territory of Ancyra Sidera, in the form of honorific statue bases for Claudius and the three sons of Constantine;[150] that the only honorific statue base found to date at Cadi was put up not by the civic organization of the Roman period but by the tribal Mysian Abbaeitans in the first century BC;[151] and that the city of Appia, whose name was preserved until recently by the modern village name Abya, is quite indistinguishable archaeologically or epigraphically from any other village in the upper Tembris valley. Indeed it is clear that this city, which existed in the time of Cicero and whose territory provided the basis for regional organization in the 240s AD,[152] had to yield priority to a more prosperous neighbour, the

village at Altıntaş, ancient Soa, which became a city with a council and people, by the third or fourth century.[153] As in north-east Lydia, these heavily rural market towns show virtually nothing to distinguish themselves from the larger *kōmai* or *katoikiai* of the region.

IV. *Villagers in Consort: The Organization of Large Villages*

A village was a community. Individual inhabitants and families on the bottom rung of the social and economic ladder could rarely secure the prosperity, or even the survival of their households through self-sufficiency. Mutual help and exchange were an essential feature of village life. Hesiod's *Works and Days*, whose universal proverbial wisdom can be detached from its archaic Boeotian setting with little fear of serious anachronism, makes much of the contrasting themes of autarky and neighbourliness, and the tensions that might be generated between them.[154] Conspicuous by its absence is any reliance on the rich city dwellers, the *basileis*. Class mistrust, if not class struggle, was universal.

A villager naturally turned to his neighbours for help when his own resources failed him. It is tempting to think, then, that villages themselves might, under certain circumstances, develop political structures which reflected and reinforced this community spirit. In Caria in the fourth and third centuries BC, where villages and confederations of villages provided the main form of communal organization, political authority lay with assemblies, *ekklēsiai*, which clearly took decisions in a manner akin to that of democratic city-states of classical Greece (see above, Ch. 7 § 1). Some of the larger villages or small towns of the Roman period, while they lacked a *boulē*, might hold assemblies and make formal decisions as a *demos*. There have been several collections of evidence from Roman Asia Minor which have been designed to show how the latent potential for village organization could develop in the right conditions. However, before a selection of this material is reviewed, its geographical limitations should be stressed. With a handful of readily explicable exceptions, the majority of inscriptions showing signs of elaborate village organization have been found in Lydia, with a smaller number coming from the territories of Nicaea and Nicomedia in Bithynia. These regions were integrated into prosperous market economies readily accessible to and influenced by civic culture and politics. Moreover in Lydia especially, the cities themselves—apart from such major centres as

[146] *TAM* v. 1, 2 (Lyendos).

[147] *TAM* v. 1. 228 (the Sasotreis), 234 (Kula; the mention of βραβεῦται indicates a village inscription, cf. note on *TAM* v. 1. 515).

[148] *TAM* v. 2. 868.

[149] For Aezani see F. Naumann, *Der Zeustempel zu Aizanoi* (1979) and B. M. Levick and S. Mitchell, *MAMA* ix (1988), introd. *passim*. Texts published by M. Wörrle throw new light on the development of the city between AD 125 and 175, *Chiron* 22(1992), 337–76.

[150] See *MAMA* x, Ancyra Sidera, P. 5–8.

[151] *OGIS* ii. 446.

[152] See *MAMA* x, xvi. Cicero, *Fam*. 3. 7. 2 and 9. 1 on Appia.

[153] *MAMA* x, xv–xvii.

[154] See P. Millet, 'Hesiod and his World', *PCPS* NS 30 (1984), 84–115.

Sardis, Thyateira, and on its fringes Pergamum—were late in developing and never became conspicuous centres of cultural influence. The distinction between *polis* and *katoikia* here was a legalistic one, which made easier the administration of the region but did not necessarily reflect a clear-cut hierarchy of social and economic status among the communities (see above, § III). In assessing the nature of Lydian society and settlement in the Roman period it seems more helpful to lay stress not so much on cities and villages as on organized and 'unorganized' communities.[155] The formal distinctions which can be drawn between cities and villages in Lydia, which lay in the right of the former to a *boulē* and to the privilege of minting coin, were less significant than the ways in which they resembled one another.

An assembly of all the people (πάνδημος ἐκκλησία) ratified the foundation of AD 237 at Orcistus.[156] Similar assemblies occur particularly in the larger villages of Lydia: an *ekklesia* comprising the elders and all the other villagers of Castollus near Philadelphia passed a resolution to divide up some mountain pasture belonging to the community; the inhabitants of Tyannollus in the Hyrcanian plain arranged and provided for the financing of local festivals and honoured their benefactors, providing for these to be lauded at all other village gatherings (σύνοδοι). Infractions of these decisions were punishable by fines, and the resolution was to be 'valid for all time, and inscribed at the village's expense (κωμητικῶς) on a marble stele'; at Apateira in the Cayster valley a candidate for the office of *logistes* was required to pay a *summa honoraria* of 250 denarii as a contribution to the recruiting tax (see above, Ch. 9 § III at n. 198), 'as had been decided by the villagers', and another text from the same village mentions a decision of the *syllogos*.[157] Several other inscriptions from this site illustrates how civic norms had penetrated the village environment.[158] Regular village gatherings, whether for transacting business or more likely for ceremonial and religious purposes, are implied by inscriptions from Tamasis, a village of Lydian Saittai, and from the territory of Bithynian Nicaea, which offered a front seat, *prohedria*, for their benefactors.[159] This evidence, however, cannot easily be matched elsewhere in Asia Minor and finds its best parallels in the epigraphy of the larger villages

of second- and third-century Syria, which display a remarkable autonomy and independence of civic control.[160]

It is clear in all these cases that the village assemblies should be matched with other evidence for quasi-urban development. Orcistus became a city under Constantine; Castollus was a well-developed community, if not actually an independent *polis* in the second century BC;[161] Apateira, which enjoyed close and profitable relations with Ephesos and Hypaepa, honoured emperors with statues and could boast a large (and therefore perhaps also a small) bath house; and Tyannollus likewise seems to have made the most of civic benefactors and set up a statue for Trajan.[162] Formal assemblies, one may safely conclude, were not to be found in most Anatolian villages.

Village magistrates are more widely attested and may have been ubiquitous, at least in theory. The Hadrianic inscription from Oenoanda made it one of the duties of the agonothete to see that demarchs were elected in all the villages of the territory, who would be responsible for providing the required sacrificial animals.[163] Every village, then, should have a demarch, elected presumably from and by the local community; but the duty of the agonothete to ensure that a man was in office in the festival year suggests that on some occasions candidates might not have been forthcoming. The valuable information that village headmen were elected is confirmed by the evidence for *brabeutai* in Lydia (see below) and in one other Anatolian village at least, the prosperous Lyrbōtōn kōmē in Pamphylia, where annually chosen komarchs (κατ᾿ ἔτος αἱρούμενοι) were charged with renting out village land so that the revenues could finance sacrifices to Apollo and other requirements for an annual festival.[164] Civic offices, as is now clear from the Oenoanda inscription, were also elective and it is arguable that election procedures, like the payment of a *summa honoraria* for village office at Apateira (see below, n. 172), aped the practice in the cities. Further, it would be naïve to assume that election procedures where they existed were necessarily democratic and reflected the free choice of the people. Nothing could be further from the truth in most civic elections.

Chief magistrates in villages bore a variety of titles.

[155] Price, *Rituals and Power*, 78–100 draws this distinction and illustrates its value.
[156] W. H. Buckler, *JHS* 57 (1937), 1–10 at p. 9.
[157] *TAM* v. 1, 222; v. 2, 1316; KP³ no. 110 with Rostovtzeff, *JRS* 8 (1918), 26 ff. = *I. Eph.* vii. 1. 3246; *I. Eph.* vii. 1. 3247 for the *syllogos*; see also *I. Eph.* vii. 1. 3249a for a similar text.
[158] See below, n. 172.
[159] Robert, *OMS* ii. 883–4 (Bithynia); *TAM* v. 1. 156 (Tamasis).

[160] G. M. Harper, 'Village Administration in the Roman Province of Syria', *YCS* 1 (1929), 105–68; H. I. Macadam, *Berytus*, 31 (1983), 103–15, cf. *SEG* xxxiii (1983), 1248.
[161] See Robert, *Ét. anat.* 159 ff.; *TAM* v. 1, p. 72; but see Debord, *Atti...* (1976/7), 62, and *REA* 87 (1985), 349 on the inadequacy of the evidence for this conclusion.
[162] KP³ 86 no. 116 = *IGR* iv 1666 = *I. Eph.* vii. 1. 3249; *TAM* v. 2. 1317–18.
[163] *Stadt und Fest*, 12 ll. 81–2.
[164] E. S. G. Robinson, *ABSA* 17 (1910/11), 229–31 no. 8; J. Keil, *JÖAI* 23 (1926), suppl. 93–6 no. 2; (*SEG* vi. 673).

The *demarchoi* of Oenoanda seem to be localized, with parallels only in Lycia and Caria.[165] *Kōmarchoi* were more widespread. The office is attested for Armenia in the fourth century BC in Xenophon's *Anabasis* (4. 5. 24), although this fact presumably reveals Xenophontic, not Armenian usage. It is treated as the standard term for village magistrates in the territory of Phrygian Hierapolis (*OGIS* 527), and occurs in Bithynia, in the Phrygian Highlands near Metropolis,[166] and in Lydia.[167] It would be otiose to multiply examples.

Another term which appears particularly in the larger villages of Lydia, and which is also found among the *Xenoi Tekmoreioi*, is *brabeutes*. At Maeonia the crowning of benefactors was to be the annual responsibility of the *logistes* and *brabeutes*, offices which seem to have fused in this case, conducted at a general assembly or synod.[168] The annual crowning of a particular local benefactor at the *katoikia* of Hierakōmē, probably in the first century BC, was again a charge on the annually elected *brabeutes*;[169] and virtually the same wording is used by an inscription found near Thyateira, where 'the annually appointed brabeutai' (οἱ κατ' ἐνιαυτὸν τασσόμενοι βραβευταί) crowned a priest of the imperial cult, probably under Augustus; and on a text from Mostene west of Sardis where the members of an association of Caesariastai and one of their number, who was a nomophylax, had given money to enable the annual *brabeutai* to provide bread and meat (ἀρτοκρέαι) for imperial sacrifices. At nearby Caesarea Trocetta two *brabeutai* of the *katoikia* of the Selindēnoi dedicated a building to the *theoi patrioi* and to Antoninus Pius. The elaborate village inscription from Tyanollus which has already been cited shows *brabeutai* responsible for honorific proclamations (*anagoreuseis*) in village synods.[170] The name of the office itself evokes one of the most characteristic duties of a village official, the arbitration of disputes, although, like most of the evidence for the activities of city magistrates, the surviving inscriptions typically show the *brabeutes* in uncontroversial public roles. There has been some discussion as to whether *brabeutai* should be regarded as strictly village officials, or whether, as the texts discovered at Maeonia and Mostene suggest, they were also found in cities.[171] The difference of opinion is insignificant if the practical distinctions between cities and villages were slight, and the survival of *brabeutai* as magistrates in small Lydian cities can easily be explained as a legacy of previous village status.

Several other terms occur in the large villages of the west, including *logistes* (*curator*), archon, *argyrotamias*, *grammateus*, and *agoranomos*, all of which immediately evoke the world of civic officials. Perhaps the most striking series of examples comes from the Lydian community of Apateira in the Cayster valley, part of Ephesian territory, where between AD 213/14 and 272/3 a series of candidates for the office of *logistes* paid successively 250, 500, 750, and 1,000 denarii as *summae honorariae*, which were devoted, in three cases to the construction of bath-houses.[172] Public accounting, supervising revenues, controlling markets, and documenting or supervising local administration, like the erection of public buildings such as fountains, bath-houses, stoas, and shops, were not activities to be found in most villages, and evidence for them is largely absent from the less well-developed areas of central Anatolia. These details, therefore, should again be treated as an index of the urbanization of more prosperous communities in the hinterland of Ephesus, Sardis, Nicaea, and Nicomedia, where they tend to appear.[173] They are not typically representative of village government or organized communal activity throughout Asia Minor. Elsewhere more anonymous terms for village headmen are common: πρωτοκωμήτης, πρῶτος τῆς κώμης, προάγων, or προέστως occur in unrevealing contexts which indicate neither the manner of appointment nor the usual functions of the office holder.

Even in the well-developed villages there is very little evidence for what village magistrates did, apart from the public, almost ceremonial roles commemorated in inscriptions. Arbitration would be a natural function, by analogy with the earliest magistrates of Greek cities whose tasks, in peacetime, involved not the formulation and execution of policy but the settling of disputes. However, there were obvious limits to the administration of village justice, not only because many matters passed directly to civic authorities or to Roman officials, but also because local misdemeanours were often a matter not for men but for the gods (see below). Another key task would be to represent the village, in particular before Roman officials or the emperor himself. Clearly villagers themselves could stand up and make a case before a procurator, as in the dispute between Anosa and Antimacheia (see below, n. 185, and Ch. 13 § 11 at n. 22), or probably when the village of Mandragora on the territory of Magnesia on the

---

[165] *Stadt und Fest*, 145–6.
[166] *SEG* xxxiii (1983), 980; *IGR* iv. 1669 = Haspels, *Highlands*, no. 31.
[167] KP³ nos. 109, 110; *TAM* v. 2, 868; cf. Robert, *Hellenica*, ix. 33.
[168] *TAM* v. 1. 515 with nn. See also Buresch, *Aus Lydien*, 37 ff.; Ramsay, *SERP* 319 ff. no. 2.
[169] *TAM* v. 2. 1269.
[170] *TAM* v. 2. 903; Buresch, *Aus Lydien*, 7 no. 6; *IGR* iv. 1348; *IGR* iv. 1497; *TAM* v. 2. 1316.
[171] Herrmann, *TAM* v. 1, 515 n.; v. 2, 903 n.

[172] *I. Eph.* vii. 1. 3245–9a (Apateira); 3250–2 (Almura).
[173] See Magie, *RR* ii. 1026–7 for a good sample of the evidence.

Maeander petitioned the proconsul of Asia for the right to hold its own market.[174] The emperor, however, was another matter, especially when the behaviour of his officials was in question; thus it is revealing that the *libelli* addressed to emperors in the third century which requested protection from abuses perpetrated by officials and soldiers (as well as by powerful men from the city) were delivered not by villagers themselves, but in one case by a centurion and *frumentarius*, and in another by a member of the praetorian guard,[175] both soldiers with far greater credibility as complainants than mere country folk. Here we may detect one of the origins of patronage, especially of military patronage for villages in the later empire, when even authorized state rapacity became intolerable.[176]

There is, however, relatively little evidence for city dwellers offering patronage or protection to villagers in the early empire in Asia Minor. The role of a patron in shielding country dwellers from oppression should be distinguished from that of a village benefactor who contributed to its amenities. *Euergetai* appear from time to time in village epigraphy, particularly once again in the quasi-urban communities of Lydia. The inhabitants of Moschakōmē, on the territory of Magnesia ad Sipylum, honoured a man who had been a hereditary benefactor of their village;[177] Tyanollus twice honoured *euergetai*, but in both cases this is symptomatic of the settlement's near-urban character,

and in one the honorand is described revealingly as 'benefactor of the city and of the *katoikia*'.[178] Another example comes from the territory of Mysian Hadrianoi, where the people of Dagouta set up an inscription for a benefactor. Here again, however, Dagouta was no modest village but one of the most important communities on Mysian Olympus, as close to being a city as any settlement in that remote area.[179] The benefactions conferred did not amount to protection of the poor by the rich, but comprised funding for buildings, foundations, food distributions, or other actions characteristic of civic aristocratic behaviour. Two specific examples can serve as illustration: Apateira honoured a benefactor for the bequest of land and produce which was to be used for celebrating the emperor's birthday at a festival of the imperial cult; in similar vein a village near Philadelphia passed a decree on 23 September AD 40, Augustus' birthday itself, thanking M. Antonius Dio for providing the wherewithal for imperial sacrifices.[180] It was generosity of this sort during the imperial peace, not the warding off of danger or crisis, which earned the title *euergetes*. An exception nicely demonstrates the rule. In 28/7 BC the *katoikia* of (N)akokōmē in northern Lydia passed a decree to honour the hereditary priest of Zeus, Attalus son of Apollonius, who had been the common saviour and benefactor of the *demos* and of the *katoikoi*. This was surely on account of services rendered during the troubled period from which the Roman world had recently emerged. *Sōtēr* is the *vox propria* in this case and reveals actions beyond that of a conventional *euergetes*.[181]

Euergetism therefore should not be confused with the patronage that was to emerge in the later empire. The origins of the latter may be found not only in peasants turning to soldiers to argue the case for their interests but more particularly in the relationship of landowners and their agents to the villagers on their domains. The Bithynian village of the Okaēnoi honoured a certain Doryphorus and his wife, the former the *oikonomos* of the estate owner, 'for being their unmatched patrons', διὰ τὸ ἡμᾶς πατρωνεύεσθαι ὑπὸ αὐτῶν ἀσυνκρίτως, and πάτρων appears alongside δεσπότης as a standard description of Bithynian estate-owners.[182] Domainal officials like Doryphorus

[174] J. Nollé, *Nundinas instituere et habere* (1982), 12–58; SEG xxxii (1982), 1149; the petitioner is not named in the surviving section of the inscription, but the language of address, δέσποτα, κύριέ μου, suggests humble status. It is worth noting in this connection that another Lydian text relating to the establishment of a rural market at a village called Tetrapyrgia on the territory of Philadelphia (*TAM* v. 1. 230 as restored by Nollé, op. cit., 58–96) refers to a member of the community doing business on behalf of his father, because the latter could only write slowly (διὰ τὸ βραδέως γράφειν). The inscription from Mandragoreis also mentions οἱ κηδόμενοι τῆς περὶ Μανδραγορειν κατοικίας, whose role seems to have been analogous to that of Eumelus, κηδέμων of the Pylitai, a village in the territory of Magnesia or Tralles (J. Nollé, *Epigr. Anat.* 15 (1990), 121–5). In both cases the 'carers' seem to have been city-dwellers who championed the village cause.

[175] Aragua, *IGR* iv. 528; Scaptopara in Thrace, *IGBulg.* iv. 2237. See the discussion by P. Herrmann, *Hilferufe aus römischen Provinzen*, Ber. Sitz. der Joachim Jungius-Gesellschaft der Wissenschaften, Hamburg, Jahrgang 8 (1990), Heft 4, esp. pp. 51 ff.

[176] More evidence for military officers offering protection for villages comes from an inscription of AD 263/4 on the territory of Nicaea, where a community honours a family group of centurions in return for their benefactions (S. Şahin, *I. Iznik* 1552. The key text for military patronage in the 4th cent. is Libanius' *de Patrociniis, Or.* 47; cf. Harper, *YCS* I (1929), 152 ff.; de Ste Croix, *Class Struggle*, 224 and 584 n. 42.

[177] *TAM* v. 2. 1408.

[178] *TAM* v. 2. 1316, 1317; cf. 1322 from a nearby village.

[179] *I. Hadr.* no. 50; for the settlement see the commentary on no. 27.

[180] *I. Eph.* VII. 1, 3245; KP¹ 43, cf. KP¹ 54 of AD 42/3 and 46 (24/3 BC).

[181] *TAM* v. 2. 1229.

[182] *I. Iznik* 10. 1. 1018; for the village cf. SEG xxx (1980), 859; for patrons on other inscriptions in the area see *I. Iznik*, 2. 1. 1128, 1131; cf. 701, 767, 1057, 1118. Compare perhaps the Muleitōn katoikia, under the direction of their komarchs,

emerged naturally as leaders of village communities on private estates in central Asia Minor (see above, Ch. 10 § III), and harmonious relations between the landowners, their agents, and the peasant ὄχλος,[183] gave villagers their best hope of fair treatment at the hands of government agents or *force majeure* wielded by city dwellers. Not all landowners will have behaved scrupulously, but enough did so for the *coloni* of imperial property in third-century Lydia to threaten to leave the land and work on neighbouring private estates, where they clearly hoped for a better deal.[184]

Conflict between neighbouring villages over land demarcation, grazing rights, or similar issues (see below, Vol. II, Ch. 19 § 1 nn. 65 and 68 for some later evidence) is an ageless theme of village life which surfaces occasionally in the sources. The organization of the transport service, with its heavy demands on the rural population for guides, draft and pack animals, and carts, exacerbated territorial arguments, as is clear from the famous dispute between the villages of Anosa and Antimacheia in central Phrygia, which surfaced three times in thirty years in hearings before the Phrygian procurators at Synnada.[185] A more fleeting glimpse of discord is offered by the inscription set up by a Phrygian sculptor to record that he had built a sanctuary and dedicated a statue of 'Concord of the Villages' near Nacolea, which may reasonably be taken to hint at preceding disharmony now gratefully concluded.[186]

There is a growing body of evidence to show how villages combined with one another, permanently or for shorter periods, to further their own interests. The Oenoanda inscription shows one association of twelve villages, one *trikōmia*, and five *dikōmiai*. It is unclear whether the groupings were *ad hoc* or permanent,

imposed from above by the city authorities or the result of a fusion at grass roots.[187] As with the synoecisms which produced new cities throughout Greek history the original causes might be varied, but the end product was similar, and federations of villages were common. There was a *dikōmia* of the Dablēnoi and the Pronnoētai near Prusa in Bithynia, and another near Nacolea.[188] *Trikōmiai* seem particularly widespread, on the territories of Dorylaeum, Nicomedia, Sardis, and in the upper Tembris valley.[189] There was a *tetrakōmia* on the north shore of Iznik Göl belonging to Nicaea or to Cius,[190] a pentakōmia at Tyriaeum,[191] a Pentakōma in the Cayster valley,[192] and a κωμή τῆς Πεντεφυλῆς near Nicomedia.[193] The modern toponym Mendechora, of the village which has produced the lengthiest surviving Lydian petition of the third century, conceals an ancient Pentechora, perhaps an association of five villages on the imperial estate which united in this complaint.[194] The inhabitants of another imperial estate in north-west Galatia honoured Zeus of the seven villages,[195] there were *Heptakōmētai* in Pontus,[196] and seven χῶροι in northern Mysia combined to set up an honorific statue.[197] In Lycia where the small communities often fused into sympolities of three or four members, there was even an Octapolis in the late Roman period,[198] and in Phrygia Roman administrative demands may have prompted the creation of a single community called 'New Villages', Καίναι Κῶμαι.[199]

More revealing than these lists are inscriptions which show how villages came together for a common purpose. At Oenoanda it was to provide sacrificial beasts, and there was no better reason than a festival. The more prominent rural shrines acted as magnets for the country folk, who would flock to them from dozens of neighbouring villages. The cult centre of the *Xenoi Tekmoreioi* provides the example with the most extensive clientèle, but it can easily be compared with the

---

offering a statue to their *prostates*, the Asiarch M. Aur. Manilius Alexander, at Philadelphia in AD 176 (*IGR* iv. 1635). *Prostates* (see above, Ch. 5 n. 44) suggests their champion in a legal battle.

[183] This is the term used to denote the peasants on the Ormelian estates of SE Asia; see above, Ch. 10 § v n. 200. De Ste Croix, *Class Struggle*, 584 n. 35 rightly notes that the word is not used for an assembly of the people.

[184] The Ağabeyköy inscription, KP³ no. 55: ἀνάγκη τοὺς καταλελειμένους ἡμᾶς, μὴ φέροντας τὴν τῶν κολλητιώνων... πλεονεξίαν, καταλείπειν καὶ ἑστίας πατρῴας καὶ τάφους προγονικοὺς μετελθεῖν τε εἰς ἰδιωτικὴν γῆν πρὸς τὸ διασωθῆναι. Similar circumstances can be detected at Aragua and Scaptopara, cf. Herrmann, *Hilferufe aus römischen Provinzen*, 58–9. The same story in the later empire, R. MacMullen, *Corruption and the Decline of Rome* (1988), 85.

[185] W. H. C. Frend, *JRS* 46 (1956), 46 ff.; T. Zawadski, *REA* 62 (1960), 80 ff.; T. Pekary, *Untersuchungen zu den römischen Reichsstrassen* (1968), 135–8, 148–55; *JRS* 66 (1976), 120–1; B. Levick, *The Government of the Roman Empire* (1985), 57–60 (with trans.).

[186] T. Drew Bear, *Nouvelles inscriptions de Phrygie*, p. 50 no. 26.

[187] Cf. Wörrle, *Stadt und Fest*, 138–9.

[188] Şahin, *Festschrift Dörner*, 773; but the Pronnoetai operate independently in another text of AD 210, *SEG* xxxiii (1983), 980; Drew Bear, *Nouvelles inscriptions*, 50.

[189] *MAMA* v no. 87 with nn.; *TAM* iv. 1; *Bull. ép.* (1974), 580; *IGR* iv. 1367; *IGR* iv. 535; L. Robert, *BCH* 107 (1983), 539 = *SEG* xxxiii (1983), 1150.

[190] *I. Iznik*, 2. 1. 726 = *I. Kios*, no. 7.

[191] Naour, *Tyriaion en Cabalide*, 37 ff. no. 7.

[192] *SEG* xxix (1979), 1151 = *I. Eph.* vii. 1. 3293. Note that it combined with five other villages to honour a burial.

[193] *TAM* iv. 1. 269.

[194] Cf. KP³ 26.

[195] *RECAM* ii no. 37; see above, Ch. 10 § III at n. 94.

[196] Strabo, 12. 3. 18, 548–9.

[197] LW no. 1745.

[198] L. Robert, *BCH* 106 (1982), 318–19 = *Documents*, 280–1.

[199] C. Habicht, *JRS* 65 (1975), 82; cf. L. Robert, *JSav.* (1983), 63 = *OMS* vii. 567 n. 53.

Fig. 31. Tombstone from Sevdiğin in the upper
Tembris valley, around AD 200. Now in Kütahya
Museum; E. Gibson, *TAD* 25 (1980), 68–9 no. 9
(*SEG* xxx (1980), 896). Inscription, Μάρκος κὲ
Ἀμμιὰς Ἀφία θυγατρὶ μνήμης χάριν. τίς ἂν ποσίσι χῖρα τὴν
κακὴν [οὕτως] ἀώροις [περιπέσοιτο συνφόραις]. The
dignified veiled figure of the deceased daughter
embodies the Phrygian qualities of σεμνότης and
σωφροσύνη.

Fig. 32. Late third-century tombstone for a young
girl from the upper Tembris valley. Now in
Kütahya Museum; like many tombstones for young
people the epitaph was largely in verse.

Fig. 33. Broken grave stele from Işıklar Köy, now
in Afyon Museum inv. E. 1978. Male and female
figures standing on a plinth. Below: Phrygian curse
formula.

Fig. 34. Doorstone from Orcistus. The vegetation
shown in the lower two panels contrasts sharply
with the bareness of the surroundings of the town,
shown in Fig. 2.

Rural Gravestones

sanctuary of Zeus Bussurigios in north Galatia, which drew devotees from several villages in the region (see below), or the sanctuaries close to Appia of Zeus Ampeleites, Zeus Thallos, and Zeus Andreas, which were frequented by worshippers from throughout the Upper Tembris Valley.[200] Another important example is the hilltop *hieron* of Apollo Lairbenos on the territory of Hierapolis, which was used by citizens of Hierapolis and the Hierapolitan villages of Mamakōmē and Kroula, Motella, Blaundos, and Dionysopolis.[201] Men came to such shrines not simply to pray and make offerings for themselves and their families, but also on behalf of their communities.[202] Village fraternity flourished in such an environment.

Four inscriptions found at Ihsaniye on the gulf of Izmit near Nicomedia carry the texts of decrees passed by a group of five villages between AD 93/4 and 134/5 which commemorated their own communal festival and its benefactors.[203] The territory of Nicomedia in Antiquity as today is among the most productive agricultural regions of Anatolia, and these texts throw a much rosier light on village life than the gloomy observations of Galen. An annual festival of the goddess and the people was funded by the efforts of magistrates who gave money or goods in pursuit of glory (φιλοδοξήσαντες), and were rewarded with crowns by the community. A wine festival (οἰνοπόσιον) was at the centre of the celebrations, and appears to have been a Bithynian speciality. Another *oinoposion* was held each year at Gölbazar in the territory of Nicaea, where a text honours one of the emporiarchs, Nicadas, who was lifelong oinoposiarch, gymnasiarch, agonothete, and building supervisor for a new temple.[204] Other 'leaders of the wine festival' are recorded in the territory of Nicaea or Cius and near Nicomedia.[205] At Ihsaniye, where festivities probably continued over several days, there were torchlight revelries which could last all night, and rustic jollity acquired a touch of urban sophistication in the form of games (*agōnes*) and activities in the gymnasium.

The best parallel for this folk festival is found at the village of Thiounta on the territory of Phrygian Hierapolis. Two stelai were erected by the village *demos* to honour phratries, each twenty-four strong and taking its name from its leader, whose members variously acted as *agonothetes*, provided oil (perhaps for the gymnasium or for lighting), and gave money for the all-night festival which could run for eight days.[206] The reliefs on the stele are as revealing as the text: at the top the gods are represented by a central standing figure of Zeus, carrying an eagle in his right hand and his staff of authority in the left; immediately to right and left are Demeter holding a winnowing fan and a cornucopia and Hermes with caduceus and a money bag; and beyond them on the right is Helios in a quadriga, and on the left a male god with a staff standing in a rustic cart drawn by a pair of oxen. On the shaft of the stele each of the twenty-four members of the phratry is depicted beside his name, and below stand fourteen oxen lined up for sacrifice, a musical instrument resembling an organ, a flute player and a priest pouring a libation from a phial. The whole scene illustrates communal worship and grateful celebration in honour of the gods who have brought well-being and prosperity to the people of Thiounta. Men and communities might wrangle and dispute; the gods brought them together in reconciliation.

v. *The Rule of the Gods: Authority, Order, and Morality in Village Life*

One of the more satisfactory criteria for distinguishing larger and economically sophisticated villages from small settlements appears in their cemeteries, in the form of tombstones which prescribe that violators of the grave should pay a fine to the village. Examples can be found, predictably enough, in the Cayster valley, less often in the Hermus basin of northern Lydia, and in Bithynia on the territories of Nicaea and Nicomedia.[207] Certain obvious inferences can be

---

[200] The main texts are published by Drew Bear, *GRBS* 17 (1976), 252–3 nos. 9–10; Robert, *BCH* 107 (1983), 549 ff. = *SEG* xxxiii (1983), 1144–56.

[201] For this sanctuary, see below, § v.

[202] For some recent illustrations of this very common phenomenon, see *SEG* xxviii (1978), 1170. 1200; xxxiii (1983), 1153, 1189; *TAM* iv. 1. 72 with P. Herrmann, *Gnomon*, 54 (1982), 127–8. A particularly explicit text is Mendel, *Cat, Mus. Imp.* iii no. 837 from near Cyzicus: Θραικιοκωμῆται τῷ θεῷ τὴν στήλλην καθιερῶσαν ὑπὲρ εὐκαρπίας καὶ ἀβλαβίας τῶν καρπῶν καὶ ὑπὲρ ὑγείας καὶ σωτηρίας τῶν γεοκτειτῶν καὶ τῶν συνερχομένων ἐπὶ τὸν θεὸν καὶ κατοικούντων Θρᾳκίαν κωμήν. The notion of coming together to worship on behalf of the community and its crops is here spelled out in detail. For an interesting group of village dedications found on the territory of Cyzicus, which refer to village festivals and games to be compared with those at Ihsaniye, see E. Schwertheim, *Asia-Minor-Studien* (Münster), 1 (Mysische Studien) (1990), 83–101.

[203] *TAM* iv. 1. 15–18 = *Epigr. Anat.* 5 (1985), 102–8 nos. 7–10; discussed by Robert, *Rev. phil.* (1943), 189–94 = *OMS* i. 364–72.

[204] L. Robert, *REA* (1940), 309 n. 2.

[205] *I. Iznik*, 2. 1. 726 = *I. Kios*, no. 7; *TAM* iv. 1. 20. Note also Şahin, *Festschrift Dörner*, 771–90 = *SEG* xxviii (1978), 980 for Zeus Bennios, involving sacrifice of oxen, burning of incense, the crowning of benefactors, and plentiful measures of wine.

[206] Ramsay, *CB* i. 1. 162–3 nos. 30–33 = *Asianic Elements in Greek Civilisation* (1927), 195–211 with figs. 1 and 2; Robert, *Noms indigènes*, 291–7.

[207] See e.g. *TAM* v. 2. 1296, 1299 (Chōrianōn katoikia); *TAM* v.

drawn from such texts. They show in the first place that fines were one of the means by which a village could raise revenue, they were a source of κωμητικαὶ πρόσοδοι.[208] In almost every case the formula refers to a further fine payable to the city on which the village depended or to the imperial fiscus, and the sum due to the village is always substantially the lesser. It would be misleading to build any far-reaching conclusions on the exact numerical proportion of the two fines, but the phenomenon in a general way well illustrates the subordinate status of even well-developed villages in the hierarchy of settlements.

In other areas, however, the violator of the tomb was threatened not with a fine, but with divine punishment. Religious imprecations replace a legal process. Texts of this sort, with the generalized threat that offenders and their families would be utterly destroyed, can sometimes be found in cities or areas that were largely Hellenized. The region around Cyzicus for instance contains a series of examples, among them the interesting gravestone of a young man, designated as a *mantis* and skilled in Pythagorean wisdom, called Asclepiakos; his name and attributes suggest strongly that he had connections with the oracular shrine of Asclepius at Aegeae in Cilicia, the most important centre of neo-Pythagorean religious and philosophical ideas in the second century AD, which had produced a more famous *mantis* of this period, Alexander of Abonuteichus.[209]

But the area which produced these funerary curses in greater quantities than any other was Phrygia.[210] The imprecations here have a literal directness not to be found in more civilized surroundings. 'Whoever lays his heavy hands on this tomb, may he leave behind his children as orphans, his wife a widow, and his household a desert'; 'He who brings his hand with heavy envy, may he fall victim to premature misfortunes'.

On the graves of young children, whose epitaphs were typically more elaborate as an expression of greater sorrow at their early demise, premature death was punishment to fit the crime: 'Whoever shall deface the lifeless visage of the child (alluding to the funerary bust), may he likewise fall victim to premature disasters'; or, more vividly still, 'If anyone shall plot against this memorial, may he lay out his children in early burial'. Another variant combined the notion of violent death with punishment by everlasting fire: 'If anyone bring his evil-doing hands against this memorial, may he leave behind his children orphaned, his wife widowed, his house deserted, may he run eternally in fire, may he perish at the hands of malefactors'. The Phrygian language was inscribed on tombstones of the later Roman period for a single purpose only, to deliver the threat of a curse against violators of tombs.

The gods would be responsible for inflicting such punishment. In the preceding examples their part is not made clear, but other formulae were quite explicit. 'May he be cursed by all the gods'; 'Whoever will do harm to this memorial, may he be cursed in the sight of the gods'. It was normal to invoke gods that were specific to the locality, or the divinities who specialized in divine vengeance. In the upper Tembris valley, the violator was threatened with the demons of Black Hecate; at Temenothyrae, 'if anyone committed an offence against the stele or the heroon, he would have to reckon with Heavenly Hecate in her wrath'. Nemesis was particularly qualified for this role: 'Do not damage the tomb but read it and pass on; for great is Nemesis among mortal men, and she stands guard over tombs.'[211] In the upper Hermus valley, the area of Lydia where Phrygian influence was at its strongest, there are many variations on the theme. 'If anyone offends against the tomb after my death, he shall have to reckon with the wrath of Anaeitis the goddess from the holy water' (*TAM* v. 1. 64); 'So that no one offends against the stele or the memorial, here stand the staffs of the god of Axiotta and of Anaeitis' (*TAM* v. 1. 172, for the staffs, see below); 'whoever offends against this, may he never encounter the mercy of Mēn of Axiotta' (*SEG* xxxi (1981), 1003); 'if anyone wishes to deface this monument, he shall have to reckon with Apollo enraged, and the mistress Anaeitis, unto his children's children, and his descendants' descendants' (*TAM* v. 1. 213); 'we call upon the great divinity (τὸ μέγα θεῖον) that no one offend against the stele or our memorials' (*TAM* v. 1. 434). Even the gods of Rome could be invoked: 'Whoever does anything against these tombs, may he himself, and the one who purchased it from

---

1, 608 (Iouddenoi), 776; *IGR* iv. 1603 (Chondrianoi); 1605 = *I. Eph.* vii. 1. 3292 (Thyairenoi); other Lydian examples in KP³ 67, 69, 108, 120, 127, 133 (cf. Magie, *RR* ii. 1027); *SEG* xxix (1979), 1293 (Plokettēnoi, territory of Nicaea); xxxiii (1983), 1080 (Kabianoi, territory of Nicaea); 1084 (Libyssa, territory of Nicomedia).

208 *IGR* iv. 635 from Phrygian Dioskōmē a well-developed village on the territory of Sebaste; 1491 from Kassaba in central Lydia which paid for its own public water supply; TAM v. 2. 317 from Tyanollus in N. Lydia; *IGR* iv. 582 Palox a large village N. of Aezani (cf. *MAMA* ix. p. xxix).

209 *I. Kyzikos*, 500 = *SEG* xxviii (1978), 943; for Alexander's background see Lane Fox, *Pagans and Christians*, 245–6. There is an excellent survey of funerary curses by J. Strubbe, 'Cursed be he that moves my bones', in C. A. Faraone and D. Obink, *Magika Hiera: Ancient Greek Magic and Religion* (1991), 33–59.

210 L. Robert, *CRAI* (1978), 253 (*OMS* v. 697–745): 'En effet la Phrygie est le domaine par excellence des imprécations funéraires.'

211 All these examples are simply cited from Robert's fundamental discussion. *CRAI* (1978), 253–67.

him or devised any other mischief, reckon with the wrath of the gods and goddesses of the Roman people (*TAM* v. 1. 423). It is interesting to note that the lengthy 'testament of Epikrates', which provided for the Roman custom of scattering roses in a ceremony at the tomb, concludes with the longest of all the surviving Lydian curse formulae.[212] Settlers of Italian origin clearly adopted the customs of the country as well as introducing their own.

In regions of central Anatolia which bounded on Phrygia, other invocations hailed the protection of Greek, Pisidian, Persian, or Lycaonian gods.[213] Certain formulae were also widely used by Christians and this readiness to call on God to protect and avenge the dead in their tombs was a distinctive regional characteristic of early Anatolian Christianity; 'By God, do no injury' (τὸν Θεόν σοι· μὴ ἀδικήσεις) was current among pagans and Christians in Phrygia and was diffused, apparently through Christian usage, to neighbouring areas such as Lycaonia, and beyond to Lycia, Byzantium, the Propontis, and Macedonia. The second half of the formula was also in some cases transformed from a threat against wrongdoers to an entreaty to the passer-by to offer prayers for the deceased.[214] Two other phrases, and their variants, have been found only in Christian or Jewish contexts: 'Whoever damages this tomb, he shall render account to God' (δώσει λόγον Θεῷ);[215] 'whosoever casts a bone out of here, he will have to reckon with God' (ἔσται αὐτῷ πρὸς τὸν Θεόν, e.g. *MAMA* vi. 234).[216] Here the threat is less specific; Christian or Jewish humility did not allow the writer of the curse to specify what the punishment for the offence was to be. However, the pagan notion of exacting retribution from the wrongdoer fitted comfortably with Jewish ideas of divine justice and vengeance; some colourful variations are attested.[217]

The selection of material cited in this digression offers a forcible reminder that the two most persistent themes of village epigraphy in Asia Minor are burial and religion. The most numerous inscriptions found at any village site in Anatolia are the tombstones; next come votive dedications to the gods; other types of

document are altogether rare. The rural populations of Anatolia, and the Phrygians in particular, revered their gods and honoured their dead to the point of heroization or even apotheosis.[218] Funerary architecture was certainly more sumptuous than domestic housing, as befitted graves which were to be eternal homes for their owners not simply the temporary accommodation of a transitory and impoverished peasant existence. Rural shrines, crowded as they will have been with carved reliefs, statues, and dedicatory inscriptions, were probably the only other groups of buildings in the countryside with any architectural pretensions.[219] A villager who looked around him for visible symbols of permanence in his family and community would turn to the cemetery and the family tombs; for visible symbols of authority he would turn to the sanctuary or, if his village had been prosperous enough to build one, to a temple.

The gods should then have a major role to play not simply in protecting the dead, but in regulating the conduct and relationships of the living. Traditional patterns of behaviour will have taken the places of regulations and law codes, whose custodians were not magistrates or village councils but the gods and, where necessary, their priests, prophets, and other interpreters. It is clear in general terms that the native inhabitants of central Anatolia observed a strict and conservative social morality. A passage in Socrates' *Ecclesiastical History* (4. 28) states that even in the fifth century the Phrygians appeared more restrained and decent than other races (σωφρονέστερα εἶναι τῶν ἄλλων ἐθνῶν). They were not given to high spirits or to anger, they had no time for horse-racing and theatrical shows; they abominated prostitution, and rarely swore oaths, evidently to reduce the risk of breaking their word.[220] Men were commended for their virtue (ἀρέτη) and their piety (εὐσεβεία), women for decent modesty (σωφροσύνη).[221] In the late Hellenistic period Nicolaus of Damascus had noted that the Phrygians abstained from swearing oaths.[222] The cults of the Phrygians mirror this preoccupation with a strict morality which was based on clearly defined notions of justice, proper

[212] P. Herrmann and Z. K. Polatkan, *Das Testament des Epikrates* (1969); (*Bull. ép.* (1970), 441).

[213] *CRAI* (1978), 277–86.

[214] For references to a full bibliography see Waelkens, *Türsteine*, 160 n. 402; and note Gibson, *Christians*, 62–3.

[215] See Robert, *Hellenica*, xi/xii. 406 n. 7.

[216] Ibid. 399–406.

[217] See below, Vol. II, Ch. 16 § III n. 198. A Jewish curse taken word for word from Deuteronomy was transplanted into the imprecations used by a follower of Herodes Atticus to protect a bath-house and statues which he had erected; 'May God strike him with destitution, fever, chill, earthquake, storm damage, madness, blindness, and losing his mind' (Robert, *CRAI* (1978), 244–52).

[218] *CRAI* (1978), 267; note in particular the practice around Dorylaeum and Nacolea in northern Phrygia of turning the tomb into a double dedication to the deceased and to Zeus Bronton (*MAMA* v. pp. xxxiv–xxxviii). For a full discussion see M. Waelkens, 'Privatdeifikation in Kleinasien', *Archéologie et religions de l'Anatolie ancienne: Mélanges en l'honneur du professeur Paul Naster* (1984), 259–307.

[219] For the tomb as the house of the dead, see Waelkens, *Türsteine* 21–31 with literature. For rural sanctuaries, see below, Vol. II, Ch. 16 §§ I and II.

[220] Cited by Robert, *CRAI* (1978), 267–9; see also below, Vol. II, Ch. 17 § IX at n. 385.

[221] See Robert, *Hellenica*, xiii. index svv.

[222] *FGrH* 90 F 103 i.

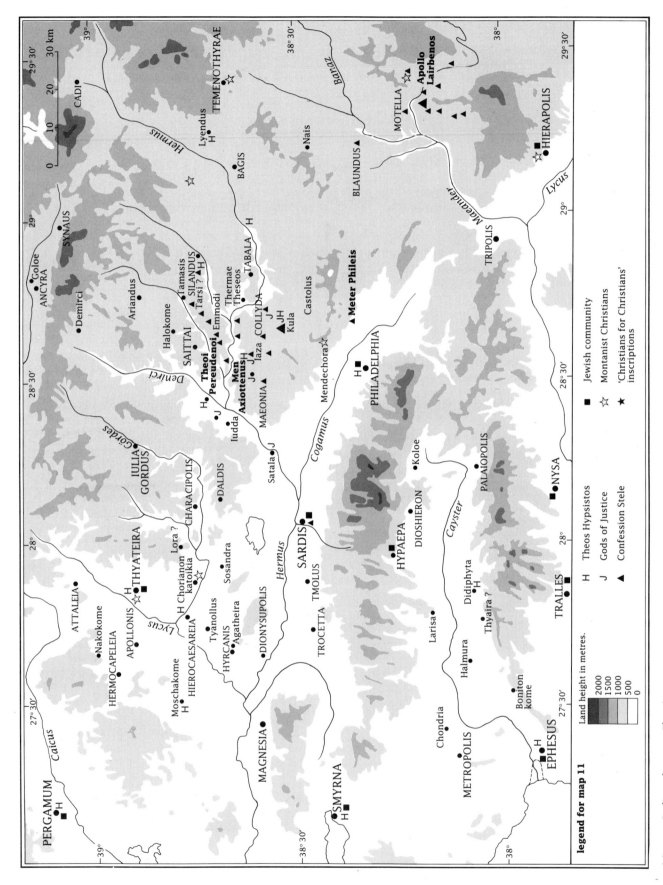

Map 11. Lydia and western Phrygia

behaviour, piety to the gods, a respect for divine authority, and a well-developed fear of divine vengeance. The gods, Ὅσιος καὶ Δίκαιος, or the abstracted divine beings of Justice and Holiness, Ὅσιον καὶ Δίκαιον, including a female counterpart Ὁσία, appear throughout Phrygia and the neighbouring parts of central Anatolia, usually in rural contexts. The principal deity at Phrygian Prymnessus was the goddess Justice, *Dikaiosyne*, and there was a priest of *Hygieia* and *Sophrosyne* at Synnada (*IGR* iv. 708, and see below, Vol. II, Ch. 16 § 11 at nn. 124–33). Apollo and the all-seeing sun Helios cast a baleful glare over man's affairs and no malefactor could escape their notice; Nemesis would ensnare anyone who thought they might transgress the limits which the gods had set (see above, n. 211). Two Phrygian inscriptions, evidently from the same sanctuary, well illustrate the range and character of this pantheon. One invokes the saviour gods, and depicts a bust of Zeus, Dionysus, a mounted god with a double axe, and a god carrying a whip in a quadriga. The latter are identified as Apollo and as Mēn Dikaios, described as the 'Eye of Justice and Moderation', Ὀφθαλμὸς Δικαιοσύνης καὶ Σωφροσύνης.[223] The other, from the region of Dorylaeum, is a strictly comparable dedication to the saviour gods by the villagers of Saklea, specifically to the Mother of the Gods, to Phoebus the Holy and Mēn the Just, and to the Eye of *Dike*, on account of their just disposition, Μητρὶ θεῶν Φοίβῳ τ' ὁσίῳ καὶ Μηνὶ δικαίῳ, ὀφθαλμῷ τε Δίκης δικεοφροσύνης χάριν ἄνδρες Σακλεανοὶ σωτῆρσι θεοῖς ὁσίοις ἀνέθηκαν. The reliefs show a bust of Zeus by a garlanded altar, Helios/Apollo riding in a quadriga, a mounted deity carrying a double axe, and Dionysus with a crown of grape clusters, carrying a thyrsus.[224]

The rule of the gods is made explicit in two series of inscriptions, the confession steles of the sanctuary of Apollo Lairbenos near Phrygian Hierapolis, and the more diffuse group of confession inscriptions found in north east Lydia. Both areas provide a clear demonstration of divine justice in action. Moreover, the case-histories which are documented in the confessions provide vivid glances at the social and economic conditions of village life.[225]

Several times in Lydia gods are described as rulers or kings of villages: Great Mēn of Petra and the Great Mother of Taza (*TAM* v. 1. 499); the Great Mother of Taza, Mis (i.e. Mēn) Labanas, and Mis of Artemidorus, the rulers of Dorou kōmē (*TAM* v. 1. 461); the Tarsene Mother, Apollo Tarsios, and Mēn Axiottenos of Artemidorus who held Koresa (Κορεσα κατέχοντα, *TAM* v. 1. 460); Great Meis Axiottenos ruling Tarsi (*TAM* v. 1. 159); Great Mother Anaeitis who holds Azitta and Meis Tiamou (*TAM* v. 1. 317); Mēn of Artemidorus who holds Axiotta (*TAM* v. 1. 526). Mēn is sometimes given the explicit name of tyrant (*TAM* v. 1, 255, 350, 536); the description 'lord tyrant' is given either to Mēn or to Zeus Masphaltēnos (*TAM* v. 1. 537). A votive text of AD 216/17 from a village near Saittae simply invokes the God King, θεῷ βασιλῖ (*TAM* v. 1. 167); in a different Anatolian context, at Galatian Ancyra, there was a sanctuary of the 'King and Queen', perhaps to be identified with Mēn and Cybele.[226]

---

223 *CRAI* (1978), 268, not fully published.

224 P. Frei, *Epigr. Anat.* 11 (1988), 26.

225 F. Steinleitner, *Die Beicht im Zusammenhange mit der sakralen Rechtspflege in der Antike* (1913) collected and discussed all the texts published up till then. Most of the Lydian material is now collected in *TAM* v. 1. 317–32, 440 (Sanctuary of Anaeitis and Mēn Tiamou, unlocated in the area of Kula); 159 (territory of Saittae), 460–1, 464–8 (Ayazviran); 492, 499, 501, 506, 509–10, 525, 527, 541, 576, 583, 592–3, 596 (all from villages of the Catacecaumene on the territory of Collyda and Maeonia); add too H. W. Pleket, *Talanta*, 10/11 (1978/9), 88–90 = *SEG* xxix (1979), 1174. L. Robert, *BCH* 107 (1983), 515 ff. publishes two confession texts from the sanctuary of 'Zeus of the twin Oak Trees', to add to *TAM* v. 1. 179a, 179b, 180 and 181. For Sardis, L. Robert, *Nouvelles inscriptions de Sardes* (1964), 23–31. From a village N. of Tripolis, see Pleket, op. cit. 90 no. 14 = *SEG* xxix (1979), 1155; The Theoi Pereudenoi texts from an unlocated site in NE Lydia, E. Varınlıoğlu and P. Herrmann, *Epigr. Anat.* 3 (1984), 1–18 (seven confessions, no. 10 identified as from Çalıbaşı köy near Kula). G. Petzl and H. Malay, *Epigr. Anat.* 6 (1985), 60 no. 4; 63 no. 5 (*SEG* xxxv (1985), 1164, 1267); G. Manganaro, *ZPE* 61 (1985), 199–203 (*SEG* xxxv (1985), 1269). Twelve confessions from the sanctuary of the Mētēr Phileis north of Philadelphia, H. Malay, *Epigr. Anat.* 6 (1985), 111–25 nos. 5, 9, 11, 12, 20, 24, 31, 34, 36, 44, with p. 125 no. 4 and *TAM* v. 1. 261. Another group of texts from the Kula area has found its way into the Museums of Bergama and Manisa, G. Petzl and H. Malay, *Epigr. Anat.* 12 (1988), 147–54 (five confessions); cf. E. Varınlıoğlu, *Epigr. Anat.* 13 (1989), 35–50 reinterpreting the longest of the texts edited by Petzl and Malay and adding five more examples probably from the same sanctuary. A long and difficult confession text said to come from Kula, Petzl and Malay, *GRBS* 28 (1987), 459–72 (*SEG* xxxvii (1987), 1001), discussed by A. Chaniotis, *Epigr. Anat.* 15 (1990), 127–31; M. L. Cremer and J. Nollé, *Chiron*, 18 (1988), 199–205 nos. 1–2 and *SEG* xxxvii (1987), 1000 and 1737 are confession texts of uncertain Lydian provenance. J. Nollé, *Epigr. Anat.* 10 (1987), 102 no. 2 (*SEG* xxxvii (1987), 1737) publishes a text which is said to come from Aeolis, between Magnesia ad Sipylum and Pergamum. There is now a corpus of these texts: G. Petzl, *Die Beichtinschriften Westkleinasiens, Epigraphica Anatolica* 22 (1994).

For further discussion see J. Zingerle, 'Heiliges Recht', *JÖAI* 23 (1926) Beiblatt, 8–72 and 24 (1929) Beiblatt, 107–24; I. Diakonoff, *Bull. Antike Beschaving* 54 (1979), 139–88; P. Frisch, *Epigr. Anat.* 2 (1983), 41–5; W. H. Buckler, *ABSA* 21 (1914/16), 169–83; A. Cameron, *Harvard Theological Review* 32 (1939), 143–79; E. Varınlıoğlu, *Epigr. Anat.* 1 (1983), 75–87; G. Petzl. *Epigr. Anat.* 12 (1988), 155–66.

226 *AS* 27 (1977), 89–90 nos. 31–2 = *SEG* xxvii (1977), 851–2; Bosch, *Ankara*, no. 189.

Often steles call not simply on the gods but also their powers, δυνάμεις (*TAM* v. 1. 317, 440, 525; see also Vol. II, Ch. 16 § v n. 259), and Leto, the mother of Apollo, is once called Δυνατὴ θεός, reminiscent of a line of an inscription from the Phrygian sanctuary of Apollo Lairbenos, where she is described as the goddess who makes possible the impossible (*TAM* v. 1. 250 with note).

These powers were concretely and specifically deployed to punish wrongdoers. The mechanics of the procedure are set out in more detailed cases:

Hermogenes and Apollonius . . . from Syros Mandrou, when three pigs belonging to Demainetus and Papias from Azita wandered off and got mixed up with the sheep belonging to Hermogenes and Apollonius, while a 5-year-old boy was pasturing them, and they were herded back inside, and therefore Demainetus and Papias were looking for them, they did not confess through some ingratitude. The staff of the goddess (Anaitis) and the lord of Tiamou (Mēn) was therefore set up, and when they did not confess the goddess duly showed her powers, and when Hermogenes died, his wife and child and Apollonius brother of Hermogenes implored her mercy and now bear witness to her and with the children sing her praises. In the year 199 (AD 114/15) (*TAM* v. 1. 317).

The authors of the offence, or their relatives, set up such inscriptions and confessed to their misdeeds typically, as here, in an artless narrative which often left the substance of what had happened obscure. This was evidently the written version of a statement made or extracted in the god's shrine. In this, and in many cases divine authority was symbolized by a staff, σκῆπτρον, which had been formally set up and provided the centrepiece of the confession procedure. Violators of tombs also had to answer for their crimes before the staff or staves of the gods (*TAM* v. 1. 160, 167a, 172, cf. p. 63). Pressure to confess came in part, no doubt, from the community or from the victims of the crime, but this was reinforced by the gods' own action in afflicting criminals with loss, disease, or, as here, with death. Reparation in such cases was clearly due to the victims, but the gods themselves demanded that atonement be done not simply by public confession but by erecting a stele which revealed their powers and praised them. A few of the inscriptions also carry a relief depicting the confession scene itself: a priest stands holding a wreath in one hand and the god's staff resting on a low base in the other; the confessor confronts him holding up his right hand as a pledge of honesty while he makes the confession; in a second case a woman confessor places an object on an altar while other figures, with right hands raised, look on, either as witnesses or to join in the praises of the god.[227] Similar

formulae recur throughout the whole corpus of inscriptions. Confessors bore witness to the god's power (μαρτυρεῖν), supplicate for mercy (ἰλᾶσθαι), and sing his praises (εὐλογία, εὐλογεῖν); the gods sought out or prosecuted offenders (ἐπιζήτησις, ἐπιζητεῖσθαι), and inflicted punishment (κόλασις), which might take the form of disease and death of their livestock, or, in more serious cases the death of the offenders or their close kin.

The range of offences found in the Lydian texts opens a small window on to village life. There are confessions to the theft of clothes from a bath house (*TAM* v. 1. 159), weapons from or by an eirenarch (*TAM* v. 1. 180), a sum of 412 denarii from a granary (*TAM* v. 1. 257), pigs and sheep (*TAM* v. 1. 317 quoted above, 460), fishing- or hunting-nets (*Epigr. Anat.* 10 (1987), 102–4 = *SEG* xxxvii (1987), 1737), and animal hides from a temple (*Epigr. Anat.* 12 (1988), 147 ff. no. 2).

Family disputes were commonplace: in one case the god punished the attempt of a group of villagers to cheat three orphans out of their inheritance by stealing documents and conniving with predatory money-lenders. The community set up the staves of the god Mēn against them and the god sought them out, punishing and destroying the plotters.[228] In another inheritance case three brothers had divided up the family vineyards left to them, disregarding a promise that part was promised to the god, until they were brought into line by a punishment which the surviving text fails to specify (*SEG* xxxiv (1984), 1212–13). A stepmother, accused by all the village of having driven her stepson mad by poisoning him, tried to rebut the charge by setting up the staff and dedicating altars in the temple, in the belief that this and her confession would give adequate satisfaction; but the gods inflicted on her a punishment, presumably death, which she did not escape.[229] A man was compelled to take back his sister into his household (*TAM* v. 1. 329, AD 244/5). There were tensions with *threptoi* (foster-children): one woman mounted a charge against her *threpte*, but when she achieved nothing the gods turned the tables against her leading her to atone with a stele which praised them (*SEG* xxxiv (1984), 1218; AD 209/10). In a bleaker tale a woman had done violence to her *threptos*; both had died and the god had asked for amends to be made by her grandson (*TAM* v. 1. 492, AD 224/5).

Perjury and deception most obviously conflicted with the gods' justice. A woman's idle talk and perjury were the cause of a breast complaint until duly confessed and atoned for (*TAM* v. 261); when a man borrowed a sum of money which he then claimed on oath to have

---

227 L. Robert, *BCH* 107 (1983), 515–20 = *Documents* 359–64 with illustrations.

228 *TAM* v. 1. 231.
229 *TAM* v. 1. 318.

repaid, he was punished by death and his daughter had to redeem the oaths, repay the money, and erect a stele to Mētēr Atimis and Mēn Tiamou (*TAM* v. 1. 440 cf. 525 for another bad debt). The *Theoi Pereudenoi*, whose sanctuary lay on the territory of Saittai, seem to have exacted a portion of property bequests made in the area, and non-payment of this debt is the subject of three or four confessions (*SEG* xxxiv (1984), 1211, 1219; cf. 1212–13). These detailed stories hint at the circumstances which caused one man on his confession stele to advise others not to swear oaths or exact them unjustly (*TAM* v. 1. 465), and which led others to offer vows to a god ὑπὲρ παρορκίας.[230]

Many of the texts concern offences against the gods and their sanctuaries as such. Men were called to account for cutting down or selling wood from sacred groves (*TAM* v. 1. 179a, 179b, 592), stoning sacred pigeons,[231] illegally pasturing flocks in a sacred grove (*Epigr. Anat.* 12 (1988), 147 ff. no. 3); visiting the sanctuary in rags (*TAM* v. 1. 238) or in a state of defilement (*SEG* xxix (1979), 1155). An elaborate confession, delivered in language of the utmost opacity, may refer to sexual offences against women attached to a sanctuary or otherwise under the god's protection (*Epigr. Anat.* 12 (1988), 147 ff. no. 5, with commentary 155–60). The fact that there is no formal distinction between the handling of these offences against sacred law and others of a secular nature simply underlines the point that in these Lydian villages divine authority and justice was accepted across the whole spectrum of human activity.

Two Lydian confession steles allude to failures to provide service, in the form of so many days' labour to the god (*TAM* v. 1. 593; *SEG* xxxiv (1984), 1210). Serving the god by cultivating his land, harvesting his crops, or maintaining temple property was presumably commonplace in Anatolian communities where the temple or sanctuary dominated all other forms of community organization. The system is seen in an extreme form in the temple-states of Cappadocia and Pontus, where whole populations were made up from *hierodouloi*, sacred slaves or serfs (see above, Ch. 7 § 1 nn. 11–12). Sacred slaves, *hieroi*, were not uncommon elsewhere in Roman Asia Minor, although they never formed more than a small minority of the population

of a given region.[232] Some may have been born to this condition, others were consigned to it by parents, relatives, or slave-owners who put them down (καταγράφειν) for temple service. The largest concentration of evidence in the Roman period comes from the sanctuary of Apollo Lairbenos, which is also the source of the only other major series of confession texts from Anatolia.

Unlike the Lydian sanctuaries, none of which has ever been excavated or even identified in ruined form, the material remains of the *hieron* Apollo Lairbenos can at least be briefly described. It stands on a mountain ridge overlooking the deeply incised bed of the upper Maeander, which flows past it on the northern side. It was approached by a sacred way from the east, which led up to the *temenos*. Here stood a substantial temple, measuring 27 × 12 metres at ground level, and probably built, to judge by the surviving decorated fragments, in the second or third century AD. The *temenos* also included other structures, including a vaulted room opposite the west end of the temple.[233] As the inscriptions show, the sanctuary attracted devotees from the small cities in the neighbourhood, Motella, Dionysopolis, and Blaundos, as well as from several villages on the territory of Hierapolis.[234]

The inscriptions themselves are written in a crude and popular form of Greek, typical of rural Anatolia.[235] As in the Lydian texts the style of the confessions is untutored and the stories are told with little logical connexion: 'I went up to the place and I went through the village twice unpurified. I forgot. I went back into the village. I announce that no one will despise the god since he will have the stele as an example. The aforementioned Eutycheis did this of his own accord and confessed and has supplicated.' The translation itself considerably clarifies the Greek of an inscription which pays virtually no heed to the orthodox forms of *koine*: ἐπεὶ τὸ χωρὶ πισετύχει καὶ διῆθα τὴν κώμη β′ ἄναγνα· λημόνησα· παρήμην εἰς τὴν κώμη· παραγέλω μηδεὶς καταφρεινήσει τῶ θεῶν ἐπεὶ ἔξει τὴν σείλην ἐξοπράφειν. ἐπόϊσ' ἐτόνμετον ἡ προγεμένε Εὐτυχεις καὶ ἐξομολογησάτο καὶ εἰλάθη (*MAMA* iv. 285). Thirty-six texts can be attributed to the site,[236] most of which are either

---

[230] T. Drew Bear, *GRBS* 17 (1976), 262–6 no. 17 (*SEG* xxvi (1976/7), 1386; *Ath. Mitt.* 29 (1904), 331; perjury plays a large part in the unprovenanced confession text from Lydia *SEG* xxxvii (1987), 1000. Note also an inscription from Philomelium which ends τὶς ἂν ὧδε ὀρκίσει εἶναι πρὸς Διὸς κατάρῃ, Calder, *AJA* 36 (1932), 456 no. 11.

[231] Cf. *MAMA* iv. 279 (discussed below); 295. Robert, *JSav.* (1971), 81 ff. = *OMS* vii. 159 ff. on the edict of Silius Italicus from Aphrodisias (J. M. Reynolds, *Aphrodisias and Rome* D. 46 with further bibliography).

[232] ἱεροί/ἱεροδουλοί in central Anatolia: *TAM* v. 1. 459, 593 (N. Lydia); *MAMA* ix. P61 (Aezanitis); x, 437, 492 (Tiberiopolis).

[233] See Calder and Buckler, *MAMA* iv p. 98 fig. 22 for a plan, and A. Strobel, *Das Heilige Land der Montanisten* (1980), 208–18 for a recent description.

[234] For the geography of the area see Robert, *Villes*[2], 127–49, 356–63.

[235] Cl. Brixhe, *Essai sur le grec anatolien*; H. Oppermann, *RE Suppl.* VA (1931), 535.

[236] Oppermann, *RE Suppl.* VA (1931), 521–35 provides the best discussion of the sanctuary and lists all the published texts,
[*cont. on p. 195*]

confessions or *katagraphe* documents, dedicating children or slaves to the service of Apollo or Leto, with whom the shrine was shared. The only significant difference from the Lydian sample is that a much higher proportion of these confessions relates to offences against the regulations of the sanctuary itself.

Four confessions concern the swearing of oaths and perjury (*MAMA* iv. 283 = Oppermann 17; Ramsay, *CB* i. 1. 149, 41 = Oppermann 22; *MAMA* iv. 279 = Oppermann 29; *MAMA* iv. 280 = Oppermann 30). The third of these is an offence concerning pigeons which were presumably connected with the sanctuary, while the last provides an interesting detail in its engraving. The confessor originally omitted his name from the stele, but added it afterwards in small letters squeezed in at the top of the stone, perhaps at the insistence of the priest, for public acknowledgement of faults was essential to the whole procedure. Two or three examples may refer to offences against a code of sexual conduct demanded by the god: a woman set up a stele in atonement after being forced, probably to have intercourse with her husband at a forbidden time (*JHS* 8 (1887), 381, 12 = Oppermann 13); a husband confessed after punishment to having wished to 'remain with his wife', doubtless also to have intercourse (*MAMA* iv. 282 = Oppermann 14), and one of the perjurers seems to have admitted also to having masturbated, perhaps in the *hieron* (Oppermann 17). There are other accounts of ritual impurity: the man who passed through the village and up to the *temenos* (ἄναγνα, cited above); another who had eaten goat's meat which had not been properly sacrificed, and atoned by ritual purification (κάθαρμα) and sacrifices (θυσίαι) (Ramsay. *CB* i. 1. 150, 43 = Oppermann 18); and two who admit to 'impure' (ἄναγνα) behaviour which is not further specified in the surviving texts (*MAMA* iv. 288–9 = Oppermann 33–4). One man admits to having been unwilling to approach the god and take part in his mysteries (*MAMA* iv. 281 = Oppermann 30), a text reminiscent of a Lydian example in which a woman confessed that she had not believed in the god for four years until punishment came to her in a series of disasters and she publicly declared her recantation (*BCH* 107 (1983), 520; AD 252/3). The most intriguing admission of the series was made by a woman who had brought soldiers into the sanctuary wishing to revenge herself on an enemy (ἐπὶ ἀνήγαγα στρατιώτας ἐπὶ τὸ ἱερὸν ἐχθρὸν θέλουσα ἀμύνασθαι). The item provides evidence from an unexpected quarter for the presence of Roman soldiers in civilian Asian communities during the later second or third century (*MAMA* iv. 287 = Oppermann 32).

The lengthiest confession involved four offences: perjury concerning pigeons, breaking into the sanctuary, stealing sheep, and failing to transfer to the god

ownership of a slave who had been promised by the καταγραφή procedure. The god's displeasure had been made clear in dreams and also by the physical actions of temple staff who had seized the promised slave as he was sitting at the sanctuary gates and brought him inside (*MAMA* iv. 279 with commentary = Oppermann 29). This text, despite several obscurities, provides a link between the two types of document which make up the bulk of the inscriptions from the sanctuary: confessions and *katagraphai*. The former show how the god controlled his people's behaviour, the latter illustrate how he used their services. Slaves or others registered with the god presumably devoted their whole lives to work for the temple, ploughing its lands or otherwise realizing its assets. One *katagraphe* of a slave-girl specifies a substantial fine to be exacted from anyone who tried to take her away from the temple (*MAMA* iv. 278 = Oppermann 28). But, as in Lydia, free peasants were also expected to contribute labour at fixed times and a confession survives made by a man who was late in doing this (*MAMA* iv. 286 = Oppermann 23).

It is impossible to say how far the formal procedures revealed by the confession documents of northern Lydia or the *temenos* of Apollo Lairbenos were replicated in other villages or at other sanctuaries in Asia Minor, except to say that this probably did not include inscribing the transactions on stone as a permanent public reminder of wrongdoing. However, the Lydian texts are far from confined to a single sanctuary but form part of the religious culture of most of the middle Hermus basin and come from the territories of several cities—Sardis, Philadelphia, Maeonia, Collyda, Tripolis, and Saittai. Moreover, the other inscriptions relating to cult activities in these areas, for the most part votive steles offered by individuals or communities on behalf of themselves, their families, livestock, crops, and villages, are essentially identical to those found all over inland Anatolia, and the types of sanctuary and the personnel attested in Lydia do not differ significantly from those found elsewhere (see below, Vol. II, Ch. 16 §§ I and II). Given these important broad similarities it is implausible to imagine that the gods of northern Lydia or Apollo Lairbenos played a radically different part in men's lives than the gods elsewhere.

Organization and authority beyond the individual household in the villages of Roman Anatolia was a matter not for village councils and magistrates but for the gods and their representatives in their sanctuaries. This does not necessarily point to a hierarchy of priests or holy men who obtained high status in the community. Ἱερεῖς commonly appear in the village inscriptions of Anatolia but never as figures of great importance and their presence was by no means essential for regulating men's relations with the gods. Any individual could make an offering or conduct a sacrifice at an altar if he saw fit to do so; the confession inscriptions never mention any intermediaries between the god and the offender, although the Lydian reliefs depict figures who had a part to play in regulating the ritual, as would be natural (see above). The gods' presence and power could be seen or felt by anyone; interpreters or mediums such as prophets, who do intermittently appear in surviving texts,[237] had their place but it was not at the centre of the picture. The counterpart of man's direct experience of the divine powers was that the gods could exercise direct control over man's affairs.

VI. *Worlds Apart*

The villages of rural Asia Minor lived a life that differed radically from that of the cities. Language and nomenclature, diet and lifestyle, cults and patterns of authority marked them off as worlds apart. Villagers will have been regarded with a mixture of contempt, suspicion, and incomprehension by most city dwellers. To Aelius Aristides they appeared to pose a distinct threat, and while individual landlords might sometimes exercise a benign form of patronage over villages in their domains, cities in general sought to control and exploit their rural territories.

The realities of this relationship are best shown by a decree of Phrygian Hierapolis, found in a village on its territory, which tried to regulate the behaviour of its gendarmerie the *paraphylakes*. These 'guardians', in future, were to provide the cost of their visits to villages from their own pockets; the villages should give nothing more than firewood, fodder, and lodging; nor were they obliged to honour the *paraphylakes* with a crown as a matter of course, but only if special favours had been rendered and acknowledged. We may legitimately infer not only that illegal extortion had formerly been widespread, but that the decree would have been more honoured in the breach than the observance. For who but the police themselves could regulate their behaviour in the villages? The obvious parallel for these provisions is to be found in the many regulations which were designed to stop Roman officials and soldiers from making oppressive demands of communities as they travelled through the provinces and lodged on their way. In other words the relation-

ship between city authorities and the villages was analogous to that between Roman provincial officials and their subjects.[238] That particular story is well known as one of relentless corruption and oppression, becoming endemic to the extent that it provided the model by which Rome in the third and fourth centuries extracted its demands from and imposed its authority on the whole empire.[239] The cultural gulf, therefore, which divided city from village will have been made wider by the hostility between villagers and the section of the civic magistracy which had most to do with their affairs.

Even while the Hellenistic kingdoms and the expanding Roman republic encroached deeply on to the autonomy and freedom of action of the cities of Hellenistic Asia Minor, these retained their old right to self-defence and organized forces to protect their territory. Aphrodisias and other cities of Caria annually appointed a *strategos epi tēs chōras*;[240] Smyrna, among others, established a network of small fortresses in the hilly country that guarded the approach to the city;[241] Ionian Teos organized a well-paid home guard under a phrourarch numbering not less than twenty *phrouroi*, equipped with shield, spear, dirk, and helmet —and three dogs.[242] Ill-documented categories such as *dekaniai* and *phylakitai* may represent a rural militia which survived in the territory of Oenoanda and other remoter parts of the interior into the Roman period.[243] Periods of emergency, such as the Galatian invasion of the 270s or the revolt of Aristonicus in the 130s BC threw up local leaders who coped with the crisis and were honoured for their efforts to protect citizens and property in the countryside.[244]

The need to control and secure territory remained, even though the threat of external war receded under the Roman empire. Officers of the law were to be

which I cite with his number as well as that of the most accessible or recent publication.

[237] For rural prophets in Lydia and Phrygia see *MAMA* ix. 60 with notes and below, Vol. II, Ch. 16 § v at nn. 272–5. The prophet was an eponymous official at Mysian Hadrianoi, see *I. Hadr.* p. 70 index s.v. Cf. *TAM* v. 1. 535, and 2. 1411 (a prophet at a sanctuary of Apollo Pandemos on the territory of Magnesia ad Sipylum).

[238] *OGIS* 527; Robert, *Ét. anat.*, 103–4; for the parallels see *JRS* 66 (1976), 106–31.
[239] R. MacMullen, *Corruption and the Decline of the Roman Empire* (1988).
[240] See Reynolds, *Aphrodisias and Rome*, D.2–3 with *CR* n.s. 30 (1984), 85.
[241] G. E. Bean and R. Duyuran, *JHS* 67 (1947), 128–34, with bibliog. at 134 n. 20.
[242] J. and L. Robert, *JSav.* (1976), 153–235 (*SEG* xxvi (1976/7), 1306) = *OMS* vii. 297–379, 3rd cent. BC. Y. Bequignon, 'Les pyrgoi de Téos', *Rev. Arch.* 28 (1928), 185–208; J. M. Balcer, 'Fifth-century Ionia: a frontier re-defined', *REA* 87 (1985), 31–42.
[243] Wörrle, *Stadt und Fest*, 147–50.
[244] For Galatians see above, Ch. 2 § 1. For local initiatives during the revolt of Aristonicus see *TAM* v. 1. 528 (129 BC) referring to Hephaistion son of Alcaeus from Sardis set in charge of an ὀχύρωμα in Lydia by the Roman legate Q. Servilius Caepio. See too the two inscriptions from the Mysian-Lydian borderland discussed in *Bull. ép.* (1984), 384 and 385.

found in most cities, most commonly eirenarchs, appointed in consultation with the provincial governor.[245] Two recently published texts from the territory of Appia in the upper Tembris valley reveal that a freedman of Vespasian on the Imperial estate in that area held the post of εἰρηνοφύλαξ τῆς ἐπαρχείας, showing that such senior officials were also to be found as part of the personnel that controlled large estates.[246] Although there are cases where the post was held by children, thus indicating that the holder and his family merely took financial responsibility for duties that were executed by others,[247] there is evidence enough that the post involved active service. Xenophon of Ephesus' novel, in an episode characteristic of the genre, depicts an eirenarch of Tarsus leading a band of horsemen to rescue the heroine who had been kidnapped by brigands;[248] there was an eirenarch of the upper villages and of Drymos (a fort?) at Pisidian Termessus (*TAM* iii. 1. 204), and the dangerous realities of enforcing order in the Pisidian Taurus appears most clearly from the collection of inscribed dedications offered to the Mountain Mother on Hisar Dağ east of Ariassus, and carved in the rock by eirenarchs, antieirenarchs,[249] and their *diōgmitai*.[250] The interface between the coastal plain of Pamphylia and the rugged highlands to the north was predictably a focus for police activity. Another eirenarch of Termessus set up a dedication at Evdir Han in the plain at the eastern extremity of the city's territory, to Eleuthera, Apollo Patroos, Tyche Agathe, Nemesis Adrasteia, and Artemis Agrotera, the last two a clue to duties undertaken in wild and violent country.[251] Similar concerns led the inhabitants of Lyrbōtōn kōmē north of Perge to build a two-storey fortified tower in their village as late as the reign of Domitian.[252]

Paraphylakes had lower ranking than eirenarchs in the cities where both offices are attested.[253] Perhaps, therefore, they more frequently patrolled the territory in person, as the Hierapolis decree implies. They certainly did not travel alone, but at the head of a well-armed mounted posse. A relief found in the relatively secure environment of the Cayster valley shows the *paraphylax* accompanied by three mounted *diōgmitai* all wearing short swords, small round shields, and a curved baton.[254] Still more revealing is a dedication from upper Caria made to another local Mountain Mother, *Mētēr Theōn Oreia*, by a mounted troupe made up of the *paraphylax* himself, ten youths, neaniskoi, under their neaniskarch, and six slaves to tend the horses.[255] The constabulary under phylarch or eirenarch were more usually termed 'pursuers', *diōgmitai*, a word which readily shows that their business extended beyond euphemistic 'protection' to hot pursuit and harassment. In an emergency they supplied ready recruits for Rome's own forces. When the barbarian Costoboci invaded Greece and threatened Athens under Marcus Aurelius, *diōgmitai* were active in the defence, and others at this time were enlisted in at least one Asian city to reinforce the hard-pressed legions of the Danube.[256]

The task in which they are best attested, due solely to the survival of the evidence, is the rounding up of Christians; *diōgmos* thus became the word the Christians themselves used to refer to state persecution. One description is archetypal, the account of the arrest of Polycarp bishop of Smyrna around AD 155, a narrative which takes as its model the gospel versions of the arrest of Jesus, but which at the same time reveals what were certainly the standard policing arrangements of an Asian city in the second century AD. After Polycarp was persuaded by his friends to withdraw from the city, first to a nearby and then to a more distant farm, the authorities, headed by the proconsul Statius Quadratus, tortured two of his

[245] Aristides, *Or.* 50. 72 (Keil); *Dig.* 50. 4. 18. 7; *Cod. Just.* 10. 77; see Magie, *RR* ii. 1514–15.

[246] T. Drew Bear, *ANRW* ii. 18. 1, 1967–81. In his commentary (1969 n. 214) on the stele set up by the imperial freedman he observes that the man was a native of the region where he held office, and thus provides evidence to contest the view of K. Hopwood (see n. 253 below) that law officers came from a completely different cultural background than the people whom they controlled. However, although there were doubtless exceptions to the general picture which Hopwood portrays, this is not one of them. The quality and size of the steles, and the length and pretensions of their inscriptions, are easily distinguished from the bulk of dedications found in this region: 'la fortune de l'affranchi et de sa femme, mais aussi *leur culture*, les différenciaient des paysans parmi lesquels ils vivaient' (1979, my emphasis).

[247] Children as eirenarchs, I. Lévy, *REG* 12 (1897), 288.

[248] Xenophon of Ephesus 2. 13. Banditry in ancient novels: P. A. Mackay, *G&R* 10 (1963), 147–52; J. Winckler, *JHS* 100 (1980), 155–81; Shaw, *Past and Present*, 105 (1984), 44 n. 123.

[249] Perhaps to be explained along the same lines as *antistratiotai*, see J. Linderski, *JRS* 74 (1984), 74–80.

[250] L. Robert, *BCH* 1928, 408–9; *SEG* vi. 686–714.

[251] Robert, *Rev. Hist. Rel.* (1928) = *OMS* ii. 58 n. 2; cf. R. Heberdey, *Termessische Studien*, 7–9, 13–15.

[252] See above, n. 164. The inscriptions have also been collected by R. Merkelbach and S. Şahin, *Epigr. Anat.* 11 (1988), 158–69, with map. The tower is in no. 151. Similar fortified towers are a feature of the rural settlements of the Melas river in Rugged Cilicia: Bean and Mitford, *Journeys in Rough Cilicia 1964–68*, 29; information from K. Hopwood).

[253] K. Hopwood, 'Policing the Hinterland: Rough Cilicia and Isauria', in *Armies and Frontiers*, 173–89.

[254] Robert, *Ét. anat.*, 103; M. Speidel, *Epigr. Anat.* 5 (1985), 159–60.

[255] *Ét. anat.* 106; *La Carie*, ii. 281–3 no. 162.

[256] *Script. Hist. Aug. Marcus Aurelius* 21. 7 (*armavit et diogmitas*); *MAMA* ix. P50 and xxxi.

domestic slaves to discover his whereabouts. Pursuit was taken up by the eirenarch, Herodes, anxious to bring his quarry to the stadium for public trial, and he set out, guided by the slave, with armed *diōgmitai* and horsemen as though to catch a brigand.[257] Only the sympathy shown to the old bishop, who was allowed time to pray after his arrest, and the eirenarch's anxious concern that he should recant and save himself, distinguished this arrest from that of common criminals. With variations the scene became a commonplace in hagiographic writing; the lives of saints are our best source of knowledge of how the Roman empire was policed.[258]

The policing of rural parts of the Roman empire, and of Asia Minor in particular, is usually discussed in relation to the phenomenon of banditry, which was naturally a widespread phenomenon and occasionally a matter for serious concern even in relatively untroubled periods of the *pax Romana* (see above, § 1). But police activity extended beyond the repression of banditry to cover many other aspects of keeping order in rural areas. In particular eirenarchs, *paraphylakes*, and their small forces of armed men were in the last analysis the only means available to compel the peasant inhabitants of city territories to make their material contribution to the administration and prosperity of the community, and to the taxes and other demands imposed by Rome. When a landlord or creditor demanded his due from a villager and met an obdurate response, the only recourse open to either party was violence. The gendarmerie brought the law of the city to bear on the side of urban dwellers and landowners against villagers

whose main interest lay in avoiding their attentions as far as possible.

The old euphemism that a police force exists to maintain law and order rarely appears more hollow than in the communities of Roman Asia Minor. The villages of Phrygia, Lydia, and Pisidia never lacked the ability to regulate the conduct of their inhabitants, and indeed imposed austere standards of morality which few townsmen of Ephesus or Pergamum could have endured. Disputes, even violent ones, were handled by traditional means. It was as dangerous for a villager to turn to outside authorities as it was later for Christians to be forced into using civil courts, not their own (see below, Vol. II, Ch. 17 § IV at nn. 136–9). When a woman introduced Roman soldiers to the sanctuary of Apollo Lairbenos to settle a private quarrel, she was forced by the god to admit and atone for her fault. Soldiers, and police, imposed no law but the old Thucydidean law of nature that the strong rule the weak. The laws and institutions of the cities provided few formal means of effecting a rapprochement between the cities and their villages other than the threat or the reality of state violence. There were too few common strands of tradition and culture to ease the relationship between town and country. Indissoluble bonds of economic necessity bound the cities of Asia Minor to their hinterland, but no partnership emerged. The oppressive role of the rural gendarmerie is the most conspicuous symptom of a general condition, that Hellenized city dwellers and native villagers lived in worlds apart. The terminology of Roman inscriptions which tend to suppress or marginalize the formal distinctions between urban and rural inhabitants may suggest otherwise, but the remainder of the evidence confirms that the divide between the citizens and the *perioikoi* of the Hellenistic period remained as pronounced as ever.

---

[257] *Mart. Polycarpi* 5–7 with the excellent notes of J. B. Lightfoot, *The Apostolic Fathers Pt. II. Ignatius and Polycarp*, iii (2nd edn. 1889), 370–4.

[258] P. Franchi dei Cavalieri, *Studi e testi*, 49 (1928), 203–38.

12 The Development of the Cities

1. Changing Characteristics of City Life

By the period that most of the cities of Anatolia were founded, the possibility that a *polis* might still be a genuinely autonomous or independent community was long since extinct. At the beginning of the second century AD Dio Chrysostom and Plutarch reminded their upper-class contemporaries and their fellow citizens that it was no longer possible to act as though they lived in the days of Pericles and Demosthenes.[1] A community's freedom of action was always constrained by the superior power of Rome, which was represented, at a distance, by the limitless authority of the emperors,[2] and embodied, near at hand, by their legates, proconsuls, and procurators (Ch. 5). If necessary, and in the last resort, Roman will could be enforced by military intervention.[3]

At the same time, however, the Roman empire depended almost entirely on the cities for its stability and coherence. Except in frontier and mountainous areas, where there was a large military presence, Rome was not able to impose direct control over her subjects for more than very short periods. The emperors had to rely on pre-existing or newly created organized communities, precisely *poleis*, to provide an administrative framework for the provinces. Cities were founded and fostered, but circumstances called for forms of city organization, and above all for an ideology of civic life that were radically different from earlier days.

The nature of the shift in the idea of the city between the classical period and the time of the Roman empire has already been briefly sketched (Ch. 7 §1). As autonomy and independence from external rule became increasingly irrelevant during the late Hellenistic and early imperial periods, public buildings emerged as the dominant and essential characteristic of cities. Such buildings were, and are, the most conspicuous evidence for the material culture of civic life. The use of a cultural, rather than a political criterion to define a civic community was characteristic of the Roman period. The great age of urban building in Asia Minor, running from the beginning of the principate to the Severan period, with the most intense activity in the second century, marks the climax of Roman civic life in the provinces.

During the Severan period there are indications of a further change, or rather a gradual transition to a new civic ideology. By this time the network of cities that covered the eastern provinces had reached its widest extent. New city foundations, or the radical transformation of old cities by new building programmes, rarely occurred between the second quarter of the third century and the reign of Constantine. Indeed new construction of any sort is sparsely attested during this period. In place of building, another development was very marked, the creation of *agones*, sporting, musical, and theatrical competitions, which took place in the cities within the framework of religious festivals. The history of these competitive festivals, like that of public building, can be traced back to the origins of Greek city life, and they had become increasingly widespread in Asia Minor and other parts of the Greek East under the Roman empire.[4] However, the phenomenon expanded enormously between the time of the Severans and the third quarter of the third century. New games, with international status, were founded in hitherto inconspicuous cities; smaller cities enthusiastically promoted their own local festivals along comparable lines. The emperors of the third century played an active role in encouraging the foundation of *agones*, as their first- and second-century predecessors had promoted public building.[5] Agonistic motifs frequently dominated the types chosen by cities for their bronze coinage,[6] and sculptured monuments and inscriptions for victors and for sponsors of the games came to fill

---

[1] Plutarch, *Mor.* 813d–e; J. H. Oliver, *Hesperia*, 23 (1954), 143–7; C. P. Jones, *Plutarch and Rome* (1971), 133; *The Roman World of Dio Chrysostom* (1978), esp. 95–103.
[2] Price, *Rituals and Power*, 54–62, 78–100.
[3] Aelius Aristides, *Or.* 26. 67; above, Ch. 9 at end.

[4] See L. Robert, *Eighth Congress*, 35–45.
[5] See S. Mitchell, *JRS* 80 (1990), 189–91 with literature.
[6] K. Harl, *Civic Coins and Civic Politics in the Roman East A.D. 180–275* (1987), esp. 63 ff.

the places hitherto occupied by the statues of civic magistrates and other benefactors. It does not seem too hazardous to suggest that in the third century *agones* took over the role of public building, and provided the best demonstration of the civic status and pretensions of a community. In like manner, the participants and victors in agonistic contests more and more enjoyed the esteem which had been accorded to public benefactors in the earlier empire. This development may have been as much to the liking of the benefactors, who were finding it increasingly difficult to maintain high levels of voluntary contribution to city life, as it was gratifying to the competing sportsmen and artists themselves.

II. *Administration and the Civic Community*

In the background to this changing ideology of city life, certain factors remained constant. Two aspects of city life were so essential and unavoidable that they are too readily taken for granted. Firstly, during the Roman period cities remained effective centres of administration, overseeing the production and distribution of resources within the urban centre and its rural territory. Secondly, and even more fundamentally, they were, in a very positive sense, communities. Whatever role a city played in the larger structure of the Roman empire, it brought together a population, usually between 5,000 and 30,000 citizens and non-citizens, whose collective behaviour and intricate interrelationships were regulated and controlled by the institutions of the polis itself.

Seen from a narrow Roman perspective, the *poleis* of the eastern provinces were units in a large imperial system of administration and control. For this to work, the cities had to fulfil their functions as smoothly as possible. They had to supervise production and consumption of goods through a well-regulated market system, maintain order in the community, and meet Roman demands for taxes and other services. According to this mechanistic model, the cities were in essence simply cogs in a larger machine.[7]

Annually elected magistrates assumed direct responsibility for these very general requirements. A formally complete list of magistrates from a Greek city in Asia Minor is now known for Oenoanda in northern Lycia, and we can reasonably conjecture the duties which they were supposed to fulfil. The list is headed by the civic priest and priestess of the emperors, and the priest of Zeus. Then come three panegyriarchs, who would have supervised festival gatherings; a secretary to the council and five prytaneis, who were also probably council officials; two city market-controllers; two gymnasiarchs, who would have been responsible for training in the gymnasia as well as the supply of oil and other necessities; four treasurers to collect and disburse revenue; two *paraphylakes* to maintain order in the countryside; an ephebarch and a teacher, who oversaw the education of boys from citizen families both in their late teens, during the ephebeia, and beforehand. The list is concluded by a supervisor of public buildings, a post made necessary by the almost unceasing construction of the Hadrianic period, to which the text dates.[8] The inscription also shows in detail how *agonothetai*, sponsors of games, enjoyed the status and privileges of public magistrates.

Although no similar exhaustive roster survives elsewhere in Asia Minor, cities which have yielded large numbers of public inscriptions usually indicate most of their magistracies. Inscriptions which have already been cited for another purpose (Ch. 7 § III), provide excellent evidence for the civic magistracies, which were probably organized in Bithynia according to the terms of the *lex Pompeia* of 63 BC. All the cities seem to have had a first archon with a small college of associates; a secretary; a market-controller; treasurers, sometimes with specific responsibility for the grain-fund and the oil-fund; an *ekdikos*, or notary responsible for putting the city's case in legal disputes; and a censor (*timetes*) or an official in charge of the roster of citizens (*politographos*), these being a distinctive feature of Bithynian city life which may be attributable to direct Roman influence.[9] The cities of Galatia appear to have had very similar constitutions. There is abundant evidence in the cities of both provinces for gymnasiarchs and agonothetes, which were virtually a requirement of any Greek city.

At Phrygian Aezani, in a region where city magistrates follow a less homogeneous pattern, there was a board of *strategoi* under a first *strategos*, one or more secretaries, a group of dogmatographi responsible for

---

[7] See A. H. M. Jones, *The Greek City* (1940), 58 (on Pontus): 'In Pontus the Roman government, through its agent Pompey, thus for the first time founded Greek cities. The motive for the innovation was not elevated. Pompey may have prided himself on his enlightenment in introducing Greek city life into the backward regions of north-eastern Asia Minor, but it is plain that his principal concern in creating a substructure of local self-government was to lighten the burden of administration that had hitherto been carried by the central executive. The foundation of these cities was in fact simply a confession of the incapacity of the Roman provincial system to administer the provinces.' Cf. S. Mitchell, *Eighth Congress*, 121.

[8] Wörrle, *Stadt und Fest*, ll. 70–2, with commentary on pp. 101–23 in which he argues that the Roman period saw the city constitutions in Lycia becoming increasingly standardized, perhaps as a result of a *lex provinciae* (cf. n. 71 below).
[9] On Bithynian constitutions see above, Ch. 7 § III at nn. 92–8. For the role of censors in Bithynia see Mitchell, *Eighth Congress*, 123–4.

drafting civic decrees, market-controllers, and, more unusually, a special magistrate responsible for the decorum of girls. A senior group of officials called *stephanephoroi*, who are particularly attested in the former Seleucid realm, may have had religious and ceremonial duties. There were panegyriarchs, as at Oenoanda, and, as almost everywhere, gymnasiarchs and agonothetes. Civic treasurers as such are not attested, but the sacred treasurer (*hierotamias*) may have supervised much of the public finances of Aezani since the city derived a significant part of its income from the lands attached to the temple of Zeus.[10]

In this small sample of civic constitutions, the citizens of Aezani, Ancyra, and the Bithynian cities were divided into tribes, each with their own magistrates, the phylarchs. No tribal divisions have yet been attested at Oenoanda. From time to time individual tribes decided to erect honorific statues to their benefactors in the cities, but there is no evidence that they met in their own assemblies to do so. Rather, such decisions would have been reached at a full assembly, where the members of a tribe could register their own wishes distinct from that of the whole people.[11] Many inscriptions from Prusias ad Hypium in Bithynia and from Ancyra provide information about civic careers. No holder of one of the higher magistracies is also known to have been a phylarch. The latter were evidently drawn not from the first rank of the local aristocracy, the 'first men' as they were sometimes known,[12] but from the next level of the hierarchically stratified citizen population.[13] At Ancyra phylarchs also regularly held the office of *astynomos*, with responsibility for maintaining streets and public squares, watercourses, and drainage in the town. Since these 'city-wardens' appear to have been tribal officials, it is safe to conclude that the tribes themselves occupied distinct quarters of the city, and that tribal membership, at least at Ancyra, was based on place of residence.[14] This corresponds to the division of two of

the larger Roman colonies in Asia Minor, Pisidian Antioch and Alexandria Troas, into *vici*, evidently modelled on the *vici* of Rome.[15]

It would serve no useful purpose to multiply examples of civic constitutions; the evidence has been assembled and lucidly analysed elsewhere.[16] The similarities in function, if not always in name, between the various city authorities are important. It is safe to say that all the cities of Roman Asia Minor had public priests to take charge of the main city cults, and a board of annually selected senior magistrates without specified responsibilities, who surely presided at meetings of the council and people, and represented the city in its dealings with other bodies, especially the Roman authorities. Regular meetings of city bodies required documentation, hence the need for a secretary (a senior and highly responsible position) as well as a secretariat to draft proposals and decisions and to maintain archives and records of city transactions. The executive arm of the magistrature operated in a limited area of public life. Treasurers administered public finances, although responsibility for raising income and decisions about spending priorities were matters for the senior city politicians and for the political assemblies. The economic well-being of the community depended above all on the smooth running of a market system. Hence the need for market-controllers whose basic role was to mediate, where necessary, between producers and consumers. Bread for basic survival and oil for the gymnasia were the only commodities whose supply was essential at any cost, and cities commonly created special magistrates (such as the *sitonai*) or special funds to ensure that they were available when needed at a reasonable price.[17] Cities usually had special magistrates responsible for maintaining law and order, notably the eirenarchs and *paraphylakes* who played an active role in keeping rural areas under control (see above, Ch. 11 § VI). There is virtually no evidence for law-enforcement and the administration of criminal justice in the cities. The assize system run by Roman governors, who often conscripted provincial juries to assist them, catered for major cases, but certainly did not deal with routine law-breaking by the lower

---

[10] See *MAMA* ix, pp. xxx–xxxii.

[11] See I. Lévy, 'Études sur la vie municipale d'Asie Mineure sous les Antonins I', *REG* 8 (1985), 203 ff. The implication is that when the assembly met, it was seated by tribes.

[12] For terms such as οἱ πρωτεύοντες or οἱ πρῶτοι used to describe the ruling clique, see de Ste Croix, *Class Struggle*, 538; J. Strubbe, *Anc. Soc.* 15/17 (1984–6), 245 n. 5.

[13] For Prusias, see W. Ameling, *I. Prusias*, pp. 23–4; in *Epigr. Anat.* 3 (1984), 27 n. 63 he observes that no phylarch there is known to have received an honorific statue. At Ancyra the highest honour recorded for a phylarch is to have been τειμηθεὶς ἐν ἐκκλησίαις (πολλάκις) and/or in the *boulē*, Bosch, *Ankara*, nos. 202, 262. One phylarch is specified to have been a *bouleutes*, no. 357. Even late in the second century, phylarchs were often not Roman citizens (Bosch, *Ankara*, nos. 201, 202; *AS* 27 (1977), 77 ff. nos. 9 and 10).

[14] Bosch, *Ankara*, nos. 201, 202, 357.

[15] Levick, *Roman Colonies*, 76–8.

[16] A. H. M. Jones, *The Greek City*; W. Liebenam, *Städteverwaltung im römischen Kaiserreiche* (1900). The three articles by I. Lévy on municipal life in Asia Minor under the Antonines, published in *REG* 8 (1895), 203–50, 12 (1899), 255–89, and 14 (1901), 350–71, although bibliographically outdated, remain very useful. There is a very full collection of evidence relating to city administration in Magie, *RR* ii. 1501 n. 24–1524 n. 58.

[17] See the evidence for Asia Minor collected and discussed by J. Strubbe, *Epigr. Anat.* 10 (1987), 45–82 and 13 (1989), 99–122.

classes.[18] It is reasonable to assume that regular city magistrates, like their equivalents at Rome, had powers of jurisdiction within their own spheres of responsibility. Certainly the *lex de astynomis* from Pergamum, which was drafted under the Attalids but still enforced in the second century AD, gave city-wardens the right to punish those who infringed the regulations with fines. Senior magistrates certainly enjoyed similar powers, and were able to enforce their rulings with fines, floggings, or (rarely) imprisonment.[19]

It is clear, then, that the administrative framework of the cities was relatively simple, but adequate (in theory) to maintain the order, stability, and financial viability that was expected by Rome. Exact population figures are notoriously hard to establish, but few of the cities of inland Anatolia will have contained more than 30,000 urban inhabitants, and most were much smaller (see below, Ch. 14 § 11). Elaborate machinery was inappropriate for communities that were no larger than a modern European country town.

The small size of the cities, and their simple political structure, makes it more necessary to appreciate their role as communities. It is commonplace to argue that by the Roman period all genuine political power was focused on the magistrates, annually replaced but drawn from a very restricted sector of the population. The city councils (which might number between 100 and 600 members) enjoyed increasing prominence in the Roman period, usurped the role of the people's assembly, and offered a defining criterion of city status itself (above, Ch. 11 § III n. 137). The people's assembly itself was reduced to a mere cipher. It is naturally not difficult to find evidence to support this appraisal. When the council and people took the commonplace action of voting honours to an individual, the council was invariably named first, no doubt implying that it had initiated the action, and the verb describing the action is frequently inscribed in the singular, ignoring the presence of the people

altogether.[20] Extended records of the transactions of political meetings are relatively rare, and those that have survived in inscribed form usually simply explain the background to enthusiastic honorific decisions. Even these show that the *demos* collectively, or private individuals other than magistrates, rarely initiated political action.[21]

However, the common assertion that the people's assemblies of the Roman period seldom took a political initiative by no means proves that they were of no political account. Peoples' assemblies continued to meet in the cities of Asia Minor at least until the later third century. Indeed, inscriptions of this period record some of the proceedings of these meetings in the form of the public acclamations which greeted particular proposals and hailed the men or women responsible for them.[22] Most of those that have survived naturally show an enthusiastic, positive response, but that is no more strange than the fact that most of the inscribed decisions of civic assemblies are honorific. Such texts were regularly inscribed on statue bases or on other monuments that adorned the public areas of the city. Negative or critical decisions belonged in the city archive.

The few literary sources that describe or allude to such meetings convey a much livelier impression of

---

[18] For the assize system, see above, Ch. 5 at nn. 30–6. Routine civic law enforcement by magistrates in the 1st cent. is best illustrated by Acts. See F. Millar, *JRS* 71 (1981), 68–72 for the evidence of Apuleius and its relevance to the empire of the 2nd cent. AD. G. P. Burton, *Chiron* 9 (1979), 477–8 points out that the account of the martyrdom of Pionius in 250 (*Acta Pionii*, 3–9) provides the most detailed evidence for examination by a local magistrate before a capital trial in the assizes. Note τοπικὰ δικαστήρια on an inscription from Pogla in Pisidia, *IGR* iii. 409; see Liebenam, *Städteverwaltung*, 485 ff., and Magie, *RR* ii. 1517–18.

[19] See G. Klaffenbach, *Lex de astynomis Pergamenorum* (1954). A provincial governor was empowered to give rights of jurisdiction to the magistrates of the emporium of Pizus in Thrace (*IGBulg.* iii. 2. 1690, 41–2). It follows, *a fortiori*, that city magistrates enjoyed similar if not wider powers.

[20] *MAMA* ix. 27 n.

[21] Cf. Lévy, *REG* 8 (1895), 203 ff.

[22] On the increasing frequency with which acclamations were recorded in the epigraphy of the later empire see Robert, *Hellenica*, x. 62 n. 1. For discussion see C. Roueché, 'Acclamations in the Later Roman Empire: New Evidence from Aphrodisias', *JRS* 74 (1984), 181–99, and 'Floreat Perge', in M. M. Mackenzie and C. Roueché (eds.), *Images of Authority: Papers presented to Joyce Reynolds* (1989), 206–28 on a series of acclamations dated to AD 275. For another example from Tralles, see H. Malay, *Epigr. Anat.* 11 (1988), 53–8, with J. Nollé, *Epigr. Anat.* 15 (1990), 121–5 (3rd–4th cent. AD). An inscription from Tlos shows how the public promise of a benefactor, Lalla, provoked a storm of acclamations in the ecclesia demanding that the priest of the imperial cult bring forward a specific proposal that Lalla be given the title 'mother of the city' (ἐφ' οἷς ἀμειβομένη ἡ πόλις τὴν Λάλλαν ἐπεβοήσατο ἐν τῇ ἀρχαιρεσιακῇ ἐκκλησίᾳ τῷ ἱερεῖ τῶν Σεβαστῶν προβουλεύσασθαι ὥστε χρηματίζειν τὴν Λάλλαν μητέρα τῆς πόλεως, C. Naour, *ZPE* 24 (1977), 265–71 no. 1 (*SEG* xxvii. 938)). Here is a rare example where we can be certain that a particular decision to honour a benefactor was taken precisely by the people in the people's assembly (*contra* de Ste Croix, *Class struggle*, 533). Other inscriptions from Asia Minor that preserve references to acclamations in the assembly include the Mylasan decree against black-market monetary dealing (*I. Mylasa*, no. 605, 55–7; perhaps restore *succlam(atum) est*: ἱς αἰῶ[να] / [τοὺς κυρίους· μεγάλοις ἡμ]ῶν ἀνεικήτοις τοῖς κυρίοις· ναοῖς [τοὺς] / [ἡμῖν σώζοντας τὸ κόλλ]υβον (cf. the Tralles inscription for placing (a statue of) the benefactors in the temples). See also Anderson, *JRS* 3 (1913), 284 no. 11 (which should be dated to the 2nd or 3rd, not the 4th cent.) from Pisidian Antioch.

political involvement. The most famous example of all comes from the Acts of the Apostles. The people of Ephesus, meeting in the theatre, were stirred up to a fever pitch by Paul's preaching, and were barely restrained from rioting by the presiding *grammateus*, who reminded them that their tumultuous behaviour might lead the Roman proconsul to restore order.[23] The opposition to Paul at Ephesus had been fomented by the guild of silversmiths under Demetrius, who saw the attack on Artemis of Ephesus as a threat to the living they earned from making silver statuettes of the goddess, and was endorsed by other associations.[24] A century later a famous proconsular edict from Magnesia on the Maeander reveals how the guild of bakers had stirred up riot and disturbance among the people when they gathered in the agora.[25] In both cases trouble had begun with a well-organized group within the citizen body, which feared that its livelihood was at risk.

Such associations, known as *syntechniai*, *homotechniai*, *synergasiai*, or by similar terms, existed in other smaller cities of Asia Minor. Often, no doubt, they were based in rows of shops; the term *plateia*, which was used to describe the colonnaded street which ran along the front of their shops (*ergasteria*), was sometimes combined with the name of a profession, to describe this Roman equivalent of the Islamic bazaar. At the great inland market-city of Apamea in Phrygia, honorific monuments were set up by 'the inhabitants of the colonnaded street by the Bath-House', by the workshop owners (*ergastai*) of the same street, and by the craftsmen in the street of the shoemakers.[26] In the smaller city of Saittai in Lydia the trade associations regularly operated as funeral societies which buried their members.[27] There is abundant evidence for trade organizations in this market town, including a *synergasia* of linen-workers, who occupied their own *plateia*, a *synodos* of the

plateia of shoemakers, as well as further craft guilds, variously titled, of weavers, wool-carders, wool-workers, felt-makers, and carpenters, to say nothing of the young and old men's associations and the town's own neighbourhood groups.[28] It is noteworthy that the gravestones which these associations set up for their members, who appear to have been free citizens not slaves, make no mention of other kinsfolk. We should presumably conclude that, in life as well as in death, members looked to them as a central part of their social life.

These groups of working people and tradesmen usually played a positive role in city life. When the *plateia* of the Paspareitai, a street at Pergamum named after Diodorus Pasparos the great civic benefactor of the 60s BC, honoured the Roman consul L. Cuspius Pactumeius Rufinus with a statue in the mid-second century, it helped to cement good relationships between the leading men of the city and common people.[29] Dio Chrysostom had, after much wrangling and dispute with other leading citizens, completed a portico and a row of *ergasteria* by the theatre at Prusa. He would no doubt have expected to be honoured in the same way by the shop-keepers who had benefited by his generosity.[30] However, the potential for disruption, as revealed by the behaviour of guilds at Ephesus and Magnesia, was equally clear and certainly weighed heavily with Trajan, when he issued his *mandatum* to Pliny in Bithynia around AD 110 that all such associations (called by the general term *hetaireiai*) should be disbanded, however beneficial they might appear, since they invariably formed the focus for political disturbance.[31]

---

[23] Acts 19: 35–42.

[24] See the discussion by Horsley, *New Docs.* iv. 7–10 no. 1.

[25] W. H. Buckler, *ASRamsay*, 30–3; R. Merkelbach, *ZPE* 30 (1978), 164–5; *I. Eph.* ii no. 215. See too the evidence for disturbance at Tarsus caused by the *linourgoi*, where there is evidence for general civic unrest, *Or.* 34 *passim*, esp. 24–31, and C. P. Jones, *The Roman World of Dio Chrysostom*, 80–1.

[26] *IGR* iv. 789–91.

[27] For the character of Saittai as an important regional centre of textile manufacture, see H. Pleket, *Epigr. Anat.* 12 (1988), 32–3, with C. Naour, *ZPE* 44 (1981), 18 ff. F. Kolb, *Epigr. Anat.* 15 (1990), 105–29 publishes a series of inscriptions from the stadium which name several city tribes. These included the inhabitants of two important outlying villages, Tamasi and Satala. Another tribe was the φυλὴ Συναίδος whose name suggests a connection with the small city of Synaos in Mysia Abbaeitis, NĒ of Saittai. These tribal names help to confirm the view that Saittai had a large territory and was the most important city of NE Lydia.

[28] See *TAM* v. 1. 79–81, 146; *SEG* xxix, 1183 (σκυτέων); *TAM* v. 1. 82–4; *SEG* xxix. 1189, xxxi. 1026, 1036, xxxii. 1034 (λινουργῶν); *TAM* v. 1. 85 (λαναρίων); *TAM* v. 1. 86; *SEG* xxix. 1184 (γναφέων); *TAM* v. 1. 91–2 (ποδάριοι); *TAM* v. 1. 90; *SEG* xxxi. 1034, xxxiii. 1020 (γειτοσύνη, γειτονία); *TAM* v. 1. 93 (Χρυσανθῖνοι); *SEG* xxxiii. 1017 (ὑφαντῶν); *SEG* xxxiii. 1018 (unspecified πλατεία); *SEG* xxix. 1186 (τεκτόνων); *SEG* xxix. 1195 (πιλοποίων); *SEG* xxix. 1198 (ἐριουργῶν). The *linourgi* had their own seats in the stadium, F. Kolb, *Epigr. Anat.* 15 (1990), 105–19. Perhaps they also sat together in civic assemblies (cf. n. 11).

[29] *I. Pergamon*, 434; *OGIS* 191; *IGR* iv. 425. One of the supervisors of the dedication was a dyer. Cf. *OGIS* 495 = *IGR* iv. 907 from Cibyra, where the guild of shoemakers (ἡ σεμνοτάτη συνεργασία τῶν σκυτοβυρσέων) honoured an equestrian benefactor ἀνθ' ὧν τῶν δημοσίων ἔργων μετὰ ἐπιμελείας προενοήσατο.

[30] C. P. Jones, *The Roman World of Dio Chrysostom*, 111–14 for the story.

[31] The catch-all nature of Trajan's ban is perfectly illustrated by the fact that it prevented both the formation of a voluntary fire brigade at Nicomedia (Pliny, *Ep.* 10. 34. 1), and Christians from sharing a common meal after worship (10. 96. 7). Trajan allowed social clubs (*eranoi*) to continue at the free city of Amisus, 'facilius si tali collatione non ad turbas et ad

The cities of Bithynia, as is well known, provide the best evidence for political turmoil in the cities of the Greek East in the second century, a phenomenon which is well illustrated by several speeches of Dio Chrysostom and by the letters which Pliny sent to Trajan concerning the province's problems. Two proconsuls had been prosecuted by the Bithynian *koinon* in the senate at Rome in the first decade of the second century. Iulius Bassus was condemned; the fate of Varenus Rufus is uncertain.[32] Such prosecutions, even when clearly justified by the corruption or violence of Roman officials, were unwelcome evidence for disorder: Dio Chrysostom warned the inhabitants of another unruly city, Tarsus in Cilicia, not to arouse Roman resentment by over-zealous prosecution of provincial governors.[33] Trajan's response to the Bithynian difficulties had been to send Pliny and later his friend, Cornutus Tertullus from Perge in Pamphylia, as special legates to the province with particular instructions to eliminate political disturbances and to investigate city finances.[34] In the long term this action hints at a reappraisal of the strategic importance of Bithynia, but the two extraordinary appointments between 110 and 115 were more obviously a response to recent events, and a clear example of how civic unrest might lead to restrictions on civic freedom of action.

Only one fragmentary inscription from Nicomedia alludes to the disturbances in Bithynia which are so familiar from Dio and Pliny.[35] This serves as a warning of how political turmoil simply disappears from view in the absence of literary evidence. An inscription from Cibyra of the Flavian period alludes to the role played by a leading citizen, Q. Veranius Philagrus, in suppressing conspiracies. This had led to the prosecution of a political enemy, whose property together with 107 slaves became public property. Without this last cause for public celebration, the fact would have gone unmentioned on Philagrus' statue base.[36] A letter of Pliny casually mentions that Ti. Claudius Aristio, the leading

figure at Ephesus during the 90s AD, was tried by the emperor's *consilium* in AD 104, and acquitted of charges brought by political opponents. Pliny described Aristio as *innoxie popularis*, which suggests that his political influence rested on his popularity with the common people, a fact that was resented by his enemies.[37] In the same period Plutarch mentions how the hostility between a certain Pardalas and Tyrrhenos at Sardis had almost ruined the city, since a small private quarrel had swelled to rebellion and warfare.[38]

The case of Aristio, the fear of widespread political conspiracies, and the seriousness of some of these disturbances are signs that this political trouble was not confined to the rivalries of city aristocrats. Disputes were conducted in public and involved the whole community. Dio's speeches to Tarsus, and his political advice to the Bithynian cities, were addressed to meetings of the whole people. Their collective reaction was surely as important as the heed paid to him by individual politicians. Dio knew the power of the people and the strength of its feelings at first hand, for years earlier a rioting mob, which demanded that he release grain from his stores during a famine, had been repelled by force from his house in Prusa, and when he spoke in the assembly afterwards to explain that he had no grain to give, he was frequently interrupted by clamorous opposition.[39]

In a Greek city of the Roman empire political meetings were public not private affairs. With rare exceptions,[40] the whole free adult male population was entitled to attend assemblies. It is worth remembering that no such official political meetings had been allowed in Rome itself since the accession of Tiberius. Meetings of the council were not private, but could be

---

inlicitos coetus, sed ad sustinendam tenuiorum inopiam utuntur' (10. 93).

32 Pliny, *Ep.* 4. 9; 5. 20; 6. 5, 13; 7. 6, 10.

33 *Or.* 34. 9, 15; C. P. Jones, *The Roman World of Dio Chrysostom*, 78–80. For the background, see P. A. Brunt's classic paper on provincial maladministration under the principate, *Historia*, 10 (1961), 189–227 (now *Roman Imperial Themes* (1989), 53–95 with substantial addenda on legal aspects, 487–506).

34 For the immediate and longer term implications, see B. Levick, *G&R* 26 (1979), 119–31.

35 *TAM* iv. 1. 3.

36 Robert, *Ét. anat.* 375–8 and *BCH* 102 (1978), 407–8 on *IGR* iv. 914 (J. Nollé, *ZPE* 48 (1982), 267–74) ll. 5–6 (δημοσίους δούλους ἐγνεικήσαντα ἑκατὸν ἑπτὰ καὶ κτῆσιν χώρας), 9–10 (καταλύσαντα συνωμοσίαν μεγάλην τὰ μέγιστα λυποῦσαν τὴν πόλιν).

37 Pliny, *Ep.* 6. 31. 3. See D. Knibbe, *ANRW* ii. 7. 2. 774, 786, W. Alzinger, ibid. 821–2, and esp. R. A. Kearsley, in Horsley, *New Docs.* iv. 49–50; he was the most active promoter of public building in Ephesus between the last years of Domitian and the beginning of Hadrian's principate; hence, no doubt, his popularity.

38 *Mor.* 825c–d; cf. note on *MAMA* ix. 21.

39 *Or.* 46, with C. P. Jones, *The Roman World of Dio Chrysostom*, 19–25.

40 At Sillyon in Pamphylia inscriptions distinguish the members of the ecclesia from mere *politai*; the former received 18 and 77, the latter 2 and 9 denarii in distributions (*IGR* iii. 800 and 801; the same distinction in *IGR* iii. 409 (Pogla, Pisidia); cf. Lévy, *REG* 8 (1895), 203 ff.; A. H. M. Jones, *The Greek City*, 174; de Ste Croix, *Class Struggle*, 528–9. Dio Chrys. *Or.* 34. 21–2 shows that the linen-workers who had been partly responsible for political disturbance at Tarsus (see above, n. 25) were not allowed to attend the assembly as full citizens, although they were natives of the city. In 34. 23 Dio implies that citizenship at Tarsus could be purchased for 500 drachmas. However, this presumably refers not to a wealth qualification for natives but to the price at which Tarsian citizenship had been sold to outsiders.

overheard by any interested citizen who cared to stand in the galleries by their doorways. The councils themselves, several hundred strong and often made up of elected members, at least until the time of Hadrian,[41] comprised a wide cross-section of the middle-ranking citizens, if not of the poorer class. In the face-to-face society of a small town there could have been no political secrets, and the knowledge of what its magistrates and councillors were doing gave the people its strongest political card. Government had to be conducted by consensus; decisions, in reality as well as in the formulae of inscriptions, had to be taken by the council and the people. It was not without reason that when Roman officials sent letters to a city, they addressed the whole collective community—the magis-trates, council, and people. Men, or citizens, still made a *polis*.[42]

Another aspect of civic turbulence under the empire is the well-known and widely attested phenomenon of inter-city rivalry. Although the reconciliatory speeches of Dio Chrysostom and Aelius Aristides indicate no close connection between internal political turbulence and the intense inter-city disputes that broke out over the ranking of cities within provinces and the privileges to which they were entitled, it is remarkable that the regions where strife was most conspicuous were exactly those where the cities were disturbed by their own internal problems. In Bithynia, Nicomedia and Nicaea vied acrimoniously for first rank in the province,[43] and there was no love lost between Nicaea and Cius and

[41] For the size of councils see the evidence collected by Liebenam, *Städteverwaltung*, 229 n. 5, Broughton, *Roman Asia Minor*, 814, and Magie, *RR* ii. 1505. Hadrian's letter to Ephesus commending Lucius Erastus, the ship's captain who had conveyed him across the Aegean in AD 124, as a recruit to the council, implies that members were at least nominally elected (SIG³ 838 = *I. Eph.* iii. 1487). Of course there is also ample evidence for (virtually) hereditary council membership during the second century; cf. Wörrle, *Stadt und Fest*, 133 for Lycia, and de Ste Croix, *Class Struggle*, 529–37.

[42] For a small collection of references to civic decrees on substantive matters (including the raising and spending of revenue), see Magie, *RR* ii. 1504 n. 28.

[43] L. Robert, *HSCP* 81 (1977), 1–39 = *OMS* vi. 211–49; C. P. Jones, *The Roman World of Dio Chrysostom*, 83–94; W. Weiser, *Schweizerische Numismatische Rundschau*, 68 (1989), 55–8, shows how Nicaea and Nicomedia vaunted their titles and privileges on their coin legends under Domitian but, with one exception at Nicomedia, ceased to do so abruptly under Trajan, perhaps, as Wieser assumes, at the behest of a

Fig. 35*a*. Hierapolis celebrates *homonoia* with Ephesus. Obv. Bust of Apollo Lairbenos with radiate crown, *ΛΑΙΡΒΗΝΟΣ*; rev. Two hands clasped, *ΙΕΡΑΠΟΛΕΙΤΩΝ Κ ΕΦΕΣΙΩΝ ΝΕΩΚΟΡΩΝ ΟΜΟΝΟΙΑ*. Mid-third century AD. For Apollo Lairbenos, see Ch. 11 § v at nn. 233–4. *SNG von Aulock*, 3662. 1626.

(*b*) Smyrna in concord with Pergamum. Obv. Wreathed bust of Caracalla; rev. Asclepius (of Pergamum) standing before enthroned Cybele, *ΠΕΡΓΑΜΗΝΩΝ ΣΜΥΡΝΑΙΩΝ ΟΜΟΝΟΙΑ Α ΕΣ ΓΕΜΙΝΟΥ*. Magistrate M. Aur. Geminus, AD 213–16. D. Klose, *Die Münzprägung von Smyrna* (1987), 340 with discussion at 51–3. Caracalla had given Ephesus the right to a third imperial temple; her rivals Smyrna and Pergamum were under pressure to settle their own differences. 8619.

(*c*) Perinthus in concord with Ephesus. Obv. Bust of Gordian III; rev. Ephesian Artemis facing Tyche of Perinthus who carries a cornucopia, *ΠΕΡΙΝΘΙΩΝ Β ΝΕΩΚΟΡΩΝ ΚΑΙ ΟΜΟΝΟΙΑ ΕΦΕΣΙΩΝ*. H. Schönert, *Die Münzprägung von Perinthos* (1965), no. 314. 10641.

(*d*) Antioch on the Maeander. Obv. Armed portrait of Gallienus; rev. Bridge with six arches with river flowing beneath; left, monumental archway with bird on top; above, river god with reeds and cornucopia. The main Roman road to the interior of Asia from Ephesus crossed the Maeander from north to south at Antioch. See Strabo, 13. 4. 15, 630; Robert, *Hellenica*, ii. 95 n. 7. *BMC Caria*, no. 57; M. Price and B. Trell, *Coins and their Cities* (1977), fig. 82. 4494.

(*e*) Diocaesareia (Rugged Cilicia). Obv. Draped bust of Otacilia Severa (AD 244–9); rev. Triumphal arch with four statues above and two standing on consoles, *ΑΔΡ ΔΙΟ[ΚΑ]ΙΣΑΡΕΩΝ Μ ΚΕΝΑ*. Ziegler, *Münzen Kilikiens*, 59 no. 395. A very similar unadorned arch with imperial statues from the same period, probably put up to celebrate imperial victories in eastern campaigns, survives at Ariassus in Pisidia (S. Mitchell, *AS* 41 (1991), 162–4). 10892.

(*f*) Caesareia in Cappadocia. Obv. Wreathed bust of Septimius Severus; rev. two elephants pulling a wagon which carries the cult image of Mount Argaeus. The oriental element in Caesareia's religious culture is abundantly clear from this coin type. See P. Weiss, *JNG* 35 (1985), 21–48 (35 no. 41 for this coin type); for the elephants, compare J. Guey, *REA* 49 (1947), 248–73. 10946.

(*g*) Syedra. Obv. Bust of Lucius Verus; rev. Statues of Dike, Ares, and Hermes with money bag and kerykeion, *ΣΥΕΔΡΕΩΝ*. The statue group was set up at Syedra on the recommendation of an oracle given by Apollo at Claros. L. Robert, *Documents de l'Asie Mineure méridionale* (1966), pl. 14, 2; Ziegler, *Münzen Kilikiens*, 26 no. 121. 12306.

(*h*) Alexandria Troas. Obv. Wreathed bust of Caracalla; rev. Three-quarter view of temple of Apollo Smintheus, with cult statue and tripod inside, COL AUG TROAD. *SNG Copenhagen* 135. 8615.

Coins depicting civic concord, buildings, and cults

between Prusa and Apamea, as they conducted their own disputes.[44] Cilicia at the opposite side of the peninsula, whose history in the second and third centuries had much in common with that of Bithynia, offered a very similar picture. In the time of Dio the metropolis, Tarsus, jealously disputed its position with all its neighbours, including Adana, Mallos, Soloi, and Aegeae.[45] After the Severan period this rivalry was focused on the rising city of Anazarbus. During the civil wars, which began with the usurpation of Septimius Severus in 193 and became endemic in the third century, the stakes in the competition for civic supremacy became higher. As the cities pledged their loyalty to competing imperial rivals, their fortunes rose or fell according to the fortunes of the candidates for the principate and their armies.[46] Inscriptions and in particular coins show exactly the same phenomenon in the leading cities of third century Pamphylia, Perge and Side, which claimed privileges, wooed imperial approval for new honorific titles, and pitched their tutelary goddesses, Artemis and Athena, in competition against one another.[47]

In Asia, the evidence comes above all from the three largest cities, Ephesus, Smyrna, and Pergamum, whose supremacy was clearly unchallenged by others even though it was vigorously disputed among themselves.[48] However, the cities of the Maeander region were also involved in competition. Laodiceia on the Lycus was involved in a dispute over *prōteia*, its place in the status hierarchy, and Nysa and Magnesia on the Maeander claimed the sixth and seventh rank respectively.[49] The positional claims of Magnesia and Nysa may not have related to the whole province of Asia, since neither could lay claim to the eminence that sixth or seventh place implies; there may have been some separate 'league table' for the cities which excluded Ephesus, Pergamum, Smyrna, and perhaps the other assize centres. These disputes over primacy were not merely disputes about titles. At major provincial festivals, seating and processional arrangements certainly made a city's position in the hierarchy clear for all to see. More important still, a city which acquired the right to celebrate an important festival, or to hold assizes,

thereby gained a vital economic advantage for itself. Visitors on such occasions were an important source of local revenue.[50]

III. *Civic Patriotism and Benefactions*

Civic tranquillity, stemming from the politics of consensus, was not a fact that could be taken for granted. The contrast between rich and poor in society was sharply marked, and access to the magistracies, the overt source of political authority, was monopolized by the local nobility. Justice before city magistrates, which was no doubt broadly in line with Roman law, doubtless dealt more kindly with the rich than the poor.[51] Often enough it is likely that the only rule applicable was that the powerful did as they wished with the weak.

These are commonplace observations that can be made of the Roman empire in general and Asia Minor in particular, yet there is startlingly little evidence for direct class-conflict in so unequal a world. Lower-class uprisings in Asia Minor are almost unexampled.[52] A partial explanation lies in the fact that society had always been accustomed to these sharp hierarchical divisions; men knew their place. But order in society was not the result of accident or inertia. Structural features underlay the stability of city life. With the evidence that has survived it is beyond our grasp to analyse the sociological structure of Roman cities in any detail. In the context of Roman Asia Minor it seems appropriate to emphasize two aspects of civic life which are well documented, and can be identified readily as factors that reinforced the unity and stability of the community.

One factor was patriotism. Even the newly founded cities of Asia Minor were regarded by their inhabitants with devotion and pride. In the second century AD Ancyra, Nicaea, or Aphrodisias commanded the loyalty of their citizens as surely as Athens, Sparta, or Argos in the fifth and fourth centuries BC. Artemidorus, the author of the *Analysis of Dreams*, wrote that he preferred to call himself a man of Daldis, his mother's city,

---

proconsul. The legends illustrate precisely the conditions which formed the background to Dio's speeches to both cities.

[44] L. Robert, *HSCP* 81 (1977), 35 n. 171; *Stud. clas.* 16 (1974), 61–9 (*OMS* vi. 275–310).

[45] C. P. Jones, *The Roman World of Dio Chrysostom*, 71–82.

[46] Ziegler, 21–50; 125–9; cf. *JRS* 80 (1990), 192.

[47] On the rivalry of Side and Perge, see esp. J. Nollé, *Antike Welt*, 21 (1990), 244–65, esp. 259 ff.

[48] See R. Merkelbach, *ZPE* 32 (1978), 287–96. The key inscription is the letter of Antoninus Pius to Ephesus, *SIG*³ 849 (*I. Eph.* iv. 1489).

[49] L. Robert, *BCH* 101 (1977), 64–77 = *Documents* 22–35; *Laodicée du Lycos*, 287 on *MAMA* vi. 6.

[50] See further Ch. 14 § vii below.

[51] P. Garnsey, *Social Status and Legal Privilege in the Roman Empire* (1970).

[52] The exceptions occur either at moments of acute political disturbance, such as the revolt of Aristonicus or during the Mithridatic Wars, or in frontier areas where neither civic life nor Roman control was well established. For a good, but almost unparalleled example of a *bellum servile* in Anatolia under the Empire, see Tacitus' account of the uprising in E. Pontus in AD 69, led by a freedman of King Polemo, 'praepotens olim, et postquam regnum in formam provinciae verterat, mutationis impatiens' (*Hist.* 3.48–9). Tribesmen in the area in the mid-2nd cent. still refused to pay their taxes, see below, Vol. II, Ch. 17 § 1 n. 28.

not an Ephesian, since Ephesus could already boast many famous citizens and he thought fit to honour the small Lydian town where he had passed his early years.[53] Dio Chrysostom declared in a speech to his fellow citizens that he would not have chosen Athens, Sparta, or Argos, the first and most distinguished cities of Greece, in preference to Prusa as his home city.[54] The gravestones of men and women who died away from home almost invariably, as far as we may judge, named the city from which they came.[55] At home, countless inscriptions recalled the benefactions which wealthy men gave to their *patris*. Love of one's city went hand in hand with love of honour as a motive for political activity. Moreover, without such patriotic enthusiasm the whole phenomenon of inter-city rivalry would be completely incomprehensible.

Patriotism cannot have been supported on thin air: to have commanded affection and loyalty as they did the new cities of Asia Minor could not have resembled the faceless new towns of the modern world. They were therefore not simply urban conglomerations, or economic units of town and country, but embodied cultural and religious traditions which were specific to each city yet also helped to relate them to the broader environment of Greek culture. On the Black Sea coast Cromna, the tiny sub-colony of Dorian Heracleia Pontica, asserted on its coins that it was the birthplace of Homer himself, while Abonuteichus, after it assumed new importance as the home of the cult of Glycon the new Asclepius, laid stress on its supposed Ionian connections and took the new name Ionopolis.[56] Areas, which had been virtually untouched by Greek civilization before the Roman empire, transformed themselves into literal extensions of the Greek world.

The new cities of the Hellenistic world were already accustomed to establish their credentials by establishing Greek cults and by producing local myths and legends, usually involving the Olympian gods or relating to the city's foundation, which tied their history and mythological past firmly to that of old Greece.[57] But the Greek city of the third or second century BC might still claim to be an autonomous community, and the character of a city was also marked in a concrete and immediate way by adopting an appropriate constitution, erecting the city walls, council chambers, market buildings, and gymnasia that proclaimed that it was a true polis, not an oriental town under despotic rule, or a nondescript village.[58] When political autonomy was no longer an option, still more stress had to be placed on the cultural ties which could be established through history, myth, and religious practices with old Greece.

The emphasis on the cultural heritage of Hellenism is a marked feature of civic life throughout Asia Minor. It took distinct regional forms. In Cilicia, for instance, the leading cities of Aegeae and Tarsos claimed that they had been visited or even founded by the hero Perseus, and claimed kinship with his birthplace, Argos.[59] Argive founders including the seers Calchas and Mopsus played a part in the legendary early history of the cities of Pamphylia, particularly Perge; but the region's name proclaimed the fact (which may be well founded) that it had originally been settled by a mixture of Greek races; and in fact kinship with Athens, demonstrated for instance by cults of Athena Polias, was stressed by several cities.[60] In contrast, the Pisidians of the mountainous hinterland often asserted a relationship with Sparta.[61] Similar claims were elaborated by the cities of north-west Asia Minor and old Greece. The legends attached to the voyage of the Argonauts through the Propontis to the eastern end of the Black Sea provided a peg on which cities of Bithynia could hang out their own claims to Greek origins. Cius and Nicaea both advertised the fact that they had been founded by Heracles, and the latter's connection with Dionysus is familiar from a detailed description in Nonnus, coins, and the Hadrianic inscription on the city's East Gate, which proclaimed Nicaea's descent from the two gods (cf. Fig. 36a).[62] Cities of the interior went so far as to give names to features of their territory that deliberately recreated a Greek environment: the eastern part of the territory of Bithynium-Claudiopolis became Mantinea; the river

---

[53] Artemidorus, *Oneirocritica* 3. 66 (235 Pack); L. Robert, *Rev. phil.* 50 (1976), 188 (OMS v. 342) n. 31.

[54] *Or.* 44. 6.; cf. Mitchell, *Eighth Congress*, 132.

[55] Contrast the practice in late Antiquity, where men preferred to name their village; see Vol. II, Ch. 19 §1 nn. 36–7.

[56] Robert, *A travers l'Asie Mineure*, 132–46; 183–90; 208–90.

[57] For an example, *exempli gratia*, from Paphlagonia, see Robert, *A travers l'Asie Mineure*, 15. The whole subject in the imperial period is surveyed by J. Strubbe, 'Gründer kleinasiatischer Städte. Fiktion und Realität', *Anc. Soc.* 15–17 (1984–6), 255–304, an invaluable guide.

[58] See S. Mitchell, *Mediterranean Archaeology*, 4 (1991), 26.

[59] Cf. Robert, *BCH* 101 (1977), 96–132; A. J. Spawforth and Susan Walker, *JRS* 76 (1986), 101–4.

[60] See *Historia*, 28 (1979), 433. For Perge, see especially P. Weiss, 'Lebendiger Mythos', *Würzburger Jahrbücher*, 10 (1984), 179–208. For the Hellenistic period, see P. Herrmann, *Eighth Congress*, 115–16.

[61] For Spartan connections see Spawforth and Walker, *JRS* 76 (1986), 88–96, with 95 n. 63 for links with Pisidia, which extended back to the 3rd cent. BC.

[62] For claims made by cities of Bithynia see *Eighth Congress*, 130–2, summarizing much detailed work by L. Robert; Robert, *HSCP* 77 (1981), 9–16 and R. Merkelbach, *Nikaia in der römischen Kaiserzeit* (1987) on the foundation legends of Nicaea.

that linked it with Tium on the Black Sea coast was the Ladon, named after the chief river of Arcadia, and a tributary of the Halys on the territory of Gangra in Paphlagonia was called the Xanthus, the alternative name given by Homer to the Scamander in the plain of Troy.[63]

Foundation legends stood at the heart of these civic traditions. Some Phrygian cities traced their origins to Phrygian heroes who had fought on the Trojan side at Ilium, others to king Midas and the age of Phrygia's own greatness.[64] Obscurer connections surface above all in the Dionysiaca of Nonnus, which drew heavily on local legends and foundation stories to enhance its learned and antiquarian flavour.[65] Two foundation myths survive from Ancyra. One attributed the city to the Phrygian king Midas, who had discovered the city's eponymous anchor and dedicated it in the temple of Zeus where it was still to be seen in the later second century AD.[66] The other suggested that the Galatians themselves founded the city and named it after the anchors which they had captured from a Ptolemaic fleet.[67] The etymological connection between the name

Ancyra, which occurs elsewhere as an indigenous place-name both in and outside Asia Minor, and the Greek word for an anchor is fictitious, but the anchor was inevitably adopted as a symbol of the city and displayed on its coins.[68] The legends of Lycaonia made similar play on the resemblance between the name, lykos the Greek word for a wolf, and a legendary founder Lykaon. These stories were blended at Iconium not only with a local tradition of a disastrous flood, but also with the legends of Perseus and the Gorgon Medusa, whose image (eikōn) explained the city's name.[69]

This invention of the past provided the cities with a much firmer sense of their own identity than the creation of workaday administrative structures and institutions. The latter may have served Roman government demands well enough but could not help

[63] Robert, Ét. anat. 262–6; A travers l'Asie Mineure, 411–14.
[64] See Strubbe, Anc. Soc. 15–17 (1984–6), 258–60.
[65] L. Robert, JSav. (1975), 153–92 (= OMS vii. 185–224), esp. 168 (200) ff. with references to earlier discussions.
[66] Pausanias, 1. 4. 5.
[67] Stephanus Byz. s.v. Ankyra.

[68] Both legends are discussed by Bosch, Ankara, pp. 1–7, who adduces parallels for the name (in some of these cases the name is simply and correctly derived from the Greek word for an anchor). A particularly good example of the anchor on the city coins is provided by an unpublished bronze medallion in the collection of the American Numismatic Society, carrying the inscription Ἰούλιος Σατορνῖνος Ἀνκυρανοῖς, comparable to the medallion depicting Antinoos, which was also struck by this Galatian governor (cf. Bosch, Ankara, nos. 131–2).
[69] See Strubbe, Anc. Soc. 15–17 (1984–6), 271 and P. Weiss, Chiron, 20 (1990), 271.

Fig. 36a. Nicaea. Obv. Portrait of Vespasian, ΑΥΤΟΚΡΑ]ΤΟΡΙ ΣΕΒΑΣΤΩ ΟΥΕΣΠΑΣΙΑΝΩ ΝΕΙΚΑΕΙΣ; rev. Head of Dionysus, wreathed in ivy, ΕΠΙ ΜΑΡΚΟΥ ΠΛΑΝΚΙΟΥ ΟΥΑΡΟ[Υ] ΑΝΘΥΠΑΤΟΥ. SNG von Aulock, 536. Dionysus and Heracles were regarded as the two divine founders of Nicaea; see Ch. 12 §III at n. 62. 8767.

(b) Laranda. Obv. Philip I wearing radiate crown; rev. Heracles with lion's skin, right hand resting on club. Aulock, Lykaonien, 71 nos. 117–19; cf. Robert, OMS i. 356–63 at 358. 10975.

(c) Mallos. Obv. Bust of Trajan Decius; rev. The emperor, standing on a yoke of plough oxen, the traditional symbol of a colonial foundation, offers a statuette of Marsyas, which also symbolized the traditional freedom of a Roman citizen, to the Tyche of Mallos. He himself is offered a crown by Amphilochus, the original Argive founder of the city. COLONIA MALLOTON FELIX S.C. SNG Levante, 1291–4; Ziegler, Münzen Kilikiens, 914–15. 15009.

(d) Pergamum. Obv. Bust of Commodus, ΑΥΤΟ ΚΑΙ Μ ΑΥΡΗ ΚΟΜΟΔΟΣ; rev. Scene showing childhood of Telephus, founder of Pergamum. Heracles (who had raped Telephus' mother Auge) surveys mount Parthenion, where the child Telephos is suckled by a doe. Eagle above, and salamander on rocks. ΕΠΙ ΣΤΡ Μ ΑΙ ΓΛΥΚΩΝΙΑΝΟΥ ΠΕΡΓΑΜΗΝΩΝ Β ΝΕΩΚΟΡΩΝ. This highly detailed illustration of the birth of Pergamum's founder was perhaps modelled on a painting. Lederer, Berliner Münzblätter (1909), 4325; cf. H. von Fritze, Die Münzen von Pergamon (1910), 69. 14161.

(e) Tarsus. Obv. Bust of Caracalla in the dress of chief magistrate (demiourgos); rev. Perseus and Heracles, divine founders of Tarsus, carry a bust of Caracalla, the city's new founder, ΑΝΤΩΝΕΙΝΙΑΝΗΣ ΣΕΥ [ΑΔ] ΤΑΡΣΟΥ ΑΜΚ ΓΒ. R. Ziegler, Chiron, 14 (1984), 223 no. 10. Cf. L. Robert, BCH 101 (1977), 96 ff. 10121.

(f) Tarsus. Obv. Draped bust of Caracalla with wreath, star above; rev. Freighter and fish, ΑΝΤΩ[ΝΕΙ]ΝΙΑΝΗΣ ΣΕΥΗ ΑΔ[Ρ] ΜΗΤ ΤΑΡΣΟΥ ΣΕΙΤΟΥ ΓΒ ΑΜΚ. The type refers to the provision of Egyptian grain for Tarsus when Caracalla's troops mustered there for this Parthian expedition. R. Ziegler, JNG 27 (1977), 34 no. 1 (pl. 3.2); cf. Ch. 14 §v n. 71. 3072.

(g) Aegeae. Obv. Wreathed bust of Caracalla; rev. Warship, Α ΑΙΓΕΩΝ ΑΝΤΩΝΕΙΝΟΥ ΠΟΛ ΑΣΟ (= AD 214/15). Aegeae played a key role as a military port, especially in the third century AD. R. Ziegler, JNG 27 (1977), 63 n. 207 (pl. 6.10). 4471.

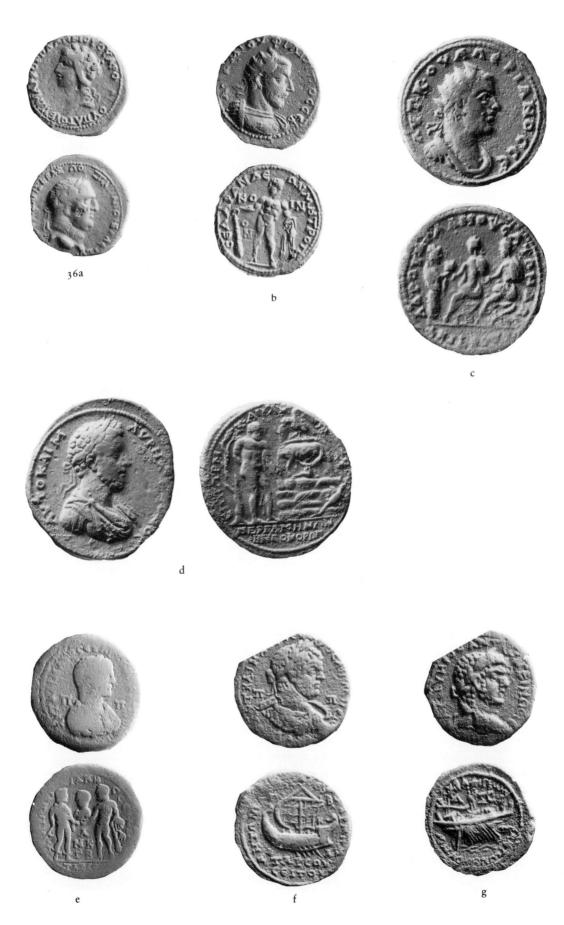

36a

b

c

d

e

f

g

Coins depicting foundation legends and the impact of imperial politics

to focus the loyalty and affection of citizens. Only by harnessing Greek tradition and legend was it possible to create genuine *poleis* in Anatolia.

The second major structural feature of the city life of the imperial period, which secured stability within the community, was the development of a systematic pattern of benefactions by the aristocracy, precisely within the context of civic life. The role of city benefactors began to change noticeably in the Greek world in the later Hellenistic period, especially after the power of Rome began to be felt directly in the communities of Greece and Asia Minor. It has been suggested that there were overriding political reasons for this evolution. Rome preferred to deal with oligarchic rather than democratic regimes and accordingly took steps to encourage a narrow ruling class. Reciprocally, those who henceforward enjoyed the greatest influence and received the greatest honours at home in their cities, were individuals who had most influence with the Romans.[70] The evidence for this is in fact very tenuous. Except on a small number of specific occasions, such as the moment when Pompey regulated the administrative arrangements of the cities of Pontus and Bithynia by the *lex Pompeia*, Roman provincial governors—still less the Roman senate—did not seek an active role in determining the shape of civic politics.[71] Before the Augustan period, and even thereafter, Rome lacked the necessary means to bring about radical and abrupt changes in the balance of power within the cities of the empire.

It is more likely that the real reasons for the shift in the balance of power from democracy to oligarchy in Greek cities were economic. From the later second century BC cities in the Roman provinces ceased to have the right to raise substantial revenue by directly taxing their subjects. Or rather, perhaps, Rome took so much for herself, that there was little room for further taxation locally. Poll and land taxes went either through the hands of *publicani* or directly to the Roman treasury (see below, Ch. 14 § VI). Cities were confined to less lucrative methods of raising revenue, for instance by renting out public land, imposing sales' taxes, or small-scale import and export duties.[72] However, civic aspirations did not decline with civic income. The gap had to be filled by contributions from another source, namely the generosity of the richer citizens, whose political standing naturally rose as they became increasingly responsible for the economic well-being of their communities. By the time of the Roman empire, most cities were dominated by a relatively narrow coterie of rich citizens, who monopolized the magistracies and were active agents in public life.

The conditions of political life in a small city during the second century are well illustrated by the lengthy inscription from Oenoanda which describes the arrangements for a new musical festival founded in AD 125. The sponsor of the festival was a distinguished local man, C. Iulius Demosthenes, who had returned to his native city after a career partly spent in imperial service as an equestrian official. Other members of his family had previously made generous contributions to city life, and he himself had already more than matched them by subsidizing the purchase of grain and building a new food market for the city. He now made a public promise to pay for the foundation of a musical and theatrical festival, eventually by donating land to the city, whose rents would cover the cost of the prizes and other expenses. Although he himself had worked out the financial arrangements and the festival programme in detail, the scheme was definitively drafted by a small committee consisting of three members of the city council; they broadened the terms of the foundation by incorporating a subsidiary promise of Demosthenes to donate an altar and a golden crown for the agonothetes, by stipulating that city magistrates and the surrounding villages should provide sacrificial victims, by arranging that no taxes should be levied on transactions during the festival, and by organizing that the agonothete of the festival should be exempt from holding other offices and liturgies during his tenure. Although all these arrangements were approved by a decree of the council and people, the original initiative lay with the generosity of one man, and the detailed arrangements were worked out by a committee of three councillors. It is important to note that the role played by higher Roman authorities was confined to the possible financial implications of the foundation. The emperor Hadrian confirmed all the arrangements, subject to the provision that the expense fell exclusively on Demosthenes: and the governor of Lycia, Flavius Aper, confirmed the tax-free status of commercial transactions and exemption from other duties for the agonothete, provided that the city's own revenues were in no way impaired.[73]

---

[70] P. Gauthier, *Eighth Congress*, 87–92.

[71] The *lex Pompeia* almost certainly laid down an administrative framework in Pontus and Bithynia (see above, Ch. 7 § III), but the evidence of Dio Chrysostom and Pliny for Bithynia itself shows that Rome did not thereby control political behaviour in the cities.

[72] See A. H. M. Jones, *The Greek City*, 135, 244 ff.

[73] Wörrle, *Stadt und Fest*, passim. See the English trans. in *JRS* 80 (1990), 183–7. I do not agree with the suggestion of G. M. Rogers, *JRS* 81 (1991), 42–51 that the worked-out proposals for the festival significantly altered the founder's original intentions or expectations. The major novelties introduced by the probouleutic committee are easily explained: Demosthenes himself donated a processional statue of Hadrian in response to Hadrian's letter which authorized the foundation; the magistrates and the villages of Oenoanda agreed to contribute sacrificial animals as a reciprocal gesture of thanks to Demosthenes, acknowledging his benefaction (cf. *Stadt und Fest*, 255–6).

The foundation of Demosthenes can be paralleled by dozens of other examples from cities of the Greek East, where wealthy men donated a source of income to their native city, which was to support an important contribution to civic life: public building, grain distribution, expenditure in the gymnasium, or a new festival. The integration of such donations into the framework of urban life shows that there was no practical distinction between activities supported by public revenues and those that were dependent on private acts of euergetism. The three councillors saw fit to extend the scope of Demosthenes' own promise so that it imposed additional obligations on magistrates and villagers to contribute to the festival; non-compliance with the regulations were made punishable by fines to the imperial treasury and to the local sanctuary of Apollo; the newly created post of agonothete enjoyed exactly the same privileges as existing public magistracies.

Two other points deserve emphasis. Firstly, the arrangements of the festival were inherently complicated and required not only careful thought but also doubtless considerable negotiation; especially between the council committee which drafted the document, the city officers, and the villages who were required to contribute sacrificial animals. Their decision was known as a *probouleusimon*, a preliminary proposal, a term which was apparently standard in the cities of Lycia.[74] Such proposals were too elaborate to have been worked out in a full council, and it is clear that most cities must have been prepared to appoint small committees for such purposes. In fact, in southern Asia Minor the office of *proboulos* seems to have become virtually universal.[75] The members of these committees clearly represented an élite within the governing class and illustrate the way in which active political power was increasingly the prerogative of a very small number of citizens.

Secondly, the attitude of the Roman authorities was entirely typical. The initiative in itself was thoroughly admirable: the whole festival represented an enhancement in the life of the city, specifically in the cultural sphere, and it was also combined with forms of homage and cult to the emperors. On the other hand, the active concern of emperor and governor was exclusively with city finances, and the revenue which Oenoanda contributed to Rome. Exactly the same preoccupation characterizes other imperial documents. For instance a third-century proconsul of Asia granted permission for a new rural market to be held on the territory of Magnesia on the Maeander, provided that city revenues were not impaired; and when the city of Mylasa passed new regulations to prevent unofficial conversions from imperial to local currency which

evaded the local levy (*collybos*) on such transactions, they alluded to the fact that otherwise the ready provision of taxes to the emperors was impeded.[76]

It is impossible to estimate what proportion of public expenditure in a Greek city depended on private generosity and benefactions, but it seems clear that no city could hope to thrive without substantial benefactors. Plutarch describes how meanness was a source of powerful resentment, and how public opinion brought great pressure to bear on the rich to spend their wealth on the community.[77] The tensions which these demands generated are occasionally laid bare by narratives which show bargaining at work between the community and its wealthy members about how much the latter should contribute.[78] Nothing, however, more clearly illustrates the expectation that the rich would redistribute their wealth to the benefit of their cities than the idealized descriptions of honorific inscriptions, which endlessly ring the changes on the patriotic zeal, open-handedness, generosity, and public extravagance of magistrates and other benefactors. Although such inscriptions may often have concealed murky scenes of bargaining and dispute between donors and recipients, their very phraseology did more than anything else to create a political climate and showed every aristocrat what was expected of him in public life.

IV. *Public Buildings*

Posterity has not dealt kindly with the public buildings of the cities of central Anatolia. In the whole of Phrygia only the imposing ruins of Aezani survive to impress a visitor. Only a mound indicates the site of the great Asian city of Synnada, the head of an assize district and the administrative centre of the imperial estates and marble quarries of Phrygia. Its fate is typical, and the sparseness of visible remains has led even specialists to conclude that Anatolia was a wilderness in architectural terms.[79]

At the least, there are substantial exceptions to this judgement. As has already been shown, three leading

---

[74] See Wörrle, *Stadt und Fest*, 27–31.

[75] Robert, *Hellenica*, xiii, 64.

[76] J. Nollé, *Nundinas instituere et facere*, 12–58; *SEG* xxxii (1982) 1149 ll. 18–19; *I. Mylasa*, no. 605, 52–3, καὶ διὰ τοῦτο καὶ ἡ εὐπ[ορία ἡ] / [πρὸς τοὺς κυρίους ἀυ]τοκράτορας τῶν φόρων βραδύνει. Compare, of course, Trajan to Pliny, *Ep.* 10. 24: 'Si instructio novi balnei oneratura vires Prusensium non est, possumus desiderio eorum indulgere, modo ne quid ideo aut intribuatur aut minus illis in posterum fiat ad necessarias erogationes.' Both illegal exactions and unnecessary expenditure threatened imperial revenues; so too Cl. Athenodorus, the procurator of Syria under Domitian, *IGLS* v. 1998.

[77] *Mor.* 822.

[78] A. H. M. Jones, *The Greek City*, 185–8; Mitchell, *Eighth Congress*, 125–6 on Dio of Prusa twice declining to take magistracies that were offered to him.

[79] [A. Boethius] and J. B. Ward-Perkins, *Etruscan and Roman Architecture* (1970), 389.

cities of Galatia possessed impressive sanctuaries of the imperial cult by the middle of the first century AD, mostly built under Augustus and Tiberius. These precincts were presumably matched, if not outshone by the Bithynian imperial temples which Octavian had authorized in Nicaea and Nicomedia as early as 29 BC (above, Ch. 8 n. 2). Pliny's letters from Bithynia, in fact, offer the test case by which to measure the progress of public building in Asia Minor during the early empire. As is well known they show that in the cities of Bithynia and Pontus there was a virtual epidemic of uncontrolled, and insecurely financed construction around AD 110. Pliny's evidence of course only provides a sample of information about public buildings in the province, even in his own day, and it is valuable to compare his information with what is known from other sources.

At Prusa substantial sums of money were potentially recoverable from the building supervisors, if proper architectural surveys were made (10. 17b). A new building to replace the old and dirty bath-house was under way, financed by private donors (10. 23–4). This new project involved renovating a notably squalid part of the city, including a large house which had been bequeathed to the city with instructions that it be converted into a temple for Claudius (10. 70). Nicomedia had suffered the loss of many private houses, a temple of Isis and a Gerusia in a recent fire (10. 33); 3,318,000 HS had been spent on an aqueduct, which had to be abandoned before completion, and another 200,000 HS on a second one (10. 37); a new Forum was being added to the old one, involving the repair or relocation of a temple of Magna Mater (10. 49). At Nicaea, the theatre was rumoured to have cost 10,000,000 HS, and more had been promised by private individuals to build basilicas around it and a covered walk-way above the cavea. Here too a bath-house, which had been destroyed by fire, was being replaced with a new building. At Claudiopolis excavation and construction was also in progress for a large bath-house, financed by the entrance fees paid by new members of the city council. There was evidence of poor workmanship and construction problems in all three projects (10. 39). A legacy had been entrusted to Pliny's care, to be spent either on public buildings or on founding quadrennial games at Heraclea and Tium (10. 75). Sinope had the means to finance a new sixteen-mile aqueduct, which was badly needed (10. 90). Likewise, Pliny judged that Amastris had sufficient money to pay for a pavement to cover a polluted stream which ran through the middle of its long and beautiful colonnaded street (10. 98). Archaeology has revealed the theatre at Nicaea and perhaps the Sinope aqueduct; the street at Amastris can be located, but no visible remains have been traced. As has many times

been observed, the problems of Bithynia were evidently those of a booming economy, marked by uncontrolled spending on ill-thought-out and badly executed projects, accompanied, inevitably, by corruption.[80]

Inscriptions from the cities of Bithynia suggest that there had been an earlier peak in building activity in Vespasian's principate. During the proconsulship of M. Plancius Varus, in the 70s AD, two of the city gates of Nicaea were completed and the ship-owners of Nicomedia had started to build a sanctuary and 'a ship-owner's house' (oikos nauklerikos) which was dedicated to Vespasian a year later by Plancius Varus' successor.[81] A private benefactor, Ti. Claudius Nestor, erected a gymnasium at Prusias ad Hypium in the same decade under the proconsul Salvidienus Asprenas.[82] Dio Chrysostom has much to say about building in Prusa at the beginning of the second century, in the decade before Pliny's governorship. He talks of removing a ruined smithy in order to build a new portico, and buying up old property in order to erect a stoa with workshops by the old bath-house. He and others had promised money for these projects, and he was anxious to avoid ugly and useless construction in seeking to make Prusa 'a neat city, more open to the air, with wider spaces, shade in summer, shelter in winter, and instead of mean and sordid ruins, lofty buildings worthy of a great city'.[83] Despite the controversy which his own speeches document, the workshops and stoa were certainly finished by the time that Pliny arrived in the province, and the plan to build a new bath-house, which Trajan and Pliny authorized, fits admirably into this pattern of urban renovation.

Building continued apace after Pliny's term of office. A Latin inscription from the colony of Apamea, Prusa's rival, records the dedication of a bath-house built with civic funds in AD 128/9, and the theatre at Claudiopolis, if not also a large temple on the city acropolis, dates to the same period.[84] Hadrian himself was said

80 For Nicaea's theatre, see S. Mitchell, JHS Arch. Reports (1989–90), 89; Sinope, D. M. Robinson, AJPhil. 27 (1906), 131; Amastris, Robert, A travers l'Asie Mineure, 151–63; C. Marek, Ist. Mitt. 39 (1989), 373–89 at 382.
81 Nicaea: Robert, HSCP 81 (1977), 7–8 = OMS vi. 217–18; SEG xxvii. 819 (Vespasianic), 820–1 (Hadrianic); I. Iznik, i nos. 25–8; Nicomedia: TAM iv. 1. 22.
82 I. Prusias, no. 42.
83 Dio Chrys. Or. 40. 3–9; 45. 11–12, 15–16; 47. 15, 21. See Broughton, Roman Asia Minor, 773; C. P. Jones, The Roman World of Dio Chrysostom, 111–14.
84 I. Apamea, no. 4 (ILS 314); I. Klaudiupolis, nos. 1–2 and pp. 22–3 on the visible remains. N. Fıratlı, Florilegium Anatolicum: Mélanges E. Laroche (1979), 110–20 conjectured that the large imperial temple which dominated the city had been dedicated to Antinous. Dio Chrys. Or. 47. 13 even mentions building at the small city of Caesareia Germanice, which has recently been located at Yaylacık köy near Apamea (T. Corsten, Epigr. Anat. 15 (1990), 19–48).

to have refurbished the agoras, main city streets, and probably the city walls of Nicaea and Nicomedia after a serious earthquake in AD 120. This is partially confirmed by several inscriptions. The East Gate of Nicaea carries a long text with a dedication to Hadrian.[85] Another text, inscribed in Latin, indicates that Hadrian was the dedicatee of an aqueduct, erected between 119 and 137;[86] and a fragmentary career inscription provides information about a local man, Patrocles, who had supervised building in the city in accordance with Hadrian's instructions.[87] An architrave found in Nicomedia carries part of Hadrian's name in the nominative, suggesting that he was responsible for putting up the building to which it belonged.[88]

After the death of Hadrian there is little evidence for new building in Bithynia until the Severan period. Nicomedia obtained the right to build a second imperial temple (a second neocorate) under Commodus and with it permission from the senate to found a new festival and build a temple for the imperial cult.[89] Less reliable sources speak of new building in the city after earthquakes under Antoninus Pius and Marcus Aurelius.[90] Lucian's *Alexander* and local coins are evidence for the temple of the New Asclepius, Glycon, at Abonuteichus on the Black Sea, which was completed by the early 160s,[91] and an inscription mentions an exedra at Heracleia Pontica, built at private expense, in AD 167.[92] There was more activity in the first decades of the third century. Shortly before AD 212, during a year when he acted as civic censor, M. Aurelius Philippianus Iason provided money for building a colonnaded street at Prusias ad Hypium, which should perhaps be identified with remains of such a street which have been observed at the site.[93] In the same period another city notable, M. Iulius Gavinius Sacerdos, responded to the honours and offices which he had received by sponsoring building work: money for the restoration of the bath-house of

Domitius when he was *agoranomos*; 50,000 denarii for the agora when he was priest of the imperial cult; and money for the construction of a new aqueduct on the occasion of an important imperial festival.[94] An inscription of the second century refers to a certain P. Domitius Iulianus, who had 'brought water into the city', evidently by constructing an earlier aqueduct.[95] Since aqueducts were almost invariably built to supply public bath-houses, it is economical to identify this Domitius as the original donor of the bath-house that bore his family name. The theatre at Prusias, whose remains have survived, has been dated to the first century, with refurbishments in the second and third.[96] Another Severan text refers to buildings erected at Dia, Prusias' coastal emporium, by M. Aurelius Chrysenius Damatrius.[97] The presence of the emperor Caracalla during the winter of 214/15 brought numerous tribulations to Bithynia, as Cassius Dio observed, but may have also introduced some imperial patronage of public building. A Latin inscription of Nicomedia indicates that the *lavacrum Thermarum Antoniniarum*, evidently a bath-house named after Caracalla, and perhaps built with help from imperial funds, was reconstructed and enlarged, also at imperial expense, by Diocletian.[98]

The only new public buildings attested in Bithynia in the middle of the third century are the city walls of Nicaea and Prusias, erected around 260 to protect the cities from Gothic invasions and other threats. Although their purpose and nature differed vastly from the agoras, theatres, and bath-houses of earlier times it is revealing that they evinced genuine civic pride and were depicted on the city coinage.[99] Thereafter, the only attested public construction in the province belongs to the period when Diocletian made Nicomedia his eastern capital, refurbishing not only the baths of Caracalla but much else besides, and created a city that still impressed Libanius in the 360s.[100]

The evidence for public building in central Anatolia is sparser even than the inadequate record for Bithynia,

[85] See L. Robert, *BCH* 102 (1978), 395 ff. = *Documents* 91 ff. According to the *Chronicon Paschale* Ἀδριανὸς ἐν Νικομηδείᾳ καὶ Νικαίᾳ ἀγορὰς ἐποίησε καὶ τετραπλατείας καὶ τὰ τείχη τὰ πρὸς τῇ Βιθυνίᾳ. The East Gate of Nicaea, restored under Hadrian, led directly into the heart of Bithynia (see above, n. 81 for the inscriptions).
[86] *I. Iznik*, i no. 55.
[87] See T. Corsten, *Epigr. Anat.* 10 (1987), 111–14; but the restoration of the last line must be wrong. Patrocles was too eminent to have been a phylarch (see above, §11 at n. 13). Perhaps read [τιμηθέντα ὑπὸ φυλῆς] Διονυσιάδος *vel. sim.*
[88] *TAM* iv. 1. 10.
[89] Cassius Dio (epitome of Xiphilinus), 73. 12. 2.
[90] Cassius Dio (epitome), 70. 15. 4; Aur. Vict. *Caes.* 16. 12.
[91] Lucian, *Alex.* 14–16.
[92] *IGR* iii. 1428; another building which cost 20,000 denarii is mentioned in *JÖAI* 28 (1933), Beibl. 100.
[93] *I. Prusias*, no. 9, with Ameling's n.

[94] *I. Prusias*, no. 20.
[95] *I. Prusias*, no. 19.
[96] Ameling, on *I. Prusias*, no. 20 remains agnostic on the identity of the bath-builder. For discussion and illustrations of the ruins of Prusias, see Ameling, *I. Prusias*, 12–13, pls. i–ix.
[97] *I. Prusias*, no. 29.
[98] *TAM* iv. 1. 29 (*ILS* 613); Magie, *RR* ii. 1562 n. 42. The baths, which were very large, were restored again by Justinian, Procopius, *Aed.* 5. 3. 7.
[99] M. Price and B. Trell, *Coins and their Cities* (1977), 104–5 with figs. 190–2 for Nicaea; *SNG von Aulock*, 915 for Prusias. See W. Wieser, *Katalog der bithynischen Münzen der Sammlung des Instituts der Universität zu Köln. Band 1. Nikaia* (1985), 90–1 and pl. xxviii.
[100] *Not. Dign.* 32; Lactantius, *Mort. Pers.* 7; Aur. Victor, *Caes.* 39, 45; Libanius, *Or.* 41. 5 ff.

but it broadly confirms the pattern that can be observed there. At Ancyra, there is virtually no datable building activity between the reign of Augustus, which saw the construction of the temple of Rome and Augustus and probably the theatre (above, Ch. 8 at nn. 35–7), and the large bath-house built by Ti. Iulius Iustus Iunianus in the time of Caracalla.[101] City walls were added in the mid-third century (below, Ch. 13 § IV n. 54). At Pessinus there is evidence that the Tiberian imperial temple was reconstructed after an earthquake in the early second century, and an arch was built over the main street, which is perhaps second century, in the Severan period.[102] At Pisidian Antioch, the imperial precinct in the city centre was constructed between the time of Augustus and Claudius, while the northern end of the city, including colonnades along the *cardo maximus*, a nymphaeum, bath-house, and aqueduct, probably all date to the late first and early second century. The stage-building of the theatre was built, or rebuilt, under the Severans. Antioch became the metropolis of the new province of Pisidia under Diocletian, and this development, like the promotion of Nicomedia to the status of a capital, was also marked by important new building projects next to the theatre.[103] It must be stressed that even in these cities where excavations and detailed surveys have taken place, only a few of the public buildings have been identified, still less accurately dated.

Our knowledge of unexcavated cities, where virtually nothing survives above ground, is naturally scantier still. More or less by chance, inscriptions have survived which mention a theatre of the Julio-Claudian period at Iconium, built partly with imperial funds and partly by the contributions of local citizens,[104] a temple of the imperial cult at Cana dedicated in AD 104/5,[105] a Hadrianic temple at neighbouring Perta,[106] and a bath-house of the same period at Sidamaria.[107] No precise date can be offered for other buildings in the cities of the plateau, such as a theatre, an aqueduct, and a nymphaeum at Laodicea Catacecaumene,[108] and a temple at Neapolis in the Cillanian plain.[109] A similarly haphazard picture of building could be

sketched in other areas of Anatolia, such as northern Lydia or much of Phrygia, where urban development only began under the Roman empire. The evidence is so patchy that it can tell us virtually nothing about the overall development of any particular city. Taken as a whole, however, it suggests that the development of urban public building was virtually complete by AD 220.[110] A survey of imperially sponsored public building in the eastern provinces leads to very similar conclusions. Imperially funded construction began with notably intense activity under Augustus and continued until the middle of the second century AD, with a second conspicuous peak in the principate of Hadrian, whose active interest in the development of cities is well documented. Thereafter, there is a sharp decline and virtually the only new constructions supported by the emperors in the third century, apart from roads and military installations, were city walls.[111]

Two large and well-studied cities exemplify the pattern admirably. Although they had undoubtedly been preceded by small-scale Hellenistic construction, the earliest datable buildings of Aezani do not belong before the Flavian period. The crucial period in its history, when it was transformed from a small Phrygian city into an architectural show-piece, occupied fifty years of the second century from about 125 to 175. During this time the temple and sanctuary of Zeus, the theatre, the main civic gymnasium, and the stadium were all built on a scale that matches almost anything to be seen in Ephesus, Smyrna, or Pergamum. The stadium, which was last of this series to be built, appears never to have been completed. Money, we may assume, was running short and by the early third century Aezani was forced to live more modestly within its means.[112] Sagalassus, the metropolis of

[101] C. Foss, *DOP* 31 (1977), 62–3, with the inscriptions published by Bosch, *Ankara*, nos. 255–8 and AS 27 (1977), 72–3 no. 6.

[102] See M. Waelkens, *Fouilles de Pessinonte*, i (1984), 78–94 summarized in *Archaeological Reports*, 31 (1984–5), 99.

[103] AS 33 (1983), 9–11 and 34 (1984), 8–10, anticipating Mitchell and Waelkens, *Pisidian Antioch: The Site and its Monuments*, forthcoming.

[104] *IGR* iii. 262 and 1474.

[105] *MAMA* viii. 211; for the date see above, Ch. 7 § v n. 185.

[106] See Ch. 7 § v n. 178.

[107] *IGR* iii. 273.

[108] *CIL* iii. 13637; *Klio*, 10 (1910), 235 = *MAMA* vii. 11.

[109] *MAMA* viii. 350.

[110] See the material collected by Broughton, *Roman Asia Minor*, 734–94.

[111] *HSCP* 101 (1987), 333–65.

[112] See R. Naumann, *Der Zeustempel zu Aizanoi* (1979). M. Wörrle argues in *Chiron* 22 (1922), 337–76 that the intensive building activity in the Hadrianic and Antonine period should be attributed largely to the initiative and generosity of the city's main benefactor, M. Ulpius Appuleius Eurycles. Reports on the recent excavations have been summarized, with full references to the original publications, in *Arch. Reports*, 31 (1984/5), 96–8 and 37 (1989/90), 127. For a historical résumé, see *MAMA* ix. pp. xxiii–xxix, and B. Levick, 'Aspects of Social Life at Aezani: A Preview of MAMA ix', in E. Frézouls (ed.), *Sociétés urbaines, sociétés rurales dans l'Asie Mineure et la Syrie* (1987), 260–70. In *MAMA* ix. 10, the dedication to Zeus of Aezani and Antoninus Pius, which refers to the construction of an aqueduct, perhaps restore τὸ βαλανεῖον or τὸ γυμνάσιον in l. 4; in which case the inscription should be connected with the large bath-house of this period recently excavated at the site (reports in *Arch. Anz.* 1980, 1982, 1984, where no dating is suggested. The architectural mouldings illustrated there, and

Fig. 37. Aezani. A view from the Hadrianic theatre along the stadium, which was under construction through the midde of the second century AD, looking towards the centre of the city where the temple of Zeus is visible among the trees.

Fig. 38. The north gate of Nicaea. The lower part of the structure dates to the Flavian period in the first century AD. The upper parts were built in several phases between the third and sixth centuries AD, but the brick construction is characteristic of Roman building techniques which were introduced to Asia Minor throughout the imperial period and became a staple of early Byzantine architecture. See A. M. Schneider, *Die römischen und byzantinischen Denkmäler von Iznik* (1943) and C. Foss and D. Winfield, *Byzantine Fortifications.*

Civic buildings

Pisidia, shows a much longer history of active public building, with a tradition that began at least as early as the second century BC. Several large projects belong to the Julio-Claudian period, especially the temple of Apollo Clarios and the monumental arches and propylons around the upper and lower agoras. It too enjoyed spectacular growth in the second century AD, with an enormous new temple precinct for Antoninus Pius and a massive bath-house, both probably complete by AD 150, which dominated the lower part of the city. But the latest datable construction before the church buildings of the late empire is a Severan gateway. The rest of the third century saw no significant additions.[113]

The exceptions to this pattern come mainly from cities in southern Asia Minor, especially in and around Pamphylia: triumphal arches for Severus Alexander at Isaura and Ariassus in Pisidia, a nymphaeum from the reign of Gordian III, and even a new aqueduct after AD 250 at Side.[114] Pamphylia, in particular, seems to have enjoyed a charmed life in the middle and later third century, relatively insulated from the upheavals and invasions that threatened the rest of Asia Minor (see below, Ch. 13 § IV at n. 75).

In the early years of the principate, particularly during the reign of Augustus himself, the urban landscape of Asia Minor had been changed by the construction of temples and sanctuaries for the imperial cult. Monumental sanctuaries came to dominate the city centres.[115] After the middle of the first century another development is equally conspicuous, the introduction of bath-houses. The bath-house, and its inevitable corollary the aqueduct, set the style for the cities of the empire in the later first and second centuries. The evidence reviewed above, and much more that could be quoted in addition, contains more references to bath-houses than to any other form of building. 'Gymnasiis indulgent Graeculi'—'today's Greeks have a weakness for gymnasia.' Trajan's famous remark to Pliny, when confronted with the projects to build a gymnasium at Nicaea and the bath-house at Claudiopolis, is usually cited as evidence for the emperor's amused tolerance of the habits of his Greek subjects. What the remark really reveals is a key aspect of the transformation, and precisely the Romanization of cities in the empire. By the second century AD the term gymnasium had become effectively synonymous with *balineum*, for by this period an exercise area without an attached bath-house was inconceivable.[116] This development was accelerated, if not actually caused by technological innovations. New methods of heating and insulating bath buildings had been introduced to Rome in the Julio-Claudian period and began to be disseminated in Asia Minor from the middle of the first century.[117] Another vital precondition was confidence in the *pax Romana*. The aqueducts that brought water from outside the cities and fed the bath-houses had to cross the boundary of the city walls, thereby negating their defensive value. The Roman aqueduct was made possible only by universal peaceful conditions.[118]

Thereafter it became a practical possibility to replace very modest Greek bathing establishments with increasingly palatial structures. Virtually the earliest major example in Asia Minor is the large bath-house built at Miletus in AD 43 by Vergilius Capito, equestrian procurator of Asia and prefect of Egypt, a local resident of Italian extraction.[119] The example he set was infectious. Between AD 70 and 150 a profusion of bath buildings sprang up in every city, conforming to a number of clearly defined regional styles.[120] Their importance can be illustrated not only by the massive remains at great cities like Sardis, where the bath–gymnasium complex covered an area measuring 120 by 170 metres and was 'undoubtedly the most monu-

the statue of Hygieia found in the building appear to belong to the mid-2nd cent.).

[113] See M. Waelkens, AS 37 (1987), 37–43; 38 (1988), 60–5; 39 (1989), 67–74; 40 (1990), 185–98.

[114] Isaura: Swoboda, *Denkmäler*, 74 no. 150; Ariassus: AS 41 (1991), 162; Side: see below, Ch. 13 § IV at n. 76. Note a bath-house at the Hyssēnōn *katoikia*, a village of northern Lydia, dedicated to Severus Alexander in AD 231, by a woman who was the daughter of a centurion from Ephesus and granddaughter of a *matrona stolata*, TAM v. 1. 758.

[115] Price, *Rituals and Power*, esp. 133–79; H. Hänlein-Schäfer, *Veneratio Augusti: Eine Studie zu den tempeln des ersten römischen Kaisers* (1985), with the comments of Price, JRS 76 (1986), 300–1; above, Ch. 8 at nn. 2–20.

[116] J. Delorme, *Gymnasion* (1960), 243–50; R. Ginouvés, *Balaneutikè* (1962), 147–50.

[117] The technological innovations, particularly new types of hot-air pipes (*tubuli*), and later larger windows, and their implications are examined in detail by A. Farrington, in his Oxford D.Phil. thesis on Lycian bath-houses. My remarks owe much to this, and to his 'Imperial Bath Buildings in South-West Asia Minor', in S. Macready and F. H. Thompson (eds.), *Roman Architecture in the Greek World* (1987), 50–9. For a recent general review, see J. Delaine, JRA I (1988), 11–32.

[118] J. J. Coulton, 'Roman Aqueducts in Asia Minor', in *Roman Architecture in the Greek World*, 72–84: 'I suggest, therefore, that the countless aqueducts of Asia Minor are not due to Roman know-how, nor, for the most part, to imitation of Rome. They were made possible by the Roman peace and its associated urban expansion, but the motivating force for their construction was to a large extent the spread of the Roman bathing habit.' My own observations of aqueducts and bath-houses in Pisidia coincide exactly this judgement. See too E. J. Owens, G&R 38 (1991), 41–58.

[119] Published by A. von Gerkan and F. Krischen, *Milet*, I. 9 (1938). Note the observation of M. Waelkens, in *Roman Architecture in the Greek World*, 97, that this building saw the first use of Roman construction techniques at Miletus.

[120] Defined by Farrington, opp. citt.

mental public structure' in the city;[121] or at Ephesus where no less than three great bathing palaces, similar in design to the Sardis structure, occupied over twenty acres of the urban landscape;[122] but also in the back-country of Lydia, where baths were built, usually with private funds, throughout the small towns and the larger village communities.[123] Faced with this evidence, we need have no hesitation in assuming that baths were also ubiquitous in the unexcavated cities of Phrygia, Galatia, and Lycaonia.

Large scale bath-houses offered a sharp visible contrast to the existing public buildings of the city. Structural considerations made it necessary to erect buildings with massive exterior walls, usually constructed from undecorated ashlar, brick, or concreted mortar, whose humdrum appearance clashed with the elegance of a city's temples and colonnades. The utilitarian design considerations which produced ugly exteriors did not extend to the interiors, which were sumptuously fitted with marble panelling and decorated with statuary.[124]

The bath-house, therefore, more than any other building type, can be taken as the architectural symbol of the new cities of the imperial period, more especially of the great age of construction during the second century AD. It was naturally accompanied by a cultural shift in the nature of city life. Providing for the gymnasium was as important for the cities as the original construction of buildings, and the gymnasiarchate became one of the most important, and expensive civic magistracies.[125] In one year at Phrygian Apamea, annual expenditure on oil for the gymnasium came to 34,000 denarii, a sum which would have covered the cost of the quadrennial musical festival founded by Iulius Demosthenes at Oenoanda more than seven times over.[126] Prosperity, as well as peace and technological progress, was the third essential requirement to support the new bathing habit.

Public building in the cities of Asia Minor was the touchstone for civic life. More specifically, the buildings which were especially typical of the imperial period, notably imperial cult sanctuaries and bath-houses, created an entirely new urban environment. The Graeco-Roman cities of the high empire were unmistakably different from the Hellenistic cities which they supplanted. The cities of Anatolia, for all their claims to kinship with famous Greek prototypes, were products of a radically different culture.

v. *Agonistic Festivals*

By the second century AD almost every city of Asia Minor had at least one bath-house, and beside it an exercise area, usually a palaestra surrounded by colonnades. Public bathing habits, which had become prevalent, were intimately connected with the cultural and physical training of the gymnasium. The terms bath and gymnasium, when they refer to buildings at least, were indistinguishable. The gymnasium was an institution whose origins can be traced virtually to the beginnings of city life; its complex history, therefore is an essential strand in the history of the development of the *polis* itself.[127] In a famous episode, rigorist Jews interpreted the founding of a gymnasium in Jerusalem by Antiochus IV as tantamount to the creation of a Greek, not a Jewish community, and broke out into open revolt against the Seleucids.[128] Gymnastic training, involving musical as well as physical exercise, prepared young men for citizenship. The gymnasium was closely linked with competitive *agones*, athletic or musical competitions, which had been staged in the context or religious festivals since the beginnings of organized Greek society. It is accordingly not a coincidence that the development and dissemination of bath-house/ gymnasia complexes was accompanied by an enormous increase in the number of agonistic festivals in eastern cities.

Under the Roman empire these competitive festivals emerged as one of the dominating features of civic life throughout the Hellenized East, but above all in the cities of Asia Minor.[129] Analysis of the abundant evidence for these games has revealed their complexity and bewildering variety. Competitions might be athletic, artistic, or both. Lesser festivals sometimes allowed competitors only from the host city,[130] but the

---

[121] F. K. Yegül, in G. Hanfmann, *Sardis from Prehistoric to Roman Times* (1983), 148–60, who also emphasizes the importance of the baths of Capito in the tradition of Asia Minor baths. See now his *Sardis 3: The Bath–Gymnasium Complex at Sardis* (1986).

[122] See, in brief, W. Alzinger, *RE* suppl. xii (1970), 1618 ff. Plans of the main Ephesian bath-houses are conveniently collected by Boethius and Ward-Perkins, *Etruscan and Roman Architecture*, 400 fig. 151. See too F. Kolb, *Die Stadt im Altertum* (1984), 178.

[123] The evidence is summarized by Broughton, *Roman Asia Minor*, 767–87; *TAM* v. 1. 611 n. on l. 22; H. W. Pleket, *Talanta*, 2 (1970), 80 ff.

[124] For the structural imperatives of bath design, see Yegül, *Sardis 3*.

[125] Delorme, *Gymnasion*.

[126] *IGR* iv. 788.

[127] See H. W. Pleket, 'Games, Prizes, Athletes and Ideology: Some Aspects of the History of Sport in the Graeco-Roman World', *Stadion*, 1 (1975), 49–89 for discussion of the disputed origins of the gymnasium in the archaic and classical Greek city.

[128] Schürer[2], i. 148.

[129] L. Robert, *Eighth Congress*, 35–45; S. Mitchell, *JRS* 80 (1990), 189–93; Pleket, *Stadion*, 1 (1975).

[130] So, for instance, at Side, Bean, *The Inscriptions of Side*

important ones were open to all-comers. From the early Hellenistic period the international guilds of competitors had a crucial role to play in the administration of a growing 'circuit' of games, which might be staged annually, or at intervals of two or more commonly four years.[131] The smaller competitions were known as *themides*, prize games, for which the victor's reward, apart from personal glory, was a money prize or *thema*. The most prestigious competitions were known as *hieroi* or *hieroi kai stephanitai agones*, sacred or sacred crown games, so-called because the victor's reward in these cases was a crown, which was dedicated to the gods.[132] The competitors' guild, indeed, took the name of 'the sacred winners of crowns and their fellow competitors associated with Dionysus'.[133] In fact, the distinction between the two types of festival is far less clear-cut than this suggests. Not only did the same competitors take part in similar events at both types of festival, but there is incontrovertible evidence to show that money prizes were also offered at the sacred games.[134]

The prestige of victors was not only on display at the games themselves. Victors in the sacred games enjoyed the privilege of making a triumphal processional return to their home town, thereby parading their success in front of their fellow citizens and allowing the city itself to bask in their reflected glory. They were also entitled to claim a material reward from the city. The term used to describe this, *opsonia*, suggests free meals at public expense rather than some form of cash pension.[135]

Games and competitions were naturally ubiquitous in the new cities of the Hellenized East. It is reasonable to assume that most if not all communities staged competitions for their citizens, and especially for the young men, in the context of the life of the gymnasium. Naturally only a very sparse record of these small domestic competitions has survived.[136] On the other hand evidence both for sacred games, and for *themides* which served as major civic festivals and attracted outside competitors is abundant, and it is possible to trace the main lines of the diffusion of this agonistic activity with reasonable clarity.

There are, of course problems. Despite the large number of relevant inscriptions that have come to light,[137] newly discovered epigraphic and numismatic evidence continues to reveal hitherto unattested contests. For example, a single inscription from Ancyra, erected in honour of a successful competitor at the *Isopythia Asclepieia Sotereia* around AD 218, mentions two previously unknown sacred festivals where he had also won victories, the *Commodeion* at Cappadocian Caesareia and the *Actia* at Antioch.[138] The abundant numismatic evidence also only offers a partial picture. With a few exceptions,[139] agonistic legends and coin types found on civic issues relate only to *hieroi agones*, and provide no information about the numerous smaller *themides*. Indeed not all cities which staged sacred games necessarily advertised the fact on their coins. Moreover, agonistic coin types do not appear at all before the reign of Commodus.[140] As many examples demonstrate, this cannot be taken to show that the games in question did not exist at an earlier date. For instance, numismatic evidence of the mid-third century from Ancyra and from Side refers to *agones mystikoi* which were celebrated at this period. An inscription from Ancyra happens to survive which shows that the festival was created under Hadrian, and there are sound reasons for believing that Side's competition started at the same time (see below, n. 154). It was also common for *agones* to change their names, in particular by acquiring new imperial titles, or for two festivals to be fused into one, either for a particular occasion or on a permanent basis. The effort required to unravel such complexities in local history can

(1965), 44 no. 146, and perhaps at Laertes, Bean and Mitford, *Journeys in Rough Cilicia 1964–8* (1970), 103 no. 88. Discussion of the meaning of the phrase πολιτικὸς ἀγών by Wörrle, *Stadt und Fest*, 241–2.

[131] Pleket, *ZPE* 10 (1973), 197–227.

[132] For the explanation of ἱερὸς στέφανος, see L. Robert, *Rev. arch.* (1978), 202–6 = *OMS* vii. 686–90.

[133] Magie, *RR* ii. 1402 n. 12 with earlier literature.

[134] See esp. Pleket, *Stadion*, 1 (1975), 56–71.

[135] Hence the term εἰσελαστικοί, see P. Weiss, *ZPE* 48 (1982), 125 ff.

[136] So, for instance, at Mylasa in Caria a group of inscriptions, in the form νίκη followed by the name of a winner, were carved on various blocks which presumably once stood in the gymnasium (*I. Mylasa*, i. 541–63). An inscription from Hyde near Mylasa provides interesting details of a local competition for boys endowed by a *paidonomos*, *I. Mylasa*, ii. 909, 15–19: ἔθηκεν δὲ τοῖς παισὶν πλεονάκις καὶ ἆθλα τὰ καθήκοντα τοῖς

ἀγῶσιν τοῖς τε ἐν παλαίστρᾳ τετελεσμένοις διαδρομῆς καὶ πάλης καὶ πυγμῆς καὶ παγκρατίου· ὁμοίως δὲ ἔθηκεν ἆθλα καὶ τῆς ἐν γράμμασιν ἁμίλλης καὶ ἀναγνώσεως τε καὶ καλλιγραφίας καὶ φιλομαθίας.

[137] L. Moretti, *Iscrizioni agonistiche greche* (1953) can naturally now be supplemented.

[138] *AS* 27 (1977), 75 no. 8; cf. *Bull. ép.* (1978), 489.

[139] Coin legends which allude to local *themides* occur in Pisidia at Palaiopolis (von Aulock, *Pisidien*, i. 1107–8, Elagabalus); Baris (Aulock, *Pisidien*, ii. 266–8, Severus Alexander); Prostanna (*Pisidien*, ii. 1809, cf. 1816–17, Severus Alexander); Seleuceia Sidera (*Pisidien*, ii. 1902–4, Elagabalus); Ariassos (*Pisidien*, i. 482–4, Gordian III, Otacilia Sebaste; in 484 ΙΕΡΟC ΑΓΩΝ should not be read). Similar legends occur on coins of Aspendos and Perge in Pamphylia, and Corycus and Syedra in Cilicia Tracheia (references in Karl, 57–8). See the study of H. Gaebler, 'Die Losurne in der Agonistik', *ZfN* 39 (1929), 271–312.

[140] See Karl, a useful, although incomplete collection of agonistic coin legends on 'Greek imperial' bronzes. His catalogue does not include agonistic types without an inscribed legend.

sometimes make it difficult to appreciate important points about the history of *agones* as a whole.[141]

Agonistic festivals occupy so large a place in the surviving evidence for the Greek cities of Asia Minor under Roman rule that a sketch, if not an exhaustive account of their development, is essential to an understanding of the development of cities in general. During the first century AD the systematic establishment of the imperial cult was the most important vehicle for the dissemination of new agonistic festivals. Augustus authorized new sacred games, the *Romaia Sebasta* to be held at Pergamum in connection with the provincial temple of Rome and Augustus; likewise *Romaia* were founded in Lycia.[142] Games of the *koinon* of Asia were held annually in Ephesus, Smyrna, Pergamum, or, in the fourth year, in one of five other cities.[143] Similar, though less elaborate cycles were doubtless established in the other provinces. The *koinon* games of Bithynia were staged at Nicomedia and Nicaea; of Galatia at Ancyra and Tavium; of Pontus at Neocaesareia; of Cappadocia at Caesareia; and of Lycia in Myra and Limyra.[144] Many games with the name *Sebasteia* or *Augusteia*, sometimes added to previous titles, are attested in individual cities, although it cannot always be assumed that they were all founded under Augustus.[145] Although they did not eclipse or replace several important agonistic festivals that had existed in the Hellenistic period, most of the prestigious *agones* of the first century AD were directly linked to emperor worship.

During the remainder of the first century AD, the only emperors who gave their names to agonistic festivals in Asia Minor were Claudius in three Asian cities,[146] and Vespasian in the province of Lycia and Pamphylia.[147] The absence to date of any festival named after Nero, connoisseur and competitor in musical and equestrian competitions, is unexpected and striking evidence that his enthusiasm for Greek culture was largely restricted to Greece in the narrow sense. However, the emergence of new imperial games in this period was accompanied by important private foundations. Two of the great nabobs of Asia in the Julio-Claudian period, Cn. Vergilius Capito at Miletus, and Ti. Claudius Balbillus of Ephesus, both in their time prefects of Egypt, founded festivals in their native cities, the *Capitoneia* and the *Balbilleia*, of which the latter established itself as one of the major sacred games.[148]

Only two agonistic festivals are known which were named after Trajan, one at Xanthos in Lycia,[149] the other at Pergamum. Between 113 and 116 C. Antius A. Iulius Quadratus, twice consul, endowed the *Diiphileia Traianeia*, a quadrennial festival which was given sacred status and parity with the *Romaia Sebasta* by a decision of the senate and a letter of the emperor himself. The *senatus consultum* contains the characteristic reminder that the cost of the games should be borne by the founder.[150]

Hadrian was as active in promoting new imperial festivals as he was in endowing public buildings in the Greek East. Aelius Aristides, *more suo*, announced that he had turned his empire into a vast festival procession,[151] and the rhetoric may be thought justified not only by three major agonistic festivals which he established in his 'Hellenic capital' Athens,[152] but also by games which took his name at six other eastern cities.[153] Hadrian was also personally involved in the creation of a group of *mystikoi agones*, whose programme was probably restricted to artistic events. These are attested at Pamphylian Side, Iconium,

141 See Pleket's just remarks on the voluminous studies of L. Robert, *Stadion*, 1 (1975), 52–3.
142 Pergamum: Magie, *RR* ii. 1295–6 n. 57; Xanthos: Robert, *Rev. arch.* (1978), 277 = *OMS* vii. 681; Balland, *Xanthos*, vii, no. 18; Wörrle, *Stadt und Fest*, 238.
143 See L. Moretti, *RFIC* 82 (1954), 276–89 (= *Tra epigrafia e storia* (1990), 141–54).
144 Deininger, *Provinziallandtage*, 61, 64, 66, 68. For Lycia, see *Stadt und Fest* 238–40. At Patara and Telmessus local games known as the *megala Kasseia* and *Sarpedoneia* were on occasion at least treated as festivals of the Lycian *koinon* (ibid., 239 n. 73). For Cilicia, see Ziegler, 58–66.
145 See Ziegler, 118 n. 314 for *Augusteia*, which seem all to be 3rd cent. creations, in contrast to *Sebasta* which can usually be traced back to Augustan times.
146 At Magnesia, *I. Magnesia* 163; Laodicea on the Lycus, *REG* 19 (1906), 253 ff. no. 148; the *Sebasta Claudieia* at Aezani were perhaps a development of earlier games, the *Sebastoi Neoi Homobōmioi*, an imperial cult festival which was also attested in Cadi see (E. Babelon, *Inv. Wadd.* 5789) and Tiberiopolis (*IGR* iv. 556); see *MAMA* ix, pp. xxii–xxiv.
147 Oenoanda, *IGR* iii. 487 with *Stadt und Fest*, 239. Wörrle argues against Balland, *Xanthos*, vii. 234 that these games were mounted by the Lycian *koinon*. If so, it should perhaps be added to the other evidence which indicates that Vespasian undertook a major reorganization of Lycia, perhaps even promulgating a *lex provinciae* (*Stadt und Fest*, 97–100). There is evidence that Vespasian directly or indirectly encouraged public building; see *HSCP* 91 (1987), 347 and 353; C. Naour, *Anc. Soc.* 9 (1978), 167–70; J. Coulton, in *Roman Architecture in the Greek World*, 80.
148 *Magie, RR* ii. 1398–9 n. 5.
149 Balland, *Xanthos*, vii. 235.
150 *CIL* iii. 7086. The games were of course associated with the new temple of the imperial cult, the so-called Traianeion, for which see the important discussion by W. Radt, *Pergamon* (1988), 239–50.
151 Aelius Aristides, 1. 304d; cf. *Script. Hist. Aug. Hadr.* 19. 2; Cassius Dio, 69. 10. 1.
152 Spawforth and Walker, *JRS* 75 (1985), 78–104 esp. 90–1; Mitchell, *JRS* 1990, 190; D. J. Geagan, *TAPA* 103 (1972), 133–56.
153 M. Lämmer, *Olympien und Hadrianeen in antikem Ephesos* (Diss. Cologne, 1967), 39; Karl, 5: Anazarbus, Tarsus, Magnesia ad Sipylum, Synnada, Thyateira, Ephesus.

perhaps at Pessinus, and at Ancyra. An Ancyran inscription set up in honour of the first agonothete by the association of Dionysiac artists indicates that Hadrian had given permission for games of this type here and in a few other cities. The name which these festivals shared, and which is unparalleled elsewhere in agonistic terminology, points to a central organizing authority, presumably the emperor himself, whose cultural interests are reflected in the musical and theatrical competitions included in the programme.[154] It has been pointed out that these interests may well be reflected in the foundation of C. Iulius Demosthenes at Oenoanda, who endorsed a festival which was exclusively confined to such events, in contrast to the great majority of local competitions in south-west Asia Minor, which were exclusively athletic and placed a heavy emphasis on wrestling. If this interpretation is right, the example shows how the emperors' own tastes in such matters could have a direct effect even on private agonistic foundations, and might help to establish a general cultural climate.[155]

In contrast with Hadrian, his two successors made efforts to curb the spread of agonistic festivals. No new sacred games in Asia Minor were named after Antoninus Pius or Marcus Aurelius. In a letter to the Ephesians, Antoninus Pius commended the generosity of Vedius Antoninus, who preferred to spend money on buildings, rather than distributions, shows, or prizes for *agones*. Indeed, on another occasion he expressed the view that it was better to renovate old buildings than to erect new ones. Here, as in other aspects of his regime, the reaction against the practice of Hadrian is palpable. He personally established only one new festival, the *Eusebeia* at Puteoli in southern Italy, which were designed precisely to honour the memory of his predecessor.[156] Of course it was impossible for an emperor's views alone to change the habits of a whole society, and private agonistic foundations continued to be a common characteristic of civic benefactions. Although there was no requirement that they should do so, the people of Balbura sought approval from Pius for an athletic and musical festival called, after its founder, the *Meleagreia*, which was explicitly modelled on the *Demostheneia* of neighbouring Oenoanda.

In his letter of reply the emperor acknowledged the precedent set by Hadrian and gave his blessing.[157] Pius was also perhaps the emperor who approved the creation of an *agon* at Phrygian Apollonia known as the *Aelia Cornuteia*, which was still perpetuated in the third century AD as a 'prize contest granted by the emperor'.[158]

A *senatus consultum* of AD 177 attempted to set a limit to expenditure on gladiatorial shows in the provinces.[159] In the same year the senate assented to a petition from Miletus, which had been referred to it by Marcus Aurelius, that the *Didymeia*, which had been celebrated since the third century BC, should be promoted to the status of sacred games in honour of the accession of Commodus. However, the emperor himself, in a speech to the senate which was appended to their decision, stated firmly that cities in general should not feel obliged by this precedent to undertake the financial burden of such festivals. The sentiment was not a new one, but the warning must have been thought timely.[160] Commodus' sole reign in fact saw a reversion to Hadrianic expansiveness and from this time on it became common for cities to make direct allusions to their sacred festivals on coin issues. *Commodeia* are attested on coins or inscriptions for Miletus (the festival approved by Marcus Aurelius), Nicaea, Phrygian Laodicea, Tyre in Phoenicia, Caesareia in Cappadocia, Tarsus, and at an unidentified city in south-west Asia Minor.[161] According to Cassius Dio, the Nicomedians used the influence of their citizen Saoterus to obtain permission from Commodus to erect a new imperial temple and found an agonistic festival. This earned them for a few years the title of 'twice neocorus', until the award was retracted by Commodus himself when Saoterus fell from grace.[162] To date no coin or inscription has been identified which mentions the games which surely took place on the occasion of the grant, but the episode well illustrates a point that has been made about such neocory grants in general:

---

154 For Ancyra see Bosch, *Ankara*, nos. 127–9, esp. 128. 8–12, ἐπειδὴ προταθεὶς ὑπὸ τῆς ἱερωτάτης βουλῆς Οὔλπιος Αἴλιος Πονπειανὸς ἀγωνοθετήσας τὸν ἀγῶνα τὸν μυστικὸν δοθέντα ὑπὸ τοῦ αὐτοκράτορος ἐν ὀλίγαις τῇ πόλει; for Iconium, see Bosch, *Ankara*, no. 130, 9; Pessinus, *IGR* iii. 231 (which does not explicitly mention an *agon mystikos*); Side, J. Nollé, *Chiron*, 16 (1986), 204–6.

155 See C. P. Jones, *JRA* 3 (1990), 486–8, and already Magie, *RR* ii. 1392–3 n. 63.

156 *SIG*³ 880 (*I. Eph.* iii. 1479). For his remark on building, see *Dig.* 50. 10. 7 praef.; cf. 50. 8. 7; he himself contributed heavily to rebuilding in Asia Minor after the earthquakes of 139 and 151/2, see *HSCP* 1987, 351–2.

157 K. J. Rigsby, *AJPhil.* 106 (1979), 401–7, and N. Milner, *AS* 39 (1989), 51–2; *AS* 41 (1991), 23–62.

158 *MAMA* iv. 154; *BCH* 27 (1893), 256 no. 35; *Stadt und Fest*, 227 n. 135. Games named after Hadrian usually took the title *Hadriana*, so Pius seems a more likely founder for these *Aelia*.

159 See Millar, *ERW* 195.

160 P. Herrmann, *Ist. Mitt.* 25 (1975), 149–66 (*AE* 1977, 801); new fragment in *Ist. Mitt.* 39 (1988). For the precedent, see esp. F. K. Dörner, *Das Erlass des Paullus Fabius Persicus* (1935), 15 l. 11, with L. Robert, *Rev. phil.* 51 (1977), 8 = *OMS* v. 426 n. 5.

161 Nicaea: Robert, *HSCP* 81 (1977), 32–3 = *OMS* vi. 242–3; Laodicea: Robert, *Laodicée du Lycos*, 283–4; Tyre: Ziegler, 71 n. 31; Tarsus: Ziegler, 28–9; Caesareia, see above, n. 138; unidentified city: Moretti, *Iscr. agon. gr.* no. 87.

162 Dio, 72. 12. 2, with *HSCP* (1977), 34, following Cl. Bosch.

the reward for the cities of a successful petition was not simply the right to erect a prestigious temple, but to stage a magnificent imperial agonistic festival.[163] In fact the *Commodeia* at Tarsus and at Laodicea were also unquestionably inaugurated to celebrate the grant of neocorates,[164] and the same could be true at Cappadocian Caesareia also.[165]

Since Augustus it had been necessary for an emperor to give his approval for the creation of a new sacred festival. Among his successors Hadrian alone had taken a major initiative, and had founded new festivals as part of a programme to foster Hellenic culture and civic life. Commodus' reign marks a new departure. It is clear not only from the story of Saoterus and Nicomedia that the emperor's own predilections played a significant part in determining where festivals should be founded. Commodus identified himself with Heracles; imperial neocories or imperial *agones* were granted to cities such as Tarsus and Tyre, where Heracles was the chief God, and Nicaea where he was worshipped as a founder. From now on particular and specific considerations which linked a city to the reigning princeps tended to determine the award of the right to stage new *agones*.

Under Severus, the main group of new *agones* were the *Philadelphia Severeia*, founded in Perinthus, Nicaea, Caesareian Cappadocia, and Anazarbus in 204/5 to celebrate the fraternal affection of Caracalla and Geta.[166] The *Commodeia* at Tarsus and the *Deia Commodeia* at Laodicea on the Lycus were renamed *Severeia*; *Megala Severeia* were founded at Nicomedia, probably when the second neocorate, which it had acquired and lost under Commodus, was restored to the city.[167] Other games which took Severus' name are attested at Perinthus and Anchialus in Thrace, Hierapolis Castabala in Cilicia, Pisidian Olbasa, and Smyrna.[168] It is important to note that although the initiative for celebrating a new festival may have come

from the local community, they were now firmly tied to the needs of imperial propaganda. The Severan *Philadelpheia* served the explicit purpose of promoting the image of the dynasty as a harmonious ruling family, and the games and second neocory awarded to Nicomedia were the reward for the support which the city had given to Severus in the war with Pescennius Niger. Agonistic festivals cannot be studied in isolation but belong in the mainstream of third-century imperial history.

Under Caracalla and his successors the spread of new festivals accelerated. Sacred games were established in important provincial cities, but especially in regions frequently visited by the emperors and their troops, such as Bithynia, Cilicia, and later Pamphylia. In these cases it is usually possible to point to a close connection between the emperor and the new festival. Troop movements, imperial *adventus*, and victory celebrations form the background for new agonistic festivals for Caracalla at Byzantium, Cyzicus, Syrian Laodicea, and Tarsus.[169] Caracalla himself was seriously ill during these years and it is no coincidence that festivals at Ancyra and Laodicea on the Lycus dedicated to the god of healing, the *Asclepieia Sotereia*, were also called *Antoneineia*, although both cities discarded the dynastic title after Caracalla's death.[170]

Elagabalus rewarded Anazarbus in Cilicia, which had declared for him at the outset of his challenge to Macrinus in 218, with a second neocory, bringing it level with its rival Tarsus, and with the right to celebrate new games, the *Antoneina Olympia Epinicia*. Adana also introduced a sacred ecumenical contest at this time.[171] On the other side of Anatolia, Nicomedia reacted likewise, received a third neocory, and celebrated the *Demetria Antoneia*, apparently celebrating the divine union of the new sun god Elagabalus with its own principal goddess, Demeter.[172] In Lydia Thyateira inaugurated its *Agon Augusteios Isopythios*,[173] and Sardis responded to the new emperor's cult of the sun god with a festival called the *Elagabalia*, in honour not of the emperor himself but of his divine patron.[174] Games in honour of Severus Alexander's victories over the Sassanians were also founded in Thyateira, the *Severeius Agon* for the victory festivals, and at Anazarbus, where he probably revived the still

[163] R. Merkelbach, ZPE 32 (1978), 287–96.

[164] This enormous temple has recently been identified; see JHS Arch. Reports (1989/90), 131; Ziegler, 63 n. 249 cites the coin evidence.

[165] Caesareia's neocory is not attested before the Severan period, when she celebrated a festival called the *Philadelphia Severeia* (see below). In principle, however, there is no reason why the neocory should not have been awarded when the city celebrated the *Commodeion* (above, n. 138).

[166] Karl, 131–2. L. Robert established that the *Philadelphia* at Phrygian Eumeneia (*Ét anat.* 164) and at Lydian Philadelphia had a much earlier origin in the fraternal harmony of Eumenes II and Attalus II.

[167] Tarsus: Ziegler, 75–7; Laodicea: Robert, *Laodicée du Lycos*, 284; Nicomedia: HSCP 1977, 30.

[168] Karl, 124–6 for Perinthus, Anchialus, and Smyrna; Ziegler, 53–4 for Hierapolis; the *Severeia* at Hierapolis may be mentioned in the agonistic inscription from Ancyra of c. AD 218, AS 27 (1977), 75 no. 8, 22 (no other restoration seems possible). Olbasa: IGR iii. 411, 414 and Ziegler, 148 n. 13.

[169] See Karl, 16–17; Ziegler, 80–5.

[170] Robert, *Laodicée du Lycos*, 291–4; *Hellenica*, xi/xii. 350–68, esp. 362–5.

[171] Ziegler, 42 ff., 88, 55–6 (Adana). See for other festivals for Elagabalus, *Bull. ép.* (1958) 180 pp. 192 and 195; CRAI (1970), 22–5.

[172] C. Bosch, *Die kleinasiatischen Münzen der Kaiserzeit: Bithynien*, i (1935), 231–3.

[173] TAM v. 2. 945, 982, 1018, 1019, 1022; see KP² 35.

[174] L. Robert, *Rev. num.* 18 (1976), 49–54 = OMS vi. 161–6.

appropriately titled *Severeia Olympia Epinicia*, which dated originally to the period of Septimius Severus' second Parthian expedition between 198 and 200.[175]

The brief reign of Maximinus Thrax between 235 and 238, who never visited the eastern provinces, saw no new sacred games, but Gordian III re-emphasized their cultural and political importance. When he created an *agon* at Rome in honour of Athena Promachos in 242 on the eve of his expedition against the Persians, he not only revived in symbolic form the historic opposition between Greeks and Persians which had been forged in the fifth century BC (see below, Ch. 13 §1), but also brought to the capital a form of festival, combining civic pageant with the presence of the emperor or his armies, which was by now a familiar phenomenon in the major cities which lay on the routes to the eastern frontier.[176] Gordian's reign also saw the foundation of new Pythian games at Side, ushering in a generation of resplendent agonistic activity in

Pamphylia,[177] *Actia* at Pontic Neocaesareia,[178] at Thessalonica, and at Aphrodisias where the *Attaleia Capetolia*, which had perhaps existed since the first century AD were promoted to the status of sacred games and took Gordian's name also.[179] Agonistic activity under Gordian is not only shown by the foundation of new sacred games, but also by the frequency of agonistic coin types minted by the cities during his reign.[180]

There was another pause under Philippus Arabus and his son, with no new sacred games attested. One is tempted to speculate that a non-Hellenized emperor may have had little taste for Greek games,[181] but a better reason may be that after the débâcle of Gordian's expedition in 243 Philip only retrieved the situation by signing a peace treaty and by paying an enormous

[175] Thyateira: *TAM* v. 2, 949, 1007–9; Anazarbus: Ziegler, 46, 90–2.

[176] Robert, *CRAI* (1970), 6–27 = *OMS* v. 647–68; also on Athena Promachos at this time, see Nollé, *JNG* 36 (1986), 127–43 at 129 n. 14. This study offers further examples of the way in which city coin types in southern Asia Minor reflected the iconographic motifs of imperial success in the wars with the Sassanians. City and imperial politics were inextricably mixed.

[177] J. Nollé, *Ant. Welt* 21 (1990), 258–9; P. Weiss, *Chiron*, 11 (1981), 315–46; *Bull. ép.* (1982), 450.

[178] R. Lane Fox, *Pagans and Christians* (1986), 538.

[179] Thessalonica: *IG* x. 1. 38, and Robert, *Ét. ép. phil.*, 53–61; Aphrodisias: C. Roueché, *JRS* 71 (1981), 119.

[180] See L. Robert, *Rev. num.* 19 (1977), 12 n. 33 with further refs. See now B. Harmacker, *MNZ* 13 (1983), 19–32, 39–50 for the activity of city mints under Gordian III.

[181] So Robert, *CRAI* (1982), 229 = *OMS* v. 791–839 emphasizing the absence of games at Arab Palmyra, in contrast to their presence in more Hellenized cities of Syria and Arabia.

Fig. 39*a*. Hierapolis-Castabala. Obv. Bust of Diadumenian, *M ΟΠΕΛΛΙ ΑΝΤΩΝΙΝΟΣ ΔΙΑΔ Κ*; rev. Prize crown between two torches, *ΙΕΡΟΠΟ ΚΑΣΤΑΒΑΛΕ ΙΕΡΟΣ*. The type shows that these sacred games were associated with a festival of the fire-walking cult of Artemis Perasia; Ziegler, 54 E6 and *Münzen Kilikiens*, 163 no. 1311; A. Dupont-Sommer and L. Robert, *La déesse de Hiérapolis-Castabala* (1964).

(*b*) Side. Obv. wreathed bust of Trebonianus Gallus; rev. Prize crown on table, *ΠΡΩΤΑ ΠΑΝΦΥΛΩΝ ΣΙΔΗΤΩΝ ΙΕΡΟΣ*. Games and festivals played a large part in Side's rivalry with the other Pamphylian cities, above all Perge. See J. Nollé, *Ant. Welt* 21 (1990), 244–65 esp. fig. 18 nos. 92–9 for types similar to this one. This coin is published by P. Weiss, *Chiron*, 21 (1991), 391 pls. 5, 7. 10109.

(*c*) Neocaesareia. Obv. Bust of Severus Alexander; rev. Two prize crowns with palm branches on a table with two palm branches; underneath, vase (for drawing lots) with palm branches. Two sacred games. Cf. *SNG von Aulock*, 105. 13594.

(*d*) Sardis. Obv. Bust of Elagabalus; rev. Table with four prize crowns; edge of table inscribed *OIKOYMENI*; under the table a vase with four palm branches; *ΕΠΙ ΟΥΛΠ ΕΡΜΟΦΙΛΟΥ ΑΡΧ ΑΓΑ ΣΑΡΔΙΑΝΩΝ Γ ΝΕΩΚΟΡΩΝ*. Four sacred games. Similar to *BMC Lydia*, 265 no. 170. 10882.

(*e*) Anazarbus. Obv. Armed portrait of Valerian; rev. Six prize crowns, one with palm branch, *ΜΗΤΡΟΠ Γ ΕΤ ΒΟΣ Γ ΑΝΑΖΑΡΒΟΥ* (AD 253/4). Six sacred games. Ziegler, 42 B57; *Münzen Kilikiens*, 148 no. 1164. 7833.

(*f*) Cremna. Obv. Bust of Aurelian; rev. Temple front with inscription DONAT(io) SACR(i) CERTAM(inis); COL IULI AUG FEL CREM. Aulock, *Pisidien*, ii no. 1574. The games at Cremna, like those at Neocaesareia and Anazarbus, were certainly associated with the presence of Roman troops. See Ch. 12 §v at n. 189. 10387.

(*g*) Mopsuhestia. Obv. Bust of Valerian; rev. Tyche of city holding a prize crown standing in front of the emperors Gallienus and Valerian, each seated on a *sella curulis*. *ΑΔΡ ΟΥΑ ΓΑΛ ΜΟΨΕΑΤΩΝ ΔΩΡΕΑΙ ΕΤ ΓΚΤ* (= AD 255/6). The scene illustrates the emperors making a gift (*dorea*) of games to the city. Ziegler, 53 D6. 15010.

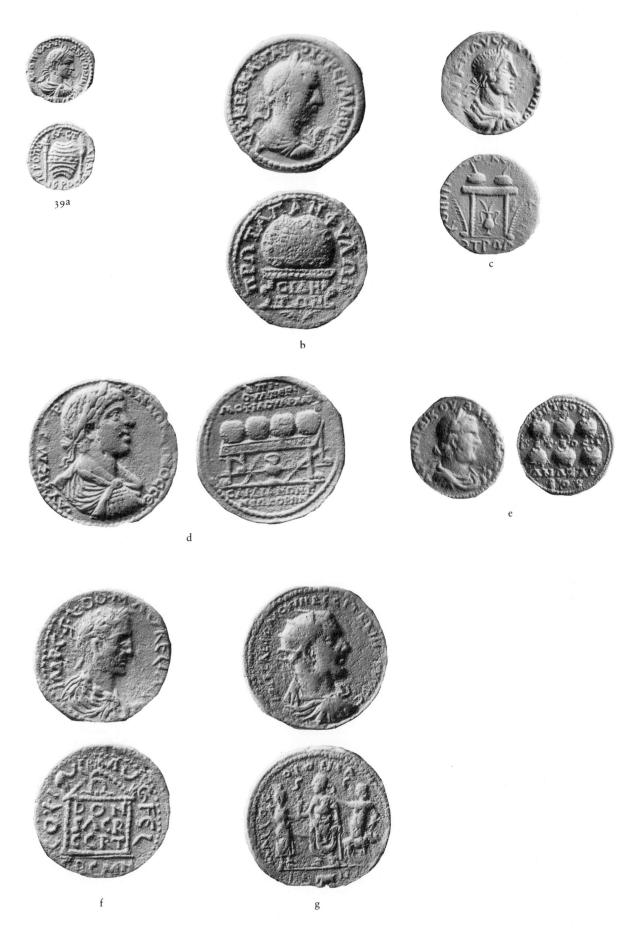

39a

b

c

d

e

f

g

Coins and festivals

indemnity to the Sassanians; Roman troops were inactive in the eastern theatre until his death in 249. The two Philips were displaced by the uprising of Trajan Decius; Anazarbus, at the hub of strategically crucial Cilicia, declared for Decius even before the civil war had been resolved, and received a third neocory and permission to celebrate an *Agon Decius Oecumenicus*, making a total of five such festivals held in the city. When coins shown that a sixth festival was introduced to their calendar only two years later under Volusian and Trebonianus Gallus, the only reasonable interpretation to hand is that they were minted in connection with a projected, if not actually realized military expedition against the Sassanians. An agonistic festival may again be explained by the presence of the army.[182]

The age of Valerian and Gallienus saw a proliferation of sacred games to match anything that had taken place under the Severans; as then, they were not confined to the strategically important zones. *Olympia* were introduced at Side,[183] and *Augusteia* or *Augusteia Actia* at Ancyra, Perge, Prusias ad Hypium, and Tarsus.[184] The *Valeriana* of Nicaea are attested by an abundant coinage.[185] In Cilicia, Mopsuhestia and Aegeae celebrated sacred games for the first time in 253/4, the former perhaps called *Eusebia*, and the latter connected with the famous local temple of Asclepius.[186] At Aphrodisias the *Valeriana Pythia*, explicitly introduced as a gift of the emperor, ranked above those founded by Gordian. They were matched locally by *Galliena Capetolia* at Antioch on the Maeander.[187] It is difficult to argue that all these festivals were closely linked with major troop movements or with the emperor's personal presence, but contemporary papyrus evidence from Egypt indicates that two new sets of sacred games in the Delta region were founded precisely to celebrate imperial victories, and thus emphasize the continuing connection between civic life and the fragile central regime.[188] The sacred games were not merely, or even principally, a demonstration of local pride and self-confidence but also an important new extension of the imperial cult,

promoted, as in earlier centuries, as much by the emperors themselves as by their subjects.

In Asia Minor the latest sacred games to be founded conform to this pattern. A *sacrum certamen*, attested by an abundant coinage, was founded by Aurelian at the colony of Cremna in Pisidia. It should be connected with the emperor's massing of troops against Zenobia of Palmyra, whose breakaway empire had briefly extended as far as Ancyra in AD 270.[189] Perge, Cremna's neighbour in the Pamphylian plain, shortly afterwards celebrated the presence of Aurelian's successor Tacitus, and its own new importance in a remarkable series of acclamations. Predictably this was accompanied by another agonistic festival, the *Taciteia*, revealed by the very last bronze coins issued by a city of the eastern Roman empire.[190]

This chronological survey has been limited in the main to the introduction of sacred games, which required imperial permission. The term *dorea* sometimes occurs on coins or inscriptions to describe this grant of permission, and the use of so positive a term—describing an imperial gift, not merely assent—further underlines the point that emperors were actively concerned to promote the games, even if they did not necessarily support them financially.[191] The spread of sacred games, over the century that divides Commodus from Tacitus, can only be understood against a background of imperial policy, the emperors' own journeys to the eastern war zones, military movements, Roman victories, and, overall, with new developments in the imperial cult. Whereas in the second century emperor worship was most frequently expressed through new temple-building, or by sacrifice and ceremony on significant imperial anniversaries throughout the year, in the third century the emphasis lay on ceremonies such as *adventus* and *profectio*, where the

---

[182] Ziegler, 99–113.

[183] J. Nollé, *Chiron*, 17 (1987), 254.

[184] Ancyra: Bosch, *Ankara*, no. 287; Robert, *Hellenica*, xi/xii. 366; Prusias: Ameling, *I. Prusias*, p. 230 and pl. x. 18; others: Ziegler, 118 n. 314.

[185] C. Bosch, 'Die Festspiele von Nikaia', *Jb. für kleinasiatische Forschung*, 1 (1950), 90 ff.

[186] Ziegler, 51–3.

[187] Roueché, *JRS* 1981, 119–20; *Aphrodisias in Late Antiquity*, 3–4; Gaebler, *ZfN* 39 (1929), 298 no. 76 for Carian Antioch. See also the *Pythia Olympia* of Tabae, on a coin of Salonina, *SNG von Aulock*, 2733; Robert, *La Carie*, ii. 146.

[188] Lane Fox, *Pagans and Christians*, 578–9 with *POxy.* 3116, 3667; cf. P. Frisch, *Zehn Agonistische Papyri*.

[189] See Aulock, *Pisidien*, ii. 1554–725 (22 types including 6 which are explicitly agonistic, *Don(atio) Sac(rum) Cert(amen)* etc.); for Zenobia at Ancyra, and Aurelian's riposte, see Zosimus, 1. 50. 1–2 and other sources cited by Magie, *RR* ii. 1574 n. 43 and 1575 n. 45. The episode and the Cremna connection will be argued for in a forthcoming study by R. Ziegler. For an earlier explanation, see Levick, *Roman Colonies*, 152.

[190] See below, Ch. 13 § v at n. 76, and the study of P. Weiss, *Chiron*, 21 (1991), 353–92; for the *Taciteia* see *BMC Cat. Lycia etc.*, 140 nos. 103–4.

[191] The term has been frequently discussed by L. Robert, e.g. *CRAI* (1982), 228 n. 1 with further refs. It remains an open question whether such a 'gift' might also entail financial subvention (*JRS* (1990), 191), but it is worth noting that the term, and its Latin equivalent *donatio*, imply a much more active imperial role than earlier granting of permission, or confirmation of local practice (cf. Wörrle, *Stadt und Fest*, 175–82), and the expressions are not attested in these agonistic contexts before the 3rd cent.

emperor himself was present, and on the new agonistic festivals.[192]

The sacred games took place against a background of more modest agonistic activity in the eastern cities, which is especially marked in southern Asia Minor. Contests for money prizes, which never acquired sacred status, are to be found throughout the Hellenized East. Some were closely linked with a local cult, others were clearly new private foundations endowed by civic benefactors. They represent an important, but not necessarily dominant part of civic culture in the second and third centuries, which was particularly marked in the mountainous regions of the south and south-west. It is notable that almost every city of Lycia, Pisidia, the inland areas of Caria, and Cilicia Tracheia has produced a plethora of evidence for prize games, usually confined to athletic competitions, above all in wrestling, boxing, and pankration. Almost all of these were the result of private foundations, and the contests bore the name of the founder who had provided the funds. The most striking evidence has been collected from Pisidian Termessus, where over thirty different contests are named on inscriptions dating between 150 and 230 AD.[193] A similar picture can be reconstructed for Lycia during the later second and early third centuries, and Caria, especially at Aphrodisias.[194] In Pisidia most of the evidence for agonistic activity seems to belong to the third century: inscriptions show that these local contests in Selge, Ariassus, and Baris were still being celebrated during the 260s AD.[195] This reflects the general picture of sustained prosperity in the region in the third century. However, the distribution of this evidence in the mountainous parts of southern Asia Minor, which contrasts with much fewer inscriptions of this type from central or northern Anatolia, suggests that it was a regional phenomenon.

For this reason it is prudent not to make too close a connection between the sacred games of the late second and third centuries and the contemporary enthusiasm for local *themides*. It is revealing, for instance, that the one Pisidian city which celebrated sacred games in the mid-third century, the Roman colony of Cremna, has produced no epigraphic evidence for the *themides* which were so popular among its neighbours. As a Roman colony it seems to have adopted this aspect of regional culture less enthusiastically than its neighbours. Aurelian's *sacrum certamen* was a novelty, not a natural growth from an existing stock. Furthermore, the *themides* were not only geographically restricted, but catered exclusively for athletes, often perhaps only for boxing and wrestling. Most of the competitors were evidently natives of the city where the event took place. They should obviously be interpreted as a key element of the civic culture that developed in these mountain zones, but we cannot infer that similar agonistic festivals were to be found everywhere. They played a much smaller part in the civic life of Lydia, Phrygia, and Galatia.

VI. *Central Anatolia: An Exception?*

The picture of city life in Asia Minor, which has been put together in the previous pages, draws on evidence from all its provinces.[196] In fact, the communities of the central regions have contributed comparatively little to the composition. The omissions have not been made deliberately. Inscriptions and coins from Lydia, Phrygia, Galatia, and Lycaonia provide information about their constitutions, and the coins are as rich a source of legend and local mythology as the coins of Greek cities elsewhere. However, there are not many signs of large-scale civic benefactions by leading families, except at Ancyra and the larger Phrygian cities of Synnada, Apamea, Hierapolis, and Laodicea. As already noted (above, Ch. 11 §III), the epigraphy of the smaller cities of northern Lydia and northern Phrygia is often almost indistinguishable from that of the villages which surrounded them. There is little evidence for internal political turbulence or for acute inter-city rivalry. The tenor of life appears to have been notably more placid than in Bithynia or Asia. The reasons perhaps lie in the self-disciplined moral codes which governed Anatolian society rather than in more intensive Roman supervision and control. Cities of Phrygia and Lydia celebrated local agonistic festivals,[197]

---

[192] Price, *Rituals and Power, passim* paints a picture of the imperial cult which seems largely convincing for the 1st and 2nd cents., but does not take account of the changing condition of 3rd-cent. Asia Minor. The imperial ceremonial of this period, which was constructed around the physical presence of the emperors or his armies, developed further in the 4th cent. See further S. G. MacCormack, 'The Ceremony of Adventus', *Historia*, 21 (1972), 721–52 and Michael McCormick, *Eternal Victory: Triumphal Rulership in Late Antiquity, Byzantium and the Early Medieval West* (1986).

[193] R. Heberdey, *TAM* iii. 1, p. 293; *ASRamsay* 198 ff; *Termessische Studien*, 42 ff. None of the contests dates before AD 150, but only four are later than 212.

[194] For *themides* in general, see Laum, *Stiftungen*, i. 94 ff.; in Lycia: Magie, *RR* ii. 1392 n. 63; Aphrodisias: Reynolds, *Aphrodisias and Rome*, 184–97; C. Roueché, *Entertainments at Aphrodisias* (forthcoming).

[195] Selge; J. Nollé, *I. Selge*, nos. 46–60, all after AD 212; Ariassos, unpublished inscription of AD 265/6 (*AS* 39 (1989), 65); Parlais: *SEG* ii. 745.

[196] The same is true of the survey of the material by J. M. Reynolds 'Cities', in D. C. Braund (ed.), *The Administration of the Roman Empire* (1988), 15–53.

[197] Note games at Cadi (*Homobōmia Sebasta*), Aezani (*Homobōmia Sebasta?* later *Sebasta Claudieia*), Synnada (*Panathenaia Athenaia*), Attuda (*Olympia Heracleia Adrasteia*), Eumeneia (*Eumeneia Philadelphia*, of Hellenistic

but civic centres were not thronged with statues of successful athletes in the local *themides*, like those of Cilicia, Pisidia, and Lycia. Even the evidence for public building remains very patchy, although the buildings that are attested, and their chronology, broadly fit with the picture of civic construction that can be observed in better-documented areas.

These reservations perhaps suggest that the smaller urban communities of central Anatolia, which greatly outnumbered the larger cities,[198] matched the model of Greek civic organization only in part. Many cities may have resembled Pausanias' picture of Panopeus. Is it possible that some did not even aspire to better things? Conditions were not always favourable for the emergence of a governing class of rich landowners who sustained the community by patriotic euergetism. The evidence is not so strong as to allow definite conclusions in either direction. The character of the majority of the Roman cities of central Anatolia is likely to remain a mystery until one or more have been subjected to careful archaeological investigation. During the Roman empire the claim to civic status rested very heavily on material appearance. Until we can envisage what a small city of Phrygia, Lydia, or Galatia actually looked like, speculation about the progress of civilization in the region can only be tentative.

origin), Tripolis (*Letoeia Pythia*), Metropolis (*Sebasta Caesareia*), as well as at Apamea, Laodicea and Hierapolis.

[198] See below, Ch. 14 § II.

13 Crisis and Continuity in the Third Century

1. Introduction

In AD 242 the doors of the temple of Janus at Rome were thrown open, *more veterum*, to announce the declaration of war. The emperor Gordian III set forth in a solemn *profectio* to lead an army through the Balkans and Asia Minor to Syria and Mesopotamia against the Sassanian king Shapur I. The triumphs of that campaign at Carrhae, Nisibis, and Singara were celebrated with particular fervour in Asia Minor. At Ephesus Gordian and his empress Tranquillina were honoured by inscriptions which claimed that they had restored and enhanced the ancient peaceful lifestyle throughout their whole empire.[1] At Rome itself, in a gesture that strikingly and deliberately symbolized the unity of Graeco-Roman history, the emperor inaugurated games in honour of the goddess Athena Promachos, who had protected Athens from the same Persian threat over 700 years earlier.[2] Two years later Gordian had been killed, his successor Philip signed a humiliating peace treaty with Shapur, and within a decade the whole of Syria and much of south-east Anatolia had been overrun from the east, as the fabric of provincial society was torn apart.

It is vain, in the continuity of history, to look for specific turning points that mark the end of one era and the beginning of the next, but the history of the empire from Augustus to the second quarter of the third century is rightly treated as a unity. The imperial frontiers held firm; the administrative structure erected by Augustus survived recognizably intact; the cities of the provinces, the essential cells from which the empire was built, and the aristocracies which manned and maintained their public institutions, still functioned broadly as they had done for two and a half centuries,

in the manner which was the necessary complement to the imperial administration. Religious practices and rituals, in the context both of traditional paganism and of Emperor worship, had admitted developments but no fundamental change. Signs of uncertainty could be detected in all these barometers of the political and cultural climate, and some had been noticeable for two or three generations, but outside the hothouse of the imperial court, where every change of ruler provoked a crisis for those close to the seat of power, it was hardly apparent that the structure was on the verge of collapse or radical change.

The events of the middle of the third century, from the 230s to the 280s, involved changes that have been interpreted as a decline, sometimes even as an extreme crisis, by contemporaries and modern observers alike.[3] Perhaps the most telling, because least self-conscious observation made by contemporaries is the admission of all parties in a lawsuit before the prefect of Egypt in AD 250 that the era of prosperity, *euporia*, still prevalent under the Severans, was now over. The prefect himself pronounced in the dispute that 'the argument from prosperity, or rather from the transformation of prosperity, is the same for villages and cities alike.'[4] Political tact and conventional rhetoric led one of the disputants to express high expectations that the current emperor would set matters on their feet again,[5] but this was little more than a pious hope, echoed in many other contemporary documents.[6] We cannot, of course, draw general conclusions from remarks made in a particular Egyptian court, but they do at least reveal a

---

[1] *I. Eph.* 4336, cf. 302–4. For the expression τῆς ἰδίας οἰκουμένης see Habicht, *Alt. von Perg.* viii. 3 7; J. Vogt, *Orbis Romanus*, 19 n. 8.

[2] See L. Robert, 'Deux concours grecs à Rome', *CRAI* (1970), 6–27, esp. 11–17; X. Loriot, *ANRW* ii. 2 (1973), 757 ff.; R. Lane Fox chose this episode to begin his book *Pagans and Christians*. Note also that the same statue of Athena Promachos was invoked to defend Rome against Alaric the Goth in 410, Zosimus, 5. 6. 2.

[3] For contemporary reactions see G. Alföldi, 'The Crisis of the Third Century as seen by Contemporaries', *GRBS* 15 (1974), 89–111 (*Die Krise des römischen Reichs* (1989), 319–43); R. MacMullen, *The Roman Government's Response to a Crisis A.D. 235–337* (1976), 1–23.

[4] T. C. Skeat and E. P. Wegener, *JEA* 21 (1935), 224–47 at 231 ll. 70, 76 (ὅτε ἦν ἐν εὐπορίᾳ τὰ πράγματα), 232, and especially ll. 101–2 where the prefect himself says ὁ τῆς εὐπορίας λόγος, ἢ τῆς ἀπὸ τῆς εὐπορίας μεταβολῆς, ἴσος ἐστιν καὶ ταῖς κώμαις καὶ ταῖς πόλεσιν.

[5] Ibid. ll. 102–3, μετὰ Σεουῆρον γέγονεν τὸ καινὸν τοῦτο ἀπότακτον, ὃ ἡ θεία τύχη Δεκίου τοῦ Σεβαστοῦ ἐπανορθώσεται.

[6] See L. Robert, *Rev. phil.* 51 (1977), 7–14 = *OMS* v. 425–32.

perception of widespread malaise, and the word used by the last speaker to describe his hopes that the emperor would set things to rights, ἐπανορθώσεται, becomes part of official terminology. It is significant that in the twenty years before and after 250 provincial officials with the powers of governors, but with the additional title of *epanorthōtes* or *diorthōtes*, were appointed with the aim of putting provinces or regions on their feet again. They appear from the 230s in the Asia Minor provinces.[7] M. Antonius Memmius Hiero held the post in Galatia in the 230s or early 240s;[8] M. Domitius Valerianus a native of Prusias ad Hypium was *diorthōtes* of the cities of Pamphylia during the reign of Severus Alexander, and another anonymous holder of the post is attested at Side;[9] inscriptions from Aphrodisias have revealed Aurelius Appius Sabinus and T. Oppius Aelianus Asclepiodotus as *epanorthōtai* in Asia in the 250s and 280s respectively, and another office-holder is mentioned at Carian Sebastopolis.[10] Another Aphrodisian inscription honours an unknown person who was *comes*, friend of the emperors, saviour of the provinces, founder and *epanorthōtes* also of Aphrodisias itself. While the use of the term *comes* points to the fourth century for this text, the title *epanorthōtes* is more at home in the third, and the expression 'saviour of the provinces' is paralleled by two third-century inscriptions of Ancyra, one set up by the *koinon* of Cyprus for an anonymous *consularis* who was hailed as 'after the emperor the saviour of the whole province', the other commemorating a benefactor who had set the city to rights after food shortages and barbarian invasions.[11] Similar concerns may be reflected in other administrative changes of the period. The creation of the new provinces of Phrygia and Caria, Pontus, and Isauria all took place before or around the middle of the third century, although no contemporary source makes clear the reasons for these alterations. The first attested governor of Phrygia and Caria, Clodius Celsinus, who held office *c.* AD 250, was hailed like his Galatian counterparts at Ancyra as saviour of the provinces and the surrounding districts (*eparcheiai*).[12]

II. Militarization

Setting matters right was a bland piece of official euphemism; the word *epanorthōtes* was no doubt deliberately chosen to suggest that crisis could be averted by sound management and administration. In practice the most conspicuous changes lay not in civilian government but in military presence. Soldiers emerge from their way-stations, frontier garrisons, and the more dangerous mountain areas to become virtually ubiquitous in cities and the countryside. There were extraordinary appointments of centurions to keep the peace in the Maeander basin at Aphrodisias, and around Pisidian Antioch, both normally peaceful areas;[13] as well as the appearance of specialized military commanders, such as a *dux* at Pisidian Termessus where trouble from recalcitrant highlanders might more readily be predicted.[14] Such officers, and even more the men they controlled or failed to control became a key element in the social changes of the period.

The increased militarization of the empire has rightly been traced back to the Severan period, and therefore anticipates by some two generations the most acute symptoms of crisis and decline in the mid-third century.[15] In fact there is also considerable evidence for a significant military presence away from the frontiers in Asia Minor during the halcyon days of the second century (see above, Ch. 9) and one document in particular serves as a warning against laying too much stress on the civil wars of 193 as a catalyst in the process of change. An inscription found in the obscure Lydian city of Tabala contains part of a letter written

[7] The Latin equivalent is *corrector*. For a general survey see *Diz. Epigr.* ii. 2. 1242–8.
[8] *RECAM* ii. 414.
[9] E. Gabba, *Athenaeum*, 34 (1956), 273–83 and full bibliography cited by K.-H. Dietz, *Senatus contra Principem* (1980), 143–6. For another anonymous holder of the post see E. Bosch, in A. M. Mansel, *Vorläufiger Bericht über die Ausgrabungen in Side 1974* (1951), 67–70 no. 19.
[10] C. Roueché, *JRS* 71 (1981), 103–20, esp. 109 nn. 23–7 (*SEG* xxxi (1981), 908–9); for Asclepiodotus, see *JRS* 71 (1981), 108, no. 6 with Roueché and D. H. French, *ZPE* 49 (1982), 159–60 for the date (*SEG* xxxi (1981), 910). The Aphrodisian text is now re-edited by Roueché, *Aphrodisias in Late Antiquity* (1989), 16–19 no. 7. For the example from Sebastopolis, see J. and L. Robert, *La Carie*, 325 no. 174.
[11] Roueché, *Aphrodisias in Late Antiquity*, 12–13, 17–18, and 29–30 no. 14, a text she dates to the fourth century, perhaps the 330s. The Ancyra parallels, supporting a third century date, are S. Mitchell, *AS* 27 (1977), 70–2 no. 5 corrected in *Bull. ép.* 1978, 488 and *SEG* xxvii (1977), 845, and Bosch, *Ankara*, no. 289 (*IGR* iii. 206).
[12] See Vol. II, App. 2, n. 1. Note also on Pontus, M. Christol and X. Loriot, 'Le Pontus et ses gouverneurs dans le second tiers du IIIᵉ siècle', *Mémoires VII: Recherches épigraphiques* (1986), 13–40 (not seen by the author). For Clodius Celsinus, see D. H. French, *Epigr. Anat.* 17 (1991), 57–9.
[13] Two such centurions are known at Aphrodisias, *MAMA* viii. 508 = *ILS* 9474 = Roueché, *JRS* (1981), 113 no. 7; *CIG* 2802 = *JRS* (1981), 114 no. 8 (*SEG* xxxi (1981), 905). For Pisidian Antioch see *IGR* iii. 301 = W. M. Calder, *JRS* 2 (1912), 80.
[14] M. Christol, *Chiron* 8 (1978), 529–40 = *TAM* iii. 1. 88 (*SEG* xxviii (1978), 1214): τὸν διασημότατον δοῦκ(α). Λ. Αὐρήλιον Μαρκιανόν . . . εἰρήνης προστάτην. For the date see Roueché, *JRS* (1981), 116 n. 91.
[15] Rostovzeff, *SEHRE²*, chs. 9–11 remains the classic and by far the best exposition.

by the emperor Pertinax, who ruled for eighty-seven days before he was assassinated on 28 March 193, thereby setting in motion the ruinous events which led to the accession of Septimius Severus. The excerpt, which was published after Pertinax's death by the proconsul of Asia Aemilius Iuncus, shows that the emperor had been approached with complaints that soldiers had been molesting the city. His reply throws light on the details of the affair. Since soldiers in transit to other destinations had turned off the highway and approached the town for no other reason except to take the so-called *supplementa*, the provincial governor, who had also been informed about this, would set right the offences which the soldiers had apparently committed. The proconsul attached his own letter to the emperor's and promised that if any soldier had left the road to go to Tabala, being not one of those despatched to Aezani, but had simply wandered off with a view to extorting money, he would be punished. It was not one of the obligations of hospitality to provide such things as *supplementa*.[16] It is a simple matter to reconstruct what had happened by looking at the abundant parallels for similar abuses in the third century (see below). Soldiers had left the military highway, ἡ λεώφορος (ὁδός), and entered the town intent on extortion. The proconsul speaks of men wandering, πλανώμενον, in order to get money, ἐπὶ τῷ ἀργυρίζειν. The emperor no doubt echoed the petitioners' complaints that they were trying to take τὰ καλούμενα σουπληµέντα. *Supplementa* was standard Latin for newly recruited reinforcements, but the inscription shows that the soldiers in question were not press-ganging recruits, but collecting a cash payment in their lieu (a practice not unknown outside the Roman Empire[17]). This was quite simply an illegitimate version of the tax known as *synteleia teirōnōn* which is attested by a slightly later inscription found in another Lydian community, and was doubtless widely exacted in the early third century (see above, Ch. 9 § III at nn. 198–201). There are other clear portents of later conditions.

The governor's task was to put matters right, ἐπανορθώσεται. His reply allowed a legitimate reason why soldiers might have visited Tabala, if they were *en route* to Aezani. By 193, at least, soldiers had proper cause to visit a city where there is no earlier record of a Roman military presence, another example of their intrusion into the peace of a *provincia inermis*.[18]

The complaints of the civilian population of Asia Minor against military oppression and extortion are familiar from an impressive, if depressing series of inscriptions of the early and middle third century.[19] At Demirci close to the northern border of the territory of Lydian Saittai in the foothills of Mount Temnos a magistrate issued an order to prevent exactions by *stationarii*, the secret agents known as *frumentarii*, and military tax collectors, *colletiones* (*TAM* v. 1. 154); a village of the Lydian Catacecaumene sent a petition to the two Philips in AD 247/8 to protest against *frumentarii*, praetorians, and *colletiones*, who treated the inhabitants like wartime enemies, προφάσει εἰρήνης . . . πολέμου τρόπῳ (*TAM* v. 1. 419; cf. 430); *frumentarii*, *colletiones*, and perhaps *stationarii* had been responsible for the shake-down of a village near Lydian Satala, which had been deprived of the necessities of life by the unending demands of these unwelcome visitors (*TAM* v. 1. 611); at Ağabeyköy on the territory of Philadelphia *colletiones* had dragged off nine workers from an imperial estate, and returned one on payment of a hefty ransom. The fate of the others who had been arrested was uncertain and their colleagues, the petitioners, now threatened to leave their homes and find other landlords (KP[3] 55); nearby at Mendechora a petition singles out *frumentarii* and others of similar station as responsible for extortion, and highlights the problems inherent in a situation where men charged with the protection of the empire themselves preyed on it (KP[3] 28). 'Quis custodiet ipsos custodes?' The culprits are not named but the abuses were the same at Güllüköy whose poor farming community, oppressed by criminal extortion, was unable to meet the legitimate demands for taxes and services and sought protection from eirenarchs or other authorities (*D. Ak. Wien* 77 (1959) no. 9; *SEG* xix. 718).

The situation seems to have been much the same outside Lydia. In AD 211/12 at Carian Euhippe soldiers and officials had left the main highways in search of

---

[16] H. Malay, *Epigr. Anat.* 12 (1988), 47–52. The main part of the text runs: ἐξ ἐπιστολῆς θεοῦ Πε[ρτίνα]/κος· "ἐπεὶ δὲ καὶ στρατιώτας [ἐν] / ὁδῷ πορευομένους ἐ[κτρέ]/πεσθαί φατε ἐκ τῆς λεωφόρο[υ] / (5) καὶ ἀνιέναι πρὸς ὑμᾶς οὐδε/νὸς ἑτέρου χάριν ἢ τοῦ λαμβά/νειν τὰ σουπληµέντα καλού/μενα, καὶ περὶ τούτου διδαχθεὶς / ὁ κράτιστος τοῦ ἔθνους ἡ/(10) γούμενος ἐπανορθώσεται / τὰ δοκοῦντα ὑπὸ τῶν στρατιω/τῶν πλημμελεῖσθαι εἰς ὑμᾶς." / Αἰμίλιος Ἰοῦνκος ἀνθύπατος Ταβα/λέων ἄρχουσιν βουλῇ δήμῳ χαί/(15)ρειν· ἄν τινα στρατιώτην ἐλέγξητε εἰς τὴν πόλιν ὑμῶν ἐκτρα/πέντα τῶν μὴ πεμφθέντων / εἰς Αἰζανούς, ἀλλ' ἐπὶ τῷ ἀργυρί[ζειν] / πλανώμενον, κολασθ[ήσεται·] / (20) οὐ δεῖ δὲ νῦν τὰ τοιαῦ[τα δίδοσθαι·] / ὡς ξένα· διείρητα[ι γὰρ καὶ δι]/ώρισται ὑπὸ πά[ντων ὅτι μὴ] / ἐξεῖναι ἀπὸ τῆς λεωφόρου] / ἀποχωρεῖν. My own restorations in ll. 20, 22, and 23.

[17] Take for example the recruiting scene from Shakespeare, 2 *Henry IV* III. ii (Bardolph: 'I have three pounds to free Mouldy and Bullcalf.')

[18] The road to Aezani from the west coast ran up the valley of the Hermus, passing Tabala as it headed for Cadi (*MAMA* ix. p. xx with n. 73). There was an important Byzantine castle at Tabala which reflected its strategic importance, see C. Foss, *J.öst.Byz.* 28 (1979), 302–4.

[19] See the bibliographical note in *JRS* 66 (1976), 112 (D. 13–21), which should be updated and emended with reference to nn. 20, 21, and 24; note also P. Herrmann, *Hilferufe aus römischen Provinzen* (1990).

their victims, as they had done at Tabala;[20] one year later at Tacina in the south-east corner of Asia complaints were directed against solders who appear to have been part of the governor's *comitatus*; they had penetrated into areas where they had no authority to go and requisitioned draft animals and wagons;[21] the particular abuse here is reminiscent of the long-running dispute between the villages of Anosa and Antimacheia in Phrygia concerning their obligations to the state transport service. The same official, a freedman procurator M. Aur. Philokyrios, had a part to play in arbitrating both disputes.[22] Inhabitants of imperial estates may have been particularly vulnerable, exposed to collusion between domainal procurators, soldiers, and other officials, without even city magistrates to offer some protection; and the long petition from Aragua in the upper Tembris valley, from the time of the two Philips, recalls the text from Ağabeyköy and incorporates the same threat to abandon the land if the pressure was not relieved. The oppressors here were soldiers, big men from the city, and imperial slaves and freedmen, who had once again left the main highways in search of plough-oxen and their owners who were pressed into illegal service.[23] Another unpublished text from the territory of Phrygian Metropolis records the efforts of a proconsul to prevent pillage and extortion by soldiers.[24]

This dossier of texts, which continues to expand with new discoveries, provides prime evidence for the supposedly ruinous condition of the empire in the third century. Above all it offers a striking picture of the militarization of hitherto peaceful regions. The villages of Lydia and Phrygia had up to this date barely been touched by a Roman official presence, still less by large bands of soldiers. It made matters worse that the latter were to all appearances beyond the control of their commanders. Peaceful and prosperous Asia Minor was reverting to a condition of anarchy that had not been known since the first century BC. It is important to stress, moreover, that the malaise was deeply endemic even in the early years of the Severan period. Even apart from the inscription of 193 from Tabala, complaints against military and official abuse were common by the second decade of the third century. The most telling evidence of all for these conditions extends back to the reign of Septimius Severus. In AD 204 the Roman senate, looking after its own members as it was accustomed to do, passed a decree which exempted all senators from the duty of providing hospitality to soldiers in their homes. this *senatus consultum* was duly published locally by senators anxious to advertise their privilege and protect their livelihood from the threat. The distribution of these inscriptions is confined to the Asia Minor provinces. In Asia itself copies have been found on the island of Paros, in central Lydia, in the Phrygian plain of Sandıklı, at Ephesus, and at Alexandria Troas. In Galatia it was published at Pisidian Antioch and perhaps at Ancyra.[25] The pattern shows firstly some of the unexpectedly remote places from which the Roman senate now recruited its members, but it also demonstrates again how soldiers now made their presence felt where they had been unknown before. The boast of Aelius Aristides that the inhabitants of the cities of the empire never saw a soldier, and were unaware of the forces that protected them, would have rung with a hollow note only sixty years after he first uttered them.

It is unlikely that other areas of Anatolia saw fewer

---

[20] L. Robert, *CRAI* (1952), 592 ff. (= *OMS* i. 345–55). For the date see W. Eck, *RE suppl.* xiv (1974), 125 no. 14b (AD 211/12); cf. Waelkens, *Türsteine* no. 236.

[21] S. Şahin and D. H. French, *Epigr. Anat.* 10 (1987), 133–42. There is room for significant improvement in the text. M. Aur. Philokyrios appears in ll. 14–15 and 30; cf. the text from Sülmenli, *JRS* 46 (1956), 46 ff.

[22] *JRS* 46 (1956), 46 ff.; trans. in B. Levick, *The Government of the Roman Empire* (1985), 57–9.

[23] The best text is in *SEHRE*² 741 n. 26; it will be re-edited with a photograph in *MAMA* x, no. 114.

[24] Copied by M. H. Ballance and to be published by him and T. Haukan. This is doubtless the unpublished inscription from the Çöl ova mentioned by T. Drew Bear, *Chiron*, 7 (1977), 363; he also publishes a fragmentary text from the territory of Eumeneia which seems to have a similar content, *Nouvelles inscriptions de Phrygie*, 16 no. 8.

[25] For references see above, Ch. 9 § II n. 108.

Fig. 40. The petition of the villagers of Aragua in the upper Tembris valley to the two Philips, AD 244–9. MAMA x, no. 114. Photo by C. W. M. Cox (1926).

Fig. 41. Dedication to Zeus Anpeleites. Above a bearded, long-haired bust of Zeus, typical of the region; below, in two registers, two pairs of yoked oxen and seven individual beasts. The inscription reads Ἀρτεμᾶς Ἀμμιάδος Ἀραγοκωμήτης Δεὶ Ἀνπελείτη εὐχήν. The use of the metronymic suggests that Artemas was an imperial slave born of a servile mother. Work of about AD 220–40, now in Kütahya Museum (L. Robert, *BCH* 107 (1983), 532). The villagers of Aragua complained in their petition that soldiers, powerful men, and imperial officials had removed them from their tasks and pressed their plough oxen into service, ἀπὸ τῶν ἔργων ἡμᾶς ἀφίσταντες κὲ τοὺς ἀροτῆρας βόας ἀνγ[αρεύοντες].

40

41

Aragua

military detachments at this period. The civil war of 193–4 in which the forces of Septimius Severus defeated Pescennius Niger three times in Asia Minor, near Cyzicus, between Cius and Nicaea, and at Issus in the Cilician gulf, marked the beginning of a period when the East saw active war on its frontiers and regular troop movements on a huge scale. The battles of the civil war almost predictably occurred at the two extremities which controlled the approaches to Asia Minor, from the north-west and the south-east, exactly echoing the victories of Alexander the Great over Darius at the Granicus and at Issus in 332 BC. Bithynia and Cilicia duly emerged with unexpected prominence as key military areas, the former because all traffic from the Balkans, troops and emperors in particular, funnelled along its main roads in transit to Syrian Antioch or to the Euphrates frontier; the latter because it served as a crucial region for concentrating and supplying troops as they prepared for war against the Parthians or Sassanians.[26]

In Bithynia the impact of the army is best seen in the inscriptions of Prusias ad Hypium, whose magistrates and people repeatedly had to provide lodging, supplies, transport, and winter quarters for troops and emperors between the 190s and 230s.[27] Soldiers involved in these eastern campaigns duly turn up in the cities of the region, notably a group of seven legionaries of Celtic or Germanic origin whose gravestones have been found in Chalcedon, Prusa, Nicomedia, and Galatian Ancyra. It seems that they died returning to the West after the Parthian campaigns of Caracalla and Macrinus in 218/19.[28] In Cilicia the epigraphic record is less complete, but coins issued by the main cities of the region —Tarsus, Anazarbus, Mopsuhestia, and Aegeae—peak at times of intense military activity suggesting that they were minted to serve the increased demands of soldiers passing through or occupying winter quarters.[29]

Bithynia, Cilicia, and the central Anatolian provinces between them have not to date produced examples of the complaints against soldiers and officials which are so conspicuous in Asia at this period. No doubt some protection was provided on these important transit routes to the frontiers by centurions and other officers stationed in the cities to keep the peace between the armies and the civilian population (see above, Ch. 9 § 11). But the record of army officers and officials effectively policing their own men, rather than joining in the plunder, is not an impressive one, and it may be safer to infer that all these roads were defined as major military highways (λεωφόροι ὁδοί) where, by definition, hospitality, provisions, transport, and other contributions could be claimed by right. The implications for the civilian inhabitants are clear: they were liable to suffer without even the faint hope of redress which was available to the cities and villages of Asia, which could at least claim some measure of immunity.

The soldiers and officials who made themselves so unwelcome in peaceful corners of rural Asia must originally have been sent to improve control over these areas. Security from external or internal enemies does not explain their presence in such numbers; it is more plausible that their chief purpose was the exaction of taxes and other contributions to the state. It is argued that in the Severan period it was increasingly common for the state to demand contributions in kind, as a convenient method of providing for the armies' needs, to replace money taxes.[30] In fact there is no compelling evidence to accept this view (see below, Ch. 14 §§ III–IV). The state had collected contributions in kind on a huge scale from the rural districts of Asia Minor as a matter of course since the late republican period, while urban communities continued to pay money taxes through the third and fourth century. The view that the economic basis of the empire was radically transformed during the third century from a system based on cash taxation to one dependent on the forced exaction of goods and supplies will not bear examination.

What did change, however, were the methods of tax collection. This became increasingly a matter for state officials. Especially during the prolonged warfare of the third century ever larger contributions were demanded of the population, especially in the eastern provinces. City magistrates and *publicani*, however, played a diminishing role in the collection and delivery of cash and goods. Financial pressures may have made many

[26] For renewed Roman imperialism against Parthia under the Severans, see F. Millar, *Journal of Jewish Studies*, 38 (1987), 146–7. The frontier itself was pushed out to include the new provinces of Mesopotamia and Osrhoene across the Euphrates. Two recent studies in particular mark an advance in our knowledge of Rome's wars with the Parthians and Sassanians in the third century: E. Kettenhofen, *Die römisch-persischen Kriege des 3 Jahrhunderts n. Chr.* (1982), which provides the basic documentation for his splendid map illustrating these campaigns published as the *Tübinger Atlas des Vorderen Orients* B. V. 12; for the impact on Cilicia see Ziegler.

[27] See above, Ch. 9 § 11. The liturgy of παραπόμπη or παραπέμψις is discussed by W. Ameling, *Epigr. Anat.* 1 (1983), 68 ff.; *I. Prusias* pp. 16–17.

[28] M. Speidel, *Epigr. Anat.* 5 (1985), 87–92; ibid. 7 (1986), 35–7 for an auxiliary of *ala II Lucensium* at Chalcedon who was also probably brought there by similar troop movements.

[29] For the abundant and complex numismatic evidence see Ziegler, esp. 130–43 on the relationship between troop movements and minting patterns. Useful observations in the review of H. Halfmann, *Gnomon*, 60 (1988), 520–3; some of the important results of this study are summarized by S. Mitchell, *JRS* 80 (1990), 191–3.

[30] D. van Berchem, *L'Annone militaire au troisième siècle de l'empire romain* (1952).

more reluctant to fulfil their old functions as tax gatherers, especially as they were generally expected to stand as guarantors for the sums they handed over to Rome. Wavering loyalty during the civil wars may also have helped to undermine the traditional system. In times when it was uncertain who was really in charge of the empire, it would be understandable if representatives of the local aristocracy hesitated to show their allegiance too clearly by collecting taxes for a particular imperial candidate. When the co-operation of the cities could no longer be taken for granted, emperors had no alternative but to use their own men, and send in soldiers or other officials to collect military supplies and money dues. This is a sign that already under the Severans duties which had previously been in the hands of civic officials were taken over by the state. It heralds the age of Diocletian and Constantine, when the number of state officials had multiplied out of hand, and many earlier civic responsibilities had simply vanished from view. This, rather than the supposed transformation from a cash economy to an economy in kind, was one of the real changes between the worlds of the early and later empire.

These new circumstances readily explain the presence of official intruders into the Asian countryside. Their main function to gather taxes and supplies for the state is often borne out by the titles and ranks which they bore. The Lydian inscriptions in particular single our *frumentarii, colletiones, stationarii,* and praetorian soldiers for special mention. *Frumentarii* by origin were officers concerned with securing supplies of grain for military units, and thus naturally assumed the role of tax collectors in regions where exactions in kind had always been commonplace. Their presence in rural districts should be linked originally to the task of obtaining grain for the *annona militaris*. In due course, as trusted men accustomed to working away from their units, they acquired other duties. Aurelius Gaius, the centurion who was praised at Aphrodisias for his decency around the middle of the third century, was a *frumentarius*, as were the soldiers who carried the petitions of Aragua and Scaptopara to Gordian and Philip in the 230s and 240s. Not all such men were necessarily corrupt and oppressive. However, they often undertook missions of a secret nature, which are well attested in the literature of the third and fourth century.[31] It is little surprise that soldiers who combined the roles of secret agent and tax collector should have been feared and hated by civilians. The Greek

term κολλητίων has less clearly defined associations. It appears to be connected with the Latin *collatio* meaning the payment of tribute or tax, and that etymology would chime exactly with their likely duties.[32] *Stationarii*, the gendarmes originally posted at stations along the main roads of the empire, were more widely distributed than other soldiers outside frontier regions, and thus a natural choice for tax collection duties when more manpower was required. It is a predictable irony that the *stationarii*, who on at least two occasions were sent to protect local populations from abusive behaviour and to keep the peace, themselves became the object of complaints.[33]

Alongside the demands for taxes in kind there existed the option of commuting payments to cash by the process of *obaeratio*. For communities with money available to them this would have been convenient and attractive. Even if they had enjoyed a productive harvest, peasant instincts will have told them that it was better to save up their surplus than sell it or hand it over as tax.[34] In a poor year surrendering their produce might mean starvation in this year or the next, when there was not enough seed corn to ensure a future crop. But agreeing to pay in cash not kind opened the door to further abuses of the system by the tax collectors. The temptation to extort extra quantities of grain, clothing, or other supplies for their own benefit was far less than that to demand coin, enough to satisfy the government, and more with which to line their own pockets. The endemic corruption of the Roman empire in the third century AD belonged to a society where cash still played a major role.

It is fruitless to speculate too far about the ways in which extortion and oppression were inflicted on the civilian population within the framework of legitimate but ill-controlled tax collection. There were few bounds to human greed or ingenuity, and no obvious way to control them. It was not simply the common people who suffered and resented the extortion. The use of soldiers to ensure that local populations paid their

[31] M. Clauss, *Untersuchungen zu den Principales des römischen Heeres von Augustus bis Diokletian* (Diss. Bochum, 1973), 86 ff.; F. Paschoud, 'Frumentarii, Agentes in Rebus, Magistriani, Curiosi, Veredarii: problèmes de terminologie', in J. Straub (ed.) *Bonner HA Colloquium 1979/81. Beiträge zur Historia-Augusta Forschung*, xv (1983), 215–43.

[32] See L. Robert, *Rev. phil.* (1943), 11 = *OMS* i. 368; *Oxford Latin Dictionary* s.v. *collatio* 2; note also Levick, *The Government of the Roman Empire*, 233 suggesting that there may be a punning association with the Greek verb κολλᾶν, to stick.

[33] *Stationarii* were posted to protect locals at Tacina, *Epigr. Anat.* 10 (1987), 133 ff. l. 36, and at Anosa, *JRS* 46 (1956), 47 l. 32; they are counted among the oppressors near Satala (*TAM* v. 1. 611) and at Demirci (*TAM* v. 1. 154). Note too that they sometimes collected fines payable for the desecration of tombs (above, Ch. 9 §1 at nn. 39–44).

[34] A rural population which was accustomed to seeing not only their surplus production but much of the basic livelihood removed by city dwellers (see above, Ch. 11 §1) would not have needed to be instructed in this basic peasant wisdom. Cf. L. Foxhall, *History Today*, 36 (June 1986), 35–43.

dues in cash or kind was matched by the inability or unwillingness of the civic aristocrats to carry out the tasks which they had traditionally performed. In fact, as the principal landowners such men had as much to lose as the peasants. Their support hitherto had been crucial to the smooth running of Rome's provinces. Losing the sympathy of municipal aristocracies carried grave risks for the stability of the empire. Even if they had been engaged in legitimate business the presence of soldiers was disruptive and a sign that the administration of the empire was not based on peaceful cooperation between the Roman authorities and the important element in the local populations which saw profit and advantage in Roman rule. Indiscipline, unruly behaviour, and systematic extortion widened the gap between soldier and civilian and increased the resentment between the government and its subjects. A vicious spiral of oppression and alienation was set in motion which was one of the key elements of the third-century crisis.

III. *Brigandage and Insurrection*

As alienation grew in the cities and villages of Asia, it took palpable and violent forms in the mountains of the south and south-west, where geography and history conspired to produce more serious forms of revolt against officialdom. The facility with which the *montagnards* of Rugged Cilicia, Isauria, Pisidia, and Lycia resisted the imposition of any authority on them is a *leitmotif* of Anatolian history. The calm intermission of the later first and second centuries AD was a striking exception to a pattern of turbulence which can be traced within the confines of Graeco-Roman Antiquity alone from the fourth century BC to the time of Justinian.[35] Even in the high empire the eirenarchs of the cities of these mountainous regions had strenuous tasks to perform, and they and their *diōgmitai* patrolled remote mountains, where they offered dedications to the local deities, nervous homage in the midst of natural and man-made dangers (see above, Ch. 11 § VI). Matters became worse. In the middle or later third century the citizens of Termessus in Pisidia set up a statue to honour a *dux*, L. Aurelius Marcianus, who had been a patron, a benefactor, and a champion of peace, εἰρήνης προστάτην, phraseology which is recalled by the praise given to the centurions Aurelius

Gaius at Aphrodisias and Aurelius Dionysius at Pisidian Antioch at about the same date. The title *dux* is prophetic of developments in the later empire, although it was already current in the command structure of the eastern frontier along the Euphrates.[36] The homonymous city of Termessus Minor in northern Lycia, which should be identified for all practical purposes with Oenoanda, set up a comparable inscription for Valerius Statilius Castus, who had ensured peace both on land and sea, and during a twelve-day stay in the city had presided over a festival held to celebrate the promotion of the younger Valerian to Caesar in November 256.[37] He held the position of *praepositus vexillationum* and bears the anomalous and unparalleled title, σύμμαχος τῶν Σεβαστῶν, which surely implies that the troops under his command were local levies, his own private army which enabled him to claim to be no simple officer under their command, but an independent ally.[38] The military precautions in both cases were surely directed at mountain uprisings in regions where brigandage, as in some of the north-western provinces of the empire, could swiftly develop into more serious forms of disaffection. The emperor Commodus had commended the citizens of Oenoanda's neighbour Bubon when they had ambushed a group of bandits, putting some of the survivors to death outright, and taking the rest prisoner.[39] Brigands indeed were not mere criminals but public enemies, to be suppressed by warfare not simply apprehended by police action. By the middle of the third century this type of warfare was no longer a legal fiction but vivid reality.

Better than any inscription are the dramatic remains of the siege of Pisidian Cremna, which had been seized by Lydius, the Isaurian brigand leader of a major Pisidian insurrection which threatened the province of Lycia and Pamphylia during the reign of Probus in AD 278. Zosimus' detailed account of this rebellion, which was only crushed after a prolonged Roman siege, has often been treated as a fantasy, but the essential features of what was clearly a major campaign are

---

[35] Justinian, *Nov.* 24, which entrusted Pisidia to a governor of higher rank, ἐπειδήπερ καὶ κῶμαι μέγισται κατ' αὐτήν εἰσι καὶ πολυάνθρωποι καὶ πολλάκις πρὸς αὐτοὺς στασιαζούσαι τοὺς δημοσίους φόρους· καὶ τοῖς λῃστρικοῖς ἐκείνοις καὶ ἀνδροφόνοις χωρίοις, ἅπερ ἐπί τινος ἀκρωρείας Λύκου κεφαλῆς καλουμένης ἵδρυται... κτλ. For the whole subject, see B. D. Shaw, *Journal of The Economic and Social History of The Orient*, 33 (1990), 199–233, and 237–70.

[36] See above, nn. 3–4. For *duces* at Dura Europos at this period see J. F. Gilliam, *TAPA* 72 (1941), 157–75; also in Egypt, idem, *Chronique d'Egypte*, 36 (1961), 386–92 (*Roman Army Papers*, 23–41; 257–63).

[37] *ILS* 8370 with the commentary of Lambertz, *RE* viiiA (1955), 226–8.

[38] For another anomalous text with certain similarities from this period, see *I. Eph.* 737.

[39] F. Schindler, *Die Inschriften von Bubon* (1972), 11 no. 2 with the commentary of J. and L. Robert, *Bull. ép.* 1973, 451 pp. 170–1. Note the phrases ὁρμήσαντας ἐπὶ τὴν τῶν λῃστῶν συνλήμψιν καὶ περιγενομένους γε αὐτῶν καὶ τοὺς μὲν ἀποκτείναντας τοὺς δὲ καὶ ζωγρήσαντας. B. D. Shaw, *Past and Present* 105 (1984), 3–51 expounds the identification of bandits with enemies of the state in detail.

confirmed by archaeology. Cremna had to be invested with two lines of siege walls, heavy artillery was used to soften up resistance, and the final assault was mounted from the top of a vast siege mound, which spanned the valley which ran along the west wall of the city and was raised twenty-five metres above the valley floor to dominate the fortifications. Standing in the shadow of this huge monument of military engineering, which had been heaped up stone by stone by Roman troops under the command of the provincial governor, it is impossible to dismiss this brigand uprising as a minor episode in a troubled period. Lydius' adventure has the appearance of an attempt to throw off imperial rule altogether.[40]

IV. *Goths and Sassanians: The External Threat*

The deployment of troops throughout Asia Minor during the third century paradoxically left it more exposed to incursions from the outside than at any time since the late republic. Towards the end of the second century AD the Pontic fleet, previously stationed at Trapezus and at Sinope,[41] was transferred to Cyzicus, leaving a notable gap in the naval defence of the northern seaboard.[42] In the second and early third centuries the Euxine had become a Roman lake, no less than the Mediterranean itself, and the scene of a widespread trading network which linked Asia Minor with the west Pontic and south Russian coasts.[43] The prospect of barbarian invasion from these directions, or even the piracy of the first century BC, was clearly not seriously contemplated. Nevertheless, in the 250s and 260s the way lay open for Gothic invasions.

The accounts and documentary evidence for these invasions are irresistibly reminiscent of the testimony to the Galatian arrival in Anatolia in the 270s BC, but still harder to disentangle. According to Zosimus, who probably drew on the third-century Athenian historian Herennius Dexippus, two important raids, tentatively dated to 254 and to 255–8, were directed against the east end of the Black Sea, overwhelming the Roman garrison at Pityous and, at the second attempt, capturing Trapezus. Large quantities of booty and prisoners were taken since the inhabitants of the sur-

rounding countryside had gathered in the city for protection.[44] Later invasions brought the Goths to central and western Asia Minor. Valiant attempts to reconstruct the topography and chronology of these razzias have still failed to make sense of all the literary sources.[45] Zosimus suggests that they sacked most of the major cities of Bithynia between Chalcedon and Prusa, including Nicomedia itself, but failed to cross the Rhyndacus, the boundary with Asia, and take Cyzicus.[46] The Byzantine writer Syncellus, who confirms that Nicomedia fell, has them invading Bithynia, overrunning Asia and Lydia, destroying the towns of Ionia, sacking Troy, and attacking Phrygia, Cappadocia, and Galatia.[47] It is impossible to believe that his account follows a topographical order, and highly likely that it is exaggerated. Zosimus, in another passage that is chronologically misplaced but should go back to a good source, confirms part of this by reporting that the Goths crossed into Asia and ravaged areas as far apart as Cappadocia, Pessinus, and Ephesus.[48] An independent fragment of the Athenian Dexippus, who defended his own city against Gothic attack, refers to a siege of Side, which should be put in the context of sea-borne raids against Pamphylia.[49]

Inscriptions from Miletus, Didyma, and Sardis suggest that they barely avoided being overwhelmed by the invaders, and the citizens of Carian Stratonicaea sought the reassurance of an oracle that their city would not fall in the coming year.[50] There is archaeological evidence that city walls were built or restored at Pergamum, Ephesus, Sardis,[51] and at Nicaea in Bithynia where the fortifications appear on coins of Gallienus and whose gates carry an inscription of Claudius Gothicus dated to 269.[52] The walls of Prusias ad Hypium also contain much reused material, typical of mid-third-century work, and are probably

---

[40] S. Mitchell, 'The Siege of Cremna A.D. 278', in D. H. French and C. S. Lightfoot, *The Eastern Frontier of the Roman Empire* (1989), 311–28.

[41] For Sinope see D. H. French, *Epigr. Anat.* 4 (1984), 53–60; cf. French and Speidel, *Epigr. Anat.* 6 (1985), 97–102.

[42] D. Kienast, *Untersuchungen zu den römischen Kriegsflotten* (1966), 106–9.

[43] M. I. Rostovzeff, 'Pontus, Bithynia and the Bosporus', *ABSA* 22 (1916–18), 1–22; L. Robert, *A travers l'Asie Mineure* (1980), 74–86 is now essential on the trading network of the 2nd and 3rd cents. AD.

[44] Zosimus 1. 31–3 with Paschoud's notes.

[45] See especially M. Salaman, 'The chronology of the Gothic invasions into Asia Minor in the 3rd century A.D.', *Eos*, 59 (1971), 109–39, and Magie, *RR* ii. 1566–8; cf. L. Robert, *Hellenica*, vi. 117 ff.

[46] Zosimus, 1. 34–36. 1; cf. Ammianus Marcellinus 31. 5. 16.

[47] Syncellus, 1. 700 (Bonn).

[48] Zosimus, 1. 28. 1.

[49] *FGrH* 100 F. 29.

[50] Miletus: A. Rehm, *Milet* i. 9 no. 339a; Didyma: *SEG* iv. 467 i and iii, with L. Robert, *Hellenica*, iv. 25, 74–5, 82 n. 1; and *Hellenica* vi. 117 ff.; Sardis: *IGR* iv. 1510, with Robert, *Hellenica*, iv. 35–47; Stratonicaea: *I. Stratonikaia*, ii. 1 no. 1103.

[51] Magie, *RR* ii. 1566–8; for Ephesus see J. Keil, *JÖAI* 30 (1937), Beibl. 204 no. 10; 36 (1946), 128–9; for Sardis see C. Foss, *Byzantine and Turkish Sardis* (1976), 3; for Pergamon, W. Radt, *Pergamon* (1988), 79.

[52] *IGR* iii. 39–40; *I. Iznik*, nos. 11–12; see S. Mitchell, *HSCP* 91 (1987), 342. For the coins see above, Ch. 12 §IV n. 99.

contemporary.[53] They were doubtless built in the aftermath of the Gothic raids that had devastated neighbouring cities. The Anatolian plateau also did not escape the attention of the barbarians. An inscription of Ancyra honours a benefactor who constructed the city walls in a time of famine and barbarian raids, and archaeological evidence suggests that they followed the same line as the sixteenth-century fortifications of the Ottoman city.[54] The walls of Dorylaeum, built largely with spoils from the Roman city, are remarkable for reusing a series of eight statue bases set up for a prominent civic benefactor, Q. Aelius Voconius Stratonicus which themselves were erected sometime between AD 212 and the middle of the century.[55] The readiness of the people of Dorylaeum to despoil the public buildings of their city of statues, which had been erected barely a generation before for a man whom they hailed as their second founder, makes the nature of the emergency vividly clear. The manner of their response to the threats hints that civic pride had almost collapsed.

The human side of the Gothic invasions is more poignantly revealed by two contemporary inscriptions. One, from the area between Iulia Gordus and Daldis in Lydia, is the tombstone of a slave who had died in April 263 soon after returning from six months' captivity among the barbarians; exhausted, no doubt, by the privations he had undergone.[56] The second is a grave epigram for a 14-year-old girl buried in Karzene, a community in western Paphlagonia, where she had been killed resisting the assaults of the barbarians, rather than submit to abduction and rape as her contemporaries had.[57] A second epitaph from the same site which was set up for their own daughter by grieving parents is dated to the year 268 of the local era, that is AD 262/3. She too might have died at the hands of the Goths. If the point could be established for certain, this would be an invaluable chronological indication that the Goths were present in this region in the same year as they had captured the slave in Lydia.[58]

The conditions of the Gothic raids in northern Anatolia are also vividly illuminated by an unexpected source—the canonical epistle of Gregory Thaumaturgus, bishop of Pontic Neocaesarea—whose first ruling concerned the guilt or otherwise of women who had been raped by the barbarians, and which continued in a similar vein to define the church's attitude to those who had against their will committed forbidden acts in captivity, collaborated with their captors, or taken advantage of the chaos caused by the invasions to loot the possessions of others.[59]

The Goths evidently took many prisoners, both pagan and Christian. According to Christian legend the latter set about converting their captors, and the first bishop of the Goths, Ulfilas, could trace his ancestry back to the Cappadocian village of Sadagolthina near Parnassus on the border of Galatia and Cappadocia.[60] A century later in AD 371 Basil of Caesareia recalled in a letter to Pope Damasus at Rome that his predecessor Dionysius had sent envoys to ransom Asiatic brethren from captivity among the Goths, and the memory of this was preserved both in written documents and the oral traditions of the church.[61]

During the same period that the Goths wrought havoc and instilled fear in the communities of northern and western Anatolia, an equal danger emerged in the south and east. Under the Severans Roman ambitions on the eastern frontier had been rekindled; Septimius Severus created new provinces in Osrhoene and Mesopotamia under equestrian governors, and took vigorous offensive action against the Parthians. Caracalla in 215–16, Elagabalus in 218–19, Severus Alexander from 231 to 233 maintained the initiative with variable success.[62] The failure of the Parthians to offer effective resistance was at least partly responsible for the eclipse of their dynasty and the rise of the Sassanians as a new force in Persia under Ardashir, who ousted the last Parthian ruler during the late 220s.

[53] I. Prusias, p. 17; W. Ameling, Epigr. Anat. 3 (1984), 21.

[54] Bosch, Ankara, no. 289, cf. nos. 290, 292, and 293, with C. Foss, 'Ankara', 32 n. 14 and 62 n. 139 discussing the meagre archaeological evidence.

[55] Weiss, JÖAI 16 (1913), suppl. 73–4 nos. 1–8 for the texts. A. Körte, Gött. Gel. Anz. 159 (1897), 391 ff. and Cox and Cameron, MAMA v. pp. xii–xiii discuss the walls.

[56] L. Robert, Hellenica, vi. 117 ff. no. 48. I agree with Robert, against the doubts of G. Walser and T. Pekary, Die Krise der röm. Welt (1962), 33, that the death of the slave, which the tomb dates, was a proximate outcome of the captivity and did not take place long after his release. The document is thus crucial for the chronology of the invasions.

[57] I. Kaygusuz, Epigr. Anat. 4 (1984), 61–2; (W. Lebek, ZPE 59 (1985), 7–8; SEG xxxiv (1984), 1271).

[58] Kaygusuz, Epigr. Anat. 4 (1984), 66 no. 8; (SEG xxxiv (1984), 1278).

[59] Text in PG 10. 1019–47. See below, Vol. II, Ch. 17 §1. The implications are carefully explored by Lane Fox, Pagans and Christians, 539–41. W. H. C. Frend, Martyrdom and Persecution in the Early Church (1965), 423 supposes that the Christians had been more prone to disloyalty than their pagan counterparts as an open gesture of defiance of Roman authority. There is no ground for this view.

[60] Philostorgius, HE ii. 5, cf. Sozomen, HE ii. 6; his successor had a Phrygian mother, see Socrates, HE v. 23, Sozomen, HE vii. 17. For the site and an inscription alleged to have been found there, at a village near the north-east corner of Tuz Göl, see Belke, TIB iv, s.v. The inscription, which refers to Sadagolthina as a polis is surely a fake, and has not been seen since the first report in 1903.

[61] Basil, Ep. 70. For the connections between the Scythian and the Cappadocian churches note M. H. Jellinek, Festschrift Kluge (Tübingen 1926), 61–5 (not seen by the author), who argues against any genuine link before the fourth century.

[62] See A. R. Birley, Septimius Severus: The African Emperor² (1988), 129–45; Magie, RR ii. 1542–4, 1551–4, 1560; C. S. Lightfoot, JRS 80 (1990), 115–26.

He was succeeded by his son, the greatest of Sassanian rulers Shapur I, who dealt three devastating military blows to Rome between 240 and 260. Around 236 Ardashir, it seems, had launched raids into Cappadocia and seized the Mesopotamian cities of Nisibis and Carrhae. This invited a Roman reprisal; preparations may have been under way during the brief joint reign of Balbinus and Pupienus in 238, but they came to nothing while the Sassanians continued the offensive, taking Hatra in 240 and advancing through Mesopotamia and Syria almost to the gates of Antioch in 241/2. Finally Rome was ready to respond and Gordian III led a great counter-attack in spring 242.[63] The expedition proved disastrous. Roman sources alleged that the emperor won a victory at Resaina in Mesopotamia, but was murdered on the return march by his praetorian prefect and successor, Philip, shortly before crossing back into Roman territory.[64] The Sassanians claimed otherwise. The inscription known as the *Res Gestae Divi Saporis* carved at Naqs-i-Rushtam in north-west Iran states that when Gordian invaded at the head of a great army of Goths and Germans, he was defeated and killed in battle at Meshike. Philip his successor sued for peace and paid a huge ransom to reclaim the prisoners of war.[65]

Philip agreed to peace terms with Shapur which included a non-aggression pact and the abandonment of Roman claims to Armenia. It seems likely that he stuck to this agreement. Indeed he may have had little option if a passage in the thirteenth Sibylline Oracle, which refers to a Syrian usurper, a ληστής who invaded Cappadocia, captured the cities of Mazaca and Tyana, took refuge in lofty Selge, and eventually fled across the Euphrates to the Sassanians, should be dated to the late 240s.[66] Internal disorders precluded further action beyond the frontiers.

Philip's successors Trajan Decius, Trebonianus Gallus, and Volusianus resumed the offensive. The *Res Gestae* of Shapur speak of the Caesar carrying out a deceit and committing injustice in Armenia, while coins from Anazarbus have been interpreted to show large troop movements and even the arrival of Gallus or

Volusian in person during 251/2 to direct military preparations in Cilicia Pedias.[67] These warlike gestures provoked a decisive Sassanian attack; Shapur claims to have annihilated a Roman army of 60,000 men at Barbalissus in Syria, a battle which newly published inscriptions from Syrian Apamea date to 252. There followed a devastating raid on Syria. The Roman garrison town of Dura Europos fell and Sassanian troops were installed in their place; cities had to fend for themselves and only Emesa is known to have offered successful resistance.[68] The invasion extended north of the Taurus into Cappadocia. The legionary fortress at Satala and other obscure places in Pontus fell victim to one advance, while another Sassanian force reached a place called Phreata, The Wells, in the Garsauritis around Cappadocian Archelais.[69]

The final round in Shapur's assault on the eastern provinces came in 259. Syrian Antioch had been attacked and perhaps sacked during the raids after Barbalissus. The new co-emperor Valerian advanced from the west through Cilicia, occupied the city and made it his base. Six years of delay and preparations followed. The Gothic invasions of Bithynia led him to send an army north to Byzantium while he himself marched into Cappadocia, but the only effect, according to Zosimus, was to exhaust the cities by the passage of his troops. More positively there were attempts to revive morale by the creation of many new games and festivals (see above, Ch. 12 §v at nn. 183–8). Like Gordian in 242 Valerian saw the need for vigorous propaganda in preparing the Greek cities of Asia Minor for another confrontation with Persia. Finally in 259 he crossed the Euphrates and led a force of 70,000 men into battle. Again the outcome was a catastrophe. Shapur inflicted a crushing defect on the Romans between Carrhae and Edessa, captured the emperor, his praetorian prefect, and many other commanders, and deported them as prisoners to Persis.[70] It is small wonder that the dynasts of Palmyra, Odènathus and his wife Zenobia, chose this moment to throw off their allegiance to Rome and declare an independent empire in the East, claiming a frontier which extended deep into Anatolia as far as Ancyra itself.[71]

[63] For Carrhae and Nisibis, see Magie, *RR* ii. 1560–1; the preparations of Balbinus and Pupienus, Ziegler 139; Hatra, the Syrian invasion, and Gordian's *profectio*, above, nn. 1–2, and X. Loriot, *ANRW* ii. 2. 757 ff.

[64] The sources have been collected and translated by M. H. Dodgeon and S. C. Lieu, *The Roman Eastern Frontier and the Persian Wars A.D. 226–363* (1991). Discussion of conflicting versions by Loriot, *ANRW* ii. 2. 770 ff. See also Kettenhofen, *Die römisch-persischen Kriege*.

[65] *Res Gestae Divi Saporis* (*RGDS*) published by A. Maricq, *Syria* 35 (1958), 395–442 = *Classica et Orientalia* (1965), 37–84 ll. 6–10 (Greek version).

[66] *Oracula Sibyllina* 13. 81–102, interpreted by Ziegler 99–104. But D. S. Potter, *Prophecy and History in the Crisis of the Roman Empire* (1990), 277 suggests that he took refuge in Syrian Soura.

[67] *RGDS* l. 10, where the Caesar is usually wrongly identified as Philip. Ziegler, 108–13 for the coin evidence of 251/2.

[68] *RGDS* l. 11. For Barbalissus see now J. Balty, *JRS* 78 (1988), 102–3; Emesa, *IGLS* 1799–81; Malalas, *Chron.* xii. 296. 10–297. 20 (Bonn); Dura, M. I. Rostovtzeff, *Dura Europos and its Art* (1935), with Balty, *CRAI* (1987), 229–39.

[69] *RGDS* ll. 12–19. Strabo notes that the wells near Savatra, close to the Garsauritis, were the deepest in the world, 12. 6. 1, 568.

[70] *RGDS* ll. 19–26. For Valerian at Antioch see Ziegler, 114–19. The march against the Goths, Zosimus, 1. 36, τῇ παρόδῳ δὲ μόνον ἐπιτρίψας τὰς πόλεις.

[71] See Magie, *RR* ii. 1574–5.

The defeat of Valerian was followed like the battle of Barbalissus by wide ranging Sassanian raids, which now extended over most of south-east Asia Minor. The catalogue of cities captured includes all the main settlements of Cilicia Pedias—Aegeae, Mopsuhestia, Mallos, Adana, Tarsus, Anazarbus, and Hierapolis-Castabala—many places in the mountains or along the coast of Rugged Cilicia, including Seleuceia on the Calycadnus, Antiochia, Anemurium, Kelenderis, Selinus, Domitiopolis—the major Cappadocian centres of Caesareia, Tyana, Comana, Kybistra, and Sebasteia in Pontus—as well as Laranda and Iconium in Lycaonia.[72]

These incursions were as alarming as the Gothic raids from the north, and provoked similar responses. Cities hurriedly demolished their public buildings and put up fortifications from the spoils. This clearly happened at Cremna where the western city wall had been rebuilt with reused material before the Roman siege of AD 278. The late Roman fortifications of Cibyra and Iconium, the latter now entirely demolished, probably date to the same period. The most precisely dated evidence for hasty rebuilding is found at the small Cilician fortress of Adanda, where the lintel of the main gate was inscribed with a dedication to Gallienus during the governorship of Voconius Zeno between 260 and 268. It is built into a wall which for the most part seems to be contemporary with the inscription, and is flanked by a tower which contains four reused statue bases, including dedications to Geta and to Caracalla.[73]

The fortifications which were built throughout the peninsula in these years offer the best illustration of the terror and insecurity which these invasions brought to Asia Minor. Almost all the major cities threw up their own fortifications, having often obtained the material to do so by the systematic demolition of the major public buildings of the city centres. The epigraphic evidence from the period shows that local initiatives, the efforts of provincial governors, and even imperial assistance all had a part to play in providing for the defence of Asia Minor now that its frontiers had collapsed.[74]

The fall of Rome's linear defences in the East profoundly affected geopolitical realities in Asia Minor. Between the principates of Septimius Severus and Valerian, Cilicia Pedias (previously an insignificant backwater) emerged as an area of vital strategic importance. This was reflected in the history of its cities which were required to sustain the war effort by providing winter quarters for troops, and were rewarded with prestigious, if hollow new titles. Inter-city rivalry flourished against this background as Tarsus, Anazarbus, and Aegeae competed for the favour of emperors, supporting one or another in the frequent civil wars.[75] The history of Pamphylia was even more remarkable. This enclave of coastal plain, dominated by the cities of Attaleia, Perge, Aspendus, and Side, was protected from Sassanian and Gothic attack by the mountain barrier of the Taurus. After the great Sassanian invasion of south-east Anatolia in the early 260s it appeared to be the only safe base from which resistance and counter-attacks could be mounted. Side and Perge in particular became the headquarters of large numbers of troops. Side's commercial harbour, which had always been at the hub of a thriving trade network linking Egypt, Syria, and Cyprus with southern Anatolia, now became an important naval station and a key to the movement of troops and supplies. The city achieved the unique distinction of acquiring six imperial neocories, two more even than Ephesus and Pergamum at the height of their prosperity. Perge equally enjoyed the spotlight. In AD 275/6 the emperor Tacitus made the city his headquarters, and its prominence is highlighted by a spectacular series of acclamations inscribed on a stele:

Viva Perge, the one asylum! Viva Perge, where Tacitus...! Viva Perge, *neocorus* since Vespasian! Viva Perge, honoured with the sacred standard! Viva Perge, honoured with silver coinage! Ephesian Games celebrated fifty six times, and more to come! Viva Perge, the treasury of the emperor! Viva Perge, four times *neocorus*! Viva Perge, the first of the assize cities! Viva Perge where consulars make their reputations! Viva Perge, where consulars sponsor the festivals! Viva Perge, the crown of Pamphylia! Viva Perge which has always been true to all the privileges granted by decree of the Senate![76]

Pamphylia had prospered mightily in the second and early third century, but few would have predicted this eminence amid the shambles of civic life in the rest of Asia Minor during the later third century.

---

[72] *RGDS* ll. 27–34.

[73] For Cremna, see above, n. 40; The late Roman walls of Iconium, excavated beneath the main mosque of the city in 1910, contained much reused material but were demolished forthwith; cf. W. M. Calder, *Rev. phil.* (1912), 48 ff. publishing the inscriptions found in it. For Adanda, see *Mon. Ant.* 23 (1914), 148 and Bean and Mitford, *AS* 12 (1962), 207–8.

[74] See *HSCP* 91 (1987), 339–42.

[75] Ziegler, *passim*.

[76] J. Nollé, *Chiron*, 16 (1986), 202 for Side and Pamphylia in general. For the Perge acclamation see I. Kaygusuz, *Epigr. Anat.* 4 (1984), 1–4 (*SEG* xxxiv (1984), 1306); P. Weiss, *Chiron*, 21 (1991), 353–92; and above, Ch. 12 § 11 n. 22. Note too C. J. Howgego, *Roman Imperial Countermarks* (1985), ch. 4 on the resilient local bronze coinage of Pamphylia up to the 270s, and Nollé, *JNG* 36 (1986), 127–43 for coin types of southern Asia Minor minted in the 250s and 260s which reflect the eastern conflict.

v. *The Resilience of the Countryside*

The Anatolian countryside offers a different picture. The rural peasantry had been accustomed to privations even amid the prosperity of the high empire; it made little difference to them whether they were victims of exploitation by rich local aristocrats, civic councillors, or soldiers and officials. Life in the third century might certainly be uncomfortable, and riddled with injustice, but it was not necessarily worse than it had been before. The country people also had less to lose from the dislocation caused by war and invasion. A tiny example offers an illustration. The parents of the young girl killed by Goths in Paphlagonia commemorated her with a well-carved verse epitaph which was no different, except for the account of the manner of her death, from hundreds of other comparable gravestones of the imperial period. This rural community had swiftly resumed its traditional pattern of life once the raid was over. It is reasonable to argue that rural communities in general in Asia Minor remained relatively untouched by the crises of the third century.

A brief sampling of the evidence from the country districts confirms that life continued without serious interruption. Rural central Anatolia is astonishingly well-endowed with funerary and votive inscriptions, themselves a generally unremarked tribute to the spread of literacy to the country districts.[77] These inscriptions tend to form reasonably homogeneous regional groups, reflecting local styles of workmanship and tastes in funerary monuments. There is rarely any indication that the sequence of inscribed stones in a given area was seriously interrupted for any reason, and editors have dated the vast bulk of this material, sometimes admittedly on very impressionistic grounds, between the early second and late fourth century AD. If this very crude characterization of the rural epigraphy of Roman Anatolia is true to the facts, it strongly suggests that the decline or 'crisis' of the third century was primarily an urban phenomenon, which did little to trouble the country districts.

A closer examination of some of these rural areas helps to sharpen the picture. The central Anatolian plateau between Ancyra and Iconium has produced well over a thousand inscriptions.[78] Almost none of the text bears an absolute date, but the earliest are funerary doorstones of the mid-first century AD or a little before.[79] A certain number of texts can be placed in the second century, especially after much of this area

became imperial property under Hadrian (see above, Ch. 10 §III at nn. 122–31); but a larger number, dated by the presence of Aurelii, belong to the third century after AD 212 or later. A high proportion of these may also be dated to the fourth century on account of their unambiguous allusions to Christianity in the form of distinctive Christian names, prominently engraved crosses, or clerical titles such as presbyter, deacon, or reader (see below, Vol. II, Ch. 17 §X at n. 453). In the absence of more precise dating criteria it is impossible to establish a clear-cut picture of the chronological distribution of these numerous texts, but nothing even hints at a break in the sequence through the period as a whole, least of all during the third century.

The same impression is given by the funerary inscriptions from the valley of the Çarşamba, in the borderland between Lycaonia and Isauria south of Iconium. The epitaphs of this region, carved on a distinctive series of decorated gravestones, have for the most part been dated to the third and fourth centuries.[80] Although many of these texts refer explicitly to clergy, and should be attributed to the fourth century, the vocabulary and style of the inscriptions is rooted in the tradition of the early imperial period and many certainly belong to the third century. The material is even more obviously homogeneous than the inscriptions from the central plateau.

Two other well-known groups of inscriptions, one from Phrygia Paroreius the other from the south-west corner of the province of Asia, make a similar point and demonstrate that decent levels of rural prosperity continued throughout the third century. The first are the records of the *Xenoi Tekmoreioi*, found at Sağır and Kumdamlı on the territory of Pisidian Antioch. This religious association erected a series of lengthy inscriptions, usually on behalf of the health and safety of the emperors and commemorating the erection of cult statues or associated buildings. They also list the subscriptions of the associates of the cult. One group of these texts should be dated around AD 238, the other belongs to the 260s. In the first case the level of contributions ranges from 161 to 1,090 denarii, in the second from 280 to 6,001 denarii. Allowing for the impact of inflation, these two sets of figures show that subscribers, who lived in villages which extend from central Pisidia to northern Phrygia, were maintaining their donations at an even level through the middle of the century. It is also significant that they continued to donate cash. Significant peasant surpluses were still

[77] L. Robert, *Hellenica*, xiii. 65 ff.

[78] A representative sample of the total is *MAMA* i. 1–383; vii. 311–593; *RECAM* ii. 220–405.

[79] *MAMA* vii. 14a = Waelkens, *Türsteine*, no. 662. See also the doorstone from Philomelium, *Türsteine*, no. 671 which may be a little earlier.

[80] The principal publications are A. M. Ramsay, *JHS* 24 (1904), 200–92; cf. eadem, *SERP* 1–58; W. M. Ramsay, *JHS* 25 (1905), 163–80; Buckler, Calder, and Cox, *JRS* 14 (1924), nos. 43–95; *MAMA* viii. 52–210, 304–10. See below, Vol. II, Ch. 17 §II at nn. 39–44.

being converted into cash and coinage remained the main medium for exchange within the market section of the economy.[81]

A very similar impression of continuity emerges from the inscriptions relating to the large private estates on the territory of the Ormeleis between Cibyra and Olbasa, which span the period from the late second century to around AD 270.[82] Although the picture is not as complete as in the case of the *Xenoi Tekmoreioi*, these texts contain a series of dedications made on behalf of the community and the estate owners, often involving cash expenditure on ceremonial crowns or altars associated with the cult of Zeus Sabazius as well as money distributions to the people, dating to *c*.200, 207/8, 215, 217/18, and 279/80. Around AD 200 a sum of 200 denarii was given to the people for investment, so as to furnish annual interest; in 270 the same sum sufficed only to pay for the erection of an altar. Despite the ravages of inflation, cash transactions continued to play a part even in the rural economy.[83]

The upper Tembris valley exhibited the same pattern of rural well-being throughout the third century. Here it has proved possible to assemble a typology of between 500 and 600 grave monuments, either local doorstones or highly decorated steles, which can be assigned to specific workshops and dated, usually to within a decade. They present a picture of continuous development extending into the second decade of the fourth century. Although we know that the area suffered abuse and injury at the hands of soldiers and others in the 240s (see above), this was not serious enough to disrupt the equilibrium of rural life.[84] The inscriptions of neighbouring Aezani may help to prove the rule that the countryside remained relatively untouched by the troubles which afflicted the cities.

The doorstones found at Aezani and throughout its territory were all produced by a single workshop, using stone from the local quarries of Göynükören, between the first and third centuries. The series dwindles to a thin trickle towards the end of this period, and few if any gravestones appear to be as late as AD 250. The explanation may lie in the fact that the workshop was almost certainly located in the city itself, and thus shared in the general urban decline, which was if anything more conspicuous at Aezani than in other cities of central Asia Minor in the third century.[85] The rural Tembris valley, which had never been so dependent on a flourishing urban centre, prospered in contrast.

The explanations for this rural continuity and the contrast with urban decline are doubtless complex, and varied from region to region. But they may share a simple truth. City life was based on an elaborate and artificial culture, which was brought to life by a combination of the administrative requirements of the early empire and local aristocratic ambitions. Both of these fundamental requirements of city life were in flux after the Severan period. Administration relied less on the co-operation of the local ruling classes and more on a new and expanding military officer class and troops, who intervened directly to take what they needed in the interests of the armies' and the emperors' well-being. At the same time fiscal and other pressures alienated the provincial aristocrats and middle-ranking inhabitants of the cities, who ceased to offer the active partnership on which the prosperity of the second century depended. The cities and their institutions were the first to suffer in this changed climate.

In the countryside, on the other hand, the population as ever was making a living as best it could from the land, by the application of traditional peasant crafts and skills that could scarcely be forgotten or neglected by a community concerned with its own survival. The countless villages and innumerable peasant families had always been the fundamental resource of the land of Anatolia. Their resilience held the eastern provinces together through the disasters of the middle and later third century, and ensured that solid foundations survived on which the empire could be rebuilt in the fourth century.

---

[81] For the texts and their interpretation see, above all, W. Ruge, *RE* va (1934), 158–69.

[82] For full references see above, Ch. 10 §v n. 198. The clearest discussion is by W. Ruge, *RE* xviii (1939), 1098–105.

[83] *IGR* iv. 887 (gift designed to be loaned out at interest, *c*. AD 200); 888 (c. AD 200); 889 (AD 207/8, set up by the mystai of Zeus Sabazius); 890 (c. AD 215); 891 (AD 217/18); 892 (c. AD 220–40, gifts from a list of individuals at either 50 or 25 denarii per head); 893 (c. AD 270, 200 denarii spent on an altar).

[84] See the chronological analysis of the material published in *MAMA* x by M. Waelkens.

[85] See *MAMA* ix. pp. xliv–liii; cf. xxvi for the exiguous record in the 3rd cent.

14   Tax, Grain, and the Economy

1. Reconstructing the Ancient Economy

The appearance of Anatolia changed fundamentally between the second century BC and the second century AD. Cities took the place of fortified refuges; settled village populations superseded transhumant groups; cereal agriculture spread to areas previously devoted to pasture and stock-raising, and thus supported a growing population. Roman rule brought a network of all-weather roads, which transformed overland communications; permanent garrisons guarded the eastern frontier, and Roman soldiers became a common sight on the roads and in the small towns. Although the small number of Roman officials and administrators made only a slight impact on the majority of the population, Roman power was acknowledged everywhere, on coins bearing the emperors' portraits, on building inscriptions which carried their names, by imperial statues in public places, and by sanctuaries of the imperial cult which existed in every city and in important rural centres. The cultural horizons of the inhabitants had also been vastly enlarged. Greek had become the common language of education and of political and commercial life in the cities, pushing the native languages of Anatolia into the country regions. Even here Greek language and culture made substantial headway. Cities were organized on a Graeco-Roman model and thus produced a new form of society, which was readily adopted by the indigenous population, and which enabled them to join a cultural and political system which now covered the whole Mediterranean basin.

These political and social transformations imply or entailed fundamental economic developments. The new forms of settlement and the increased population went hand in hand with economic growth. The exploitation of the land, the distribution of wealth, and the methods of state taxation all took new forms. Coinage, which had played only a marginal part in the economic life of central Anatolia before the Roman period, assumed a significant role by the second century AD, when most cities minted bronze money to oil the wheels of their own market systems.

It remains extremely difficult to characterize these economic changes in detail. The historical sources which are usually marshalled to illustrate the history of the Roman empire and in particular of its provinces, including the material gathered in earlier chapters of this study, rarely throw direct light on the underlying economic or fiscal structures. Effectively there was no science of economics in Antiquity, and no conscious intellectual analysis of the nature of economic forces in society. This does not mean that economic motivation was unknown, or that economic considerations did not play a significant part in determining human action. Rather, such considerations were not identified and subjected to contemporary scrutiny and analysis, except in exceptional cases, or at an immediate practical level. Reconstructing the overall pattern and principles of ancient economic systems, therefore, is a modern science.[1]

Faced with little direct ancient evidence, except the lists of products that can usually be compiled of a region's products, and in particular by a lack of reliable quantifiable data, modern reconstructions have usually been based on different forms of indirect evidence, used singly or in combination. Archaeological data, that is material remains preserved more or less by chance rather than by human intention, offer the most obvious way of compensating for the lack of documentary or literary evidence for economic activity. It is possible, for instance, to identify the sources of production and patterns of distribution of certain durable products, such as marble or pottery, and thereby assemble a partial picture of ancient trading activity. The study of pottery amphoras has been particularly important since it reveals information not simply about pots, but about the goods which they contained. Analysis of amphora finds from shipwrecks, and from Monte Testaccio, the huge waste dump in Rome's docklands, now underpins

---

[1] M. I. Finley, *The Ancient Economy* (1974), and H. W. Pleket, 'Wirtschafts- und Sozialstruktur', in F. Vittinghoff *et al.*, *Handbuch der Europäischen Wirtschafts- und Sozialgeschichte*, i (1990), 79 ff. should suffice from a huge bibliog.

our understanding of maritime trade in the ancient Mediterranean.[2] To date amphora finds have thrown no direct light on the economy of inland Anatolia. Indeed the pottery storage jars, or pithoi, whose remains can be found at most Roman or late Roman sites on the Anatolian plateau, are manifestly too large to have been easily transported and instead provide evidence for how local agricultural produce was often stored. Moreover, no serious study of Anatolian pottery production in the Hellenistic and Roman periods has been published, and this avenue of enquiry remains closed.[3] On the other hand much energy has been devoted to the study of Anatolian quarries, above all the Phrygian marble quarries around Docimeium, and this has significantly changed perceptions of the economic importance of the area, above all in the Roman period.

The distribution of coin types is even more relevant for the reconstruction of the economy. Coin-finds reflect patterns of trade and exchange, at least within the monetized sector of the economy. Since the bronze coins minted by the cities of western Asia Minor are rarely found outside the assize districts to which those cities belonged, at least in the province of Asia, it is reasonable to assume that most commercial activity stemmed from short-haul trade and transport of goods from country to city, between neighbouring cities, or between a smaller city and the larger assize centre on which it was juridically dependent. In contemporary Turkey traders offer their goods for sale in weekly markets, moving in a fixed circuit from one rural centre to another, returning after seven days to their starting point. These small networks are usually confined within a single administrative area.[4] Inscriptions refer to the creation of periodic markets in rural areas of western Anatolia during the Roman period, regulated so as not to damage existing, town-based markets. The longer, three-week cycle which they usually observed presumably reflects the relative slowness of transport between one market pitch and another, compared to modern conditions where motorized transport has virtually eliminated journey times. Regulated periodic markets within the confines of a Roman assize district offer an attractive explanation for the usual distribution pattern of civic bronze coinage in the imperial period.[5] On the other hand, coins minted by the imperial authorities primarily to meet the needs of soldiers along the eastern frontier are found more widely distributed across eastern Asia Minor from the Black Sea to northern Syria, and imply that these troops, who were naturally far less sedentary than the peasant population of most of Anatolia and who had access to better systems of transport, were supported by a much wider economic hinterland.[6]

Specific archaeological or numismatic evidence can profitably be supplemented by a third approach, namely by using detailed and careful observation of conditions in the present day, or in the recent, pre-mechanized past, to build up a picture of a regional economy which can validly be transferred to Antiquity. In many parts of Anatolia there is good reason to believe that patterns of settlement and methods of rural exploitation were broadly similar in Roman and late Ottoman times, and the observations of European

[2] See J. J. Paterson, 'Salvation from the Sea', JRS 72 (1982), 154 ff., reviewing recent work; further bibliography at N. Purcell, JRS 75 (1985), 7 n. 26. Amphoras Dressel types 1–4, which were produced in Italy and the western provinces, hardly ever reached eastern Mediterranean ports (D. W. Rathbone, JRS 73 (1983), 163). Their place was obviously taken by eastern types, but to date almost all the work on amphoras in the eastern Mediterranean has been devoted to the Hellenistic period. See J. Y. Empéreur (ed.), Recherches sur les amphores grecs, suppl. to BCH (1986), and the full bibliog. by Empéreur and Y. Garlan, REG 100 (1987), 58–109.

[3] Amphoras were transported overland in Gaul, see P. Middleton, in P. Garnsey and C. R. Whittaker, Trade and Famine in Classical Antiquity (1983), 76, with Cicero, Font. 19–20; it would be reasonable to expect at least some finds on inland sites in Asia Minor. Amphoras were often depicted on votive and funerary monuments in Phrygia; T. Drew Bear, ANRW ii. 18. 3, 2009–10 rightly associates them with local viticulture. According to Galen, peasants brought grain to market in large jars, saturating the contents with water to increase the weight, Nat. Fac. I. 14. 56, cited by P. Garnsey, Famine and Food Supply in the Graeco-Roman World (1988), 48. As for other ceramic production, the fine pottery produced in the Arretine workshops of central Italy in the 1st cents. BC and AD rarely reached eastern markets. It follows that the Greek world used its own products. In Asia Minor large-scale production centres have only recently been identified at Pergamum (Arch. Reports (1984/5), 79) and at Sagalassus (M. Waelkens et al., XII Kazı Sonuçları Toplantısı (Ankara, 1991), 119–54, and AS 41 (1991), 206–12. For Pergamene wares see JHS Arch. Reports (1989/90), 92; Radt, Pergamon (1988), 317–19 and bibliog. p. 381; and esp. C. Meyer-Schlichtmann, Die pergamenische Sigillata aus der Stadtgrabung von Pergamon, Perg. Forsch. 6 (1988).

[4] For the circulation of bronze coin within assize districts, see Robert, Villes[2], 410, Monnaies grecques (1967), 86–105, and compare his remarks in Études de numismatique grecque (1951), passim. C. J. Howgego, Greek Imperial Countermarks (1985), 34 emphasizes that this should not be treated as a strict rule, but the pattern seems clear in several cases. For the contemporary markets, see W.-D. Hütteroth, Türkei (1982), 459–63, with a fascinating map, fig. 113.

[5] J. Nollé, Nundinas instituere et habere (1982) publishes two long inscriptions relating to markets at Castolupedion, NE of Lydian Philadelphia (cf. Ch. 11 §IV at n. 174), and between Tralles and Magnesia on the Maeander (Ch. 12 §III at n. 76), both areas where the rural economy was monetized to a considerable degree.

[6] Howgego, Greek Imperial Countermarks, 27, argues that the presence of Pontic issues in Syria was part of the normal pattern of coin circulation along the eastern frontier.

travellers (in particular of the eighteenth and nineteenth centuries) freqently provide vivid illustrations of conditions that are likely to have prevailed in Antiquity also. Although no ancient writer alludes to the fact, and timber is a perishable product which leaves few archaeological traces, the observations of travellers and geographers leave no room for doubt that the prosperity of the Bithynian city of Prusias ad Hypium, in Antiquity as in the nineteenth century, rested on the forests which surrounded the city, which could be exploited to full effect because the city could easily transport the timber to ports on the Black Sea, and thence export it to profitable markets.[7] In innumerable cases local knowledge of modern conditions provides a basis for understanding the nature, and sometimes even the scale of ancient economic activity. What it cannot reveal are the precise mechanisms by which individuals, local communities, or the Roman state exploited and profited from the area's resources.

Another line of enquiry is unabashedly theoretical. Models of economic behaviour can be constructed on the basis of factual knowledge, or more often on the basis of assumptions about important variables such as levels of population, available means of transport, rates and methods of taxation, and similar relevant factors. Such models are used to predict or at least suggest patterns and levels of economic activity, which can be checked (usually only very partially) against direct surviving evidence. These models have proved to be powerful interpretative tools, but their use is only valid if the assumptions on which they rest are made explicit and can stand up to critical scrutiny. If these key assumptions are precarious, the whole edifice may collapse like a house of cards.[8]

The archaeological investigation of Anatolia remains at a very primitive stage. Pottery is often—even usually—entirely neglected by the excavators of Roman sites, and reliable publications of well-dated material are virtually unknown. Coin-finds from hoards and controlled excavation have been sporadic and poorly reported. It is not surprising, therefore, that the comparative approach, relying on analogies between late Ottoman and Roman times, has been more widely used than any other in attempts to reconstruct the regional economy. The detailed observations of travellers and scholars of recent times have been indispensable in evoking a traditional life-style, especially in the rural areas, where little need have changed since Antiquity. However, while this information enables one to envisage a localized pattern of economic activity, usually at the level of primary production, it rarely helps with the understanding of the wider structures of the ancient economy. The important questions in this regard do not concern what the land produced, but the subsequent patterns of distribution which determined who profited from the exploitation of these resources, and how those profits were used. Even the most detailed catalogues of the products of Asia Minor, and the most accurate definition of the areas from which they came, reveal nothing in themselves of the economic pattern by which these products were exploited, still less of the ways in which such regional activity fitted into the framework of the Roman economy as a whole.[9]

In this predicament there is little recourse except that of modelling a hypothetical pattern of activity, and testing it against the few relevant concrete data that can be established. Any such model must distinguish between the production and distribution of goods through private trade and commerce, which will have been governed by market considerations, and similar economic activity carried out by the state, whose own interest in supplying the city of Rome, its officials, and above all its armies outweighed purely commercial considerations.

II. *City and Country: The Economic Relationship*

By the mid-second century, the areas of Anatolia with which this book has been mainly concerned, Bithynia, Paphlagonia, and Pontus, Galatia and Lycaonia, Asian Phrygia, Mysia, and Lydia, probably contained about 130 cities.[10] No population figures are available for any of these except for Galen's well-known total of 120,000 inhabitants for Pergamum, calculated as

[7] L. Robert, *A travers l' Asie Mineure*, 11–128; cf. *Eighth Congress*, 128–9.

[8] K. Hopkins, with 'Taxes and Trade in the Roman Empire (200 BC–AD 400)', *JRS* 70 (1980), 101–25, and 'Models, Ships and Staples', in P. Garnsey and C. R. Whittaker, *Trade and Famine in the Ancient World* (1983), 84–109, has provoked more thought and discussion on these topics than any amount of more conventional economic history, and my debt should be obvious. However, the models themselves are not immune to criticism: see S. Mitchell, *Armies and Frontiers*, 135–7 on mining as a source of bullion for coin, standing outside the tax-trade circle; R. MacMullen, *Corruption and the Decline of Rome* (1988), and *Historia*, 35 (1986), 744–5 following R. W. Goldsmith, *Revue of Income and Wealth*, 30 (1984), 273 ff., who argues that Hopkins underestimates the GNP of the empire by perhaps 50%; R. D. Duncan-Jones, *Structure and Scale in the Roman Economy* (1990), 30–47 counters two key assumptions, that most taxation was raised in cash, and that inter-regional trade was the principal mechanism for distributing coined money through the empire. See too H. Pleket, *Gnomon* (1985), 148–54 on Hopkins' later paper.

[9] For a splendid collection of such evidence—and much shrewd comment—see, of course, Broughton, *Roman Asia Minor*, 599 ff.

[10] Bithynia 13; Pontus 11; Paphlagonia 6; Galatia and Lycaonia 20; Phrygia about 45; Mysia 11; Lydia 20.

40,000 male citizens with wives and slaves. If the young of both sexes up to the age of 18 are added, the total population should have been between 180,000 and 200,000.[11] It is uncertain whether this figure included only the city dwellers, as most probably rightly assume, or also the dependent rural population. Pergamum, in any case, was one of the three largest cities of western Anatolia,[12] and no other city in the areas listed above is likely to have matched it for size. Analogies with other parts of the empire suggest that few cities had more than about 25,000 urban inhabitants—Nicomedia, Cyzicus, Ancyra, Thyateira, and Sardis would certainly have come into this category—and the majority would have fallen in a range between 5,000 and 15,000.[13] Indeed some small cities, on the scale of Caesareia Germanice in Bithynia, Perta and Kana in Lycaonia, or Stectorium and Otrous in the Phrygian Pentapolis, were perhaps hardly bigger than large villages, with populations of 3,000 or less. If we assume an average figure of 7,000 inhabitants in each city the total urban population of these areas will have been around 910,000. Rural inhabitants in the Roman world as a whole certainly outnumbered city dwellers, by a margin of up to ten to one. Even a small city like Oenoanda had thirty-five dependent villages on its territory. The villages on Ancyra's territory should certainly be numbered in hundreds, and a rural to urban population ratio of ten to one is recorded for the late nineteenth century. The area around Ancyra was less heavily urbanized in the second century AD than most of Phrygia or Lydia, and it is probably more realistic to allow an eight to one ratio for central Anatolia as a whole.[14] This would imply a rural popu-

lation of about 7,280,000, and a total of 8,190,000, rather more than half the population of the whole of Asia Minor.[15] If anything, this figure is probably an underestimate.

Each city and village, it is safe to assume, attempted to live as far as possible on its own products, above all on the grain which it was able to grow. Bithynian Apamea, which apparently used the income derived from its olive plantations, fisheries, and maritime trade to pay for grain, imported from Thracian Perinthus, and building timber from Prusa, was a rare exception to the general rule.[16]

In some parts of Asia Minor, for instance in Lydia where large estate-owners are rare, the curial class inconspicuous, and where large, prosperous villages operating with a monetized economy are hardly to be distinguished from the smaller cities, it seems probable that peasant smallholders were able to sell surplus grain and other products to satisfy the modest local urban markets (see above, Ch. 10 § IV at nn. 171–9, and Ch. 11 § III at nn. 139–48). It is unlikely that this pattern was widespread in much of the rest of the Anatolia, where the peasants working the land were unable to profit directly from the fruits of their labour. The evidence cited from Galen in Chapter 11 § I, which presumably reflects conditions in Mysia or the Caicus valley, shows that city dwellers had first pick of the harvest, taking the best grain for themselves and often leaving the villagers to face severe shortages. Similarly, the edict of Antistius Rusticus from Pisidian Antioch implies that during a grain shortage wealthy land-owners were able to hoard grain in order to force up its price and increase their profits. Peasant smallholders or tenants in these areas did not supply the urban market in their own right, and were sometimes even unable to retain what they needed for their own sub-sistence. The implications of this are further illustrated below (§ v).

The curial class often owned much of the cereal-producing land in the immediate city hinterlands, for instance at Ancyra, Pisidian Antioch, and Iconium in Galatia (above, Ch. 10 § III at nn. 57–67). The owners of larger and remoter estates, like those in the central Anatolian plateau or the eastern part of the territory of Nicaea, enjoyed an even more powerful position in

[11] Galen, 5. 49 (Kühn); cf. Radt, *Pergamon*, 175, who estimates 160,000 compared to perhaps 25,000–40,000 in the Attalid period.

[12] With Ephesus and Smyrna. The belief that there were 40,000 male citizens at Ephesus in the 2nd cent. rests on a misunderstanding of an inscription; see P. D. Warden and R. S. Bagnall, *Class. Phil.* 83 (1988), 220–3.

[13] These figures are based on a comparison with those for North Africa, discussed by R. D. Duncan-Jones, *The Economy of the Roman Empire*² (1973), 259–87. After careful analysis B. Levick concludes that the urban population of Pisidian Antioch, one of the larger inland cities, probably did not exceed 10,000 (*Roman Colonies*, 92–6); Hanfmann, *Sardis from Prehistoric to Roman Times*, 146, with 278 n. 92 suggests 60,000–100,000 for Sardis, which seems generous. Th. Wiegand, *Milet VII*, suggested 100,000 for Hellenistic Miletus.

[14] Hopkins, 'Models, Ships, and Staples', suggests that one in ten inhabitants of the empire lived in towns. This is probably an underestimate of the urban population. Oenoanda: see above, Ch. 11 § III at n. 125; Ancyra: V. Cuinet, *La Turquie d'Asie*, i (1894), 249 lists 1,021(!) villages in the sancak of Angora, which then covered the ancient territories of Ancyra, Pessinus, Phrygian Midaeion(?), Iuliopolis, Germa, and Kinna, with a

total population of 283,133 (27,825 in Angora itself, the only substantial town; average size of other settlements 250 per village). In this very thinly urbanized region this 10:1 rural–urban ratio is plausible for the Roman period also.

[15] This is close to the population estimate of Broughton, *Roman Asia Minor*, 619, calculated on a different basis, which for the regions covered here comes to 7,300,000. He too took this as a low estimate. His total for all Asia Minor is 13,000,000, compared to the 1935 Turkish census figure of 13,657,661.

[16] L. Robert, *Stud. clas.* 16 (1974), 61–9 = *OMS* vi. 283–91.

relation to their tenants (Ch. 10 § III at nn. 68–113; § IV at nn. 161–70). No doubt economic dominance lay behind the ability of city councillors and grander landowners to oppress dependent communities with *force majeure*. When Q. Sicinius Clarus, governor of Thrace in AD 202, founded an emporium at Pizus, he took pains to specify that the inhabitants, former villagers, should not suffer insult and injury (ὕβρις and ἐπήρεια) at the hands of the curiales from the nearby cities. Similarly, when Orcistus petitioned Constantine for the right to city status, independent from Nacolea, its inhabitants complained that they had suffered *depraedatione potiorum*, and even after their independence had been granted they alleged that Nacolea still continued to exact a tax *pro cultis*, which had to be abolished by a further imperial ruling.[17]

Under such conditions of landownership, the transfer of the harvest from grain-lands to the cities will not have been a commercial operation, and the same rules will have applied to other products, which would usually have been smaller both in quantity and commercial value. Landlords or their agents simply took what they required from the peasants as a form of rent, surely without cash payment. In parts of North Africa, where conditions may have been analogous, imperial tenants had their obligations defined by a Roman law (above, Ch. 10 § V n. 196). Most private tenants, whether in Asia Minor or in Africa, enjoyed no such protection. Often, therefore, villages were in no position to earn money and enter the monetized economy, by selling their primary products. Large parts of central Anatolian society were not integrated into the monetized economy of the wider Roman world.

III. *Central Anatolia under Grain and the Problem of Transport*

If the picture of landownership in central Anatolia offered earlier (Ch. 10 § III) is broadly accurate, large tracts of territory formed private or imperial estates. The wealthy Italian immigrants and the Asian aristocrats who had acquired these properties had clearly done so with a view to profit. During the second and third centuries AD the populations of these estates lived in established villages, and practised an agricultural regime which combined dry cereal farming on a large scale with the raising of sheep and cattle. This is shown by the evidence of grave reliefs and confirmed

by incidental details: free grain distribution was a central feature of the festival foundation of AD 237 at Orcistus, and of the testamentary benefactions given to Nacolea by an imperial freedman in the late second century.[18] Orcistus was notable in the early fourth century for the abundance of water-mills on its territory, which certainly processed grain not simply from the local harvests but brought from further afield in the central plateau, and was perhaps *en route* to the sea ports of the Propontis.[19] The economics of cereal farming on a scale which clearly exceeded the needs of local urban markets require discussion.

It is important to stress that the use of the land for growing cereals in Roman times was exceptional, and contrasted with the normal pattern of land utilization in the central steppe. Today, to be sure, central Turkey is almost entirely under cereal cultivation. Three large state-run enterprises control the production of most of the arable land between Kadınhan (near ancient Laodicea Catacecaumene) and Polatlı (near Gordium), and large-scale collective silos for storing the harvest of smaller producers are located at regular intervals throughout the rest of the region. From here it is transported to the large urban markets. Modern mechanized transport by road or rail makes the whole process cost-effective.[20] This, however, is a recent development. Between 1927 and 1960 the proportion of pasture and rough grazing land in the plateau fell from 60 per cent to 37 per cent, while arable rose in the same period from 9 per cent to 30 per cent.[21] Before the end of the nineteenth century the area was almost entirely devoted to pastoralism, a tradition which can certainly be traced back through the Ottoman and Seljuk to the later Byzantine period.[22] We can deduce similar conditions before the arrival of Roman rule (see above, Ch. 10 § 1). The Roman imperial period offers the only historical parallel for modern land usage. We need to identify the specific political and economic considerations that made it practical to practise large-scale arable farming in the region without the benefit of modern mechanized transport.

Transport represents the nub of the problem. It is commonplace in the study of the ancient world to argue that overland transport of bulky, low-cost goods,

---

[17] For the interpretation of *IGBulg.* iii. 2. 1690, ll. 34–49, see Mitchell, *Festschrift Mihailov*, forthcoming; Orcistus: *MAMA* vii. 305 i. 37–8; iii. 20. See further *JRS* 1976, 115; P. Herrmann, *Hilferufe aus röm. Provinzen* (1990), 44–6, 58–60. For the 4th cent., see the splendid patristic evidence cited by MacMullen, *Corruption and the Decline of Rome*, 85.

[18] Buckler, *JHS* 57 (1937), 1–10; *MAMA* v. 202 = *ILS* 7196 (see above, Ch. 10 § IV n. 154); cf. Garnsey, *Famine and Food Supply*, 264–5.

[19] A. Chastagnol, *MEFRA* 1981, 408 correctly makes this point; cf., on water mills, Pleket, *Epigr. Anat.* 12 (1988), 26–8, and P. Roos, *Festschrift für Jale Inan* (1989), 495–7, illustrating an example at Orcistus, pl. 189 fig. 2.

[20] Hütteroth, *Türkei* 367–71.

[21] M. F. Hendy, *Studies in the Byzantine Monetary Economy* (1985), 34.

[22] See above, Ch. 10 § II nn. 43 and 51.

whether by pack-animals or in carts, was simply too expensive to be economically feasible except in very exceptional circumstances. This view is usually based on the figures for land transport found in Diocletian's Price Edict, which have been calculated to show that transporting 1,200 pounds of wheat a hundred miles by wagon would add 55 per cent to the cost of the goods; forty times more than the equivalent load carried by sea.[23] Support for this analysis may be found in more recent data. In the late nineteenth century grain transported 346 kilometres (c.233 Roman miles) from Sivas was valued three or four times more at its destination, Samsun, than it had been on the threshing floor; grain carried 132 kilometres (c.89 miles) across Ilgaz Dağ from Çankırı to Kastamonu more than doubled its price.[24]

These figures suggest that hauling low-cost goods for long distances overland was simply out of the question. This, however, makes nonsense of the pattern of estate-ownership just described and also conflicts with the impression given by a variety of items from the Roman evidence, which suggest that land transport along the main roads was a major feature of regional life. Cities and villages of inner Anatolia were notably conscious of the importance of the road network to them, and indeed the contribution they made to it. Orcistus' petition to Constantine stressed that it stood at the junction of four major routes, and that it possessed a way-station (*mansio*). A little to the south the Phrygian villages of Anosa and Antimacheia were also dominated by the roads that ran through them, carrying traffic from and to Ancyra, as well as to Amorium, Meirus, and neighbouring cities.[25] They complain of being overburdened by official requisitioning, and in particular of having to provide heavy ox-drawn wagons (*protēla*). These were specifically needed for the transport of marble, which was quarried nearby in the huge quarries at Docimeium. Although imperially owned, these supplied architectural pieces, sarcophagi, and statuary, usually in a half-finished state, not only for official building projects but also for private customers during the second and third centuries. Provided that a customer could afford the price, both the road system and existing transport technology were capable of

delivering very heavy loads overland (Fig. 30). The distribution of Docimian sarcophagi indicates the main routes they followed: south into Pamphylia and west along the Maeander valley to Ephesus, allowing shipment to Italy and the West.[26] The road network throughout the plateau was designed for wheeled transport and built to a high specification. Wagons would run on well-drained gravelled surfaces; hill climbs were carefully graded so as to minimize the difficulties faced by draft animals with heavy carts. Particular attention was paid to the mountainous sections that linked the interior with the coast. The early imperial highways that crossed the Taurus at the Cilician gates, at the Döşemealtı Pass north of Perge, and below Termessus on the route to Side in Pamphylia, were all designed for wheeled traffic, unlike the majority of Roman roads in mountainous areas, and unlike the late Roman roads built across the same passes. Road transport of bulk goods was certainly slow, but it never travelled faster in Antiquity or at any period before the introduction of the railways, than on these routes.[27] They were obviously regularly used by military and official traffic, and by the marble trade from state-run quarries, none of which was fettered by the same commercial constraints as private enterprises, but the cost-free maintenance of an excellent transport infrastructure produced at least an encouraging environment for private use.

It is also possible to modify the impression made by the figures in the Price Edict. Firstly, the comparative costs of sea transport are certainly underestimated, since they take no account of the substantial additional expense entailed by transporting grain from threshing floor to the docks, storage, loading and unloading, and further land transport to a final destination. Correspondingly the price increase between threshing floor and consumer recorded in the late Ottoman figures takes account not only of transport costs but also of the profits of middlemen.[28] It is unlikely also that the Diocletianic figures reckon with the costs of insuring the cargo, a necessary expense for most private shippers. The 40:1 cost ratio should be at least halved in most instances. Secondly, the peasants and their animals who provided the means of overland transport may well have been prepared to do so at very favourable rates, if the service provided them with a rare opportunity to earn cash and their animals were otherwise idle. Often, too, they will have been simply forced

[23] Duncan-Jones, *The Economy of the Roman Empire*[2], 366–9. Garnsey, *Famine and Food Supply*, 22–3 cautions against over-stating the cost.

[24] Hendy, *Studies in the Byzantine Monetary Economy*, 557 cites these figures from Cuinet, *La Turquie d'Asie*, i. 637 and iv. 431. Note, however, that this is not the whole story. Half the cereal production of landlocked Angora, despite transport difficulties, was exported (Cuinet, i. 256–7 and 259). The explanation is presumably large-scale exactions for the provisioning of Constantinople.

[25] *MAMA* vii. 305 i. 23; *JRS* 46 (1956), 46 ff. (*SEG* xvi. 754), ll. 3–7, also mentioning a *mansio* (μονή).

[26] M. Waelkens, *Dokimeion: Die Werkstatt der represäntativen kleinasiatischen Sarkophage* (1982), with Fig. 7; 'Carrières de marbre en Phrygie', *Bulletin des musées royaux d'art et d'histoire* (Bruxelles), 53 (1982), 50–3.

[27] I owe these observations, mostly made in the field, to David French. For the mountain roads, see above, Ch. 6 at nn. 3–6.

[28] Hopkins, 'Models, Ships, and Staples', 104–5.

to provide transport, just as they were compelled to give up the best of their crops.[29] Thirdly, as Cicero observed, there were very significant differentials in the price of wheat across Asia Minor. He implies that costs at Ephesus around 70 BC were much higher than at Philomelium in Phrygia, although the difference was not so great as to justify transporting grain the 250 Roman miles that separated them.[30] Such variations might have provided an inducement to inter-city grain trading over shorter differences.

There are indeed some hints in the ancient evidence that bulk grain was transported from the Anatolian plateau to the coast, and thence to other markets, even occasionally by private merchants. The Tiberian regulations for requisitioning wagons and pack-animals for official transport from the territory of Sagalassus state that private individuals carrying grain or similar products on a commercial basis were not entitled to requisition transport at the favourable official rates. The Greek text uses the verb διακομίζουσιν, which implies that these convoys, accompanied by freedmen or slave managers, were not simply moving goods from country to city but crossing Sagalassian territory, almost certainly along the *via Sebaste* which linked Phrygia and the central plateau with the Pamphylian coast. In the late nineteenth century a precisely parallel situation is documented in this region. The goods exported from Isparta, Sagalassus' modern equivalent, consisted 'chiefly of wheat, of which a large quantity is sent to Adalia on camels. The cost of transport is thus rendered enormous', rising from between 6 and 8 piastres per *kile* in the interior to 25–30 piastres at the sea ports.[31] There were important coastal harbours, at Perge, Attaleia, and notably at Side. Grain exports passed in particular through Aspendus. An anecdote told by Philostratus recalls how Apollonius of Tyana remonstrated with the rich merchants of the city and forced them to open their granaries during a time of famine; the market buildings on either side of the main agora appear substantially larger than would be necessary merely for local needs; and the Roman bridge across the river Eurymedon immediately below the city stood nine metres above the water level, to allow the passage of large transport ships up the river to the commercial docks.[32] It is unlikely that the Pamphylian plain itself, with four major cities sited close to one another and extensive olive culture, had much grain surplus to export; the port surely handled produce, in particular grain, from the plateau.[33]

Nevertheless, it seems impossible to build a coherent argument on this evidence for a commercial grain trade from Anatolia. Both the cost and the logistic problems of transport would have confined most private merchants to a radius of perhaps fifty miles from the threshing floors, three days' journey for a loaded wagon. Merchants who seized carts illegally from the villages near Sagalassus simply underlined by their action the fact that transport over longer distances was only possible with relays of draught- or pack-animals along the route, something that must almost always have been beyond their means. The evidence from Aspendus shows only that Anatolian grain was collected and shipped there, not that it was a commercial trade.

An alternative and a better explanation for the bulk of this traffic is that a large part of the surplus production of the central plateau was extracted as a tax contribution. Here, transport costs could simply have been reckoned as part of the tax liability. This notion is neatly illustrated by a well-documented practice of corrupt provincial administration. Roman provincial governors and their staff were entitled to claim a grain tax for their own use in the province, *frumentum aestimatum*, or *frumentum cellae nomine*. This contribution, however, was frequently commuted to a demand for cash, whose estimate included not only the value of the grain but also the cost of delivering it to wherever the Roman official might be stationed. Verres as quaestor in Asia, and governors of Britain before

[29] Note Aelius Aristides attempting to commandeer native guides in Thrace *en route* to Rome, 48. 60 (K); and unauthorized persons (probably chiefly soldiers) taking men and animals from the fields in Syria, *IGLS* v. 1998. However, the ability of private landowners to press peasants into their service must have decreased the further they travelled from their properties.

[30] *Verr.* 2. 33. 191–2.

[31] *JRS* 66 (1976), 127 ff. In the discussion of the Sagalassus edict, I would now place more emphasis on the requisitioning of heavy transport in connection with taxation in kind, much of which might have been handled by the imperial freedmen and slaves indicated in the text (ll. 24–5, 50–1). The quotation is from E. J. Davis, *Anatolica* (1874), 152–3.

[32] Philostratus, *Vit. Apoll.* 1. 15; for the market-buildings of Aspendos, see H. Cüppers, *BJb.* 161 (1961), 25–35 and H. Lauter, *BJb.* 170 (1970), 77–101; for the bridge, see *JHS Arch. Reports* (1989/90), 120–1. Large Roman *horrea* have survived at Andriake in Lycia (Hadrianic, J. Borchhardt *et al.*, *Myra: Eine lykische Metropolis* (1975), 66–71; cf. *HSCP* 91 (1987), 354) and perhaps at Amastris in Paphlagonia (A. Hofmann, *Ist. Mitt.* 39 (1989), 197–210; the identification of the building is uncertain). Their economic role would bear further investigation. For the port at Side, which was important as a naval station but crucial in the supply of *annona* to Syria in the 3rd cent., see Nollé, *Chiron*, 17 (1987), 258 ff. and H.-J. Drexhage, *Asia-Minor-Studien*, 3 (1991), 75–90.

[33] In modern times Pamphylia is split into an area of poor land at the foot of the Taurus, only 20% cultivated (cereals, olives), and intensively worked, heavily irrigated land near the coast, over 70% cultivated, often with cash crops. Compare the central plateau, with 50–70% of the land under cereals. Hütteroth, *Türkei*, 361–7 with fig. 92. For Side's territory in Antiquity, see Nollé, *Epigr. Anat.* 1 (1983), 119 ff.

Agricola, made a point of ordering grain to be brought from inconveniently remote and inappropriate areas, so that the cash conversion would include very high estimates for the expense of transport. The basic principle that gave a veneer of legality to this form of extortion was that when the state demanded grain or other goods as a tax, it also required their delivery to some official collecting point. In practice, no doubt, there would have been wide local variation in the way that transport costs were distributed between producers and *conductores*, or other state officials responsible for collection. An excerpt from the *Digest*, originally derived from Modestinus in the second quarter of the third century, cites a fictitious case that might arise in a community where it had long been the custom for landowners themselves, and not *conductores*, to undertake the burden of delivering tax-grain (*annonae*) and irregular contributions. The text implies that both methods were familiar.[34]

Is it in fact plausible that Anatolia in the second century AD met a substantial part of its tax liability by contributions in kind? Between the annexation of the province of Asia in 129 BC and the principate of Augustus, much of the revenue extracted from Asia Minor had been in kind. According to Cicero the three main sources of income in the 60s BC were from customs dues, from tithes, and from a tax on pasture.[35] The use of the second term is best understood as covering at least some contributions in produce as well as in cash. Other evidence confirms that this was regular practice in the late republic. Naturally during the wars of the period supplies were directly commandeered by Roman commanders, for instance by Lucullus who supported his campaign against Mithridates in 74 BC on Galatian grain.[36] But the publicani, who had acquired the rights to collect the Asian taxes by the *lex Sempronia* of Gaius Gracchus in 123 BC, also extracted goods as well as cash; Cicero says that they maintained slave establishments in the salt mines, in the countryside (presumably to supervise the collection of produce),

and at harbours and at frontier posts to collect the *portoria*.[37] Collecting tax in kind put the publicans in the business of handling, transporting, and selling natural products, and in this connection they were given various immunities and privileges by the Roman senate. For instance, the custom's law for the province of Asia, drawn up in 75 BC and republished with additions in AD 62, exempted the publicani from paying duty on slaves or goods which they transported in or out of Asia, and the *lex Antonia de Termessis*, drafted a few years later, made it illegal for the free city of Termessus to impose tolls on the *vectigalia*, evidently goods rather than cash, which were carried by the publicani through their territory.[38]

Large parts of Asia Minor in the first century BC, notably Bithynia and Pontus, faced an acute shortage of cash. According to the *Pro lege Manilia* of 66 BC, the outlying Anatolian provinces yielded insufficient *vectigalia* to sustain the cost to Rome of protecting them. By contrast Asia was so fertile in the richness of its lands, the variety of its natural products, the extent of its pastures, and the quantity of goods which were exported, that it stood head and shoulders above all the other regions.[39] The wording of Cicero's rhetoric suggests that the revenues which he had in mind, perhaps particularly after Asia Minor had been drained of cash by Sulla and during the Mithridatic campaigns, came directly from the land. Certainly in a speech to the cities of Asia delivered in 43 BC Mark Antony argued that by asking not for fixed totals but for specific proportions of their crops, the Roman authorities shared the risks of variable harvests with the producers.[40]

It is not likely that the situation changed radically in the early principate. Nero's commissioners in AD 62

---

[34] e.g. Cicero, *Verr.* 2. 33. 191–2; Tacitus, *Agr.*, 19; *CTh.* 11. 1. 22 (AD 386). See L. Neesen, *Untersuchungen zu den direkten Staatsabgaben der römischen Kaiserzeit* (1980), 110–12. P. Herz, *Studien zur römischen Wirtschaftsgesetzgebung: Die Lebensmittelversorgung* (1988), 181–4 also argues for tax exactions in kind as a source of army supplies, and cites *Dig.* 26. 7. 32. 6 (Modestinus), 'L. Titius, coheres et curator sororis suae, cum esset ex civitate, in qua usitatum erat ipsos dominos praediorum, non conductores onera annonarum et contributionum temporariarum sustinere, morem hunc et consuetudinem semper observatam secutus et ipsi pro communi et individua hereditate annonas praestitit.'

[35] *Manil.* 15. In what follows I draw selectively from the evidence collected by Broughton, *Roman Asia Minor*, 511 ff.

[36] Plutarch, *Lucullus*, 14. He had imposed a 25% tax on crops, Appian, *Mith.* 83.

[37] *Manil.* 16, 'publicani familias maximas quas in salinis habent, quas in agris, quas in portibus, quas in custodiis.' See Broughton, *Roman Asia Minor*, 540. The salt mines are worth a comment. Salt from Tuz Göl and other central Anatolian sources was readily available for preserving carcasses; the region could export meat (cf. above, Ch. 10 §1 at nn. 38–40).

[38] Asian Customs' Law (*Epigr. Anat.* 14 (1989)), ll. 74–8; *ILS* 38, 31–6. See, most recently, J.-L. Ferrary, *Athenaeum*, 63 (1985), 419–57, and the acute discussion of Sherwin-White, *JRS* 66 (1976), 1–14 at 11.

[39] See above, Ch. 3 §II. Cicero, *Manil.* 14, 'Nam ceterarum provinciarum vectigalia, Quirites, tanta non sunt ut eis ad ipsas provincias tuendas vix contenti esse possumus. Asia vero tam opima est ac fertilis ut et ubertate agrorum et varietate fructuum et magnitudine pastionis et multitudine earum rerum quae exportentur facile omnibus terris antecellat.'

[40] Appian, *BC* 5. 4, οὓς γὰρ ἐτελεῖτε φόρους Ἀττάλῳ, μεθήκαμεν ὑμῖν, μέχρι δημοκόπων ἀνδρῶν καὶ παρ' ἡμῖν γενομένων ἐδέησε φόρων. ἐπεὶ δὲ ἐδέησεν, οὐ πρὸς τὰ τιμήματα ὑμῖν ἐπεθήκαμεν, ὡς ἂν ἡμεῖς ἀκίνδυνον φόρον ἐκλέγοιμεν, ἀλλὰ μέρη φέρειν τῶν ἑκάστοτε καρπῶν ἐπετάξαμεν, ἵνα καὶ τῶν ἐναντίων κοινωνῶμεν ἡμῖν, τῶν δὲ ταῦτα παρὰ τῆς βουλῆς μισθουμένων.

essentially reproduced a scheme for collecting the *portorium* in Asia which had been drawn up by the consuls in 75 BC, and incorporated a number of additional clauses from the period which separated them. Not only does the law show that the methods of extracting custom's dues were essentially unchanged, but it incorporates allusions to other forms of taxation which remained unaltered. In particular it was still relevant to specify under Nero that publicans were to collect a tithe of crops produced, or a tenth part of oil and wine production from cultivators who were liable to this form of taxation.[41] Dio of Prusa implies that the normal levy on the produce of Bithynian Nicaea was a tithe. Writing in the early second century AD, Hyginus indicated that in some provinces a proportion of the crop, sometimes one-fifth or one-seventh, was paid in lieu of the money tax on land (*tributum soli*), which had been introduced to other regions. Careful surveying was necessary, for it was common to underestimate the area of land in order to reduce the tax liability, and this had specifically occurred in Pannonia, where the tribute was paid in cash, as well as in Phrygia and in the whole of Asia, where by implication levies were widely raised in kind.[42] Indeed, an inscription of the Claudian period from Cibyra has been interpreted to show that the city paid a fixed proportion of the harvest from its arable land in tax to Rome.[43] In rural areas where the economy may have barely been monetized (see above) such procedures would have naturally recommended themselves.

It is worth speculating about some of the processes which may have occurred in the exploitation of rural Anatolia as a source of tax revenue in kind. In the late republic the *publicani* used *familiae* of slaves and freedmen to extract an appropriate tithe from local harvests, transport it to the coast, and sell it, either to the state for its armies and for the Roman corn dole, or on the open market. The financial pressures of the first century BC caused much land in Asia and the adjacent provinces to be sold to Roman or Italian buyers, many

no doubt *publicani* themselves (see above, Ch. 3 § 11 at nn. 26–9), so that they were now paying a tax on their own property rather than exacting a tithe from others. It would be natural for the slaves and freedmen who had operated the taxation system to handle other aspects of estate management. Thus it is no surprise that this became one of their primary functions in the first and second centuries AD.

The Roman state also acquired considerable tracts of land through conquest, notably after the campaigns of Servilius in Pamphylia, Isauria, and eastern Pisidia, and these became *ager publicus*. Perhaps much of this too was leased by *publicani* in the late republic. From the time of Augustus it became feasible for the state to exploit public land more directly, through imperial procurators, freedmen, and slave managers, and such land as was not used for the settlement of veterans was usually incorporated into imperial estates. Legacies and confiscations increased the number and size of imperial properties throughout the principate (see above, Ch. 10 §§ III–IV). Such properties may not have been taxed in the normal sense, but the state derived revenue from them through rents. The status of a *colonus* on one of these estates might often have appeared attractive since the tenant presumably paid only a single levy on his harvest, not a tax to the state followed by a rent to the landlord.[44] On the other hand, the rents for imperial land could be set higher than those for private tenants. If the analogy with agricultural estates in North Africa is valid, individual imperial tenants may have rented land on these estates by contracting to pay up to one-third of their crops either directly to the emperor's agent, a procurator, or to a leaseholder (see above, Ch. 10 § V). In Egypt rents in kind raised from imperial property varied between one- and two-thirds of the crop.[45] No doubt the cost of delivering the grain or other crops to appropriate collecting centres was a charge that fell on the *colonus*, while the state undertook long-distance distribution.

To conclude, large parts of Asia Minor still paid a

---

[41] Asian Custom's Law, ll. 72–4; Dio Chr. 38. 26.

[42] Hyginus, 205 (Lachmann), 'agri . . . vectigales multas habent constitutiones. In quibusdam provinciis fructus partem praestant certam, alii quintas alii septimas, alii pecuniam, et hoc per soli aestimationem. Certa enim pretia agris constituta sunt, ut in Pannonia arvi primi, arvi secundi, prati, silvae landiferae, silvae vulgaris, pascuae, his omnis agris vectigal est ad modum ubertatis per singula iugera constitutum. Horum aestimatio nequa usurpatio per falsas professiones fiat, adhibenda est mensuris diligentia . . .'

[43] Duncan-Jones, *Structure and Scale*, 187–98 on *IGR* iv. 914, 11–15, which should now be consulted in the edn. by J. Nollé, *ZPE* 46 (1982), 267–74. I suspect (*contra JRS* 1976, 124 n. 113) that Tiberius Nicephorus, who had been oppressing the people of Cibyra by illegal exactions, was an imperial freedman procurator, like the Maximus of Pliny, *Ep.* 10. 27–8.

[44] The Latin term for imperial tenants, *coloni dominici*, appears precisely in the early 3rd-cent. inscription from Takina in Asia, *Epigr. Anat.* 10 (1987), 133 ff., 16 and 32 (*SEG* xxxvii. 1186). The condition of tenants is illuminated by late Ottoman conditions, summarized by W. M. Calder and quoted by W. H. Buckler, *JHS* 37 (1917), 115: 'The larger Turkish estates in Anatolia have part of the land worked by labourers hired by the year who get 7–800 piastres a year as their keep. Day labourers are hired in addition at harvest time. Another part of the land is handed over to "partners" who receive from the landlord buildings, implements, seed and according as they cultivate 50 or 100 dönüms of land, one or two pairs of oxen. *After deduction of the tithe, they divide the crops with the landlord*' (my italics).

[45] Garnsey, *Famine and Food Supply*, 244 ff.; Neesen. *Untersuchungen zu den direkten Staatsabgaben der römischen Kaiserzeit*, 101–4.

significant part of its tax liabilities in grain, wool, hides, raw salt, salt meat, and other produce. In essence much of the cost of gathering and transporting these goods lay with the taxpayers, who would have had to deliver them to appropriate designated collecting points. The collection and subsequent distribution was handled in the late republic by *publicani*, who sometimes themselves became landholders in these regions on very favourable terms. Under the empire they shared responsibility for collecting Asian produce for the state with the managers of imperial estates, who were usually slave or freedmen procurators. Thus taxation in kind like taxation in cash was handled both directly by imperial officials, and indirectly by private contractors.[46]

IV. *Supplies for Troops*

The destination of grain and other goods, levied as a tax or rent on rural areas of Anatolia, remains a matter for conjecture, but a simple solution comes readily to mind. There is no evidence to show that it was used to supplement the corn supplies of Rome itself. Except in unusual circumstances (see below, nn. 69–71) Roman authorities were not concerned to provide food for provincial cities, and in any case cities almost always relied on their own produce in the first instance and only looked to import grain during times of acute shortage. There was no market here for tax-grain. The only remaining large-scale customer was the Roman army.

The origins of this practice can be traced to the republican period. The mobile armies of the second century BC had been supplied on campaign by the *publicani*, who entered five-yearly contracts with the state to supply food, transport, equipment, weapons, and other military needs for the legions.[47] In the intensive campaigning of the first century BC, and especially during the civil wars, regular contracted sources of supply were certainly widely supplemented by direct levies on the local populations, but in general there is no reason to doubt that the large numbers of Roman or Italian *publicani* in Asia Minor continued to fulfil this crucial role, and it would have been logical for Augustus to have inherited at least some elements of this method of army supply, certainly for the legions and other units which were active in Anatolia until as late as AD 6 (see above, Ch. 6).

During the first and early second centuries, especially after the Flavians had transformed Roman foreign policy and established permanent garrisons along the Danube and the Euphrates frontiers, the logistics of military supply underwent a radical change. The inherent problems were made more difficult by the fact that most of the troops were now stationed further away from regions with a substantial agricultural surplus to supply them; on the other hand they were eased by the creation of fixed, rather than mobile garrisons. The demand for supplies was thus stabilized and well-established transport networks could be set up, using roads, sea-routes, and a permanent transport infrastructure.

Anatolia was in a position to send grain and other goods to three military areas: the Balkans, especially the lower Danube frontier of Upper and Lower Moesia; the northern Euphrates frontier in Armenia Minor and Cappadocia; and the middle Euphrates frontier, south of the anti-Taurus, in Syria. The road system which effectively linked all three areas, and ran directly across Anatolia, was virtually in place by the beginning of Domitian's principate (above, Ch. 9 § 11).

On this hypothesis the eastern frontier garrisons should have been supported, as far as possible, by exactions imposed on eastern and perhaps central Anatolia. Coin finds from the eastern *limes* have been interpreted to show that most of the frontier zone, from the Euxine to Dura Europus, and a hinterland which embraced the thinly urbanized regions of Pontus, Cappadocia, and Commagene, formed a monetarily homogeneous zone, which was dominated by silver and bronze coinage minted locally (for instance at Cappadocian Caesareia) but under central control, in the first instance to serve the needs of the garrisons.[48] Such coinage would not have been distributed through the region in the form of direct payment for the staples which were imported for army use. *Ex hypothesi* these were tax contributions. But the enormous logistic effort required to move supplies through the area surely generated much secondary commercial activity, certainly enough to circulate coinage issued to soldiers through the whole region which supplied them.

Supplies to the Balkans would have been particularly important for central and north-west Turkey. The exchange of goods between Anatolia and the Danube provinces has been subjected to detailed study, which leaves no doubt that there was a pronounced imbalance in favour of Anatolia. Moreover, supplying the Balkan garrisons is assumed to be the chief factor underlying

[46] See P. A. Brunt, in A. H. M. Jones, *The Roman Economy* (1974), 180–3.
[47] *JRS* 1976, 129 n. 156; Polybius 6. 17; See E. Badian, *Publicans and Sinners* (1972). Also of course supplemented by requisitioning wherever necessary (and often not), Cicero, *Att.* 5. 21 (six months as governor of Cilicia without resort to requisitioning or billeting).
[48] Howgego, *Greek Imperial Countermarks*, 17–31; For Caesareia, E. A. Sydenham, *The Coinage of Caesarea in Cappadocia* (1978).

the phenomenon.[49] However, the Roman army on the Danube cannot have relied on long-distance commercial traffic to provide its basic staple needs. Even if private suppliers had a means of overcoming the problem of land transport costs (which defies all probability), it is unlikely that Roman commanders would have tolerated a source of supply which was potentially so unreliable, and which placed them directly at the mercy of the vagaries of market forces. Moreover, crucially, there is absolutely no evidence that private merchants from advantageously placed cities such as Nicomedia did undertake the task of supplying the armies with staples.[50]

In practical terms the crucial advantage of a state-run military supply service over private enterprise was that the state could organize its transport in relays. Under ancient conditions, as has been wrily observed, draft animals carting grain between two widely separated regions would have eaten their load before reaching their destination.[51] The problem vanished if teams of animals worked back and forth over short distances, passing on their burden to other teams for the onward journey. This was the common feature of all state transport under the empire. For some purposes, especially for couriers requiring fast, well-trained mounts, it was appropriate for the state to maintain its own stables, as apparently on the express overland routes between the Balkans and Syria (above, Ch. 9 § 11 at nn. 78–86);[52] more often, and especially for heavy transport, the communities along the road were required to provide animals, and also carts.[53]

In the first two centuries AD army provisioning was not exclusively supported by direct taxation in kind. In a well-known passage of the Panegyric of Trajan, Pliny hailed the justice of a regime, in which

harvests are not seized as though from an enemy and left to perish in storehouses. Imperial subjects of their own accord transport the products which the earth grows, the seasons nurture and the annual harvest brings, and do not fail to meet long-established tribute requirements under the pressure of new requisitions. The state treasury genuinely buys what it appears to buy. This is the source of general abundance, of a grain supply which is properly agreed by voluntary sales, of sufficiency and the abolition of famine.

The passage makes admirable sense as a commentary on a system of grain supply, which was based on tax contributions supplemented by state purchases.

Evidence from papyri and ostraca in Egypt shows that the army often made payments for supplies (as they were supposed to pay for requisitioned transport) and that requisitioned grain was supplemented by cereals purchased at prices fixed by the state.[54] The sources do not make it clear what proportion of regular army requirements was made up in this way. Perhaps goods extracted as direct tax and rents never sufficed for regular needs and extra purchases were standard.

Although there is little incontrovertible direct evidence from the first two centuries that taxes or rents raised in kind were dispatched more or less directly for consumption by Roman troops on the frontiers, the practice was certainly widespread in other parts of the empire, and a particularly close analogy can be drawn with relationship between the German frontier and the Gallic provinces. Although intensive estate cultivation was practised in the territory adjoining the Rhine *limes*, the frontier region's surplus production was demonstrably too small to support the legionary and auxiliary garrisons and their dependants on top of the existing population. The gap was bridged by surplus produce from the agriculturally rich Gallic hinterland, which was transported to the frontier region by a river and road system just as elaborate as Asia Minor's.[55]

Detailed re-examination of all the evidence for the interregional movement of goods between Anatolia, the Balkans, and the eastern frontier would be inappropriate at this point. The logic of the argument implies that traffic in staples between these areas can only have been organized by the state. Even the extra grain purchased to make up the tax short-fall was presumably transported by the same means and along the same

---

[49] E. Gren, *Kleinasien und der Ostbalkan in der wirtschaftlichen Entwicklung der römischen Kaiserzeit* (1941); cf. Mitchell, *Armies and Frontiers*, 133–9.

[50] Robert, *BCH* 102 (1978), 419–28.

[51] Hopkins, 'Models, Ships, and Staples', 104–5.

[52] On mounts for couriers, see further Rostovtzeff, *SEHRE*[2] 704 n. 40.

[53] *JRS* (1976), 120–1.

[54] Pliny, *Pan.* 29, 'nonne cernere datur, ut sine ullius iniuria omnibus usibus nostris annus exuberet? Quippe non ut ex hostico raptae perituraeque in horreis messes nequiquam quiritantibus sociis auferuntur. Devehunt ipsi, quod terra genuit, quod sidus aluit, quod annus tulit, nec novis indictionibus pressi ad vetera tributa deficiunt. Emit fiscus quidquid videtur emere. Inde copiae, inde annona, de qua inter licentem vendentemque conveniat, inde his satietas nec fames usquam.' Rostovtzeff, *SEHRE*[2] 608 n. 23 shrewdly comments that such a claim would not have been easy to make after Trajan's Dacian and Parthian wars. For the evidence from Egypt, see *SHERE*[2] 721 n. 45; Garnsey, *Famine and Food Supply*, 252. Duncan-Jones, *Structure and Scale*, 147–8 (= *Chiron*, 6 (1976), 247–8) estimates compulsory purchase prices of Egyptian grain to have been about one-third lower than market prices.

[55] For Germany see L. Wierschowski, *Heer und Wirtschaft: Das römische Heer der Prinzipätszeit als Wirtschaftsfaktor* (1984), 161–73. For Gallic supplies see P. Middleton, 'The Roman Army and Long-Distance Trade', in Garnsey and Whittaker, *Trade and Famine in Classical Antiquity*, 75–83; 'Army Supply in Roman Gaul: An Hypothesis for Roman Britain', in B. C. Burnham and H. A. Johnson (eds.), *Invasion and Response* (BAR, 1979), 85 ff.; and J. F. Drinkwater, *Roman Gaul* (1983), 124–31.

routes as the main supply. Such supplies were particularly required when units were brought up to strength
in wartime, or when they were engaged in troop movements or campaigns that removed them from their
regular provisioning sources. Three well-known items
from the literary evidence illustrate the extra burdens
that war imposed. The people of Byzantium, at the
nodal point between the two regions, suffered particularly during the increased activity of wartime in AD 53,
because they occupied lands which were so convenient
for commanders and armies in transit by land and sea,
and also for the transport of supplies ('simul vehendo
commeatus opportuna forent').[56] Similar language was
used by Pliny, relaying to Trajan the complaints of
Juliopolis on the Bithynian Galatian border, which
suffered from very heavy transit traffic, particularly of
a military nature ('plurimisque per eam commeantibus
transitum praebent').[57] Another exchange of letters
between Pliny and Trajan alludes to Maximus, an
imperial freedman procurator responsible to the provincial procurator, taking an escort of six infantry
and two cavalrymen into Paphlagonia, *ad frumentum
comparandum*. It is frustrating that we cannot tell
whether the mission was directed to the coastal or
inland parts of the province, but the heavy military
escort leaves no doubt that the grain purchase of this
extraordinary mission was compulsory and not a commercial business.[58] It may not be a coincidence that
the burdens of Byzantium and Iuliopolis (and by implication of Paphlagonia too) were particularly marked
on the eve of major campaigns: Corbulo's Armenian
war of AD 54 and Trajan's operations in the same area
which began in 114. The logistics of large-scale warfare
in the East usually required preparations which began
a year or two before the outbreak of hostilities.

The troop movements themselves imposed a particular strain on cities located along the transit routes,
whose urban inhabitants were not generally directly
affected by the burden of supplying the peacetime
army. A citizen of Thyateira of Italian origin organized
supplies in one of the Anatolian provinces, probably
Galatia, to supply the winter quarters of *legiones V
Macedonica, VII Claudia, IV Scythica*, and *I Italica*
during the Parthian campaign of Trajan or Lucius
Verus.[59] Such provisions, however, had to be supported by the local communities, and wealthy men

gained credit for undertaking the task as a liturgy.
C. Iulius Severus entertained Trajan's forces as they
overwintered in Ancyra in 113/4, and his compatriot,
Latinius Alexander, performed similar services on their
return under Hadrian in 117.[60] The logistics of Verus'
Parthian war involved Ephesus, where the sophist T.
Flavius Damianus provided 201,000 medimni of wheat
over thirteen months for the victorious Roman forces
when they returned through the city in 166.[61] Like
the burdens themselves, the evidence becomes more
copious during the third century.

It is commonly argued that there was a significant
difference in methods of taxation and army supply
between the practices of the early empire and of the
third century. The Severans tended to replace money
taxes with levies in kind, and the state supplied its
armies by such levies and by direct requisition, rather
than by paying for its needs and thereby stimulating
the monetized economy of the empire.[62] If the reconstruction offered above is sound, the difference between
the two periods was far less marked than this. The basic
system of direct provisioning had been in place since
the time of Augustus, and formed an essential part of
post-Flavian frontier arrangements. It has been argued
further that Septimius Severus created a new branch
of the administration, the *annona militaris*, which
assumed responsibility for army supply. *Mansiones*
along the Roman road system, which had always
played a crucial role in transport and distribution,
were systematically designated as collection points for
provincial grain and other tax goods, which could then
easily be moved by the relay system to their destination.[63] This reads more into the evidence than is strictly

[56] Tacitus, *Ann.* 12. 62.

[57] Pliny, *Ep.* 10. 77–8.

[58] Pliny, *Ep.* 10. 27–8. For campaign preparations see Ziegler,
140–2, citing Philo, *Leg. ad Gaium*, 248 ff.; MacMullen,
Corruption and the Decline of Rome, 171–2. I have not seen
J. P. Adams, *Logistics of the Roman Imperial Army: Major
Campaigns on the Eastern Front in the First Three Centuries
A.D.* (Yale, 1976).

[59] *TAM* v. 2. 1143.

[60] Bosch, *Ankara*, nos. 105–6, 117–18; Rostovtzeff, *SEHRE*²
695–6 n. 6. Chaeremon of Nysa had done precisely the same
in supporting Roman troops quartered at Apamea in Phrygia
during the Mithridatic War, *SIG*³ 741. Cf. Siculus Flaccus, *De
cond. agr.* 165 (Lachmann). For other parallels and discussion,
cf. Garnsey, *Famine and Food Supply*, 244 ff. and
Wierschowski, *Heer und Wirtschaft*, 261 n. 601.

[61] *Forsch. Eph.* iii no. 80 = *I. Eph.* iii. 672; J. Keil, 'Ephesos und
der Etappendienst zwischen der Nord- und Ostfront des
Imperium Romanum', *Anz. Wien* (1955), 159–70.

[62] Rostovtzeff, *SEHRE*² 412–14, 469 ff.; Hopkins, 'Taxes and
Trade', 123–4. The notion is pervasive in the modern
literature, despite occasional protests, notably M. Corbier,
'Dévaluation et fiscalité sous les derniers Antonins et les
Sévères', in *Les Dévaluations à Rome* (1977), 273–309.

[63] D. van Berchem, *L'Annone militaire dans l' empire romain du
III*ᵉ *siècle* (1937); but see his 'L'annone militaire, est elle un
mythe?', in *Armées et fiscalité dans le monde antique*
(Colloque Paris, 1976), 331–6, and the subsequent
observations by M. Corbier, emphasizing that the Severans
strove to maintain money taxes rather than replace them with
levies in kind, and of J.-M. Carrié, suggesting that the *annona
militaris* (and the term is not attested as such before the
tetrarchy) was not essentially a novelty of the third century; 'le
nouveauté de l'*annona militaris* institutionalisée a donc moins

necessary, and attempts to establish a moment of change with more precision than is appropriate. There is clear evidence for compulsory grain exactions before the Severan period; correspondingly, examples can be found of payments for extra grain (*frumentum emptum*) at least as late as the 230s.[64] If the office of the *annona militaris* was indeed a Severan innovation, it may represent no more than tighter state control over a system. It is certainly possible that many new *mansiones* were established along the major routes in the early third century, but the system as a whole, and the utility of the *mansiones* as collecting points for agricultural produce destined for consumption by the armies, was much more likely to have evolved with the growth of the road system.[65] Tasks previously undertaken by private contractors or civic magistrates now fell to officials; soldiers as such came more frequently into direct contact with the civilian population as collectors of tax goods, replacing slave and freedmen agents of the emperor: in place of freedmen procurators and *conductores* the inscriptions mention *frumentarii*, *stationarii*, and *colletiones* (above, Ch. 13 § II at nn. 31–3). The mechanics of tax collection were militarized, but the underlying principles of exaction in kind remained the same.

During the third century, as the thrust of Roman foreign policy turned once again towards Persia, campaigning and troop movements in the eastern provinces were more frequent, and imposed heavier demands on the communities along the transit routes between the Balkans and the eastern frontier than before (Ch. 13 § IV). Asia Minor became a war zone. Armies based in Syria were supplied with grain sent from small cities in the Taurus mountains as well as from Bithynia and Galatia.[66] Soldiers were now conspicuous in previously peaceful areas; military discipline was laxer than before; and corruption and extortion became endemic.[67] Missions like those of Maximus,

Trajan's procurator, to buy Paphlagonian grain surely became almost routine. No doubt the practice of compulsory purchase at fixed prices was by now widely replaced by simple requisitioning, compounded by extortion. The pressures on the civilian population, urban and rural, were not produced by a new system of taxation in kind, but by the intensification and corrupt application of old practices.

v. *Grain Supply and Living Standards in Cities and Villages*

If the preceding sketch of the organization of Roman army supply is broadly correct, measures for supplying the cities can easily be fitted into place. Under normal circumstances a provincial city was responsible for feeding its own citizens with local produce. After the Roman state had collected its tax in kind, a fifth, a seventh, or more often a tenth of the crop, the harvest from a city's territory became available for sale in the market-place. Where city landlords owned or otherwise controlled most of the rural territory, they extracted their due as rent; the needs of the peasants themselves came at the end of the line (above, Ch. 11 § I). In more favourable circumstances villagers themselves might earn a cash income from surplus produce. Landowners doubtless made a profit from the surplus, but perhaps not a large one, at least from grain. Market controllers attempted to regulate the sale price of staples, particularly bread, since this was essential if civic order was to be maintained. Public-spirited magistrates often undertook the liturgy of *sitonia*, and with it the responsibility of providing an adequate corn supply, often at some cost to themselves. Shortages led to riots and other forms of protest, which were usually the best weapon in the hands of the common people against racketeering. In rare cases Roman authorities intervened when these internal mechanisms failed.[68]

The state supply system was only rarely used to help cities in difficult situations. The Roman authorities in Egypt kept a particularly close watch on the food supplies of the notoriously turbulent city of Alexandria. Normally the huge surplus production of the Nile valley, much of which was used to feed Rome itself, provided a firm buffer against shortage, but on one occasion the small Pisidian city of Pogla sent *annona* to the nation of Alexandria, no doubt to avert a famine.[69] More often Egyptian grain was diverted to Asia Minor.

résidé dans l'invention de certains procédés fiscaux que dans leur généralisation, dans un recours plus systématiques à ces procédés.' See further Wierschowski, *Heer und Wirtschaft*, 151–61.

[64] Wierschowski, *Heer und Wirtschaft*, 159–61 with nn.

[65] See also on the *mansiones* of the Antonine Itinerary, van Berchem, *Actes du IX congrès international sur les frontières romaines, Constantsa 1972* (1974), 301–7. There is no up-to-date study of *mansiones* in the early empire.

[66] Bean and Mitford, *Journeys in Rough Cilicia 1964–8* (1970), nos. 19–21; cf. Mitchell, *Armies and Frontiers*, 139 ff.

[67] See above, Ch. 13 § II; MacMullen, *Corruption and the Decline of Rome, passim*, cf. *Latomus* (1987), 753–4, 'With numbers rising in the late third century and sharply increased by Diocletian, officials also steadily increased their rates of pillage from the flow of money and goods they handled . . . the cause of this . . . was the dissolving of the effective power of the state among the scores of thousands on its pay roll, each

claiming his own part of the emperors' sovereignty—including the right to take.'

[68] See above, Ch. 12 §§ II–III.

[69] Rostovtzeff, *JÖAI* 4 (1901), Beibl. 38; *IGR* iv. 409; G. E. Bean, *AS* 10 (1960), 59 no. 104; cf. Garnsey, *Famine and Food Supply*, 254 on other efforts to keep the peace in Alexandria by ensuring the food supply.

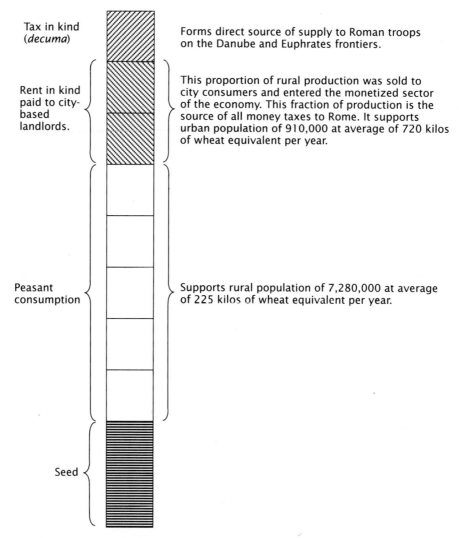

Tax in kind (*decuma*) — Forms direct source of supply to Roman troops on the Danube and Euphrates frontiers.

Rent in kind paid to city-based landlords. — This proportion of rural production was sold to city consumers and entered the monetized sector of the economy. This fraction of production is the source of all money taxes to Rome. It supports urban population of 910,000 at average of 720 kilos of wheat equivalent per year.

Peasant consumption — Supports rural population of 7,280,000 at average of 225 kilos of wheat equivalent per year.

Seed

The figures assume that the rural population produced 450 kilos of wheat equivalent per head per year.

Division of the harvest between state, city, and country

An imperial ruling of the second century granted Ephesus priority in the queue for Egyptian grain, after Rome's own needs had been supplied, and Tralles drew on the same source at least once, in accordance with a special dispensation from Hadrian.[70] Ironically the presence of large Roman forces at Tarsus in 215 and in 231, which no doubt obtained provisions in the usual way by exactions and forced purchase from local sources, led Caracalla and Severus Alexander to allow the city to import Egyptian grain to cope with the heavy extra demand.[71]

[70] M. Wörrle, *Chiron*, 1 (1971), 325–49; Garnsey, *Famine and Food Supply*, 255–7.
[71] R. Ziegler, *JNG* 27 (1977), 29–67.

The division of the harvest between state, city, and country is perhaps best illustrated by the accompanying diagram. Ten per cent of the crop went directly to the state as a tax; during warfare or other emergencies the proportion might be increased by requisition or compulsory purchase. Twenty per cent (or perhaps 25 per cent) would have to be retained annually as seed for the following year. This left a maximum of 70 per cent for local consumption, to be divided between town and country. Since Imperial tenants handed over a third of their crop to the emperor, it is realistic to assume that private tenants surrendered a similar proportion in total; so 20 per cent would go to city landlords, leaving 50 per cent for their own consumption.

It is hazardous to convert these proportions into real figures but hard to resist the temptation, especially if the experiment helps to give some notion of the possible implications of this division for the workings of ancient society. Other figures may readily be substituted for the following suggestions, and conclusions reformulated accordingly. According to a generous estimate, subsistence level for an individual may be calculated at 250 kilos of wheat equivalent per year.[72] Anatolian peasants were also obliged to support the non-productive city dwellers and soldiers with a surplus. We may guess average individual production to have been around 450 kilos wheat equivalent per year. The total produced by a rural Anatolian population of 7,280,000 would thus be 3,276 million kilos, to be divided as 327.6 million surrendered as tax, 655.2 million to the cities, 655.2 million reserved for seed, and 1,638 million for subsistence. Accordingly, average peasant consumption would be 225 kilos, average city consumption 720 kilos. The difference between the last two figures is a measure of the difference in standard of living between city and country. Of course, only about a third of the extra produce commandeered by the cities need have been in the form of grain and other products for basic subsistence. The remaining two-thirds would have been other rural produce—such as wool, meat, timber, or garden crops that could be sold for cash in the city markets, or provided the raw material for secondary products. The cash raised from this surplus was the source of money taxes to the state and the disposable income used to build and maintain the cities of the empire.

VI. *Local Coinage and Money Taxes*

Civic economies in Roman Asia Minor were undoubtedly monetized. City dwellers practised a huge diversity of trades to earn a living, and sold their products in the market-place. Prices in cities, whether for a loaf of bread or for the construction of a temple, were expressed in cash terms.[73] Most of the cities of Asia Minor felt the need to mint their own bronze coins to facilitate low-value transactions. It has always been a puzzle that such coin issues were often very irregular; some cities minted only during a single reign; others with wide intervals between issues.[74] Plainly at other times the existing supply of old, locally produced

coins, or of coins from neighbouring cities, were enough for their needs. This phenomenon becomes more intelligible if we assume that only about one-fifth of the economy was monetized, and that comparatively little coin moved out of the cities into the countryside. Small quantities of change sufficed, especially in land-locked towns which did little business outside their territories and a circle of neighbouring cities.

Civic coinage in general became more abundant in the third century. Many cities minted during this period for the first time; others minted in most (but rarely all) emperors' reigns from the Severan period up to the time of Gallienus in the 260s, and the number of types produced during individual reigns also tended to increase considerably. This gives the lie to the view that the Roman empire was already reverting to an economy in kind; urban wealth was still accumulated and disbursed in cash. One reason for the increasing use of civic coinage was certainly the progressive devaluation of the silver money minted by the Roman State. Local bronze coins also decreased in weight, but more slowly than imperial 'silver', whose intrinsic value by 260 was 2 per cent of what it had been in 200. As civic bronze gained in relative value, demand for it presumably rose, and this provides one reason why it was struck in greater quantities between 200 and about 270, when all local mints ceased.[75] Another clear reason for heavy third-century minting is that issues often coincided with the presence, or anticipated presence of Roman forces in a region, a phenomenon which can be traced with great precision in the cities of Cilicia and Pontus, where the coins are precisely dated.[76] It is unlikely that local bronze was issued to soldiers directly as pay, but cities, alerted to troop movements by imperial edicts which prepared the ground for campaigns a year or more ahead of their arrival, ensured that enough local money was in circulation to meet the extra needs of billeted or over-wintering soldiers.[77] The city itself made a small

---

[72] Hopkins, 'Taxes and Trade', *JRS* 1980, 117–18 for the figure and an explanation of wheat equivalent. The problem comes in estimating how much above minimum subsistence the average peasant produced (cf. n. 8).

[73] See Duncan-Jones, *The Economy of the Roman Empire*, and *Structure and Scale*, passim.

[74] The pattern is easily traced through P. R. Franke *et al.*, *SNG von Aulock*, index.

[75] See the excellent discussion by W. Wieser, *Katalog der bithynischen Münzen der Sammlung des Instituts für Altertumskunde der Universität Köln. Band 1. Nikaia* (1985), 161–81.

[76] Ziegler, 130–43; Dr Ziegler is preparing a fuller study of the phenomenon.

[77] For such edicts see van Berchem, *Actes du IX congrès*; for the interpretation, see Howgego, *Greek Imperial Countermarks*, 29; 'It is likely, however, that the army elicited coinages not as pay but simply by its presence. The army on the move would have created temporary increases in the level of trade and demand for coin *en route*. Coinages may have been struck to meet this need. . . . Bosch [*Arch. Anz.* (1931), 427] has shown that military types and coins of Asia Minor were concentrated on the military routes from Bithynia to Cilicia. Again this is not evidence that the coins were struck to pay the army, but is illustrative of the economic influence of the army to the cities

percentage (usually one-sixteenth or one-eighteenth part) in exchanging local bronze for Roman denarii, and the extra small change allowed traders to make the most of any market opportunities.[78] No doubt it was common to give credit to local customers at normal times; no prudent trader would voluntarily extend credit to transient soldiers; cash payments had to be made easy.

Money taxation was necessarily exacted from the monetized section of the economy, which may not have exceeded 20 per cent in much of Anatolia. Modern analyses of Roman taxation usually distinguish between indirect taxation, which was levied on specified transactions, such as the inheritances of Roman citizens (*vicesima hereditatum* at 5 per cent), the manumission of slaves, but above all the import and export of goods (*portoria*), and direct taxation on persons and property, the *tributum capitis* and the *tributum soli*. The latter are generally believed to have accounted for the bulk of tax income to Rome in the early empire.

Although Roman practice was notably diverse—and we should allow place for much arbitrariness even in officially authorized tax collection—some form of registration or census, brought up to date as necessary, lay behind the assessment of a population for its direct tax liabilities; and there is enough evidence from scattered sources to support this common-sense inference.[79] Land registration, which assessed quality and use as well as area, lay behind the tithes that were levied. Registration of individuals for the poll-tax, which covered both the free and the slave population, but excluded Roman citizens and other privileged groups, was presumably less complex. In general many city dwellers qualified for these exemptions and the bulk of revenue raised by *tributum capitis* must also have been levied on the rural population. However, since the peasants, *ex hypothesi*, had little or no cash reserves to pay their taxes, and since collection from individuals, especially from the huge numbers who lived in the countryside, would have been a practical impossibility, communities (usually cities) were held collectively responsible for paying the tax bill for their inhabitants. Normally the assessment appears to have been rounded to an exact figure, which was probably somewhat lower than the total liability of all the inhabitants; the city magistrates, or more rarely *publicani*, were responsible for collecting the money and handing it over to Roman officials.[80] It follows

that the poll-tax for rural inhabitants would in fact have been paid by their urban landlords, who of course reckoned with this obligation when they established the levels of rents in kind that they drew from their properties.

There is no useful evidence from Asia Minor for the rate at which the poll-tax was levied, or none that can be expressed in terms of cash per head. It has been suggested that overall tax rates in the Roman empire were low.[81] This may be true if money tax is calculated as a percentage of the total produce of the empire. But if in fact the state could only levy cash from the 20 per cent of production which belonged to the monetized economy, taxes (at whatever level they were raised) will have seemed notably more burdensome. Certainly from time to time a wealthy benefactor chose to underwrite a city's tax liability, either by paying the bill entirely himself, or, providing for the longer term, by establishing a foundation whose revenues could be used for paying the poll-tax.[82] On the other hand, the limited scope of money taxation in relation to economic activity as a whole will have reduced its value as a driving force in the economy. If all or most Roman taxation on agricultural production had been collected in cash, then peasants and landowners alike would have been obliged to make strenuous efforts through trade to turn their agricultural assets into a cash income, out of which to pay the state.[83] In fact, in Anatolia at least, only city dwellers felt this pressure.

If cash income from 'direct taxation' was lower than is generally assumed, Rome's indirect sources of revenue should be seen as relatively more important. In AD 58, in response to an increasing volume of complaints against the rapacity of *publicani*, Nero rashly proposed that 'indirect taxation', the *vectigalia*, of which the *portoria* formed the most important element, could be dispensed with. He was dissuaded by old hands in the senate, but a senatorial commission was charged to revise the legislation which controlled the contracts of the *publicani*. In AD 62 their proposals were ready for legislation, and the redrafted law which governed the raising of *portoria* in the province of Asia has come to light on a long inscription from Ephesus.[84]

Nevertheless it is unlikely that the legitimate collection of *portoria*, at 2½ per cent of the value of the

---

with which it came into contact.' Cf. Nollé, *Chiron*, 17 (1987), 260.

[78] See *OGIS* 484 = *IGR* iv. 352 (Pergamum); *I. Mylasa*, no. 605; Broughton, *Roman Asia Minor*, 895–7 (with trans.).

[79] Brunt, *JRS* 71 (1981), 163–6; see Ch. 5 n. 62.

[80] Brunt, *JRS* 71 (1981), 161–72, enlarging on the clear and detailed exposition of Neesen, *Untersuchungen zu den direkten Staatsabgaben der römischen Kaiserzeit*.

[81] Hopkins, 'Taxes and Trade', 116–20; called into question by Brunt, *JRS* 1981, 170.

[82] *IG* xii. 5. 946. (Tenos); *ILS* 6960 (Ibiza); *Arch. Delt.* 2 (1916), 148 (taxes paid by high priest of the Macedonian *koinon*); cf. *IGR* iv. 181 (Lampsacus, poll-tax reduced by half) and 259 (Assus, reduction of poll-tax and other dues).

[83] A central thesis of Hopkins, 'Taxes and Trade'.

[84] H. Engelmann and D. Knibbe, *Das Zollgesetz der Provinz Asia, Epigr. Anat.* 14 (1989). I have benefited from a provisional English translation of the text made by Michael Crawford and H. C. van Bremen.

goods traded, yielded a large tax income, in proportion to Rome's total revenues. It is hard to believe that more than about 10 per cent of goods that circulated in the cash economy crossed the boundaries of customs' zones and became liable for duty.[85] Exceptions to this rule may have been the luxury textile products produced in parts of Asia Minor (notably in the Phrygian cities of Laodicea and Hierapolis)[86] and slaves. Phrygia, Galatia, Cappadocia, and other central regions of Anatolia were an important source of slaves under the empire. Slave-markets are attested, or can reasonably be inferred at Acmonia and Apamea in Phrygia, and at Lydian Thyateira, and papyri indicate that Side, in particular, was an important port for the slave trade. Since the potential value of new slaves could not readily be estimated until their potential had been developed through training, the duty on slaves was expressed in different terms from those for commodities. The tax on child slaves of either sex was not to exceed five denarii (implying a notional maximum market value of 200 denarii); a further clause added in 17 BC appears to allow an increase of two and a half denarii on imported and one denarius on exported slaves.[87] The traffic in slaves from the interior of Asia Minor to the coastal ports must have been balanced to some degree by imports. It seems likely that the most important commodity to travel in the reverse direction was olive oil from the coastal regions, not so much for private consumption as for use in the gymnasia. In Phrygian Apamea, one of the larger cities, public expenditure on oil in a single year came to 34,000 denarii (above, Ch. 12 § IV n. 126).

VII. *Economic Growth and Urbanization*

The economy of Anatolia clearly grew significantly during the early empire. This is plain from the spread and development of settlements. By the second century AD the number of settled villages had grown substantially, above all in the centre of the plateau, and a pattern of cities had been superimposed on the existing rural network. The growth in population which this implies must have been supported by increased agricultural production. The most important development was the enlarged scale of cereal agriculture, and the

relative decline in pastoralism in the rural economy. There was much spare land in rural Asia Minor, methods of cultivation and types of grain were also probably improved,[88] and the scope for increasing agricultural cultivation was very large. In absolute terms, therefore, cereal production probably did little to inhibit sheep- and cattle-rearing, and wool and textiles remained central to the economy, especially to the cash sector.

Standards of living in the countryside, however, will not have risen in proportion to the overall economic growth, since most of the surplus was transferred to the cities. Here, prosperity may be gauged by the quantity of cash in local circulation, which sometimes becomes visible in the form of cash distributions to city dwellers, in the foundations established by rich citizens to support various beneficial projects and activities, including games and festivals, and in lavish public buildings, which were almost always paid for in cash, very rarely by direct labour.[89] Commercial activity, defined in the broadest sense, played a crucial role in making this possible. City dwellers, who were not primary producers of grain and other foodstuffs, had to earn enough money to buy what they needed; for most, this meant plying a trade or offering some form of retail service. The epitaphs from Corycus in Cilica indicate the enormous range of this activity, even in a modest town. Food, clothing, housing, tools, and storage were the primary needs, catered for by the butchers and bakers, weavers and tailors, masons and carpenters, blacksmiths and potters who were to be found in every city. The economic essence of urban life was that a man practised a specialized craft or trade and sold his produce or services, usually to his fellow townsmen, in order to earn a living for himself and his family.

The other key to the system was monetization. This was as central a feature of city life in the Graeco-Roman period as political and cultural criteria. The market buildings, or the shops and workshops of the city's traders, were as important as the civic agora, the imperial temple, or the bath-house. The central social and economic role played by money as such, rather than specific Roman demands for money taxes, was surely the main driving force in the economy. To live, or to live well, it was necessary to make a profit out of one's business.

---

[85] I forbear from calculating a figure. I doubt if the annual total much exceeded two million HS.

[86] See H. W. Pleket, *Münstersche Beiträge zur antiken Handelsgeschichte*, 3 (1981), 30–3; *Epigr. Anat.* 12 (1988), 33–4.

[87] W. V. Harris, 'Towards a Study of the Roman Slave Trade', in J. H. D'Arms and E. C. Kopff, *The Seaborne Commerce of Ancient Rome: Studies in Archaeology and History* (1980), 117–40, 'the great source was Asia Minor . . . over and over again we hear of the typical slave as a Cappadocian or a Phrygian' (p. 122); Asian Custom's Law, ll. 11–12, 98–9.

[88] David French reports observing dams for water collection and presumably irrigation in the territory of Laodicea Catacecaumene. Similar dams here and elsewhere were noted by W. M. Ramsay, *Luke the Physician* (1908), 129. For Anatolian grain types, and experiments to improve yields, see above, Ch. 11 § I.

[89] Duncan-Jones, *Structure and Scale*, 174–5. He notes that buildings were usually paid for in cash, and that direct labour was only used by small, poor, remote cities.

For most, this was a modest matter of earning enough to sustain a family and to obtain the raw materials for one's craft or trade. For the wealthy, the city's landlords, more was at stake. Their position as leaders of society depended ultimately on their ability to translate their landed assets into wealth, which could be used and displayed within the framework of city life. They, or rather their agents, who were often slaves or freedmen, strove to sell their surplus in bulk, either to their fellow citizens or, more crucially, to outsiders.

This could be done in two ways. Either a city exported its goods, or it attracted foreign customers. For many smaller cities, which were infrequently visited by outsiders and lay off the major routes, export might be the only means by which they could establish themselves in the wider economy of the Roman empire, and the only source of extra moneyed wealth to sustain itself as a city. Such cities in particular had an incentive to concentrate on specialized production in goods that could not be obtained elsewhere. Cities were famous not for their most abundant product, almost always cereals, but for what they could sell to others. However, lack of specialized export commodities, and above all the problems of land transport imposed a serious barrier to urban development and checked city growth. For most of the small cities of northern Lydia, Phrygia, Galatia, or Lycaonia there was little prospect of lifting themselves above the level of a small market town, and some were barely distinguishable from villages (see above, Ch. 11 § III).

Communities in more favoured situations could hope to prosper. A site on or near a Roman road, and still more on a navigable river or one along which timbers could be floated, improved the chance of competitive exports. Some cities clearly benefited from the local products or services that they could offer the wider community—Saittai and Prusias would have been of little account without, respectively, textiles and timber. When the people of Orcistus petitioned Constantine for city status, they did well to emphasize not only their position at a road junction, but also the abundance of water-mills they possessed. The emperor may not have paid much attention to so mundane a detail, but without this advantage the community had no real chance of establishing itself as more than a larger village among its neighbours.

But throughout most of the interior, a city's main hope of betterment lay in attracting wealthy foreign customers, thereby disposing of the problem of transport which bedevilled any attempt to export goods. The point is perfectly made in Dio Chrysostom's speech to the citizens of Phrygian Apamea. The city was a market centre and meeting place for an enormous region, not only Phrygia, Lydia, and Caria,

but for Cappadocians, Pamphylians, and Pisidians. Furthermore the annual assizes (to quote Dio's bright-eyed description) brought a throng of litigants, jurors, orators, governors, attendants, slaves, pimps, donkey-drivers, travelling salesmen, prostitutes, and craftsmen,

so that those who have goods for sale can sell them for the highest prices and nothing in the city lies idle, neither the animal teams, nor the houses, nor the women. This contributes greatly to prosperity; for wherever the great throng of people comes together, there necessarily is the greatest abundance of money, and the place naturally blossoms[90]

Apamea had been an important trading centre in the Hellenistic period,[91] but the economic benefits that derived from its status as a Roman assize centre were the key to its further growth under the empire.

A famous festival, an important shrine, or the status of an assize centre were crucial assets. All three would be the cause for periodic influxes of large numbers of visitors; a festival was often the occasion for a coin issue, to meet the needs of increased trade. Cities competed fiercely with one another for the right to build new temples, celebrate new imperial festivals, and indeed to acquire assize status. Especially for middle-ranking cities like Aezani, which acquired assize status in the mid-second century, or Lydian Philadelphia which was given the right to a neocorate, and thus to celebrate a major imperial festival, by Caracalla,[92] there was more at stake here than mere prestige. The new privileges provided the basis for further economic development.

In the end the cities that gained most of all were the provincial capitals. The presence of Roman administrators, and even soldiers when their rapacity could be contained, was a vital source of income, and gave provincial centres a marked advantage over other cities. Not only did the military or official presence bring cash directly into a city, but the city, as the focus of Roman power, attracted petitioners and visitors from throughout the province, in the same way as but on a larger scale than the lesser assize centres. It is no coincidence that the Anatolian cities which appear to have flourished through late Antiquity were precisely

---

[90] Dio Chrys. *Or.* 35. 14–16, with C. P. Jones, *The Roman World of Dio Chrysostom* (1978), 67–8: (15) πρὸς δὲ τούτοις αἱ δίκαι παρ᾽ ἔτος ἄγονται παρ᾽ ὑμῖν καὶ ξυνάγεται πλῆθος ἀνθρώπων ἄπειρον δικαζομένων, δικαζόντων, ῥητόρων, ἡγεμόνων, ὑπηρετῶν, οἰκετῶν, μαστροπῶν, ὀρεοκομῶν, καπήλων, ἑταιρῶν τε καὶ βαναύσων. ὥστε τά τε ὤνια τοὺς ἔχοντας πλείστης ἀποδίδοσθαι τιμῆς καὶ μηδὲν ἀργὸν εἶναι τῆς πόλεως, μήτε τὰ ζεύγη μήτε τὰς οἰκίας μήτε τὰς γυναῖκας. τοῦτο δὲ οὐ σμικρόν ἐστι πρὸς εὐδαιμονίαν· ὅπου γὰρ ἂν πλεῖστος ὄχλος ἀνθρώπων ξυνίῃ, πλεῖστον ἀργύριον ἐξ ἀνάγκης ἐκεῖ γίγνεται, καὶ τὸν τόπον εἰκὸς εὐθηνεῖν.

[91] Strabo, 12. 8. 13, 576 (with Laodicea one of the two largest Phrygian cities); 12. 8. 15, 577 (second largest Asian emporium after Ephesus).

[92] Aezani, *SEG* xxxv (1985), 1365; Philadelphia, *SIG*[3] 883.

such provincial centres: Sardis, Aphrodisias, Synnada, Caesareia, Ancyra. Although there is no evidence that the Roman authorities were responsible for anything resembling an economic policy or development planning, in this as in many other respects, the indirect contribution of the Roman state to the economic success of the empire was enormous. Not the least of Rome's achievements was to have distributed the empire's wealth throughout the provinces, preparing the way for the evolution of a new order when the capital of the world moved from Italy to Nicomedia, and to Constantinople.

General Index

This index includes the names of Roman provinces and the major cultural regions of Asia Minor. Other geographical designations are listed in the Index of Place Names (Vol. II).

acclamations *114 fig. 18g*, 201
  at Perge 238
administrative staff (of Roman governors) 69, 135
adventus 221, 224–5
ager publicus 90, 157, 249
agones, see games
agricultural productivity (under principate) 4
ala:
  Antiochiensium 74
  Augusta Germaniciana 74
  Claudia Nova 136
  Moesiaca 136
  I Augusta Colonorum 74
  I Flavia Augusta Britannica Miliaria C. R. 136
  II Lucensium 232 n. 28
  VI equitata 129
amphoras 241–2
arbitration:
  in village life 183
Argonauts, voyage of 207
Armenia:
  Nero plans invasion 40
  Roman claims abandoned 237
  under Vespasian 118
Armenia Minor 93
  annexed to Empire 118
  koinon of 116
  part of Galatia/Cappadocia 63
  under Vespasian 63
Armeniarch 116
armour:
  Celtic 16, 21
  of couriers 132
  of *diogmitai* 196
Asia (province):
  cities in 1st century 80
  extent of 72
  famine in 146
  governors in 3rd century AD 228
  imperial cult in 100
  inter-city rivalry 206
  koinon of 109
  Mithridates VI in 30
  roads in 129
  Roman military 121
Asia Minor:
  Antiochus I's precarious hold 18
  Celtic raids and extortion 23–4, 29–31
  Gothic invasion 235
  Roman control develops 29–31 and *passim*
assemblies:
  in cities 201, 203 n. 40
  at Ephesus and Magnesia on the Maeander 202
  in villages 181–2
asses and donkeys 143

assizes 200, 206
  in Asia 62
  in Bithynia 64 n. 31
  in Cilicia 64
  and coin circulation 242 n. 4
  economic importance of 248
  in Galatia 65
  in Pamphylia 238
atheism 194
Attalid kingdom 21–2, 24–6, 29, 161
  influence in western Asia Minor 85
Attis (priest):
  at Pessinus 26, 48
augury:
  of Deiotarus 34, 37

Bar-Kochva revolt 137
bath houses:
  at Aezani 214 n. 112
  at Apamea 202, 217
  at Apateira 182, 183
  in Bithynia 212–13
  and civic life 216–17
  in Galatia 214
  linked with aqueducts 213
  at Sidamaria 214
battle:
  Actium (31 BC) 34, 90
  Ancyra 20
  Aphrodisium (Pergamum) 21
  Barbalissus (AD 252) 237
  of the elephants 45–6
  Granicus 232
  Issus 232
  Kurupedion (281 BC) 13
  Lysimacheia (277 BC) 13, 15, 45, 48
  Magnesia (190 BC) 19
  Meshike (AD 244) 237
  Mt. Magaba (189 BC) 24, 45, 48, 51, 54
  Mt. Olympus (189 BC) 24, 45, 51, 58
  Nicopolis (47 BC) 34, 36
  Nisibis (AD 242) 227
  Pharsalus (46 BC) 34, 36
  Philippi (42 BC) 34, 37
  Resaina (AD 243) 237
  Singara 197
  Zela (47 BC) 36
benefactions/benefactors 117
  distinguished from patronage 184
  in Maeonia 183
  of priests at Ancyra 107–12
  sparse in central Asia Minor 225
  underwrite tax liability 256
  of village festival 187
  in villages 182
beneficiarii 69, 122, 133, 135
bequests:
  of territory to Rome 61–2

Bithynia:
  Celts in 23, 55, 57
  city constitutions 88–9
  civic turmoil in 203, 204, 206
  estates 160–1, 162
  grain production 253
  imperial cult 102
  key military area in 3rd century AD 232
  koinon of 109
  language 175
  left to Rome by Nicomedes IV 62
  lex Pompeia 162
  public building 253
  recruits from 140
  wine festivals 187
boule:
  as criterion for city status 180, 181, 182, 201
  meetings of 204
  prominent in Roman period 201
boundaries:
  between cities 94 n. 150
  natural 5–6
  of Roman provinces 5
brabeutai 182–3
brigands 77 n. 74, 197, 234–5
  in Mysia 165, 166

Cappadocia:
  annexed by Tiberius 63
  cereals in 168
  cities in 1st century BC 81, 82
  forts and castles in 84
  Galatians embroiled with 19
  Gothic invasion 235
  Hellenization promoted by kings 83–4
  lack of cities 97–8
  language 173–4
  legions stationed in 139–41
  pre-Roman epigraphy and coinage 86
  roads 129
  Sassanian invasion 237, 238
  temple states in 1st century BC 81–2
  Vespasian joins to Galatia 63
Caria:
  Gothic attack feared 235
  Hellenization 85
  language 172
  prize games 225
  province of Phrygia and Caria 228
  village base of Carian polity 181
castellum 121
  of Homonadeis 77
cereals:
  for Alexandria 254
  Anatolian grain for Syrian armies 253
  best grain taken by cities 224–5, 253
  civic funds for grain purchase 89

cereals: (cont.):
  edict of Antistius Rusticus 66, 145, 150
  distribution schemes 111, 159, 245
  Egyptian for Anatolia 254
  experimental cultivation 167–8
  farming in central Anatolia 144, 245
  in Galatia 145, 148 n. 49
  peasant consumption levels 255
  price differentials 247
  Ptolemy II sends corn to Pontic cities 20
  sitonai 250, 253
  state purchases 251, 253
  storage 168, 242
  for Tarsus 208 fig. 36f, 254
  as tax in kind 248–9
  transport costs 246
  wheat and barley for Cyzicus 16
Christians:
  in central Anatolia 239
  at Docimeium 170 fig. 30
Church organization 4
Cilicia 7
  coinage 255
  in kingdom of Polemo I 38
  military area in 3rd century AD 232
  recruits from 140
Cilicia Pedias:
  cities taken by Sassanians 238
Cilicia Tracheia (Rugged Cilicia):
  Celtic material culture in 54
  cities taken by Sassanians 238
  kingdom of M. Antonius Polemo 94
  native opposition to Roman rule 234
  prize games 225
  recruitment from 136, 139
  Roman military presence 122
citizenship, Roman 109, 113, 179, 208 fig.
  36c, 256
city administration 199–206
  see also magistrates
city foundations:
  in Cappadocia 97–8
  in central Anatolia 96–7
  Claudian policy 96
  in Hellenistic Anatolia 81
  imperial policy 98
  in North Galatia 86–7
  in Paphlagonia 92
  in Pontus 91, 178 n. 120
  in Rugged Cilicia 94–5
  in South Galatia 95
  supplant tribal groupings 176
city planning:
  at Ancyra and Pessinus 105
  at Pisidian Antioch 104, 105–6
city territories 149, 179
  in Galatia 87–8
  in Paphlagonia 93
  in Pontus 31–2, 91–2, 162
classis Pontica 124
  transferred to Cyzicus 235
climate 144
  winter: in Bithynia 168; in Thrace 166
  see also rainfall
cochineal 50 n. 85, 146
cohors:
  Apula 73
  I Augusta Cyrenaica in Galatia 121, 122
    fig. 20
  I Claudia Sygambrorum veterana
    equitata 121
  I Raetorum at Eumeneia 121
  I T . . . 139 n. 179
  II Hispanorum 121

II . . . at Dascusa 119
colletiones 229, 233
coinage/coins:
  and agonistic festivals 198, 222 fig. 39
  of Amyntas as army pay 38 n. 142
  of Ancyra 145 n. 17
  bronze, distributed by troops 242, 250
  depict fortifications 213
  economic importance 241, 255, 257
  in Galatian cities 87 nn. 80–2
  of Galatian koinon 112
  of Galatian tribes 113
  latest bronze civic (Perge) 224
  linked to military presence 255–6
  of Pessinus 103–4
  in pre-Roman Anatolia 86
  of Soatra 96
  widely used in 3rd century AD 20, 255
coloni 185, 249 n. 44
colonies (Roman and Italian):
  at Apameia 160
  at Attaleia 102, 152
  constitutions 89
  date of Pisidian 76
  foundation coin type at Lystra 114 fig. 18a
  in Galatia 77, 90
  at Heliopolis 153
  land for 90–1
  at Mallos 208 fig. 36c
  military responsibilities of 76
  at Nicopolis 32
  at Ninica 38 n. 138, 77, 114 fig. 18b
  in Phrygia Paroreius 38
  around Pisidia 71
  in Pontus 36–7, 40, 41
Commagene 177, 250
confession texts 191–5
conscription 140–1
  see also recruitment
conversion to Christianity:
  of Cappadocia 10
corvée labour 127, 163, 194
couriers 129, 164, 166
Crusaders:
  cross Anatolia 143
culture:
  Anatolian regional 7
  Celtic spreads to Anatolian population 19
    n. 80
  of cities 207
  classical 4
  gap between town and country 197
  and Greek language 174
  inscriptions and Greek 86
  material, of cities 198
  mixed in Anatolia 86; at Hanisa 83
curial class (city councillors):
  economic power of 244–5
  see also boule
curses and imprecations (on tombstones):
  Christian 189
  in Phrygia and Lydia 188
  typical of Anatolian population 174

darnel (toxicity) 168
dead, reverence for 189
Deuteronomy, Book of:
  curses invoked 189 n. 217
diet:
  rural 168–70
Dis Manibus:
  use of formula 135, 160
doreai 224
Druids 48, 49, 51 n. 93

Drynemetos (Galatian meeting place) 27, 49
dux 228, 234
dynasts 94
  reasons for 33, 34, 40
  succession and marriages among
    Galatians 28, 36
  under M. Antonius 38–9

elephants:
  on coin of Caesareia 204 fig. 35f
  used against Galatians 8
emporium:
  at Apamea 258 n. 91
  in Bithynia 187
  at Gordium 54
  at Hanisa 83
  at Pessinus 83
  at Sinope 82
  at Tavium 51, 83
epanorthotes (diorthotes) 227 n. 5, 228, 229
eparchia (hyparchia) 91, 92
estates 9
  administration of (N. Africa) 162–3
  of Aelius Aristides 165 n. 4
  Bithynian 160–1
  of Dio Chrysostom 160
  Galatian 111, 149–58
  imperial: in Cappadocia 98; at
    Tymbrianassus 67
  Lydian 161–2
  among Ormeleis 163–4, 240
  at Phocaea 166
  Phrygian 158–60
  rents exacted in kind 245
eunuchs:
  at Pessinus 48
euporia 227
Expositio Totius Mundi 145, 146

famine:
  in Asia 146
  Galen on 169
  at Pisidian Antioch 66
  at Prusa 203
  of 1873 145
feasts/feasting:
  demothoiniai 110
  among eastern Celts 44
  among Gauls 43
  in Life of St Theodore 44
  at Neocaesareia 116
festivals 182
  near Nicomedia 187
  at Thiounta 187
  see also games
fines for grave violation 122, 187
fire beacons 129
Flavian frontier policy 250
flood(s) 105
foundation legends 208
  see also myths
fortifications:
  built in mid-3rd century AD 235–6, 238
  Hellenistic, in central Anatolia 85
  in Iberia 119
  at Isaura 72 n. 32, 85
  at Nicaea and Prusias 213
  in Pamphylia and Cilicia 196
  in Pisidia 72 n. 27
frumentarii 229, 233
funerals (Celtic) 57

Galatia 1, 7, 9
  asses in 143

Augustan city foundations 77
Augustan province 61
cereal farming 144–6, 147–8, 248, 253
city foundations in S. 94–7
during civil wars 34–41
climate, landscape, and crops 143–4
estates 149–58, 164
funerary monuments 146–7, 148
garrisons in 74, 78, 121
Gothic invasions 235
imperial administration in 63–9
koinon 109, 110, 112, 113, 116
occupied by Celts 19, 51–8
Paphlagonia attached to 92–3
pottery of E. Galatia 83
pre-Roman epigraphy and coinage 86
public buildings 212, 213–14
recruitment from 136–42
roads 124, 126–9
source of slaves 30–1, 74
tribes 27–9, 42–3
urbanization under Roman rule 86–8, 89
Vespasian joins to Cappadocia 63
villages 178–9
weaving 146
wine 146–7
wool 146, 147–8
games (*agones*) 111, 198–9, 217–25
  Actia 222; (Syrian Antioch) 218
  Aelia Cornuteia (Apollonia) 220
  at Aezani 219 n. 146
  agon mystikos 218, 219–20
  Antoneineia Olympia Epinicia (Adana) 221
  Asclepieia Sotereia 221
  of Asian *koinon* 218
  of Athena Promachos (Rome) 222, 227
  Attaleia Capetolia (Aphrodisias) 222
  Augusteia Actia 224
  Augusteia Actia (Tarsus) 111 n. 71
  Augusti Actia (Nicomedia) 111 n. 71
  Augusteios Isopythios (Thyateira) 221
  Balbilleia (Ephesus) 219
  of Bithynian *koinon* 218
  in Bithynian village 187
  Caesareia (Attaleia) 152
  Capitoneia (Miletus) 219
  in Cappadocia 82 n. 13
  Commodeia 220–1
  Commodeion (Caesareia) 218
  at Cremna under Aurelian 224, 225
  Decius Oecumenicus 224
  Demetria Antoneia (Nicomedia) 221
  Demostheneia (Oenoanda) 210, 220
  Didymeia (Miletus) 220
  Diiphileia Traianeia (Pergamum) 219
  Elagabalia (Sardis) 221
  Eusebeia: (Mopsuhestia) 224;
    (Puteoli) 220
  of Galatian *koinon* 112, 116, 219
  Galliena Capetolia (Antioch on the
    Maeander) 224
  Isopythia Asclepieia Sotereia (Ancyra) 218,
    221
  Marcus Aurelius and 220
  Megala Severeia (Nicomedia) 221
  Meleagreia (Balbura) 220
  in Nile Delta 224
  Olympia (Side) 224
  Philadelphia (Eumeneia and
    Philadelphia) 221 n. 166
  Philadelphia Severeia 221
  in Phrygia and Lydia 225 n. 197
  Pythia (Side) 222
  Romaia (Lycia) 218

  Romaia Sebasta (Pergamum) 219
  Severeia Olympia Epinicia
    (Anazarbus) 222
  Severeius 221
  Taciteia (Perge) 225
  themides at Termessus 225
  Valerian promotes 237
  Valeriana (Nicaea) 224
  Valeriana Pythia (Aphrodisias) 224
  see also festivals
gerusia 212
gladiatorial shows/*venationes* 110
  at Ancyra 111
  Galen and 169
  at Neocaesareia 116
  at Pessinus 105

hecatomb 109–10
Hellenization:
  of Cappadocia 35 n. 103, 82
  of Celts in Greek cities 58
  of Galatian aristocracy 35
  of Galatian cults 49
  in Phrygia 174
  of Phrygia Paroreius 85
  of Pisidia 7
  of Pontus 82
  of western Anatolia 85
hippeis 132
  see also couriers
Historia Augusta 145
Hittite empire 175
horses:
  breeding 132
  racing not practised by Phrygians 189
hospitality and billeting 65
  Cicero avoids 250 n. 47
  at Prusias ad Hypium 232
  senators protected from 230, 234 n. 108
human sacrifice 48
hys (holm-oak) 50

imperial freedmen and slaves:
  born of servile mother 230 fig. 41
  at Laodicea Catacecaumene 153, 156
  in Lydia 161–2
  among Orondians 157
  supervise official transport 247
inns:
  near lake Manyas 167
  rare in Thrace 166
Ionia:
  Anatolia viewed from 5
  Gothic invasion 235
Iranian population in Anatolia 47
Isauria:
  conquests of P. Servilius 72
  imperial dedication symbolizes Roman
    control 66–7, 79
  new province in 3rd century AD 228
  nomenclature 75
  opposes Roman rule 234
  recruits from 136, 139, 140
  Roman military presence 122
  in time of Alexander 85
  war of AD 6 73, 78, 116

Jewish communities 172
Justinianic Code 124

koinon (commune):
  of Asia 100
  of Cappadocia 102
  of Galatia 103, 109, 110, 112–13, 116

  of Lycaonians 176
  of Milyadeis 176 n. 104
  of Pontus 116
  priesthoods of (Galatia) 112, 114

La Tène pottery 51
landscape:
  in central Anatolia 1, 2 figs. 1 and 2, 6 figs.
    3 and 4, 143
  in the Milyas 8 fig. 6
  in Pontus 8 fig. 5
languages:
  Aramaic 86, 172
  Armenian 173 n. 79
  Bessian 173 n. 79
  Carian 172, 173 n. 72
  Celtic (Galatian) 50–1, 173, 175
  Coptic 173 n. 79
  Gothic 174
  Graeco–Aramaic bilingual text 86
  Greek 50, 172, 173; rural dialects 174,
    193
  Hebrew 172
  Isaurian 173
  Latin 135, 160, 172, 173; at Ancyra 135
  Luwian 175
  Lycaonian 173
  Lycian 172
  Lydian 172, 173
  Mysian 173
  Pamphylian 172
  Phoenician 172
  Phrygian 174, 188
  Pisidian 173
  Sidetan 172 n. 67
  Solymian 173
  Syriac 173 n. 79
legio:
  I Adiutrix 133; Anatolian recruitment 138
  I Italica 122 fig. 19, 133 n. 92, 252;
    Anatolian recruitment 138; at
    Apamea 121
  I Parthica 180 n. 134; Anatolian
    recruitment 139
  I Pontica 124
  II Adiutrix: Anatolian recruitment 138
  III Augusta 136
  III Cyrenaica 73, 136; Anatolian
    recruitment 136–7
  III Gallica: builds hydraulic device 119; in
    Cappadocia with Corbulo 140
  III Parthica: Anatolian recruitment 139
  IV Flavia: Anatolian recruitment 138;
    soldiers in Phrygia 121, 139
  IV Scythica 133 n. 92, 160, 252; Anatolian
    recruitment 140; at Zeugma 119
  V Macedonica 133 n. 92, 139, 252;
    Anatolian recruitment 136, 138; not in
    Augustan Galatia 73 n. 42; in
    Pontus 135–6
  VI Ferrata: Anatolian recruitment 140;
    campaigns at Samosata 119
  VII Claudia 121 n. 28, 133 and n. 92, 137,
    252
  VII (*Macedonica*) 136, 139; Anatolian
    recruitment 137–8; under Augustus in S.
    Asia Minor 73
  X Fretensis, Anatolian recruitment 140
  X Gemina 133; veterans, perhaps at
    Iconium 74 n. 55
  XI Claudia: Anatolian recruitment 138;
    soldiers at Apamea 121, 122 fig. 19
  XII Fulminata 34; Anatolian
    recruitment 139; centurion at Caspian

legio: (*cont.*):
  Sea 121; centurions at Comana and
    Neoclaudiopolis 136; at Melitene 118;
    officers at Ancyra 134, 135; road-
    building in Phrygia 121; vexillation at
    Trapezus 124
  XIV Gemina 133; Anatolian
    recruitment 139
  XV Apollinaris 122 *fig.* 21; Anatolian
    recruitment 139; officers at Ancyra 134;
    vexillation at Trapezus 124
  XVI Flavia Firma 34; Anatolian
    recruitment 139; centurions at
    Ancyra 134; recruited in AD 70 118
  XXII Deiotariana: also known as
    Cyrenaica 136; Anatolian
    recruitment 136–7
  XXII Primigeneia 133
  XXX Ulpia Victrix 132 n. 89, 136
limes 34, 118, 119
literacy:
  in Anatolia 238
  in Phrygia 174
Lycaonia 7, 9
  ceded to Ariarathes 29
  foundation legend 208
  imperial cult 116
  language 173, 175
  in Polemo's kingdom 38
  recruitment from 136
  Sassanians in 238
Lycia 7
  grain distribution schemes 111
  Hellenization 85
  language 172
  opposition to Roman rule 234
  prize games 225
  recruitment from 139, 140
Lycia and Pamphylia, province of 79
Lydia 7, 9
  confession steles 191–3
  estates 161, 162
  Gothic invasion 235
  language 172
  soldiers in 3rd century AD 230, 233
  villages 180–3

magistrates (civic) 88, 89, 97, 199–200
  diminishing role in tax-collection 232–3
markets 242, 247
  for slaves 257
migration (Celtic) 13, 14, 42
military abuses 180, 229, 230
military presence 9
  and agonistic festivals 224
  in an Asian sanctuary 194
  becomes ubiquitous in 3rd century AD 228,
    230
  and bronze coinage 255–6
  economic impact 134
military supplies 250–3
  for Lucullus 31, 248
  from southern Asia Minor 238
  for Valerian 237
misthotes 153, 155, 156, 164
monks:
  on Mysian Olympus 165
Mysia 7
  Aelius Aristides in 167–8
  brigands 165, 166
  Celtic names in 57
  cereals and other products 169–70
  language 173
  tribes 176

Mysia Abbaeitis 181
myths:
  and civic culture 207–8

name types:
  Celtic 50, 57, 175
  Iranian 47
  Macedonian 85
  Phrygian 175
  Thracian 175
negotiatores 154 n. 99, 162
  in Bithynia 160
  in central Anatolia 35
  in Milyas 103
  in Phrygia 158
  in Pontus 32
neo-Pythagorean ideas 188
nudity (in warfare) 45

oaths 194
  abhorred by Phrygians 189, 193 n. 30
obaeratio 233
oikonomos/oikonomissa (*vilici*) 151, 155,
    156, 160, 162, 164
  as village patrons 184
olives/olive oil 169, 187
  at Bithynian Apamea 244
  civic purchase 89
  for gymnasium 109, 217
  major import to inland regions 257
  not grown in central Anatolia 109 n. 57
  in Pamphylia 247
oracle(s):
  of Glycon 173
  of Phaenno 15
  reassures Carian Stratonicaea 235
  Sibylline 237
oral culture:
  in Church 236
  in Galatia 51

Pamphylia:
  dialects 172
  diorthotes in 228
  Gothic raids 235
  importance in 3rd century AD 238
  nomenclature 125
  plain of 151
  public buildings 216
panegyris 105
Paphlagonia 7
  becomes Roman province 91–2
  Celt in 23
  Paphlagoniarch 116
  part of Galatian province 92–3
  recruitment from 136, 139
  roads 127
parapompe/prosecutio ('escort duty') 132,
    134, 232 n. 27
Parthian Wars 236
  of Lucius Verus 132, 252
  of Septimius Severus 133, 222, 232 n. 26
  of Trajan 132, 136, 251 n. 54, 252
pastoralism 148, 157
patriotism 206–10
patronage:
  of rural communities 184
peace-keeping 195–7
  diogmitai 122, 196, 234
  eirenarchs 89 n. 102, 156, 166, 192, 196,
    200, 229, 234
  eirenophylax 158, 196
  paraphylakes 195, 196, 200
  persecution of Christians 196

Perusine War 73
phrouria:
  in eastern and central Anatolia 84–5
  of Homonadeis 77
  as typical Galatian settlements 54, 58
  see also *castellum*
Phrygia 1, 7, 9
  and Caria: first governor 228
  cities in 1st century AD 81
  collapse of old kingdom 1, 58
  confession steles 191, 192
  Epictetus 20
  Gothic invasion 235
  Great 29, 30
  imperial estates 158–61, 211
  language and names 174, 175
  marble quarries 121, 211
  militarization 230
  pulses grown in 169
  tribes 126
  villages and cities scarcely
    distinguishable 181
Phrygia Paroreius 144, 175, 176
  cities Hellenized 85
  fertile soil 144, 145
  part of kingdom of Amyntas 38
  Roman military presence 122
  rural prosperity 239–40
  Seleucid settlements 20
pigs and pork 192
  favoured meat in cities 169–70
pirates 29
  in eastern Black Sea 34, 235
Pisidia 7
  Celtic presence 55
  colonies 76, 77
  Hellenization 85
  imperial cult 104, 105–6
  landscape 71
  language 173, 175
  opposition to Rome 234
  part of kingdom of Amyntas 38
  prize games 225
  Roman military presence 78, 122
plague:
  under Marcus Aurelius 133
plebs frumentaria 111
politics (civic and provincial) 65, 112, 117,
    203, 210
  inter-city rivalry 204–6
Pollia (Roman tribe) 137
Pontus 7, 9
  city constitutions under Roman rule 88–9
  coinage 255
  Darius appointed king by M.
    Antonius 38–9
  forts and castles 84
  and Galatians 19, 20, 23
  Greek colonies on coast 81
  Hellenization 82, 83–4
  koinon 116
  languages 172
  main routes 32
  part of Roman province 31–4, 91, 93, 228
  Polemo becomes king 39
  pre-Roman epigraphy and coinage 86
  recruitment from 136
  roads 124, 127–8
  Roman military presence 136
  Sassanians in 238
  temple states 82
Pontus and Bithynia (province):
  creation of 81, 160
Pontus Galaticus:

origin 94
part of Pontus 63
Pontus Polemoniacus:
origin 94
part of Galatian province 39, 63
population:
of cities 200
estimate for Roman Anatolia 243–4
growth 149
portoria (customs dues) 68, 248, 249, 256
in Asia 256–7
at Derbe 96 n. 170
pottery:
production centres 242 n. 3
power (divine) 192
Praetorian Guard 136
pragmateutes 150, 151, 155, 160, 161, 162, 164
prehistory (of Anatolia) 1
continuity from 83
private armies 234
procurators, domainal and other 149 n. 56
in Africa 162, 164
in Asia 164, 249 n. 43
in Galatia 156
in Lydia 161
in Paphlagonia 252
in Phrygia: regulates transport dispute 230
procurators, provincial:
duties of 67, 68, 97, 98
govern Cappadocia 97
property disputes 161, 192
Propontis 15
Hellenized 175
ports of 245
Thracians in 175
provincia:
meanings of 61
public buildings 117, 211–17
and Graeco-Roman culture 80–1
and Hellenism 207
supervisor at Oenoanda 199

quarries (marble) 242
of Aezanoi 240
Phrygian 159, 170 *fig. 30*
transport from 246

rainfall:
in Anatolia 144
rape:
during Gothic invasion 236
recruitment to legions 136–41
abusive 229
of *diogmitai* 196
see also conscription; *legio*
Res Gestae 73
Res Gestae Divi Saporis 237
Revelation, Book of 146
rituals:
in civic cult 113
roads:
Amaseia–Zela–Comana Pontica 129
Ancyra–Caesareia 129
Ancyra–Gangra 122 *fig. 22*
Ancyra–Sebasteia–Nicopolis 129
Apamea–Lycaonian plain 70; see also *via Sebaste* below
Bosporus to Dorylaeum–Ancyra 129
bridges Maeander at Antioch 104 *fig. 35d*
building costs 126
building from Flavians to Hadrian 124
Byzantium–Satala ('Northern Highway') 127

Caesareia–Melitene 124, 129
Caesareia–Sebasteia 129
Caesareia–Tavium 129
Cilician Gates–Syria 129
at Cremna 128 *fig. 26*
Eumeneia–Apamea 121
Eumeneia–Sebaste 121
Iconium–Isaura 122
koine hodos 1
Laertes–Syedra 122
late Roman compared to imperial 246
leophoroi hodoi 229 n. 16, 232
Lydia–Aezani 229 n. 18
Maeander Valley–Phrygia Paroreius 121
Melitene–Satala 124
military building 121
and military supplies 251
Nicaea–Dorylaeum 126 n. 62
Nicopolis–Satala 124
Olympus–Rhodiapolis–Limyra 122
Ottoman 127
Perge–Magydus 128 *fig. 25*
Persian royal (Sardis to Susa) 129
Pessinus–Ancyra–Tavium 126
in Phrygian Pentapolis 125 *fig. 23*
'Pilgrim's Road' 129, 132
republican, in Asia Minor 58 *map 4*
and routes in Taurus 70–1
Samosata–Melitene 124
Satala–Trapezus 124
Sebasteia–Melitene 129
Smyrna–Cyzicus 166
via Appia 126, 166
via Egnatia 166
via Nova Traiana 124
via Sebaste 7, 70, 76, 77, 78, 125 *fig. 24*, 247
Roman policy in Asia:
after 188 BC 26
after 133 BC 9
after 63 BC 31
rural inhabitants:
status of 162, 176–8

salt 147, 246 n. 37
Sassanians 7, 232
Gordian III and 222, 227, 237
Philip and 227, 237
raids into Asia Minor 238
rise of 236–7
threat from 236–8
Seleucids 7, 20, 22, 23, 24, 91, 161
influence in western Asia Minor 85
resurgence under Antiochus III 22
Seljuks 1
serfs 176
settlement:
patterns in central Anatolia 148–9
types (rural) 177
sheep 146, 192
in pastoral economy 148
stealing 194
shepherds:
monuments of 146 n. 29
slave trade 257
in Bithynia 30
in Galatia 47
soils 144, 145
soter:
title recognizes victory over Galatians 18, 25
staff (symbol of divine authority) 192
state formation:
contrast between Galatia and Gaul 58

in Galatia 27
stationarii/stationes 141
collect fines 122
at Dacibyza 129 n. 81
in E. Pisidia and Isauria 77 n. 78, 122
perhaps collect taxes 233
as protectors of local population 233 n. 33
responsible for abuses 229, 233 n. 33

tabellarii 129, 164 n. 209
see also couriers
taxation/taxes:
Asian after 123 BC 30
from Cappadocia under Tiberius 63
change from money taxes to material requisitions doubted 232
collection methods militarized 253
confines cities' freedom of action 210
conscription as form of 140, 229
demands lead to land acquisitions 30, 154
exactor and 159
impact and forms of 68
in kind 247–50
and land registration 256
no major change in methods in 3rd century AD 252–3
organized by cities 98
Roman concern for 211
temple architecture:
Hermogenian 103
Roman 104
temple states 81–2
and sacred slaves 176–7, 192
temples (rural) 189
of Apollo Lairbenos 193
of imperial cult 153
of Men 151, 152
tetrarchs (Galatian) 27, 29, 107, 154
Thesmophoria 17
timber and forests 7
on Mysian Olympus 166
at Prusa 244
at Prusias ad Hypium 243
time:
organization of 113
trade:
archaeological evidence for 241–2
associations 202
see also emporium; markets
transhumance 145
transport:
economic constraints and costs 245–7
of marble 159, 170 *fig. 30*
for officials 65, 67, 132, 230
organized in relays 251
see also couriers
Treaty of Apamea 23 n. 121, 24
tribute (*stipendium*), paid to Galatians 16, 19, 20, 22
trimarkisia 44

villages 9
administration in larger villages 181–2, 190–1
as bedrock of communal life 170
concord of 185
in groups 178, 185
of Hierapolis 187
living standards compared to those of cities 255
magistrates 182–3
names for 178
organization 5

villages (*cont.*):
    resilience in 3rd century AD 240
    revenues 185
    ruled by gods 187–95
    subscriptions to *Xenoi Tekmoreioi* 239
vines/wine:
    in Anatolia 146–7

in Bithynia 187
evidence of amphoras 242 n. 3
in Lydia 192

warfare:
    Galatian 22, 43, 44–6
    Pisidian 72

water mills 245
winter quarters:
    of Caracalla in Bithynia 133
    in Cilicia 238
    of legions 252
wool and textiles 146, 257
    at Saittai 180, 202 n. 27

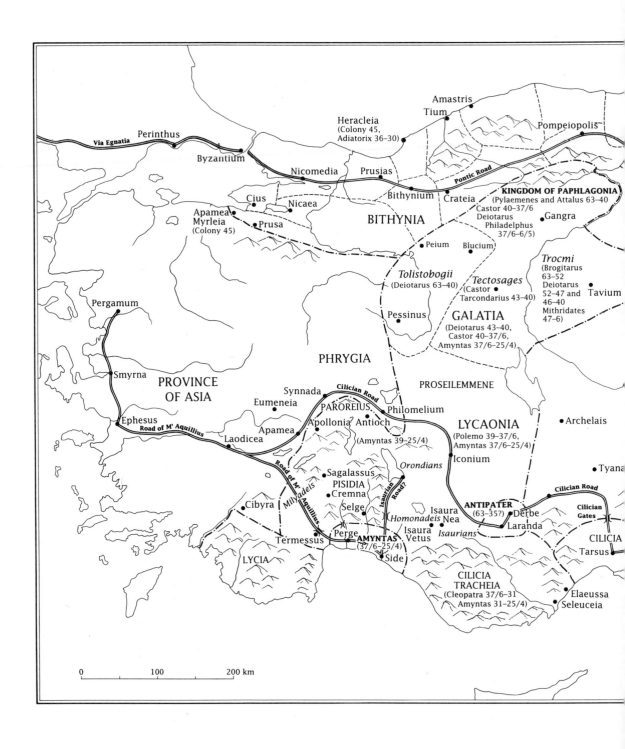

Amastris
Tium
Heracleia
(Colony 45,
Adiatorix 36–30)
Pompeiopolis

Via Egnatia Perinthus
Byzantium
Nicomedia Prusias
Pontic Road
Bithynium Crateia
KINGDOM OF PAPHLAGONIA
(Pylaemenes and Attalus 63–40)
Castor 40–37/6
Deiotarus
Philadelphus
37/6–6/5)
Gangra

Cius
Nicaea
BITHYNIA

Apamea
Myrleia
(Colony 45) Prusa

Peium Blucium)

Trocmi
(Brogitarus
63–52
Deiotarus
52–47 and
46–40
Mithridates
47–6) Tavium

Tolistobogii
(Deiotarus 63–40)

Tectosages
(Castor •
Tarcondarius 43–40)

Pergamum

Pessinus

GALATIA
(Deiotarus 43–40,
Castor 40–37/6,
Amyntas 37/6–25/4)

PHRYGIA

PROSEILEMMENE

Smyrna

PROVINCE
OF ASIA

Synnada Cilician Road
Eumeneia
PAROREIUS Philomelium
Apollonia Antioch
Apamea (Amyntas 39–25/4)
Laodicea

Archelais

LYCAONIA
(Polemo 39–37/6,
Amyntas 37/6–25/4)
Iconium

Ephesus Road of M' Aquillius

• Tyana

Orondians

Road of M' Aquillius
Sagalassus
PISIDIA
Cremna
Selge

Homonadeis Nea

Cilician Road

ANTIPATER
(63–35?) Derbe
Laranda

Cilician
Gates

Cibyra

Isaura Nea
Isaura *Isaurians*
Vetus

CILICIA
Tarsus

Termessus
Perge **AMYNTAS**
(37/6–25/4)
Side

LYCIA

CILICIA
TRACHEIA
(Cleopatra 37/6–31
Amyntas 31–25/4)

Elaeussa
Seleuceia

0   100   200 km

Sinope
(Colony 45)

Amisus
(Straton
36–30)

Gazelonitis
Deiotarus

Neapolis

P·O·N·T·U·S

Amaseia
(King
Brigatus ?
36–3/2)

Eupatoria-
Magnopolis

Pharnaceia-
Cerasus

Trapezus

Cabeira-
Diospolis

PONTIC KINGDOM
(Deiotarus 63–40,
Darius 39–37/6
Polemo 37/6–)

Zela
(Temple
State
36–3/2)

Comana
(Temple State)

Pontic Road

Caranitis

Culupene Nicopolis

Megalopolis

ARMENIA MINOR
(Deiotarus 63–47,
Ariobarzanes III 47–42)

CAPPADOCIA
(Ariobarzanes II 63–52,
Ariobarzanes III 52–42,
Ariarathes X 42–37/6,
Archelaus I 37/6 – A.D. 17)

Caesareia

SOPHENE

Tomisa
Crossing

Arsameia

COMMAGENE
(Antiochus I 69–36)

KINGDOM OF
TARCONDIMOTIDS

Anazarbus

Hierapolis-Castabala

PEDIAS

Amanus
Gates

SYRIA

Antioch

Note on Map 3

The political developments in Asia Minor during the first century BC are too elaborate to be shown in full on a monochrome map. They are illustrated with exemplary scholarship by J. Wagner, on the map *Die Neuordnung des Orients von Pompeius bis Augustus (67 v. Chr.–14 n. Chr.), Tübinger Atlas des Vorderen Orients* B. V. 7 (Wiesbaden, 1983). J. G. C. Anderson's map of Asia Minor, published by John Murray in 1903, was described as 'a little masterpiece, a solid work of learning on two square feet of paper'. The same tribute should be paid to this contribution to the *TAVO* series. Any attempt to indicate firm territorial boundaries for the provinces of Asia and Cilicia would be fundamentally misleading. The provinces were constructed around the routes that ran through them. 'Just as Macedonia may with propriety be regarded as the via Egnatia and Narbonensis as the Domitia, so Cilicia in the years 56–50 BC is the high road from western Asia to Syria' (R. Syme, *RP* i. 123). Not simply in these years, one may add. Republican Asia was built around the road which M'. Aquillius built from Pergamum to Ephesus, along the Maeander to Laodicea, south-east through Pisidia to Pamphylia and its destination, Side (as shown by the discovery of D. H. French, *Epigr. Anat.* 17 (1991), 53–4). M'. Aquillius probably at least marked out the central Anatolian route, familiar from Cicero's Cilician letters, which ran through Phrygia to Lycaonia, and was eventually extended through the Cilician Gates to Tarsus, the Amanus Gates, and the province of Syria. P. Servilius may have attempted to link the two systems by building a road across the Taurus from Side, after his victory over the Isaurians in the early 70s (cf. A. N. Sherwin-White, *Roman Foreign Policy in the East 168–1 BC* (1984), 155–6). Pompey surely established a similar route through Bithynia and Pontus, the northern highway used by all the armies of the Mithridatic Wars, thus extending the *via Egnatia* east almost to the Euphrates. Pompey's arrangements for this new province, above all the creation of a network of provincial cities and territories, make it possible to trace provincial boundaries in a way that is not feasible for Asia or Cilicia. These civic and provincial boundaries are shown on the map, inevitably in a very approximate form.

===== Major Roads
—·—· Provincial Boundaries
——— Boundaries of Civil Territories, Kingdoms, and Regions

Map 3. Kingdoms and Roman provinces in Anatolia in the first century BC

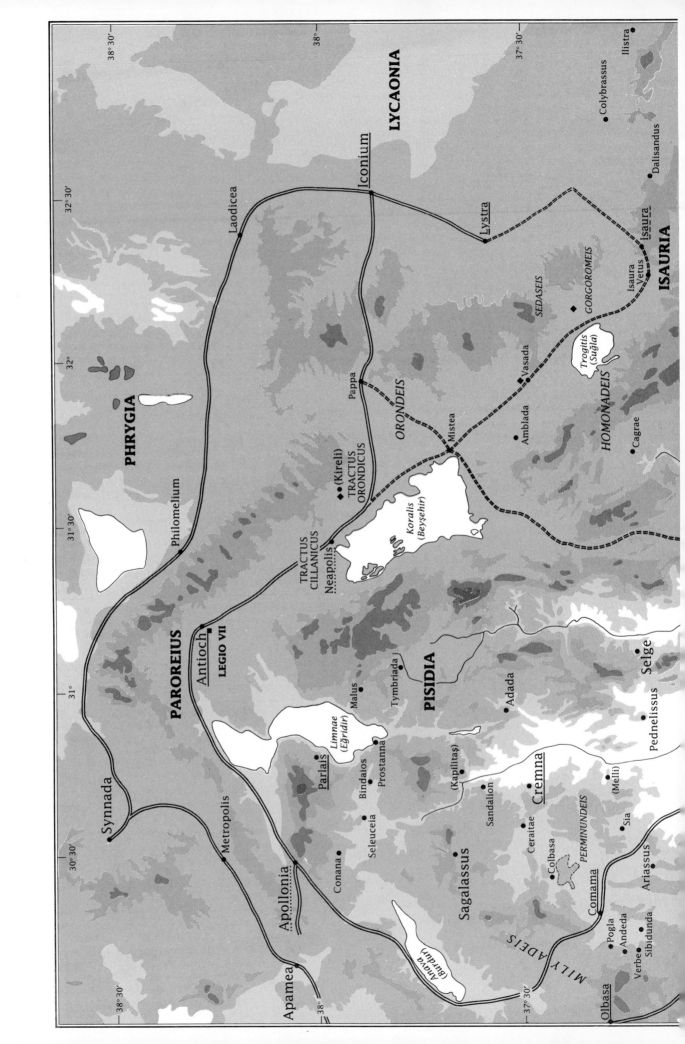

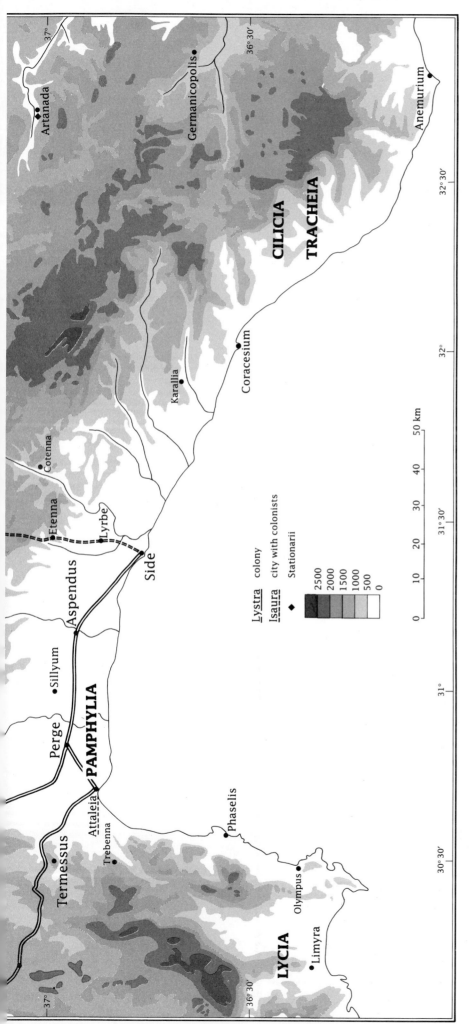

Map 5. The Pisidian Taurus

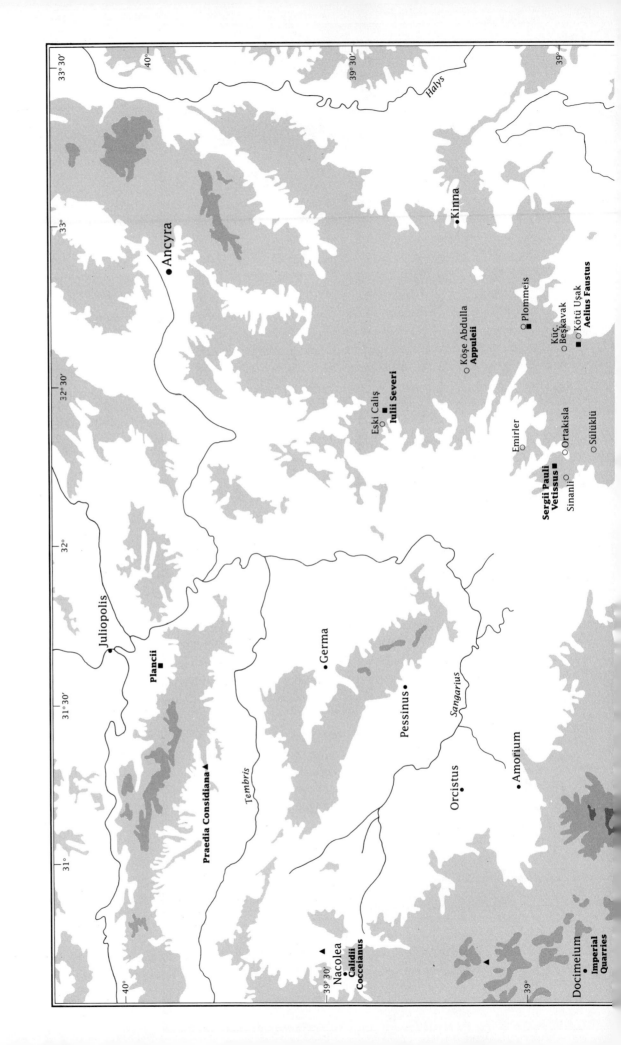

33° 30'

40°

39° 30'

33°

Halys

•Kinna

Ancyra

32° 30'

Plommeis■

○Köşe Abdulla
Appuleii

Küç.
○Beşkavak
Kötü Uşak
Aelius Faustus

Eski Calış
Iulii Severi

Emirler
○

○Ortakisla

Sülüklü
○

32°

**Sergii Pauli
Vetissus**■

Sinanli○

•Juliopolis

•Germa

Pessinus•

Sangarius

Plancii■

31° 30'

Praedia Considiana▲

Tembris

Amorium•

Orcistus
•

31°

40°

39° 30'

Nacolea▲
•
**Calidii
Cocceianus**

▲

Docimeium
•
**Imperial
Quarries**■

39°

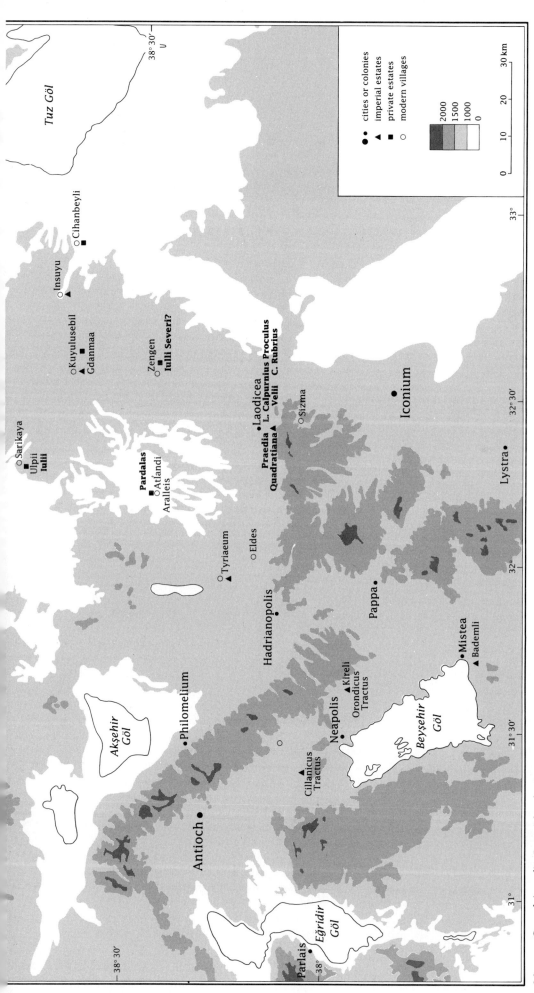

Map 10. Central Anatolia: Imperial and private estates